36: *British Novelists, 1890-1929: Modernists,* edited by Thomas F. Staley (1985)

37: *American Writers of the Early Republic,* edited by Emory Elliott (1985)

38: *Afro-American Writers After 1955: Dramatists and Prose Writers,* edited by Thadious M. Davis and Trudier Harris (1985)

39: *British Novelists, 1660-1800,* 2 parts, edited by Martin C. Battestin (1985)

40: *Poets of Great Britain and Ireland Since 1960,* 2 parts, edited by Vincent B. Sherry, Jr. (1985)

41: *Afro-American Poets Since 1955,* edited by Trudier Harris and Thadious M. Davis (1985)

42: *American Writers for Children Before 1900,* edited by Glenn E. Estes (1985)

43: *American Newspaper Journalists, 1690-1872,* edited by Perry J. Ashley (1986)

44: *American Screenwriters,* Second Series, edited by Randall Clark, Robert E. Morsberger, and Stephen O. Lesser (1986)

45: *American Poets, 1880-1945,* First Series, edited by Peter Quartermain (1986)

46: *American Literary Publishing Houses, 1900-1980: Trade and Paperback,* edited by Peter Dzwonkoski (1986)

47: *American Historians, 1866-1912,* edited by Clyde N. Wilson (1986)

48: *American Poets, 1880-1945,* Second Series, edited by Peter Quartermain (1986)

49: *American Literary Publishing Houses, 1638-1899,* 2 parts, edited by Peter Dzwonkoski (1986)

50: *Afro-American Writers Before the Harlem Renaissance,* edited by Trudier Harris (1986)

51: *Afro-American Writers from the Harlem Renaissance to 1940,* edited by Trudier Harris (1987)

52: *American Writers for Children Since 1960: Fiction,* edited by Glenn E. Estes (1986)

53: *Canadian Writers Since 1960,* First Series, edited by W. H. New (1986)

54: *American Poets, 1880-1945,* Third Series, 2 parts, edited by Peter Quartermain (1987)

55: *Victorian Prose Writers Before 1867,* edited by William B. Thesing (1987)

56: *German Fiction Writers, 1914-1945,* edited by James Hardin (1987)

57: *Victorian Prose Writers After 1867,* edited by William B. Thesing (1987)

58: *Jacobean and Caroline Dramatists,* edited by Fredson Bowers (1987)

59: *American Literary Critics and Scholars, 1800-1850,* edited by John W. Rathbun and Monica M. Grecu (1987)

60: *Canadian Writers Since 1960,* Second Series, edited by W. H. New (1987)

61: *American Writers for Children Since 1960: Poets, Illustrators, and Nonfiction Authors,* edited by Glenn E. Estes (1987)

62: *Elizabethan Dramatists,* edited by Fredson Bowers (1987)

63: *Modern American Critics, 1920-1955,* edited by Gregory S. Jay (1988)

64: *American Literary Critics and Scholars, 1850-1880,* edited by John W. Rathbun and Monica M. Grecu (1988)

65: *French Novelists, 1900-1930,* edited by Catharine Savage Brosman (1988)

66: *German Fiction Writers, 1885-1913,* 2 parts, edited by James Hardin (1988)

67: *Modern American Critics Since 1955,* edited by Gregory S. Jay (1988)

68: *Canadian Writers, 1920-1959,* First Series, edited by W. H. New (1988)

69: *Contemporary German Fiction Writers,* First Series, edited by Wolfgang D. Elfe and James Hardin (1988)

70: *British Mystery Writers, 1860-1919,* edited by Bernard Benstock and Thomas F. Staley (1988)

(Continued on back endsheets)

Dictionary of Literary Biography • Volume Eighty-nine

Restoration and Eighteenth-Century Dramatists Third Series

Dictionary of Literary Biography • Volume Eighty-nine

Restoration and Eighteenth-Century Dramatists Third Series

Edited by
Paula R. Backscheider
University of Rochester

A Bruccoli Clark Layman Book
Gale Research Inc.
Detroit, New York, Fort Lauderdale, London

Matthew J. Bruccoli and Richard Layman, *Editorial Directors*
C. E. Frazer Clark, Jr., *Managing Editor*

Manufactured by Braun-Brumfield
Ann Arbor, Michigan
Printed in the United States of America

Library of Congress Cataloging-in-Publication Data

Restoration and eighteenth-century dramatists. Third series / edited by Paula R. Backscheider.
p. cm. – (Dictionary of literary biography; v. 89)
"A Bruccoli Clark Layman book."
ISBN 0-8103-4567-6
1. English drama–18th century–Dictionaries. 2. English drama–18th century–Bio-bibliography. 3. English drama–Restoration, 1660-1700–Dictionaries. 4. English drama–Restoration, 1660-1700–Bio-bibliography. 5. Dramatists, English–18th century–Biography–Dictionaries. 6. Dramatists, English–Early modern, 1500-1700–Biography–Dictionaries. I. Backscheider, Paula R. II. Series.
PR701.R4 1989c
822.009–dc20
89-36563
[B]
CIP

To Jacob H. Adler in the year of his retirement

Contents

Plan of the Series

. . . Almost the most prodigious asset of a country, and perhaps its most precious possession, is its native literary product–when that product is fine and noble and enduring.

Mark Twain*

The advisory board, the editors, and the publisher of the *Dictionary of Literary Biography* are joined in endorsing Mark Twain's declaration. The literature of a nation provides an inexhaustible resource of permanent worth. We intend to make literature and its creators better understood and more accessible to students and the reading public, while satisfying the standards of teachers and scholars.

To meet these requirements, *literary biography* has been construed in terms of the author's achievement. The most important thing about a writer is his writing. Accordingly, the entries in *DLB* are career biographies, tracing the development of the author's canon and the evolution of his reputation.

The purpose of *DLB* is not only to provide reliable information in a convenient format but also to place the figures in the larger perspective of literary history and to offer appraisals of their accomplishments by qualified scholars.

The publication plan for *DLB* resulted from two years of preparation. The project was proposed to Bruccoli Clark by Frederick G. Ruffner, president of the Gale Research Company, in November 1975. After specimen entries were prepared and typeset, an advisory board was formed to refine the entry format and develop the series rationale. In meetings held during 1976, the publisher, series editors, and advisory board approved the scheme for a comprehensive biographical dictionary of persons who contributed to North American literature. Editorial work on the first volume began in January 1977, and it was published in 1978. In order to make *DLB* more than a reference tool and to compile volumes that individually have claim to status as literary history, it was decided to organize volumes by topic, period, or genre. Each of these freestanding volumes provides a biographical-bibliographical guide and overview for a particular area of literature. We are convinced that this organization–as opposed to a single alphabet method–constitutes a valuable innovation in the presentation of reference material. The volume plan necessarily requires many decisions for the placement and treatment of authors who might properly be included in two or three volumes. In some instances a major figure will be included in separate volumes, but with different entries emphasizing the aspect of his career appropriate to each volume. Ernest Hemingway, for example, is represented in *American Writers in Paris, 1920-1939* by an entry focusing on his expatriate apprenticeship; he is also in *American Novelists, 1910-1945* with an entry surveying his entire career. Each volume includes a cumulative index of subject authors and articles. Comprehensive indexes to the entire series are planned.

With volume ten in 1982 it was decided to enlarge the scope of *DLB*. By the end of 1986 twenty-one volumes treating British literature had been published, and volumes for Commonwealth and Modern European literature were in progress. The series has been further augmented by the *DLB Yearbooks* (since 1981) which update published entries and add new entries to keep the *DLB* current with contemporary activity. There have also been *DLB Documentary Series* volumes which provide biographical and critical source materials for figures whose work is judged to have particular interest for students. One of these companion volumes is entirely devoted to Tennessee Williams.

We define literature as the *intellectual commerce of a nation:* not merely as belles lettres but as that ample and complex process by which ideas are generated, shaped, and transmitted. *DLB* entries are not limited to "creative writers" but extend to other figures who in their time and in their way influenced the mind of a people. Thus the series encompasses historians, journalists, publishers, and screenwriters. By this means readers of *DLB* may be aided to perceive litera-

*From an unpublished section of Mark Twain's autobiography, copyright © by the Mark Twain Company.

ture not as cult scripture in the keeping of intellectual high priests but firmly positioned at the center of a nation's life.

DLB includes the major writers appropriate to each volume and those standing in the ranks immediately behind them. Scholarly and critical counsel has been sought in deciding which minor figures to include and how full their entries should be. Wherever possible, useful references are made to figures who do not warrant separate entries.

Each *DLB* volume has a volume editor responsible for planning the volume, selecting the figures for inclusion, and assigning the entries. Volume editors are also responsible for preparing, where appropriate, appendices surveying the major periodicals and literary and intellectual movements for their volumes, as well as lists of further readings. Work on the series as a whole is coordinated at the Bruccoli Clark Layman editorial center in Columbia, South Carolina, where the editorial staff is responsible for accuracy of the published volumes.

One feature that distinguishes *DLB* is the illustration policy–its concern with the iconography of literature. Just as an author is influenced by his surroundings, so is the reader's understanding of the author enhanced by a knowledge of his environment. Therefore *DLB* volumes include not only drawings, paintings, and photographs of authors, often depicting them at various stages in their careers, but also illustrations of their families and places where they lived. Title pages are regularly reproduced in facsimile along with dust jackets for modern authors. The dust jackets are a special feature of *DLB* because they often document better than anything else the way in which an author's work was perceived in its own time. Specimens of the writers' manuscripts are included when feasible.

Samuel Johnson rightly decreed that "The chief glory of every people arises from its authors." The purpose of the *Dictionary of Literary Biography* is to compile literary history in the surest way available to us–by accurate and comprehensive treatment of the lives and work of those who contributed to it.

The *DLB* Advisory Board

Foreword

The plays of the closing decades of the eighteenth century are among the most neglected and misunderstood in English literary history. This volume, which describes hundreds of them, captures a time of great theatrical activity and success. The major playhouses each held audiences of more than two thousand, and they expanded to over three thousand by the end of the century. In spite of lively competition from the opera, pleasure gardens, burlettas, puppet shows, recitals, concerts, equestrian shows, circuses, and spas, the patent theaters were filled night after night and, in most seasons, extended successful runs beyond the traditional 15 May closing.

These playwrights, who were born between Charles Macklin near the beginning of the century and James Boaden in 1762, left a huge repertory of plays that remained popular until into the twentieth century. Only a few of these plays, however, are ever performed or even taught today. The exceptions are, of course, plays by Richard Brinsley Sheridan and by Oliver Goldsmith. At least one, and usually more, of Sheridan's plays is revived every single year, and most English and American people who consider playgoing as a regular part of their leisure life have seen Sheridan's *The School for Scandal* (1777), *The Rivals* (1775), or both. Many have also seen Oliver Goldsmith's *She Stoops to Conquer* (1773). These plays deserve their longevity; not only are they brilliantly plotted and filled with wit and humor, but they use one of theater audiences' favorite strategies–dramatic irony–as well as it has ever been done and take up timeless human concerns: gossip, sibling rivalry, and respect between classes and the sexes.

The rest of the playwrights and many of their plays deserve to be better known. They are among the most successful of all the playwrights in Western history. Eleven of them saw more than a dozen of their plays performed, and all had several genuine hits that went on to be repertoire pieces for a hundred years. George Colman the Elder's *Separate Maintenance* (1779), Hugh Kelly's *School for Wives* (1773), Richard Cumberland's *The West Indian* (1771), Hannah Cowley's *Belle's Stratagem* (1780), and Arthur Murphy's *Know Your Own Mind* (1777) can hold their own in any company. Another fine play of Kelly's, *False Delicacy* (1768), was rapidly translated into French, German, Portuguese, and Italian. Over this long time period many of these plays continued to be favorite acting parts for players looking for vehicles to display their mature, virtuoso skills, for players' benefits, and for retirement performances. Names of characters became part of the language and as familiar to generations of people as "a John Wayne type" is to us. Cumberland, whose melodramatic plays include villains, maidens in distress, and last-second rescues, gave us the now much-parodied line, "Foiled again" (*The Brothers,* 1769).

Perhaps the most distinctive feature of this era is the dominance of great actor-playwrights and even actor-playwright-managers. Macklin, Foote, Holcroft, Inchbald, O'Keeffe, and Murphy all had some success on the boards, and both Colmans, Macklin, Foote, and Sheridan were successful managers. As might be expected, they created great acting parts and knew how to please their audiences. George Colman the Younger, for instance, wrote such a good part in *The Iron Chest* (1796) that great actors continued to ask for it in spite of the play's history of unsuccessful revivals. He and his contemporaries ignored screams of outrage from the Republic of Letters and mingled elements of the Gothic and the sentimental, the comic and the lugubrious, included numerous songs, and delighted in their public's applause.

This era demonstrates that great theater need not be great literature, at least if we insist that literature must be read. Although there are many reasons that these plays succeeded, four are worth describing for the modern person.

The first reason might at first seem to be a weakness. Restoration and eighteenth-century plays are notorious for their complicated plots. Every undergraduate student's nightmare is to be called upon to sketch the plot of William Congreve's *The Way of the World* (1700), George Farquhar's *The Recruiting Officer* (1706), or Sheridan's *The Rivals,* or to be faced with a final exam featuring the names of twenty-five characters to identify. It is, of course, much easier to remember the women involved with Mirabel when they are seen dressing in character, displaying particular mannerisms, and being of different ages, and to keep straight Joseph and Charles Surface when they have appeared, moved, spoken, worn various outfits, and displayed their living quarters. The vast majority of the plays of the second half of the eighteenth century have complex plots and many characters. Three couples with their friends, enemies, guardians, and relatives are not at all unusual. In order to appeal to their large audiences, playwrights found it useful to include characters of many ages, situations, and classes. Benjamin Hoadley's very popular *The Suspicious Husband* (1747) stayed near the top of the list of most performed comedies throughout the era; it stars an extravagantly suspicious father, Strictland, whose actions complicate the romances of his daughter Jacintha and their houseguest Clarinda. The play includes a rake, Ranger, who makes witty observations and complicates things by leaving his hat in Mrs. Strictland's room. Comic meetings and scurrying departures depend upon the strategies of Spanish intrigue comedy. At the end, the couples are united, and the resolution even improves the Strictlands' marriage, because Strictland recognizes his irrational and unfair distrust of his wife. Tragedies were no less complicated.[1]

Yet another reason for the popularity of many of these plays was their domestic subject matter. Important for the development of the great "problem plays" written at the end of the nineteenth century, these plays are sometimes seen to be about dated, mundane, or depressing situations. Both tragedies and comedies tended to treat similar problems. Since critics usually classify plays written before the twentieth century more rigidly according to classical genres, these are often judged "mixed" and, therefore, found inferior. In content, they are accused of suffering from "sameness." Many of the plays of the period are about problems that arise in marriage. A typical play, and one of the best, Arthur Murphy's *The Way to Keep Him* (1760), presents two couples whose marriages are in trouble. Sir Bashful Constant learns to reject the fashionable pretense of indifference to his spouse, and Mrs. Lovemore finds she must resume her vivacity and humor in order to hold her husband's interest. Edward Moore's *The Gamester* (1753), the melodramatic story of a compulsive gambler whose wife and sister watch helplessly as he destroys himself and ruins the family, gained steadily in popularity during the last quarter of the eighteenth century. The part of Mrs. Beverley, the wife, became one of Sarah Siddons's perennial triumphs. Many of Elizabeth Inchbald's best plays present families in crisis. Sir George and Lady Harriet are divorced and unhappy in her *I'll Tell You What* (1785). In *Next Door Neighbors* (1791), Eleanor and Henry struggle in poverty while their father is in prison.

Another set of plays examined the conflicts in society generated by the middle-class (or lower) men who had earned great wealth in trade. Samuel Foote, for instance, used the eighteenth-century pejorative term for the newly rich and powerful men with East Indian wealth as the title for a play that captures many of the prejudices of the time (*The Nabob,* 1772). The Nabob, Matthew Mite, drives the Oldham family into debt in order to force them to allow him to marry their daughter, but a generous pure-English merchant rescues them. Several of these plays mention the power of the returning men to buy votes and take over seats in Parliament, as Matthew Mite attempted. Of course, many of these returning men do rescue deserving people as Steele's Indiana and Sheridan's Joseph Surface were. Very often playwrights examine the proper uses of wealth and uphold many of the conservative attitudes of those confronted with the nouveau riche.

Theatergoers in this era expected a very high level of staging. As befit the heirs of scene designs by two of Britain's greatest architects (Inigo Jones and John Vanbrugh) set designers routinely created sublime wildernesses and lavish seraglios for these spoiled audiences. William Capon, scene painter at Drury Lane, studied past styles of architecture and used them to give historical authenticity to individual plays. James Boaden described one of Capon's sets as "positively a building"; it represented a fourteenth-century church and was fifty-six feet wide, fifty-two deep, and thirty-seven high.[2] Cumberland's *The Brothers* begins with a storm and a shipwreck. In fact, designers put a lot of water on the stage, and canals, cascades, and "lakes" came to be taken for granted. Even in so short a piece as a prologue or an epilogue management occasionally did something as extravagant as including a boy rowing a boat on real water. Night after night Carlo the dog jumped into water to save a small child in Frederick Reynolds's *The Caravan* (1803). For a time Covent Garden specialized in ships at sea. The ship was fixed to a moving plat-

The interior of the Theatre Royal, Drury Lane, in 1795 (watercolor by Edward Dayes; by permission of the Henry E. Huntington Library and Art Gallery)

An 1804 performance of Richard Brinsley Sheridan's Pizarro *at the Theatre Royal, Covent Garden (engraving by J. Fittler, based on a drawing by J. Pugh)*

John Philip Kemble as Richard and Dorothy Jordan as Matilda in a 1786-1787 production of Richard Coeur de Lion *at the Theatre Royal, Drury Lane (engraving by Richardson, published by A. Hogg, 1787)*

Fire-scene transparency designed by Cipriani and Richards for a 1779 production of The Mirror or Harlequin Everywhere *at the Theatre Royal, Covent Garden*

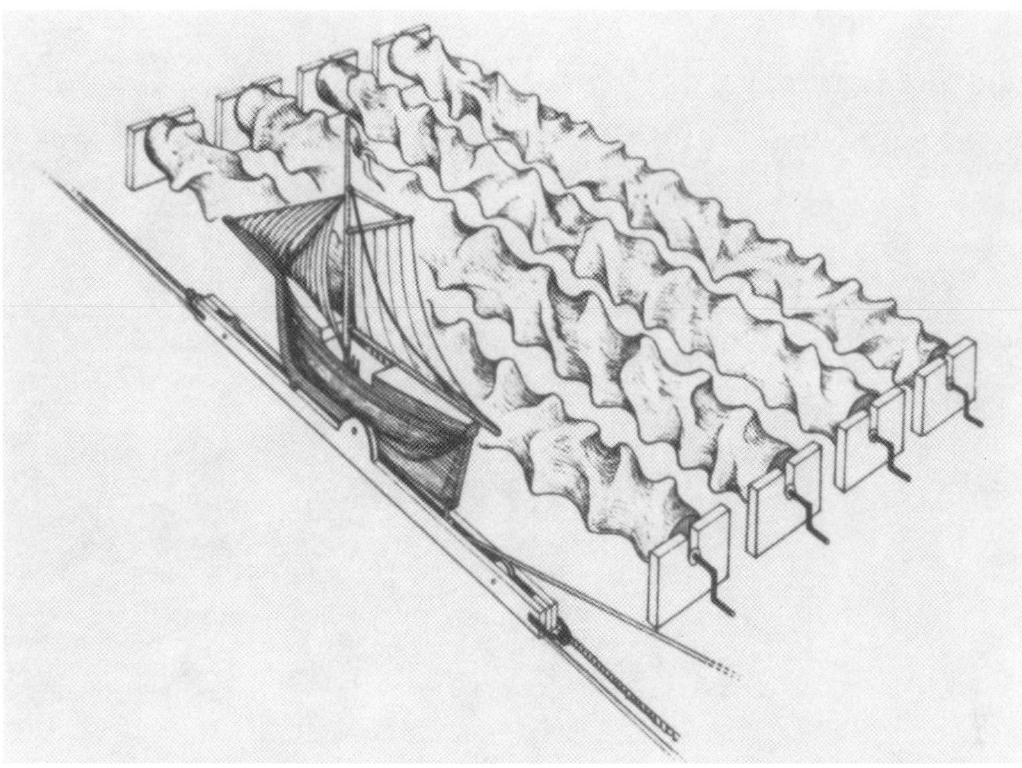

Ship and waves machines (drawing by Ken Forsyth, adapted from A. Rees The Cyclopedia; or, Universal Dictionary of Arts, Sciences, and Literature, *1819)*

The Manager and His Dog, *an 1803 caricature of Richard Brinsley-Sheridan, manager of the Drury Lane theater, satirizing his salvation from financial ruin by the success of* The Caravan, *a melodrama in which a dog saves a drowning child. Sheridan is said to have called the dog "my guardian angel."*

Hannah Pritchard as Lady Macbeth and David Garrick as Macbeth (engraving by V. Green, based on a painting by Johann Zoffany, 1776)

form and moved up and down by a cord attached to its stern. Wave machines, revolving cylinders turned by handles, supplied the rolling sea.[3]

Especially notable for their staging were the many Gothic plays. Caverns, dark forests, huge rocks, cliffs, barren seacoasts with a glimpse of an awe-inspiring castle turret or convent tower, dungeons, tombs, and torture chambers could be expected, and impressive light and sound effects thrilled the spectators.[4] Some of the best Gothic novelists, too, including Horace Walpole and Matthew "Monk" Lewis, wrote Gothic plays. Walpole, whose play *The Mysterious Mother* (1768) was never acted, participated in the adaptation of his *Castle of Otranto* (1764) that Robert Jephson saw produced at Covent Garden in November 1781 as *The Count of Narbonne*. James Boaden, whose adaptations of Ann Radcliffe's novels *The Romance of the Forest* (1791) and *The Italian* (1797) had been hits, reworked Lewis's popular novel *The Monk* (1795) into *Aurelio and Miranda* (1798). Monk Lewis's own play *The Castle Spectre* (1797) became one of the most popular plays of the age; acted sixty times in its first season, it has an abundance of spectacular scenes. For instance, the last act opens in front of "Conway Castle by moonlight" and proceeds in a vaulted chamber, complete with strange music, unusual lighting effects, and the supposedly assassinated character "Reginald, pale and emaciated, in coarse garments, his hair hanging wildly about his face, and a chain bound round his body." Lewis went on to write a number of other Gothic plays, and in his lifetime was better known for them than for his novel.

Many believe that things went too far. If Joe Haines and William Pinkethman delivered prologues on donkeys, then their successor John Quick rode an elephant (Covent Garden, 13 April 1784). If they were to have a ghost it would have to appear with special effects as James Boaden's specter did in *Fontainville Forest* (1794). This ghost appeared in a haze of blue-gray gauze with special lighting that made the figure appear to fade in and then melt away. The climax of *Alexander the Great: or, The Conquest of Persia* (Drury Lane, 1795) was the appearance of Alexander in his chariot pulled by two elephants, accompanied by Darius's car drawn by three white horses.

The most difficult aspect of this theater to recapture is that of the players; yet this fourth reason

The Apotheosis of David Garrick *(1782), by George Carter (from the RSC Collection, with the permission of the Governors of the Royal Shakespeare Theatre). As Shakespeare waits in Parnassus with the Muses of Comedy and Tragedy, Garrick is mourned by seventeen contemporary actors and actresses in costume for their favorite Shakespearean roles: (kneeling) Elizabeth Younge as Cordelia in* King Lear, *Elizabeth Hartley as Desdemona in* Othello, *John Palmer as Iachimo in* Cymbeline, *William Parsons as the gravedigger in* Hamlet; *(standing) Mary Ann Yates as Isabella in* Measure for Measure, *Frances Abington as Beatrice in* Much Ado About Nothing, *Jane Pope as Mrs. Page in* The Merry Wives of Windsor, *Robert Bensley as Prospero in* The Tempest, *William Smith as Hamlet, John Hayman Packer as Friar Lawrence in* Romeo and Juliet, *Richard Yates as Malvolio in* Twelfth Night, *Thomas Hull as Pisanio in* Cymbeline, *Thomas King as Touchstone in* As You Like It, *Joseph Vernon as Thurio in* Two Gentlemen of Verona, *Robert Baddeley as Dr. Caius in* The Merry Wives of Windsor, *John Moody as Adam in* As You Like It, *and William Brereton as Orlando in* As You Like It.

for the success of late eighteenth-century theater is surely among the most important. David Garrick did not retire until 1776, and the world has not forgotten the names of John Philip Kemble and Sarah Kemble Siddons. Garrick's acting has been well described by many eyewitnesses, biographers, and scholars.[5] It seems that what Garrick and the generation of players who followed him added to their performances was emotional interpretation. More like skilled orators than modern actors, James Quin, Theophilus Cibber, Spranger Barry, and their contemporaries used rhetorical tricks like voice modulation almost exclusively. When Laurence Sterne's Trim assumes a stance with body bent forward at an 85 1/2 degree angle and the left foot slightly forward in order to read the sermon, he is in the position actors took to deliver major speeches (*Tristram Shandy*, volume 2, chapter 17). Garrick, in contrast, was "alive in every muscle and feature"[6] and struck people as remarkably mobile. A German visitor captured the contrast between Garrick's style and that common at the time when he began his career: "He moves to and fro among other players like a man among marionettes."[7]

Garrick's own leading ladies, Hannah Pritchard (his renowned Lady Macbeth), Mary Ann Yates, and Susannah Maria Cibber, joined him in heightening and exploiting intense emotion. The greatest of these new passionate actresses was, of course, Sarah Kemble Siddons. Among her most effective techniques was to break long silences in which she appeared stunned with grief, hypnotized with horror, or insensate with emotional exhaustion, with piercing screams of agony, maniacal laughter, or portentous, almost sighing lamentations. Eyewitness accounts of her performances retain more of her power to characterize than those describing any other performer. James Boaden described the way Mrs. Siddons performed Belvidera in the scene in *Venice Preserved* (the original 1682; her first performance in 1782, her first London season) in which she first meets Jaffier's fellow conspirators: "the alarmed yet *searching* survey which she took of them, was one of those expressions in which the actress *writes* with characters of *fire:* you felt that there was a language more eloquent than speech, and saw beauty and intelligence interpret the very *silence* of the poet." James Sheridan Knowles recalled her performance as Lady Macbeth as unforgettable:

> Though pit, gallery, and boxes were crowded to suffocation, the chill of the grave seemed about you while you looked on her;–there was the hush and the damp of the charnel-house at midnight; you had a feeling as if you and the medical attendant, and lady-in-waiting, were alone with her; your flesh crept and your breathing became uneasy.

The American actor Edwin Forrest said of Siddons's sleepwalking scene in the same performance: "I have read all the high-flown descriptions of the critics, and they fall short." Knowles replied, "Well, sir, I smelt blood! I swear I smelt blood!"[8]

During this period, the beautiful actresses George Anne Bellamy, Frances Abington, and Jane Pope had dazzling careers. John Philip Kemble filled Covent Garden with his portrayals of Shakespeare's great tragic heroes and a host of melodramatic, often romantic, melancholy protagonists; among the latter were Octavian in George Colman the Younger's *Mountaineers* (1793), Penruddock in Richard Cumberland's *The Wheel of Fortune* (1795), Percy in Monk Lewis's *The Castle Spectre,* and the part that made his reputation in Dublin, Jephson's Count of Narbonne. Many major parts were reinterpreted at this time, and familiar plays made sensations. George Frederick Cooke made Shakespeare's Iago possess Othello's soul and changed Shakespeare's Richard III and Sir Pertinax in Macklin's *The Man of the World* (1781); Charles Macklin gave London a Shylock that revolutionized the interpretation of the character.

The comedians of the period were no less skilled than those who played serious parts. Garrick, of course, was a superb comic actor, and yet when he appeared with Thomas Weston or Henry Woodward, audiences felt that they were watching equals. John Quick was a tremendous favorite, and he made a number of parts, including Goldsmith's unparalleled Tony Lumpkin, his own. Kitty Clive retired, but others like Dorothy Jordan, who excelled in breeches and tomboy parts, took her place. Famous for her lovely singing and speaking voice, which was described as "liquid and mellow as the nightingale's," she enchanted those who saw her. When playing her favorite comic parts, she entered scenes with a vivacious manner and moved with what James Boaden described as "her elastic spring" and a joyous smile. She wore her beautiful naturally curly hair loose down her back throughout her career, and it bounced attractively as she moved. Her great parts were Viola in *Twelfth Night,* Peggy in Garrick's *Country Girl,* and Miss Hoyden in Richard Sheridan's *A Trip to Scarborough* (1777). Jane Green distinguished herself as Sheridan's Mrs. Malaprop and Goldsmith's Mrs. Hardcastle, and Mary Bulkley turned *The Rivals'* Julia Melville and *She Stoops to Conquer*'s Kate Hardcastle into showcase parts.

These actors, unlike today's, felt free to adlib and to modify words, phrases, or speeches to give them topicality. Pinkethman had been famous for doing so, and playwrights began to create parts to take advantage of the audience's delight in such uncensorable lines. George Colman the Elder's *Polly Honeycombe* (1760) includes many allusions to heroines in contemporary novels, and actors could easily swap the latest ones for those in the original text. Dick in Arthur Murphy's *Apprentice* (1756) has many lines that are quotations from popular plays; when Henry Woodward and other actors delivered them in the ways living actors spoke them, they brought down the house. Richard Sheridan's *The Critic* (1779) includes many of the techniques Henry Fielding had used in his great dramatic political commentaries. Samuel Foote made his reputation as actor and playwright on his ability to introduce people, subjects, and fashions of immediate interest on the stage. As Colman said of Foote, "Yet there is no Shakspeare [*sic*] or Roscius upon record who, like Foote, supported a theatre for a series of years by his own acting, in his own writings, and for ten years of the time upon a *wooden leg*!" Anyone who ever saw Foote play Mrs. Cole in his *The Minor* (1760) or as the devil in his *Devil upon*

Two Sticks (which ran fifty nights in its first season, 1768) or had seen him transform an old war horse of a part like Bayes in George Villiers, duke of Buckingham's *The Rehearsal* into a topical tour de force (the original 1671, Foote's first notable performance of the part 13 December 1745) or turn a sketchy outline with a title like "Diversions of a Morning" into a "play" expressed amazement, wonder, and delight–or amazement, wonder, and outrage. In 1770 Francis Gentleman dedicated volume 2 of *The Dramatic Censor* to Foote and wrote, "this writer we stile the dramatic noun substantive . . . strength of judgment, knowledge of life, selection of characters, application of satire, vivacity of sentiment, and terseness of dialogue. . . ." Gibbon once said, "when I am tired of the Roman Empire I can laugh away the Evening at Foote's Theatre."[9] On the work of such playwrights and performers was the theater's unprecedented success based.

–Paula R. Backscheider

1. See, for example, Robertson Davies's account of Richard Cumberland's *The Carmelite* (1784), in "Playwrights and Plays," in *The Revels History of Drama in English, 1750-1880,* edited by Clifford Leech and T. W. Craik (London: Methuen, 1975), p. 179.

2. Richard Southern, "Theatres and Stages," in *The Revels History of Drama in English, 1750-1880,* pp. 68-69.

3. Colin Visser, "Scenery and Technical Design," in *The London Theatre World, 1660-1800,* edited by Robert D. Hume (Carbondale: Southern Illinois University Press, 1980), pp. 105-106.

4. Visser gives a useful overview of some of the major techniques, pp. 107-118.

5. Alan S. Downer, "Nature to Advantage Dressed: Eighteenth-Century Acting," *PMLA,* 58 (December 1943): 1002-1037; Frederick and Lise-Lone Marker, "Actors and their Repertory," in *The Revels History of Drama in English, 1750-1880,* pp. 96-106; George Winchester Stone, Jr., and George M. Kahrl, *David Garrick: A Critical Biography* (Carbondale: Southern Illinois University Press, 1979), pp. 25-51; Alan Kendall, *David Garrick. A Biography* (New York: St. Martin's Press, 1985), pp. 34-41.

6. Richard Cumberland, *Memoirs of Richard Cumberland* (London: Printed for Lackington, Allen & Co., 1806), p. 60.

7. Quoted in Frederick and Lise-Lone Marker, "Actors and their Repertory," in *The Revels History of Drama in English, 1750-1880,* p. 98.

8. I am grateful to Associate Professor Douglas Howard of St. John Fisher College for sharing his work on Sarah Siddons; the major sources in the part of his work used here were James Boaden, *Memoirs of Mrs. Siddons,* 2 volumes (London: Colburn, 1827), I: 351; Arthur Colby Sprague, *Shakespearian Players and Performances* (Cambridge, Mass.: Harvard University Press, 1953), p. 67.

9. Paula R. Backscheider, Introduction to *The Plays of Samuel Foote,* 3 volumes, edited by Backscheider and Douglas Howard (New York & London: Garland, 1983), I: xix.

Acknowledgments

This book was produced by Bruccoli Clark Layman, Inc. Karen L. Rood, senior editor for the *Dictionary of Literary Biography* series, was the in-house editor.

Production coordinator is James W. Hipp. Systems manager is Charles D. Brower. Photography supervisor is Susan Todd. Layout and graphics supervisor is Penney L. Haughton. Copy-editing supervisor is Joan M. Prince. Typesetting supervisor is Kathleen M. Flanagan. William Adams, Laura Ingram, and Michael D. Senecal are editorial associates. The production staff includes Rowena Betts, Anne L. M. Bowman, Nancy Brevard-Bracey, Joseph M. Bruccoli, Teresa Chaney, Patricia Coate, Allison Deal, Holly Deal, Charles Lee Egleston, Sarah A. Estes, Susan C. Heath, David Marshall James, Kathy S. Merlette, Laura Garren Moore, Sheri Beckett Neal, and Jack Turner. Jean W. Ross is permissions editor.

Walter W. Ross and Jennifer Toth did the library research with the assistance of the reference staff at the Thomas Cooper Library of the University of South Carolina: Lisa Antley, Daniel Boice, Faye Chadwell, Cathy Eckman, Gary Geer, Cathie Gottlieb, David L. Haggard, Jens Holley, Jackie Kinder, Marcia Martin, Jean Rhyne, Beverly Steele, Ellen Tillett, Carol Tobin, and Virginia Weathers.

Dictionary of Literary Biography • Volume Eighty-nine

Restoration and Eighteenth-Century Dramatists Third Series

Dictionary of Literary Biography

Miles Peter Andrews

(?-18 July 1814)

Laura Morrow
Louisiana State University in Shreveport

PLAY PRODUCTIONS: *The Conjuror,* London, Theatre Royal in Drury Lane, 29 April 1774;

The Election, London, Theatre Royal in Drury Lane, 19 October 1774;

Belphegor, or the Wishes, London, Theatre Royal in Drury Lane, 16 March 1778;

Summer Amusement, or an Adventure at Margate, by Andrews and William Augustus Miles, London, Theatre Royal in the Hay-Market, 1 July 1779;

Fire and Water, London, Theatre Royal in the Hay-Market, 8 July 1780;

Dissipation, London, Theatre Royal in Drury Lane, 10 March 1781;

The Baron Kinkvervankotsdorsprakingatchdern!, adapted from Elizabeth, baroness Craven's novel of the same name, London, Theatre Royal in the Hay-Market, 9 July 1781;

The Best Bidder, London, Theatre Royal in Drury Lane, 11 December 1782;

The Reparation, London, Theatre Royal, Drury Lane, 14 February 1784;

The Enchanted Castle, London, Theatre Royal, Covent Garden, 26 December 1786;

Better Late than Never, by Andrews and Frederick Reynolds, adapted from a play by Philippe Néricault Destouches, London, Theatre Royal, Drury Lane, 17 November 1790;

Mysteries of the Castle, by Andrews and Reynolds, London, Theatre Royal, Covent Garden, 31 January 1795.

BOOKS: *A new musical interlude. called the Election. As it is performed at the Theatre-Royal in Drury-Lane* (London: W. Griffin, 1774);

Songs, chorusses &c. in the comic opera of Belphegor; or, The Wishes. Now performing at the Theatre-royal, in Drury-Lane (London: Printed for T. Becket, 1778);

Songs, trios, duetts, and chorusses, in the comic opera of Summer amusement; or, An adventure at Margate. As it is performed at the Theatre-Royal in the Hay-market (London: T. Cadell, 1779);

Fire and Water! A comic opera: in two acts. Performed at the Theatre-Royal in the Hay-market (London: T. Cadell, 1780);

Songs, duetts, trios &c. &c. in the comic opera of Fire and water. Performed at the Theatre Royal (London: Printed for T. Cadell, 1780);

Dissipation. A comedy, in five acts; as it is performed at the Theatre-Royal, in Drury-Lane (London: Printed for T. Becket, 1781);

The Baron Kinkvervankotsdorsprakingatchdern. A new musical comedy. As performed at the Theatre-Royal in the Hay-market (London: T. Cadell, 1781);

Songs, Duets, Chorusses &c. in the Musical Comedy of the Baron (London: T. Cadell, 1781);

The Charming Captain. Sung by Mrs. Wrighten, in the Best Bidder [single sheet] (Salisbury: Fowler, 1782);

The reparation, a comedy. As performed at the Theatre-Royal in Drury-Lane (London: Printed for T. & W. Lowndes, 1784);

The songs, recitatives, airs, duets, trios, and chorusses, introduced in the pantomime entertainment, of the Enchanted castle, as performed at the Theatre-

Act 2d Scene 1st ——

Bluster, Swallow — (meeting)

Swallow —

Well Captain, what Sort of Entertainment have you met with, how did you fare with Maria? —

Bluster —

Dungeons and Death, is that a Question? am I not sure of Conquest — no less the Object of Love to the Fair, than of Terror to the Foe —

Swallow —

As you say, the Proof of the Pudding is in the eating — she has then consented to marry you? —

Bluster —

Quite the reverse — my Presence made so lively an Impression on her Heart that it had a visible Effect upon her Senses, and instead of saying yes which she meant to do, she continually answer'd No —

Swallow —

I too then must have made the same lively Impression upon Harriet, for she answer'd

Page from the playhouse copy of The Conjuror *submitted to the Examiner of Plays for licensing prior to the first performance, on 29 April 1774 (Larpent Collection, LA 372; by permission of the Henry E. Huntington Library and Art Gallery)*

Royal, Covent-Garden (London: Printed for the author, 1786);

Belphegor; or, The Wishes. A comic opera: as it is acted at the Theatre-Royal, Smoke-Alley (Dublin: Printed for the booksellers, 1788);

Better Late Than Never, a Comedy. In five acts. As performed at the Theatre-Royal in Drury-Lane (London: J. Ridgway, 1790);

The mysteries of the castle: A dramatic tale, in three acts. As performed at the Theatre-Royal, Covent-Garden (London: Printed by W. Woodfall for T. N. Longman, 1795);

Songs, duets, choruses, &c. in the Mysteries of the castle. A dramatic tale (London: T. Cadell, 1795).

OTHER: Edward Topham, ed., *The Poetry of the World*, 2 volumes, includes poems by Della Crusca (Robert Merry), Anna Matilda (Hannah Cowley), Arley (Andrews), and Benedict the Bard (Edward Jerningham) (London: Printed by J. Bell, 1788).

A misapprehension with which one may emerge from the perusal of a drama anthology is that the contributions of the finest playwrights of an age typify the nature and quality of the drama encountered by contemporary audiences. It is thus useful to be acquainted with the careers of minor figures such as Miles Peter Andrews, whose dramatic efforts better represent the typical theatrical fare offered his contemporaries. Andrews was a moderately successful eighteenth-century playwright, but his contributions are now familiar only to the most ardent and specialized historians of the drama. Though his pieces were generally well received by the audiences for whom they were written, Andrews's work has, justly, faded into obscurity. He attempted a variety of forms–full-length comedy, musical interludes and farces to accompany other plays, comic ballad operas, pantomime. Each is in its way pleasant, if superficial and predictable; each surely was enhanced by performance but is almost entirely of historical interest today.

The second son of an eminently successful, theater-loving Watling Street drysalter, Andrews was educated in Utrecht with the intention of his going into commerce and expanding the family business in Aleppo. When a close relative died in Turkey, however, Andrews's plans changed, and he returned to England. There, through his father, he became acquainted with some of the prominent members of theatrical circles, chief among them Samuel Foote and David Garrick. For Andrews, as for most playwrights of his and the previous age, play writing was for him but play. A successful, highly respected businessman, Andrews assumed control of the Dartford Powder Mills–his family's gunpowder manufacturing business in Kent–when his elder brother died. Although Andrews owned Bignore Manor in Dartford, he resided in London beside Green Park, in a mansion built by and purchased from Lord Grenville.

Andrews's concern with improving the manufacture of gunpowder reflected, perhaps, not mere commercial aspiration but a genuine desire to assist in the defense of his country, particularly against the turbulent and openly hostile French–certainly his plays celebrate such patriotic fervor. Andrews's interest in the military, which is reflected in several of his plays, is based on experience: he served as lieutenant-colonel commandant of the Prince of Wales's Volunteers. His involvement with public affairs was indeed long-standing: he was a well-known "paragrapher" to the morning papers. When he pursued his interest in government actively, he became as successful in the political as in the commercial arena: in 1790, he succeeded the late Lord Westcote as the single Member of Parliament representing Bewdley (in Worcestershire). Andrews was reelected without opposition for the same office in 1796, 1802, 1806, and 1807, thereby sitting five successive Parliaments. As an M.P., Andrews is best remembered for his patriotic speeches in 1797 in support of William Pitt's unpopular proposal for trebling taxes in order to prepare for war with France. No contemporary source suggests that Andrews was considered a gifted orator; thus, his continued reelection after taking an unpopular and what could be perceived as self-serving position indicates the extent of his constituency's confidence in his integrity.

Andrews's influence in both the theater and Parliament was, however, eclipsed by that he held in society. Throughout his life, he was considered unusually good company, and his frequent parties were extraordinarily popular in the fashionable world. The most oft-repeated story about his friendships concerns that with the dissolute Lord Thomas Lyttleton, whose behavior was so reprehensible that his own family would have nothing to do with him. Lyttleton's early death contributed in a curious way to Andrews's own renown. Lyttleton left Andrews two unexpected, significant legacies–a substantial financial bequest, and a memorable encounter which served as the basis for a widely repeated (and, Andrews insisted, entirely true) anecdote. Late at night, at the moment of Lyttleton's death, Andrews was awakened from a fevered sleep by the ghost of his friend, who said, "Andrews, 'tis all over with me."

Lord Lyttleton was not Andrews's only spirited acquaintance: through the theater he met Nancy Brown (later Mrs. Cargill), with whom he had an affair which, according to *A New Catalogue of Living English Authors* (1799), "made a considerable noise in the fashionable world, and was the subject of more than one enquiry [*sic*] at Bow-street." Mrs. Cargill, a "catholic admirer of the male-sex," as the *Catalogue* deems her, "was lost by the ship going to pieces, in which she was returning to India."

Andrews died at his house on Cleveland Row 18 July 1814. His death was sudden: he had just sent out two hundred invitations to view a display of–appropriately–fireworks.

Andrews's first contribution to the drama was a farce called *The Conjuror* (1774). It did not survive its first season and was never printed. His next offering, *The Election* (1774), was more successful. This one-act musical afterpiece continued to be offered occasionally through the 1787-1788 season. It was, however, less well received critically than popularly; the *Westminster Magazine,* for example, suggested "that if the writer was serious, he has been ridiculous: and if he meant to be jocose, he should have it upon some expedient to discover his intention." The thin plot of this patriotic piece centers on John, an honest man who resists pressure, especially from his wife, to sell his vote. The doggerel contains a surprisingly familiar phrase: "ev'ry Briton's song sho'd be / Or give me Death or Liberty."

Andrews then attempted another afterpiece, *Belphegor* (1778), a two-act comic opera. Based on Jean François Guichard's *Le Bucheron; ou les trois souhaits* (1763), *Belphegor* played a dozen times its opening season and was revived occasionally until its final appearance in 1789. Although the *Biographia Dramatica* states that only the songs were printed (thereby implying that a prose text once also existed), the 1788 Dublin edition presents a full story in song, complete with stage directions; it appears, then, that the songs alone constituted this afterpiece in its entirety.

Belphegor celebrates the simplicity of pastoral life. The impoverished sophisticate Belphegor is escaping his creditors when he encounters the rustic drunkard Booze. He convinces Booze that he is a good devil sent by Pluto to determine "whether the continual complaints of married men against their wives, were well founded" and grants Booze three wishes. Booze wastes his first wish calling up a pudding; he then wishes his carping wife, Dame Din, mute; at Belphegor's advice Booze uses his third wish to restore his wife's ability to speak. The piece closes with Dame Din and her husband happily reconciled to one another and to simple village life.

Summer Amusement (1779) is a three-act comic opera Andrews wrote in collaboration with William Augustus Miles, a political pamphleteer and playwright who was fired from his post in the Office of Ordnance. An immediate success, it was revived often for more than a decade, then occasionally until its final performance in 1795. Surprisingly, *Summer Amusement* was never published; only a nineteen-page edition of the music remains. We can get a sense of its flavor from some of the characters' names–Etiquette, Shuffle, Spruce, Sprat, Cathartic–and from the following lines from one of Etiquette's songs: "Neatest of pretty feet, for dancing intended / Accept of a partner who always was commended."

In the prologue to *Fire and Water* (1780), a two-act comic ballad opera, Andrews thanks George Colman (the Younger) for his contribution to the play's success; this is unintentionally ironic, as Colman deemed Andrews "one of the most persevering poetical pests" and said his plays were, "like his powder mills, particularly hazardous affairs, and in great danger of going off with sudden and violent explosion." Though it played thirteen times the year it opened, the play was never revived.

Fire and Water is set in Portsmouth, which is awaiting attack by the French. Nancy, who loves the patriot Fred, is pressured by her father, Launch, to marry the Frenchman Ambuscade, "a capering, strutting, impudent fencing master, always teizing [*sic*] one to death with scraps of old songs." Nancy suspects, rightly, that Ambuscade is only feigning interest in her to gain information about the royal dock for unscrupulous purposes. Amid many jokes at the expense of Catholics and Americans, a conspiracy is revealed: Sulphur (an experimenter with electricity), Firebrand (an arsonist), and the Jesuit priest San Benito plan to destroy the dockyard. When Fred catches these traitors setting fire to the storehouses, they expose Ambuscade as a collaborator. The piece ends with Launch's approving Nancy's engagement to Fred and with a call for American forces to help the British punish French and Spanish intrigues.

The formulaic characterization is familiar to

33

to offer you Something more worthy your Consideration

Sir Ted:

What's that you say? Ah–but I've engag'd my Vote.

Bam.

Well, Sir Tedious, before the day of Election comes on. You shall hear from me again–at present I will only have the Honour

Enter Inkhorn hastily with a Paper:

Ink.

Here it is Sir Tedious–here it is–the Proof Sheet of your Speech, and finely worded–I shall give it if you please to a Leader in Opposition.–

Sir Ted:

Well done, Mr. Punter–how active you are!–Hail Emulation Daughter of Dilligence, & nurse to Dispatch!–by thee the Scholar gets the Dictionary, and the Statesman foregoes his Nightcap–the Soldier is taught to Stomach a Bullet, and the Author the Difficulty of Bringing out a new Piece.

Ink.

very good, very moving indeed–will you please to Step into your Study, and Correct the press?

Bam.

Sir Tedious–Only one word if you please.

Sir Ted:

Sweet Sir, I have n't a word to spare–but must attend This Honourable Gentleman to correct the Press–So beg

Page from the playhouse copy of The Best Bidder submitted to the Examiner of Plays for licensing prior to the first performance, on 11 December 1782 (Larpent Collection, LA 607; by permission of the Henry E. Huntington Library and Art Gallery)

the readers of eighteenth-century exemplary comedy, with its idealized lovers and satirized fools. Ambuscade is a predictable fop, aside from his being a genuine (if humorous) menace to national security. Andrews's insistence upon anti-Catholicism as a basis for unity among Englishmen and for improved British-American relations is, however, unusual that late in the century. Also, throughout this piece, which opened two years prior to Andrews's initial election to Parliament, Andrews calls attention to the continuing (and now apparently imminent) threat posed by France. The play opens with Launch encouraging the workmen on the Portsmouth dock to sing while they work, for "a song, in my mind, makes labour easy *in spite of* mine *and his Majesty's enemies*." The First Workman responds, "So had it need, master Launch: for we have had enough of it: these cursed French Monsieurs find us constant employment." Launch assures all the workers that "the harder you are drove now, the faster we shall drive them by-and-by. . . . you are hereby insuring the defense of our country against mine and his *Majesty's enemies*." To Launch's warning that "if the French should come, they'll take your wives away from you," the Second Workman responds, "If that's the worst, there's no harm done; but damn 'em, I was afraid for my religion; I was afraid they would have taken away our religion and left us their own." Andrews uses San Benito (especially in conversations with Sulphur) as the focus for most of his criticism of Roman Catholicism. When, for example, San Benito asks, "hav'n't I made my sanctity the means of introducing me into families in order to betray their confidence," Sulphur responds, "What signifies your sanctity? it's not the fashion here–the appearance of it, indeed, was necessary among the saints at Boston–." Through Sulphur, some amusing metaphors based on fire and electricity also strengthen this play.

Dissipation, Andrews's first full-length comedy, played fourteen performances upon opening in 1781 but was performed only three times more before it vanished from the stage. It is based, in part, on David Garrick's *Bon Ton* (1775). In the preface Andrews remarks that "The great objection to this play has been the want of a plot . . . [but my] chief aim in writing was to draw a lively picture of the manners of high life, characterized by an easy indifference to the vicissitudes of fortune, and a kind of indolent acceptance of every fashionable enjoyment." Here, too, he reveals his dissatisfaction with theater manager Richard Brinsley Sheridan, who, Andrews complains, "has taken away several *witty* things from this comedy, which probably would have had a *striking* and *very violent* effect." Given the awkward intricacy of *Dissipation*'s plot, Sheridan's deletions were probably well advised.

The title refers primarily to Lord and Lady Rentless, whose neglect of public and private responsibilities jeopardizes the reputation and fortune of the virtuous lovers Charles Woodbine and Harriet Acorn. Lord Rentless, who has misappropriated Charles's money, neglects his duties in the House of Lords for gambling and wenching. He leaves his servant Coquin in charge of his business while he pursues the daughter of Alderman Uniform, Miss Maria Uniform, who shares her father's obsession with the military. Lord Rentless and his wife express contempt for "love and conjugal affection," attributing Harriet's espousal of these values to her rusticity. The source of their marital accord, they believe, is mutual indifference: as Lady Rentless explains, "We are always chearful [*sic*] when met, and happy when separate." The sincerity of their apathy becomes apparent when each is exposed to the other during a clandestine rendezvous, Lord Rentless with Miss Uniform, and Lady Rentless with Labradore, the Jewish pawnbroker.

Much havoc results from the Rentlesses' vice. Sir Andrew Acorn breaks off Harriet's match with Charles, whom he mistakenly considers a duplicitous fortune hunter, and Alderman Uniform wants to avenge his daughter's reputation by shooting Lord Rentless. Ultimately, Coquin and Judith, Labradore's daughter, announce they have taken all Labradore's securities and are married; Lord Rentless pacifies Alderman Uniform; Charles's reputation is cleared, and his bride and estate restored.

Although the Rentlesses are interesting figures, *Dissipation* is otherwise derivative and uninspired. Country folk like the Acorns, whose wisdom surpasses that of the city sophisticates, are commonplace in period comedy; the days of the glorification of the libertine are long past. Labradore is obviously modeled on Shylock; his cry "Oh, my papers! my bonds! my deeds!" unmistakably echoes Shylock's lament for his daughter and ducats. An unusual scene is Coquin's pretending to be an ailing rabbi during his courtship of Judith; here, as in *Fire and Water,* Andrews presents the religion of "outsiders" as a basis for scornful humor.

Andrews's next offering was his least successful–*The Baron Kinkvervankotsdorsprakingatch-*

James William Dodd, who played Mr. Flurry in the first production of Better Late than Never *(engraving by R. Laurie, based on a portrait by Robert Dighton)*

dern! (1781), a three-act comic opera based on a novel of the same name by Lady Elizabeth (Berkeley) Craven, who also wrote comedies and musical pieces. According to the 12 July 1781 *London Chronicle*, the play was badly received by the audience and withdrawn by Andrews's request after three performances. In his preface to the printed edition, Andrews complains that "having been charged with bringing on a polite Theatre many low and gross indecencies, many vulgar and improper allusions, justice, and not vanity, obliges him . . . to rescue himself from so ungentlemanlike a conduct." He also explains that the phrases and terms his audience found objectionable were simply ordinary Dutch usage.

Set in Göttingen, *The Baron* centers on the attempts of Franzl, a young Dutch soldier, to marry Cecil, the daughter of an impoverished but conceited German baron. From Lady Craven's novel comes the title figure, whose absurdly polysyllabic name is never mentioned in the course of the play; the Dutch characters are Andrews's innovations. Franzl's father, Mynheer Van Boterham, brings his family along when he collects the overdue mortgage on the baron's dilapidated castle, whose walls are covered with portraits of the baron's ancestors, about whom he speaks incessantly. Whereas the baron is obsessed with his genealogy, Franzl's father is (initially) overly concerned with wealth. Neither father approves the match between Cecil and Franzl: the baron wants Cecil to marry Captain Hogrestan, an old and ugly miles gloriosus; Mynheer Van Boterham wants Franzl to wed a monied merchant's daughter.

The baron's corrupt virtues are accentuated when his innocent daughter is accused of spending the night with Franzl: the baron is relieved rather than horrified to find the couple unmarried. After Cecil marries her wealthy and beloved Franzl, the baron declares he will never forgive her for having married beneath her and thereby injuring the dignity of the family name. The play concludes with the Van Boterhams welcoming Cecil as their daughter-in-law and discouraging her from attempting to pacify her foolish father.

Although Andrews's reliance on Dutch and German stereotypes can be criticized, it is not easy to find those "vulgar" and "improper" materials to which Andrews attributes the play's failure; the situation in which Cecil is placed is indeed indelicate, but neither the language nor the action is. (Perhaps the actors' pronunciation of the "Dutchisms" was suggestive.) *The Baron* probably failed because of its weak plot and generally unsympathetic characters. One of the better scenes is that in which Cecil climbs on a pile of portraits to escape Hogrestan; Andrews's use of family portraits as a running joke in this play draws upon Sheridan's comic use of ancestral portraits in *The School for Scandal* (1777). Unfortunately, the humor in *The Baron* is otherwise largely predictable and repetitious.

Andrews's next play was a two-act farce, *The Best Bidder* (1782). After eight performances, it disappeared; only a single song was printed. *The Reparation* (1784), a slightly more successful five-act sentimental comedy, lasted a total of fourteen performances. Loveless dissuades his friend Belcour from libertinism by confessing his own entrapment of a virtuous woman, Julia, in a false marriage; when later forced into a legitimate marriage, Loveless reveals his perfidy to Julia, who by then had borne him a child. Now a widower, Loveless wants to marry Julia, whom he truly loves but has been unable to find. In accordance with the laws of the God of Happy Coincidence who rules sentimental

William Thomas Lewis, who played Hilario in Mysteries of the Castle *(engraving by J. Corner, based on a portrait by M. Brown)*

comedy, Julia (who now calls herself "Louisa") is in the area Loveless is visiting. She has just been ejected from Sir Gregory Glovetop's home, having been the (unwilling) object of the indecorous attentions of Lord Hectic, a would-be libertine. When the reformed Loveless learns of Louisa's plight, he is unaware of her actual identity but attempts to help her and her son. Louisa, however, recognizes and avoids him, although she accepts his offer to support her child. (The child is, oddly, never referred to by any name.) Loveless recognizes Louisa when he rescues her from rape by Lord Hectic, but she refuses to trust him. She forgives him just as he is about to allow her father to kill him in a duel.

The detailed exposition of Loveless's past and Belcour's temptation is long-winded and heavy-handed. Like many sentimental comedies, *The Reparation* lacks humor, especially in its major characters, who often lapse into sententiousness; Louisa's opening line is typical of her speech: "How vain is the philosophy which books would preach up to us, to assuage the real anguish of the heart." As in *Dissipation,* libertinism is presented negatively. Louisa and Loveless are terribly sensitive and terribly sincere; the scenes with the child are apt to send modern readers into insulin shock. As in *Belphegor* and *Dissipation,* happiness is associated with the rejection of "sophisticated" values. The humor is provided by the obsessions of the minor characters–by Miss Penelope Zodiac, for example, a learned lady who only pretends indifference to men, and by Captain Swagger (a comic Irishman) and the irascible Colonel Quorum. As in *The Baron,* Andrews uses paintings as the basis for humor, with Hectic's pride in his portrait gallery not of ancestors but of women he has seduced.

Andrews's next effort, *The Enchanted Castle,* was a two-act pantomime; only the songs were published. This piece was one of Andrews's most successful, playing forty-six performances in the opening 1786-1787 season; the pantomime was not revived until 1796, when its last two performances were offered. In his preface Andrews credits as sources "the Writings of Miss Aikin, and the Hon. Horace Walpole" (referring to Anna Letitia Aikin [Barbauld]'s *The Fragment of Sir Bertrand* [1775] and Walpole's *The Castle of Otranto* [1765]). Here, Andrews also indicates that he has attempted some innovation with pantomime, which he does by drawing elements of plot and characterization from Milton's *Comus* (1637) and Shakespeare's *A Midsummer Night's Dream* (circa 1595) and *The Tempest* (1611). Among the characters are Harlequin, Columbine, a Necromancer, a Virgin abducted from India, the Genius of the Wood, Hymen, Neptune, magicians, giants, and attendant nymphs. One of the more bizarre elements is the singing of "Yankee Doodle," titled in the manuscript "American Ballad."

Andrews wrote *Better Late than Never* (1790), a five-act comedy, in collaboration with Frederick Reynolds, the author of more than two dozen plays. Based on Philippe Néricault Destouches's *Le Dissipateur; ou, l'honnête friponne* (1753), it played for only a handful of performances, then disappeared. The 18 November 1790 *Gazeteer* describes how after Francis Godolphin Osborne, duke of Leeds (to whose wife the play is dedicated), Major John Scott, Mr. John Julius Angerstein, and James Boswell attended a rehearsal, Boswell composed this verse: "Andrews, your play is safe enough; / For noble Leeds endures it; / Boswell and Scott are pledged to puff, / And Angerstein ensures it."

Saville, a rake and a gambler, despairs that because of his inability to control himself, he is about to lose his estate and his beloved Augusta. His friend, Sir Charles Chouse, however, helps

Augusta with her plot to save Saville from himself by gaining control of his estate. Augusta's wit makes her more akin to the heroines of "Restoration" comedy than other of Andrews's women. She first pretends to be a Hussar officer who loans Saville gambling money for which his estate is collateral. Later, she poses as a lawyer; hers is an unusual "breeches" part in that she dons, so to speak, two different pairs of breeches. Once she explains to Saville her reasons for deceiving him, he is delighted (and, apparently, reformed) by her cleverness, and they are once again to be married.

The Mr. and Mrs. Flurry subplot, which also concludes with a happy reformation, draws heavily upon the problems of Lord and Lady Teazle in Sheridan's *The School for Scandal.* Mrs. Flurry, a young wife eager to be in fashion and tired of her elderly husband, has been flirting with Sir Charles; they meet at the studio of the painter Pallet, from whom Sir Charles has ordered a full-length portrait of her. (Thus again, portraiture is used for comic purposes.) In the course of the play, Sir Charles and Mrs. Flurry are discovered behind a curtain in Pallet's studio by Mr. Flurry; but the lawyer Mr. Flurry hired to spy on his wife testifies that she repelled Sir Charles's overtures. As the main plot provides humor mainly through wit, the subplot employs humor of situation. Additional comic moments are provided by Diary, Augusta's servant; a compulsive reader, her conversation is replete with often apt allusions to famous plays and contemporary novels.

Andrews's last play was a three-act musical "dramatic tale," *Mysteries of the Castle* (1795), also written with Reynolds. This successful piece was mounted nineteen times the year it opened and was revived occasionally until 1800. *Mysteries of the Castle* is a strange mixture of Gothic romance and broad comedy. The settings, especially the castle, reflect the period's passion for the Gothic; consider, for example, this description of one set: "A picturesque view of ruins of ancient magnificence."

At her greedy father, Fractioso's, insistence, Julia had married the evil Count Montoni, who had convinced her that her beloved Carlos was already married. But when Julia discovered the count's falsehood and refused to consummate their marriage, the count secretly imprisoned her in an abandoned castle and informed her family she was dead. He now plans to murder her, should she not give in to his lust. Carlos, the serious-minded sentimental hero, has returned to avenge Julia's death, for which he blames the count; he is accompanied by his more lighthearted friend, Hilario, who is in love with Julia's sister, Constantia. After serious and humorous plots and counterplots, the count is exposed by his own agents, and both pairs of lovers are engaged with Fractioso's blessing.

The main plot is highly melodramatic. For example, wounded in a duel with the count and believing that he has lost Julia, Carlos wishes to die and carves his own epitaph; when she discovers it, Julia screams hysterically. We can see here a distinct shift in both masculine and feminine dramatic ideals from the century before: the lovers' lack of self-possession is presented positively, as testimony to true love. Wit is no longer requisite (or desirable) in the hero or heroine.

The humorous moments are provided by Hilario, whose dialogue is often quite witty. Farce is also employed as Hilario outwits Fractioso, whose avarice provides a locus for many jokes; like Labradore in *Dissipation,* Fractioso is more concerned with his ducats than with his daughters. Additional broad humor is provided by Annette (who is modeled on the Nurse in *Romeo and Juliet*) and Cloddy, the rustic.

Andrews's work may interest those studying the depiction of the military, or of religion, or of patriotism in English drama; or the use of humours characters during the eighteenth century; or the development of sentimental comedy, the pantomime, or the comic opera. Aesthetically considered, however, the authors of the *Biographia Dramatica* are not far from the truth in deeming Andrews's works "utterly deficient in point of force and splendour."

References:

David Erskine Baker, Isaac Reed, and Stephen Jones, *Biographia Dramatica; or, A Companion to the Playhouse,* second revision, 3 volumes (London: Longman, Hurst, Rees, Orme & Brown, 1812);

John Genest, *Some account of the English stage, from the Restoration in 1660 to 1830* (Bath: H. E. Carrington, 1832).

Papers:

The Larpent Collection at the Huntington Library includes manuscripts for three unpublished plays: *The Conjuror, The Best Bidder,* and *The Enchanted Castle* (listed as "The Castle of Wonders"). The collection also includes manuscripts for *The Election, Belphegor, Summer Amusement, Fire and Water, Dissipation, The Baron Kinkvervankotsdorsprakingatchdern!, The Reparation,* and *Better Late than Never.*

Isaac John Bickerstaff

(26 September 1733-circa 1808)

Valerie C. Rudolph
Purdue University

PLAY PRODUCTIONS: *Thomas and Sally*, London, Theatre Royal in Covent Garden, 28 November 1760;

Judith, London, Theatre Royal in Drury Lane, 27 February 1761;

Love in a Village, London, Theatre Royal in Covent Garden, 8 December 1762;

The Maid of the Mill, London, Theatre Royal in Covent Garden, 31 January 1765;

Daphne and Amintor, London, Theatre Royal in Drury Lane, 8 October 1765;

The Plain Dealer, London, Theatre Royal in Drury Lane, 7 December 1765;

Love in the City, London, Theatre Royal in Covent Garden, 21 February 1767; abridged as *The Romp*, Dublin, Crow-Street Theatre, 23 March 1774;

Lionel and Clarissa, London, Theatre Royal in Covent Garden, 25 February 1768; revised as *School for Fathers*, London, Theatre Royal in Drury Lane, 8 February 1770;

The Absent Man, London, Theatre Royal in Drury Lane, 21 March 1768;

The Padlock, London, Theatre Royal in Drury Lane, 3 October 1768;

The Royal Garland, A New Occasional Interlude in Honour of His Danish Majesty, London, Theatre Royal in Covent Garden, 10 October 1768;

The Hypocrite, London, Theatre Royal in Drury Lane, 17 November 1768;

The Ephesian Matron, London, Ranelagh House, 12 May 1769;

Dr. Last in His Chariot, London, Theatre Royal in the Hay-Market, 21 June 1769;

The Captive, London, Theatre Royal in the Hay-Market, 21 June 1769;

The Maid the Mistress (published as *He Wou'd if He Cou'd; or, An Old Fool Worse Than Any*), London, Ranelagh House, 28 May 1770;

The Recruiting Serjeant, London, Ranelagh House, 20 July 1770;

'Tis Well It's No Worse, London, Theatre Royal in Drury Lane, 24 November 1770;

The Sultan; or, A Peep into the Seraglio, London, Theatre Royal in Drury Lane, 12 December 1775;

The Spoil'd Child, Ulverstone, Ulverstone Theatre, 16 October 1787.

BOOKS: *Leucothoe. A dramatic poem* (London: R. & J. Dodsley, 1756);

Thomas and Sally; or, the sailors's return. A musical Entertainment. As it is performed at the Theatre-Royal in Covent-Garden. The music composed by Doctor Arne (London: Printed for G. Kearsley & J. Coote, 1761);

Judith. A sacred drama. As it is performed at the Theatre Royal in Drury-Lane. The music composed by Dr. Arne (London: Printed for J. Coote & T. Davies, 1761);

Love in a village; a comic opera. As it is performed at the Theatre Royal in Covent-Garden (London: Printed by W. Griffin for J. Newbery, 1763);

The maid of the mill. A comic opera. As it is performed at the Theatre Royal in Covent Garden. The music compiled, and the words written, by the author of Love in a village (London: Printed for J. Newbery, R. Baldwin, T. Caslon, W. Griffin, W. Nicoll, T. Lownds & T. Becket, 1765);

Daphne and Amintor. A comic opera, in one act, as it is performed at the Theatre Royal in Drury-Lane (London: Printed for J. Newbery, W. Griffin, W. Nicoll, and Becket & De Hondt, 1765);

The plain dealer. As it is performed at the Theatre Royal in Drury Lane. With alterations from Wycherly (London: Printed for W. Griffin, T. Lowndes, W. Nicoll, and Beckett & De Hondt, 1766);

Love in the City: a comic opera. As it is Performed at the Theatre Royal in Covent Garden. The Words Written, and the Music Compiled by the author of Love in a Village (London: Printed for W. Griffin, 1767); abridged as *The Romp. A Musical Entertainment. In Two Acts. Altered from Love*

Title-page illustration from a 1767 edition of Thomas and Sally

in the City, By Mr. Bickerstaff. As it has been acted at The Theatres Royal in Dublin and York, and now performed at the Theatre-Royal in Drury-Lane (London: Printed for W. Lowndes & J. Barker, 1786);

Lionel and Clarissa. A comic opera. As it is Performed at the Theatre-Royal in Covent-Garden (London: Printed for W. Griffin, 1748 [i.e., 1768]); revised as *A School for Fathers. A comic opera. As it is performed at the Theatre-Royal in Drury-Lane. A new edition* (London: Printed for W. Griffin, 1773);

The Absent Man: A farce. As it is acted by His Majesty's Servants, at the Theatre Royal in Drury-Lane (London: Printed for William Griffin, 1768);

The Padlock: a Comic Opera: As it is perform'd by His Majesty's Servants, at the Theatre-Royal in Drury-Lane (London: Printed for W. Griffin, 1768);

The Royal Garland, a new Occasional Interlude, in honour of his Danish Majesty. Set to Music by Mr. Arnold, and performed at the Theatre Royal, Covent-Garden (London: Printed for T. Becket & P. A. De Hondt, 1768);

The Hypocrite: A comedy. As it is performed at the Theatre Royal in Drury-Lane. Taken from Moliere and Cibber, by the Author of the alterations of the Plain-Dealer (London: Printed for W. Griffin, 1769);

The Ephesian Matron. A Comic Serenata, After the Manner of the Italian. As it is performed at the Ranelagh House. The Music by Mr. Dibdin (London: Printed for W. Griffin, 1769);

Doctor Last in His Chariot: A Comedy: As it is performed at the Theatre Royal in the Hay-Market (London: Printed for W. Griffin, 1769);

The Captive, a Comic Opera; As it is Perform'd at the Theatre-Royal in the Hay-Market (London: Printed for W. Griffin, 1769);

The Life, and Strange unparallel'd and unheard of Voyages and Adventures of Ambrose Gwinett, formerly well known to the public, as the Lame Beggar (London: Printed by J. Lever, 1770)–first published in *The Gentlemen's Journal*, 26 November 1768;

The Recruiting Serjeant, A Musical Entertainment As it is Perform'd at the Theatre-Royal in Drury-Lane (London: Printed for William Griffin, 1770);

'Tis Well it's no Worse: A comedy. As it is Performed at the Theatre Royal in Drury-Lane, by His Majesty's Servants (London: Printed for W. Griffin, 1770);

He Wou'd if He Cou'd; or, An Old Fool worse than Any: A burletta. As it is performed at the Theatre Royal in Drury-Lane. The Music by Mr. Dibdin (London: Printed for W. Griffin, 1771);

Proposals for Printing, by Subscription, Fables, Philosophical and Moral, In Verse (London: W. Griffin, 1771);

The Sultan, or a Peep into the Seraglio. A farce, in two acts. By Isaac Bickerstaffe [sic]. Acted at the Theatres Royal in Drury-Lane and Covent-Garden (London: Printed for C. Dilly, 1787);

Edward Shuter as Justice Woodcock, John Beard as Hawthorn, and John Dunstall as Hodge in act 1, scene 6, of the first production of Love in a Village *(painting by Johann Zoffany; by permission of the Victoria and Albert Museum)*

Ann Cargill as Rosetta with Charles Du Bellamy as Young Meadows (left) and Mary Ann Wrighten as Margery (right), roles they played together in the September 1780 Drury Lane production of Love in a Village

The Spoil'd Child; in two acts. As performed at the Theatre-Royal, Smoke-Alley (Dublin: Printed for the booksellers, 1792).

Collection: *The Plays of Isaac Bickerstaff*, edited by Peter A. Tasch, 3 volumes (New York & London: Garland, 1981).

OTHER: *Queen Mab* [a cantata], in *Shakespeare's Garland: Being a Collection of New Songs . . . Performed at the Jubilee* (London: T. Becket, 1769);

A Select Collection of Vocal Music, Serious and Comic with a Thorough Bass for the Harpsicord, edited by Bickerstaff (London: J. Johnston, 1771-1772?);

"The Brickdust-Man and Milk-Maid," *St. James Chronicle*, no. 1784, 25 July 1772; *The London Evening Post*, no. 6952, 25 July 1772.

Between John Gay and William Schwenk Gilbert, between *The Beggar's Opera* (1728) and *The Beefeater's Bride* (known as *The Yeoman of the Guard*, 1888), there was Isaac John Bickerstaff and his bevy of musical and dramatic entertainments. Popularizer, plagiarizer, and, as his biographer Peter A. Tasch calls him, "dramatic cobbler," Bickerstaff, in the span of a dozen years (1760-1772), not only revised and revived plays by Molière, Pedro Calderón de la Barca, William Wycherley, and many more, adapting them to the more "refined" sensibilities of his era, but also pumped new life into the flagging English opera. English ballad opera, the rage of the 1720s and 1730s, had set original English lyrics to popular English tunes. With the exception of *The Beggar's Opera*, this overused form had lost its freshness for theatergoers of Bickerstaff's day. Bickerstaff's solution was a novel blending of English words and Continental-style music. His resulting "comic operas" delighted London audiences more eager for entertainment than for edification. And Bickerstaff the playwright did not disappoint them.

Bickerstaff the man, however, did. Born in Dublin on 26 September 1733, the young Bickerstaff no doubt benefited from this cultured city's musical and theatrical offerings, which included both local and imported talent, for example, George Frideric Handel. Bickerstaff's father, John, supervised Dublin's bowling greens and tennis courts. When, as lord lieutenant of Ireland, Philip Dormer, lord Chesterfield abolished John Bickerstaff's office, he mitigated the loss by appointing young Bickerstaff as one of his pages. When he was only twelve, Bickerstaff received an army commission, and he held the rank of second lieutenant for ten years. A small inheritance enabled him to resign his commission, receive half-pay, and remove himself to London to try his fortune in the theater. His first work, the dramatic poem *Leucothoe* (1756), failed to be produced, and financial necessity soon compelled Bickerstaff to enlist in the marines. During his five years in the marines, he wrote the comic opera *Thomas and Sally* (1760) and the oratorio *Judith* (1761). The success of *Love in a Village* (1762) enabled Bickerstaff to resign his marine commission and devote his talents exclusively to the theater. With one exception (*Love in the City,* 1767), his unerring sense of what would stage well kept Bickerstaff's entertainments lively and likable.

After more than a decade of success, Bickerstaff's future seemed assured. In 1772, however, scandal cut short that future. Accused of homosexuality, Bickerstaff fled to France to escape the death penalty. A letter to David Garrick from Bickerstaff indicates that he was living in poverty. Finally, he seems to have disappeared. Conflicting contemporary reports allege that Bickerstaff was living either in France, in Italy, or in England under an assumed name. The year of his death is unknown, but Bickerstaff seems to have been alive as late as 1808, the year payment of his military pension ceased. Though Bickerstaff himself disappeared, many of his entertainments held the stage well into the nineteenth century, and some have even enjoyed brief revivals in the twentieth.

Bickerstaff's chief composers were Thomas Arne and Charles Dibdin, the latter also playing the renowned role of Mungo, the black servant, in *The Padlock* (1768). Bickerstaff himself downplayed the importance of his librettos and elevated the importance of the music, which he insisted should develop plot and reflect character, instead of being a gracious, but gratuitous, insertion into the action. Most of Bickerstaff's works are sentimental. Characters who are basically good triumph over all obstacles, especially those confronting young lovers whose guardians insist on their marrying someone inappropriate. Restoration bawdiness is either tamed or banished. Intrigues are intended, but with the exception of Bickerstaff's version (1765) of Wycherley's *Plain Dealer* (1676), little happens to challenge conventional morality. When Bickerstaff began writing for the stage, the theaters were offering only a handful of musical entertainments per season and almost none of the older comedies. When Bickerstaff quit writing for the stage, however, he had already established that

Charles Dibdin as Ralph in the first production of The Maid in the Mill

Sophia Baddeley as Clarissa and William Parsons as Lionel in the first production of School for Fathers, *Bickerstaff's revised version of his* Lionel and Clarissa

no theatrical season could be successful without offering a substantial number of the kinds of works he wrote.

A brief "musical entertainment," *Thomas and Sally*, first brought Bickerstaff the acclaim of London audiences. It opened at Covent Garden on 28 November 1760. Bickerstaff claimed that his text existed chiefly for the purpose of Arne's music. This two-act entertainment resembles a nineteenth-century melodrama. The virtuous Sally, a country lass pining for her beloved Thomas, who is away at sea, is accosted by the local squire, who first tries flattery, then force, to have his way with her. Thomas returns just in time; the squire is driven off; and the happy couple is united. Clichés, both structural and verbal, abound. Vice is equated with riches; virtue with poverty. Fortune is changeable; love remains. Thomas uses nautical language, such as referring to the squire as a "pirate." Lines like "I'd work my fingers to the bone" trivialize the dialogue. Patriotic songs glorify England, and Thomas's concluding observation is that British patriotism will be rewarded by British women.

Judith, Bickerstaff's first oratorio, celebrates a different kind of patriotism. Judith, the biblical heroine, rescues her people from destruction by ingratiating herself with the enemy general Holofernes and then cutting off his head while he sleeps. Bickerstaff truncates the biblical plot, omitting Judith's prayers and preparations, her escape from Holofernes's camp, and her determination to remain a widow. Instead, he emphasizes her courage and her chastity while in Holofernes's camp. *Judith* opened at Drury Lane 27 February 1761, with music composed by Arne.

By the end of the following year, *Love in a Village* had established Bickerstaff on the London stage. This most popular of Bickerstaff's works appeared at Covent Garden on 8 December 1762. In his dedication to John Beard, who acted the sensible, country-loving Hawthorn, Bickerstaff asserts that his comic opera has little dramatic merit, but "tolerable" songs. Part ballad opera and part new music, *Love in a Village* includes a list of sixteen different composers at the end of the printed text, including, of course, Arne. In the advertisement following the dedication, Bickerstaff admits some slight indebtedness to Charles Johnson's *The Village Opera* (1729). Critics, however, charged that Bickerstaff had borrowed substantially from Johnson, and his masterpiece never did escape the taint of plagiarism.

In *Love in a Village* the course of true love takes many twists and turns before it runs smoothly. There are two pairs of lovers to be united: Lucinda and Eustace; Rosetta and Young Meadows. The former plan to elope; the latter, disguised as a maid and a gardener, imagine social-class differences that prevent their love. Despite Lucinda's quick wit and her presentation of Eustace to her father as her music master (a hint borrowed from Wycherley's *The Gentleman Dancing Master*, 1672), the elopement is thwarted, but the couple is eventually united anyway. Rosetta and Young Meadows discover that the arranged marriages each sought to escape were really to one another, thus removing class barriers to their union. Nevertheless, even the apples of a pastoral paradise must have an occasional worm, and not to be wed are the rustic Hodge and his cast-off mistress, Margery, who finally leaves the countryside for London and a life of prostitution.

Bickerstaff loved symmetry, especially balancing pairs of characters. While *Love in a Village* has three pairs of lovers, it also pairs Justice Woodcock, the country squire, with Hawthorn as appreciators of country life; Woodcock and Sir William Meadows as fathers concerned with arranged marriages; and Woodcock and his sister Deborah as adversaries in the courtship of Eustace and Lucinda. Perhaps the most unusual part of the work, though, is the hiring fair that concludes the first act. Servants go to the fair to find work, and the finale is a "Servants Medley" with songs by a house-maid, a cook-maid, a footman, and a carter, as well as a concluding servants' chorus.

The overwhelming popularity of *Love in a Village* led Bickerstaff to venture into comic opera again, and his *Maid of the Mill* premiered at Covent Garden on 31 January 1765. In his dedication to William, duke of Gloucester, Bickerstaff argued that comic opera ought not to compete with tragedies and comedies but instead provide "occasional relief" from them. Indeed, comic opera can be enjoyed without impugning either the good taste or the good sense of its audience.

The Maid of the Mill is an adaptation of Samuel Richardson's novel *Pamela* (1740). In Richardson's work Pamela, a servant girl, is pursued by her employer, Squire B----. Despite many trials, Pamela preserves her virtue, and Squire B---- finally marries her. In Bickerstaff's opera, Patty, a miller's daughter (Pamela), has been educated above her station by the late Lady Aimworth. Lord Aimworth, her son (Squire B----), is in love with Patty but engaged to marry Theodosia, a fortune. Patty, in turn, is engaged to Farmer Giles (Parson

Charles Dibdin as Mungo in the first production of The Padlock

Williams). Theodosia is in love with Mr. Mervin. The proper lovers are united at the conclusion, and barriers of social class and parental tyranny are transcended by humility, good sense, and wit. Theodosia is the most spirited character; Patty the most passive. Together they show that both action and patience are necessary in the love game. Farmer Giles, who believes gossip about Patty's relationship to Lord Aimworth, acts impatiently, and loses both Patty and her father's estate.

The success of *The Maid of the Mill* won Bickerstaff a contract with Covent Garden. He was to write three more comic operas, attend rehearsals of the same, and assist with their staging. Furthermore, he was to write for no other theater for five years, except by special license. He was to receive the profits from the third, sixth, and ninth nights' performances.

Despite this contract, when the great actor-manager David Garrick opened the new Drury Lane season, the second work he produced was Bickerstaff 's brief comic opera *Daphne and Amintor* (8 October 1765). Adapted from German François Poullain de St. Foix's *L'Oracle* (1740), Bickerstaff 's story is subordinated to his staging. Mindora, a magician, has educated the young princess Daphne to believe that no other intelligent, sentient beings exist in their world. According to an oracle, Mindora's son Amintor will suffer unnamed misfortunes if he does not receive the love of a princess who believes he is "deaf, dumb, and insensible." Mindora tricks Daphne into loving Amintor, thereby invalidating the oracle. The setting is a garden with statues, who at Mindora's bidding descend from their pedestals and dance. At a wave of Mindora's wand, this scene is transformed into that of an elaborate palace also filled with singers and dancers who entertain at the concluding feast. The music was mainly Italian, earning Bickerstaff disfavor with critics who preferred English tunes. Indeed, Bickerstaff 's preface to the printed text did not help his cause since he remarked that English and Scottish ballads "scarce deserve the name of music." Instead Bickerstaff advocated music that supported "action and character."

"Action and character" without music were Bickerstaff 's choices for his next work, *The Plain Dealer*, which opened at Garrick's Drury Lane

Thomas King as Dr. Cantwell and Frances Abington as Charlotte in the first production of The Hypocrite

theater on 7 December 1765. An adaptation of Wycherley's 1676 play, *The Plain Dealer* (itself an adaptation of Molière's *Le Misanthrope*, 1666), Bickerstaff's version catered to an audience that objected to the immorality of Restoration comedy. Without really removing immoral action, Bickerstaff had his characters talk properly about improprieties. For example, men do not talk of "ravishing" women as in Wycherley's play but, instead of being "rude" to them, though, as Bickerstaff's context makes clear, with the same intention. In the printed version Bickerstaff used inverted commas before each line of dialogue that was his and not Wycherley's, but his acknowledgments are not always exact.

Captain Manly, who scorns all forms of dishonesty, especially the social lie, trusts only one other person, Olivia. Engaged to her, he leaves money with her before going to battle at sea. By the time he returns Olivia has secretly married his best friend, Vernish, and the two plot how to get rid of Manly and keep his money. Fidelia, in love with Manly, follows him disguised as a man. In the end Manly is sexually and financially revenged on Olivia and Vernish and gives his heart to the undisguised Fidelia. At the same time, he learns to moderate his extreme demands for "plain dealing."

Bickerstaff also condensed Wycherley's subplot about the litigious Widow Blackacre, her son Jerry, and Manly's friend Freeman, who is the true "plain dealer" in the play. Honest with Manly, yet able to tolerate the social lie for its utility, Freeman is the voice of reason and moderation. He rules his passions while the other characters' passions rule them. His reward is to get an estate without the encumbrance of a wife.

In *The Plain Dealer* Bickerstaff so well understood his audience that the play was a fixture in the repertory until the end of the century. However, in his next comic opera, *Love in the City* (21 February 1767), he badly misjudged the sentiments of one important segment of his audience–the middle-class merchants. They did not appreciate Bickerstaff 's satire, and the piece failed despite a lively plot and charming music.

Priscilla Tomboy is the opera's most memorable character. She is very much her own woman, speaks her own mind, and chooses her own marriage partner, Captain Sightly. However, there is a major negative aspect to her character. Priscilla, raised in Jamaica, comes to London with her black woman slave, Quashaba, whom she treats abominably. She talks of flaying Quashaba, observing that she would probably not feel it because she is subhuman. (Bickerstaff comments more sympathetically on the plight of blacks in *The Padlock.*)

The family of the Cockneys, who are grocers, are satirized for their upstart ambitions. Their desire to marry Penelope, the daughter, to a lord allows Penelope to present her lover, a young mercer, in that guise and secure the marriage. Even Penelope's uncle, the wealthy merchant Barnacle, marries Miss La Blond, the hatter jilted by the social-climbing Young Cockney, in order to keep the Cockneys from inheriting his money. Thus, as in most of Bickerstaff 's previous works, love triumphs, but not without trickery.

In his preface Bickerstaff acknowledges the "absurdity" of "Musical Drama," but he also asserts that the mind easily "accommodate[s]" itself to the necessities of theatrical illusion with pleasurable results. Although the audience may have accommodated itself to the illusion, it did not accommodate itself to the underlying reality it depicted, and the only way this opera could keep the stage was in a shortened form as *The Romp* (1774).

Bickerstaff 's new comic opera, *Lionel and Clarissa,* debuted in the midst of a contractual controversy. George Colman, the manager of Covent Garden, held Bickerstaff 's contract to write exclusively for his theater until 1770. Bickerstaff, on the other hand, wanted to write for Drury Lane, managed by David Garrick. Colman, however, held Bickerstaff to his contract, and Bickerstaff, in turn, blamed Colman's slipshod production for *Lionel and Clarissa*'s lack of success. It opened at Covent Garden on 25 February 1768. Two years later (8 February 1770), Bickerstaff revised it and transferred it to Drury Lane under the new title *School for Fathers.*

Again, Bickerstaff uses two pairs of lovers and a threatened elopement. The madcap Diana Oldboy almost elopes with Mr. Harman, but instead returns to her father to seek a more conventional resolution to her romantic dilemma. Clarissa Flowerdale, her friend, loves beneath her station–the object of her affection being Lionel, her tutor. Finally her father comes to see Lionel's merit, and the couple is engaged. The most novel character in the work is Colonel Oldboy's son Mr. Jessamy; schooled in nothing but foppish affectation, he arrogantly woos Clarissa, expecting her to rejoice at the honor of being his bride. The finale leaves him self-absorbed and unwed.

In *The Absent Man* Bickerstaff successfully tried his hand at farce. The work was presented at Drury Lane on 21 March 1768. Pure entertainment, it focuses on the character of the absent-minded Mr. Shatterbrain. Flavia, his fiancée, and her lover, Mr. Welldon, take advantage of Shatterbrain's weakness, deceive the clergyman sent to marry Shatterbrain to Flavia, and marry one another instead. The good-natured Shatterbrain forgives. Then addressing the audience directly, he starts to talk about the meaning of the farce, but four lines later admits that he has forgotten it. The audience is free to clap or hiss but not to analyze.

Returning to comic opera at Drury Lane with *The Padlock* (3 October 1768), Bickerstaff borrowed his plot from Miguel de Cervantes's exemplary novel *El celoso extremeño* (1613). The aging Don Diego, eager to marry the young Leonora, padlocks her in his house while he goes to make wedding arrangements. The young Leander gets into the house anyway and wins Leonora's affections. A repentant Don Diego, realizing his foolishness, blesses the young couple and orders all the locks and bars removed from the house. Love, he learns, cannot be coerced, only given.

The character of Mungo, the black servant, gave the opera its tremendous popularity. Played in blackface by Charles Dibdin, one of Bickerstaff 's chief musical collaborators, Mungo reflects on the harsh lot of slaves but nevertheless maintains his dignity and his wit. The black actor Ira Aldridge kept Mungo and *The Padlock* on the stage into the second quarter of the nineteenth century.

On 10 October 1768 at Covent Garden, Bickerstaff presented entertainment fit for a king. *The Royal Garland,* a pastoral interlude with music by Samuel Arnold, was offered before the visiting king of Denmark. Shepherds and shepherdesses, Calliope and the Genius of England, praise both the pastoral life and the virtues of the Danish mon-

Frances Abington as Roxalana in the first production of The Sultan

arch. This purely occasional piece concludes with a garland dance.

The following month at Drury Lane, *The Hypocrite*, one of Bickerstaff 's most popular adaptations of Molière, opened on 17 November 1768. Based on Molière's *Tartuffe* (1664), as adapted by Colley Cibber in *The Non-Juror* (1717), Bickerstaff 's version enjoyed almost a century of popularity. Dr. Cantwell is the religious hypocrite–a villainous con artist with designs on the fortune and wife of Sir John Lambert. Sir John's piety leads him to disinherit his son, to sign over his estate to Cantwell, and to try to force his daughter to marry the hypocrite. Cantwell is finally exposed, and all ends well. Unlike in Molière's play, no king intervenes to bring about justice, though Cantwell is eventually turned over to the law. Bickerstaff 's original contribution to the Molière-Cibber plot is the character of Mr. Maw-worm, a religious enthusiast, who continues to support Cantwell even after he is unmasked, attributing all the accusations against him to the work of the devil. Excess of anything, even of religion, needs to be subjected to reason and moderation–the point of the comedy.

It is also the point of *The Ephesian Matron*, the serenata (dramatic cantata) Bickerstaff presented on 12 May 1769 at Ranelagh House, one of the London pleasure gardens. The matron refuses to leave the tomb of her recently deceased husband, vowing to die there herself. Pleas from her father and her maid avail nothing. A kindly centurion also reasons with her and in so doing wins her heart. The centurion has been guarding the body of a hanged criminal, and the body is stolen while he is consoling the matron. To save her new lover from being hanged, the matron insists that he substitute her husband's body for that of the criminal.

As the wedding date is being set, the matron protests that she must observe a decent time of mourning–at least a year. However, she not unwillingly settles at last for one day, and the piece ends with some adverse reflections on female constancy. *The Ephesian Matron* was quite successful, being produced both at the Haymarket on 31 August 1769 and at Drury Lane on 8 May 1771.

The Haymarket was managed by Samuel Foote, whose comedy *The Devil on Two Sticks* (1768) had featured the character of Dr. Last. To supply Foote with a sequel, Bickerstaff once again adapted Molière, this time *The Imaginary Invalid* (1673). *Dr. Last in His Chariot* opened at the Haymarket on 21 June 1769. Garrick's prologue was spoken by Foote himself. The imaginary invalid is Mr. Ailwou'd; the chief quack is Dr. Last with his mysterious pills and potions; and the chief deceiver is Mrs. Ailwou'd, who pretends to love her husband but who really loves only his money. All are finally exposed and depart, except for Ailwou'd himself. Slightly chastened but not totally reformed, he consents to the marriage of his honest daughter Nancy to the equally honest Mr. Hargrave. The joke was on Bickerstaff, however, for even Foote's acting could not insure the success of *Dr. Last in His Chariot.* Despite the hijinks of such scenes as that of an entire roomful of quacks attempting to diagnose Ailwou'd's illness, the comedy had relatively few performances.

As an afterpiece to *Dr. Last in His Chariot,* Bickerstaff presented a "singing farce," *The Captive.* Adapted from a comic subplot in John Dryden's *Don Sebastian* (1689), the work subordinates politics to passion. Ferdinand, a Christian slave, is in love with a Muslim princess. The princess's mother, however, is in love with Ferdinand, and the princess's father is in love with shady dealing. The latter almost costs everyone's life, but all escape and Ferdinand wins his bride. The plot is trite and the characters insipid, but five songs by Dibdin compensated somewhat for these deficiencies.

The following year (28 May 1770), Bickerstaff returned to Ranelagh House with another serenata, *The Maid the Mistress* (subsequently printed as *He Wou'd if He Cou'd; or, An Old Fool worse than Any,* 1771). Betty, the maid, prevents her employer, Mr. Goosecap, from marrying a rich widow. Instead he marries Betty. This slight piece has little to recommend it, and contemporary audiences agreed.

Two months later (20 July 1770) Bickerstaff was again at Ranelagh House with another serenata, *The Recruiting Serjeant.* A recruiting sergeant extols the pleasures of war to a rural lad, who almost enlists but thinks better of it at the last minute and does not sign up. Despite the work's patriotism (it ends with toasts to the king and queen and praise of the military), parts of it resemble a Brechtian antiwar satire, especially the recruiting sergeant's enthusiastic description of battlefield slaughter. *The Recruiting Serjeant* was well received and maintained its popularity into the nineteenth century. It was presented in Boston (1799) and in New York (1800) with similar success.

Bickerstaff's last full-length play staged before he went into exile was the Spanish intrigue comedy *'Tis Well It's No Worse.* This adaptation of Calderón's *El escondido y la tapada* opened at Drury Lane on 24 November 1770. Two pairs of lovers, Don Pedro and Aurora, and Don Ferdinand and Marcella, have their unions impeded by duels and codes of honor. Most of the action takes place in Aurora's house, where a secret panel hides Don Pedro and provides for ludicrous comings and goings, with characters often disguised. A night scene was obligatory in intrigue comedy, and the "mistakes of a night" further complicate the plot. Finally all is clarified and resolved, and the right couples are paired. The play's reception, however, was mixed. It was not often produced until 1788 when John Kemble shortened the comedy and presented it as *The Pannel.*

Only two new works by Bickerstaff were staged after he fled England. *The Sultan; or, A Peep into the Seraglio* was presented at Drury Lane on 12 December 1775. This slight piece focuses on a captured English beauty, Roxalana, whose wit and spirit dethrone the sultan's empress and lead to her ruling over the sultan himself. Roxalana is simply Priscilla Tomboy in harem clothes. The role was a favorite for Mrs. Frances Abington and a succession of actresses. In 1794 *The Sultan* was performed in New York as *The American Captive.*

The Spoil'd Child, which opened at the Ulverstone Theatre on 16 October 1787, was attributed to Bickerstaff, though the author is not really known. The work is memorable chiefly for the role of the title character, Little Pickle, who exasperates every other character, even going so far as to bake his aunt's favorite parrot and serve it to her for dinner. Little Pickle is the kind of child W. C. Fields loved to hate. Actresses, however, loved Little Pickle, and the role was much sought after throughout the nineteenth century.

The abrupt ending to Bickerstaff's career forestalls speculation about whatever new direc-

but let's have nomore of this.

Roxalana.

Oh if it offends you (respectfully) I should be sorry to offend you.

Solyman.

You may easily avoid it then.

Roxalana.

Yes, but I like to speak the truth, and do you know why you don't like to hear it, because your Ears have not been accus=tom'd to it.

Solyman.

But why won't you consider who I am, and who you are:?

Roxalana.

Who I am, and who you are! Why you are the Grand Signior, and I am —— ~~a pretty Woman, and the difference be=tween us is very well made up~~ An

Page from the playhouse copy of The Sultan *submitted to the Examiner of Plays for licensing prior to the first performance, on 12 December 1775 (Larpent Collection, LA 397; by permission of the Henry E. Huntington Library and Art Gallery)*

tions the late eighteenth-century theater might have taken had it had the services of his considerable talents. Would he have experimented with other musical forms? Would he have returned more older plays to the repertory albeit in altered form? Bickerstaff was certainly not a major playwright. He was, however, a competent artist whose works entertained the audience of his day and would, for the most part, do likewise in our own.

Biography:

Peter A. Tasch, *The Dramatic Cobbler: The Life and Works of Isaac Bickerstaff* (Lewisburg, Pa.: Bucknell University Press, 1971).

References:

René Guiet, "An English Imitator of Favart: Isaac Bickerstaffe," *Modern Language Notes*, 38 (January 1923): 54-56;

Ethel Macmillan, "The Plays of Isaac Bickerstaffe in America," *Philological Quarterly*, 5 (January 1926): 58-69;

Howard H. Russell, "The Five Chief Works of Isaac Bickerstaffe," Ph.D. dissertation, University of North Dakota, 1939;

Peter A. Tasch, "Garrick's Revision of Bickerstaff's *The Sultan*," *Philological Quarterly*, 50 (January 1971): 141-149.

Papers: The Larpent Collection at the Huntington Library includes manuscript copies of the following plays submitted to the Examiner of Plays, for licensing: *Judith* (no. 187), alterations and additions to *The Plain Dealer* (no. 250), *Lionel and Clarissa* (no. 278), *The Absent Man* (no. 280), *The Padlock* (no. 285), "An Occasional Interlude" (*The Royal Garland*, no. 286), *'Tis Well It's No Worse* (no. 312), *The Sultan* (no. 397), and *The Spoilt Child* (no. 862). The Houghton Library, Harvard University, has an undated letter from Bickerstaff to George Colman and a 14 July 1768 letter from Bickerstaff to David Garrick.

James Boaden

(23 May 1762-16 February 1839)

Temple J. Maynard
Simon Fraser University

PLAY PRODUCTIONS: *Ozmyn and Daraxa,* London, King's Theatre, 7 March 1793;

Fontainville Forest, London, Theatre Royal, Covent Garden, 25 March 1794;

The Secret Tribunal, London, Theatre Royal, Covent Garden, 3 June 1795;

The Italian Monk, London, Theatre Royal in the Hay-Market, 15 August 1797;

Cambro-Britons, London, Theatre Royal in the Hay-Market, 21 July 1798;

Aurelio and Miranda, London, Theatre Royal, Drury Lane, 29 December 1798;

The Voice of Nature, Boaden's translation of *Le Jugement de Salomon: Mélodrame en Trois Actes, Mêlé de Chants et de Danse* (1802), by Louis Charles Caigniez, London, Theatre Royal in the Hay-Market, 31 July 1802;

The Maid of Bristol, London, Theatre Royal in the Hay-Market, 24 August 1803.

BOOKS: *Songs and Chorusses, in Ozmyn & Daraxa. A Musical Romance, in Two Acts. First Performed at the King's Theatre, Hay-Market, on Thursday, March 7th, 1793* (London: Printed by C. Lowndes, 1793);

Fontainville Forest, A Play, in Five Acts, (Founded on the Romance of the Forest,) as performed at the **Theatre-Royal, Covent-Garden** (London: Printed for Hookham & Carpenter, 1794);

The Secret Tribunal: A Play. in Five Acts. By James Boaden, Author of Fontainville Forest, as performed at the Theatre-Royal, Covent-Garden (London: Printed by G. Woodfall for T. N. Longman, 1795);

A Letter to George Steevens, Esq. Containing a Critical Examination of the Papers of Shakespeare; Published by Mr. Samuel Ireland. To Which Are Added, Extracts From Vortigern (London: Printed for Martin & Bain, 1796);

The Italian Monk, A Play, in Three Acts; Written by James Boaden, Esq.; and first performed at the Theatre Royal, Haymarket, on Tuesday, Aug. 15, 1797 (London: Printed for G. G. & J. Robinson, 1797);

Cambro-Britons, An Historical Play, in Three Acts. First Performed at the Theatre Royal, Haymarket, on Saturday, July 21, 1798 (London: Printed for G. G. & J. Robinson, 1798);

Aurelio and Miranda: A Drama. in Five Acts. With Music. First Acted at the Theatre Royal, Drury-Lane, on Saturday, December 29, 1798 (London: Printed for J. Bell, 1799);

A Rainy Day, Or Poetical Impressions During a Stay at Brighthelmstone, In the Month of July 1801 (London: Printed for T. Egerton by C. Roworth, 1801);

The Voice of Nature: A Play, in Three Acts. As Performed at the Theatre Royal, Haymarket, Boaden's translation of *Le Jugement de Salomon: Mélodrame en Trois Actes, Mêlé de Chants et de Danse,* by Louis Charles Caigniez (London: Printed for James Ridgway, 1803);

The Maid of Bristol, A Play, in Three Acts. As Performed at the Theatre Royal in the Haymarket (London: Printed for Longman & Rees, 1803);

An Inquiry Into the Authenticity of Various Pictures and Prints, Which From the Decease of the Poet to Our Own Times Have Been Offered to the Public as Portraits of Shakespeare: Containing a Careful Examination of the Evidence on Which They Claim to be Received; By Which the Pretended Portraits Have Been Rejected, the Genuine Confirmed and Established, Illustrated by Accurate and Finished Engravings, By the Ablest Artists, From Such Originals as Were of Indisputable Authority (London: Printed for Robert Triphook, 1824);

Memoirs of the Life of John Philip Kemble, Esq., Including a History of the Stage, From the Time of Garrick to the Present Period, 2 volumes (London: Printed for Longman, Hurst, Rees, Orme, Brown & Green, 1825);

Memoirs of Mrs. Siddons. Interspersed With Anecdotes of Authors and Actors, 2 volumes (London:

James Boaden (mezzotint by Bell based on a portrait by Opie; courtesy of the National Portrait Gallery, London)

Henry Colburn, 1827);

The Man of Two Lives. A Narrative Written by Himself (London: Henry Colburn, 1828);

The Life of Mrs. Jordan; Including Original Private Correspondence and Numerous Anecdotes of Her Contemporaries, 2 volumes (London: Edward Bull, 1831);

Memoirs of Mrs. Inchbald: Including Her Familiar Correspondence With the Most Distinguished Persons of Her Time. To Which Are Added The Massacre, *and* A Case of Conscience; *Now First Published From Her Autograph Copies,* 2 volumes (London: Richard Bentley, 1833);

The Doom of Giallo; Or, The Vision of Judgment, 2 volumes (London: John Macrone, 1835);

On The Sonnets of Shakespeare. Identifying the Person to Whom They Are Addressed; and Elucidating Several Points in the Poet's History (London: Thomas Rodd, 1837)–an expanded version of two articles Boaden wrote for *Gentleman's Magazine* (September 1832): 217-221; (October 1832): 308-314; (November 1832): 407.

Collection: *The Plays of James Boaden,* edited by Steven Cohan (New York & London: Garland, 1980).

OTHER: *The Oracle; or, Bell's New World* [daily newspaper], edited, with contributions, by Boaden, 1789-1798 or later;

The Private Correspondence of David Garrick With the Most Celebrated Persons of His Time; Now First Published From the Originals, and Illustrated With Notes. And a New Biographical Memoir of Garrick, 2 volumes, edited, with a memoir, by Boaden (London: Henry Colburn & Richard Bentley, 1831, 1832).

James Boaden's lifelong fascination with the theater found its outlet in theatrical criticism, the writing of plays, and in the biography of actors and actresses. His contemporaries valued him for his pamphlets on Shakespeare and for his popular dramas. Boaden's theatrical biographies, produced later in his life, are perhaps his most significant contribution for us today. His plays exploited the current vogue for Gothicism and melodrama, and several of them had a considerable success, in part because of the capable performances of John Philip Kemble, Sarah Siddons, and Dorothy Jordan. However, Boaden was sensitive to the necessities of dramatic presentation, and his manipulation of stage effects certainly contributed to the enthusiastic reception of his plays.

James Boaden was born at White Haven in Cumberland on 23 May 1762, son of William Boaden, a merchant in the Russian trade, but the family moved to London while he was still a child. His early training in a countinghouse was designed to fit him for a merchant's career, but his inclination was for journalism and the theater. In the introduction to his *Memoirs of the Life of John Philip Kemble* (1825) Boaden confesses: "In the almost childish season of life, I imbibed that fondness for the stage, which, shall I say, *compelled* me to attend to it with constancy and passion;–it constituted my *sole* amusement and principal *expense*–I studied, as though I had been to make it a profession." In 1789 Boaden became editor for the *Oracle; Or, Bell's New World,* a daily newspaper reporting military intelligence, news of the royal family, real estate, stocks, sales by auction, births, marriages, deaths, and elopements, as well as art news. In the *Oracle,* under the pseudonym of Thespis, he offered dramatic criticism and theatrical gossip. Boaden is very reticent about his private life, but it is known that he married and left nine children, one of whom, John Boaden, was a painter.

Boaden's first effort for the stage was *Ozmyn and Daraxa,* a "musical romance" or opera in two acts. It was premiered as an afterpiece on 7 March 1793, produced by Kemble for the Drury Lane company at the King's Theatre in the Haymarket. In his *Memoirs of the Life of John Philip Kemble* Boaden mentions that he found the story in the *Spanish Rogue* and thought it might "afford an opportunity to display the musical science of his young friend Atwood." Most of the songs are set to music composed by Thomas Atwood, but some are by Giovanni Giornovichi, Michael Kelly, and Wolfgang Amadeus Mozart. The opera was never published in full, though the *Songs and Chorusses* (1793) were, and are included in Steven Cohan's edition of *The Plays of James Boaden* (1980); the manuscript of the entire work is in the Larpent Collection of the Huntington Library. Boaden confides that Richard Brinsley Sheridan told him "that his songs were better written, than any which he had read since *The Duenna,*" Sheridan's great success of 1775. However, Boaden was "so pleased" when Sheridan paid him for the work, that he "kept no copy." This may account for the fact that *Ozmyn and Daraxa* was never published in full, but it may have been considered too slight a work to be preserved in print. Boaden apparently got one hundred pounds for *Oxmyn and Daraxa* and, according to Michael Kelly, the work, "a very pretty operatic piece," was "well received."

Boaden's second play, *Fontainville Forest,* was first produced on 25 March 1794 at the Theatre Royal, Covent Garden. The story is derived from Ann Radcliffe's novel *The Romance of the Forest* (1791), but Boaden simplifies it, focusing on the central incidents which transpire "in an Abbey chiefly, and the adjacent parts of the Forest." Among the significant changes is a more sympathetic role for the character of Lamotte. Although he robs the marquis of Montault and is initially prepared to sacrifice Adeline to the marquis' lust, he is forced to it by necessity, and in a soliloquy castigates himself. We observe him distraught and torn by his struggles with his conscience, angry with his wife, Hortensia, and impatient with his son, Louis, who replaces Radcliffe's Theodore as the hero of the tale. The strongest character is that of Adeline, the heroine. She ventures into the secret apartment, convinced "that some mystery / Is wrapt within these chambers," and bravely stiffens her resolve:

> How, if I sink with fear?
> And so benumb'd, life freeze away in horror?
> No matter, powerful impulse drives me onward,
> And my soul rises to the coming terror.

She toys with the conventional fears of the Gothic heroine, but she acts with fortitude. Her enterprising courage leads her to the discovery of the dagger and the letter, thus precipitating the resolution of the mystery.

The tremendous success of *Fontainville Forest* was in part attributable to Boaden's correct assessment of stage business. He broke with the dramatic conventions of the day in introducing a ghost on stage. In doing so he departed from his source, as Radcliffe offers a rational explanation of the ghost and, in effect, undercuts the terror she has earlier created, an approach that Boaden characterizes as "*ungenerous* in thus playing upon poor timid human nature, and agonizing it with false terrors." Furthermore, Boaden challenges comparison with

Act Second.

Scene Pedrilla's Garden

Laida enters.

What has not been atchiev'd by Love? No, my Mistress is certainly right, stony Limits cannot Keep him out. She entreated me to look carefully about the Garden, expecting reasonably enough, that Ozmin will attempt some daring enterprize to see her. Ah! well, he is still Commander in the Citadel, though the town is in possession of the Enemy.

Attwood

Vainly Men by fetters strive
Woman's constant Heart to bind,
Absence Keeps her Love alive,
Hardship roots it in the mind.

Fancy fills the gloomy void,
Fondly views the Lover mourn,
Pride too bids, by force annoy'd,
Liberty and Love return.

Oviedo as a Labourer crossing the Stage stops.

Ov. By all my hopes, Laida's voice — I must discover myself — Laida!
Lai. Ha! what do I hear — What would You?
Ov. Why know whether I am to live? If Laida still thinks of her Oviedo.
Lai. O Mahomet! it is himself
Ov. No faith it is not — but I am Oviedo.
Lai. How my heart beats! Oviedo, tell me, tell me — How came you hither!? What's your design? How long have you been at Sevilla? How did you escape discovery? Where is your Master? I am out of breath with expectation.

Page from the playhouse copy of Ozmin and Daraxa *submitted to the Examiner of Plays prior to the first performance, on 7 March 1793 (Larpent Collection, LA 970; by permission of the Henry E. Huntington Library and Art Gallery)*

John Philip Kemble, the subject of Boaden's first biography (portrait by Martin Archer Shee; 1795, oil on canvas, 72.8 x 59.6 cm; gift of Mr. and Mrs. William O. Goodman, 1925. 587, © 1989 The Art Institute of Chicago. All Rights Reserved)

Shakespeare by insisting on the actual representation of the ghost on stage. Current theatrical practice allowed the retention of such anachronisms in old plays, such as *Hamlet* (circa 1600-1601), where they were to some extent justified by the outmoded belief in incorporeal visitations, but deplored and virtually proscribed the appearance of spirits in the "enlightened" contemporary drama. But Boaden determined to hazard the attempt and, though many of the critics were offended, the enthusiastic response of the audience fully justified the innovation. Boaden notes in his biography of Kemble that "any great effect in this play depended on the management of the ghost scene." He here introduced a technique that was to become a standard practice: "The great contrivance was, that the spectre should appear through a blueish-gray gauze, so as to remove the too corporeal effect of a 'live actor,' and convert the moving substance into a gliding essence." Boaden also persuaded Thomas Harris, the manager, to alter the traditional stage armor for a costume of "a dark blue grey stuff, made in the shape of armour, and sitting close to the person." The result fully answered the author's expectations:

> the whisper of the house, as he was about to enter, –the breathless silence, while he floated along like a shadow . . . and the often-renewed plaudits, when the curtain fell, told me that the audience had enjoyed 'That sacred terror, that severe delight,' for which alone it is excusable to overpass the ordinary limits of nature.

Finally, in the epilogue to *Fontainville Forest* Elizabeth Pope, who had played the role of Adeline, remarks, "Know you not, Shakspeare's petrifying pow'r / Commands alone the horror-giving hour?" and then she rhetorically asks the author of the play: "But Sir . . . You mean to sanction then

Sarah Siddons as the Tragic Muse (engraving based on a portrait by Sir Joshua Reynolds). In his biography of Mrs. Siddons Boaden attempted to record "some of the electric fire" of her performances.

your own pale sprite, / By his 'that did usurp this time of night:' / 'I do, he answered. . . .' " By this allusion to Horatio's words to the ghost in *Hamlet*, Boaden may have intended not just to "sanction" his own ghost, but to invoke comparison with the great dramatist. When Boaden discusses *Fontainville Forest* in his *Memoirs of the Life of John Philip Kemble* he remarks: "nothing ever was more tasteless than the stage exhibition of the Ghost in Hamlet . . . the whole of this 'gracious figure' should look as if it was collected from the surrounding air, and ready [*sic*], when its impression should be made, to melt into 'thin air' again." Boaden prided himself on doing better with his own ghost, at least insofar as stage business was concerned. His complaisance in this regard earned him his nickname of "Billy-the-Go-By Boaden," meaning that he believed he had done better than William Shakespeare. Certainly, the play was successful; it was performed thirteen times in its first season, from 25 March 1794 to 18 June 1794.

The Secret Tribunal opened on 3 June 1795, at the Theatre Royal, Covent Garden. Boaden's play, which is derived from *Hermann von Unna* (1788) by Benedikte Naubert, introduced the institution of the Secret Tribunal or Inquisition to Gothic fiction in English. The device was later employed by such writers as Ann Radcliffe in *The Italian* (1797), Mathew Gregory Lewis in *The Monk* (1795), and by Charles Robert Maturin in *Melmoth the Wanderer* (1820).

In *The Secret Tribunal* Herman, nephew of the

duke of Wirtenberg, is in love with Ida, who is pursued by Ratibor, the duke's brother. Ratibor hopes to have the duke assassinated, to poison his sister-in-law, to assume the duke's position, and to marry Ida. Going to meet the duke, Herman rescues him from Ratibor's assassins, but in the scuffle drops his sword and picks up one of theirs. He is later found with the incriminating bloody sword, accused of attacking the duke, his uncle, who is too readily credulous. Herman's trial is turned over to the authority of Ratibor. The duke's wife dies, and Ida is accused of administering poison. She is to be tried at midnight by the secret tribunal in a subterranean vault. Herman, whose innocence is indicated when an incriminating letter from Ratibor is found, attends the tribunal in disguise; and a series of revelations restores the lovers to one another and to the duke's favor. Unlike most Gothic heroes, Herman is instrumental in opposing the villain but only at the end of the play.

Despite its pervasive influence on later fictions and drama in the Gothic mode, *The Secret Tribunal* was not notably successful itself. It was performed only three times in its first season, and three times in the next year.

It was in *The Oracle* that in February and April of 1795 Boaden wrote a series of puffs concerning the Shakespeare papers being shown by Samuel Ireland, and supposedly found by his son William Henry Ireland, that involved Boaden in the controversy over the great Shakespeare forgery. Initially impressed like so many others, Boaden enthused (16 February 1795), "the conviction produced upon our mind, is such as to make all scepticism ridiculous, and when we follow the sentiments of Dr. Joseph Warton, we have no fear of our critical orthodoxy." Others were less sure, and the *Morning Herald* repudiated the find as early as 17 February. Boaden visited Samuel Ireland's house twice to inspect the manuscripts, and on 23 April reiterated his faith: "The Shakesperiana, which have been so luckily discovered, are now considered as genuine by all but those who illiberally refuse to be convinced by inspection." The controversy swelled as young William Henry Ireland continued to produce more "Shakesperean" manuscripts to please his credulous father. But the number of dissentient voices grew, and Boaden reversed his position, influenced perhaps by his friend the Shakespearean scholar George Steevens. On 11 January 1796 he published *A Letter to George Steevens, Esq. Containing a Critical Examination of the Papers of Shakespeare; Published by Mr. Samuel Ireland. To Which Are Added, Extracts From Vortigern,* by James Boaden, Esq. In this work he was among the first to repudiate in print the spurious hoax, pointing out chronological inconsistencies in some of the documents and criticizing the sentiments and the orthography of others. He writes:

> my doubts were accumulated from the reflection in my closet upon circumstances recorded; examining those facts scrupulously by the light of history; and applying to things the rule of chronology, and to persons the records of biography. I found myself speedily entangled in perplexities, and at war with known events.

Boaden concludes that he had "allowed myself to aid the cause of deception." Commenting on Samuel Ireland's preface to his edition of the so-called Shakespeare manuscripts, Boaden goes beyond refutation to exclaim, "I could scarcely believe the evidence of the sense, that presented criticism so despicably shallow, and assertion so miserably fallacious." Of the manuscript of *Lear* supposedly discovered among the other Shakespeare forgeries Boaden concludes, "that its interpolations are not in the manner of Shakspeare–and that its orthography bears the character of no period of English Literature, except indeed that when the forgeries of Chatterton were offered to the public." In short, the whole collection of Shakespeariana was an imposture. As a result of his repudiation, Boaden was roundly attacked by Samuel Ireland and his supporters in such works as John Wyatt's *A Comparative Review of the Opinions of Mr. James Boaden . . . relative to the Shakspeare MSS* (1796), and by Walley C. Oulton in *Vortigern Under Consideration; With General Remarks on Mr. James Boaden's Letter to George Steevens, Esq.* (1796).

It was in *Vortigern Under Consideration* that Oulton applied to Boaden the nickname of "Billy the Go-By," suggesting that Boaden believed that he had in his own work surpassed "Billy," that is, William Shakespeare. But this sobriquet was first used by the satirist Peter Pindar (John Wolcot?) in *The Cap . . .* (1795). He quotes Boaden as having often said, "That if HARRIS gave him proper encouragement he had no doubt but in a short time he should give BILLY (Shakespeare) *the go by.*" The date of *The Cap* would indicate that it was in connection with *Fontainville Forest* (1794) that Boaden made this claim. The story as told by Samuel Jones Arnold (1774-1852), son of Dr. Samuel Arnold, is noted by Richard Brinsley Peake in his *Memoirs of the Colman Family* (1841). Arnold recalls:

> The play I have alluded to [*The Italian Monk*] had a ghost in it, and Mrs. Gibbs looked and acted like an angel. It was of this very play that Mr. Boaden was *said to have said,* he had given Billy, (meaning William Shakespeare) the go-by. . . .

However, Peake quotes Arnold as linking the story to Boaden's play of *The Italian Monk,* which was not produced until 1797, too late for the genesis of the story, and anyway it was in *Cambro-Britons* (1798), not in *The Italian Monk,* that Boaden for the second time used a ghost.

Appended to Boaden's *Letter to George Steevens* are *Extracts From Vortigern* which, Boaden reminds his readers, had "appeared in a diurnal publication," that is, *The Oracle.* They are part of a widespread campaign to discredit the spurious play of *Vortigern,* written by William Henry Ireland, which was about to be produced as Shakespeare's play at Drury Lane on 2 April 1796. Kemble, who suspected the authenticity of the work, had proposed staging it on April first! The "Extracts" are not of William Henry Ireland's composition, however, but are Boaden's own parody. They are offered, Boaden asserts, "as faint attempts to imitate the inimitable, because, if the play of VORTIGERN, announced for representation, should, in a trifling degree resemble the great Poet, such partial resemblance may be here shewn not to be decisive of the question of ORIGINALITY." By thus implicitly claiming in print to be able to write pseudo-Shakespearean verse himself, Boaden must have reinforced the impression that he saw himself as the rival of Shakespeare. Taken together, his epilogue to *Fontainville Forest* and these *Extracts From Vortigern* sufficiently account for his nickname of Billy-the-Go-By.

The Italian Monk premiered at the Theatre Royal in the Hay-Market on 15 August 1797, with "new Musick, Scenery, Dresses, and Decorations. The Overture and Musick by Dr [Samuel] Arnold. The Scenery by Marinari, Rooker, &c." The story is derived from Ann Radcliffe's novel *The Italian* but with one major revision. Radcliffe's villain, Schedoni, commits suicide at the end of the novel and dies unrepentant; Boaden allows him a change of heart. In the play Schedoni plots to separate Vivaldi and Ellena, hoping thereby to consolidate his power with Vivaldi's mother, the marchioness. He has Ellena taken to a convent, where she is to be forced to take the vows and retire from the world. When Vivaldi rescues her and tries to marry her, the ceremony is interrupted, Vivaldi is denounced to the Inquisition, and Ellena is carried off to be killed. Later Schedoni, in the act of plunging a dagger into her breast, recognizes a picture she wears around her neck and realizes she is his daughter. Boaden had used a similar device in *Fontainville Forest,* where the marquis, snatching a picture of her mother from Adeline's neck, realizes that she is his niece. From this moment Schedoni labors to undo his elaborate stratagems, to rescue Vivaldi from the hands of the Inquisition, and to further the union of the lovers. In the play Schedoni, himself brought before the Inquisition and accused of having murdered his wife, Ellena's mother, is unexpectedly reunited with her; it is revealed that she has spent the intervening years in a convent (shades of Shakespeare's *Winter's Tale,* 1611). The monk is allowed a complete renovation of character, and the audience a happy ending to the play.

Boaden records that Palmer, who played the Monk, "said that he could not quit London without in a particular manner thanking me for the part of Schedoni." *The Italian Monk* enjoyed a considerable success, being played twelve times in its first season.

Cambro-Britons was first performed at the Theatre Royal in the Hay-Market, on Saturday, 21 July 1798. It is a historical drama set in thirteenth-century Wales. Some of the incidental songs were written by George Colman the Younger, with new music by Dr. Samuel Arnold. The reigning Welsh prince, Llewellyn, is being attacked on the flanks of Mount Snowdon by vastly superior forces under the command of the English King Edward. Llewellyn's brother, Prince David, has defected to the English side, and Llewellyn's betrothed, Elinor, has been captured by the English. Prince David endeavors to woo Elinor for himself, and when Llewellyn contrives to meet her at the shrine of his mother in an abbey at Chester the two brothers come to blows. Here, for the second time, Boaden introduces a ghost on stage. The spirit of their mother rises from her tomb to forbid the violence, thus effecting a reconciliation between her sons. As the brothers kneel to embrace each other, a chorus of spirits comments, "Dear is the incense that repentance flings." The ghost offers her blessings, as her "funeral dress falls off; drapery of a fine cerulean colour gradually unfolds itself; her figure seems glorified; and through the opening window she is drawn, as it were, into the air, while music, as of immortal spirits, attends her progress." Once again, Boaden's handling of a ghost is a source of pride to him and delight to his contemporary audi-

25

Scene 2. Aurelio's ~~Ambrosio's~~ Cell

(Enter ~~ambrosio~~ Aurelio.)

Aur: ~~Amb~~:—In vain I seek the healing power of Sleep!
Since passion grew an inmate in my heart;
Imagination stung, can sleep no more.
If worn out with the days distempering thoughts
I fling me on my restless Couch to Slumber,
Its sullen and benumbing reign is broke
By visions of licentiousness and horror.
Can Nature's impulse be unholy Fire?
Yet, what is Virtue, but surmounted Passion?
What all my merits, but strict self denial?
Would I had never climb'd this giddy height,
This Pyramid of earthly vanity!
Each mounting step is less and less secure;
And when we reach the summit of the Spire,
And deem Heav'n wonders at our steady Course,
The very eminence disturbs the brain
And down we fall, the scoff of humbler fools—(A Knocking without)
What knocking's that? Miranda ~~Matilda~~ (without)

Mir: ~~Mat~~:—Are you alone, good father?

Aur ~~Amb~~:—Come in. O, how that gentle voice thrills through me!

(Enter ~~Matilda~~ Miranda.)

Mir ~~Mat~~:—Shall I secure the door?

Aur ~~Amb~~:—Why?—O, most true!
Guilt is of dark soul, and loves privacy.

Mir ~~Mat~~:—Unkind Aurelio ~~ambrosio~~, thus to brand as Crime
A Passion your own excellence inspires.

Aur ~~Amb~~:—Thou dear deluder—Give me back myself.
Talk not to me of excellence and virtue,
I never had them—or, if once call'd mine,
My fatal fondness pluck'd them from my breast
And fill'd it with a love I had disclaim'd.

Mir ~~Mat~~:—When purity like yours embraces love,

Page from the playhouse copy of the play produced as Aurelio and Miranda, *submitted to John Larpent, the Examiner of Plays, for licensing prior to the first performance, on 7 March 1793. Based on Matthew Gregory Lewis's notorious novel* The Monk, *the play was first given the same title, but it was revised as "Aurelio" in this manuscript, where the names of the characters were also changed, probably because of objections from Larpent (Larpent Collection, LA 1232; by permission of the Henry E. Huntington Library and Art Gallery).*

ences. Subsequently, Llewellyn contrives to hold off the invading English army, and an honorable peace is secured.

Significantly, throughout the play the Welsh are referred to as "Britons," and characterized as bravely opposing a superior hostile force. In his preface to the published play Boaden emphasizes his patriotic motives in writing *Cambro-Britons,* as a topical reference to the state of war currently existing between England and France. This play was well received. It was performed twelve times between 21 July and 23 August 1798.

Aurelio and Miranda was first acted at the Theatre Royal, Drury Lane, on 29 December 1798, with music by Michael Kelly. Based on Lewis's notorious novel *The Monk,* this play greatly simplifies the plot and significantly alters the characterization. The play was originally called *The Monk,* but the title and the names of the principal characters are changed in the manuscript, presumably because the Examiner of Plays objected. Boaden uses the central incidents surrounding the monk Aurelio (Ambrosio in Lewis's work), who is tempted by discovering that a young novice in his monastery is actually a woman in disguise; the subplot involves Agnes, the reluctant nun, and Don Raymond, her lover. Whereas the powerful climax of the novel involves Ambrosio's torment and the probable damnation of this hypocritically pious villain, Boaden redraws the characters of Aurelio and Miranda so that, although tempted and lustful, he is withheld from the actual realization of his illicit passion by Miranda's virtue. In so doing, Boaden sought to avert some of the censure that was anticipated in bringing a tale of such recent notoriety to the stage, but the strategy did not answer. The public and the critics continued to reprehend the choice of subject, while simultaneously they were disappointed with the altered ending. In the play, Miranda holds Aurelio off until he is released from his clerical vows upon discovering that he is actually of noble birth, whereupon he virtuously offers to marry her. The violence and incest of Lewis's tale is omitted, and the play moves from the temptations of Aurelio by Miranda's beauty to the contrived and incredible conclusion. The monk's lust for his sister, Antonia, so prominent a feature of the novel, is omitted, as is the death of Agnes's child in the vaults beneath the convent, with all the repellent details of its putrefaction. The audience, anticipating the Gothic horrors of Boaden's source, led to expect them from the initial presentation in the first three acts, were simply disappointed in the denouement.

Boaden reports that "a storm of indignation was excited, that so *immoral* a work as the Monk should be resorted to for the purposes of an exhibition, however moral its tendency." Perhaps in this instance Kemble's dramatic sense did a disservice to the play, as his representation of the Monk was considered far too elevated. Still, the play survived for six performances in its first season.

The Voice of Nature premiered at the Theatre Royal in the Hay-Market on 31 July 1802. It was derived from Louis Charles Caigniez's *Le Jugement de Salomon* (1802), itself based on the judgment of Solomon incident in 1 Kings 3: 16-28. As the play opens, Lilla has come to observe the meeting of King Alphonso with his betrothed, the Princess Clorinda. In reality she hopes to see again Prince Rinaldo, who had been her lover in the past and was the father of her child. Rinaldo is about to get married, to Alzira, because she claims that the four-year-old child she is raising is her son by him. Lilla sees Alzira and the child and feels drawn to the boy.

As the plot unfolds we learn that her son had been stolen soon after birth and replaced with a dead child, while Alzira's sickly baby became suddenly healthy. The proofs that Lilla can offer to assert her claim are inconclusive and the decision is vital, because Prince Rinaldo will wed the mother of the child. The judgment is finally relegated to King Alphonso, who, like Solomon, ascertains the true mother by her response when the child is threatened, "Seize that infant, let him die, and be his remains divided between these women." The play is considerably less Gothic than Boaden's earlier successes, except in this climactic scene where Alphonso, Boaden's Solomon figure, orders the death and dismemberment of the boy. This scene was severely criticized as unfit for dramatic representation, in part because the disputed infant is not a baby, but a child able to comprehend the situation, and Alphonso appears cruel rather than wise.

The Maid of Bristol was first performed at the Theatre Royal in the Hay-Market on Wednesday, 24 August 1803. It is a simple tale of thwarted love. Stella has traveled to Bristol from her native Austria in order to meet her betrothed, Baron Lindorf, who has been fighting on behalf of the English in America. He is returning, wounded, from the war. When the two finally meet, he tells Stella they never can be wed, and she discovers that he has been falsely informed that she had married in his absence, and so he has contracted a loveless marriage himself. Stella's distress is such that she wanders into the fields, finding shelter under a

Dorothy Jordan as the Comic Muse, supported by Euphrosyne (Joy), one of the Three Graces (portrait by John Hoppner; Royal Collection, Buckingham Palace; by permission of Her Majesty Queen Elizabeth II. Copyright reserved). In his biography of Jordan, Boaden alludes to her relationship with the future William IV, by whom she had ten children, but defends her moral character.

shed, where she determines to live the life of a hermit. It is this aspect of the play which is supposed to have been suggested by a little-known work, *A Narrative of Facts: supposed to throw Light on the History of the Bristol-Stranger; Known by the Name of the Maid of the Hay-Stack,* translated by George Henry Glasse (1785). Some humor is introduced in the characters of two sailors, Oakum and Ben Block, and some rustic dialogue is delivered by the foolish countryman Jacob Clod. The simple conflict is resolved when Lindorf's wife dies on her way to meet him, but Stella is hesitant: "Oh, Lindorf! various emotions crowd in upon my soul! Do not imagine me insensible of the blessing I have so ardently desir'd–But this is a solemn moment. . . ." The play was, understandably, not one of Boaden's great successes.

Two further works attest to Boaden's continuing interest in Shakespeare. In 1824 he published *An Inquiry Into the Authenticity of Various Pictures and Prints, Which From the Decease of the Poet to Our Own Times Have Been Offered to the Public as Portraits of Shakespeare.* In this work he reproduces "accurate and finished engravings" to facilitate his arguments. Here he discourses knowledgeably on his material, doing pioneer work in an endeavor to establish the probable likeness of the Bard. The care with which Boaden conducts his argument and the quality of the engravings make this an important study. For the first time readers were enabled to compare the different likenesses and portraits of Shakespeare, brought together in one work. In two articles "On the Sonnets of Shakespeare" in the *Gentleman's Magazine* (1832) Boaden identifies the

"W. H." of the sonnet sequence as William Herbert, earl of Pembroke, an identification accepted by subsequent critics. The argument was somewhat expanded and republished as *On The Sonnets of Shakespeare* (1837). Boaden's several publications on Shakespeare, as much as his other writings, established his reputation as an important literary figure for his contemporaries.

Boaden wrote two novels in the course of his productive life, *The Man of Two Lives* (1828) and *The Doom of Giallo; Or, The Vision of Judgment* (1835). Of these two novels, the first has the interesting theme of reincarnation or the transmigration of souls: the hero has the chance to atone in a second life for some of the injustices he committed in a former existence. Edward Sydenham is conscious, almost from birth, of his identity with Frederic Werner, a native of Frankfurt: "I *am* the man now writing his present history, and am equally sure that I *was* that other being whose life I also record, because I know it to have been mine." In the course of the history, the narrator discourses on musicians contemporary with himself–Henry Purcell, Christoph Willibald Glück, George Frideric Handel and Thomas Augustine Arne, painters such as Henry Fuseli and Sir Joshua Reynolds, and poets such as William Cowper, William Shakespeare and John Milton. Speculations of an occult nature occur concerning the Rosicrucian philosophy and the plurality of worlds; one interesting character, who seems able to know what is passing in Sydenham's mind, turns out to be no other than Mesmer, the practitioner of a primitive psychology. We witness Sydenham's association in Germany with Francina and Leonora–the woman who had virtuously loved Frederic Werner and the beautiful opera singer who had caused him to embitter Francina's life. At first Sydenham seems as fascinated with both these women as Frederic could have been, but eventually he finds his mate in Sophia, a younger woman, who is his contemporary.

Boaden's five theatrical biographies remain an invaluable source of information about styles of acting, methods of production and staging, theaters, and audiences of the eighteenth and early nineteenth centuries. The *Memoirs of the Life of John Philip Kemble* is introduced by a "History of the Stage, from the Time of Garrick to the Present Period," in which Boaden discusses theatrical practice under such various managers as Garrick, Sheridan, and Tom King, and the performance of such players as Samuel Reddish, Spranger Barry, and Sarah Siddons. The life of Kemble is traced from his birth and early schooling to the advent of his acting career. It is interspersed with incidental descriptions of the numerous theaters at which Kemble appeared in England and Ireland and with anecdotes of his associates. Boaden's keen interest in staging, costume, setting, and stage business is everywhere apparent, and he interpolates comments and criticisms on writers and on individual plays. In this, the first of his biographies, which concerns the life of his friend Kemble, Boaden seeks "to record his progress in the art which he professed; and also to display his personal character, as it unfolded itself during an intimacy of near thirty years." But total frankness is not the author's intent, as he confesses, "On some few, a very few points, in the exercise of, I hope, a sound discretion, I have ventured to baffle the search of the malignant." In later biographies Boaden was less discrete. Boaden's own plays and his concepts of staging and production are discussed wherever appropriate in the context.

In the introduction to his *Memoirs of Mrs. Siddons* (1827), the author states his intention to record the evanescent details of stage performances. He quotes Colley Cibber's lament in *An Apology for the Life of Colley Cibber* (1740):

> Pity it is that the momentary beauties flowing from an harmonious elocution cannot, like those of poetry, be their own record! That the animated graces of the player can live no longer than the instant breath and motion that presents them; or, at best, can but imperfectly glimmer through the memory or imperfect attestation of a few surviving spectators.

But Boaden determines to attempt such a record:

> we shall always communicate by our touch some of the electric fire which we have received. It is, therefore, gratitude to the actor and duty to the public to perpetuate the character of excellence, and afford models for imitation to future artists.

In his *Life of Mrs. Jordan* (1831), together with an account of her career and her experiences in the theater, Boaden is pleased to allude to her long-standing liaison with Prince William Henry, duke of Clarence, later King William IV, and to the ten children she had by him. Boaden also seeks to elucidate the complexities of her involvement with Richard Ford. In this biography he departs very far from his earlier practice of leaving the private lives of his subjects in obscurity. But Boaden seeks here to stifle the criticism of Mrs. Jordan's moral character and to reassert the greatness of her dramatic achievement.

With his edition of *The Private Correspondence of David Garrick* (1831, 1832) Boaden includes a biographical memoir of more than sixty pages that is of a kind with his other theatrical biographies. Drawing upon the copious detail of the correspondence, he fashions a fascinating account of Garrick's acting and managerial experience, and of his private life.

In preparing his *Memoirs of Mrs. Inchbald* (1833), Boaden had access to Elizabeth Inchbald's autograph journals, and to her collection of correspondence. He details her acting career, her interaction with friends and managers, as well as her achievements in fictional and dramatic writing. Boaden is able to praise her in both public and private life.

James Boaden's achievements form a significant contribution to our knowledge and understanding of the theater in this period. His essays in *The Oracle* record contemporary responses to dramatic productions and constitute a gauge of their popular reception. Boaden's plays are keenly attuned to the taste of the day, and he broke new ground in his exploitation of Gothic themes and melodramatic devices. His writings on Shakespeare added their weight to the ongoing revaluation of the poet's place as the greatest of English dramatists even as Boaden sought to extend our knowledge of the Bard's life and works. In his biographical memoirs Boaden performed an invaluable service in recording for posterity those evanescent details of production and performance that alone allow us to comprehend the theatrical practices of an earlier age. In each of the genres in which Boaden wrote, he earned the respect of his contemporaries and merits our grateful approbation.

References:

Jeremy F. Bagster-Collins, *George Colman The Younger, 1762-1836* (New York: King's Crown Press, 1946);

Steven Cohan, Introduction to *The Plays of James Boaden* (New York & London: Garland, 1980);

Bernard Grebanier, *The Great Shakespeare Forgery* . . . (London: Heinemann, 1966);

[Samuel Ireland], *Mr. Ireland's Vindication of His Conduct, Respecting the Publication of the Supposed Shakspeare MSS. Being a Preface or Introduction to a Reply to the Critical Labors of Mr. Malone, in His "Enquiry into the Authenticity of Certain Papers, &c. &c."* (London: Published by Mr. Faulder & Mr. Robson, 1796);

William Henry Ireland, *An Authentic Account of the Shaksperian Manuscripts, &c.* (London: Printed for J. Debrett, 1796);

John Mair, *The Fourth Forger: William Ireland and the Shakespeare Papers* (London: Cobden-Sanderson, 1938);

Edmond Malone, *An Inquiry Into the Authenticity of Certain Miscellaneous Papers and Legal Instruments, Published Dec. 24, 1795 and Attributed to Shakspeare, Queen Elizabeth, and Henry, Earl of Southampton* . . . (London: Printed by H. Baldwin for T. Cadell, Jun. and W. Davies, 1796; republished, London: Frank Cass, 1970);

[W. C. Oulton], *Vortigern Under Consideration; With General Remarks on Mr. James Boaden's Letter to George Steevens, Esq. Relative to the Manuscripts, Drawings, Seals, &c. Ascribed to Shakespeare, and In the Possession of Samuel Ireland, Esq.* (London: Printed for H. Lowndes, 1796);

Richard Brinsley Peake, *Memoirs of the Colman Family. . .*, 2 volumes (London: Richard Bentley, 1841; reprinted, New York: Benjamin Blom, Inc. 1972);

Louis F. Peck, *A Life of Matthew G. Lewis* (Cambridge, Mass.: Harvard University Press, 1961);

Peter Pindar [John Wolcot?], *The Cap. A Satiric Poem. Including Most of the Dramatic Writers of the Present Day* (London: Printed for the Author, 1795);

Montague Summers, *The Gothic Quest: A History of the Gothic Novel* (London: Fortune Press, 1938);

Willard Thorp, "The Stage Adventures of Some Gothic Novels," *PMLA*, 43 (June 1928): 476-486;

[John Wyatt], *A Comparative Review of the Opinions of Mr. James Boaden (Editor of the Oracle), in February, March, and April, 1795, and of James Boaden, Esq. (author of* Fontainville Forest, *and of* A Letter to George Steevens, Esq.) *in February, 1796, relative to the Shakespeare MSS* . . . (London: Printed for G. Sael, 1796).

Papers:

The manuscripts of seven of Boaden's plays are in the Larpent Collection at the Huntington Library. These are *Ozmyn and Daraxa* (LA 970), *Fontainville Forest* (LA 1014), *The Secret Tribunal* (LA 1085), *Cambro-Britons* (LA 1222), *Aurelio [and Miranda]* (the manuscript bears the title *The Monk,* crossed out, with *Aurelio* added above) (LA 1232), *The Voice of Nature* (LA 1355), and *The Maid of Bristol* (LA 1388).

George Colman the Elder

(?15 April 1732-14 August 1794)

Sid Sondergard
St. Lawrence University

PLAY PRODUCTIONS: *Polly Honeycombe*, London, Theatre Royal in Drury Lane, 5 December 1760;

The Jealous Wife, London, Theatre Royal in Drury Lane, 12 February 1761;

The Musical Lady, London, Theatre Royal in Drury Lane, 6 March 1762;

Philaster, adapted from Francis Beaumont and John Fletcher's play, London, Theatre Royal in Drury Lane, 8 October 1763;

The Deuce is in Him, London, Theatre Royal in Drury Lane, 4 November 1763;

A Midsummer Night's Dream, by Colman and David Garrick, adapted from Shakespeare's play, London, Theatre Royal in Drury Lane, 23 November 1763; shortened by Colman as *A Fairy Tale*, London, Theatre Royal in Drury Lane, 26 November 1763;

The Clandestine Marriage, by Colman and Garrick, London, Theatre Royal in Drury Lane, 20 February 1766;

The English Merchant, adapted from Voltaire's *L'Ecossaise*, London, Theatre Royal in Drury Lane, 21 February 1767;

The Oxonian in Town, London, Theatre Royal in Covent Garden, 7 November 1767;

King Lear, adapted from Shakespeare's play, London, Theatre Royal in Covent Garden, 20 February 1768;

Man and Wife; or, The Shakespeare Jubilee, London, Theatre Royal in Covent Garden, 7 October 1769;

The Portrait, adapted from Louis Anseaume's *Tableau parlant*, London, Theatre Royal in Covent Garden, 22 November 1770;

Mother Shipton; or, The Harlequin Gladiator, London, Theatre Royal in Covent Garden, 26 December 1770;

The Fairy Prince, adapted from Ben Jonson's *Oberon, the Faery Prince*, London, Theatre Royal in Covent Garden, 12 November 1771;

An Occasional Prelude, London, Theatre Royal in Covent Garden, 21 September 1772;

Comus, adapted from John Milton's masque, London, Theatre Royal in Covent Garden, 17 October 1772;

Elfrida, adapted from William Mason's play, London, Theatre Royal in Covent Garden, 21 November 1772;

Achilles in Petticoats, adapted from John Gay's *Achilles*, London, Theatre Royal in Covent Garden, 16 December 1773;

The Man of Business (original title, *The White Lyar*), London, Theatre Royal in Covent Garden, 31 January 1774;

Epicoene; or, The Silent Woman, adapted from Jonson's play, London, Theatre Royal in Drury Lane, 13 January 1776;

The Spleen; or, Islington Spa, London, Theatre Royal in Drury Lane, 7 March 1776;

The Tailors; A Tragedy for Warm Weather (alternate title, *Wet Weather*), adapted from the anonymous play *The Tailors*, London, Theatre Royal in the Hay-Market, 16 September 1776;

New Brooms! An Occasional Prelude, London, Theatre Royal in Drury Lane, 21 September 1776;

Polly, adapted from Gay's play, London, Theatre Royal in the Hay-Market, 19 June 1777;

The Sheep-Shearing, adapted from Shakespeare's *The Winter's Tale*, London, Theatre Royal in the Hay-Market, 18 July 1777;

The Spanish Barber; or, The Fruitless Precaution, adapted from Pierre-Augustin Caron de Beaumarchais's *Le Barbier de Seville*, Lon-

George Colman the Elder (engraving by S. Fisher, based on a portrait by Sir Joshua Reynolds)

don, Theatre Royal in the Hay-Market, 30 August 1777;

The Female Chevalier, adapted from William Taverner's *The Artful Husband*, London, Theatre Royal in the Hay-Market, 18 May 1778;

The Suicide, London, Theatre Royal in the Hay-Market, 11 July 1778;

Bonduca, adapted from John Fletcher's play, London, Theatre Royal in the Hay-Market, 30 July 1778;

The Separate Maintenance, London, Theatre Royal in the Hay-Market, 31 August 1779;

The Manager in Distress, London, Theatre Royal in the Hay-Market, 30 May 1780;

The Genius of Nonsense, London, Theatre Royal in the Hay-Market, 2 September 1780; adapted as an interlude, *Blade Bone; or, The Agreeable Companion* (alternate title, *Harlequin's Frolic*), London, Theatre Royal in the Hay-Market, 20 August 1788;

Preludio (to *The Beggar's Opera Reversed*), London, Theatre Royal in the Hay-Market, 8 August 1781;

The Fatal Curiosity, adapted from George Lillo's play, London, Theatre Royal in the Hay-Market, 29 June 1782;

Harlequin Teague; or, The Giant's Causeway, by Colman and John O'Keefe, London, Theatre Royal in the Hay-Market, 17 August 1782;

Volpone (alternate title, *The Fox*), adapted from Jonson's play, London, Theatre Royal in the Hay-Market, 12 September 1782;

The Election of the Managers, London, Theatre Royal in the Hay-Market, 2 June 1784;

Tit for Tat, adapted from Joseph Atkinson's *The Mutual Deception*, London, Theatre Royal in the Hay-Market, 29 August 1786;

The Village Lawyer, London, Theatre Royal in the Hay-Market, 28 August 1787;

Ut Pictura Poesis! or, The Enraged Musician, London, Theatre Royal in the Hay-Market, 18 May 1789.

SELECTED BOOKS: *The Connoisseur*, by Colman and Bonnell Thornton, nos. 1-140 (London, 31 January 1754-30 September 1756);

A Letter of Abuse to D---d G-----k, Esq. (London:

Printed for J. Scott, 1757);

Polly Honeycombe, A Dramatick Novel of One Act. As it is Now Acted at the Theatre-Royal in Drury-Lane (London: Printed for T. Becket & T. Davies, 1760);

Two Odes, by Colman and Robert Lloyd (London: H. Payne, 1760);

Critical Reflections on the Old English Dramatick Writers; Intended as a Preface to the Works of Massinger, Addressed to David Garrick (London: Printed for T. Davies, J. Fletcher & J. Merril, 1761);

The Jealous Wife: A Comedy. As it is Acted at the Theatre-Royal in Drury-Lane. By George Colman, Esq . . . (London: Printed for J. Newbery, T. Davies, W. Jackson & A. Kinkaid, 1761);

The Musical Lady. A Farce. As it is Acted at the Theatre-Royal in Drury-Lane (London: Printed for T. Becket & P. A. Dehondt, 1762);

Philaster, A Tragedy. Written by Beaumont and Fletcher. With Alterations. As it is Acted at the Theatre-Royal in Drury-Lane (London: Printed for J. & R. Tonson, 1763);

The Deuce is in Him. A Farce of Two Acts. As it is Performed at the Theatre Royal in Drury Lane (London: Printed for T. Becket, P. A. De Hondt & T. Davies, 1763);

A Midsummer Night's Dream. Written by Shakespeare: With Alterations and Additions, and Several New Songs. As it is Performed at the Theatre-Royal in Drury-Lane (London: Printed for J. & R. Tonson, 1763); abridged as *A Fairy Tale. In Two Acts. Taken from Shakespeare. As it is Performed at the Theatre-Royal in Drury Lane* (London: Printed for J. & R.Tonson, 1763);

Terrae-Filius, nos. 1-4 (London, July 1763);

The Comedies of Terence, Translated into Familiar Blank Verse (London: Printed for T. Becket & P. A. De Hondt, W. Johnston, W.Flexney, R. Davis, & T. Davies, 1765);

The Clandestine Marriage, A Comedy. As it is Acted at the Theatre-Royal in Drury-Lane, by Colman and David Garrick (London: Printed for T. Becket, P. A. De Hondt, R. Baldwin & T. Davies, 1766);

The English Merchant, A Comedy. As it is Acted at the Theatre-Royal in Drury-Lane (London:Printed for T. Becket & P. A. De Hondt and R. Baldwin, 1767);

The History of King Lear. As it is performed at the Theatre Royal in Covent Garden (London: Printed for R. Baldwin & T. Becket, 1768);

T. Harris Dissected (London: Printed for T. Becket, 1768);

A True State of the Differences Subsisting between the Proprietors of Covent-Garden Theatre; in Answer to a False, Scandalous, and Malicious Manuscript Libel, Exhibited on Saturday, Jan 23, and the Two Following Days; and to a Printed Narrative, Signed by T. Harris and J. Rutherford. By G. Colman, signed by Colman and William Powell (London: Printed for T. Becket, 1768);

The Oxonian in Town. A Comedy, In Two Acts, As it is Performed at the Theatre Royal in Covent Garden (London: Printed for T. Becket & R. Baldwin, 1770);

Man and Wife; or, The Shakespeare Jubilee. A Comedy, Of Three Acts, As it is Performed at the Theatre Royal in Covent Garden (London: Printed for T. Becket & R. Baldwin, 1770);

The Portrait; A Burletta. As it is performed at the Theatre Royal, in Covent Garden. The Music by Mr. Arnold (London: Printed for T. Becket, 1770);

The Recitatives, Airs, &c. in the New Pantomime Entertainment of Mother Shipton As it is now performing at the Theatre-Royal in Covent-Garden (London: Sold at the Theatre, 1770);

The Fairy Prince: A Masque. As it is Performed at the Theatre-Royal in Covent-Garden (London: Printed for T. Becket, 1771);

Comus: A Masque. Altered from Milton. As Performed at the Theatre-Royal in Covent-Garden. The Musick Composed by Dr. Arne (London: Printed for T. Lowndes, T. Caslon, S. Bladon, W. Nicoll & T. Becket & Co., 1772);

Achilles in Petticoats. An Opera. As it is Performed at the Theatre-Royal, in Covent-Garden (London: Printed for W. Strahan, T. Lowndes, T. Caslon, T. Becket, W. Nicoll & R. Snagg, 1774);

The Man of Business, A Comedy. As it is Acted at the Theatre-Royal in Covent-Garden (London: Printed for T. Becket, 1774);

Epicoene; or, The Silent Woman. A Comedy, Written by Ben Jonson. As it is Acted at the Theatre Royal in Drury-Lane. With Alterations, by George Colman (London: Printed for T. Becket, 1776);

An Occasional Prelude, Performed at the Opening of the Theatre-Royal, Covent-Garden. On the twenty-first of September, 1772 (London: Printed for T. Becket, 1776);

The Spleen, Or, Islington Spa; A Comick Piece, of

Engraving, possibly by Smith, based on Thurston's copy of Johann Zoffany's portrait of Colman

Two Acts. As it is Performed at the Theatre Royal, in Drury-Lane. By George Colman (London: Printed for T. Becket, 1776);

New Brooms! An Occasional Prelude, Performed at the Opening of the Theatre-Royal, in Drury-Lane, September 21, 1776. By George Colman (London: Printed for T. Becket, 1776);

The Sheep-Shearing: A Dramatic Pastoral. In Three Acts. Taken from Shakespeare. As it is performed at the Theatre Royal in the Hay-Market (London: Printed for G. Kearsley, 1777);

Polly: An Opera. Being the Sequel of the Beggar's Opera. Written by Gay. With Alterations. As Acted at the Theatre-Royal, Hay-Market (London: Printed for T. Evans, 1777);

Bonduca. A Tragedy, Written by Beaumont and Fletcher. With Alterations. As it is Performed at the Theatre-Royal in the Haymarket (London: Printed by T. Sherlock for T. Cadell, 1778);

The Tailors; A Tragedy for Warm Weather. In Three Acts. As it is Performed at the Theatre Royal in the Haymarket (London: Printed by T. Sherlock for T. Cadell, 1778);

Airs, Duetts, Trios, and Finale introduced in the Comedy of The Spanish Barber. As Performed at the Theatre-Royal in the Hay-Market. The Second Edition (London: Printed for T. Cadell, 1779);

Elfrida: A Dramatic Poem. Written on the Model of the Antient Greek Tragedy. First Published in the Year 1751, and Now Altered for Theatrical Representation (London: Printed by H. Godney for J. Dodsley & T. Cadell, 1780);

The Manager in Distress. A Prelude On opening the Theatre-Royal in the Hay-Market, May 30, 1780. By George Colman (London: Printed for T. Cadell, 1780);

Songs, Duetts, Trios, &c. in the Genius of Nonsense: An Original, Whimsical, Operatical, Pantomimical, Farcical, Electrical, Naval, Military, Temporary, Local Extravaganza. Performed at the Theatre-Royal in the Hay-Market (London: Printed for T. Cadell, 1781);

Songs, Airs, &c. in the Entertainment of Harlequin Teague; or, The Giant's Causeway. As it is now performing at the Theatre-Royal, Hay-Market (London: Printed for T. Cadell, 1782);

The Art of Poetry: An Epistle to the Pisos. Translated from Horace. With Notes (London: Printed for T. Cadell, 1783);

The Fatal Curiosity: A True Tragedy. Written by

George Lillo, 1736. With Alterations, As revived at The Theatre-Royal, Hay-market, 1782 (London: Printed for T. Cadell, 1783);

Prose on Several Occasions, Accompanied with Some Pieces in Verse, 3 volumes (London: T. Cadell, 1787);

A Very Plain State of the Case; or the Royalty Theatre Versus the Theatre Royal (London: [T. Cadell], 1787);

Tit for Tat, A Comedy in Three Acts. Performed at the Theatres Royal Hay-Market, Drury-Lane, and Covent-Garden (London: Printed for C. Dilby, 1788);

Ut Pictura Poesis! or, The Enraged Musician. A Musical Entertainment. Founded on Hogarth. Performed at the Theatre-Royal in the Hay-market. Written by George Colman, Composed by Dr. Arnold (London: Printed for T. Cadell, 1789);

Some Particulars of the Life of the Late George Colman, Written by Himself, and Delivered by Him to Richard Jackson . . . for Publication after His Decease (London: T. Cadell, 1795).

Collections: *The Dramatick Works of George Colman*, 4 volumes (London: Printed for T. Becket, 1777);

New Brooms! (1776) and The Manager in Distress (1780): Two Preludes by George Colman, the Elder, edited by J. Terry Frazier (Delmar, N.Y.: Scholars' Facsimiles & Reprints, 1980);

Plays by David Garrick and George Colman the Elder, edited by E. R. Wood (Cambridge: Cambridge University Press, 1982);

The Plays of George Colman the Elder, 6 volumes, edited by Kalman Burnim (New York: Garland, 1983).

OTHER: *Poems by Eminent Ladies. Particularly, Mrs. Barber, Mrs. Behn, Miss Carter, Lady Chudleigh, Mrs. Cockburn, Mrs. Grierson, Mrs. Jones, Mrs. Killigrew, Mrs. Leapor, Mrs. Madan, Mrs. Masters, Lady M. W. Montague, Mrs. Monk, Duchess of Newcastle, Mrs. K. Philips, Mrs. Pilkington, Mrs. Rowe, Lady Winchelsea*, 2 volumes, edited by Colman and Bonnell Thornton (London: Printed by R. Baldwin, 1755);

The Merchant, translated by Colman, in volume 2 of *The Comedies of Plautus, Translated into Familiar Blank Verse*, 2 volumes, edited by Thornton (London: Printed by J. Lister, 1767);

Samuel Foote, *The Devil upon Two Sticks; a comedy in three acts. As it is performed at the Theatre-Royal in the Haymarket. Written by the late Samuel Foote, Esq., and now published by Mr. Colman*, edited by Colman (London: Printed by T. Sherlock for T. Cadell, 1778);

Foote, *The Maid of Bath; a comedy, in three acts. As it is performed at the Theatre-Royal in the Hay-Market. Written by the late Samuel Foote, Esq., and now published by Mr. Colman*, edited by Colman (London: Printed by T. Sherlock for T. Cadell, 1778);

Foote, *The Cozeners; a comedy, in three acts, as it is performed at the Theatre-Royal in the Haymarket. Written by the late Samuel Foote, Esq., and now published by Mr. Colman*, edited by Colman (London: Printed by T. Sherlock for T. Cadell, 1778);

Foote, *The Nabob; a comedy, in three acts. As it is performed at the Theatre-Royal in the Haymarket. Written by the late Samuel Foote, Esq., and now published by Mr. Colman*, edited by Colman (London: Printed by T. Sherlock for T. Cadell, 1778);

Foote, *A Trip to Calais; a comedy in three acts. As written, and intended for representation, by the late Samuel Foote, Esq. To which is annexed, The Capuchin; . . . altered from The Trip to Calais, by the late Samuel Foot* [sic], *Esq. And now published by Mr. Colman*, edited by Colman (London: Printed by T. Sherlock for T. Cadell, 1778);

Francis Beaumont and John Fletcher, *The Dramatick Works of Beaumont and Fletcher; collated with all the former editions, and corrected; with notes, critical and explanatory, by various commentators*, 10 volumes, edited by Colman (London: Printed by T. Sherlock for T. Evans & P. Elmsley, 1778).

The center stage of London theatrical life was home to George Colman the Elder, and he shared it with such distinguished colleagues as Samuel Foote, David Garrick, and Richard Brinsley Sheridan, acting as dramaturge and manager for the Drury Lane (1763-1765), Covent Garden (1767-1774), and Haymarket (1777-1785) playhouses. Neither so unrestrained as Foote nor so reserved as Sheridan, the fashion-conscious Colman proved himself a playwright of great wit and range, writing comedies of every conceivable length and stylization from one-act burletta to five-act satire of sentimentalism. The Oxford graduate's knowledge and love of Renaissance drama provided him a vast selection of models for eighteenth-century theatrical interpretation, a most practical perspective since nearly one-quarter of his dramatic output consisted of Renaissance adaptations. Taking apparent glee in delivering whatever his audiences required in order to laugh, whether genteel comedy of manners or burlesque self-mockery, he thrived professionally with his creed of "exposing vice and folly by painting mankind in their natural colours, without assuming the rigid air of a preacher or the Moroseness of a philosopher."

George Colman grew up laboring beneath the shadow of expectations cast by a surrogate father–his uncle William Pulteney, later earl of Bath–as his father, Francis Colman, British envoy to the grand duke of Tuscany's court at Florence since 1724, died in Pisa on 20 April 1733, a year and two days after the christening of his son George. Colman was named for King George, as his sister, born 1730 but predeceasing their father, was named for Queen Caroline. The formative influence on his youth, however, was neither diplomat nor monarch, but Pulteney–a member of the powerful clique that toppled Prime Minister Robert Walpole in 1742, a determined man who had little difficulty enforcing his will on the life and studies of his unofficial ward, Colman. Marriage in 1714 to Anna Maria Gumley, sister of George's mother, Mary, provided Pulteney the financial foundation upon which he eventually established a reputation as the wealthiest man in England, abandoning his political career upon investment as earl of Bath, 13 July 1742.

Following Francis's death, Mary Colman brought George to London, where they were provided housing near Rosamond's Pond, in St. James's Park. Along with his own son, William, Pulteney in 1741 sent Colman to Westminster School, near Westminster Abbey. Colman's comrades at Westminster included Charles Churchill, William Cowper, Richard Cumberland, Edward Gibbon, Robert Lloyd, and Bonnell Thornton, and they would figure prominently in his future literary pursuits. Attending the lower school until 1746, Colman qualified through special examinations as a King's Scholar upon entrance to the upper school, and hence became eligible to attend either Trinity College, Cambridge, or Christ Church, Oxford. Viscount William Pulteney left Westminster School at the age of sixteen to follow an army career, so the family hopes for a scholar rested entirely on George, who in 1750 qualified as second-best King's Scholar and hoped to attend Cambridge with other friends. Pressure from his Oxonian uncle, however, coerced Colman into staying another year at Westminster, after which he distinguished himself as first King's Scholar and matriculated at Christ Church, Oxford, 5 June 1751.

Colman's first extant literary effort is an eighty-line sequence of couplets jealously celebrating his cousin's selection of an exciting vocation, "Verses to the Right Honorable Lord Viscount Pulteney," not published until 1763, when George's theatrical popularity recommended it to Westminster alumnus Robert Lloyd's *St. James's Magazine*. While at Oxford, Colman anonymously published an essay, "A Vision," in Dr. John Hawkesworth's 15 September 1753 *The Adventurer*. The essay exhibits a collegiate admiration of neoclassicism, depicting a dream vision of famous authors burning elements of their works or styles at a sacrificial bonfire "in proportion as the author had ventured to deviate from a judicious imitation of Homer." During his Oxford years Colman maintained a variety of interests related to belles lettres; *Poems by Eminent Ladies* (a hastily culled variety of seventeenth- and eighteenth-century poets) co-edited with Bonnell Thornton came out in 1755, the year Colman earned his Oxford B.A.

Continuing to direct his nephew's education, Pulteney made arrangements for George to study law following graduation, and Colman records the imperative nature of his patron's charge in "The Law Student," a poem written in 1757: "Now Christ-Church left, and fixt at Lincoln's Inn, / Th' important studies of the Law begin." When dissenting vocational options are offered, the earl's voice insistently cries to him, "stick close; close, Coley, to the Bar!" While studying and occupying Lincoln's Inn chambers, Colman partially resisted this advice through two significant pursuits. With the assistance of Bonnell Thornton, he continued to write and edit *The Connoisseur*, a weekly journal of light satiric commentary on popular fashions, tastes, and cultural activities, begun at Oxford and published every Thursday between 31 January 1754 and 30 September 1756. The two Westminster cronies wrote collectively as "Mr. Town," and treated topics such as playhouse behavior, sarcastically observing theatergoer types like "the gentlemen who draw the pen from under their right ears about seven o'clock, clap on a bag-wig and sword, and drop into the boxes at the end of the third act, to take their half-crown's worth with as much decency as possible." *The Connoisseur*'s contributors included former Westminster

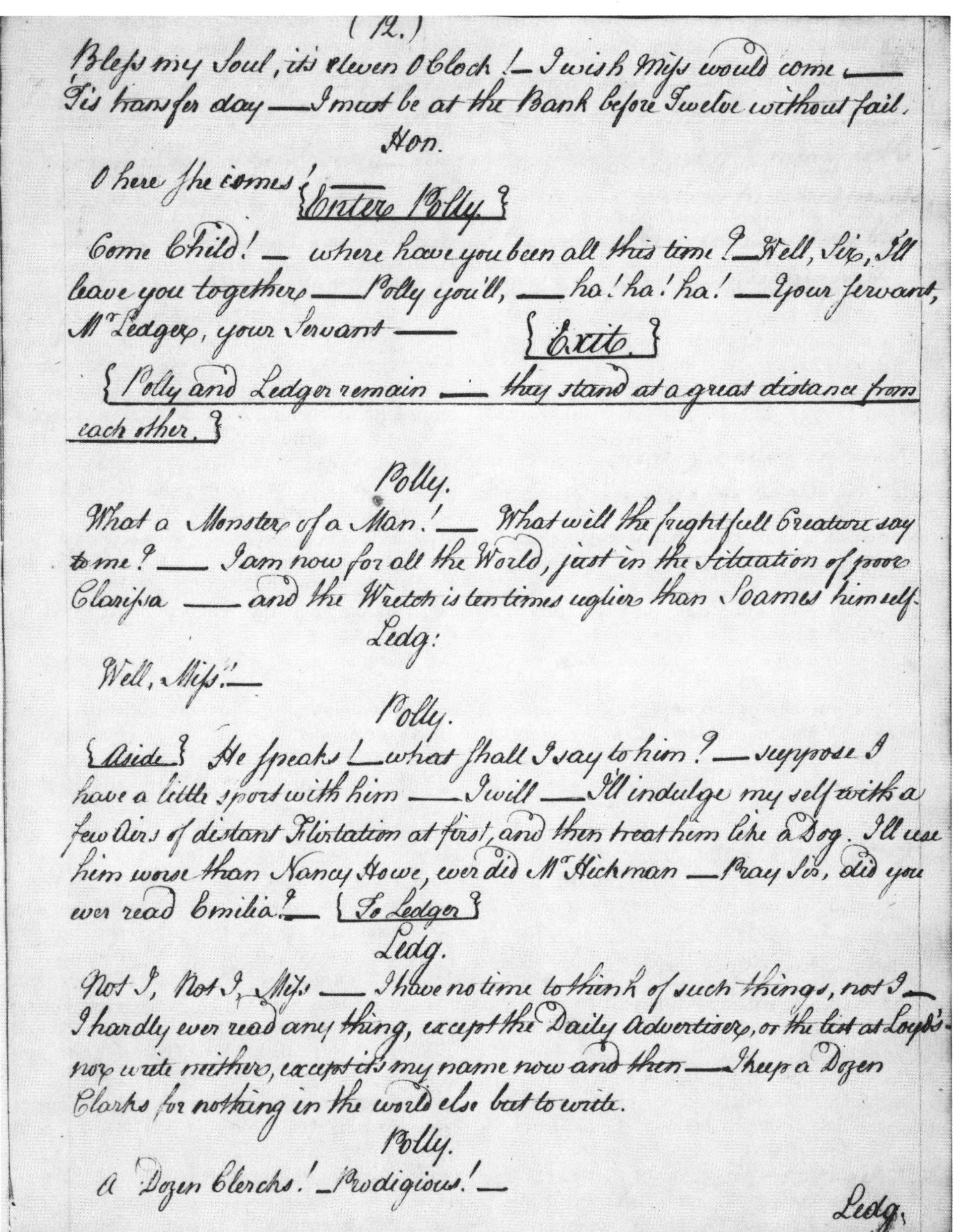

(12.)

Bless my Soul, it's eleven O'Clock! — I wish Miss would come — 'Tis transfer day — I must be at the Bank before Twelve without fail.

Hon.

O here she comes! {Enter Polly.}

Come Child! — where have you been all this time? — Well, Sir, I'll leave you together — Polly you'll, — ha! ha! ha! — Your servant, Mr Ledger, your Servant — {Exit.}

{Polly and Ledger remain — they stand at a great distance from each other.}

Polly.

What a Monster of a Man! — What will the frightfull Creature say to me? — I am now for all the World, just in the Situation of poor Clarissa — and the Wretch is ten times uglier than Soames himself.

Ledg:

Well, Miss!—

Polly.

{Aside} He speaks! — what shall I say to him? — suppose I have a little sport with him — I will — I'll indulge my self with a few Airs of distant Flirtation at first, and then treat him like a Dog. I'll use him worse than Nancy Howe, ever did Mr Hickman — Pray Sir, did you ever read Emilia? — {To Ledger}

Ledg.

Not I, Not I, Miss — I have no time to think of such things, not I — I hardly ever read any thing, except the Daily Advertiser, or the list at Loyd's - nor write neither, except it's my name now and then — I keep a Dozen Clarks for nothing in the world else but to write.

Polly.

A Dozen Clerchs! — Prodigious! —

Ledg.

Page from the playhouse copy of Polly Honeycombe *submitted to the Examiner of Plays for licensing prior to the first performance, on 5 December 1760 (Larpent Collection, LA 179; by permission of the Henry E. Huntington Library and Art Gallery*

colleagues Cowper and Lloyd, and the periodical's popular influence is reflected by favorable reviews and reprinted material in other publications such as *The Gentleman's Magazine*, *The London Magazine*, *Gray's Inn Journal*, and *The Monthly Review*.

The other major distraction in which Colman indulged while at Lincoln's Inn was the Nonsense Club, composed of seven members (including Thornton, Lloyd, and Cowper), which met on Thursday evenings; these mid-century Merry Pranksters staged burlesques and elaborate public practical jokes. Despite his divided interests, Colman did complete his studies and was called to the bar 24 January 1757; he apprenticed on the Oxford legal circuit from 1758 to 1761, and later lampooned the self-serving circuit appointments of legal peers in *The Clandestine Marriage* (1766), where his Counsellor Trueman admits to traveling the western circuit to serve Lord Ogleby "merely because his Lordship's interest and property lie in that part of the kingdom." George's adherence to Pulteney's educational directives was rewarded when the earl granted sufficient funding for him to complete an Oxford M.A. (though making it clear in a letter that the twenty guineas he advanced his nephew were eventually to be "refunded, with what interest you think fit"); Colman received the degree in 1758.

The reluctant lawyer secured his entrance into the London theatrical world by slipping a clever encomium, *A Letter of Abuse to D---d G-----k, Esq.* (1757), into the popular proliferation of pamphlets criticizing the Drury Lane master's selection and direction of plays. Garrick had a good eye for comic talent–as when he signed the mercuric Samuel Foote to act his *The Author* for eighteen performances during the 1756-1757 season–and was probably impressed withColman's satirical skills, further demonstrated in *Two Odes* (1760), co-written with Lloyd, parodying Thomas Gray ("Ode to Obscurity") and William Mason ("Ode to Oblivion").

Colman successfully transferred his talent for satire to the drama, and his "Dramatick Novel in One Act," *Polly Honeycombe*, became the most popular afterpiece of the decade, playing regularly for the next six years and receiving sporadic revivals throughout the three decades following its Drury Lane opening, 5 December 1760. Polly, craving the excitement that is routinely experienced by the heroines of popular romance novels, rejects Ledger, the dull broker selected by her parents as a suitable husband. Her choice is the self-proclaimed writer Scribble, who satisfies her desire for intrigue by sending secret messages: "Will he squeeze it, as he did the last, into the chicken-house in the garden? Or will he write it in lemon-juice, and send it in a book, like blank paper? Or will he throw it into the house, inclosed in an orange?" The allusions to popular characters, novels, and novel devices are numerous, and topicality merges with absurd excess to yield a typically implausible romance resolution: Scribble, revealed as a kinsman of the Honeycombe family's nurse, and not a gentleman, retains Polly's love since "Who knows but he may be a Foundling, and a gentleman's son, as well as Tom Jones?" He wins his beloved by default when Ledger decides "She'd make a terrible wife for a sober citizen," and Mr. Honeycombe rants, "a man might as well turn his Daughter loose in Covent-Garden, as trust the cultivation of her mind to A CIRCULATING LIBRARY." The afterpiece was presented anonymously–primarily in deference to Pulteney–until 12 December, when Garrick then inserted an entreaty into the Prologue for the audience to "Exert your favour to a young Beginner, / Nor use the Stripling like a Batter'd Sinner!"

The *Critical Reflections on the Old English Dramatick Writers . . . Addressed to David Garrick* (1761), published separately and as a preface to an edition by Thomas Davies of Philip Massinger's dramatic works, placed Colman even more solidly in Garrick's favor, and the manager initially played the lead role of the suspected husband, Mr. Oakly, when Colman's mainpiece, *The Jealous Wife*, opened to great success on 12 February. Acknowledging the popularity of sentimental comedy, Colman has Mrs. Oakly's tearful recognition in act 5 reconcile her to her husband; yet the play's opening scene challenges the formula with a marked reversal, as Oakly informs his brother the major of the domestic chaos caused by his wife's jealousy: "Her Love for Me hath confined Me to my House, like a State Prisoner, without the Liberty of seeing my Friends, or the Use of Pen, Ink, and Paper; while my Love for Her has made such a Fool of me, that I have never had the Spirit to contradict Her." Meanwhile, the romantic subplot between Oakly's ward, Charles, and Harriot reflects a nostalgia for Restoration comedy stylistics. The published drama included a fervent apology to Pulteney for "having written a Play entirely without your Knowledge" and for presently attempting "to vindicate one Act of Presumption with

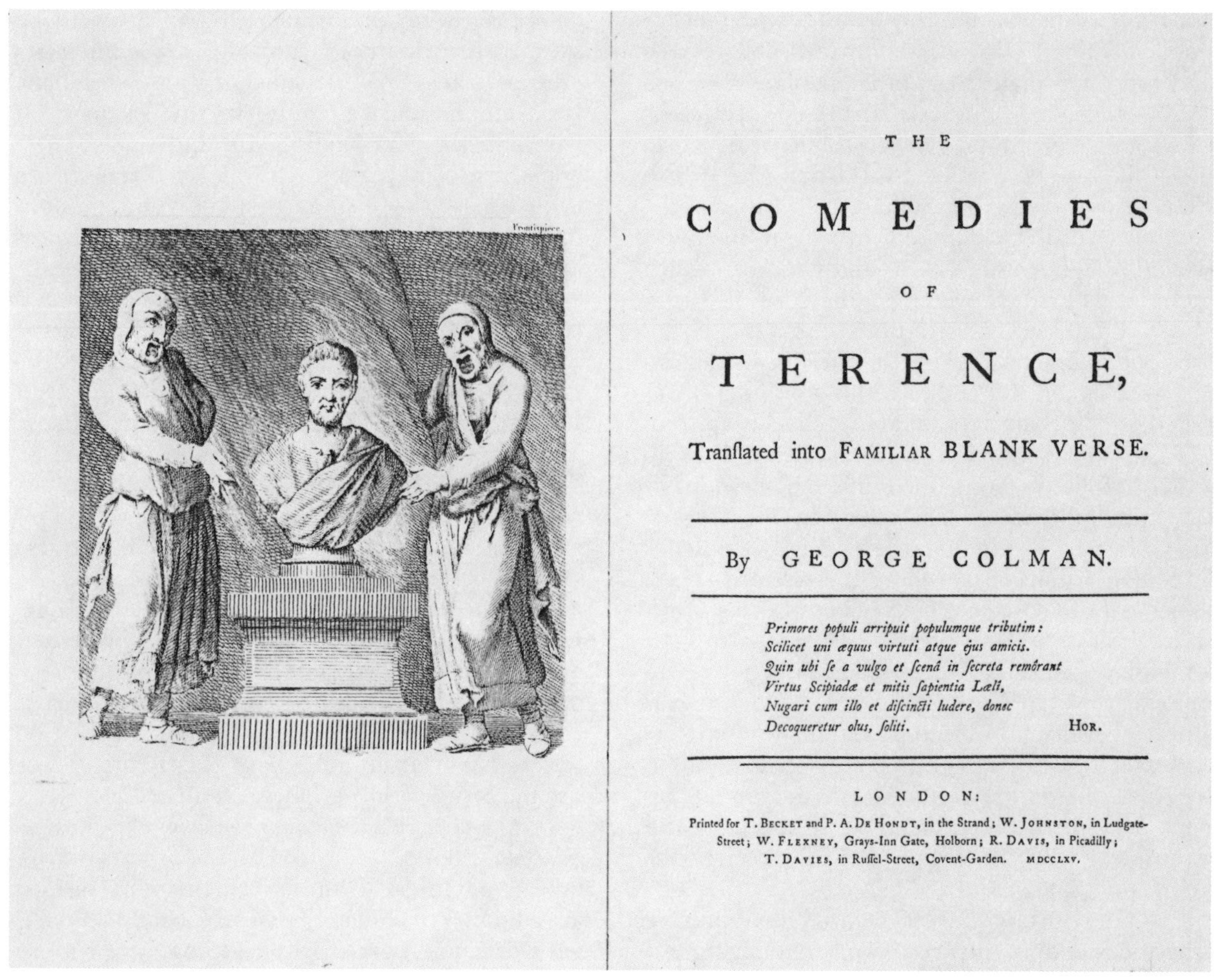

THE

COMEDIES

OF

TERENCE,

Tranflated into FAMILIAR BLANK VERSE.

By GEORGE COLMAN.

Primores populi arripuit populumque tributim:
Scilicet uni æquus virtuti atque ejus amicis.
Quin ubi ſe a vulgo et ſcenâ in ſecreta remôrant
Virtus Scipiadæ et mitis ſapientia Læli,
Nugari cum illo et diſcincti ludere, donec
Decoqueretur olus, ſoliti. HOR.

LONDON:

Printed for T. BECKET and P. A. DE HONDT, in the Strand; W. JOHNSTON, in Ludgate-Street; W. FLEXNEY, Grays-Inn Gate, Holborn; R. DAVIS, in Picadilly; T. DAVIES, in Ruſſel-Street, Covent-Garden. MDCCLXV.

Frontispiece and title page for the translation in which Colman departed from the English tradition of rendering tragedy in blank verse and comedy in prose. In his preface Colman asserts, "Menander and Apollodorus wrote in measure; Terence, who copied from their pieces, wrote in measure; and consequently they, who attempt to render his plays into a modern language, should follow the same method."

another"; Colman adroitly shifts focus to the earl, however, observing that his practice of keeping company with certain "wicked Wits" has obviously not compromised his honor–nor has his nephew's work in the theater.

In addition to his fame, Colman's notoriety also increased in 1761 when Charles Churchill's *Rosciad* satire appeared on 14 March and provoked immediate controversy. While attacking many members of the London literati, it reserved praise for a select few including Colman, Lloyd, and Garrick. The ensuing pamphlet war evoked responses like that published in Tobias Smollett's *Critical Review*, wishing "Long Life, and redundancy of carrion, to the leash of staunch hounds, the ravenous C------ll, the yelping C----n, and the howling L---d!" A vehicle for counterattack was launched by Colman, Garrick, and Thornton with the 18 April publication of the *St. James's Chronicle*, while George spent the spring riding his last Oxford legal circuit. Colman's *Chronicle* contributions cover many subjects, and include, beginning in June, fifteen installations of "The Genius" (1761-1762), a light entertainment series that avoided the controversies addressed by the journal and included the telling "Portrait of the Author, and Description of his Person," describing his height as "little more than five feet" and noting the common reaction that "As I walk along the street, I hear the men and women say to one another, *there goes a little man*!" Also contributing to Colman's notoriety–perhaps acknowledged in the accusations of *The Jealous Wife*'s Mrs. Oakly that Oakly was "keeping" Harriot–

was his maintenance of Sarah Ford, an actress he met in 1760, who had formerly lived with Henry Mossop the actor, by whom she had a daughter–Harriet. Miss Ford perpetuated the Colman dramatic tradition by giving birth to another George Colman, 21 October 1762.

Colman returned to parody of popular affectations in *The Musical Lady*, which premiered in the 1761-1762 season, but was even more popular the following season and was regularly revived for a decade. Originating in the excess of material generated during the composition of *The Jealous Wife*, Colman's third play turns to satire of English infatuation with Italian music and musicians, yet also contains significant autobiographical content. Mask, furnished by his father with "a handsome set of chambers in King's Bench Walks" to study law, settles for a garret, in Old Mask's opinion, "with a worse smell than the county gaol," and sells off all his law books. The earl of Bath's attitude (or George's own guilt) toward his rejection of the legal profession could hardly have been more explicitly portrayed. Mask rests his hopes on marrying Sophy, a young woman of such affected Italianate taste that "I should hardly be surprized at her marriage with one of the *Sopranos* at the opera." Old Mask rails against his son until Freeman informs him of Mask's fortunate marriage to a woman of wealth–at which point he reverses his polemic and compliments the lad's resourcefulness, "Ods-my-life–strip him stark naked, and throw him into the sea, he would rise up again with a sword and bag-wig." Colman must certainly have hoped for similar support from Pulteney as he settled into the professional life of an author.

Colman faced a frenetic year in 1763, both disappointing and encouraging, beginning with the death of his cousin, Viscount Pulteney, 12 February, in Madrid–more than twenty thousand pounds in debt. This discovery convinced the earl of Bath to alter his original will radically, perhaps out of fear of similar profligacy from George. Early in July, while attending an Oxford celebration with Thornton and Churchill, Colman composed a series of four satiric essays entitled *Terrae-Filius*, university wit directed at the institution as well as its playfully "anonymous" author, who "means once more to convert the Tennis-Court into a Playhouse" in order "to present us with new JEALOUS WIVES, and new POLLY HONEYCOMBES, of his own composition." Colman did receive the opportunity to present new theatrical entertainments–not from Oxford, but from an exhausted Garrick, who left him as performance director and James Lacy as business manager of Drury Lane when he departed 15 September to tour the Continent.

Colman exploited the opportunity of including his own material in the 1763-1764 season, filling over twenty percent of the assigned production slots with his original plays or adaptations. His mainpiece adaptation of Francis Beaumont and John Fletcher's pastoral tragicomedy *Philaster* (1609) opened 8 October 1763, featuring the impressive debut of William Powell in the title role, and it played sixteen more times that season. Alterations in the play are typical of eighteenth-century "improvements" on Renaissance drama; it is generally compacted, and act 4's violence is excised, Colman rationalizing that "The Hero's wounding his Mistress [Arethusa] hurt the Delicacy of most; and his maiming *Bellario* [Euphrasia] sleeping, in order to save himself from his Pursuers, offended the Generosity of all." The acting director unveiled an original farce, *The Deuce is in Him*, 4 November, and prompter William Hopkins recorded in his diary that it "gave the Audience such entire Satisfaction, that I never heard such Bursts of Applause." As with Colman's previous stage successes, the play is eclectic in mixing laughing comedy with a small portion of sentimentalism, effectively mocking the latter. Its mainplot describes Colonel Tamper's method of testing the faith of Emily–by pretending to have lost an eye and a leg in recent battle–and its subplot seeks to reunite Mlle. Florival, disguised as a man, with her English lover, Major Belford. Tamper's histrionics ("I would not part with this wooden leg for the best flesh and blood in Christendom") are rewarded with confirmation of his jealousy, once the women learn of his dissembling and convince Mlle. Florival to play the part of a rival, Captain Johnson. Properly shamed in the end, he confesses his pettiness and is forgiven by Emily, providing the formula resolution of the reform comedy.

The season was a success, but Colman suffered some serious setbacks during its run. A collaborative adaptation of *A Midsummer Night's Dream* with Garrick had been in the planning stages for at least a year, and despite some reservations on his absent partner's part, Colman produced it 23 November–his first failure at Drury Lane. Songs are interpolated throughout the text, which omits Shakespeare's act 5 entirely, and Hopkins reported that "never was a Piece so

Sophia Baddeley as Fanny, Thomas King as Lord Ogleby, and Robert King as Canton in a 1770 command performance of The Clandestine Marriage. *George III was so delighted by Mrs. Baddeley's performance that he ordered Johann Zoffany to paint this picture (by permission of the Garrick Club).*

murdered as this was by the Singer-speakers." Ever practical, however, Colman performed radical surgery on the adaptation, and it was successfully performed three nights later as *A Fairy Tale*, its two acts retaining only the mechanicals, the fairies, and twelve songs by Michael Arne, Charles Dibdin, Charles Burney, John Christopher Smith, and James Hook; it appeared sixteen times that season. The remainder of the year was equally difficult for Colman, as exhaustion forced him to follow Garrick to Europe and to recuperate at Paris in May, though he returned to work within two months. His patron Pulteney died 7 July, and George learned to his great disappointment that the bulk of Bath's estate had been left to his disagreeable brother, Gen. Henry Pulteney, while Colman's anticipated inheritance of forty thousand pounds had been reduced to an annuity of nine hundred guineas (this disappointment increased when the estate did not go to Colman upon the general's death in 1767). Other losses followed: the deaths of friends Charles Churchill, 7 November, and Robert Lloyd a few weeks later.

Occupying Colman's attentions in the interim, and filling a need perceived by students of dramatic history, *The Comedies of Terence, Translated into Familiar Blank Verse*, complete with an extensive technical introduction, was published 25 April 1765. He justifies his blank-verse translation as the respect comedy deserves: from almost all forms but tragedy "that measure is now excluded; and since the days of Milton, it has been thought to relish so much of the sublime, that it has scarce ever been suffered to tread the stage, as an attendant to the Comick Muse." His dedication of *The Eunuch* to the King's Scholars of St. Peter's College, Westminster, nostalgically acknowledges his youthful experiences in acting Latin plays there. The collection was well received, and Colman also contributed a translation of Plautus (*The Merchant*) to a collection edited by Thornton in 1767.

It seems ironic that Colman, whose earlier plays generally eschewed or openly mocked the literature and culture of sensibility, should be praised by his contemporaries for the sentimental content of *The Clandestine Marriage*, a full-length mainpiece co-written with Garrick and inspired by the first of six plates in William Hogarth's *Marriage à la Mode*, depicting a marriage brokerage between wealthy parties. Begun before Garrick's departure in 1763, the comedy could not be completed before his return to London, April 1765, and did not open until 20 February 1766. The self-serving lawyers introduced in act 3 (who serve to distance Colman further from his former vocation), the addition of Fanny's pregnancy ("a little tell-tale") to the title's secret union, and the comic range of the amorous though generous Lord Ogleby all contributed to the immediate popularity of the play–traditionally considered Colman's best–performed nineteen times that spring. Colman was forced to make another recuperative journey to Paris later that year, accompanied by Sarah and Harriet, while young George remained behind at Northumberland House, the playwright's new villa.

Lady Alton takes Spatter of *The English Merchant* (1767) to task for alleged ingratitude: "Did not I draw you out of the garret, where you daily spun out your flimsy brain to catch the town flies in your cobweb dissertations? Did not I introduce you to Lord Dapperwit, the Apollo of the age?" Virtually prophesying sentiments Garrick would express to its author later that year, this passage is suggestive of factors contributing to the decision that Colman's unambiguously sentimental (and consequently popular) mainpiece would be his last new play at Drury Lane for nine years. The first problem was a prior disagreement when Garrick had refused to play Ogleby in *The Clandestine Marriage* despite early assurance to his co-author that he would; the more significant schism, however, occurred when Colman became a partner with Thomas Harris, William Powell, and John Rutherford in purchasing the Covent Garden theater and patent from John Beard, thanks in part to money he inherited from Mary Colman, who died 3 May. This transaction resulted in Garrick losing his most popular playwright, and, in Powell, his most popular young actor.

Although the 1767-1768 season at Covent Garden opened officially under Colman's management, disputes with his co-patentees erupted almost at once, primarily over choice roles and separate dressing rooms for actresses "sponsored" by Harris (Mrs. Jane Hemet Lessingham) and Rutherford (Mrs. George Anne Bellamy), while the Covent Garden company routinely supported their director / manager. A pamphlet war between the rival parties ensued, and hostilities remained active until a suit brought by Harris and Rutherford's successors, solicitor Henry Dagge and James Leake the bookseller, against the manager was judged in Colman's favor, 20 July 1770. Despite such distractions, Colman scheduled two plays from his own pen that first season, one original and one adaptation. *The Oxonian in Town* played over twenty times, despite an interruption of its third night, 10 November, based on complaints that the character of McShuffle, one of the London sharpers attempting to swindle Oxonian Frank Careless, was an Irish slur. Since the other crooks, Rook and Shark, are clearly *not* Irish, the play's antigambling stance is unequivocably portrayed, and a statement declaring no intention of anti-Hibernianism was published the next day, there were no subsequent interruptions. Colman's adaptation of *King Lear*, opening 20 February 1768, sought to retain the positive resolution of Nahum Tate's adaptation without inventing the Edgar / Cordelia romance Shakespeare never intended. The play concludes with Goneril and Regan mutually poisoned at a banquet, Lear happily surrounded by friends Cordelia, Kent ("Thou Kent, and I, in sweet tranquility / Will gently pass the evening of our days"), Edgar, and Gloucester ("My poor dark Glo'ster!"). It played but three times that season.

Colman was too practical a businessman to fail to exploit the unrestrained Bardolatry inspired by Garrick's Shakespeare Jubilee at Stratford, 6-7 September 1769. After surviving the rain that plagued that celebration, the Drury Lane manager advertised the Jubilee's transference to the stage–but not before 14 October. In the interim, Colman capitalized on the delay by opening his own *Man and Wife; or, The Shakespeare Jubilee* on 7 October. Dapperwit, the Colman persona, explains in the prelude that he is mourning "for a dear and worthy friend, and a most valuable partner–a man, whose goodness of heart was even superior to his admirable tal-

Elizabeth Hartley, who created the title role in Colman's adaptation of a play by William Mason (frontispiece to the 1796 edition of Elfrida*)*

ents in his profession": the reference is to Powell, who had died 3 July 1769 of complications resulting from a cold caught playing cricket. The comedy quickly moves to the chaos of severely overbooked Stratford and the attempts of Colonel Frankly and Charlotte to marry despite her quarreling parents, Mr. and Mrs. Cross (a conflict anticipating the moral conclusion "that nothing is so necessary as harmony among those whose interests are so intimately connected as those of Man and Wife"). A spectacular "Pageant, Exhibiting the Characters of Shakespeare" parades between acts 2 and 3, including delicious juxtapositions such as Richard III marching with the two Princes in the Tower, or Coriolanus with the "Roman Ladies–dishevelled." Garrick eventually had the greater triumph with his extremely popular and extravagant *The Jubilee;* as of 24 January 1770 Colman stripped his comedy of its prelude and pageantry, reducing it to an afterpiece.

A tragic accident marked Colman's Easter week, 1771, as Sarah Colman–who had become his wife sometime between 1767 and 1769–mistakenly swallowed the wrong medicine for a slight ailment and died of its effects. The Covent Garden master had created two new pieces for the 1770-1771 season, both effectively supported with music by Samuel Arnold. *The Portrait,* a one-act burletta, warns against May / December marriages (with Pantaloon in the latter role) and raises the musical question, "Can the young e'er agree with

George Mattocks in the first production of Achilles in Petticoats

the old / To form a ridiculous pair; / Or ladies endure to be sold / Like the cattle expos'd at a fair?" Renewed interest in harlequinades, like the topical *Harlequin's Jubilee*, or traditional favorite *Harlequin Doctor Faustus*, which had more than fifty performances in the 1768-1769 season, contributed to making Colman's pantomime, *Mother Shipton; or, The Harlequin Gladiator*, a similar success, running fifty-seven times before the end of the 1770-1771 season and earning its author the popular sobriquet "Mother Shipton."

Differences with co-patentee Harris were finally resolved in December 1771, when he became a member of the Sublime Society of Beefsteaks–of which Colman had been a member since 1767–a fraternal coterie of movers and shakers in London society and letters whose founders included John Rich and William Hogarth, and whose membership was graced with luminaries such as Sir Joshua Reynolds, Dr. Johnson, the Prince of Wales, and Richard B. Sheridan. Colman's only new authorial contribution to the Covent Garden season was *The Fairy Prince*, an adaptation of Ben Jonson's *Oberon, the Faery Prince* (1611), employing the masque's extravagant form to take advantage of popular interest in the installation of the Knights of the Garter. The second part of the masque, staged at "*The Lower Court of Windsor Castle, with a View of the Round Tower, the outside of St. George's Chapel, &c.*," ends with a procession of knights and their entourages at St. George's Chapel. The Grand Chorus ends the piece declaring "Great GEORGE's name / Shall be the Theme of Fame. / Record the GARTER's Glory! / A badge for Heroes, and for Kings to bear." The popular afterpiece ran consecutively for twenty-two nights following its 12 November premiere, though this triumph was marred on 30 November, when Colman experienced an epileptic seizure while at the theater that necessitated several weeks of complete rest before he could resume his responsibilities.

An Occasional Prelude, composed to open the 1772-1773 season, is a rich document revealing much about the realities of working professional theater. At once self-deprecatory and disparaging of the popularity of puppet shows, the playwright has two chairmen (men sent in advance literally to "hold" chairs for performances) discuss the Covent Garden manager: "To be sure he is no bigger than one of the Outlandish poppits at the Hole in the Wall yonder." The manager asks his carpenter if he has "Brush'd up Mother Shipton" and "laid by the Fairy Prince," and the harried laborer complains about "the Gentleman Managers now-a-days," each of whom are so "full of Fly-traps and Somersets, and Trick upon Trick" one would think "he had been born and bred a Harlequin." Lamenting the deluge of unsolicited manuscripts pouring into his playhouse, the manager waxes philosophical: "The theatre is a Foundling Hospital for wit–limited indeed–for we can no more take in all that are brought, than the other Foundling Hospital." In the same season Colman also introduced two new adaptations, of Milton's *Comus* (1634) and William Mason's *Elfrida* (1751), both incorporating music by Dr. Thomas Arne. Colman justified his excision of the "divine arguments on temperance and chastity" in *Comus* because even "the most accomplished declaimers have been embarrassed in recitation of them." It did not, however, popularly displace John Dalton's 1738 adaptation, which had retained the masque's didactic portions. *Elfrida*, written more than twenty years earlier but not for performance, was adapted without its author's knowledge; outraged, Mason wrote Lord Nuneham (2 December 1772) that "little Colman and old fumbling Dr. Arne have committed a rape on the body of my poor daughter *Friddy*." Perhaps spurred by the controversy, theatergoers returned to see the play twenty-seven times that season.

Covent Garden coffers benefited unexpectedly from one Colman experiment in 1773, while its manager gained a valuable lesson in practical dramaturgy from the other. Colman guaranteed his place in literary history by offering the premiere of Oliver Goldsmith's *The Mistakes of a Night, or She Stoops to Conquer* on 15 March, a play he–and Garrick, and virtually everyone else in London theatrical circles–little suspected capable of averaging more than two hundred fifty pounds per night through its twelve spring performances. Further demonstrating his willingness to take risks, he rewrote John Gay's opera *Achilles* (1733), inserting new songs to music by Thomas Arne, simply for the opportunity of presenting an entirely transvestite cast. While *Achilles in Petticoats* proved a pointless addition to Colman's list of personal adaptations in terms of theatrical revenue–the audiences apparently agreed with Ajax, "Spare your jokes, Periphas, for my courage wants no farther provocation"–it did demonstrate the comedic potential of cross dressing, potential he would find profitable several years later at the Haymarket.

The 1773-1774 season ran one more Colman original, *The Man of Business*, which provoked reviews like the February 1774 *Westminster Magazine*'s that condemned it as "dull, tedious, uninteresting and improbable," an interesting response to the comedy's polemical focus on the unreliability and vindictiveness of the press. Bad reviews led Colman to play the martyr for freedom of expression in the drama's published dedication: "Better were it that thousands and ten thousands of such insignificant individuals as myself should be maliciously slandered, than that sacred right of Englishmen should be violated or infringed." Its reform-comedy plot combines a comedy of manners structure with the prodigal son motif of Terentian comedy, featuring an essentially good but fashionably frivolous young man (Beverly) who fritters away a fortune before being shown the errors of his ways and thereby becomes eligible to marry his virtuous beloved (Lydia) thanks to help from a parent / patron (Golding, Lydia's real father). Onto this structure are grafted vehement attacks on the newspapers' gossip and society columns (Tropick says of them "there are not a more silly, empty, insolent, impudent, ignorant, lying vermin, than your framers of common reports and collectors of personal paragraphs") and on abuses of the law, as displayed by the unscrupulous Denier ("A Caesar, a Machiavel, sir! You know all the turnings and windings and narrow back stairs of the law too"). Though not a failure per se, this frustrated effort toward more serious comedy played only thirteen nights and signaled to Colman that it was time to resign as Covent Garden's manager. He was succeeded by Thomas Hull (who continued Colman's practice of personally adapting a wide variety of theatrical pieces) later that spring and was given an official farewell at the end of the season, 26 May, when a mock elegy he had composed was read as an epilogue, encouraging "Thus having buried him let's waive Dissection! / 'Tis now too late to give his faults correction."

Besides writing reviews for *The Public Advertiser* and *The London Chronicle*, between 10 July and 4 December 1775 Colman was also a regular

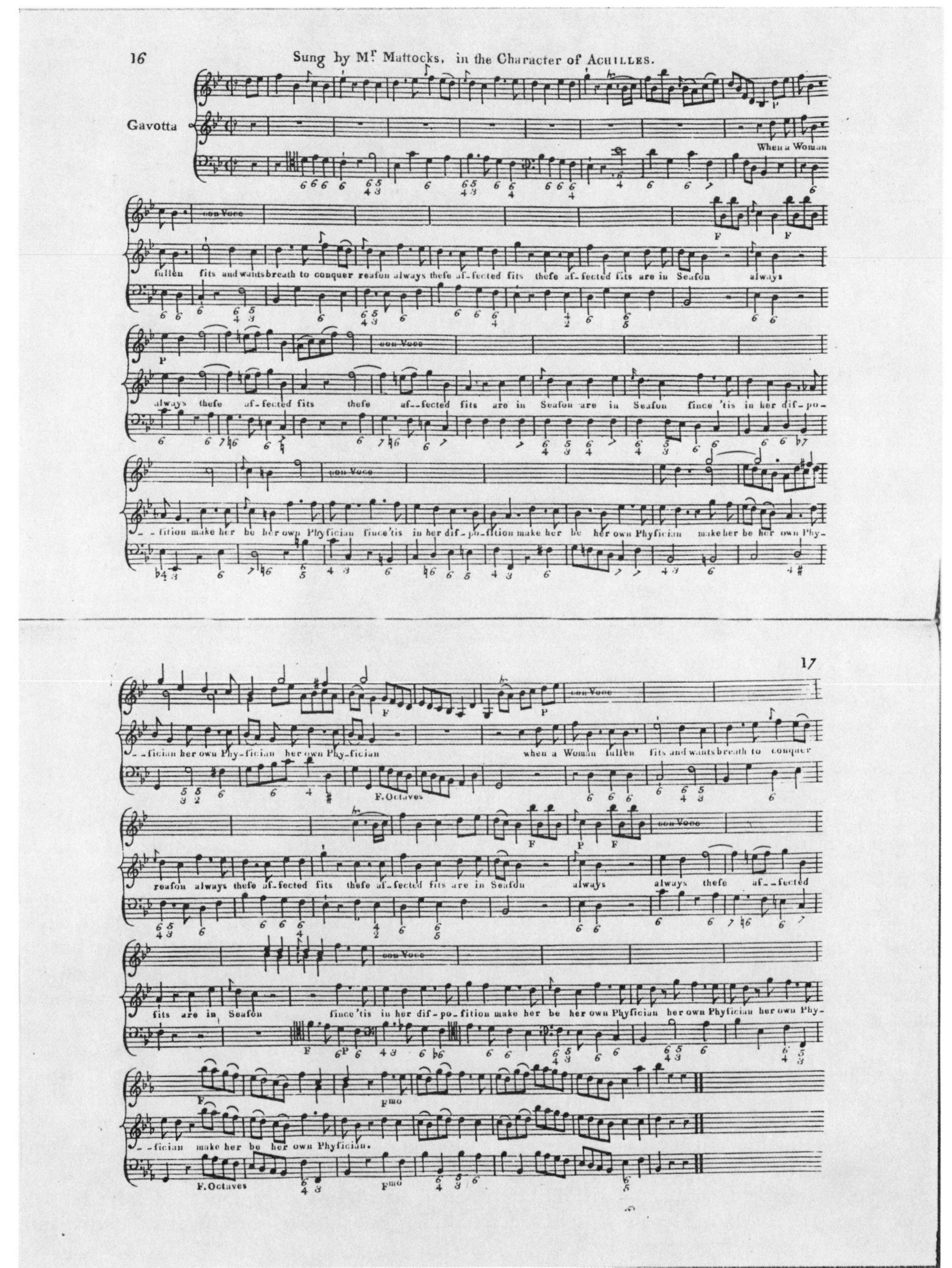

Song written by Thomas Arne for Achilles in Petticoats *(from* The Overture, Songs &c. in the Opera of Achilles in Petticoats, *1774)*

Hester Colles as the title character in Colman's adaptation of John Gay's Polly *(drawing by J. Roberts; by permission of the Trustees of the British Museum)*

contributor to *The London Packet*; these pieces included biographical impressions and six essays entitled "The Gentleman," playfully signed with pseudonyms such as "Chiaro Oscuro" and "The Blackguard." Their old wounds finally healed, Garrick produced Colman's adaptation of Ben Jonson's *Epicoene; or, The Silent Woman* (1609) on 13 January 1776, but without success, despite the presence of the inimitable Mrs. Sarah Siddons in the lead. Author and manager undaunted–perhaps in an effort to build a clientele for the manager Garrick hoped would succeed him–an original Colman farce premiered at Drury Lane on 7 March; *The Spleen; or, Islington Spa* played only seven times, largely because of its late entry in the season. Its delightful dramatis personae–featuring a hypochondriac (D'Oyley), quack apothecaries (Rubrick and MacHoof), and a phony doctor (Laetitia, disguised as Dr. Anodyne, who tells the querulous D'Oyley he need not avoid the juices of red meats: "Without them, Sir, instead of beef or mutton, you might as well eat mahogany")–combine with more media criticism (in the shape of a redundant journal called the *Noon-Post*, which "is the only time of day, you know, left open for an additional news-paper") and a feasible love plot to produce a very compact, full comic entertainment that seems mysteriously to have failed–not unlike some of the "spas" it satirizes.

Colman's career was not damaged by this lull because it coincided with the confusion caused by vital personnel shifts in London theater management. Garrick left Drury Lane at the completion of the 1775-1776 season and was succeeded by Richard Brinsley Sheridan. Commemorating the event, Colman wrote *New Brooms! An Occasional Prelude*, which opened on 21 September to inaugurate the 1776-1777 season. It begins admid the bustle of playgoers from every social station ("Have a care of your pockets, gentlefolks!"), but it moves quickly away from this setting; the drama critic Catcall decides he would prefer to visit Mr. Crochet the author rather than to see the scheduled piece. The entertainment at Mr. Crochet's is pompous and topical–but also reflective of some of the very tastes that Colman himself encouraged in London audiences, as Crochet's new opera, *Topsy-Turvy*, is set in the

115

Enter Squib & Nancy.

Tob. Oh! your servant, Gentlemen! Come, we have no time to lose. Let's to business immediately. The Pops are much of a length, I hope. Where are yours, Bounce?

Bou. Here, sir, here are my instruments — um — um —

Tob. And yours, Squib?

Squib. Here — heigho!

Tob. All fair — well, how far off will you stand? not less than ten paces, I hope. Let me see — (beginning to measure

Nancy. Stay, sir! Just before we arriv'd, Mr Squib said something of an accommodation.

Tob. Accommodation? impossible, Rattle. You know to what lengths matters have been carried between them.

Bounce. Let's hear what the gentleman has to say, however, Mr Tobine!

Page from the playhouse copy of The Suicide *submitted to the Examiner of Plays for licensing prior to the first performance, on 11 July 1778 (Larpent Collection, LA 450; by permission of the Henry E. Huntington Library and Art Gallery)*

Antipodes where "The ladies judge, fight, swear, drink, ravish" while "the gentlemen knit, spin, scold, pout." Another shift in the theatrical world was initiated when Samuel Foote, master of the Haymarket, formalized agreements with Colman in late 1776 to make the former Covent Garden manager the new manager of the Haymarket–at a potentially risky price of sixteen hundred pounds per year. Appropriately, on 16 September 1776, Colman's first piece to be performed at the Haymarket had been his adaptation of *The Tailors; A Tragedy for Warm Weather*, an anonymous blank-verse farce detailing the Tailors' War between the Flints and the Dungs, a play designed to provide a backdrop for contemporary allusions and literary satire. The unruly Haymarket crowd of 1767 had already forced Foote to reduce the play from three acts to an afterpiece, but it still had not pleased.

Colman officially received the Haymarket lease on 16 January 1777 and opened his first summer season with *The English Merchant*, at the same time his adaptation of *The Tailors* proved an audience favorite. An adaptation of Pierre-Augustin Caron de Beaumarchais's *The Spanish Barber; or, The Fruitless Precaution* (1775), supplemented with music by Samuel Arnold and premiering 30 August, became an immediate and permanent Haymarket standard. Its depiction of the loyal Lazarillo's endeavors to assist Count Almaviva's courtship of Rosina was performed each season for the following twenty-two years (except in 1795, when it played exclusively at Drury Lane). Without serious damage, the new manager also produced two unsuccessful adaptations, one of John Gay's opera *Polly*, the other of Shakespeare's *The Winter's Tale*, entitled *The Sheep-Shearing*. Foote died 21 October, after receiving only one of Colman's semi-annual payments of eight hundred pounds, and the new manager secured the Haymarket lease annually thereafter from the lord chamberlain. Although Foote had made the Haymarket profitable, and was universally applauded for his talents at "taking off" public figures, Colman brought experience and professionalism with him–acquiring established performers to reinforce the flux of players from the winter patent houses, and replacing "certain decayed and moth-eaten articles, which Foote dignified by the collective name of a wardrobe"–that earned the little theater greater popularity, if less notoriety.

Two important projects appearing in 1778 received the benefit of Colman's editorship: an assortment of six plays by Samuel Foote and *The Dramatick Works of Beaumont and Fletcher*, the latter reflecting critical facility with the Renaissance texts for which he demonstrated a lifelong enthusiasm–while respecting traditional standards of quality, as when he judiciously notes that the best drama of Francis Beaumont and John Fletcher "would hardly disgrace the stage which has exhibited *The Two Gentlemen of Verona*." Supporting his critical edition, Colman produced his adaptation of Fletcher's *Bonduca* (circa 1611) on 30 July 1778, prudently supported with music by Henry Purcell; it had twelve performances that summer. No text remains for Colman's adaptation *The Female Chevalier*, which opened the 1778 Haymarket season, but the reasons for its failure (eight performances scheduled, never revived) may be hinted in *The London Chronicle*'s comments that the original, William Taverner's *The Artful Husband* (1717), issued from a writer whose works "are now little known but by the sweepers of dramatic cobwebs."

The Suicide, a work as unconventional as its four-act structure suggests, opened 11 July 1778; it exhibited once again the inventive wit of Colman's early comedies even as it addressed London's fashionable proclivity toward self-destruction. Tobine, a mercer by fate though a masquerader by choice, decides to commit suicide once it becomes clear that his finances are all but exhausted and he has guaranteed that none of his partners will suffer from his loss–although his abandoned love, Nancy, disguised as Dick Rattle, is consulted for advice on the most effective method. She procures a narcotic from concerned Dr. Truby–theatrical reincarnation of Friar Lawrence–thereby setting up the Shakespearean intertextuality of Tobine's suicide soliloquy:

> To be or not to be, that is the question–To be a Gentleman, a man of the world, a man of property, a man of pleasure–*tis a situation devoutly to be wished*–But then to be ruin'd, to be a Bankrupt, to be in the Gazette, ay, *there's the rub! Come, cordial, & not poison!*

Black humor (Juggins the tavern owner, thinking Tobine dead, accuses Tom Cellerman of putting "too much arsenick into the Sherry"), the vicarious pleasure of attacking the entire dramatic community with impunity (Catchpenny the author complains about playgoers to Ranter the actor: "Their taste is vitiated by the barbarity & ignorance of the Managers, & corrupted by the

Charles Bannister as Polly Peachum in Colman's 1781 production of The Beggar's Opera Reversed, *John Gay's popular opera with the roles played by members of the opposite sexes (etching based on a drawing by J. Sayer)*

badness of the Actors"), and a jolly resolution (Dr. Truby exacts promises from the lovers that "you Madam, will never more quit the Petticoat, nor you, Mr. Tobine ever die again as long as you live") contribute to the finest play of Colman's later years.

Colman produced another provocative four-act original during the Haymarket's 1779 season, *The Separate Maintenance*, which appeared 31 August and was revived each summer for eight subsequent seasons. Criticizing the eighteenth century's genteel version of the trial separation, it concludes "A woman, parted from her husband, her natural protector, is always in danger"–although that danger is limited to damaged reputation, as Lady Newbery and her sister Miss English are more than a match for the self-fashioned beau, Leveret. With occasionally barbed humor, Colman treats topical concerns like fashionable indifference (Leveret declares "Sulkiness ever attends Dignity. It's vulgar to talk, and more vulgar to be civil"), bluestockings, tyro dramatists, and London entertainment year round (Lady Fustian storms out when no one will indulge a reading of her turgid *Cyrus Son of Cambyses*, screaming "Tragedy is as much above your sphere, as dancing is below mine . . . I shall therefore leave private Society to Cards, Dice, and trivial Dissipation–and public Amusements to shew, Song, and Dance in the Winter, and Gross Buffoonery in the Summer").

With the summer season opening on 30 May 1780 of *The Manager in Distress*, the Haymarket recovered from the 1 March 1780 miscalculation on Colman's part when he rented the theater for Charles Dibdin's *Pasquin's Budget;* when it was discovered to be a puppet show, the angry spectators rioted. *The Manager in Distress* addresses the perennial Haymarket problem of personnel shortages that resulted whenever the patentees of the large playhouses decided "that *one* house shou'd withdraw their performers, and the *other* forbid theirs from supplying their places." The "Little Manager" milked sympathy successfully from his patrons, as his distress played for thirty performances that summer. Though en-

George Colman the Elder (portrait by Thomas Gainsborough; by permission of the National Portrait Gallery, London)

tered late in the season, *The Genius of Nonsense* was another hit and ran frequently the following year. The farce opens with Harlequin determining to sew his mouth shut since "the Managers of the Playhouse have put so much Nonsense into my Mouth, that I have resolved never to open it again." Pantomimes, nonsense songs (such as the "*Animal Accompaniments*" to Harlequin's "I'm master of *Forte, Piano*: / Notes suited to every case. / Like puppies, I yelp in *Soprano*, / Or growl, like a bull-dog, in base"), and harlequinade physical humor were confirmed as foolproof ingredients for success at London's summer playhouse.

The summer of 1781 turned topsy-turvy on 8 August, when Colman began reaping the box-office rewards of his earlier experimentation with *Achilles in Petticoats*. Hitchcock the Prompter, in the manager's *Preludio*, complains that the production of *Beggar's Opera* (so called because its author's name is Beggar) may be delayed because "Polly is but half shaved; and besides, Mr. Bannister's Jumps are so tight, that the Carpenter is not able to lace them." This comic chaos preceded *The Beggar's Opera Reversed*, with Gay's roles played by members of the opposite sexes, an innovation that, according to the *Preludio*'s Townly, was "not half absurd enough either"–so the nonsense bill was completed by *Medea and Jason*, a burlesque ballet. The entertainment that George Colman the Younger called a "monstrous exhibition" also played the following summer, in addition to the manager's new adaptations of George Lillo's *Fatal Curiosity* and Ben Jonson's *Volpone*, and an original pantomime, *Harlequin Teague; or, The Giant's Causeway*, co-written with John O'Keefe. *Harlequin Teague* was a particular favorite with the 1782 Haymarket patrons, as it features the "Characters Out of Character" (such as the Disinterested Lawyer and the Fighting Quakers), the Dwarf who claims to be Cormack the Irish Giant, and The Man With Two Heads (named Unicorpudunocapitalapidus). It played twenty-three times for their pleasure.

Colman reaffirmed his talent for translation when he published *The Art of Poetry: An Epistle to the Pisos* (1783), a rendering of Horace's *Epistola ad Pisones, de arte poetica* into heroic couplets (and occasional triplets). He also proved himself still capable of raising controversy, as his prelude, *The Election of the Managers*, initially was refused a license for its allusions to alleged election bribery but finally opened 2 June 1784. "Little Bayes," the Colman persona, returns to a familiar theme when he cries, "The Press is a most powerful Engine, & must ever retain its dignity & influence in a free country," and Type asserts that the newspapers have been fully liberated: "No terrors of Newgate or the Pillory now–None of your stars & your dashes! but names and titles at full length." The playful manager displays his endearingly self-deprecatory humor once again in the final scene's anti-Bayes rally, at which certain posters depicting a child and a rod are inscribed "*Birch for little Bayes*."

After facing the recurrent torments of gout for several years, Colman suffered a stroke in October 1785 that left him partially paralyzed and unable to speak without difficulty. His health deteriorated steadily after that. More-frequent epileptic seizures eroded his mental condition until it finally became necessary in 1790 to institutionalize him at Paddington, where he died 14 August 1794. Surprisingly, this final period of Colman's life yielded additional literary output. His adaptation of an unsuccessful Joseph Atkinson play, which he entitled *Tit for Tat*, earned him the original author's thanks as it opened 29 August 1786 and continued to be popular for the next four years. *Prose on Several Occasions, Accompanied with Some Pieces in Verse* appeared in 1787, collecting his satires, newspaper contributions, essays, and many of his legions of prologues and epilogues. A play credited to Colman by the 29 August 1787 *Public Advertiser* the day after its opening, *The Village Lawyer* perhaps discourages such attribution in its gleeful pardon of the cozening lawyer, Scout; Colman's lawyers rarely fared so well. His final dramatic piece, *Ut Pictura Poesis! or, The Enraged Musician*, ran for fifteen performances during the Haymarket's 1789 season, its short burlesque action culminating in a *tableau vivant* recreation of Hogarth's painting *The Enraged Musician*.

Curiously repeating history, Colman had compelled his son to study law as he had been similarly compelled by the earl of Bath–with the same result, for young George rebelled and became a successful playwright. Pulteney, however, never encouraged his protégé's theatrical ambitions, while Colman the Elder gave his son most prudent help–by playing young George's first drama, *The Female Dramatist* (16 August 1782), anonymously (prudent as "it was uncommonly hissed!" according to the author), and by watching anxiously in the wings while the first play publicly acknowledged as the work of George Colman the Younger, *Two to One* (19 June 1784), played successfully to the Haymarket crowd. His career well founded, the son managed the Haymarket for his father in absentia from 1790 to 1794, at which time he became the official licensee.

Colman's dramatic canon is a mine of successful eighteenth-century comedic stylizations. His talent for dramatic satire–of fashions, of social distinctions–transcends the immediately topical and contemporary, as plays such as *The Deuce is in Him*, *The Suicide*, and *The Separate Maintenance* remain sharp and authentic in their depictions of human foibles, not the least because they are more brooding and cynical than most of the dramatic surprises in "Mother Shipton's" repertoire. As revelations of the tribulations routinely faced and conquered by the theater manager, Colman's preludes (*An Occasional Prelude*, *New Brooms!*, *Preludio*, *The Manager in Distress*, and *The Election of the Managers*), written both at large Covent Garden and at the Haymarket's "Little nutshell," are invaluable. "Little Coley" has been unfortunately ignored by modern literary critics, a neglect which can only be explained by the unavailability (until Burnim's 1983 edition) of the dramatist's works–for they are literate, funny, and accessible, certainly worthy of revival on our contemporary stage.

Letters:

Posthumous Letters, from Various Celebrated Men: Addressed to Francis Colman and George Colman the Elder: with Annotations and Occasional Remarks, &c., edited by George Colman the Younger (London: Cadell & Davies, 1820);

Richard Brinsley Peake, *Memoirs of the Colman Family, Including Their Correspondence with the Most Distinguished Personages of Their Time* (London: R. Bentley, 1841).

Biography:

Eugene Richard Page, *George Colman, the Elder: Essayist, Dramatist, and Theatrical Manager 1732-1794* (New York: Columbia University Press, 1935).

References:

Theodore Baird, "The Life and Works of George Colman the Elder," Ph.D. dissertation, Harvard University, 1929;

Joseph M. Beatty, Jr., "Garrick, Colman, and *The*

Clandestine Marriage," *Modern Language Notes*, 36 (March 1921): 129-141;

Frederick L. Bergmann, "David Garrick and *The Clandestine Marriage*," *PMLA*, 67 (March 1952): 148-162;

Richard Bevis, *The Laughing Tradition: Stage Comedy in Garrick's Day* (Athens: University of Georgia Press, 1980);

Terence M. Freeman, "With Arched Brow and Leering Eye: The Resurgence of Satiric Drama in the British Theatre of the Third Quarter of the Eighteenth Century," Ph.D. dissertation, University of Pennsylvania, 1986;

Ross Allen Grossman, "Two Unpublished Plays by George Colman the Elder," Ph.D. dissertation, Claremont Graduate School, 1976;

Kathleen M. Lynch, "Pamela Nubile, *L'Ecossaise* and *The English Merchant*," *Modern Language Notes*, 47 (February 1932): 94-96;

Harry William Pedicord, "George Colman's Adaptation of Garrick's Promptbook for *Florizel and Perdita*," *Theatre Survey*, 22 (November 1981): 185-190;

George W. Stone, Jr., "*A Midsummer Night's Dream* in the Hands of Garrick and Colman," *PMLA*, 54 (June 1939): 467-482;

Paul Stanley Varner, "The Comic Techniques of George Colman the Elder," Ph.D. dissertation, University of Tennessee, 1982;

Howard P. Vincent, "Christopher George Colman, 'Lunatick,' " *Review of English Studies*, 18 (January 1942): 38-48.

Papers:

Manuscripts of many of Colman's plays are housed in the Larpent Collection of the Huntington Library, San Marino, California. The British Museum holds a collection of Colman's letters.

George Colman the Younger

(21 October 1762-26 October 1836)

Martin J. Wood
University of Wisconsin–Eau Claire

PLAY PRODUCTIONS: *The Female Dramatist*, based upon a character in Tobias Smollett's *Roderick Random*, London, Theatre Royal in the Hay-Market, 16 August 1782;

Two to One, London, Theatre Royal in the Hay-Market, 19 June 1784;

Turk and No Turk, London, Theatre Royal in the Hay-Market, 9 July 1785;

Inkle and Yarico, based upon Richard Steele's *Spectator* no. 11, London, Theatre Royal in the Hay-Market, 4 August 1787;

Ways and Means; or A Trip to Dover, London, Theatre Royal in the Hay-Market, 10 July 1788;

The Family Party, possibly by Colman, London, Theatre Royal in the Hay-Market, 11 July 1789;

The Battle of Hexham, or Days of Old, London, Theatre Royal in the Hay-Market, 11 August 1789;

The Surrender of Calais, London, Theatre Royal in the Hay-Market, 30 July 1791;

Poor Old Hay-Market, or Two Sides of the Gutter, London, Theatre Royal in the Hay-Market, 15 June 1792;

The Mountaineers, London, Theatre Royal in the Hay-Market, 3 August 1793;

New Hay at the Old Market, London, Theatre Royal in the Hay-Market, 9 June 1795; adapted by Colman as *Sylvester Daggerwood*, London, Theatre Royal in the Hay-Market, 7 July 1796;

The Iron Chest, adapted from William Godwin's novel *The Adventures of Caleb Williams*, London, Theatre Royal, Drury Lane, 12 March 1796;

The Heir at Law, London, Theatre Royal in the Hay-Market, 15 July 1797;

Blue-Beard, or Female Curiosity, adapted from Grétry's *Barbe bleue*, London, Theatre Royal, Drury Lane, 16 January 1798;

Blue Devils, a translation and adaptation of Joseph Patrat's *L'Anglais, ou Le Fou Raisonnable*, London, Theatre Royal, Covent Garden, 24 April 1798;

Feudal Times, or The Banquet Gallery, London, Theatre Royal, Drury Lane, 19 January 1799;

The Castle of Sorrento, by Henry Heartwell, revised by Colman, London, Theatre Royal in the Hay-Market, 13 July 1799;

The Review, or the Wags of Windsor, London, Theatre Royal in the Hay-Market, 1 September 1800;

The Poor Gentleman, London, Theatre Royal, Covent Garden, 11 February 1801;

John Bull, or the Englishman's Fireside, London, Theatre Royal, Covent Garden, 5 March 1803;

Love Laughs at Locksmiths, London, Theatre Royal in the Hay-Market, 25 July 1803;

Gay Deceivers, or More Laugh than Love, London, Theatre Royal in the Hay-Market, 22 August 1804;

Who Wants a Guinea?, London, Theatre Royal, Covent Garden, 18 April 1805;

We Fly by Night, or Long Stories, a translation and adaptation of *Le Conteur, ou Les Deux Postes*, London, Theatre Royal, Covent Garden, 28 January 1806;

The Forty Thieves, by Colman and C. W. Ward, London, Theatre Royal, Drury Lane, 8 April 1806;

The Africans, or War, Love, and Duty, an adaptation of Jean-Pierre Claris de Florian's *Selico, Nouvelle Africaine*, London, Theatre Royal in the Hay-Market, 29 July 1808;

X.Y.Z., London, Theatre Royal, Covent Garden, 11 December 1810;

The Quadrupeds of Quedlinburgh, or the Rovers of Weimar, adapted from "The Rovers; or, The Double Arrangement," a parody by George Canning and John Hookham Frere, Lon-

George Colman the Younger (engraving by W. Greatbach, based on a portrait by De Wilde)

don, Theatre Royal in the Hay-Market, 26 July 1811;

The Travellers Benighted, possibly by Colman, based upon a story from M. G. Lewis's *The Monk*, London, Theatre Royal in the Hay-Market, 30 September 1811;

Doctor Hocus Pocus, or Harlequin Washed White, London, Theatre Royal in the Hay-Market, 12 August 1814;

The Actor of All Work, or First and Second Floor, London, Theatre Royal in the Hay-Market, 13 August 1817;

The Gnome-King, or The Giant-Mountains, London, Theatre Royal, Covent Garden, 6 October 1819;

Shakespeare versus Harlequin, possibly by Colman, a revision of David Garrick's *Harlequin's Invasion*, London, Theatre Royal, Drury Lane, 8 April 1820;

The Law of Java, London, Theatre Royal, Covent Garden, 11 May 1822;

Stella and Leatherlungs, or A Star and a Stroller, London, Theatre Royal, Drury Lane, 1 October 1823.

BOOKS: *Two to One. A Comic Opera, in Three Acts. As Performed at the Theatre-Royal, Hay-Market, and Smock-Alley* (Dublin: Printed for W. Wilson, 1785);

Turk, and No Turk. A Comic Opera. For the Voice, Harpsichord; Violin, or German Flute. Composed by Dr. Arnold [songs only] (London: Skillern, 1785);

Inkle and Yarico: an Opera, in Three Acts. As Performed at the Theatre-Royal in the Hay-Market, on Saturday, August 11th, 1787 (London: Printed for G. G. J. & J. Robinson, 1787);

Prose on Several Occasions; Accompanied with Some Pieces in Verse (London: Printed for T. Cadell, 1787);

Ways and Means; or, A Trip to Dover. A Comedy, in Three Acts, As it is Performed at the Theatre-Royal, Hay-Market (London: Printed for G. G. J. & J. Robinson, 1788);

The Family Party; a Comic Piece, in Two Acts, as Acted at the Theatre Royal, Haymarket, anonymous, possibly by Colman (London: Printed for J. Debrett, 1789);

The Battle of Hexham. A Comedy. In Three Acts, as Performed at the Theatre-Royal, Crow-Street [pirated edition] (Dublin: Printed by P. Byrne, 1790); republished as *The Battle of Hexham; or, Days of Old. A Play, in Three Acts. First Perform'd at the Theatre-Royal, Hay-Market, on August 11, 1789* [authorized edition] (London: Longman, Hurst, Rees & Orme, 1808);

The Surrender of Calais. A Play. In Three Acts. By George Colman, Jun., Esq. As Performed at the Little Theatre Haymarket [pirated edition] (Dublin: P. Byrne, 1792); republished as *Surrender of Calais: a Play, in Three Acts. First Perform'd at the Theatre Royal, Hay-Market, on Saturday, July 30, 1791* [authorized edition] (London: Longman, Hurst, Rees & Orme, 1808);

The Mountaineers. As it is performed, with the utmost Applause, at the Theatre Royal, Hay-Market, London; and the Theatre Royal, Crow-Street, Dublin [pirated edition] (Dublin: Thomas McDonnel, 1794); republished as *The Mountaineers; a Play, in Three Acts; Written by George Colman; (the Younger.) And First Performed at the Theatre Royal, Hay-Market, on Saturday, August 3, 1793* [authorized edition] (London: J. Debrett, 1795);

New Hay at the Old Market; an Occasional Drama, in One Act: Written by George Colman, (The Younger,) on Opening the Hay-Market Theatre on the 9th of June, 1795 (London: Printed by W. Woodfall for T. Cadell & W. Davies, 1795); abridged as *Sylvester Daggerwood; or, New Hay at the Old Market. An Occasional Drama, in One Act. Written By George Colman, (the Younger,) on Opening the Hay-Market Theatre, on the 9th of June, 1795* (London, 1796);

The Iron Chest: a Play; in Three Acts. Written by George Colman, the Younger. With a Preface. First represented at the Theatre-Royal, in Drury-Lane, on Saturday, 12th March, 1796 (London: Printed by W. Woodfall for Cadell & Davies, 1796);

My Night-Gown and Slippers; or Tales in Verse. Written in an Elbow-Chair, by George Colman, the Younger (London: Printed for T. Cadell, Jun. & W. Davies, 1797);

Blue-Beard; or, Female Curiosity! A Dramatick Romance; First Represented at the Theatre Royal Drury-Lane, on Tuesday January 16, 1798 (London: Printed by T. Woodfall for Cadell & Davies, 1798);

The Heir at Law: a Comedy in Five Acts. As Performed at the Theatre-Royal, Crow Street [pirated edition] (Dublin: T. Burnside & G. Folingsby, 1798); republished as *The Heir at Law: a Comedy: in Five Acts. Written by George Colman, the Younger; and First Performed at the Theatre-Royal, Hay-Market, on Saturday, July 15, 1797* [authorized edition] (London: Longman, Hurst, Rees & Orme, 1808);

Feudal Times; or, The Banquet-Gallery: a Drama, in Two Acts. First Presented at the Theatre-Royal, Drury-Lane, on Saturday, Jan. 19th. 1799 (London: Printed by T. Woodfall for Cadell & Davies, 1799);

The Poor Gentleman; a Comedy, in Five Acts: Written by George Colman, the Younger. As Performed at the Theatres-Royal, London and Dublin, with Universal Applause [pirated edition] (Dublin: Printed by Thomas Burnside, 1801); republished as *The Poor Gentleman: A Comedy, in Five Acts, As Performed at the Theatre-Royal, Covent-Garden. (First Acted on the 11th of February 1801)* [authorized edition] (London: Printed by A. Strahan for T. N. Longman & O. Rees, 1802);

The Review; or, the Wags of Windsor. A Musical Farce, In Two Acts. As Performed at the Theatres-Royal, London and Dublin, with the Greatest Applause [pirated edition] (Dublin: Printed by Thomas Burnside, 1801); republished as *The Review, or the Wags of Windsor; a Musical Farce, in Two Acts* [authorized edition] (London: Printed by D. Deans for J. Cawthorn, 1808);

Broad Grins; by George Colman, (the Younger;) Comprising, with New Additional Tales in Verse, Those Formerly Published under the Title of "My Night-Gown and Slippers" (London: Printed for T. Cadell, Jun. & W. Davies, 1802);

Love Laughs at Locksmiths. A Comic Opera, in Two Acts. As It Is Performed at the Theatre-Royal, Dublin [pirated edition] (Dublin: Printed by T. Burnside, 1803); republished as *Love Laughs at Locksmiths; A Farce, in Two Acts* [authorized edition] (London: Printed by D. Deans for J. Cawthorn, 1808);

John Bull, or, An Englishman's Fire-Side: a Comedy, in Five Acts, as Performed at the Theatre-Royal, in Dublin [pirated edition] (Dublin: O'Brien & sold by every bookseller, 1803); republished as *John Bull; or, The Englishman's Fire-side: a Comedy, in Five Acts. First Performed at the Theatre-Royal, Covent-Garden, on the 5th of March, 1803* [authorized edition] (London: Printed for Longman, Hurst, Rees & Orme, 1805);

Epilogue to the New Play of The Maid of Bristol. Written by George Colman, the Younger, (Being an Address to the Patriotism of the English.) And Spoken by Mr. Elliston, in the Character of a British Sailor [broadside] (London: Printed by Cox, son & Baylis for J. Debrett, 1803);

Who Wants a Guinea? A Comedy, in Five Acts, as Perform'd at the Theatre-Royal, Covent-Garden. First Acted April 18, 1805 (London: Longman, Hurst, Rees & Orme, 1805);

We Fly by Night; or, Long Stories, a Musical Farce, Performed at the Theatre Royal Covent Garden (London: Ridgeway, for M. Kelly, 1806);

The Africans; or, War, Love, and Duty. A Play, in Three Acts. First Perform'd at the Theatre-Royal, Hay-Market, on July 29, 1808 (London: Longman, Hurst, Rees & Orme, 1808);

Blue Devils; a Farce, in One Act. By George Colman, the Younger. First Acted at the Theatre Royal, Covent Garden, on the 24th of April, 1798 (London: Printed by William Burton for John Cawthorn & James Cawthorn, 1808);

The Forty Thieves: A Grand Romantic Drama, in Two Acts, by Colman and C. W. Ward, but attributed to Colman and Richard Brinsley Sheridan (New York: David Longworth, 1808);

The Gay Deceivers, or More Laugh Than Love. A Farce, in Two Acts. By George Colman, the Younger. First Acted at the Theatre Royal, Haymarket, on the 22nd of August, 1804 (London: J. Cawthorn & James Cawthorn, 1808);

Poetical Vagaries; Containing an Ode to We, a Hackney'd Critick; Low Ambition, or the Life and Death of Mr. Daw; A Reckoning with Time; The Lady of the Wreck, or Castle Blarneygig; Two Parsons, or the Tale of a Shirt (London: Printed for the Author, 1812);

Vagaries Vindicated or Hypocritick Hypercriticks: A Poem, Address'd to the Reviewers (London: Printed for Longman, Hurst, Rees, Orme & Brown, 1813);

Eccentricities for Edinburgh, Containing Poems, Entitle'd, A Lamentation to Scotch Booksellers. Fir; or the Sun-Poker. Mr. Champernoune. The Luminous Historian; or, Learning in Love. London Ruralty; or, Miss Bunn and Mrs. Bunt (Edinburgh: Printed by J. Ballantyne and Co. for J. Ballantyne, 1816);

The Gnome-King; or, The Giant-Mountains: a Dramatick Legend, in Two Acts. First Performed at the Theatre Royal, Covent Garden, on Wednesday, October 6th, 1819 (London: John Miller, 1819);

X.Y.Z. A Farce, in Two Acts (London: for W. Simpkin & R. Marshall, 1820);

The Actor of All Work; or, The First and Second Floor. A Farce. In One Act. With the Comic Song of The Picture of a London Playhouse, as Introduced by Mr. Mathews, at the New-York Theatre (New York: E. M. Murden, 1822);

The Law of Java: a Play, in Three Acts; First Perform'd at the Theatre-Royal, Covent-Garden, Saturday, May 11, 1822. The Overture, and Musick, by Mr. Bishop (London: Printed for W. Simpkin & R. Marshall, 1822);

Random Records, 2 volumes (London: H. Colburn & R. Bentley, 1830);

Barney Benithine and Billy Bowling–Written by George Colman, for Mr. Harley, possibly by Colman (London: Clementi, Collard & Collard, n.d.);

The Elder Brother, possibly by Colman (London: Benjamin Steill, n.d.).

Collections: *The Dramatic Works of George Colman the Younger. With an Original Life of the Author*, edited by J. W. Lake, 4 volumes (Paris: Malepeyre, 1823-1824);

The Plays of George Colman the Younger, 2 volumes, edited by Peter A. Tasch, (New York & London: Garland, 1981).

OTHER: Henry Heartwell, *The Castle of Sorrento. A Comick Opera in Two Acts. First Represented at the Theatre Royal Hay-Market, on Saturday July 13th, 1799. Altered from the French, and adapted to the English stage*, revised by Colman (London: Printed by T. Woodfall for Cadell & Davies, 1799);

Posthumous Letters, From Various Celebrated Men; Addressed to Francis Colman, and George Colman, the Elder: With Annotations, and Occasional Remarks, by George Colman, the Younger. Exclusive of the Letters, Are, an Explanation of the Motives of William Pulteney (afterwards Earl of Bath) for His Acceptance of a Peerage; and Papers Tending to Elucidate the Question Relative to the Proportionate Shares of Authorship to be Attributed to the Elder Colman and Garrick, in the Comedy of The Clandestine Marriage (London: T. Cadell & W. Davies, 1820).

The most popular English dramatist at the turn of the nineteenth century, George Colman the Younger earned his fame as a gifted writer of comedy and farce. Of course he was funny; everyone knew that. His sense of humor was legendary. People sought his company, invited him to dinner, and followed his conversation just to enjoy the pleasure of his warm wit. They found him an extremely convivial, charming, generous man. Neither his comedy nor his humor were cruel–low, broad, vulgar at times, but never cruel. He felt a benevolent affection for his most pitiful comic characters. On the other hand, he was also perhaps too vain, too fond of fine clothes and drink, too extravagant in satisfying his tastes. In some sense his best plays were a reflection of himself: solid, honest, a bit too busy or theatrical, and usually disorganized, but full of robust, good humor, and very funny indeed. He wrote plays exactly as his audiences wanted them: brisk, lighthearted, fast-moving pieces with just enough complication, confusion, and momentary anguish to make their impossibly happy endings all the more enjoyable. His was not an age that wanted realism, and when the taste of his time began to seek the melodramatic flavor that was to characterize the nineteenth-century English theater, Colman sensed the change and adjusted his plays accordingly. He aimed to please not the literary scholars but the public.

George Colman the Younger was destined for the theater. His father wanted him to study law, but George Colman the Elder was hardly the man to compel anyone to follow a profession at the bar. Intended for law himself by his uncle William Pulteney, earl of Bath, he earned that guardian's displeasure by declining such a career in favor of drama. His considerable talent as a playwright did nothing to placate his guardian, and what was worse Colman the Elder shared his bed but not his name with a little-known actress whom the earl detested. The result of the young man's double obstinacy was the loss of his chance at the earl's large fortune. Perhaps this caused hardship, but Colman was quite happy. Sarah Ford remained his mistress for six or seven years, and in 1767 he married her. George the Younger, born in October of 1762, was almost certainly Colman's natural son, and Sarah Ford was probably the boy's mother, but no definitive record has survived. In any event the couple legitimized the boy with their marriage, and he considered Mrs. Colman his only mother. The father went on to a successful career as a playwright and theatrical manager. Author of some thirty-five plays that saw production, Colman the Elder also helped manage the Drury Lane theater from 1763 to 1765, the Covent Garden theater from 1767 to 1774, and in 1776 obtained the right to operate London's Haymarket theater. He moved in theatrical and literary circles all his life, including David Garrick, Richard Sheridan, and Oliver Goldsmith among his closest friends, while Samuel Johnson, Edmund Burke, and Sir Joshua Reynolds were occasional callers.

Thus the boy's early home life was imbued with a theatrical and literary spirit. But his father did not want drama to be the boy's career. When he was eight years old, Colman entered London's Marylebone Seminary, where like all the other pupils he could expect to pass his time pleasantly until he was ready to go on to one of the finer public schools. He had little inclination to study industriously, but it made no difference because he had to leave after only three months. His mother had accidentally poisoned herself with a dose of the wrong medicine, and she died on 29 March 1771, Good Friday. His grieving father took him from London to their home in Richmond; the boy did not return to Marylebone.

Eventually his father returned to his plan of having Colman educated for the bar. In June of 1772 Colman entered Westminster, the public school his father had attended. Among the boy's acquaintances there was Frederick Reynolds, who became a playwright himself and Colman's lifelong friend. Colman was no better a student here than he had been at Marylebone; he simply was not interested, working just enough to avoid failure. He preferred the life at Richmond and the fascinating people who visited there, so he returned to his father's villa at every opportunity. It is no wonder that he retained a greater affection for the theater than he ever developed for law. Even when he was obliged to remain in London he had ready access to the theaters, especially the one at Covent Garden, where his father worked as production manager from 1767 until 1774. More interesting still was the elder Colman's acquisition in 1776 of the right to produce dramas in the Theatre Royal, Haymarket–the so-called Summer Theatre. He rented this theater for about a year from the patentee Samuel Foote, with whose unexpected death in 1777 the royal patent expired; thereafter Colman was able to continue operating the Haymarket under a license renewed for him each year by the lord chamberlain.

At about this time young George got his first actual stage experience with some very small roles in a series of amateur productions sponsored by Sir Watkin Williams Wynn, a benefactor of Westminster. Otherwise he came no closer to theatrical life than he could get by visiting the Haymarket every time his Westminster obligations would allow. His father still intended him for a career at law, enrolling him at Christ

Mrs. Met.

Why yes, as you say, the public was unanimous in that particular.

Dash.

Perfectly so – But I have a trifling Jeu de' Esprit of my own to offer you.

Mrs. Met.

O Let me see it by all means – I adore all Sacrifices to the Muses be they ever so trifling.

Dash.

I am afraid it is not worth your Alteration. The Lines do but disgrace the Subject (takes out a paper & Reads.)

Whoe'er my Widows Works peruses
Whoe'er acquainted with her Face is,
Must in the first behold the Muses
And in the later View, the Graces.

Mrs. Met.

Well, that is very prettily turn'd upon my Liturature, with no less Elegance than accuracy.

Dash.

Thus then I offer it at the Shrine of your Beauty, but when shall we Name the happy Day. When shall the Flambeaux of Hymen be lighted up, thou combination of Venus and Minerva Unworthy as I am, when is the Name of Metaphor to dwindle into Dust?

Mrs. Metap.

For heavens sake Sir desist, you make me expire with Confusion.

Page from the playhouse copy of The Female Dramatist *submitted to the Examiner of Plays for licensing prior to the first performance, on 16 August 1782 (Larpent Collection, LA 598; by permission of the Henry E. Huntington Library and Art Gallery)*

E P I L O G U E,

Written by the Author of the COMEDY.

Spoken by Mr. PALMER, *in the Character of a News-Paper Writer.*
(Squabbling behind the Scenes.)

I TELL you I muſt and will ſpeak. How—not fit?
Pooh! prithee—I will but harangue 'em a bit. *(comes forward)*
Excuſe me, good folks—I'm juſt popt from the Pit.
I'm a Critick, my maſters! I ſneer, ſplaſh and vapour:
Puff Party: Damn Poets: in ſhort—*Do* a Paper.
My name's *Johnny Grub*—I'm a vender of Scandal,
My Pen, like an Auctioneer's Hammer, I handle;
Knocking down Reputations by one inch of candle!
I've heard out the Play: But I need not have come.
I'll tell you a ſecret, my maſters—but, mum!
Tho' ramm'd in amongſt you, to praiſe or to mock it,
I brought my *Critique*, cut and dry, in my pocket.
We, great, Paper Editors,—ſtrange it appears!
Can often, believe me, *diſpenſe with our Ears.*
The Author—like all other Authors—well knowing
That *We* are the People to ſet him a-going,
Has begg'd me, juſt now, in a flattering tone,
To publiſh a *friendly Critique* of his own.
Ev'ry good has its evil: We don't pay a *Souſe*—
Neither We, nor our friends, to come into the Houſe;
But then 'tis expected, becauſe we are *free*,
We are bound to praiſe all the damn'd nonſenſe we ſee:
Hence comes it, the Houſes, their emptineſs ſcorning,
At low ebb at Night *overflow* in the Morning!
Hence Audiences, ſeated at eaſe, at the Play,
Are ſqueez'd to a mummy, poor devils, next day!
Even Actors themſelves, will extort ſomething from us;
And the vileſt Performer's an Actor---of *promiſe.*
While ſelf-praiſing Authors, write Volumes on Volumes,
And Puffs, every morning—like ſmoke—riſe in columns!

Our

E P I L O G U E.

Our Bard of to-night,—I had tickl'd him ſweetly!
Foiſts *his* Puff upon me—damn it, mine was ſo neatly
Work'd up—it's a pity—an excellent Pill!
Some ſweet—three Parts ſour—ſhall I read it?—I will!
" Laſt night: *Little* Theatre: Comedy,—Name,
" *Ways and Means*—unproductive—Plot blind, Language lame!
" As the Author *has* Parts—*Our* Advice, in this Play,
" Is—New model the Story—*but this by the way*,
" His Dialogue too,—he may truſt to *Our* Print,
" Is, tho' poor, groſs and vulgar—*but this is a hint.*
" Impartial's our Motto—There's really no end
" To his Puns and his Quibbles—*We ſpeak as a Friend.*
" That the Actors had doubts on't, we cannot help thinking,
" For they all did their utmoſt to keep it from ſinking.
" *Young Banniſter* buſtled, in hopes of it's riſing,
" And *Palmer*'s exertions were really ſurpriſing."
So much for *Ourſelves.*—What the Author advances,
To ſupport *Ways and Means*, will ne'er mend his Finances.
He calls it a light, Summer thing,—and, with him,
His Pun is all Laugh,—and his Quibble all Whim—
In ſhort his Critique would ſo tire you to hear it,
I muſt publiſh my own—or elſe ſomething that's near it.
If therefore, in any one Paper you ſee
An abuſe of the Play,—whatſoever it be,—
Wherever the Poet ſhall find a hard rub,
That Paper, depend on't, is *done* by—JOHN GRUB.

Colman's characterization of drama critics in this epilogue to Ways and Means *helped to ensure poor reviews for the play (from the 1788 edition)*

Church College at Oxford in 1780. But young Colman could not stay away from the Haymarket long enough to do creditable work at Oxford, and after a few futile terms his father took stronger measures. Hoping that remoteness from London would foster a life that did not mirror his own, he transferred the boy in the autumn of 1781 to King's College at Old Aberdeen in Scotland. But as the son later wrote in his autobiography, *Random Records* (1830), "Alas! this happened too late;–a dramatick fever, not to be subdued by the cool temperature of the Northern climes, was already lurking in my veins; it lay dormant for the first months of my exile, and then began to rage."

Predictably enough, Colman's dedication to his studies was no greater at King's than at Christ Church or anywhere else. He began to cause minor trouble in the town and to ride around the countryside for days at a time. One night, stopping at a country inn, Colman found the album in which travelers customarily recorded their thoughts and fancies, generally with no great art. Although Colman's contribution on this occasion was probably juvenile and tasteless, he remembered it as his first composition, his "virgin offering to the Muse." Soon after, he published a poetical satire upon the English statesman Charles Fox, entitled *The Man of the People*, most copies of which he was obliged to purchase himself, and all of which now appear to be lost. Nonetheless, a writing career had begun, and it was not long before Colman combined his literary talents with his greatest love, the drama. The very next spring saw the birth of *The Female Dramatist*, a two-act musical farce. Colman sent it to his father at the Haymarket, where the manager allowed it to debut, anonymously, on 16 August 1782.

The Female Dramatist played only one night;

it offered little to its audience, and less to posterity. The actress Sarah Gardner, in her performance as Mrs. Metaphor (an adaptation of Mrs. Melpomene from Tobias Smollett's novel *Roderick Random,* 1748), gave the farce its only vital moments. It is a tale of a hack writer hoping to trick Mrs. Metaphor, an admirer of the drama, into a marriage beneficial only to himself, until all is discovered and his hopes rightfully dashed. For her efforts Mrs. Gardner earned the dubious distinction of being supposed the author, an error perpetuated by bibliographic sources well into the twentieth century.

The failure of *The Female Dramatist* did not daunt Colman, who immediately began work on a full three-act play. Charged with energy and enthusiasm for the first time, he demonstrated a degree of industry his studies had never inspired. His father might have other ideas, but Colman knew what he wanted. Thus he left the university and moved to the town of Montrose, where he completed his second dramatic piece, *Two to One,* in the spring of 1783. After a few more months in Montrose, he moved back to New Aberdeen for the rest of the year, studying history more or less on his own. Early in 1784 he was recalled to England by his father, who may have begun to realize the futility of his hopes for his son's future.

In London Colman waited eagerly for 19 June, the opening of *Two to One* at the Haymarket theater. Much more successful than its predecessor, this play continued for nineteen performances before enthusiastic audiences. Its theme of young love crossed by parents' intentions, perpetuated by trickery and disguise, finally to be blessed by everyone, is a venerable one; its author's undeveloped talent did not interfere too much with such a pleasing vehicle. Colman's confessed method of composition, haphazard scribbling with no plan or direction, leaves the play with a species of incoherence less satisfying to readers than to audiences. But its commercial success pleased his father, and its reception among critics and audiences pleased the son. In the resulting warmth of spirit Colman's father sent him on a brief tour of Paris, just before one last attempt at preparing him for the bar. In Paris, of course, Colman visited the theaters as often as he could. Back home in London a month later, he entered the fall term as a law student at Lincoln's Inn. This time the experiment lasted less than a term; besides a secret marriage to the actress Catherine Morris, who had played a significant role in *The Female Dramatist,* Colman resumed secret work on his true career, writing *Turk and No Turk* in December of 1784. Neither commitment could be revealed to his father immediately; indeed, the marriage was not disclosed for four years. But the play was sent to the elder Colman early in 1785, and he scheduled it for production in July. Now no illusions remained; like it or not, the son was following the father. Thus ended the formal education of George Colman the Younger.

Though it ran ten nights, which meant it probably broke even, *Turk and No Turk* was not the success Colman might have wished. It pleased its audiences, but only the songs ever saw print in book form; the reviewers refrained from damning it, but were more kind than enthusiastic in their praise. A musical comedy in three acts, *Turk and No Turk* is another tale of crossed love that uncrosses, miraculously, by the end. The wanton young hero, Ramble, cannot marry his Emily: all the parents forbid it. Emily's father does approve of the rich Turk who shows up to sue for her hand, and who is of course Ramble himself. The inevitable discovery comes during the wedding ceremony, but somehow everything works out, and the marriage is blessed.

It is impossible to know whether this play reveals Colman's yearning for his father's blessing upon his clandestine marriage. The most significant feature of Colman's personal life is the extent to which he strove to keep it private. Not even his autobiography yields much personal information. Little is known of Mrs. Catherine Colman; after her marriage she acted no more. By the time Colman began an affair with the actress Maria Gibbs in 1795 or so, Mrs. Colman had been invisible to the public for years. The new liaison was no secret, and Colman was frequently criticized in the press on moral grounds, but so were nearly all theatrical people. Colman refused to reply to these attacks, perhaps because reply would have been fruitless, but more likely because he consistently refused to make his personal life a matter of public record. He and Catherine Colman separated in 1801, and he married Maria Gibbs in 1809, but whether his first wife's death or a divorce made the marriage possible is still unknown. So carefully did he guard his privacy that not even his remarriage was mentioned in the newspapers of the day.

Not long after the Haymarket closed for the season in September of 1785, the elder Colman suffered a severe stroke. His son rushed to his

George Colman the Younger

side and arranged for competent care, and the elder Colman soon began to improve. But the illness changed young Colman's life forever: it marked the beginning of his participation in the management of the Haymarket theater. Even in illness his father jealously guarded the business, but details here and there required more attention than he could command. Colman helped his father, not obtrusively or publicly, but when and where he thought he must. Eventually his father's recovery was complete enough that Colman could leave; by the Haymarket's summer season, 1786, he returned to his rooms near Lincoln's Inn. There he started work on *Inkle and Yarico*, finishing it by the summer of 1787; it opened at the Haymarket on 4 August.

This play, another three-act musical comedy, is an adaptation of Richard Steele's *Spectator* no. 11, though it features some significant deviations from Steele's tale. Inkle, a young Englishman seeking his fortune in the West Indies, becomes lost in the forest, where he meets the Indian maid Yarico. Together with Inkle's man and the man's own Indian maid, the couple flees hostile natives and arrives in the Barbadoes. There Inkle decides to seek the wealthier hand of the English governor's daughter Narcissa, and for this reason tries to sell Yarico as a slave (in Steele's version this treachery was motivated entirely by prospects of profit, not marriage). Unfortunately for Inkle, the would-be purchaser is the governor himself, who soon discovers the betrayal. In his indignant anger he condemns the slave trade in general and Inkle in particular. But all is well by the end, for Inkle repents and marries Yarico. *Inkle and Yarico* became an instant success. Audiences loved its blend of comedy and sentiment, wit and moral, and the music that accompanied each scene. It continued to play twenty nights that season, and many more nights in the succeeding years. Although it is by no means remembered as a masterpiece, the play was clearly superior to Colman's first three. More significantly, something in this mix of genres appealed to audiences of the day, and Colman was to make frequent use of the pattern in his future work.

Farce, however, remained young Colman's favorite kind of play, and he returned to this form for his next work the following season.

Ways and Means; or A Trip to Dover contains no sentiment at all but plenty of spirited action and humor. Its opening on 10 July 1788 treated the audience at the Haymarket to a lively and enjoyable, though hardly original, story in which a baronet invites two young gallants, Random and Scruple, to his manor, mistaking them for rich tradesmen instead of secret suitors to his two daughters. The couples, realizing that one of the daughters is to be married off to someone else the next evening, take advantage of Sir David Dunder's hospitality by planning to elope. Their plans misfire humorously when Random's servant, drunk and confused, moves a chair from its hallway position marking the daughters' door to a position outside Sir David's room. The resulting scene in Sir David's chamber leads to his discovery of the plot just as Random's estranged father arrives at the manor. Of course, all ends happily, and the right marriages ensue. Perfect as it was for its time, *Ways and Means* did not thrive on its opening night, and thanks partly to an epilogue in which Colman attacked theatrical critics for wantonly damaging writers' reputations, did poorly with the reviewers as well. For whatever reason, despite the play's great popularity in years to come, this was not to be its year of success; it ran only nine nights. Worse yet, Colman now had enemies among the critics.

Though summer had seemed cruel, the next winter season brought a new kind of success for the young playwright; his *Inkle and Yarico* opened on 26 January 1789 in Covent Garden theater, one of the two great winter houses. This opening brought Colman new audiences and a new measure of respectability. The Haymarket had operated at a disadvantage since its inception as the third Theatre Royal in 1766. For many years what was considered legitimate drama could only be produced in the two theaters possessing Royal Patents, the winter theaters at Drury Lane and Covent Garden. When Foote received a patent making the Haymarket the third Theatre Royal in 1766, he was limited to operating it during the winter theaters' customary closed season, the summer months from 15 May to 15 September. When Foote died the elder Colman was granted a continuing license with the same restrictions. The summer theater offered its productions at the Little Theatre in the Haymarket. But the Little Theatre's audiences were necessarily much smaller than those at the other patented houses, and the wealthier patrons were usually absent from London during the summer months anyway.

An even greater disadvantage for the Haymarket arose from the jealousy the winter theaters felt over this new competitor, however small. No licensing restriction prevented either Covent Garden or Drury Lane from operating whenever their proprietors wished; custom and the market alone had enforced the summer closings. Thus the larger houses never felt obliged to stop a successful run on 15 May simply because that was the Haymarket's legal opening night. These intrusions often ran on into June, delaying the Haymarket's opening for a month or more, a ruinous circumstance not only in the competition for receipts but also in the rivalry for actors. The Summer Theatre found itself constrained to wait until actors and audiences were freed by the tyrannical winter houses.

The Haymarket also needed to earn respect, to get rid of a "summer-crowd" stigma. Its only summer competition came from the unlicensed houses, where the "illegitimate" drama could play year round. This kind of drama, generally anything without spoken dialogue, consisted of pantomimes, animal acts, and other spectacles performed with musical accompaniment. To counter these entertainments, as well as the summer heat, the Haymarket had emphasized comedies, especially farces, and much greater use of music accompanying the spoken dialogue than ever before. Although this practice by Colman's time was also becoming established at Covent Garden and Drury Lane, those theaters played to more elite audiences than could be found in London in the summer. A Haymarket playwright might still feel inferior to his Covent Garden counterpart. But whatever stigma may have attached to Colman's talents because of his plays' summer venues, the winter production of *Inkle and Yarico* at Covent Garden removed. George Colman the Younger was now a significant dramatist.

He soon became a significant theater manager as well. Colman's unobtrusive assisting position at the Haymarket changed in June of 1789 when his father's condition degenerated badly. The Haymarket licensee was now incapable of conducting his business; he had become deranged. The son took control of operations in mid season and managed them so smoothly that none on the outside guessed what had happened. Colman made his managerial debut with a couple of new plays, *The Family Party* on 11 July and *The Battle of Hexham, or Days of Old* a month later. *The*

Family Party is a farce Colman may have written but offered anonymously. It is not memorable, poking fun both at an old, dull tradesman who, though quite wealthy, is not particularly eager to become a gentleman, and at a ridiculous, recently knighted fop. It saw only six performances, received moderate applause, and died quietly. The second play was undoubtedly his own. Furthermore, *The Battle of Hexham,* an historical drama, was something quite new.

The story of Edward the Fourth's defeat of Henry the Sixth and Queen Margaret, and their subsequent escape aided by the captain of a band of robbers, was well known to Colman's audience. What they did not expect was the addition of music throughout. Colman also embellished the story with a completely fictional subplot concerning domestic fidelity. Thus we meet Adeline, disguised, searching for her fugitive husband, Gondibert, and arriving at Henry's camp at Hexham just before the decisive battle. Gondibert had fled six months earlier because his support of Henry's cause had put his life in danger; he now lives in the forest, captain of robbers. The battle is a disaster, and the principal players escape to the forest separately. Gondibert captures a new victim, the defeated Queen Margaret, then learns her identity and offers his assistance; after all, they are on the same side. When his men bring him another captive, the disguised Adeline, she recognizes him and tests his faithfulness; when his answers suit her, she reveals her identity, and the emotional reunion scene plays out. The Queen and her child, the Prince of Wales, escape to France, and Gondibert enjoys an amnesty declared by the victorious Edward.

The mixture of genres in this play provided a new experience for its audience. Though comic opera had long been a profitable commodity in the licensed theaters, and while nothing would have surprised audiences in the illegitimate ones, the addition of music to the near-tragic drama of *The Battle of Hexham* offered a new experience to audiences in a Theatre Royal. Indeed, together with the high drama of battle and flight, the use of spectacle and sentimentality, and the miraculously happy ending, the play's musical embellishments have caused scholars to consider it the first successful example of English melodrama, the form that was to dominate the stage over the next century. And successful it was. Audiences and critics alike praised the play; it ran for twenty nights in 1789, and was revived many times in the succeeding years. This reception, and the critics' sympathy on learning of his father's incapacity, helped close the breach Colman had opened during the *Ways and Means* affair.

By the summer season of 1790, Colman was the official licensee for the Haymarket, and he opened the season on 14 June with an address to the audience complaining of the habitual encroachment by the winter houses upon his nominal opening date of 15 May. The address earned him sympathy from the public and the critics, but made no change whatever in the practices of the other Theatres Royal. Instead it marked the beginning of a long and costly battle between the theaters that was to frustrate Colman's life as manager of the Haymarket. But the season was very successful despite its accustomed loss of one month, and Colman established himself as an adept manager. His duties must have kept him busy, for he did not bring out another piece of his own until the 30 July 1791 opening of *The Surrender of Calais.*

Another musical historical drama, *The Surrender of Calais* gets its central story from an old tale by Jean Le Bel in *Vrayes Chroniques,* in which six citizens of Calais, in response to an offer from the attacking English King Edward, volunteer to sacrifice themselves so that their fellow townspeople might be spared. To this framework Colman added the sentimental and romantic touches so popular in *The Battle of Hexham:* Julia and Ribaumont, crossed in love by her father, the governor, separately plan to volunteer for hanging, he in secret and she, learning of his intentions, in disguise. Before King Edward, Julia reveals that Ribaumont is not really a citizen of Calais, and offers herself instead. Edward condemns both, whereupon Julia discloses her identity, Edward softens and frees them, and his Queen Philippa convinces him to free all the volunteer prisoners. And, of course, Edward rules that Julia and Ribaumont may now marry. The play is not noble or grand, and in a sense may even be considered, like *The Battle of Hexham,* to exploit serious and tragic events for the sake of easy emotion and sentiment. But that judgment ignores the public's enthusiastic response. Although not quite melodrama, Colman's work was its immediate predecessor, and exactly what audiences wanted. Its enormous popularity was reflected in *The Surrender of Calais*'s twenty-eight performances that season alone, and the critics celebrated Colman's genius.

Colman further developed this formula

with *The Mountaineers,* which opened on 3 August 1793. Once again he freely adapted and embellished his source, a pair of stories in Miguel de Cervantes' *Don Quixote* (1605), to yield the kind of sentimental, emotional, musical blend he knew could succeed. Set during the fifteenth-century Spanish siege of Granada, the play features two sets of crossed lovers: the Spaniard Virolet and his Moorish beloved Zorayda, who wishes to convert; and Virolet's sister Floranthe and her beloved Octavian. Octavian haunts the mountains near Granada, out of his wits with melancholy for Floranthe, whose father had forbidden their marriage in favor of another suitor. Octavian thinks he has killed this suitor and thus must hide in the mountains; Floranthe searches for him with the news that the rival recovered and married another. During the siege, meanwhile, Virolet has escaped, with Zorayda's help, from his imprisonment by her father, Bulcazin, and they too flee across the mountains. Everyone eventually arrives at the same place, including Bulcazin, who then attempts to kill his daughter. Octavian intervenes and threatens to kill Bulcazin, but Virolet arrives and spares him. Gratefully Bulcazin awards Zorayda to Virolet, and everyone rejoices. Colman's addition of the wild mountain scenery to the endearing features of his earlier musical dramas nearly completes the formula for melodrama, and audiences of the era loved *The Mountaineers.* It played more than twenty-five nights its first season.

Colman's next major drama did not appear until 1796. He busied himself with theatrical management most of the time, and what little respite the winters normally offered was lost to him during the theatrical season of 1793-1794, when the Drury Lane company occupied his Little Theatre. The Drury Lane house had been closed for rebuilding, and its company temporarily relocated to the King's Theatre, Haymarket, in 1791. Two years later, displaced even from its temporary house, the company arranged for Colman to conduct its business from his Little Theatre. He did so in popular fashion, keeping prices well below what the public would have paid for admission to either winter house in a normal season. But again he could not open the summer season as early as the law allowed, waiting until July of 1794 for a reasonable chance at a profitable season. His father's long-expected death in August of that year made Colman the sole manager and proprietor of the Haymarket, a fact ratified by the Crown when he obtained the license in his own right. Both the critics and the town were compassionate, praising Colman's very genuine filial affections and attentions during his father's long decline.

During these years of little original composition he nonetheless found occasion to compose a pair of brief preludes satirizing the great winter houses. *Poor Old Hay-Market, or Two Sides of the Gutter* opened with the season on 15 June 1792. On the other side of the gutter was his chief target, Drury Lane and its temporary residence across the Haymarket from his own. The prelude contains only one scene; it was performed only seven times, and though well received, it may never have seen print, existing today only in manuscript. *New Hay at the Old Market* is more stable stuff. This two-scene piece mocks both the tremendous size and the pompous performances of the other two theaters and introduces the character of Sylvester Daggerwood, a fictitious actor who quotes Shakespeare in his sleep, and who was so popular that Colman later shortened the play to one act and named it after him. *New Hay at the Old Market* played thirty-two times that season, and its revised version, *Sylvester Daggerwood,* was frequently performed well into the next century.

In 1796, after a lapse of three years, Colman brought out another full-length drama, this time for one of his competitors. In evident recognition of Colman's abilities as a playwright, Sheridan asked him to convert William Godwin's political novel, *The Adventures of Caleb Williams* (1794), into a tragedy to be performed at Drury Lane. The task was formidable; *Caleb Williams* is a lengthy and complex work, more a study of character, principle, and the abuse of power than the tale of murder and justice it may at first appear to be. A tragedy that would have challenged any playwright, it taxed Colman's talents severely. He himself preferred to write farces, though he composed musical comedies because they succeeded so well with the public. Why he agreed to adapt the novel is not clear, unless the allure of writing for one of the winter houses proved more temptation than his reputed vanity could withstand. But agree he did, and *The Iron Chest* opened at Drury Lane on 12 March.

Opening night was a disaster–Colman had been late with the script, rehearsals had been scheduled too suddenly and were too rushed, principal actors fought illness both during rehearsals and the opening performance–and succeeding performances were scarcely better. An

Set design by Thomas Greenwood, Jr., for the 1798 production of Blue-Beard

excellent play might have survived these and other setbacks, but *The Iron Chest* is not an excellent play. Sir Edward Mortimer (Falkland in the novel) is a reclusive, moody squire whose steward Wilford (Caleb Williams) learns of the squire's past acquittal for the murder of a man who had persecuted and tormented a young woman. Later Wilford innocently provokes Sir Edward by a casual reference to murder and is so startled by the squire's violent departure that he tries to open the man's locked iron chest, only to be caught in the act when Sir Edward returns. Sir Edward confesses that the crime was indeed his and warns Wilford not to leave the house or reveal the secret. Wilford escapes anyway and becomes a prisoner to a band of robbers, with whom he remains until Sir Edward's men find him and bring him back to face false charges of thievery. The squire has planted jewels in Wilford's trunk, but a search reveals that he has also quite stupidly left the original murder weapon, a bloody knife. As if this were not enough, he somehow left a detailed narration of his guilt, which he intended to destroy before his death. Confronted by such irrefutable evidence, he confesses, looking toward the next world.

This incredible ending alone did not destroy the play; the songs and musical interludes throughout must have poorly complemented its bleak story, and the mischances of the opening night simply ensured its destruction. The play lasted four performances at Drury Lane, none of them very well liked. Now Colman's vanity served him ill. This failure he could not accept, blaming everything but his own pen. Understandable as this reaction may seem, his recriminations were not confined to private conversations; he spelled them out in a peevish preface to the published version of the play later that same year. Chiefly he attacked the renowned actor John Philip Kemble, who played Sir Edward despite an illness that he was treating with opium. Colman was probably correct in thus ascribing some of the blame–Kemble had also set the rehearsal schedule and opening date–but he clearly breached decorum and taste with the manner of his complaint. If the critics disliked the play, they hated the preface and reviled its author.

Convinced of his own innocence, however, Colman bided his time until the summer season,

Maria Gibbs as Grace Gaylove in The Review, or the Wags of Windsor, *a role created for her by Colman (engraving based on a portrait by A. Buck). The playwright also wrote the parts of Cicely in* The Heir at Law, *Annette in* Blue Devils, *and Mary in* John Bull *for Gibbs, whom he married in 1809.*

when he opened the play again in his own theater. On 29 August a somewhat different cast (certainly without Kemble) presented *The Iron Chest* to a receptive Haymarket audience. It was a slightly shorter version, but most of its flaws remained; credit for its success on this occasion must go to the company, whose loyalty to Colman may have brought forth extra effort. Although it succeeded it did not thrive; its run this time was thirteen nights, and the play probably lost money. However, as a vehicle for great actors it kept its popularity for nearly a century. In any event *The Iron Chest* is as close as Colman's melodramatic method ever approached to the genre of tragedy.

The following summer Colman returned to comedy with *The Heir at Law*. It proved a hit and must have convinced him never to stray into tragedy again. The story had elements with which Colman and his audiences were quite familiar: social climbers, a foolish gallant, a virtuous country lass, a greedy eccentric, and a familiar theme of lovers crossed, this time by the young man's suddenly elevated social status. In this version when a wealthy but distant relation dies and his son is lost at sea, the inheritance and title fall to an unlikely husband and wife who suddenly become Lord and Lady Duberly—though the lord loses none of his malapropist charm. Their sudden elevation prompts them to hire the eccentric scholar Dr. Pangloss as tutor to their son Dick. Dr. Pangloss seems unable to speak without quoting and giving attribution; Dick prefers yearning for his beloved Cicely, the country lass, to studying and pays Pangloss a bonus salary not to bother him with studies.

Soon, however, Dick convinces himself that to marry Cicely, common as she is, would demean him, and suggests that she become his mistress; naturally, their love is finished. But wait–the true heir, Moreland, is not lost at all. He returns, unaware of his father's death, to locate his fiancée, who has fallen on hard times and moved to a new address, and who also happens to be Cicely's employer. When at last Moreland finds her, there also is Dick, repentant, betrothed to Cicely. Dick's parents, the temporary lord and lady, have come along, and now everyone finds out who is who (the lord exclaims, "Eh? what? Henry Moreland! Why zounds! the late Lord Duberly's lost heir!"). The reunited couples are happy, Cicely has won a lottery, and the former lord and lady feel relieved to be common again. Only Dr. Pangloss loses out; he realizes, quoting Otway, "That I'm not worth a ducat."

Audiences were delighted. After its opening on 15 July 1797, it played twenty-seven more times, the first signs of a truly enduring popularity that was to last more than a hundred years. The scheming, alluding Pangloss; the general fun and humor; the sentiment; the perfect ending: all contributed to its appeal and secured the high esteem of its public. Today it must be regarded as one of his finest achievements. The critics' complaints about its low humor, sentimentality, and tendencies toward farce made no difference to Colman, whose eye was as always on the gross receipts, especially since his obsession with proving *The Iron Chest* a good play appears to have left him in poor financial shape.

This kind of distress probably contributed to Colman's willingness to hire his talents out to the winter houses for his next three compositions. After all, the competitors paid better. Covent Garden commissioned a farce, *Blue Devils*, and Drury Lane ordered what must be called two melodramas, *Blue-Beard, or Female Curiosity* and *Feudal Times, or The Banquet Gallery*. Covent Garden opened *Blue Devils* on 24 April 1798 but did not do well with it. A translation of *L'Anglais* (1781), a farce by the French playwright Joseph Patrat, *Blue Devils* is a tale of misunderstandings. A waiter with no money, James, has been fired for falling in love with Annette, his employer's daughter. James meets a suicidal but wealthy Englishman who thinks at first that James would like to join him in death. But when he learns that James is only broke, the Englishman, Megrim, gives him money. Megrim also misunderstands Annette, thinking she loves him, and her father mistakes Megrim's request for her hand as an offer to relieve him from bankruptcy. James then provides that relief with Megrim's gift. The lovers are happy, the father is out of debt, and Megrim has found, in acts of benevolence, the pleasure he has been seeking to make his life worthwhile. As a farce *Blue Devils* is nothing special, and Covent Garden performed it only twice. But Colman's Haymarket worked its magic again; using virtually the same cast as Covent Garden's he opened it on 12 June of that same year and eight more times that summer.

The Drury Lane dramas were a different matter altogether. The Drury Lane company wanted an attractive vehicle with which two of its members, a talented composer and an imaginative stage machinist, could take advantage of the public's growing appetite for grand spectacle. *Blue-Beard, or Female Curiosity* is that vehicle and little more. Its story is insignificant; sinking doors, sepulchers, skeletons, cracks in the earth, collapsing buildings, and constant musical numbers hold the audience fast. Once again it made no difference that critics objected to the mixture; *Blue-Beard* was performed no fewer than sixty-three times that winter season after its debut on 16 January 1798. *Feudal Times, or The Banquet Gallery* is similar if not quite as successful; it offers a ruthless baron, his forbidding castle, a kidnapped and imprisoned lady, a siege, and a last-minute escape before the castle's tower explodes. This entertainment opened during the following season, on 19 January 1799, and played thirty-nine times. His audiences content, Colman ignored the critics and counted his money.

Colman did not write again for the Haymarket until the summer of the following year, and then he gave them a farce. Evidently summer audiences did not have quite the winter crowds' appetite for spectacular melodrama; furthermore, the winter houses could pay better for Colman's hard work. When next he wrote a five-act comedy, he sold it to Covent Garden. More suitable for the Haymarket, farces were also much easier for Colman to write. *The Review, or the Wags of Windsor*, a hastily made piece written to conform to songs that had already been composed, was performed nine times after its opening on 1 September 1800. Its major contribution to the stage was the character Caleb Quotem, an eccentric jack-of-all-trades who has little to do with the story but whose constant chatter keeps

13

gales of Adversity will make women weep, a woman's tear falls like the dew that Zephyrs shake from Roses—Nay, confide in me.

Mary I will, sir; but—(looking around)

Pereg Leave us a little, honest friends.

Dennis Ahem! Come, Mrs Brulgruddery! let you & I pair off, my Lambkin!

Mrs Bru Ah! she's no better than she should be, I'll warrant her.

Dennis By the powers! she's well enough tho' for all that

Ext Dennis & Wife.

Pereg Now, sweet one, your name?

Mary Mary, Sir.

Pereg What else?

Mary Dont ask me that, Sir. My poor father might be sorry if it was mention'd now.

Pereg Have you quitted your father, then?

Mary I left his house at day-break this morning, Sir.

Pereg What is he?

Mary A Tradesman in the neighbouring Town, sir.

Pereg Is he aware of your departure?

Mary No, sir.

Pereg. And your mother?

Mary I was very little when she died, Sir.

Pereg: Has her father, since her death, treated you with cruelty?

Mary He? Oh, bless him! No! He is the kindest father that ever breathed, Sir.

Pereg How must such a father be agonized by the loss of his Child!

Page from the playhouse copy of John Bull *submitted to the Examiner of Plays for licensing prior to the first performance, on 5 March 1803 (Larpent Collection, LA 1371; by permission of the Henry E. Huntington Library and Art Gallery)*

the farce from moving forward too quickly.

The comedy for Covent Garden, *The Poor Gentleman*, contains little to surprise Colman's audiences, unless its large share of sentiment was unexpected. The gentleman of the title, Lieutenant Worthington, a poor, retired, wounded officer on half pay, refuses offers of assistance in his financial distress, which only increases as the play progresses. His daughter Emily, meanwhile, is the target of a young rake, whose assault on her is frustrated by Bramble, one of Worthington's would-be benefactors. The rake challenges Bramble, but the duel is interrupted by Worthington, arriving to fight his own battles of honor. The rake repents. Then Bramble's uncle, Sir Robert, reveals that he has paid Worthington's debt to forestall the poor gentleman's arrest; in return he demands Worthington's blessing on a marriage between Bramble and Emily, and the play ends happily. The emphasis throughout on expressions of virtue on the one hand and villainy on the other feels once again like melodrama; once again the audiences enjoyed what they saw. Its opening on 11 February 1801 was the first of twenty-five performances that season.

It must have been a curious time for Colman, finding himself in the position of writing plays for competitors who seemed determined to harm him. Though the great winter houses purchased his plays, they continued their injurious practice of allowing successful plays to run well beyond the Haymarket's 15 May opening. No law prevented them from playing as long as they liked, but the tradition was irksome to Colman as it cut out as much as a third of the Haymarket's entire season. His irritation was in some respects well justified. Even at full capacity the Little Theatre would seat some eighteen hundred patrons, compared to three thousand or so at each of the other Theatres Royal; Colman needed his four months more than either winter house needed its eight or nine. Furthermore, the extension of a successful run at either competitor deprived Colman each year of the actors he needed to form his summer company. He saw this as grossly unfair and decided to change things.

Because his earlier satirical complaints had made no difference, he took stronger measures. In an address to his audience after the final curtain had fallen on the 1802 summer season, Colman announced his plan to form a new company wholly independent of the other theaters; each actor in his new company must begin on 15 May. This seemed a gamble, because few established actors would trade a lucrative long season for a short one. But Colman found an abundance of fine talent. Although the established did indeed remain with the winter theaters, including his acting manager, Colman had his pick of all those who were new to town, new to acting, or for some other reason not attractive to Covent Garden and Drury Lane. He also traveled the countryside, recruiting attractive talent when he found it in the provincial theaters. With the apparent support of the King, and the enthusiastic backing of Haymarket audiences and most of the critics, Colman launched his new company before the public on 16 May 1803 and before the Royal Family in a command performance on 17 May. The first month was lean, as might be expected, and the company of newcomers had its expected share of difficulties, but the season was finally successful and encouraging.

In the end, however, the assault on the winter theaters caused a much more serious change in the management of the Haymarket than merely the formation of an independent acting company. Although the move added greatly to the Little Theatre's prestige, it added also to Colman's personal mound of debt. His creditors had been asked to wait while he spent his own money on the competition; after a while they grew impatient. He had always kept the business solvent, though his own financial affairs suffered from his excessive taste in clothing and entertainment, and now the business was his only asset. The creditors demanded a part of it. One of these, Colman's brother-in-law David Morris, may even have extended large sums to Colman in a calculated hope of gaining some managerial control over the theater. If that is so, he was correct; late in 1804 Morris and two others became Colman's partners, and the Colman dynasty at the Haymarket ended after twenty-eight years.

Meanwhile, he continued to write for the winter houses–a practice destined to cause him trouble with his new partner Morris. On 5 March 1803 Covent Garden staged his latest comedy, *John Bull, or The Englishman's Fireside*. For this grand hymn to the English national spirit Colman pulled out all the stops. Mary Thornberry, seduced and abandoned by Frank Rochdale, has fled home lest her father learn of her sin. Near a public house, she is saved from a ruffian by Peregrine, recently shipwrecked off the coast. Peregrine brings her into the pub, hears her story, and registers special interest when he learns that Frank has abandoned her upon orders from his father, Sir Simon Rochdale, who has already chosen a wealthy bride for Frank. Determined to intervene, Peregrine leaves Mary with the landlord and sets off. While he is away, Tom Shuffleton arrives, sent by his friend Frank to help Mary if he can. Frank truly loves her but cannot disappoint Sir Simon. Far from aiding her, as soon as he sees her, Tom wants her for his own mistress and gives her the name of a woman in London, an old friend.

Just then Peregrine arrives and, after a brief dispute, Tom leaves. Behind Peregrine comes Mary's father, Job Thornberry, whom Peregrine has met in town and whom a trusted friend has just bankrupted; Peregrine then gives Job the money he needed, revealing that thirty years earlier Job had given Peregrine, then a boy, a gift of money himself. Now Job and his daughter are reunited, and Job goes to Sir Simon to insist upon justice for Mary. Sir Simon refuses, whereupon Peregrine reveals that Sir Simon is his younger brother. As a boy Peregrine had run away to sea; he has returned as the rightful Rochdale heir. Sir Simon gives his assent, which pleases Mary and Frank, and Peregrine's ship is suddenly discovered and his great wealth restored. And as for John Bull, according to the prologue,

> John Bull is–*British Character* at large;
> 'Tis he, or he,–where'er you mark a wight
> Revering law, yet resolute for right;
> Plain, blunt, his heart with feeling, justice full,
> That is a Briton, that's (thank heaven!) John Bull.

Audiences found much to love in this play. They identified with the honest Job, despised Tom the cad, sympathized with the ruined maiden, and rejoiced at her redemption. They laughed heartily at the minor comic characters always sprinkled throughout Colman's plays. Moralists objected that Mary's vice was rewarded, but they missed the point; Colman portrayed her as a victim. Critics, on the other hand, thought very well of the play, recognizing it as the best comedy in many years. *John Bull* played forty-eight times that season, enough to make it a tremendous success. It must also be considered his finest work. Colman wrote more dramas in the next twenty years, but he never again wrote one so good.

The next two summer seasons at the Haymarket each featured a new farce by Colman, *Love Laughs at Locksmiths* in 1803, and *Gay Deceivers, or More Laugh than Love* in 1804. The first was very successful, playing thirty-one nights that season, but the next was only moderately so; it saw only fifteen performances its first year. The following winter season he wrote another five-act comedy for Covent Garden, but *Who Wants a Guinea?* was no *John Bull.* Colman wrote it in haste, and most critics agreed that it seemed too much a reworking of all his old tricks. After its opening night on 18 April 1805, it was performed only nine times. When next he sold a play to Covent Garden it was a farce, *We Fly by Night, or Long Stories.* Typical of his farces, it became quite popular, playing thirty-one times in the 1806 winter season.

In addition to writing plays Colman had his theater business and personal finances to worry about. Despite resorting to a partnership at the Haymarket, Colman never did get quite ahead of his creditors. One of them finally caught him with the force of law in 1807, and he was arrested and confined to a debtors' house. There he lived for more than three years, until he was moved to a similar but more pleasant residence; he was not entirely freed from custody until 1817. But this custody was not unbearable to him, for he could receive visitors and occasionally leave the house. It is testimony to his unfailing charm and wit that even as a prisoner he frequently received and accepted invitations to dine out, to spend evenings in drink and conversation. And because he could still manage the theater from where he was detained, his existence there was tolerable, even comfortable.

The partnership, on the other hand, was never a comfortable one for the partners and least of all for Colman. Morris proved to be a difficult person in his manner and business dealings, and sought greater and greater control over the minute operations of the theater. Much to Colman's dismay this led to arbitration and legal battles that threatened to ruin his beloved Haymarket. Morris further antagonized Colman by bringing suit against him for breach of contract when the playwright sold a new farce to Covent Garden in 1806, and again with a second farce in 1810. Both times Colman was acquitted; he had never agreed to write exclusively for the Haymarket. The suits appear to have been brought as a nuisance–or even an attempted intimidation of a man already in distressed circumstances. Although Morris conducted his part of the dispute in public, Colman characteristically tried to come to terms with him behind the scenes.

Meanwhile he kept writing. The Haymarket

did well with *The Africans, or War, Love, and Duty*, a three-act musical comedy that played thirty-one times in the summer of 1808. But Covent Garden's 1810 purchase, the farce *X.Y.Z.*, was halted by one of Morris's suits after only two performances. Even selling his plays was becoming more difficult for Colman.

During one of the partners' rare truces they decided once again to take on the winter houses, this time by requesting and receiving from the lord chamberlain a license to remain open a month later, until 15 October. The longer season took effect in 1811, opening 15 May, and not with an entirely independent company. Colman had carefully arranged the schedule of plays to take advantage of gaps in the winter theaters' use of certain star players. Despite another suit by Morris over whether he had been sufficiently consulted in the management of the theater and despite his attempts to remove Colman as manager, the season was successful, and ended on the last legal day. The following season was nearly as long and successful as well, hampered though it was by yet more legal action from Morris; but the next summer, 1813, thanks to more dissension and litigation, the Little Theatre at the Haymarket did not open at all.

Although the partners were able to agree sufficiently to offer a season in 1814 and thereafter, their financial circumstances convinced them to stop trying to compete head-on with the larger theaters. They returned to their original summer venue, opening in June or July, closing in mid September. During these litigious years Colman had written another pair of comic pieces, *The Quadrupeds of Quedlinburgh, or the Rovers of Weimar*, in 1811, and *Doctor Hocus Pocus, or Harlequin Washed White*, in 1814. Both were very well received by their Haymarket audiences, as was *The Actor of All Work, or First and Second Floor* three years later. His light comic touch had not deserted him. But he gradually tired of managing, especially of managing with Morris as a partner. The season of 1818 was Colman's last one as the man in charge of productions at the Little Theatre, Haymarket.

Colman wrote at least three more pieces for the stage: *The Gnome-King, or The Giant-Mountains*, a "Dramatick Legend" in two acts for Covent Garden's 1819-1820 season; *The Law of Java*, a three-act musical comedy, performed at Covent Garden in 1822; and *Stella and Leatherlungs, or A Star and a Stroller*, an afterpiece for Drury Lane in 1823. None of these proved very popular, and Colman wrote no more dramas by himself. He probably assisted in the revision of many others, for he was often called upon by friends and associates for just such work. But in any real sense he was more or less done with writing. Furthermore he no longer needed the income; in 1824 George IV appointed Colman Examiner of Plays, more commonly called Licenser, a post made vacant by the death of John Larpent. In effect this gave him complete authority to censor any plays or parts of plays that he deemed immoral, overly political, blasphemous, or otherwise dangerous.

This office provided steady income but nothing else beneficial to George Colman. He could hardly have ended his career with a less fortunate appointment. He became extremely unpopular with critics and playwrights by performing his duties with excessive zeal and moralistic fastidiousness. Any reference in a play that even hinted of a political subject was ruled out, as were all references to the Deity or to biblical figures or verses. Calling a woman on stage "an angel" was not to be tolerated under Licenser Colman; the word "damn" was condemned. Even more puzzling were his consistent objections to hints of sexual matters, even such mild transgressions as the use of the word "thigh." Under such strictures, of course, references to immoral sexual conduct, however tastefully made, were automatically forbidden if that conduct were not punished in the manner deserved by such a vice.

Colman's friends puzzled over such an approach to an office that could have brought England's foremost living dramatist the kind of revered status his declining years so richly deserved. They looked to his own work and saw countless examples of the very abuses he now corrected in others. Indeed, much of the life and humor of his best work would have been prohibited had Larpent wielded the censor's pen the way Colman did. His behavior as Licenser thus appears hypocritical. Although some excuse can be made for him on the grounds that the audiences in general were beginning to speak out against the excesses of the stage and that theater owners were not so upset with him as the critics and playwrights were, nonetheless his behavior still defies explanation. His biographer Jeremy Bagster-Collins provides the most plausible explanation when he suggests that Colman had lost his sense of humor, and was "overzealous in the performance of duties for which he was by nature unfitted." On the other hand, some evidence suggests that Colman performed his duty as strictly as he could in the full knowledge that, at performance, his erasures would be ignored. His position as manager for so many years should have left him in the position of knowing pretty well what other managers would do with his emendations. If this is what happened, then Colman has been misunderstood for a century and a half. Whatever the explanation, the result was that Colman was much reviled–in his official capacity–by the theatrical community he had loved and helped build for more than forty years.

Regardless of their reaction to him as an official, however, few if any old associates maintained their hostility in social surroundings. Colman was universally reputed to be as charming in his old age as he had been all his life. Actors recalled his generosity and humanity, friends remembered his readiness to help them, and proprietors his straightforward business manner. He was as always a frequent guest at the tables of the great, the one person everyone found agreeable. He probably drank too much and certainly kept late hours, but he did so to the delight of his hosts and companions. Because he had observed such excesses all his life they are unlikely to have contributed greatly to the gradual decline he suffered during his twelve years as Licenser. He was quite simply wearing down. Frequent bouts of ill health accompanied by severe pain gradually kept him more often at home, where his second wife was his constant companion. He concealed his discomforts from the public, however, and most were surprised to learn of his poor condition or, later, of his death. Indeed, despite the suffering of which they remained ignorant, friends found him wittier than ever in his last months. He pursued his duties as Licenser nearly to his end, which came at home, quietly, in late October of 1836. He was seventy-four.

George Colman the Younger was not a great dramatist, though he was the funniest, the most enjoyed, indeed the best of his day. Instead of greatness he sought popularity. Critics complained that, writing what the public liked, he never wrote as well as he was able, never dared to try new forms; yet he can be credited–or blamed–for starting melodrama on its first tentative steps. He was criticized for not upholding the great literary traditions of his country; yet Colman knew that the drama, a performing art, is the most immediate of the literary genres. Any standard of greatness that loses sight of the drama's popular appeal risks irrelevance. Scholars argued that he was simply vulgar or sentimental, preferring farce and low comedy, mixing different dramatic forms. If they were right about this, he did not care; he had made his point. Colman is best remembered, and should be remembered, for *The Heir at Law, John Bull,* and *The Poor Gentleman.* But equally important in some sense are his other thirty dramas, more or less, that shaped and reflected the taste of his time, and the hundreds of his contemporaries' plays he produced on the Haymarket stage. He made people laugh, year after year, and he had great fun doing so.

Biography:

Jeremy F. Bagster-Collins, *George Colman the Younger, 1762-1836* (New York: King's Crown Press, 1946).

References:

David Erskine Baker, Isaac Reed, and Stephen Jones, *Biographica Dramatica; or, A Companion to the Playhouse*, second revision, 3 volumes (London: Longman, Hurst, Rees, Orme & Brown, 1812);

William Hazlitt, *A View of the English Stage* (London: Stodart, Anderson, et al., 1818);

Hubert C. Heffner, "The Haymarket Theater Under Colman the Younger, 1789 to 1805," *Speech Monographs*, 10 (1943): 23-29;

Charles Beecher Hogan, *The London Stage, 1776-1800: A Critical Introduction* (Carbondale: Southern Illinois University Press, 1968);

Raymond Mander and Joe Mitchenson, *The Theatres of London* (London: New English Library, 1975);

Richard Brinsley Peake, *Memoirs of the Colman Family, Including Their Correspondence with the Most Distinguished Personages of Their Time*, 2 volumes (London: R. Bentley, 1841);

Peter A. Tasch, Introduction to *The Plays of George Colman the Younger*, 2 volumes, edited by Tasch (New York & London: Garland, 1981), I:xi-lvii;

Howard Payton Vincent, "George Colman the Younger: Adopted Son," *Philological Quarterly*, 15 (April 1936): 219-220.

Papers:

The Larpent Collection at the Huntington Library, California, holds the manuscript copies submitted to the Licenser John Larpent for the original English productions of the following plays and verses: *The Female Dramatist, Two to One, Turk and No Turk, Inkle and Yarico, The Battle of Hexham, or Days of Old, The Surrender of Calais,*

Poor Old Hay-Market, or Two Sides of the Gutter, The Mountaineers, New Hay at the Old Market, The Iron Chest, My Night-Gown and Slippers, The Heir at Law, Blue-Beard, or Female Curiosity, Blue Devils, Feudal Times, or The Banquet Gallery, The Review, or the Wags of Windsor, The Poor Gentleman, John Bull, or The Englishman's Fireside, Love Laughs at Locksmiths, Gay Deceivers, or More Laugh than Love, Who Wants a Guinea?, We Fly by Night, or Long Stories, The Africans, or War, Love, and Duty, X.Y.Z., The Quadrupeds of Quedlinburgh, or the Rovers of Weimar, Doctor Hocus Pocus, or Harlequin Washed White, The Actor of All Work, or First and Second Floor, The Law of Java, and *Stella and Leatherlungs, or A Star and a Stroller.*

Hannah Cowley

(14 March 1743-11 March 1809)

Jean Gagen
University of Kansas

PLAY PRODUCTIONS: *The Runaway*, London, Theatre Royal in Drury Lane, 15 February 1776;

Who's the Dupe?, London, Theatre Royal in Drury Lane, 10 April 1779;

Albina, London, Theatre Royal in the Hay-Market, 31 July 1779;

The Belle's Stratagem, London, Theatre Royal, Covent Garden, 22 February 1780;

The School of Eloquence, London, Theatre Royal in Drury Lane, 4 April 1780;

The World As It Goes; or A Party at Montpelier, London, Theatre Royal, Covent Garden, 24 February 1781; revised as *Second Thoughts are Best*, London, Theatre Royal, Covent Garden, 24 March 1781;

Which Is the Man?, London, Theatre Royal, Covent Garden, 9 February 1782;

A Bold Stroke for a Husband, London, Theatre Royal, Covent Garden, 25 February 1783;

More Ways than One, London, Theatre Royal, Covent Garden, 6 December 1783;

A School for Greybeards, London, Theatre Royal, Drury Lane, 25 November 1786;

The Fate of Sparta, London, Theatre Royal, Drury Lane, 31 January 1788;

A Day in Turkey, London, Theatre Royal, Covent Garden, 3 December 1791;

The Town Before You, London, Theatre Royal, Covent Garden, 6 December 1794.

BOOKS: *The Runaway, A Comedy: As it is Acted at the Theatre-Royal in Drury-Lane* (London: Printed for the Author & sold by Mr. Dodsley, Mr. Becket, Mr. Cadell & others, 1776);

Who's the Dupe? A Farce: As it is Acted at the Theatre-Royal in Drury-Lane (London: Printed for J. Dodsley, L. Davis, W. Owen, S. Crowder & others, 1779);

Albina, Countess Raimond; A Tragedy, By Mrs. Cowley: As it is Performed at the Theatre-Royal in the Hay-Market (London: Printed by T. Spilsbury for J. Dodsley, R. Faulder & others, 1779);

The Maid of Arragon, A Tale. By Mrs. Cowley, Part I (London: Printed by T. Spilsbury for L. Davis, T. Longman, J. Dodsley, T. Cadell & others, 1780)–includes "Lines in Imitation of Cowley" and a "Monologue," a poem on Chatterton;

The Belle's Stratagem, A Comedy, As Acted at the Theatre-Royal in Covent-Garden (London: Printed for T. Cadell, 1782);

Which is the Man? A Comedy, As Acted at Theatre-Royal in Covent-Garden (London: Printed for C. Dilly, 1783);

A Bold Stroke for a Husband, A Comedy, As Acted at the Theatre Royal, in Covent Garden (London: Printed by M. Scott for T. Evans, 1784);

More Ways Than One, A Comedy, As Acted at the Theatre Royal in Covent Garden (London: Printed by J. Davis for T. Evans, 1784);

A School for Greybeards; Or, The Mourning Bride: A Comedy, In Five Acts. As Performed at the Theatre Royal, Drury-Lane (London: Printed for G. G. J. & J. Robinson, 1786);

The Scottish Village; or, Pitcairne Green (London: Printed for G. G. J. & J. Robinson, 1786);

The Poetry of Anna Matilda (London: Printed by John Bell, 1788);

The Fate of Sparta; or, The Rival Kings. A Tragedy. As it is Acted at the Theatre-Royal in Drury-Lane (London: Printed for G. G. & J. Robinson, 1788);

A Day in Turkey: or, The Russian Slaves. A Comedy, As Acted at the Theatre Royal, in Covent Garden (London: Printed for G. G. & J. Robinson, 1792);

The Town Before You, A Comedy, As Acted at the Theatre-Royal, Covent-Garden (London: Printed by G. Wood Fall for T. N. Longman, 1795);

The Siege of Acre: An Epic Poem in Six Books (Lon-

Hannah Cowley (engraving by James Fittler, based on a portrait by Cosway)

don: Printed at the Oriental Press by Wilson and Co. for J. Debritt, 1801).

Collections: *The Works of Mrs. Cowley, Dramas and Poems*, 3 volumes (London: Wilkie & Robinson, 1813)–comprises Cowley's final revisions of her published plays;

The Plays of Hannah Cowley, 2 volumes, edited by Frederick M. Link (New York & London: Garland, 1979).

OTHER: Poems by Anna Matilda (Hannah Cowley) to Della Crusca (Robert Merry), in *The World*, 10 July, 4 August, 23 November, 22 December 1787; 3 January, 22 February, 1 April, 26 May 1788 (Della Crusca's responses in intervening issues); this correspondence between Anna Matilda and Della Crusca was republished (with several other poetic pieces) in *The Poetry of Anna Matilda* (London: J. Bell, 1788) and in *The Poetry of the World*, 2 volumes, compiled by Edward Topham (London: J. Bell, 1788);

Edwina, a Poem, in *The History of the County of Cumberland*, by William Cumberland (London: Printed by F. Jollie, sold by H. Law & Son, W. Clark, and J. Taylor, 1794), II: 5-15.

The brief biographical information we have about Hannah Cowley centers on her life after she had begun writing for the theater and after her retirement in 1801 to Tiverton, Devonshire, where she was born on 14 March 1743. It is likely that she spent her childhood and years before her marriage there. Her father, Philip Parkhouse, was a bookseller and was reputed to be a highly educated classical scholar, who had originally trained to be a clergyman. It is likely that her father encouraged her literary interests and supervised her education, although it apparently did not include the study of any foreign languages.

After her marriage in 1772 to Thomas Cowley, a newspaper writer and clerk in the Stamp Office, the couple moved to London, which became her home until after her retirement from the stage. They had at least three children, Thomas, Mary Elizabeth, and Frances. Her husband died in

TO

DAVID GARRICK, Efq;

SIR,

AMIDST the regrets I feel for your quitting the Stage, it is peculiarly gratifying, that a Play *of mine* clofes your *dramatic* life—It is the higheft pleafure to me, that *that* Play, from its fuccefs, reflects no difhonour on your judgement as a Manager.

Pofterity will know, thro' a thoufand Channels, that Mr. GARRICK was the ornament of the eighteenth Century, that he poffeffed the friendfhip of thofe whofe Names will be the glory of Englifh Hiftory, that the firft ranks in the kingdom courted his fociety—may my fmall voice be heard amongft thofe who will inform it, that Mr. GARRICK'S *Heart* was no lefs an honour to him, than his *Talents!*

Unpatronized by any *name*, I prefented myfelf to you, obfcure and unknown. You perceived *dawnings* in my Comedy, which you *nourifh'd* and *improved*. With attention, and follicitude, you *embellifh'd*, and prefented it to the world—*that* World, which has emulated your generofity, and received it with an applaufe, which fills my heart with moft lively gratitude. I perceive how much of this applaufe I owe to my *Sex*.—The RUNAWAY has a thoufand faults, which, if written by a Man, would have incurred the fevereft lafh of Criticifm—but the Gallantry of the Englifh Nation is equal to its Wifdom—they beheld a *Woman* tracing with feeble fteps the borders of the Parnaffian Mount——pitying her difficulties (for 'tis a thorny path) they gave their hands for her fupport, and placed her *high* above her level.

All this, Sir, and whatever may be its confequences, I owe to you. Had you rejected me, when I prefented my little RUNAWAY, depreffed by the refufal, and all confidence in *myfelf* deftroyed, I fhould never have prefumed to dip my pen again. It is now my tafk to convince You and the World, that a generous allowance for a young Writer's faults, is the beft encouragement to Genius—'tis a kindly Soil, in which weak Groundlings are nourifh'd, and from which the loftieft Trees draw their ftrength, and their beauty.

I take my leave of you, Sir, with the warmeft wifhes for your felicity, and Mrs. GARRICK'S—to whofe *tafte*, and follicitude for me, I am highly indebted. May your recefs from the Stage be attended with all the bleffings of retirement and eafe—and may the world remember, in its moft diftant periods, that 'tis to Mr. GARRICK the Englifh Theatre owes its emancipation from groffnefs, and buffoonery—that to Mr. GARRICK'S *Judgement* it is indebted for being the firft Stage in Europe, and to his *Talents* for being the delight of the moft enlightened and polifh'd age.

I am, Sir, your moft devoted,

and obedient humble Servant,

THE AUTHOR.

PROLOGUE.

Written by the AUTHOR.

Spoken by MR. BRERETON.

O The fweet profpect! what a fine Parterre!
Soft buds, fweet flowers, bright tints, and fcented air! [*Boxes*.
A Vale, where critic wit fpontaneous grows! [*Pit*.
A Hill, which *noife* and *folly* never knows! [*Gallery*.
Let Cits point out green paddocks to their fpoufes;
To me, no profpect like your crouded houfes—
If, as juft now, you wear thofe fmiles enchanting;
But, when you frown, my heart you fet a panting.
Pray then, for pity, do not frown to-night;
I'll bribe—but how—Oh, now I've hit it—right.
Secrets are pleafant to each child of Eve;
I've one in ftore, which for your fmiles I'll give.
O lift! a tale it is, not very common;
Our Poet of to-night, in faith's a—Woman,
A woman, too, untutor'd in the School,
Nor Ariftotle knows, nor fcarce a rule
By which fine writers fabricate their plays,
From fage Menander's, to thefe modern days:
How fhe could venture here I am aftonifh'd;
But 'twas in vain the Mad-cap I admonifh'd;
Told her of fqueaking cat-calls, hiffes, groans,
Off, offs, and ruthlefs Critics' damning moans.
I'm undifmay'd, fhe cry'd, critics are Men,
And fmile on folly from a Woman's pen:
Then 'tis the Ladies' caufe, there I'm fecure;
Let him who hiffes, no foft Nymph endure;
May he who frowns, be frown'd on by his Goddefs,
From Pearls, and Bruffels Point, to Maids in Boddice.
Now for a hint of her intended feaft:
'Tis rural, playful,—harmlefs 'tis at leaft;
Not over-ftock'd with repartee or wit,
Tho' here and there *perchance* there is a hit;

PROLOGUE.

For fhe ne'er play'd with bright Apollo's fire,
No Mufe invok'd, or heard th' Aönian lyre;
Her Comic Mufe—a little blue-ey'd maid,
With cheeks where innocence and health's difplay'd;
Her 'Pol—in petticoats—a romping Boy,
Whofe tafte is trap-ball, and a kite his joy:
Her Nurfery the ftudy, where fhe thought,
Fram'd fable, incident, furprife and plot.
From the furrounding hints fhe caught her plan,
Length'ning the chain from infancy to man:
Tom plagues poor Fan; fhe fobs, but loves him ftill;
Kate aims her wit at both, with roguifh fkill:
Our Painter mark'd thofe lines—which Nature drew,
Her fancy glow'd, and colour'd them—for you;
A Mother's pencil gave the light and fhades,
A Mother's eye thro' each foft fcene pervades;
Her Children rofe before her flatter'd view,
Hope ftretch'd the canvas, whilft her wifhes drew.
We'll now prefent you drapery and features,
And warmly hope, you'll like the pretty creatures;
Then Tom fhall have his kite, and Fan new dollies,
Till time matures them for *important* follies."

⁂ The dotted lines in the Play are omitted at the Theatre.

Dedication and prologue to Cowley's first play (from the 1776 edition of The Runaway*)*

1797 in India, where he had lived since 1783, when he had joined the East India Company. Her two surviving children, Thomas and Frances, were settled far from England. The biographical sketches of Cowley that were written not long after her death (in the preface to the 1813 edition of her works and in the edition of *Biographia Dramatica* published in 1812) reflect the Hannah Cowley of her later years. They emphasize her quiet domesticity, her indifference to fame, and even her lack of interest in attending the theater often. The remark that she wrote mainly for the pleasure of writing is undoubtedly partly true but ignores evidence that she needed to supplement her husband's meager income. The description of her in the *Biographia Dramatica* as lively and unassuming in manner, with a face animated and expressive, may well be true, as may the observation that she did not like to go out in the evening in her later years but often had large parties at her home.

Her significant achievement as a dramatist has not been adequately recognized in our day though there are indications that this neglect is beginning to change. From her time to our own, there have been critics who have recognized her excellence, notably Allardyce Nicoll in our century. More recently, David W. Meredith has asserted that Cowley's works are unmatched before her time by any woman except Aphra Behn. Though this statement ignores Susanna Centlivre's more widely recognized achievement as a playwright earlier in the century, there is no question that Cowley deserves a place of honor on the roll of eighteenth-century playwrights. In fact, the reviewer of *The Belle's Stratagem* in 1782 in *The Critical Review* praised this play as the "best dramatic production of a female pen . . . since the days of Centlivre, to whom Mrs. Cowley is at least equal in fable and character, and far superior in easy dialogue and purity of diction." The reason for the neglect of Cowley's plays in this century is not easy to understand. But the appearance in 1979 of the two-volume Garland edition of her plays, edited by Frederick Link, now makes her dramas much more readily accessible than formerly.

Mrs. Cowley wrote thirteen plays–two of them tragedies–but her reputation rests on her comedies. The way in which she began writing for the stage has often been repeated. While attending a theatrical performance with her husband, she remarked, "Why I could write as well myself." She took her husband's laughter as a challenge, and the next day she began to write a play that became *The Runaway*. She finished it quickly and sent it to David Garrick to read; he encouraged her and suggested revisions. On 15 February 1776, Garrick premiered the play at the Theatre Royal in Drury Lane, where it met with more success than she dreamed possible. In fact, *The Critical Review* marveled at the skill which this "untutored genius" displayed.

The Runaway is a lively comedy, entertaining and amusing, even though it may not often provoke outbursts of actual laughter. The easy, natural dialogue for which Cowley is often singled out for special praise makes its appearance in this first dramatic production. The play is only lightly touched by sentimentalism. It avoids any suggestion of approval of moral impropriety and certainly places a premium on goodness and benevolence but not at the expense of high-spirited fun.

Set at the country estate of Mr. Hargrave, it concerns the romantic dilemmas of two pairs of young lovers. George Hargrave, home from college on vacation, decides to have some fun at the expense of his sister, Harriet, and her fiancé, Sir Charles Seymour, his motivation (notably weak) being the fact that neither had confided in him their love. He accordingly persuades Harriet that Charles is in love with another woman and Sir Charles that Harriet loves another man. This situation creates coolness and tension between the two lovers but little laughter.

Much of the laughter in the play actually centers on George himself when he ironically fails to realize that his father has selected Lady Dinah, a wealthy, arrogant, and pretentious "Lady Philosopher," to be George's bride. Knowing that Lady Dinah's age fits her much more appropriately to be his father's bride rather than his own, he reacts favorably to what he assumes is his father's announcement of his approaching marriage to Lady Dinah. There is more ironic laughter at George's expense when he generously congratulates Lady Dinah, who is sufficiently astute to sense that George does not realize that he rather than his father is the prospective bridegroom. All the while George is falling more deeply in love with the young runaway Emily, who has been entrusted to the Hargraves by their close friend Mr. Drummond, to whom she has fled for sanctuary from her uncle, who is trying to force an uncongenial marriage on her.

Lady Dinah is quick to realize that George is in love with Emily and that Emily threatens her marriage to George. At first Lady Dinah has been an object of satire simply because, in her pompous parade of her knowledge of the classics, she fits the stereotype of the learned lady in drama. For example, Bella, George's cousin, delights in interrupting Lady Dinah's "harangues" because she claims that she cannot endure so much wisdom! But the folly of Lady Dinah's pretentious display of her learning fades into the background as the viciousness of her character is increasingly revealed. Out of jealousy for Emily, Lady Dinah concocts a scheme to discredit her reputation. George runs into difficulties too when he finally understands the import of his father's matrimonial negotiations and refuses to marry Lady Dinah. His irate father then threatens to disinherit him. Mr. Hargrave's plan to marry George to a woman much older than he, a woman whom he does not love and who has nothing to recommend her but what Mr. Hargrave values unduly–her wealth and social position–is implicitly criticized but also overtly condemned by George's godfather, Mr. Drummond, the embodiment of good sense and benevolence.

Mr. Drummond wins the consent of both Emily's uncle and Mr. Hargrave to the marriage of George and Emily by offering to make George the heir of his fortune and to surrender to Emily the jointure left to him by his dead wife. Meanwhile, the treachery of Lady Dinah has been exposed; she leaves shamed and angry; and Mr. Hargrave finally admits that he has been wrong in his attitude toward her. The difficulties between Harriet and Charles have been cleared up too. The play ends with the prospect of two happy marriages and possibly a third, for we learn that Bella's suitor is posting hastily from Dover in the hope of an engagement to her. Though Bella claims that she could never be induced to honor and obey her husband, there is a strong suggestion that she will weaken when Belville appears. Bella, who remains on the periphery of the action during most of the play, heralds in her wit and independence the later emergence of a type of witty heroine who would become the most delightful of all Cowley's characters.

The play's initial run of seventeen performances during its first season and its frequent revivals were an auspicious beginning for Mrs. Cowley's career. The occasional improbabilities in the plot and weaknesses in motivation (faults which Cowley never completely overcame) were easily forgiven because the play very obviously pleased and entertained its audiences.

The next play that Cowley attempted to have produced was the tragedy *Albina*, which ran into many difficulties. In the meantime she had written a farce, *Who's the Dupe?*, which also encountered some difficulties since it was not produced until late in the season on 10 April 1779. Nevertheless, *Who's the Dupe?*, her second play to be produced, became one of Cowley's most popular plays, with *The London Stage* recording 126 performances between its opening in 1779 and 1800. Though Cowley borrowed extensively from the subplot of Centlivre's *The Stolen Heiress* (1702), she has added distinctive touches of her own which strengthen the satire and heighten the humor.

The prefatory note in the 1813 edition of *Who's the Dupe?* remarks that in addition to satirizing pedantry the play satirizes "the disgusting vulgarity in an upstart citizen." In the prologue to the same edition Cowley also remarks that since learned men and writers have often satirized the "petty foibles" and faults of women and exposed their "whims and vanity," she as a woman asks leave to laugh at these same learned men "whose sarcastic pen" has spared neither "Matron Maid or Bride." All this is precisely what Cowley has done in this broadly amusing farce.

Old Doiley is the vulgar "upstart citizen," wealthy and ignorant but so enamored of "Larning" that he is determined to have a son-in-law who is "Larned." Although he has chosen the pedant Gradus from Oxford to be his daughter Elizabeth's husband, Elizabeth dupes her father and Gradus and wins for her husband Granger, the man she loves. Neither Doiley nor Gradus is mean or vicious. Yet both deserve to be duped. Doiley is not merely a tyrannical father who believes that his will should determine whom his daughter marries, but he patronizingly laments wasting money on educating daughters in French and dancing, "Jography" and "Stronomy." Gradus, moreover, seconds these opinions and extols those "immortal periods" when women could neither read nor write.

Elizabeth, however, has the wit to engineer the ruse by means of which Gradus is discredited in her father's eyes. Granger then successfully poses as a scholar who buries himself in his books, reads Greek and Latin, and has mastered the English philosophers.

The scene in which Granger supposedly demonstrates his superiority to Gradus in ancient tongues is one of the best in the play. On the spot he composes a bogus oration consisting entirely of obscure, polysyllabic English words, none of which Doiley recognizes as his mother tongue. Gradus, of course, recognizes the hoax but his protests are in vain. Entranced by Granger's "Larning," Doiley

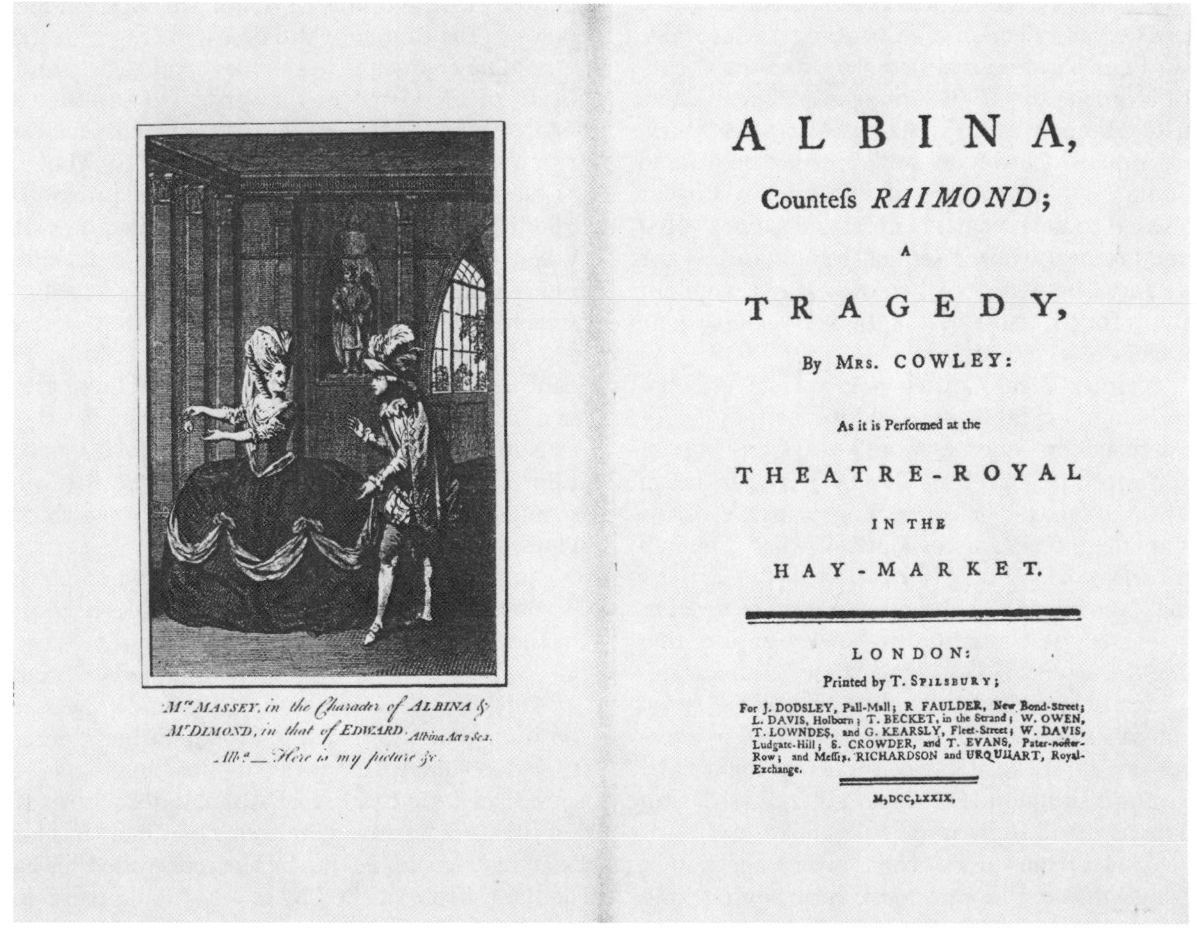

ALBINA,

Counteſs *RAIMOND*;

A

TRAGEDY,

By Mrs. COWLEY:

As it is Performed at the

THEATRE-ROYAL

IN THE

HAY-MARKET.

LONDON:

Printed by T. Spilsbury;

For J. DODSLEY, Pall-Mall; R. FAULDER, New Bond-Street; L. DAVIS, Holborn; T. BECKET, in the Strand; W. OWEN, T. LOWNDES, and G. KEARSLY, Fleet-Street; W. DAVIS, Ludgate-Hill; S. CROWDER, and T. EVANS, Pater-noſter-Row; and Meſſrs. RICHARDSON and URQUHART, Royal-Exchange.

M,DCC,LXXIX.

Frontispiece and title page for Cowley's first tragedy, which became the center of controversy when, before its first performance, Cowley discovered strong similarities between Albina *and two plays by Hannah More*

offers to leave Granger every farthing he has if he will marry Elizabeth. Moreover, he patronizingly suggests that Gradus trot back to Oxford to learn the difference between Greek and English.

Elizabeth is the first of Cowley's fully developed witty and resourceful heroines, a type of character in which she increasingly excelled. Gradus realizes that he has been duped not once but twice and is willing to admit that he may need to know more of the real world. But Doiley, declaring himself the happiest man alive at the prospect of Elizabeth's marriage to a learned man, never realizes that he has been duped–hence the relevance of the question in the title: who *is* the dupe?

Cowley's next play, the tragedy *Albina*, which premiered on 31 July 1779, was preceded and accompanied by a long controversy, which Cowley relates in detail in her preface to the first edition of the play. Cowley had first presented *Albina* for consideration to Garrick at about the time he resigned as manager of Drury Lane. When Richard Brinsley Sheridan, who succeeded Garrick, failed to respond to her queries about the play, she presented *Albina* to Thomas Harris at Covent Garden, only to have the play rejected as unfit for performance.

Not long afterward, Hannah More's *Percy* was presented, and to Mrs. Cowley's astonishment and distress she realized that the father of the heroine of Hannah More's play was placed in a situation almost identical to that of Westmoreland in her own play; and not only did he behave in a similar manner when the honor of his daughter was impugned, but "even spoke several lines nearly verbatim." Moreover, Cowley subsequently discovered that the French play on which More's play was closely modeled did not have in it a scene in which a father defends his defamed daughter and even offers to champion her in a duel.

Despite her suspicions, Cowley's prudence suggested a cautious silence because Sheridan at

Drury Lane, to whom she had presented *Albina* after Harris's rejection of it, had taken a favorable view of her play and had virtually promised to produce it during the 1779-1780 season. The production of Hannah More's *The Fatal Falsehood*, however, aroused Cowley to public protest because in attending a performance of this tragedy Cowley professed to have heard "with astonishment" what seemed to her "every essential circumstance of the Plot, and Character" of her own play except for changes for the most part in the very places which had been objected to in hers.

Neither Mrs. Cowley nor anyone else has been able to explain with certainty the reasons for the similarities between More's plays and *Albina*. The conjectures that Mrs. Cowley herself makes in her preface are probably the most plausible. *Albina* was in the possession of Garrick when Hannah More was working on *Percy* and living at Garrick's home. Knowing the habit of managers to give advice and suggest alterations, Cowley implies that amid "the croud of Plots, and Stage Contrivances, in which a Manager is involv'd, *recollection* is too frequently mistaken for the suggestions of *imagination*." The most charitable construction that can be put on this situation is to assume that Garrick and/or Harris made suggestions to Hannah More that were drawn from their unconscious recollection of Cowley's *Albina* and that More incorporated into her plays with no knowledge of their ultimate source.

Eventually Cowley's play was presented by George Colman the Elder at the Haymarket on 31 July 1779. Its success could scarcely be expected to be great considering Cowley's public outcry and Hannah More's reputation for integrity. Nevertheless, after a short run that was at least sufficient to prevent the play from being damned as an utter failure, Cowley received three benefits. *Albina*, however, never received enthusiastic plaudits. About the best that can be said for it is that worse tragedies had been performed during this period and that it was as good as many that had appeared.

From an historical point of view the play is interesting in its embodiment of many of the theories of tragedy popular in the Restoration and eighteenth century. What modern readers of *Albina* may find at fault in it is often what eighteenth-century audiences wanted to find in the tragedies they viewed–edifying moral instruction, generous doses of pathos, a series of highly emotional crises, and poetic justice at the conclusion of the "tragedy." The historical framework of Albina (set in the reign of Richard I), as well as the conflict between love and duty or honor are both commonplace in the drama of the time.

The characters in the play tend to be simplistically divided between the very good and the very bad, though there are partial exceptions to this rule. Albina, the widowed daughter of the earl of Westmoreland, represents female purity and goodness, while Editha, who is the daughter of a fallen enemy, is full of bitterness at her dependence on Albina and capable of vicious deceit and treachery even though she has received nothing but kindness and consideration from Albina. The contrast between Albina and Editha is highlighted in a scene where Albina insists that the choicest gift of Nature to woman is the capacity to love, whereas Editha angrily retorts that love will be forever a stranger to her heart because the fire which animates *her* heart is "bright ambition."

The conflict in the play arises when Albina is about to marry Edward, a valiant soldier chosen by the king to lead his warriors against the "sacrilegious Turk." Since Editha had hoped to marry Edward herself as a means of regaining the social position that she had lost by her father's defeat, she determines to prevent this marriage. In Gondibert, the brother of Albina's dead husband, Editha finds a convenient tool. Gondibert has long been in love with Albina but has controlled his passion and been satisfied by seeing Albina daily. But news of Albina's imminent marriage to Edward arouses his long-suppressed passion for Albina. Editha exploits Gondibert's anguish by persuading him to participate in a plot to prevent Albina's marriage to Edward by convincing Edward of Albina's infidelity.

The plot succeeds temporarily, but Egbert, a loyal retainer who has overheard the details of the plot, reveals the truth. The king banishes Gondibert, and the remorseful Edward is reconciled with Albina. Realizing that he has been robbed of his reputation and his country and that the love of Albina is forever beyond him, Gondibert goes mad. In his madness he attempts to kill both Albina and Edward but by mistake kills Editha instead and then stabs himself. Before he dies he asks for and receives pity and forgiveness from both Albina and Edward. At the close of the play Albina's father, Westmoreland, moralizes over the fact that, through unrestrained passion, vice in the shape of love has crept into Gondibert's heart. Although Editha is the more active force in their villainy, Gondibert, her tool, is the more interesting of the two "villains" in that he has a genuine conscience, is capable of moral conflict and of

Sarah Siddons, who created the role of Chelonice in The Fate of Sparta

remorse. His mad scenes are the most spectacular in the play and in their tempestuousness undoubtedly aroused terror and a degree of pity. The unjust accusation leveled against Albina was undoubtedly designed to arouse pity too, while her father's unhesitating defense of her fidelity inevitably arouses admiration. The tragedy conforms to many of the expectations of eighteenth-century audiences without excelling in any particular respect. The blank verse is without distinction as is the entire play. Reading it is a harmless diversion, which at least illustrates the popular taste in eighteenth-century tragedy.

Mrs. Cowley waited nine years before presenting another tragedy, *The Fate of Sparta*, which opened on 31 January 1788 at Drury Lane. It fared somewhat better than *Albina* for a number of reasons, one of them being the fact that the famous Mrs. Sarah Siddons played the part of Chelonice, a role perfectly designed to display Siddons's talents for portraying scenes of pathos and distress. In her dedication to the first edition of the play Cowley admits that, although she is indebted to Plutarch's *Life of Agis* for the characterization of several of the principal figures in the tragedy, the "fable and events" are "all invention–except in the conduct of Chelonice, and the scene in the Temple," though even in this scene Cowley admits that she has "taken some liberties."

The tragedy thus has a historical framework to which much "invention" has been added. The conflict centers on possession of the throne of Sparta. Although the throne has been bestowed jointly on Leonidas and Cleombrotus, a bitter struggle over sole control of the throne ensues. Because Leonidas is Chelonice's father and Cleombrotus her husband, she is inevitably caught in an agonizing struggle to be true both to her duty to her father and to her husband.

Mrs. Cowley was aware that Chelonice's virtue might seem "too perfect," and she invokes the authority of Plutarch for her portrayal of Chelonice's perfections, with the comment that she does not believe that Plutarch has been "suspected of writing fiction to compliment women." Undoubtedly the most dramatic scene in which Chelonice demonstrates her loyalty to her father occurs when Leonidas has placed her on trial for treason against him. When Leonidas's faction had nearly been defeated by Cleombrotus, Chelonice in disguise as a priestess succeeded in crossing the enemy lines and procuring an interview with her husband. Though Cleombrotus was not persuaded

Elizabeth Hartley as a Nymph with a Young Bacchus (portrait by Sir Joshua Reynolds; by permission of the Tate Gallery). She created the role of Lady Frances Touchwood in The Belle's Stratagem.

easily to spare Leonidas, he finally consented to withdraw his troops for a twenty-four-hour respite.

But when Leonidas hears that his daughter has visited her "rebel" husband, he assumes that she is a traitor, and his suspicions of her loyalty are fanned into such a hot flame by the unscrupulous Amphares (motivated by his ambition to win the throne and Chelonice for himself) that he is deaf to Chelonice's claims of innocence and tries and condemns her as a rebel and traitor leagued with Sparta's foe. Though the people plead for her, Chelonice sternly admonishes them not to pity her or spare her lest the door for treason be opened. She exhorts the people to be proud that in their sovereign they have a hero who will punish those most precious to his heart. She even clasps her chains and calls on the gods to witness that these chains are dear to her as a father's gift. However much pity and admiration this scene may have been designed to arouse, to any modern reader (and perhaps, one hopes, to some members of her original audiences) Chelonice's loyalty to her father seems ludicrous and even perverse here rather than admirable.

Nevertheless, as a "paragon of female excellence," Chelonice continues to pass every strenuous test of her virtue, proving her double loyalty to both her father and her husband. At the conclusion Amphares receives poetic justice in failing in his ambitions and in finally being killed by Cleombrotus, after Amphares has given Leonidas his death wound. Though Leonidas's cruelty and tyranny have been progressively revealed throughout the play, Cleombrotus has proved himself capable of increasing magnanimity and had even fought to save Leonidas's life not long after Leonidas had ordered Cleombrotus's head to be cut off.

Before Leonidas dies, he finally recognizes the perfections of his much maligned daughter, blesses her, and assigns the throne to both Chelonice and Cleombrotus.

As in *Albina*, virtue finally triumphs and vice is punished by defeat and death. The plot is much more complex than that of *Albina* and has more intense emotional crises as Chelonice is torn between her suspicious, tyrannical father and her ambitious but essentially just and loving husband. The play had a run of nine days, and Cowley received three benefit performances. The production, however, had mixed reviews and could scarcely be claimed as a success. This second attempt at tragedy apparently convinced Cowley that her forte lay in comedy.

In fact, her most popular comedy, *The Belle's Stratagem*, was produced immediately after *Albina*, premiering on 22 February 1780. *The Belle's Stratagem* is clearly a comedy of manners, mirroring fashionable London society as it was viewed through the eyes of a playwright concerned to entertain without giving moral offense. The main plot deals with a problem in courtship, the other with a problem which develops within a marriage. The title is taken from the stratagem by means of which Letitia Hardy wins the love of the young gentleman Doricourt, to whom she was contracted in marriage when they were both children, though there has been a lapse of years since they have seen one another. When Doricourt's arrival in England from Rome is described, it is apparent that he is a fashionable young gallant with a carriage, liveries, and dress which have become the rage of the day. Doricourt, however, is not impressed by Letitia's reputation as a beauty, for she seems to have none of the spirit, the fire, "*l'air enjoué*," which had attracted him to the resistless charmers of Italy and France.

Despite his lack of enthusiasm for Letitia, Doricourt intends to do the honorable thing and marry her. But Letitia has no intention of marrying a man who is as indifferent to her "as a husband of fifteen months." Her stratagem consists of repelling him by pretending to be a loud, garrulous, crude simpleton and then to win his love as a masked beauty at a masquerade. Doricourt notices how divinely this unknown beauty dances and soon learns how bewitching as well as beautiful she is and how spirited and wild.

Though Doricourt pretends madness to avoid marrying Letitia in her role as a repulsive simpleton, in the end his honor persuades him to marry her, only to be tormented afterward by the appearance of the masked beauty who claims that Doricourt swore eternal love to her and that, believing him, she surrendered to him her virgin heart. She also insists that her honor is spotless, her birth equal to his, and her fortune large. Only after Doricourt has been desperate with misery for a short time does Letitia reveal her identity to him in a dramatic moment attended by great rejoicing. Her stratagem has proved that English women have as much charm and spirit as their European counterparts, and by her initiative and resourcefulness she has not only won the man *she* loves but a man who also loves her.

The secondary plot has a long dramatic history stretching back not merely to the earlier eighteenth century and Restoration period but to the drama written before 1640. It focuses on the problems encountered by a married couple from the country when they visit London and are introduced to the habits and recreations of fashionable life. The problems of Cowley's couple, Sir George and Lady Frances Touchwood, are not, however, very serious even though Sir George does not wish his wife to adopt the habits of fashionable life and is eager to return to the country. In fact, he is so passionately and possessively in love with his wife that he does not even want her to see Doricourt because he has heard that Doricourt is very handsome.

When Lady Frances meets two fashionable London ladies, the widow Mrs. Racket and Miss Ogle, they urge her–against her husband's wishes–to go shopping with them for a new gown (without her husband), to go to an exhibition and auction, and then take a turn in the park with them. Lady Frances disobeys her husband and goes with them, though without any unfortunate results since both Mrs. Racket and Miss Ogle are innocent of any evil designs. In fact, in spite of her name, which suggests superficiality and frivolity, Mrs. Racket defines a fine lady in the first scene of the second act in a manner clearly showing that she does not associate fashionable elegance and poise with any species of immorality or folly. Moreover, on her return Lady Frances, though she had enjoyed her outing, remarks that she would rather be with Sir George for fifteen minutes than have fifteen days of amusement without him. Unlike earlier ladies from the country who become foolishly and extravagantly obsessed with London recreations and fashions, Lady Frances remains unusually stable and sensible. She therefore does not need to be shocked or frightened into reforming. Yet Cowley follows this pattern, though with only the gentlest

27

St. Geo... I am particularly engag'd —

Dori... Oh! lord, that shall be no excuse in the world. (rises from the Sopha) Lead the way, John... Exit, following the Servt.

St. Geo... What devil possess'd me to talk about her! here, Doricourt! runs after him.

Enter Mrs. Racket, and the Miss Ogles follow'd by a Servant.

Mrs. R... Acquaint your Lady, that Mrs. Racket, and the two Miss Ogles are here. .... Exit Servant.

Miss O... I shall hardly know Lady Frances, 'tis so long since I was in Shropshire.

Mrs. R.. And I'll be sworn you never saw her out of Shropshire, her father kept her lock'd up with his Caterpillars and Shells, and lov'd her beyond any thing. but a blue butter fly and a petrified frog.

Miss O.. Ha! ha! ha! well, 'twas a cheap way of breeding her — you know he was very poor, tho' a Lord a very high Spirited, tho' a — Virtuoso. In town, her Pantheon, Operas, and Robes de Cour, would have swallow'd his Sea weeds, Moths and Monsters in six weeks.

Lucy O... How can you speak so contemptuously, Sister? He was a Noble=man of a most amiable Character, and gave Lady Frances a most elegant Education.

Miss O... Pray Miss Lucy, don't be so voluble, Sir George, I find, thinks his wife a most extraordinary Creature! He has taught her to despise every thing like fashionable life, and boasts that Example will have no effect on her.

Page from the playhouse copy of The Belle's Stratagem *submitted to the Examiner of Plays for licensing prior to the first performance, on 22 February 1780 (Larpent Collection, LA 513; by permission of the Henry E. Huntington Library and Art Gallery)*

suggestion that Lady Frances needs to be more wary.

At the masquerade, which both Lady Frances and her husband attend that evening, the rakish Courtall, who has been attracted to Lady Frances, disguises himself in a habit identical to that which Sir George has chosen to wear. In that disguise Courtall, with strictly dishonorable intentions, plans to carry Lady Frances off with him. But Saville, a virtuous friend and gentleman, learns of this scheme and determines that Lady Frances shall not be victimized by Courtall. He not only outwits Courtall but so shames him that he flees to France.

When Lady Frances learns of the danger she had been in, she confesses that she was perhaps too much inclined to adopt a new system of conduct and in the future Sir George will be her constant companion and protector. Sir George, on the other hand, is urged not to retire to Hampshire because Lady Frances "was born to be the ornament of Courts." Now that she has been sufficiently warned not to wander beyond the reach of her protector, even the most anxious husband would not wish to banish her from the British court, the implication being that no harm could touch her in that sacrosanct place. Thus there is a compromise in both directions and a bit of the flattery of the royal house, in which Cowley rather frequently indulged. This plot may seem to some readers more interesting than the main plot because of the way in which Cowley's benevolent attitude toward human nature and her admiration for London fashions that are both elegant and innocent has softened the conflict between Lady Frances and Sir George and altered the resolution.

Fortunate in having been performed by an excellent cast of actors and actresses, the play ran for 28 nights during its first season. It became a part of the standard repertory of Covent Garden and by 1800 had been acted 118 times in London theaters.

In spite of the success of *The Belle's Stratagem*, Cowley's next three comic productions all failed, were never printed, and survive only in manuscript. *The School of Eloquence*, intended as an interlude or afterpiece, was first presented by Sheridan on 4 April 1780. It was withdrawn after one performance. On 24 February 1781 Cowley's five-act comedy, *The World As It Goes; or A Party at Montpelier*, was presented at Covent Garden but so unsuccessfully that Cowley quickly withdrew it for alterations. As *Second Thoughts are Best*, it was presented on 24 March but again met with severe objections.

Success returned to Mrs. Cowley, however, with *Which Is the Man?* It opened on 9 February 1782 and had a run of twenty-three performances its first season, with occasional revivals for many years thereafter. Though its popularity never equaled that of *The Belle's Stratagem*, it has been recognized from its initial performance as a good play. A comedy of manners, it draws on many stereotyped characters but not without some vitality. It reflects the moral climate of the theater of Cowley's day but without tedium.

One of the strengths of the play lies in the parade of characters who inhabit the London scene on which the comedy focuses. Lord Sparkle is in the tradition of Lord Foppington but less amusing and more discreditable than his original. He has flattered and deceived two rustics from Cornwall–Bobby Pendragon and his sister Sophy–in order to win their influence, which "got him the borough." The laughter at the gaucherie and naiveté of the Pendragons, who have followed Sparkle to London, enlivens a number of scenes, though some sympathy is directed to them because of Sparkle's unscrupulous exploitation of them, especially Sophy, who expects Sparkle to marry her because he had called her a bewitching and adorable girl and talked to her precisely like all the lovers in romances such as *The Constant Lover* and *The Reclaimed Rake*.

A somewhat darker and less comic side of Sparkle's character is seen in his relation with Julia, the ward of his "honourable cousin" Mr. Fitzherbert. Fitzherbert is the voice of rectitude and benevolence in the play, though Sparkle refers to him as "old Cato the Censor." For the sake of fashion, Sparkle hopes to win as his bride the witty and wealthy young widow Lady Bell Bloomer; yet he has also decided to make Julia his mistress because fashion now dictates that one's mistress should be drawn from a higher social order than seamstresses or mantua makers.

Julia, however, had been secretly married in France to Belville, a fashionable young man who is a friend of Fitzherbert yet does not know that Julia is Fitzherbert's ward–a glaring improbability on which other improbabilities are progressively heaped. For reasons never explained, Belville cautions Julia to continue to keep their marriage secret even after they have independently returned to England. This secrecy involving the marriage of Julia and Belville, including their ignorance of the fact that they have unknowingly married precisely in accordance with Fitzherbert's wishes, becomes the source of numerous complications. On one occasion Julia narrowly escapes being raped by Lord Sparkle, and later she is found by Belville in what seems to be a compromising position with another man. Belville is so shocked that he promptly says farewell forever to her. It hardly needs to be said that in the final act these misunderstandings are all cleared up.

Lady Bell Bloomer, the young widow who is just emerging from mourning and eager to enter the world of pleasures which her fortune, youth, and beauty will open to her, behaves at times like a giddy coquette interested in nothing beyond the admiration she will arouse and the conquests she will make. But her promise to herself to keep innocence and honor as her handmaids strikes the moral note that Cowley is careful to include in her version of this stereotyped character. That Lady Bell is not what she seems is also underscored by the thoughtful assessments of her character by Fitzherbert and Julia, both of whom realize that a "fine understanding" and "sensible heart" are concealed behind Lady Bell's giddiness.

Because Lady Bell professes to believe that caprice is absolutely essential to a fine lady, she teases Lord Sparkle and does not allow him to know what her attitude toward him really is. Even when she has admitted to herself that it is the poor but honorable soldier Beauchamp whom she loves, her vanity tells her that it would be preposterous to give up a coronet for Beauchamp, and she teases Beauchamp even more mercilessly than Lord Sparkle, since Beauchamp truly loves her and suffers deeply over what he regards as her rejection of him. But after Lady Bell has learned progressively of the many vices of Sparkle, she openly announces that she prefers to give her heart to a poor soldier "who boasts only worth, spirit, honour, and love" than to one who has been unable to resist "vice in the seductive form of fashionable dissipation." Fitzherbert so thoroughly approves of Lady Bell's choices that he makes Beauchamp his heir, though Beauchamp decides to continue as a soldier and to divide his heart between his love for Lady Bell and his love for his country.

There is more serious moralizing in this play than in Cowley's previous plays–for example, on the disgracefulness of Lord Sparkle's behavior to the Pendragons and Julia; on the union of souls, the "elegant attentions of polish'd manners" and mutual respect necessary in any happy marriage; and on the glory of the profession of the soldier who loves and guards his country against her foes.

There is much delightful wit in many of the scenes, especially those involving Lady Bell Bloomer and the fashionable ladies and gentlemen who assemble in her apartment. Unlike many of Cowley's witty heroines, Lady Bell does not need to display much initiative and resourcefulness because she does not find herself in a deplorable situation from which she must find a way to rescue herself. She simply has to decide which man she will choose as her husband–Lord Sparkle or Beauchamp, and there is never much suspense over what her final choice will be.

The various strands of plot are woven together because of the close relationships among the principal characters. Lord Sparkle, for example, is Fitzherbert's cousin, plots to make Fitzherbert's ward, Julia, his mistress, and hopes to marry Lady Bell Bloomer, who is a close friend of both Julia and Fitzherbert. Even Bobby Pendragon's crude attempt to woo Julia Manners (suggested to him by Fitzherbert, who feels the need to punish Julia for marrying without his consent) integrates Bobby into the plot centering on Julia and the predicaments to which her "rash" behavior gives rise.

In spite of the title of the play, which presumably refers to Lady Bell's choice of a husband, one would be hard put to say where the focus of interest lies–on Sparkle and his various discreditable schemes, on the improbable predicaments of the long-suffering Julia Manners, or on the engaging wit and joie de vivre of Lady Bell. If the play seems to lack a focus, its merits are obvious in the swift movement of the various strands of the plot, in the interesting and varied cast of characters, and in the easy, natural, and often witty flow of the dialogue.

The title of Cowley's next play, *A Bold Stroke for a Husband* (25 February 1783), was obviously suggested by Susanna Centlivre's *A Bold Stroke for a Wife* (1718), but is otherwise not indebted to it. Set in Spain, there is little, if anything, distinctly Spanish about the play except some of the proper names. It differs in no essentials from an English comedy of romantic intrigue except for the fact that women rather than men are the principal intriguers, and in one of the two interwoven plots there is a large injection of sentimentality. For a number of elements in the plot Cowley is indebted to Thomas Otway's *The Atheist* (1683) and Thomas Durfey's *The Virtuous Wife* (1679).

Although its two plots differ markedly in tone in that one is serious and moralistic in a sentimental fashion while the other is full of wit, gaiety, and laughter, the play is able to accommodate these two diverse plots without any sense of disharmony since they are closely interwoven structurally

Elizabeth Kemble, who created the role of Arabella in More Ways than One *(engraving by J. Goldar)*

and thematically. Most of the characters in both plots know each other and even have a share in the action of both plots. Moreover, bold strokes are demanded not only of Victoria, who reclaims her philandering husband in the serious plot, but also of Victoria's cousin Olivia, who gains a husband in the high-spirited comic plot. Both women are daring and resourceful and responsible for rescuing themselves from the miserable situation in which the men in their lives (Victoria's husband and Olivia's father) have placed them.

Victoria's husband, Don Carlos, has not only succumbed to Laura, an unscrupulous fortune hunter, but in a state of intoxication has condemned himself and his wife and children to financial ruin by deeding to Laura the estate which came to him through his wife. With modest reluctance but a firm sense of necessity, Victoria sets out to recapture her faithless husband and her fortune. Disguised as Florio, a handsome young gentleman, Victoria wins the fickle affections of Laura, who promptly discards Carlos but refuses to surrender the estate. Nearly insane with anger at Laura and remorse over his treatment of Victoria, Carlos plans to get revenge by killing Laura's new paramour in her arms. But when Carlos rushes in with his sword drawn, Victoria (Florio) pulls off her hat, drops to her knees, and urges him to strike his sword deep into her heart, where dwells all the anguish of betrayed love. She then flies to his arms, protesting her love for him, and begging *him* to pardon *her* "too severe reproaches." Though she does not at this juncture reveal all the details of how, with the cooperation of her friend Gasper, she has recovered their estate, Carlos learns enough to rejoice wholeheartedly in their reconciliation. Now a repentant sentimental hero, he declares that to look at and listen to and love his wife is "like the bliss of angels cheering whispers to repentant sinners."

Before Olivia initiates the stratagem by means of which *she* wins the man she loves, she has first had to devise ways to repel the many unwelcome suitors her father, Don Caesar, has presented to her as prospective husbands. Finally desperate to have Olivia marry and produce a male heir, Don Caesar presents Olivia with an ultimatum–if by her "perverse humour" Olivia drives away the final two suitors that he is willing to present for her inspection, he will send her to a convent, and he will marry a young wife and produce the desired male heir himself.

During this crisis, Olivia never loses her wit and sense of fun. She is obviously as exhilarated by teasing and duping her frantic father as she is in bewildering and even outraging her suitors. When she has driven away the first of these last two suitors–Don Garcia–by her shrewishness and then the second, the musician Don Vincentio, by insisting that her favorite musical instrument is the Jew's harp, Don Caesar can only glare at Olivia in speechless rage. But Olivia remarks, with impudent delight, that she sees "a young mother-in-law [stepmother], and an old lady abbess in every line of his face."

Olivia's lively wit and sense of fun are equally in evidence in her successful pursuit of Julio, the man who so bewitched her when she had seen him two years previously (though until recently he has been out of the country) that his image has been constantly in her mind ever since. This is the reason no other suitor can please her. Pressured into action by her father, Olivia arranges a meeting in the Prado with Julio, though she is veiled, as is her "exemplary cousin" Victoria, who accompanies her. Olivia's wit and beauty immediately attract

Julio, though he does not know her identity until close to the end of the play. This fast-paced courtship has many amusing complications. Its sprightliness is heightened by the fact that Olivia's maid, Minette, is very nearly as witty and skillful at deception as her mistress. Although she decides to woo Julio for herself, her scheme fails, and Julio soon discovers the identity of the one woman who has enraptured him and whom he is eager to marry. When Don Caesar learns that there is a man who actually is willing to marry Olivia, he receives the news with shocked delight. Both plots are thus happily resolved through the bold strokes taken first by Victoria and then by Olivia.

Most readers probably find the liveliness and wit of the comic plot more delightful than the serious plot. In both plots, however, Cowley's moralistic emphasis is in evidence–explicitly in the "excessive" goodness of Victoria to her scapegrace husband and in the lush fulsomeness of Don Carlos's repentance in the serious plot; implicitly in the absence of any licentiousness in the dialogue or any morally questionable situations in the comic plot.

The play's initial run of eighteen performances marked it as a success. There were revivals during the next three seasons and, on rare occasions, thereafter until 1828.

More Ways than One, which opened at Covent Garden on 6 December 1783, was dedicated to Mrs. Cowley's husband, who had departed for India for service in the East India Company. The poem emphasizes the paradox of her grief and sadness over the absence of her husband and the comfort and joy that writing this comedy has brought her. The satire in the play ranges over a fairly wide variety of social types and social evils but with the broad, good-natured humor characteristic of Cowley.

Like most of Cowley's comedies, this one ends with the prospect of a happy marriage–more specifically, two happy marriages involving two young women who are sharply contrasted throughout the play. One is Miss Archer, who is sophisticated and witty, has a well-cultivated mind, the experience of travel in Europe, and the conquest of many adoring lovers, all of whom she has rejected. The other is Arabella, raised in the country by two spinsters, who taught her only such household arts as sewing and "making seed-cake, and stewing codlings." She cannot read or write, has never heard of "Point or Brussels," and her only card game is "beggar my neighbour." Arabella knows so little about the ways of the world that she supposes she has to marry the old man Evergreen, whom her guardian, the physician Feelove, has chosen for her. Feelove never allows her to stir from his home, and Evergreen intends to continue this kind of incarceration in his own home. The portrayal of Arabella is reminiscent of that of Margery Pinchwife in William Wycherley's *The Country Wife* (1675) and Agnes in Molière's *School for Wives* (1667), to which, of course, Wycherley's play is clearly indebted. But whatever Cowley borrowed from Wycherley or Molière or other playwrights who have been suggested she has skillfully adapted to her own purposes and inclinations.

Both Feelove and Evergreen are satirized for their avarice, since Feelove wishes to pay as small a dowry as possible to dispose of Arabella (so that he can keep as much of her fortune as possible), while Evergreen wants to receive as large a dowry as possible. Both men regard Arabella as merely a pawn in their financial negotiations. Feelove is also the butt of broad satire because of his incompetence as a doctor and his bland indifference to anything about his patients except the money he can extract from them. Evergreen, on the other hand, is also ridiculed because at his age (he has a grown son) he is planning a January-May marriage, his only concern being to keep his new property cloistered from any man except himself. Although Arabella's youth and beauty have a powerful sensual appeal to Evergreen, there is nothing overtly licentious in his behavior to her.

Miss Archer, who is the ward of old Evergreen, twits Evergreen mercilessly about this marriage and vows that, no matter how stringently Evergreen tries to protect his young bride from the dangers of young men and the infections of fashionable life, she herself will teach this "pretty young cherub" to captivate the whole town and to acquire a greater desire for laces, feathers, diamonds, and fops than can be satisfied in six years. But what Miss Archer actually does for Arabella is even more important. She champions her love for young Bellair, who has fallen so desperately in love with her that he has feigned an illness in order to gain entrée into Feelove's home and be nursed by Arabella, who sheds tears over his supposedly imminent death. Arabella's childlike frankness in expressing her distaste for Evergreen and her quite natural attraction to Bellair is the source of several pleasant comic scenes.

Bellair finally seizes an opportunity to declare his love to Arabella and to secrete her from Feelove's home. Unfortunately, not knowing the identity of her prospective husband, Bellair takes her to Evergreen's home, thinking that this "grave gentleman" will provide a sanctuary for her until Bellair can arrange the elopement. Cowley makes good comic use of Bellair's mistake and Evergreen's glee over it. But through the help of Miss Archer, Arabella escapes from her threatened marriage to Evergreen and later wins Feelove's consent to her marriage to Bellair.

In the meantime Bellair's friend Carlton has decided to court Miss Archer in spite of her reputation for rejecting her adoring lovers. He is attracted to her partly because of her cultivated mind but also because no man has yet won her love, and he wishes to be the first to capture the heart of the woman he marries. But because Carlton knows that adoration has so far failed to win Miss Archer, he decides to use indifference, slights, even insults. He tells himself that these methods will punish her pride and shame her into reformation. Here Cowley is making use of an old plot formula–the reformation of a headstrong young woman who mistreats her suitors or a young wife who refuses to be restrained by prudence until she is shocked or shamed into seeing the error of her ways. As Cowley handles this situation, however, it is unconvincing since Miss Archer's need for reformation is never realized within the course of the play. We have never seen her mistreat a lover. Rejecting a lover whom she does not love is scarcely a crime against love. Her ridicule of Evergreen is delightfully appropriate and could not be more thoroughly deserved, and certainly her championship of the nearly helpless Arabella wins our sympathy. Carlton, on the other hand, seems at times inexcusably rude as well as stiff and egotistical. Admittedly his methods work in that they at times reduce Miss Archer to tears or indignation and in either case arouse her interest in him. When eventually Miss Archer and Carlton are reconciled, one cannot help feeling that Miss Archer deserves better. Cowley should have portrayed Miss Archer less attractively and sympathetically or Carlton less offensively.

There is some incidental satire on Sir Marvel Mushroom, who represents another comic type with a long ancestry–a freshly made knight from the country who comes to London to acquire all the arts and manners of fashionable life. But Mushroom also wishes to be considered a learned man, and in his frantic attempt to stuff his mind with poetry, philosophy, and history he often comically garbles his newly acquired learning. Mushroom is connected with the Archer-Carlton plot in that out of pique over believing that he has been rejected by Miss Archer, he writes a verse satire on her, but allows Carlton to claim authorship of it as part of his program to reform her pride. Later Miss Archer persuades Mushroom to assist Arabella in escaping from Evergreen's home.

Throughout the play, Cowley has obviously tried to avoid giving moral offense, for she has scrupulously altered anything in the plot formulas and stock characters which she uses that might suggest immoral behavior. Yet the many improbabilities in the plot aroused some adverse criticism. In fact, the play was both praised and damned, although it pleased many members of the audience, and it ran initially for fifteen performances. But it was only rarely revived thereafter. Possibly the plot seemed overloaded with episodes, though they are generally well integrated into the main design. In spite of its only modest success, the play has the usual easy, natural dialogue that is one of Cowley's special merits and also has a good share of wit and broad comedy. It deserves more attention than it has usually received.

A School for Greybeards (25 November 1786), set in Portugal, is like *More Ways than One* in attacking the folly and conceit of old men who marry or plan to marry young and beautiful girls who do not love them. Besides satirizing the inappropriateness of marriages of youth and age, it also condemns enforced marriages between young people whenever mutual love is absent. Avarice, however, is not an issue in the marriage alliances that have been contracted or are projected in this play.

Don Alexis, who has recently acquired a young wife, Seraphina, realizes by this time that he has made an ass of himself in marrying a girl and warns his friend Don Gasper, who is on the verge of marrying the eighteen-year-old Donna Antonia, that it will be easier for him "to spin cables out of cobwebs . . . than to manage a young rantipole wife." Though Don Gasper refuses to be deterred, the two men remain on friendly terms, and when Don Gasper tells Don Alexis that his son Octavio, who has hitherto shown little interest in matrimony, is sufficiently attracted to Don Alexis's daughter Viola to be willing to marry her, Don Alexis happily agrees to the marriage. Without a thought for Viola's feelings (she is in love with Don Sebastian), Don Alexis remarks, "Ay, ay, let boys and girls marry." His own marriage has taught him that youth and age do not mix well in matrimony. But it never enters his mind that love as well as suitable ages should also be a factor in matrimony.

The main intrigue in the comedy focuses

on thwarting Don Gasper's marriage to Donna Antonia. Her rescuer is Don Henry, to whom she has formerly been betrothed. After having been banished from Portugal for participating in a duel, Don Henry returns in disguise. He discovers the lie by means of which Don Gasper has won Donna Antonia's reluctant consent to marry him. Then, after procuring his pardon from the queen herself, he reveals his identity and Gasper's base trickery in a highly dramatic scene and boldly insists that Antonia is his contracted wife. Don Gasper, realizing that his perfidy has been starkly disclosed, surrenders Antonia to him without a struggle.

The other intrigue centers on the rescue of Don Alexis's daughter Viola from the marriage to Don Octavio which her father is forcing on her. Through the wit and resourcefulness of her father's witty, young wife, Seraphina, she escapes from her father's home and marries Don Sebastian, whom she loves. The scheme by means of which Seraphina fools Don Alexis into helping his own daughter elope and marry Don Sebastian has some reminiscences of Sheridan's *The Rivals* (1775) or of earlier plays dealing with maidens whose ideas of courtship and marriage have been molded by reading too many romances. When Octavio comes for the first time to woo Viola, he mistakes Seraphina for Viola. Seraphina at first merely enjoys the mistake, then decides to use it to rescue Viola from an enforced marriage to Octavio. Now deliberately posing as Viola, she convinces Octavio that she despises the sober, quiet prudence of a marriage approved by her father. Only if her father opposes the marriage and she will have to face all sorts of "blissful difficulties," such as scaling ladders to elope and being pursued, will she believe that Octavio really loves her. Don Octavio then informs Don Alexis that they must plot against the lovely, capricious "Viola" and that Alexis must order Viola to see him no more. Of course he must allow an elopement to take place. Alexis not only agrees but is vastly amused to think that he is assisting in the plot to have his daughter marry the very man he has chosen for her.

Of course, it is the veiled Seraphina who climbs down the ladder accompanied by Viola, whom Seraphina has simply identified as a friend whom she wishes to be with her. The marriage with Don Sebastian takes place quickly, and soon both Don Alexis and Don Octavio learn to their chagrin how they have been duped. The play ends, however, with a general amnesty on the part of the old men who have been outwitted and happiness on the part of the united lovers. Even Octavio is content–in fact, relieved to find that at least he is not married–for he had never been enthusiastic about matrimony from the start and had been willing to marry Viola simply because he thought he could endure to be married to her.

Seraphina is by all odds the most delightful character in the play. She is one of the most interesting of Cowley's witty, resourceful heroines. Although married to an old man, she has not become embittered. In fact, she sometimes reminds us of Sheridan's Lady Teazle in *School for Scandal* (1777) as she playfully torments Don Alexis by her many pointed references to his age. She admits that she loves to sit on her balcony while "all the impudent young face-hunters in Lisbon" fall "prostrate" before her. In fact, she insists that she will enjoy admiration until she becomes "old, shrivell'd" and "grey-pated" as Don Alexis is now. When Alexis threatens to block up all the windows and nail shut the doors to secure his honor, she retorts that if he cannot find better security than these devices, he will be one of the herd of cuckolds. The best security for *his* honor, she tells him, is *her* honor: "It is due to my own feelings to be chaste–I don't condescend to think of yours in the affair. The respect I bear myself, makes me necessarily preserve my purity–but if I am suspected, watch'd, and haunted, I know not but such torment may weary me out of principles, which I have hitherto cherish'd as my life."

The enthusiasm with which she carries out the trick by means of which she outwits Don Alexis and Don Antonio and rescues Viola demonstrates her joie de vivre, her initiative, and her disapproval of failing to respect a woman's wishes in the choice of her husband. Moreover, her own refusal to be dominated or intimidated by her husband exemplifies that inner strength and respect for her own integrity that is one of Cowley's recurring statements about women and the position they should occupy in marriage.

In her prefatory address in the first edition of the play, Cowley remarks that the idea of the business concerning Antonia, Henry, and Gasper was suggested to her by "an obsolete Comedy," the work of "a poet of the drama, once highly celebrated." This comedy is *The Lucky Chance* (1686) by Aphra Behn. The reputation of Aphra Behn for licentiousness may have been the reason why Cowley did not wish to mention her name. Nevertheless, Cowley's indebtedness to Behn was considerably greater than she admitted, even though she made many changes in her adaptation and certainly tried to purge everything she borrowed from Behn of any suggestion of licentiousness. Nevertheless, she was severely criticized by John Genest for not acknowledging more openly and fully her indebtedness to Behn. But even before her lack of candor with regard to her use of *The Lucky Chance* was known, the play ran into difficulties.

There was apparently a hostile faction in the first-night audience. At least her prefatory address notes that the reviews of the first-night performance observed that there had been people in the theater "who went there *determined* to disapprove at all events." One of the objections was "the indecency of some of the expressions." Only because one of the papers recorded the passages to which objections had been raised was Cowley able, so she claims, to know what passages were found offensive. Apparently the prudery of late eighteenth-century audiences exceeded Cowley's own. Though she removed the offending passages, in the printed version she restored them in order to let the obvious meaning speak for itself and absolve her of the charge of indelicacy. She does object, however, to the fact that playwrights are allowed to portray vulgar or low-bred persons and "disgusting folly," but such characters must converse elegantly, and no expressions which deviate in the least from politeness can be allowed. In this respect, Cowley argues, restrictions are placed on the dramatist that the novelist is not obliged to observe, and she implies that these restrictions have been applied to her play with particular stringency simply because she is a *woman* playwright.

Though Cowley proudly insisted that every expression reputed to be indecent has been restored to the printed text, in one respect she has yielded and kept in the printed text the change dictated by the objections of the first-night audience: instead of having Viola rescued from a hated marriage immediately after the ceremony but before the marriage became valid, she was rescued before the ceremony could take place.

In the final paragraph of Cowley's preface she mentions the "many oppressive circumstances" with which this comedy has had to struggle but maintains that neither these circumstances nor the "sterile month of December" when the play was running has prevented it from having "many brilliant and crouded nights." There were, however, only nine performances, and some of these had had to be postponed because of the illness of the actors. Nevertheless, from Cowley's day to ours, *A School for Greybeards* has been recognized as an entertaining comedy of intrigue. In addition to some of Cowley's usual virtues, such as easy, lively dialogue, Allardyce Nicoll praises it for "capturing some of the verve which characterized in previous eras the plays of Mrs. Behn and Mrs. Centlivre."

A Day in Turkey: or, The Russian Slaves is unlike any other of Hannah Cowley's plays in that it could be called a musical comedy or comic opera. Its music, songs, and dancing, together with its exotic costumes and spectacular stage effects, were designed to appeal to current popular tastes and undoubtedly contributed to the initial appeal of the play. It was first produced at Covent Garden on 3 December 1791, but its roots go back much earlier in Cowley's career.

In 1779 Mrs. Cowley had sent to Garrick a sketch of a comedy she had written dealing with Turkish manners and drawing in part on a story, "Soliman II" (1761), by the French novelist Jean Françoise Marmontel (1723-1799). When Cowley learned, however, that Charles Dibdin the Elder had written a musical version of Marmontel's tale (*The Seraglio*) and that it had been presented at Covent Garden on 14 November 1776 as an afterpiece, she discarded her own unfinished play as needlessly repetitive. She returned to it, however, when she was writing *A Day in Turkey*, which is a revised and expanded version of the earlier play and consists of five acts. She appealed to the current taste for music and spectacle but also made good use of her flare for comedy and of the widespread interest in the recent Russo-Turkish war. In contrasting the manners and mores of Turkey with those of Europe, Cowley demonstrates the importance of freedom and the degradation of its loss in a variety of contexts that mingle the comic with the serious.

The action of the play centers chiefly on the experiences of four war prisoners of the Turks, all of whom are taken to the seraglio of the Turkish Bassa, Ibrahim: Orloff, a Russian army officer; his newlywed wife, Alexina, who was captured immediately after the ceremony and before their marriage was consummated; Paulina, the daughter of Alexina's father's vassal (who has also been taken captive along with Paulina and her brother); and A La Grecque, a French emigrant who was the valet of Orloff. A La Grecque is the principal comic character in the play. Though he does not have a central role in the predicaments of Paulina or Orloff or Alexina, his witty comments on their experiences in the seraglio, as well as his allusions to the revolution in France, are scattered throughout the play and do much to enliven it.

Paulina is also a good source of comedy.

Beautiful but ignorant, she is nevertheless quick-witted, blunt, crude, and fearless in her protests against the slavery in the seraglio. When she has been groomed and lavishly dressed in Turkish garb, the Bassa sees her and mistakes her for Alexina, whom he is eager to enjoy as a new love. Paulina, on the other hand, mistakes the Bassa for merely another slave. In her anger at finding herself in such a wretched place, she showers contempt on this stranger's claim to love her. But her scorn and insults only increase the Bassa's raptures. Not until he has gone does she learn that it is the powerful Bassa who has fallen in love with her.

Alexina, who has secretly witnessed this first meeting of Paulina and the Bassa, is enormously relieved because she has done all in her power (helped by slaves friendly to her) to avoid being brought before the Bassa, who has eagerly summoned her. In fact, she has told Lauretta, the slave girl who has been assigned to her as her servant, that she would kill herself rather than yield to the Bassa. Though Lauretta is amused at the thought of a woman preferring to rush into the arms of death rather than into the arms of a man who loves her, she cooperates with Alexina to the extent of her ability. Azim, however, a slave who is by nature malicious, conceives a particular hatred for Alexina and puts her in solitary confinement in a room where he says the last prisoner stayed fourteen years.

In the meantime Orloff is so furiously angry over his capture that he forces his way into the presence of the Bassa and demands that his bride be restored to him as chaste as when he led her to the altar. When Orloff is told that Orloff 's wife is "the lovely Russian who adorns your harem," the Bassa assumes that this "lovely Russian" is Paulina. Although he believes that, as his slave, Paulina is his by "undoubted right," he also believes that, as the wife of another, "she is sacred." To avoid temptation, the Bassa stops seeing Paulina, and Paulina, who by now has fallen deeply in love with him, fears that she has lost him.

When by chance the two do meet, Ibrahim's virtuous determination not to love another man's wife fades as he gazes at his "cruel charmer," while Paulina cannot refrain from admitting that she loves him and no other. In a dramatic moment the Bassa embraces Paulina as he exclaims, "Transcendent moment! O, bliss too exquisite." At this moment Orloff, thinking the woman embraced by the Bassa is his wife, rushes in shouting "Base woman! adulterous villain!" and threatens the Bassa with a dagger. Slaves then rush to his defense, and the Bassa decrees death that very day for Orloff.

It should be obvious that melodramatic and sentimental elements are blended with the comic in the imbroglio of mistaken identities involving Paulina, the Bassa, Orloff, and Alexina. In fact, Alexina has been in her way as melodramatic in her fears for her honor and her grief over her separation from her husband as Orloff has been in his indignation over his capture and the threat to his wife's chastity once he learns that she is in the Bassa's seraglio.

The happy ending is effected when Orloff learns that it was Paulina in the Bassa's arms and Alexina has truly remained chaste–and also when the Bassa learns that Paulina is not Orloff's wife and he may love her without crime.

In a rather hasty ending, the Bassa frees Paulina's brother and father, forgives and frees Orloff and also Alexina, and then announces that he intends to make Paulina his by the sacred rites of marriage, for without the dignity given to love by marriage, he now sees that love "sinks into the lowest appetite." Orloff praises the Bassa for learning through love to revere marriage and predicts that marriage will teach him "to honour love." When Alexina, who has been cruelly treated by Azim, asks the Bassa to forgive him also, the Bassa remarks that this "Charming magnanimity" must come from Christian doctrines, which he intends to study closely. The play thus ends with general happiness and rejoicing.

In the revised version of the play published in the 1813 edition of Cowley's works, substantial changes are made, particularly in the treatment of female slaves. The degradation of women who are regarded only as sex objects without minds to cultivate and respect is particularly emphasized. In spite of mixed reviews the original version of *A Day in Turkey* delighted audiences sufficiently to permit fourteen performances during the first season and three during the early months of 1794.

The character of the Bassa Ibrahim is probably the least believable of all the characters in the play, being throughout a fool for love, though his concept of love has been elevated by the conclusion of the play. A La Grecque, on the other hand, is undoubtedly the most delightful. Yet Cowley was criticized for the political allusions which A La Grecque was accused of making. In her advertisement to the first edition, Cowley vehemently denied that her comedy is "tainted with Politics," about which she claimed to know nothing. She in-

PREFACE.

THE following is rather the Comedy which the Public have choſen it to be, than the Comedy which I intended. Some things have been left out, and ſome have been added ſince the firſt repreſentation: In ſhort, the Comedy has been *new claſs'd*—it has been torn from its genus.

It is hoped, however, that there may be found characters, in THE TOWN BEFORE YOU, to intereſt, and ſituations to attach; and that thoſe events which were vivacity in the Theatre, will not be dulneſs in the cloſet.

But it muſt be noticed, that the ſcene, in the ſecond act, between TIPPY and his Landlady, and that in the fifth act, between TIPPY and the Bailiff, were no part of my original deſign. They were written during the illneſs of MRS. POPE, after the Piece had been played ſeveral nights. Alas! I am ſorry to remark, that no ſcenes in the Comedy (to uſe the Stage idiom) *go off* better.

An

x PREFACE.

An acute Critic lately ſaid, in one of thoſe aſſemblies where converſation, though ſometimes light, is ſeldom without meaning, "A Comedy to pleaſe, in the preſent day, muſt be *made*, not written." It requires no great expanſe of comprehenſion to perceive the meaning of this dogma; the truth of which I am equally ready to acknowledge, and to deplore: But ſhould it *want* illuſtration, it may be found every week in a popular Piece, where a great Actor, holding a ſword in his left hand, and making aukward puſhes with it, charms the audience infinitely more than he could do, by all the wit and obſervation which the ingenious Author might have given him; and brings down ſuch applauſes, as the bewitching dialogue of CIBBER, and of FARQUHAR pants for in vain!

The patient developement of character, the repeated touches which colour it up to Nature, and ſwell it into identity and exiſtence (and which gave celebrity to CONGREVE), we have now no reliſh for. The combinations of intereſt, the ſtrokes which are meant to reach the heart, we are equally incapable of taſting. LAUGH! LAUGH! LAUGH! is the demand: Not a word muſt be uttered that looks like inſtruction, or a ſentence which ought to be remembered.

From a Stage, in ſuch a ſtate, it is time to withdraw; but I call on my younger cotemporaries, I invoke the riſing generation, to *correct* a taſte which, to be gratified, demands neither genius or intellect;—which aſks only a happy knack at inventing TRICK. I adjure them to reſtore to the Drama SENSE, OBSERVATION,

PREFACE. xi

VATION, WIT, LESSON! and to teach our Writers to reſpect their own talents.

What mother can now lead her daughters to the great National School, THE THEATRE, in the confidence of their receiving either poliſh or improvement? Should the luckleſs Bard ſtumble on a reflection, or a ſentiment, the audience yawn, and wait for the next tumble from a chair, or a tripping up of the heels, to put them into attention. Surely I ſhall be forgiven for ſatiriſing myſelf; I have *made* ſuch things, and I bluſh to have made them.

O! GENIUS of a poliſh'd age, deſcend!——plant thy banners in our Theatres, and bid ELEGANCE and FEELING take place of the *droll* and the *laugh*, which formerly were found only in the Booths of *Bartlemy* Fair, and were divided between *Flocton* and *Yates!* With actors capable of giving force to all that is intellectual, is it not *pity* to condemn them to ſuch drudgery? THEY are no longer neceſſary. Let Sadler's Wells and the Circus empty themſelves of their performers to furniſh our Stage; the expence to Managers will be leſs, and their buſineſs will be carried on better. The UNDERSTANDING, DISCERNMENT, and EDUCATION, which diſtinguiſh our modern actors, are uſeleſs to them;—ſtrong muſcles are in greater repute, and grimace has more powerful attraction.

PROLOGUE.

Preface to Cowley's last play (from the 1795 edition of The Town Before You*)*

sisted that the allusions which A La Grecque makes to the revolution in France were demanded by fidelity to the definition of comedy as "a picture of life–a record of passing manners–a mirror to reflect to succeeding times the characters and follies of the present." In accordance with this conception of comedy, she asks how she could fail to have A La Grecque "hint at the events which had just passed, or were then passing in his native country." Moreover, all of these comments are made in a comic context. But the parallels between the lack of freedom of the Russian captives and Turkish slaves and the prominence of the ideal of freedom in the revolutionary fervor in France could scarcely be missed. Of course, Cowley need not have included A La Grecque in her comedy, but without him she would have sacrificed the wittiest and most thoroughly comic character in the entire play.

The Town Before You (6 December 1794) was Cowley's farewell to the theater, as she explains in her preface to the first edition. The emphasis on nothing but laughter, the loss of interest in "bewitching dialogue," in the "patient development of character," in "strokes which are meant to reach the heart," or in anything "that looks like instruction" has alienated her from the theater. "What mother," she asks, "can now lead her daughters to the great National School, THE THEATRE, in the confidence of their receiving either polish or improvement?" The negative answer is obvious.

Mrs. Cowley's lament over the degeneration of theatrical fare is not without confirmation by historians of drama. The theater for which Cowley's comedies were well suited had largely disappeared. In fact, the public reaction to the first performance of *The Town Before You* forced her to make excisions and additions that obviously displeased her. In the opening sentence of her preface she remarks tartly that her play is "rather the Comedy which the Public have chosen it to be, than the Comedy which I intended."

Whatever her regrets about the changes that she consented to make in the play, there is much that is typical of Cowley in it. The play is a return to the comedy of manners with a large measure of intrigue–a mixture not in the least unusual. The play also has generous doses of moralistic sentimentalism, with decency and goodness given a full representation along with villainy, which has comic as well as serious dimensions.

Various representatives of London society are portrayed and interact in the play. Lady Horatio Horton represents the old London aristocracy. Lady Horatio, however, has largely rejected the wearisome and demanding social round of fashionable life and has instead devoted herself to the study and practice of sculpting. Only to her friend and confidante Lady Charlotte does she admit briefly that her enthusiasm for sculpting has waned because she is in love with Sidney Asgill but fears that he does not return her love. Actually Sidney is much in love with Lady Horatio but has not spoken to her of his love because she is wealthy and he is financially dependent on his prosperous uncle Simon Asgill, a London businessman who has put him through Cambridge.

Mr. Conway, who belongs to Lady Horatio's circle, is a gentleman of fashion who has avoided the vices of fashionable life, or so Lady Charlotte, who describes him, asserts. She admits that he has some vanity but even more good sense, that he has chosen his friends well and loves goodness. Recently he has fallen in love with Georgina, the lively young daughter of a rich, newly made knight from Wales, Sir Robert Floyer. Georgina is thoroughly intoxicated by the fashionable life of London but is especially attracted to Lady Horatio and her sculpting. Mr. Conway describes Georgina as "wild as one of the kids on her father's mountains," though he hopes that he will be able to catch this "little Welsh fawn."

Sir Robert Floyer, in his attempts to establish himself in the fashionable life of London, is an old comic type, but the satire that is directed at him is gentle rather than contemptuous. His gullibility and social aspirations make him an easy dupe of the two scoundrels Fancourt and Tippy. Sir Robert, however, is alert to the dangers of dissipation in the London social whirl which his daughter Georgina is eager to enter. In fact, in a speech heavily sentimental in tone he calls dissipation the enemy of female honor and prays that his child may be shielded from its corruption.

Fancourt and Tippy are not content, however, with merely duping Sir Robert of one thousand pounds. They have far more sinister plans to "ruin" Georgina. Fancourt's wife, however, learns of these plans and determines to save the girl. Mrs. Fancourt has long been disillusioned with her husband, who has squandered her own small fortune and with Tippy his partner in crime is now intent on living by duping other men of their money. She is thoroughly aware of her husband's hard heart and complete lack of scruples. Disguised as a Savoyard fortune-teller, she gains access to Georgina's home, where, in reading Georgina's fortune, she is able to warn her of the two evil men who are dangerously threatening her. The reality of this threat is soon brought home to Georgina, and she is deeply grateful to Mrs. Fancourt for her timely warning. Tippy is the more amusing of the two scoundrels. As a look-alike of Lord Beechgrove, he dines at Beechgrove's clubs, is treated with deference, and is allowed to charge his bills to his lordship's account. He also poses as a well-traveled connoisseur of fine art, but in an amusing scene set in Lady Horatio's studio, he comically reveals his ignorance by failing to recognize Georgina, who is posing as a statue, and by pronouncing this work that of a mere block-chopper. Mr. Conway eventually succeeds in winning his "little Welsh fawn." In the scene where she breaks down and admits her love, it is a relief that her conversion to good sense and prudence has not stifled her wit and playfulness.

As is usual in Cowley's plays, at the conclusion two couples face the prospect of a happy marriage. Lady Horatio and Sidney Asgill finally overcome the barriers that have kept them apart. Sidney's uncle Simon Asgill is proud of his heritage and deeply suspicious of fine ladies like Lady Horatio. He therefore decided to test her to see if she had an upright mind and innate goodness as well as birth, beauty, and riches. He had previously tested his own nephew and discovered that Sidney, believing his uncle had lost his entire fortune, had generously turned over to him the small amount of property he owns in his own right. Sidney then decided to serve his country by becoming an English sailor, and he ends the third act with a sentimental flourish of patriotism as he invokes the blessings of heaven on his country.

In spite of serious misunderstandings and conflicts that developed between Lady Horatio and Simon Asgill, in the end the two see one another in truer and more favorable lights. Lady Horatio still regrets Sir Simon's philistine failure to appreciate fine art. Yet when he exhorts her to put aside her chisel and marble blocks and set about making a good wife, neither she nor anyone else protests. Though Lady Horatio's interest in sculpture and sculpting has never been explicitly satirized, there is a gentle implication that such activity is at least harmless and a good alternative to idleness or participation in a frantic social life. Sidney, of course, joyously accepts Lady Horatio's vows of love but promises that, if his country ever needs his services, he will resume the habit of a sailor since "whilst the sea flows ... ENGLAND MUST BE THE MISTRESS OF THE GLOBE."

In the meantime, Fancourt and Tippy have been thoroughly exposed. Though Sir Robert has lost a thousand pounds, he is otherwise unharmed and has been alerted to the presence of plotters and deceivers everywhere. In gratitude to Mrs. Fancourt, whose "husband" has just confessed that their marriage was a sham since the ceremony was conducted by none other than Tippy himself, Georgina offers her everlasting protection under her father's roof and addresses Mrs. Fancourt now as her mother, sister, and friend.

Though Tippy and Fancourt have been arrested and brought to Sir Robert's house by constables, Sir Robert dismisses the constables and implies that the only punishment these scoundrels will receive will be the exposure of their villainy. When Sir Robert orders them to "Go! turn out upon the world!" the two seem utterly unrepentant. Fancourt says to Tippy, "Come, Tippy, the field before us is a wide one.... *Talents* are our armed forces, with which we encounter Vanity and Folly. Wherever *they* appear, we wage war.... Be of good heart, my boy! The foe is numerous, but weak. Conquest and pillage are our own!"

The jingoism that concludes the third and fifth acts may be offensive to modern ears, as may some of the sentimentalism of the play. And certainly the complications in the courtship of Sidney Asgill and Lady Horatio seem in part contrived and implausible. Yet Mrs. Cowley's talent was not in serious decline in this comedy. In spite of the initial protests that induced her to make changes, the play had a modest run of ten performances. From Cowley's day to ours the play's merits have been recognized. In addition to Cowley's continuing skill in the handling of dialogue, she has enlivened the play with interesting portrayals of a variety of social types inhabiting the changed London of the late eighteenth century. While not the best of her comedies, *The Town Before You* is a reputable work to mark the end of her writing for the stage.

After her retirement to Tiverton, Hannah Cowley, who had written poetry throughout her adult life, continued to write additional poetry. She died in Tiverton on 11 March 1809. The 1813 edition of her works includes all of Cowley's published plays as she had revised them and aimed also to publish all of her varied kinds of poetry.

Cowley's claim to fame does not rest, of course, on her poetry but on her comedies, all of which succeeded in varying degrees on the stage, some of them having remarkably long runs over a period of years. Like other playwrights of her age and earlier ages, she borrowed repeatedly from the works of earlier playwrights but always altered what she borrowed to fit the context and tenor of her own plays. She made use repeatedly of a variety of stereotyped characters, situations, and motifs but was able to infuse them with vitality and a measure of individuality. She joins the throng of playwrights who over the centuries have satirized the tyranny of parents or guardians who choose mates for their children with a total disregard for the preferences of the young people. And she excelled in the portrayal of witty, resourceful, independent, young heroines who refuse to be victimized by the tyrannical power of fathers or guardians or even husbands. Moreover, some of these strong-minded heroines rescue their weaker sisters from the tyranny that threatens them and their happiness.

Cowley was no reformer and not a feminist in any militant sense of the word. She had nothing specific to say about how women's education should be improved or their position in marriage. Yet she repeatedly emphasizes the importance of cultivating and respecting women's minds and of treating women as responsible human beings who should have much more control over their lives, particularly in the choice of a husband. She also viewed marriage as a loving partnership rather than a union of a ruler and his subject.

While the range of her plays is not great, her major preoccupation–courtship and marriage–is typical of her age and many other ages as well. She eschewed politics but on a number of occasions engaged in a flag-waving patriotism that to modern readers may seem inappropriate. Although her plays inevitably show some influence of sentimentalism, she avoided its excesses and never allowed it to stifle her sense of humor. Her plays continue to be surprisingly entertaining and pleasant to read. She never reaches the comic heights of Richard Sheridan or Oliver Goldsmith at their best. But neither do other eighteenth-century dramatists.

In her "masterly portraiture of manners," Nicoll ranks her with such contemporaries as George Colman the Elder and Richard Cumberland, though he praises other qualities in her art too. Acquaintance with her comedies should persuade increasing numbers of critics that Hannah Cowley deserves a position of distinction among those dramatists who fall short of being first-rate, but whose plays are far above the average, worth reading and possibly worth reviving.

Joyce East's doctoral dissertation, "The Dramatic Works of Hannah Cowley" (University of Kansas, 1979), is, so far as this writer knows, the only work to present thorough critical analyses of all of Cowley's plays, even those never published. Based on extensive research both in England and this country, East's dissertation provides valuable information, including the results of wide reading of reviews of Cowley's plays in the periodical literature of the time. This writer is deeply indebted to Professor East for the information her research has enabled her to provide.

The only other sustained (though much shorter) discussions of Cowley's plays appear in Frederick M. Link's introduction to his edition of *The Plays of Hannah Cowley*. These discussions are astute and helpful. This writer has frequently made use of Link's careful enumeration of the performances of Cowley's plays, especially during their first seasons but also during subsequent revivals.

Bibliography:

J. E. Norton, "Some Uncollected Authors XVI: Hannah Cowley, 1743-1809," *Book Collector*, 7 (Spring 1958): 68-76.

Biographies:

David Baker, Isaac Reed, and Stephen Jones, *Biographia Dramatica: A Companion to the Playhouse*, 3 volumes, second revision (London: Printed for Longman, Hurst, Rees, Orme & Brown, 1812), I: 152-154;

Preface to *The Works of Mrs. Cowley, Dramas and Poems*, 3 volumes (London: Wilkie & Robinson, 1813), I: v-xxi;

Frederick M. Link, Introduction to *The Plays of Hannah Cowley*, 2 volumes, edited by Link (New York & London: Garland, 1979), I: v-xlvi;

David W. Meredith, Entry on Hannah Cowley, in *Dictionary of British and American Women Writers 1660-1800*, edited by Janet Todd (Totowa, N.J.: Rowman & Allanheld, 1985), p. 94.

References:

Ernest Bernbaum, *The Drama of Sensibility: A Sketch of the History of Sentimental Comedy and Domestic Tragedy, 1696-1780* (Boston & London: Ginn, 1915);

James Boaden, ed., *The Private Correspondence of David Garrick*, 2 volumes (London: H. Colburn and R. Bentley, 1831-1832);

Joyce East, "The Dramatic Works of Hannah Cowley," Ph.D. dissertation, University of Kansas, 1979;

John Genest, *Some Account of the English Stage*, 10

volumes (London: C. Chapple, 1808);

Clarence C. Green, *The Neo-Classic Theory of Tragedy in England During the Eighteenth Century* (Cambridge, Mass.: Harvard University Press, 1934);

Robert Hume, *The Development of English Drama in the Late Seventeenth Century* (Oxford: Clarendon Press, 1976);

Shirley Strum Kenny, "Humane Comedy," *Modern Philology*, 75 (August 1977): 29-43;

David M. Little and George M. Kahrl, eds., *The Letters of David Garrick*, 3 volumes (Cambridge, Mass.: Harvard University Press, 1963);

Frederick Peter Lock, "Mrs. Cowley's Comedies," M.A. thesis, McMaster University, 1972;

John Loftis, *Sheridan and the Drama of Georgian England* (Oxford: Basil Blackwell, 1976);

Allardyce Nicoll, *A History of Late Eighteenth Century Drama, 1750-1800*, second edition (1952; reprinted, Cambridge: University Press, 1955);

R. Crompton Rhodes, "The Belle's Stratagem," *Review of English Studies*, 5 (April 1929): 129-142;

Eric Rothstein, *Restoration Tragedy: Form and the Process of Change* (Madison: University of Wisconsin Press, 1967);

Arthur Sherbo, *English Sentimental Drama* (East Lansing: Michigan State University Press, 1967);

Stuart M. Tave, *The Amiable Humorist: A Study in the Comic Theory and Criticism of the Eighteenth and Early Nineteenth Centuries* (Chicago: University of Chicago Press, 1960).

Papers:

The Larpent Collection in the Henry E. Huntington Library holds fair-copy manuscripts for *The Runaway, Who's the Dupe?, Albina, The Belle's Stratagem, The School of Eloquence, The World As It Goes, Which Is the Man?, A Bold Stroke for a Husband,* "New Ways to Catch Hearts" (produced and published as *More Ways than One*), *A School for Greybeards, The Fate of Sparta, A Day in Turkey,* and "The Town as It Is" (produced and published as *The Town Before You*).

Richard Cumberland

(19 February 1732-7 May 1811)

Joseph J. Keenan, Jr.
Duquesne University

PLAY PRODUCTIONS: *The Summer's Tale*, London, Theatre Royal in Covent Garden, 6 December 1765; revised and abridged as *Amelia*, London, Theatre Royal in Covent Garden, 12 April 1768;

The Brothers, London, Theatre Royal, Covent Garden, 2 December 1769;

The West Indian, London, Theatre Royal in Drury Lane, 19 January 1771;

Timon of Athens, altered from Shakespeare's play, London, Theatre Royal in Drury Lane, 4 December 1771;

The Fashionable Lover, London, Theatre Royal in Drury Lane, 20 January 1772;

The Squire's Return, Kelmarsh, Northamptonshire, November 1773;

The Note of Hand, London, Theatre Royal in Drury Lane, 9 February 1774;

The Princess of Parma, Kelmarsh, Northamptonshire, October 1774;

The Election, Kelmarsh, Northamptonshire, October 1774;

The Choleric Man, London, Theatre Royal in Drury Lane, 19 December 1774;

The Battle of Hastings, London, Theatre Royal in Drury Lane, 24 January 1778;

The Critic, London, Theatre Royal, Covent Garden, 20 March 1779;

Calypso, London, Theatre Royal, Covent Garden, 20 March 1779;

The Bondman (lost except for prologue), adapted from Philip Massinger's play, London, Theatre Royal, Covent Garden, 13 October 1779;

The Duke of Milan (lost except for prologue and epilogue), adapted from Massinger's *The Duke of Milan* and Elijah Fenton's *Mariamne*, London, Theatre Royal, Covent Garden, 10 November 1779;

The Widow of Delphi, or The Descent of the Deities, London, Theatre Royal, Covent Garden, 1 February 1780;

The Walloons, London, Theatre Royal, Covent Garden, 20 April 1782;

The Mysterious Husband, London, Theatre Royal, Covent Garden, 28 January 1783;

The Carmelite, London, Theatre Royal, Drury Lane, 2 December 1784;

The Natural Son, London, Theatre Royal, Drury Lane, 22 December 1784; significantly revised and shortened version, London, Theatre Royal, Drury Lane, 10 June 1794;

The Arab (probably a revision of the lost and unperformed *Salome* and itself the basis for the unperformed *Alcanor*), London, Theatre Royal, Covent Garden, 8 March 1785;

The Country Attorney, London, Theatre Royal in the Hay-Market, 7 July 1787;

The Imposters, adapted from George Farquhar's *The Beaux Stratagem*, London, Theatre Royal, Drury Lane, 26 January 1789;

The School for Widows, in large part a revision of Cumberland's *The Country Attorney*, London, Theatre Royal, Covent Garden, 8 May 1789;

Prelude for the Opening of the Theatre Royal Covent Garden, London, Theatre Royal, Covent Garden, 17 September 1792;

The Armorer, London, Theatre Royal, Covent Garden, 4 April 1793;

The Box-Lobby Challenge, London, Theatre Royal in the Hay-Market, 22 February 1794;

The Jew, London, Theatre Royal, Drury Lane, 8 May 1794;

The Wheel of Fortune, London, Theatre Royal, Drury Lane, 28 February 1795;

First Love, London, Theatre Royal, Drury Lane, 12 May 1795;

The Dependent, London, Theatre Royal, Drury Lane, 20 October 1795;

The Days of Yore, London, Theatre Royal, Covent Garden, 13 January 1796;

Don Pedro, London, Theatre Royal in the Hay-Market, 23 July 1796;

Richard Cumberland

The Last of the Family, London, Theatre Royal, Drury Lane, 8 May 1797;

The Village Fete, London, Theatre Royal, Covent Garden, 18 May 1797;

False Impressions, London, Theatre Royal, Covent Garden, 23 November 1797;

The Eccentric Lover, London, Theatre Royal, Covent Garden, 30 April 1798;

A Word for Nature (similar to *The Passive Husband* in *The Posthumous Dramatic Works*), London, Theatre Royal, Drury Lane, 5 December 1798;

Joanna of Montfaucon, based on August von Kotzebue's *Johanna von Montfaucon*, London, Theatre Royal, Covent Garden, 16 January 1800;

Lovers' Resolutions, London, Theatre Royal, Drury Lane, 2 March 1802;

The Sailor's Daughter, London, Theatre Royal, Drury Lane, 7 April 1804;

A Melo-Dramatic Piece: Being an Occasional Attempt to Commemorate the Death and Victory of Lord Viscount Nelson, London, Theatre Royal, Drury Lane, 11 November 1805;

A Hint to Husbands, London, Theatre Royal, Covent Garden, 8 March 1806;

The Jew of Mogadore, London, Theatre Royal, Drury Lane, 3 May 1808;

The Widow's Only Son, London, Theatre Royal, Covent Garden, 7 June 1810;

The Sybil; or, The Elder Brutus, London, Theatre Royal, Drury Lane, 3 December 1818.

BOOKS: *An Elegy Written on St. Mark's Eve* (London: Printed by M. Cooper, 1754);

The Banishment of Cicero. A Tragedy (London: Printed for J. Walter, 1761);

The Summer's Tale. A Musical Comedy of Three Acts. As it is Performed at the Theatre Royal in Covent-Garden (London: Printed for J. Dodsley, W. Johnston & J. Walter, 1765);

A Letter to the Right Reverend the Lord Bishop of O----d, Containing some Animadversions upon a character given of the late Dr. Bentley, in a letter, from a late professor in the University of Oxford, to the Right Rev. Author of The Divine Legation of Moses Demonstrated (London: Printed by J. Wilkie, 1767);

Richard Bentley D.D., the playwright's maternal grandfather

Amelia. A Musical Entertainment of Two Acts. As it is Performed at the Theatre Royal in Covent-Garden (London: Printed for J. Dodsley, 1768);

The Brothers: A Comedy. As it is performed at the Theatre Royal in Covent-Garden (London: Printed for W. Griffin, 1770);

The West Indian: A Comedy. As it is Performed at the Theatre Royal in Drury-Lane (London: Printed for W. Griffin, 1771);

Timon of Athens, Altered from Shakespear. A Tragedy. As it is Acted at the Theatre-Royal in Drury-Lane (London: Printed for the Proprietors of Shakespear's Works & sold by T. Becket, 1771);

The Fashionable Lover; A Comedy: as it is acted at the Theatre-Royal in Drury-Lane (London: Printed for W. Griffin, 1772);

The Note of Hand; or, Trip to Newmarket. As it is acted at the Theatre-Royal in Drury-Lane (London: Printed for T. Becket, 1774);

The Choleric Man. A Comedy. As it is performed at the Theatre-Royal in Drury Lane (London: Printed for T. Becket, 1775);

Odes (London: Printed for J. Robson, 1776);

Miscellaneous Poems consisting of Elegies, Odes, Pastorals, &c. together with Calypso a Masque (London: Printed for F. Newberry, 1778);

The Battle of Hastings, A Tragedy. By Richard Cumberland, Esq.: As it is acted at the Theatre-Royal in Drury-Lane (London: E. & C. Dilly, 1778);

Calypso; A Masque: in three acts. As it is performed at the Theatre-Royal in Covent-Garden (London: Printed for T. Evans, 1779);

The Songs in The Widow of Delphi; or, The Descent of the Deities, A Musical Drama, of Five Acts. Set to Music by Mr. Thomas Butler. As it is performed at the Theatre-Royal, Covent-Garden (London: Printed for G. Kearsly, 1780);

Anecdotes of Eminent Painters in Spain, during the Sixteenth and Seventeenth Centuries, with cursory remarks upon the present state of arts in that kingdom, 2 volumes (London: Printed for J. Walter, 1782);

A Letter to Richard Lord Bishop of Landaff on the Subject of His Lordship's Letter to the Late Archbishop of Canterbury (London: Printed for C. Dilly & J. Walter, 1783);

The Mysterious Husband. A Tragedy in five acts. As it is acted at the Theatre-Royal, Covent-Garden (London: Printed for C. Dilly & J. Walter, 1783);

The Carmelite: A Tragedy. Performed at the Theatre

Richard Cumberland, Lord Bishop of Peterborough, the playwright's great-grandfather (engraving by C. Picart)

Royal Drury Lane (London: Printed for C. Dilly & G. Nicol, 1784);

The Natural Son: A Comedy. Performed at the Theatre Royal Drury Lane (London: Printed for C. Dilly & G. Nicol, 1785);

Character of the Late Lord Viscount Sackville (London: Printed for C. Dilly, 1785);

The Observer, 5 volumes (London: Printed for C. Dilly, 1786-1790);

An Accurate and Descriptive Catalogue of the Several Paintings in the King of Spain's Palace in Madrid; with some account of the pictures in the Buen-Retiro (London: Printed for C. Dilly & J. Walter, 1787);

Arundel. By the Author of The Observer, 2 volumes (London: Printed for C. Dilly, 1789);

The Imposters: A Comedy. Performed at the Theatre Royal Drury Lane (London: Printed for C. Dilly, 1789);

Curtius Rescued from the Gulph; or, the Retort Courteous to the Rev. Dr. Parr, in Answer to His Learned Pamphlet, Intitled, A Sequel, etc. (London: Printed for Hockham & Carpenter, 1792);

Calvary: or the Death of Christ. A Poem, in Eight Books (London: Printed for C. Dilly, 1792);

Songs and Choruses in the Comic Opera of the Armorer. As performed at the Theatre Royal, Covent-Garden (London: Printed for C. Dilly, 1793);

The Box-Lobby Challenge, A Comedy. As performed at the Theatre-Royal, Hay-Market (London: Printed for J. Debrett, 1794);

The Jew: A Comedy. Performed at the Theatre-Royal, Drury Lane (London: Printed for C. Dilly, 1794);

The Wheel of Fortune: A Comedy. Performed At the Theatre-Royal, Drury-Lane (London: Printed for C. Dilly, 1795); modern edition, edited by Thomas Joseph Campbell (New York: Garland, 1987);

Henry . . . By the author of Arundel, 4 volumes (London: Printed for C. Dilly, 1795);

First Love: A Comedy. Performed At the Theatre-Royal, Drury-Lane (London: Printed for C. Dilly, 1795);

The Days of Yore: A Drama in three Acts. Performed at the Theatre-Royal, Covent-Garden (London: Printed for C. Dilly, 1796);

False Impressions: A Comedy in Five Acts. Performed at the Theatre Royal, Covent Garden (London: Printed for C. Dilly, 1797);

The Observer, volume 6 (London: Printed for C. Dilly, 1798)–includes Cumberland's translation of *The Clouds*, by Aristophanes;

Joanna of Montfaucon; A Dramatic Romance of the Fourteenth Century: As Performed at the Theatre-Royal, Covent-Garden. Formed upon the Plan of the German Drama of Kotzebue: And adapted to the English stage by Richard Cumberland (London: Printed by Luke Hansard for Lackington, Allen & Co., 1800);

A Few Plain Reasons Why We Should Believe in Christ and Adhere to His Religion: Addrest to the patrons and professors of the new philosophy (London: Printed for Lackington, Allen & Co., 1801);

A Poetical Version of Certain Psalms of David (Tunbridge Wells: Printed for J. Sprange, 1801);

The Sailor's Daughter: A Comedy, in five acts. Now Performing at the Theatre-Royal, Drury Lane (London: Printed by Luke Hansard for Lackington, Allen & Co., 1804);

A Melo-Dramatic Piece: Being an Occasional Attempt to Commemorate the Death and Victory of Lord Viscount Nelson (London: Printed by L. Hansard for Lackington, Allen & Co., 1805);

A Hint to Husbands: A Comedy, in five acts, Now Performing at The Theatre-Royal, Covent-Garden (London: Printed by R. Taylor & Co. for Lackington, Allen & Co., 1806);

Memoirs of Richard Cumberland Written by Himself containing An Account of his Life and Writings

Interspersed with Anecdotes and Characters of Several of the Most Distinguished Persons of his Time, with whom he has had Intercourse and Connection (London: Printed for Lackington, Allen & Co., 1806); second edition, with supplement and index, 2 volumes (London: Lackington, Allen & Co., 1807);

The Exodiad. A Poem, by Cumberland and Sir James Bland Burgess (London: Printed by J. Wright for Lackington, Allen & Co., 1807);

The Jew of Mogadore. A Comic Opera in Three Acts. Now Performing at the Theatre-Royal, Drury Lane (London: Printed for S. Tipper, 1808);

The London Review, nos. 1-4 (London: Samuel Tipper, February-November 1809);

John de Lancaster: a Novel, 3 volumes (London: Printed for Lackington, Allen & Co., 1809);

Retrospection, A Poem in Familiar Verse (London: Printed by T. Bulmer & Co. for the author and sold by G. & W. Nicol, 1811).

Collections: *The Posthumous Dramatic Works of the Late Richard Cumberland*, with a preface by his daughter, Frances Marianne Jansen, 2 volumes (London: Printed by W. Bulmer and Co. for G. and W. Nicol, 1813)–volume 1: *The Sybil; or, the Elder Brutus, The Walloons, The Confession, The Passive Husband, Torrendal, Lovers' Resolution;* volume 2: *Alcanor, The Eccentric Lover, Tiberius in Capreae, The Last of the Family, Don Pedro, The False Demetrius;*

The Plays of Richard Cumberland, edited by Roberta F. S. Borkat, 6 volumes (New York & London: Garland, 1982)–includes first printings of "An Impromptu . . . after the play of *Hamlet*"; prologue and epilogue to *The Squire's Return; The Princess of Parma* (fragment); *The Election* (fragment); *The Critic, a prelude;* prologue to *The Bondman;* prologue and epilogue to *The Duke of Milan; The Widow of Delphi, or The Descent of the Deities; The Arab; The Country Attorney; The School for Widows; Prelude for the Opening of the Theatre Royal Covent Garden; Richard the Second; The Armorer; The Dependent; The Village Fete;* and *A Word for Nature.*

OTHER: *The British Drama: A Collection of the Most Esteemed Dramatic Productions, with Biography of the Respective Authors, and Critique on Each Play*, edited, with commentary, by Cumberland, 14 volumes (London: Printed for C. Cooke, 1817).

Richard Cumberland, who has been called the most insistent of the sentimentalists, the grandfather of melodrama, the founding ancestor of the problem play, began his literary career in 1744 when he enrolled at Westminster School and then went on to Trinity College, Cambridge, in 1747. No doubt greatly influenced by his maternal grandfather, the great classical scholar Dr. Richard Bentley, Richard Cumberland set about mastering the classics. When Oliver Goldsmith dubbed him the Terence of England in *The Retaliation* (1774), it is small wonder Cumberland was so pleased as to overlook the implications of the rest of the portrait, which suggested that he failed to imitate nature in his plays, that his characters were all paragons beyond satire, and that his comedies were more appropriately tragedies; for first and foremost Cumberland is a classicist.

While his first play, "Shakespear in the Shades," known to us only from the passage Cumberland included in his *Memoirs* (1806), is primarily an example of Cumberland's insistence upon poetic justice–bringing back Shakespeare to rectify some of his "errors" relative to Hamlet and Ophelia, Romeo and Juliet, Lear and Cordelia–young Richard Cumberland was primarily a scholar of Latin and Greek. In his *Memoirs* he recalled profiting from the solid moral teaching of his esteemed and beloved mother, Joanna Bentley, but even more he boasted that he walked in his august grandfather's footsteps within his very college. Well grounded in the classics at Westminster, he entered Trinity and shortly thereafter received as a gift "a valuable parcel of my grandfather's books and papers." Among these were a number of Greek plays, "particularly of the Comic Poets now lost," which Cumberland studied and eventually commented upon in his *Observer* essays (1786-1790, 1798).

Predisposed by family toward an attitude of benevolence, his paternal great-grandfather, Richard, being an eminent Shaftesburian philosopher and his own father, Denison Cumberland, a clergyman who tamed the wild Irish by an open justice and generosity, Cumberland immersed himself in the study of the classics, and through this combination evolved a theory of comedy that would serve him through his life. Indeed, he *wanted* to be the Terence of England. Wholeheartedly embracing the idea that the end of drama was to instruct and then amuse, he held plot based upon unswerving poetic justice to be the drama's cornerstone. Moreover, characters in comedy and in tragedy had to be exemplary, for instruction was better accomplished through em-

George Germain, viscount Sackville, whose help in securing Cumberland's appointment as clerk of reports in the Board of Trade (1762) was the beginning of his lifelong friendship toward the playwright. In his Memoirs *Cumberland wrote that Sackville had "no trash in his mind; he studied no choice phrases, no superfluous words, nor ever suffered the clearness of his conceptions to be clouded by the obscurity of his expressions. . . ."*

ulation than ridicule. He accepted the divisions of Greek comedy as old, middle, and new, and found excellence in the new.

His classical studies, recorded in *The Observer*, in which he also translated Aristophanes' *The Clouds* from his Bentley papers, showed Aristophanes to be the best of the writers of old comedy. While granting that "the corrupt and abominable manners" of Aristophanes' times deserved severe satire, Cumberland regretted that Aristophanes yielded to the deplorable taste of his audience and indulged himself in needless obscenity and in a reckless depiction of folly. Cumberland could admire the vitality of early Aristophanes, but found his last two plays, wherein he moved away from bawdy personal invective toward Euripidean sentiment, infinitely preferable. Ridicule was acceptable only when wholly good natured and when linked with positive moral example. Greek middle comedy had value to Cumberland because it was no longer obscene, but that negative virtue was countered by the fact that it was all idle amusement, diversion without education.

The writers of Greek new comedy became Cumberland's idols: Menander, Diphilus, Apollodorus, Phillippides, and Posidippus. Their aim was a realistic presentation of life with its mixture of pleasure and pain underscored by the reassuring view that all was part of a benevolently ordered universe. Cumberland found this new comedy most congenial because it took itself seriously; it even took on a sublime quality. As he observed in his "Dedication to Detraction," prefaced to *The Choleric Man* (1775), the comedies he admired contained "sententious passages, elegant in their phrase, but grave, and many of them, especially those of Diphilus, of a religious cast."

Braced with this classical background and armed with his commitment to the truth of benevolence, Cumberland left Cambridge, degree in hand in 1751, and became private secretary to George Montague, lord Halifax, president of the Board of Trade. It was a pleasant occupation allowing ample leisure for literary study. Halifax became lord lieutenant of Ireland; Cumberland became Ulster secretary; later Cumberland was appointed crown agent for Nova Scotia and provost marshall for South Carolina. Riding the coattails of Halifax, Cumberland, now married (1759) to Elizabeth Ridge and starting a family (he would have four sons and three daughters), was well on his way to a successful political career. When Halifax became secretary of state in 1762, however, Cumberland was passed over for the post of his private secretary. He had lost his position as favorite by his ill-advised refusal of a baronetcy. At that point he availed himself of the good offices of George Germain, later lord Sackville, and accepted a position as clerk of reports in the Board of Trade. So it was that in 1762 Cumberland found himself a comfortable bureaucrat, a bureaucrat who had published a play, *The Banishment of Cicero* (1761), but had not yet had a play produced.

David Garrick did not find *The Banishment of Cicero* suitable for staging, even though Halifax supported it. The play possessed a complicated plot that took great liberties with Roman history and clouded the central issue of Clodius's diabolic machinations to bring down Cicero with a complicated love plot in which Clodia (Clodius's sister) lustfully pursues Frugi, the hero, who is inspired to nobility by a pure passion for Tullia. The two plots are not well integrated in that Cicero's fall

thousand things to say to you: Before you go, tell me I conjure you where you are to be found? Here give me your direction, write it upon the back of this Visiting Ticket — have you a Pencil?

Charles.

I have: but why shou'd you desire to find us out? 'tis a poor, little, inconvenient place; my Sister has no apartment fit to receive you in.

Servant. enters. O. P.

Madam my Lady desires your company directly.

Charlotte.

I am coming — well have you wrote it? give it me, — O Charles! either you do not, or you will not understand me.

(Ext. severally.

End of the First Act.

Act 2. Scene 1.

A Room in Fulmer's House. Enter Fulmer & Mrs. Fulmer. P.S.

Mrs. Fulmer.

Why how you sit musing & moping, sighing & desponding, I am ashamed of you Mr. Fulmer: Is this the Country that you described to me, a Second Eldorado, Rivers of Gold & Rocks of Diamonds! you found me in a pretty snug retir'd way of Life at Boulogne, out of the Noise & Bustle of the World, & wholly at my ease; you indeed was upon the wing

Page from the playhouse copy of The West Indian *submitted to the Examiner of Plays for licensing prior to the first production, on 19 January 1771 (Larpent Collection, LA 315; by permission of the Henry E. Huntington Library and Art Gallery)*

and the romantic subplot are not thematically or historically connected. Though judged unstageworthy, the play reflects certain of Cumberland's tendencies and values that would contribute to his reputation as a sentimentalist. He creates single-minded villains who loom darkly over the plot, and he brings in a romantic love interest. In keeping with his commitment to the goodness of heart and to the value of feeling, poetic justice prevails.

Four years later Cumberland's first play was produced, the three-act comic opera entitled *The Summer's Tale*. Surviving charges of plagiarism leveled against him by Isaac Bickerstaff (and no doubt giving rise to Richard Sheridan's portrait of him in the 1779 *Critic* as Sir Fretful Plagiary), Cumberland savored the success of nine nights.

Despite its being elaborately overplotted, *The Summer's Tale* shows Cumberland's comic ability to blend the moral and the laughable. The complex love plot is replete with sententious statements to the effect that true love and virtue are the only basis for marriage. To this moral seriousness Cumberland added his first sympathetic portrait of a character usually the subject of national or ethnic prejudice: his first noble Irishman, Paddy. Paddy, who had resigned his faith to bear arms for England, robs lawyer Shifter of money Shifter had bilked out of the honest Bellafont. Bellafont pronounces Paddy's blessing in sweeping terms of the Irish character: "To trace actions apparently good from dishonourable motives is no uncommon thing; but it is the peculiarity of his nation to commit the wildest extravagancies upon principles of the most exalted magnanimity."

The pointing of morals in stilted language, the championing of the downtrodden, and the worldly rewarding of the noble hearted are the hallmarks of Cumberland's sentimentality, but there is much of *The Summer's Tale* that is very funny: good satire of lawyers in the person of the disreputable Shifter and some rather bitter satire of the government's mistreatment of soldiers during peacetime, but the greatest fun lies in the character of Sir Anthony, who sees all events in light of the good reading they will make in his diary. This blend of the serious and the humorous is what Cumberland found in Greek new comedy, and it is what he brought to the late eighteenth-century stage.

Cumberland followed in 1768 with *Amelia*, a two-act revision of *The Summer's Tale* that devoted more time to the emotional state of Henry, a rather underdeveloped character, whose love for Amelia was doomed by disparity in social rank. In *Amelia* Cumberland gives this theme more attention. Once Amelia's high rank is made known to Henry, he is supposed to be content, but his heart does not heal. Cumberland flirted here with the theme of the human heart and the power of social rank, but he did not fully engage it. He provided Henry with a comfortable living and a suitable girl to marry in the wholesome Patty, but the theme of social disparity was not resolved, neither for Henry, nor for a modern reader. *Amelia* then did little more than suggest the sentimental potential and the social problem inherent in this plot.

In the three years following *Amelia* Cumberland enjoyed his greatest success as a dramatist. Adhering to the values of Greek "new" comedy and insisting on the instructional potential of all drama, Cumberland produced *The Brothers* in 1769 and *The West Indian* in 1771. In these two plays he established the two major trends of all his work: *The Brothers* as serious comedy that develops into melodrama and the problem play; *The West Indian* as the comedy of manners or laughing comedy in the manner of Oliver Goldsmith, Richard Sheridan, George Colman, and Arthur Murphy. Since most of his work belongs to the school of *The Brothers*, Cumberland's reputation is generally that of a sentimentalist, a playwright who indulges in the falsely emotional and mawkish. But there is another side to Cumberland: the comedian.

The Brothers in 1769 had been a modest success, but *The West Indian* in 1771 ran twenty-seven nights at Drury Lane and was transferred to the Haymarket for a summer performance. Moreover, contemporary reviewers, well aware of the tension between the moralistic, preachy comedy called sentimental and the satiric, laughing comedy–well before Goldsmith's famous essay on the subject–heaped praise upon the piece as a comedy as comedy should be. Said John Hawkesworth in *The Monthly Review*, *The West Indian* "excites a curiosity strongly interested, and has so blended the pathetic and ridiculous, that if the spectator or reader has sensibility and discernment, he will be kept almost continually laughing with tears in his eyes." An anonymous correspondent to *The Whitehall Evening Post* put the matter into a single sentence in praising *The West Indian* as a return to true comedy: "at a comedy I expect and love to laugh; and I took up the pen to make my acknowledgments to an author who has gratified this inclination,–who has introduced laughter without dismissing sentiment,–and who has showed morality and mirth to be far from incom-

Portrait of Cumberland by George Romney, to whom Cumberland dedicated his Odes *(1776)*

patible!" In *The West Indian* Cumberland realized his goal of comedy in the style of Menander.

The play has a serious moral purpose: to dispel the prejudice that existed against those British who lived in the West Indies and the long-standing prejudice against the Irish. Belcour is the most engaging of West Indians; although impetuous and improvident, he is never cruel. His blood may run too warm from the island sun, but his heart is open and sensitive to human virtue and suffering. Not only is he a man of feeling, but he is a laughable one. His fight with the customs officials over his menagerie proves funny because it illustrates Belcour's naiveté as well as the oversophistication of Londoners; his impetuousness and gullibility in mistaking the most virtuous Louisa for a whore produce comic incidents and laughable cross-purpose dialogue.

O'Flaherty takes up where Paddy of *The Summer's Tale* left off. A robust example of the noble-hearted Irishman, O'Flaherty's zest for life, marriage, fighting, and drinking makes him a comic, but wholly sympathetic character. He sees the values of life in their true light, and he pursues them despite conventions, ranks, and titles. O'Flaherty and Belcour are naive proponents of the goodness of heart; their clumsiness is amusing; their triumph is satisfying. Before them fall the affectations of society–from the hypocrisy of the puritanical Lady Rusport to the false delicacy of Louisa and Charles Dudley. Cumberland steers clear of the sentimental and the melodramatic not only through laughter, but by maintaining a lighthearted tone throughout.

Primarily, he creates no false suspense. From page one, the audience knows that Stockwell is Belcour's father, and this knowledge creates delightful opportunities for dramatic irony. Belcour's being duped of jewels and being misled as to Louisa's character pose no serious threat, for Belcour has plenty of money, and Charlotte Rusport could dispel the misunderstanding in an instant, but she

Act 3d: Scene 1st:

{Enter Frederick & Mrs: Ratcliffe}

Fred:_ Can you forgive me? has my lovely advocate sued out my pardon, and may I now invoke a blessing on my love and me?

Mrs R. Heaven in its bounty, bless you both! may all good fortune follow you, all comforts light upon you and love and happiness ever subsist between you!

Fred.- Such piety can never pray in vain - Where is Eliza?

Mrs R.- She does not know you are here, shall I call her?

Fred.- Not yet, I have a little sum, and you must be our Banker; Charles is too proud to touch it; his spirit is of a pitch too high to stoop to worldly matters We have been warm and cordial friends, how we may fare as brothers, heaven only knows; I have some fears.

Mrs R.- Eliza is impress'd with the same apprehensions, but if Sir Stephen acquiesces, all will be well; I hope this money is a token of his forgiveness.

Fred.- 'Twill serve to set us out; I have provided lodgings more commodious; I hope you will permit Eliza to remove, and I make further suit, that you will have the goodness to accompany her.

Mrs R. Well but you don't answer to my question of the money. Hav'nt you seen your father?

Fred.- I have seen him.

Mrs R.- And explain'd to him?-

Fred.- I have.

Mrs R.- Well! what says he?

Fred.- If he had said what wou'd have done him honour and given ease to my Eliza's mother, I shou'd not have waited for your question: But nature must have time to work, I have only stir'd the dregs. may I now see Eliza? There is a cloud on my heart also, which only her bright presence can dispel.

Mrs R.- Ah, Sir, she can be only bright henceforward by reflection! her

Page from the playhouse copy of The Jew *submitted to the Examiner of Plays for licensing prior to the first performance, on 8 May 1794 (Larpent Collection, LA 1018; by permission of the Henry E. Huntington Library and Art Gallery)*

John Philip Kemble as Penruddock in the first production of The Wheel of Fortune

(and the audience) are rather enjoying the folly. Without serious suspense, the audience is free to laugh–especially since there are no serious villains.

The Fulmers have wicked intentions, but they bicker and complain of their long history of failures in business and in evil. One cannot take them seriously. Nor can one take Lady Rusport seriously; she may intend to deprive the Dudleys of their just inheritance, but she is vain, cheap, and petty. Putty in the hands of O'Flaherty, Lady Rusport poses no genuine threat.

Free from serious suspense and effective villains, *The West Indian* satirizes human folly and weakness, extols the human heart, brings all of its characters to a recognition of the value of benevolence, and sends the audience home pleased, amused, and contented–just as does *She Stoops to Conquer* (1773) or *The Rivals* (1775). Delighted with *The West Indian*, Garrick wrote to Dr. John Hoadly in May of 1771 that Cumberland's prospects as a comic writer were limitless.

Cumberland followed with *The Fashionable Lover* (1772), a piece more akin to *The Brothers* than to *The West Indian*. Then, in 1774, he produced *The Note of Hand*, his first effort at farce. In it he employs once more his noble-hearted Irishman, this time named MacCormuck–an upstanding young man who will not tolerate affectation or cheating, and one who is outspoken in his grievance about England's treatment of Ireland. MacCormuck is Cumberland's Irishman who not only works toward dashing the prejudice against his nation, but who brings an element of political satire to the play. Overall, *The Note of Hand* is an attack against gambling and other frivolities that distract members of Parliament (Revell) from their duties and obligations. While the play contains some sententiousness regarding gambling, it is mostly a piece of comic situation and character, even making a satiric comment on plays like *The Brothers* when Revell accuses Rivers, after a particularly sententious speech, of being "as dull as a sentimental comedy." Although *The Note of Hand* shows some genuine comedic skill in Cumberland, it is too short to sustain a weighty moral message against gambling, and it becomes a rather unhappy blend of platitude and comic character.

Also in 1774, Cumberland produced *The Choleric Man*, a solid comedy in the laughing tradition. Despite an instance of self-deprecation in his line against sentimental comedy in *The Note of Hand*, Cumberland was highly pleased with *The Brothers* and *The Fashionable Lover*, and he found the word *sentimental* onerous when applied by others to his works. In his "Dedication to Detraction," Cumberland made his strongest statements in favor of sentimental comedy, petulantly responding to his critics, overstating his own case at the expense of the actual classic values he espoused. Then, as if to prove a point, he wrote *The Choleric Man*, a play as free from sentimentality as any of his. He borrowed his plot from Terence's *Adelphi*, but eschewed even those sentimental scenes that were in his source.

The Choleric Man, a solid laughing comedy, builds on the conventional theme of demonstrating correct social values based on humanitarian benevolence; it laughs at the folly of those who have incorrect values while presenting the right way through exemplary characters. Its strength lies in its satire. At the heart of the play is the question of education: which brother will be the better man, the one grounded in the classics and the grand tour (Charles), or the one brought up to the fowling piece and the stable (Jack)? The answer is that a humanistic education improves natural goodness, but a country education creates a booby unprepared for and insensitive to the world. This theme is further embodied in the educators: Manlove, the town lawyer, has learned the value of humanity while his half-brother, Nightshade, has lived so long in the country that he thinks a pheasant as important as a man.

The plot of the play turns upon a series of mistaken identities caused by Jack's disguising himself as Charles, proving himself a booby and creating one comic situation after another, culminating when the irascible Nightshade hits the postman on the head, and everyone avows he has killed him. The whole business is a ruse to make Nightshade aware of humanity, and as he stands aside to ponder his action, Laetitia, the heroine, reflects "that even the worst of men have moments of compunction." While this seems a natural opportunity for sentimental reformation, Cumberland instead shows Nightshade's mind wherein there is no repentance but a scheming to have his servant Gregory take his place at the trial.

This most pleasing play enjoyed as much success as Sheridan's *The Rivals*, but it marked a falling off from Cumberland's extraordinarily popular *West Indian* and *Fashionable Lover*. Perhaps in an effort to recapture that popularity Cumberland spent the next several years in modest experimentation outside comedy. He saw his tragedy *The Battle of Hastings* staged, wrote a flimsy curtain raiser in *The Critic*, did two adaptations of plays by Philip Massinger (*The Bondman* and *The Duke of Milan*, both lost except for their prologues and the epilogue for the second), and unsuccessfully attempted lyric theater. Of his *Calypso* he candidly owned in his *Memoirs* that his lyrics "buried" the fine music, and in the midst of preparing for his mission to Spain he did a slapdash job in *The Widow of Delphi*, leaving critics in accord that the play is weak, sentimental, and far beneath Cumberland's abilities. When he returned from Spain, Cumberland went back to serious comedy in *The Walloons* (1782) and then wrote two tragedies in two years (*The Mysterious Husband* in 1783 and *The Carmelite* in 1784). None of these proved a financial success adequate to Cumberland's needs. His desire to relive his former popularity caused him to reprise O'Flaherty in *The Natural Son* (1784). The critics rightly found the piece to be underplotted, and while it possessed good, witty dialogue, it suffered from being, at least in part, a sequel. O'Flaherty appealed to those who already liked him, but there was little new in terms of satire, plot, or character in the piece.

Writing with great rapidity in these years, Cumberland continued to produce a variety of plays, borrowing sometimes from his own earlier works, sometimes from others. When in 1789 he turned to George Farquhar's ever popular *The Beaux Stratagem* (1707), Cumberland was taking advantage of what the late eighteenth century found to be the best of the comedy of manners: an open satiric humor, solid poetic justice, and moral rectitude. Cumberland rewrote *The Beaux Stratagem* as *The Imposters*, turning the fortune hunters from noblemen into upper middle class and from sympathetic to unsympathetic; their cleverness and wit are cause for much laughter as they outsmart the social-climbing Sir Soloman Sapient and his antiquated cousin Dorothy. In the end, however, the imposters are exposed by the noble Sir Charles Freemantle, who truly loves Eleanor, the object of the imposters' scheme. Although most of the play is satiric, Cumberland returns to some sentimental moments: Eleanor throwing herself between two duelists, the imposters' being transported for their

Hither the immediate Hand of Heaven has led me.
Hopeless of Pardon, to expire before you.
And cast your Husband's Murderer at your feet.

Mat.

Ah! Scorpion, is it thou? I shake with horror
Thee have I pitied? Thee have I preserv'd
Monster, avaunt! Go to the Rocks for Food
Call to the Winds for Pity! lay thee down
Beneath some blighted Yew, whose pois'nous leaf
Kills as it falls; there howl thyself to death
Hang's the Roof o'er us yet? I am astonish'd
Art not asham'd, O Earth, to bear him yet?
Oh, Sea to cast him up again? Begone.

Hild.

I do not wait for Pardon – but for Death
Call to your Servants; whelm me with their Swords
Heav'n throws me on your Mercy; You receiv'd
And gave me Shelter, hospitably tender'd
Food and restoring Medicines; I refus'd them;
My Thirst is unallay'd my Wounds undress'd
No particle of Food has pass'd my Lips
For I disdain a Fraud upon your pity
And where I can't have pardon scorn Support
The only Mercy I implore is Death.

Matil.

Page from the playhouse copy of The Carmelite *submitted to the Examiner of Plays for licensing prior to the first performance, on 2 December 1784 (Larpent Collection, LA 674; by permission of the Henry E. Huntington Library and Art Gallery)*

crime. *The Imposters* is within Cumberland's range as a writer of comedy of manners, but by this point in his career he is clearly more comfortable with the serious play, and when the audience supported the piece for only six performances, he had little reason to return to the spirit of *The Choleric Man*.

In fact, Cumberland returned to the type only once more, in *The Box-Lobby Challenge*, a very pleasant play that ran twelve nights at the Haymarket in 1794. It is most remarkable for its excellent delineation of low-class characters, the Crochets. Its satire good-naturedly scoffs at the old lady who thinks she is still a beauty, at the country bumpkin who thinks the Grand Tour a big game safari, at the hack poet, and at the lady novelist. All of this laughter–and there is a lot–is balanced by the good sense of Captain Waterland, whose love for the beautiful and virtuous Laetitia is delicately, but not sentimentally, handled. *The Box-Lobby Challenge*, like *The Choleric Man*, is a rollicking good comedy–filled with incident and humor, but Cumberland was now committed to his serious comedies.

These serious comedies had had their beginning in *The Brothers* of 1769, a play in which Cumberland puts forward one of his strongest themes: worldly wisdom pales in the light of natural virtue. Worldly wisdom is embodied in Belfield, Senior, a thoroughgoing villain, a man of infinite avarice, a man capable of bigamy, a man so caught up in vicious machinations that he utters the now stereotypical line of "foil'd again" when his plans go awry. Cumberland introduces this darkest of villains into comedy, and in the fifth act brings about his reformation, one of the falsities that mark sentimental comedy, one of the exaggerations that mark melodrama.

Cumberland treats Belfield, Senior, with unrelenting seriousness. For four and one-half acts Belfield, Senior, is a successful villain. There is no laughter at his expense, nor can there be. His perverted view of the world's values has elevated evil and punished good, and there is real danger that his view will prevail. He cannot simply be sent offstage at the end of the play to the laughter of the other characters; he must either be incarcerated or converted. In keeping with benevolence Cumberland has him become aware of his meanness and promise a life of restitution. What laughter there is in the play lies in the subplot of Sir Benjamin and Lady Dove and in the noble British tar Ironsides. These, however, are more comic relief than essential comedic or satiric elements in the play.

In short, this is a serious comedy that even Cumberland recognized as having some tiresomely moralistic scenes. Apparently, Cumberland owed much to the actors for making the play work; he gives particular credit to Richard Yates and Henry Woodward for comic embellishments, and in a letter to George Montagu, Horace Walpole says of *The Brothers:* "It acts well, but reads ill."

Unfortunately, we cannot recover the acting, and these serious comedies of Cumberland strike us much more as melodramas than as comedies of any kind. In his *English Melodrama* (1965) Michael R. Booth observed that the world of melodrama is an idealized and simplified one, a world audiences crave but cannot find. Of this world he said, "character, conduct, ethics, and situations are perfectly simple, and one always knows what the end will be, although the means may be temporarily obscure." Good triumphs; evil is usually punished, though sometimes it is redeemed, as villains occasionally repent.

Melodrama best describes *The Brothers* and many of Cumberland's serious comedies. Opening with a storm and a shipwreck, an atmosphere of suspense and excitement, *The Brothers* begins with the mystery of Violetta's lost husband and the adjacent mystery of the plight of Belfield, Junior. Ironsides brings in a theme of jingoistic patriotism, and the ingredients of melodrama are all in place. Only the subplot of the Doves with its satire of jealousy and dueling brings genuine comedy into the play. With *The Brothers* Cumberland moved strongly in the direction of plays of social reform and benevolence.

After *The West Indian* of 1771 Cumberland returned to serious comedy with *The Fashionable Lover* (1772), his favorite play, so stated in his *Memoirs*, where he labeled it a drama "of a moral, grave, and tender cast." Although the language is much less stilted than that of *The Brothers, The Fashionable Lover* still possesses an overly complicated plot of coincidence and intrigue. Lord Abberville, the fashionable lover, must learn the true value of human virtue by first falling to a baseness in which he attempts to rape Augusta and in which he gambles to the brink of bankruptcy. The Bridgemores must learn that fraud and cruelty bring true emptiness, and Augusta's virtue must be rewarded with an honest lover, the return of a long-lost father, and a fortune: pure virtue, unmitigated evil, and moral sentiment pervade the whole in a setting as melodramatic, though different, as that of *The Brothers*. The mysterious seascape (nature's brooding violence) is replaced by the opulence of Lord Abberville's mansion, and the menace of the interior of a house of prostitution (the violence of human corruption).

Rape, bankruptcy, and plotted murder underlie the central action of the play, and, whatever comedy there is, is secondary. Cumberland introduces the Welshman, Dr. Druid, to take advantage of a comic stage accent and to point the satire of scientific pedantry. While Cumberland uses the stage Welshman for comic effect, he does present the generous, benevolent Colin Macleod, who challenges the English aversion to Scots. As such he joins Paddy, O'Flaherty, and Belcour as an example of Cumberland's humanitarian crusade against national prejudice. Macleod's integrity and ingenuity eventually lead to the destruction of Bridgemore and the conversion of Lord Abberville, but he is comic in his addiction to Scotland and in his outspoken, openhearted view of the world. He is the element of comic relief, the forerunner of the comic man so much a part of melodrama.

Cumberland's concern with showing the triumph of virtue and the purity of poetic justice led him to develop antagonists for his heroes who were the vilest of villains, capable of placing innocence in the most unwarranted distress. His belief in benevolence caused him to make these villains redeemable once virtue touched them. And his commitment to Greek comedy led him to keep satire as part of the fabric of his serious comedies; so he created comic characters to control and lighten the action with some degree of social satire: lawyers, scientists, fashion-conscious women. Self-satisfied with these serious comedies of instruction and amusement, he returned to the same basic formula in 1782 with *The Walloons*.

During the ten years between *The Fashionable Lover* and *The Walloons*, Cumberland became secretary to the Board of Trade, had the first London production of his tragedy *The Battle of Hastings*, wrote several comedies (of particular importance were *The Note of Hand* and *The Choleric Man*), became embroiled in a critical war with those who attacked him as a sentimentalist, and went to Spain in 1780-1781 on a secret mission to negotiate a peace between that country and England. Not only did the negotiations fail, but Cumberland discovered that his expenses were not to be reimbursed, and upon his return to England he learned that the Board of Trade was abolished and along with it his comfortable bureaucratic position. Disappointed, in debt, out of a position, Cumberland retired to Tunbridge Wells and embraced the idea that he now had to write to live.

One would imagine a dark period in Cumberland's drama, the product of a man embittered by literary, political, and personal disappointment, even betrayal. But such did not occur. His sense of the basic goodness of the human heart, his deep commitment to teaching positive values through exemplary character and poetic justice, and his desire to abolish dark prejudice carried him forward with themes and patterns of composition quite similar to those of a more leisured period.

Strikingly, *The Walloons* is most patriotic, reflecting Cumberland's own disappointment only in the failure of England to appreciate fully the loyalty of its sons. Written at the request of John Henderson, an excellent actor in search of a "fine bald-faced villain," *The Walloons* offered him Father Sullivan, a priest who breaks the seal of confession, practices extortion, moves to betray English military secrets to the Spanish, and finally betrays his fellow conspirators. In the end all of his machinations are discovered, and he goes off to execution without the slightest repentance. In contrast to Father Sullivan are Montgomery and Drelincourt, both Catholic, who serve with Spain against England only because English anti-Catholicism will not allow them in the English service. Their true patriotism, however, is never in question, and for their refusal to carry out Father Sullivan's plan, poetic justice smiles on them when the king in his mercy restores their estates and accepts them as full-privileged citizens.

What humor there is in *The Walloons* lies in a farcical subplot of Pat Carey, a fop, who fruitlessly tries to elope with the serving maid Kitty, and in Davy, a sailor whose language is all "salt" and who manipulates the action so that the true patriotism of his friends Montgomery and Drelincourt is made known and so that Father Sullivan's plot is exposed. In both cases the humor serves as comic relief. The good feeling the audience has at the conclusion is not from laughing at folly, but rather from witnessing virtue triumph over vice, which has been exposed not to ridicule but to execution.

Cumberland followed *The Walloons* with a series of not-very-successful comedies, and then found his register in serious comedy again in *The Jew* (1794). This play is in its own way a remarkable blend of comedy, melodrama, and the drama of social purpose. Certain melodramatic qualities continue in the piece: the virtuous, distressed heroine and hero; the sensitive mother; the sententious language; the comic man–here the always-famished servant, Jabal. But there is no villain, no Belfield, Senior, no Bridgemore, no Father Sulli-

Richard Cumberland (engraving by Scriven, based on a portrait by Clover)

van. The play's problems are caused by people momentarily blinded to genuine values, not by men devoted to evil. There simply is no need for black villainy in the play, for Cumberland's concern is not so much with virtue triumphant as it is with presenting the essential benevolent humanity of the Jew.

In earlier plays Cumberland employed conventional eighteenth-century stage Jews–sly, usurious, miserly men. For example, Napthali, a veritable Shylock, fully participates in the wicked conspiracy of *The Fashionable Lover*. But in *The Observer* he had called upon his countrymen to wash themselves clean of bigotry and recognize in the Jew a fellow human being filled with feelings. In *The Jew* he deliberately set out to convince the English Christians that Jews were people capable of the greatest of human dignity and compassion. Cumberland's attitude toward Jews at this time may have been influenced by the success of Daniel Mendoza, the Jewish boxer, who defeated Humphries, the British champion, in 1789; by the granting of citizenship to Jews by France in 1791; and by his firsthand experience of the persecution of Jews during his time in Spain. Whatever Cumberland's complex of motivation, he presented for the first time a Jewish character whose generosity, feeling, and wit dashed the stereotype of the Jew that Christian Britain so loved to hate, thereby softening public opinion and preparing the way for pro-Jewish legislation.

Unlike O'Flaherty and Macleod, Cumberland's other creations to destroy ethnic prejudice, Sheva is not a minor character; he dominates the play with his great generosity. Masked by a pretense of miserliness, Sheva lends to the rich at usurious rates, but secretly shares his fortune with the oppressed. Recognizing the sentimental value of love over money as a basis for marriage, Sheva supplies the fortune for Frederic and Eliza that the Christian father withholds because it is not prudent. Further, he recognizes that true honor is to pay one's just debts, not to run one's friend through the guts; so, he condemns a duel between Frederic and Charles. Most important, he is human–lonely, persecuted, feeling.

While the seriousness of Cumberland's theme leads him to heighten the emotional scenes of the play, to exaggerate characters, and to deal in sententiousness, he supplies *The Jew* with sardonic, self-deprecating humor. A good actor could do much with the accent and understatement to highlight the absurd injustice of the Christian world as perceived by the Jew. Unlike his other serious comedies in which Cumberland relegated comedy to the subplot, he allows it to be part of the main action in *The Jew,* making the play less a melodrama and more a play of social commentary, a commentary to which he returned in *Tiberius in Capreae* (written in 1797) and *The Jew of Mogadore* (1808).

If *The Jew* foreshadowed the play of social comment, Cumberland's next serious comedy clearly anticipates the drama of T. W. Robertson. Except for a brief scene involving servants (III.ii) there is nothing funny in *The Wheel of Fortune* (1795). Its theme is that gambling destroys happiness, that revenge is shallow, that contentment is ideal, and that true happiness lies only in the knowledge that one has been benevolent. The plot concerns itself with Penruddock, who lives alone in a forest because twenty years earlier his great friend Woodville, through deception and slander, had stolen the beautiful Arabella from him. Life has made him a philosopher; he has learned the value of contentment. In this state of mind he first refuses the enormous estate left him by his cousin; then, when he learns that Woodville's gambling has deeded over all his own property to this cousin, Penruddock accepts the inheritance, the prospect of revenge having overwhelmed all his philosophy.

No one, of course, has any sympathy for Woodville's behavior; a man who gambles away his family's happiness is beneath contempt: Mrs. Woodville now lives in poverty; Henry, his son, just returned from a French prison, finds his family honor destroyed and his prospects of marrying Emily gone. Emily will marry the wealthy bore David Dow so that she will have enough money to alleviate the Woodvilles' distress. Penruddock is not affected. Eventually brought to perceive his cruelty by Henry, who greatly resembles his mother, Penruddock becomes secretly benevolent to the Woodvilles and restores the property to Henry, makes a handsome settlement on Mrs. Woodville, and arranges for Emily to be free to marry Henry.

The play presents a serious moral lesson through a thrilling plot and a happy ending. What Cumberland began in 1769 with *The Brothers,* based on the values of Greek "new" comedy and the sense of benevolence and poetic justice, had moved from sentimental comedy through heavy melodrama to the social-problem play. Now, hard pressed to produce even a play or two a year, Cumberland found himself both out of time and ahead of his theater. To save time, Cumberland borrowed from himself and reworked old ideas, but the theaters were not ready for the serious problem play. They were suffering true growing pains; they increased in size, but acoustics and lighting could not keep pace. The audience wanted spectacle, not wordy moral treatises. Cumberland was unable to please his audiences. *First Love* (1795) enjoyed moderate success by once again extolling the values of love and romance over economic concerns, and lightening the dramatic central plot with a comic subplot in the marital bickerings of the Wrangles. *The Dependent* (1795), however, had only one performance, and *The Days of Yore* (1796), an Arthurian piece, ran only a few nights.

More successful was *False Impressions* (1797), wherein Cumberland attempted his sometimes successful blending of the melodramatic and the comic. Beginning the play with the very comic Scud, an apothecary more interested in the shilling than the curing of patients, Cumberland established a lighthearted tone that counterbalanced the melodramatic villainy of Lawyer Early, who seeks to have or ruin the beautiful Emily Fitzallen, even to the point of attempting rape. The two plots do not fit well together, but their juxtaposing shows Cumberland's desire to find a formula to win back the audience. While complaining bitterly of the deteriorating taste of the times and of the unabashed theatrical surrender to spectacle, Cumberland still experimented. In 1804 he suggested that *The Sailor's Daughter,* unappreciated in the theater, might have been more appropriate in the closet, and in 1806 he offered *A Hint to Husbands,* a comedy in blank verse. In these experiments he came closest to the right formula for success in his *Joanna of Montfaucon* (1800), a play whose roots are more in his tragedies than in his regular or serious comedies.

Cumberland's first tragedy, *The Banishment of Cicero,* had been rejected by Garrick in 1761. Following that he worked on *Salome*–never produced or published, though parts of it were later incorporated into *The Arab* (1785)–and did a romantic and sentimental adaptation of *Timon of Athens* (1771). It was 1778 before Cumberland's first tragedy was performed. In *The Battle of Hastings* Cumberland sentimentalizes the heroic. To the historical facts of the Norman invasion, Cumberland adds a romantic intrigue involving Edgar, rightful heir to the crown, and Edwina, while Harold, the usurper, tries to marry his daughter Mathilda to Edgar for political reasons. The sentimental preference for the value of personal love over public need rings false when Harold is defeated, but Edgar assumes leadership, calling for the remainder of these Anglo-Saxons to follow him forever against the Norman invader. Since the audience is well aware of historical truth, Edgar's enthusiasm for love seems hollow. When Antony and Cleopatra choose love over honor, Dryden has them die, perhaps gaining honor in a better world. When Edgar and Edwina choose love and have their reward here, despite the historical collapse of their cause, the effect of the tragedy is greatly diminished.

Cumberland's next tragedy of merit was *The Mysterious Husband* (1783). The line that separates Cumberland's serious comedies–sometimes seen as sentimental comedies, melodramas, or plays of social purpose–and his sentimental tragedies is fine indeed. For in truth the problems of *The Mysterious Husband* and *The Brothers* are not greatly different. In *The Mysterious Husband,* Davenant, a gamester, has married Mrs. Davenant under false pretenses, and then he turns to bigamy to gain funds and to pretended death for peace to pursue his pleasure. He has executed the very crimes Belfield, Senior, contemplates. In both plays Cumberland focuses on the moral issues of fidelity and generosity. But *The Mysterious Husband* has neither quarreling Doves nor noble Ironsides for comic relief; it has only extended reflections on the wronged woman and on the deceptions of evildoers. When Davenant is finally confronted by the goodness of his wife and by the incestuous result of his double marriage (the son of his first marriage has married his second wife, whom Davenant had abandoned), Lord Davenant first poisons and then stabs himself. When Belfield, Senior, in *The Brothers* is confronted by the goodness of Violetta and by the narrow escape he has had from bigamy, he converts. Both actions show a fundamental goodness of heart in the most vile of characters, and the difference between Cumberland's serious comedies and his tragedies lies not in human motivation, but in how far evil action has proceeded before discovery. This, of course, is fully within the bounds of Cumberland's insistence upon poetic justice and benevolence, and one fears the invited implication of this poetic is that comedy gives us a reformed villain who becomes a saint on earth while tragedy produces a reformed villain who, despite suicide, is ripe for sanctity in heaven.

In *The Carmelite* (1784), Cumberland's next and most popular tragedy, the theme of sanctity continues in that the villain Hildebrand, moved by guilt for his treachery, actually repents before his death. He attains great dignity in his dying, and heaven surely awaits the repentant. On earth, Saint Valori and Mathilda conquer evil and life's trials through a thorough commitment to selfless love. Neither theme nor plot is startling, but Cumberland's full-scale excursion into the Gothic made the play work. There is the opening shipwreck (as in *The Brothers*) and the gloomy castle occupied by Mathilda and Montgomeri; there is Saint Valori disguised as a Carmelite; and there is Mathilda's precarious mental state. This is a fine Gothic tale for the stage, using all of the conventions to suggest the darkness of the human soul–the full range of passion and violence that lies in the dark mystery beyond the conscious. Cumberland created a character in Mathilda for Mrs. Sarah Siddons that allowed her an emotional range far beyond Lady Randolph in John Home's *Douglas* (1756), usually regarded as one of the finest of the eighteenth-century romantic tragedies. *The Carmelite* takes advantage of the burgeoning enthusiasm for the Gothic and in setting, plot, and character carried romantic tragedy to exciting lengths. Melodramatic as it is, *The Carmelite* might well be revived today because the Gothic conventions allow the imagination to accept greater degrees of heightened emotion without challenging the essential suspension of disbelief.

Unfortunately, Cumberland never repeated his success in the Gothic. He returned to tragedy in 1785 with *The Arab,* which was another of his sentimental tragedies and lasted only one night; he apparently revised it as *Alcanor,* but that version never saw performance. Of the rest of Cumberland's tragedies there is little to be said. He developed more spectacular effects to adjust to increasingly large theaters that needed gimmicks to hold the attention of larger, less educated audiences, who had to struggle both to hear and to see the plays clearly. In *Don Pedro* (1796) Cumberland created a leader of robbers who brings about his own death after fearing he has killed his brother. It is another chance for Cumberland to develop the theme of essential human benevolence, this time among the more violent. In *Tiberius of Capreae* he returns to another Sheva-like Jew, a Samaritan magician named Simon, who uses his magic to bring about Tiberius's moral conversion, but more important, perhaps, the magic gives the theater a liveliness in spectacular effect that the drama of moral purpose could not. Cumberland may not have approved of the theaters' surrender to the trick or the stunt, but he was shrewd enough to go along with the trend. In the Gothic, natural to his sensitivities since *The Brothers*, he had some success with integrating the spectacular with his themes and characters, but his other tragedies of spectacle, *Tiberius of Capreae* and *Torrendal*, did not make a happy blend of stage sensationalism and the benevolent, sentimental themes they presented. *Torrendal* (never acted and not published until the posthumous works) suffers particularly from this problem.

In 1800, however, Cumberland attempted something new in *Joanna of Montfaucon*. Reluctantly and complainingly, he abandoned his principles of classic drama, and with painstaking apology to head off further accusations of plagiarism, he offered an adaptation of August von Kotzebue's *Johanna von Montfaucon* (also 1800). His version is an action-packed romance complete with music by Thomas Busby. There was much fighting, much melodramatic passion, a strong sense of divine providence, and a hero wholly deserving of the philosophy of benevolence. Cumberland saw the piece as a surrender to poor taste because the setting, business, and music overwhelmed his theme and characters. He was right. He was an established literary playwright being eclipsed by theater technology, but his script for *Joanna of Montfaucon* worked; he just could never become enthusiastic enough about these new trends to develop them into genuinely literary efforts.

From 1800 to his death on 7 May 1811 at the age of seventy-nine, Cumberland wrote constantly. He published religious poems, his third novel, and his memoirs. Moreover, he undertook a Johnsonian task in writing biographical and literary commentaries for a fourteen-volume edition of the English playwrights, and he began *The London Review*. It was a reaction against those young men in the north who were being so effective and influential in determining literary merit with their *Edinburgh Review*. To Cumberland, they were irreverent and insolent, and they hid behind anonymity. In *The London Review*, all articles would be signed. John Murray and Sir Walter Scott found Cumberland inexhaustible but doomed; he was out of touch with literary value; his plays were curiosities, not mainstays of the theater; his novels were sentimental and old-fashioned; and no one could survive with signed reviews. They were right.

The London Review failed after four numbers. But the integrity of signed reviews caught on. This is Cumberland's legacy in little. His ideas were always good; his execution was most often short of the mark. His desire to teach the doctrine of benevolence and patriotism was commendable; so was his desire to reawaken comedy by imitating Greek "new" comedy. Nothing could be more worthy than his commitment to themes of social justice: his taking up the cause of the Irish, the Scot, the West Indian, and especially the Jew.

Unfortunately, his plots were overcomplicated, his characters too good or too bad, his dialogue sometimes too preachy and artificial. His reputation continues to be that of a sentimentalist–a practitioner of the maudlin. Mrs. Hester Thrale Piozzi found him hard to like; Horace Walpole found him dull; Goldsmith made fun of him; Garrick and Colman tolerated him. Modern readers have the same reactions, for much of his work is tedious, pretentious, and unrealistic. And yet *The West Indian, The Choleric Man, The Imposters, The Jew,* and *The Carmelite* deserve literary consideration and perhaps another chance on the stage. Cumberland simply wrote too much. Had he written only these few plays he would be ranked with Goldsmith, Sheridan, Colman, and Murphy. As it is, he is remembered more for what he foreshadowed than for what he wrote: the melodrama, the problem play of social protest, and the romantic musical drama.

Biographies:

William Mudford, *The Life of Richard Cumberland, embracing a Critical Examination of his Various Writing*, 2 volumes (London: Sherwood, Neely & Jones, 1812);

George Paston (pseudonym for Emily Symonds), "Richard Cumberland," in *Little Memoirs of the Eighteenth Century* (New York: Dutton, 1901), pp. 57-116;

J. Homer Caskey, "Richard Cumberland's Mission to Spain," *Philological Quarterly*, 9 (January 1930): 82-86;

Samuel Flagg Bemis, *The Hussey-Cumberland Mission and American Independence* (Princeton: Princeton University Press, 1931);

Richard J. Dircks, "Richard Cumberland's Political Associations," *Studies in Burke and his Time*, 11 (Spring 1970): 1550-1570.

References:

Ethel Beck, *The Sources of Richard Cumberland's Comedy The Choleric Man* (Bern: University of Bern Press, 1912);

Richard Bevis, *The Laughing Tradition: Stage Comedy in Garrick's Day* (Athens: University of Georgia Press, 1980);

Roberta F. S. Borkat, Introduction to *The Plays of Richard Cumberland*, volume 1 (New York & London: Garland, 1982);

Thomas J. Campbell, "Penruddock Recreated: John Philip Kemble's Alterations of Cumberland's *The Wheel of Fortune*," *Theatre Survey*, 25 (May 1984): 83-94;

Campbell, "Richard Cumberland's *The Wheel of Fortune:* A Critical Review," Ph.D. dissertation, University of Oregon, 1982;

Campbell, "Richard Cumberland's *The Wheel of Fortune:* An Unpublished Scene," *Nineteenth Century Theatre Research*, 11 (Summer 1983): 1-11;

James E. Cox, *The Rise of Sentimental Comedy* (Springfield, Mo.: Published by the author, 1926);

Robert J. Detisch, "The Synthesis of Laughing and Sentimental Comedy in *The West Indian,*" Educational Theatre Journal, 20 (October 1970): 291-300;

Richard J. Dircks, "Cumberland, Richardson, and Fielding: Changing Patterns in the Eighteenth-Century Novel," *Research Studies*, 38 (December 1970): 291-299;

Dircks, *Richard Cumberland* (Boston: Twayne, 1976);

John W. Draper, "The Theory of the Comic in Eighteenth-Century England," *Journal of English and Germanic Philology*, 37 (1938): 207-223;

Kurt Fehler, *Richard Cumberland. Leben und dramatisch Werke, ein Beitrag zur Geschichte des englischen Dramas in 18 Jahrhundert* (Erlangen: Junge & Sohn, 1911);

Ivan Kyrle Fletcher, "Cumberland's *The Princess of Parma,*" *Times Literary Supplement*, 15 March 1934, p. 187;

Joseph J. Keenan, Jr., "The Poetic of High Georgian Comedy: A Study of the Comic Theory of Murphy, Colman, and Cumberland," Ph.D. dissertation, University of Wisconsin, 1969;

M. J. Landa, "The Grandfather of Melodrama," *Cornhill Magazine*, new series 59 (1925): 476-484;

Louis I. Newman, *Richard Cumberland, Critic and Friend of the Jews* (New York: Block, 1919);

Olaf S. Olsen, "*The Choleric Man:* A Laughing Comedy by Richard Cumberland," Ph.D. dissertation, New York University, 1969;

Regis Ritz, "Le Voyage souterrain dans les tragédies gothiques de Richard Cumberland," *Bulletin de la Société d'Études Anglo-Americaines des XVIIe et XVIIIe Siècles*, 8 (1979): 113-125;

Donald Onis Rogers, "The Comedies of Richard Cumberland," Ph.D. dissertation, University of Southern Louisiana, 1979;

Sybil Rosenfeld, *"Princess of Parma," Times Literary Supplement*, 16 April 1938, p. 264;

G. Barnett Smith, "The English Terence," *Fortnightly Review*, 73 (1900): 243-257;

Wylie Sypher, "The West Indian as a 'Character' in the Eighteenth Century," *Studies in Philology*, 36 (July 1939): 503-520;

Linus Travers, " Nature's Spoilt Children: A World of Extended Innocence in the Comedies of Richard Cumberland," Ph.D. disstertation, Boston University, 1972;

William Van Lennep, *"The Princess of Parma," Times Literary Supplement*, 24 October 1936, p. 863;

Eugene M. Waith, "Richard Cumberland, Comic Force, and Misanthropy," *Comparative Drama*, 12 (Winter 1978-1979): 283-299;

Oskar Wellens, "The London Review, 1809," *Neophilologus*, 69 (July 1985): 452-463;

Stanley T. Williams, "The Dramas of Richard Cumberland, 1779-1785," *Modern Language Notes*, 36 (November 1921): 403-408;

Williams, "The Early Sentimental Dramas of Richarch Cumberland," *Modern Language Notes*, 36 (March 1921): 160-165;

Williams, "The English Sentimental Drama from Steele to Cumberland," *Sewanee Review*, 33 (October 1925): 405-426;

Wiliams, *Richard Cumberland: His Life and Dramatic Works* (New Haven: Yale University Press, 1917);

Williams, "Richard Cumberland's West Indian," *Modern Language Notes*, 35 (November 1920): 413-417;

Frederick T. Woods, "The Beginning and Significance of Sentimental Comedy," *Anglia*, 55 (1931): 368-392;

Elizabeth M. Yearling, "Cumberland, Foote, and the Stage Creole," *Notes and Queries*, 25 (February 1978): 59-61;

Yearling, "Victimes of Society in Three Plays by Cumberland," *Durham University Journal*, 74 (December 1981): 23-30;

Wolfgang Zach, "Richard Cumberland: *The West Indian,*" *Das englische Drama im 18. und 19. Jahrhundert: Interpretationen* (Berlin: Schmidt, 1976).

Papers:

The manuscripts of Cumberland's plays, with one exception, are housed in the Larpent Collection at the Huntington Library. Only the manuscript for the nonproduced *Palamon and Arcite* is in the British Museum. Cumberland's political papers and correspondence are scattered. His writings on his diplomatic work in Spain are in the British Museum. Several letters on the American Revolution are at Princeton University, Princeton, New Jersey, and at the University of Michigan, Ann Arbor.

Samuel Foote

(January 1721-21 October 1777)

Douglas Howard
St. John Fisher College

PLAY PRODUCTIONS: *The Diversions of the Morning* (variously advertised and performed with revisions as *A Dish of Chocolate* and *A Cup of Tea*), London, Little Theatre in the Hay-Market, 22 April 1747;

An Auction of Pictures, London, Little Theatre in the Hay-Market, 18 April 1748;

The Knights, London, Little Theatre in the Hay-Market, 3 April 1749;

Taste, London, Theatre Royal in Drury Lane, 11 January 1752;

The Englishman in Paris, London, Theatre Royal in Covent Garden, 24 March 1753;

A Writ of Inquiry . . . executed on the Inquisitor General by Mr. Foote (lost skit), London, Little Theatre in the Hay-Market, 16 December 1754;

The Englishman Returned from Paris, London, Theatre Royal in Covent Garden, 3 February 1756;

The Green-Room Squabble or a Battle Royal between the Queen of Babylon and the Daughter of Darius (lost skit), London, Little Theatre in the Hay-Market, summer 1756;

The Author, London, Theatre Royal in Drury Lane, 5 February 1757;

Tragedy a-la-Mode, Dublin, Crow-Street Theatre, 4 January 1760; first performed in London as *Modern Tragedy*, Theatre Royal in Drury Lane, 6 April 1761;

The Minor, two-act version: Dublin, Crow-Street Theatre, 28 January 1760; three-act version: London, Little Theatre in the Hay-Market, 28 June 1760;

The Lyar, London, Theatre Royal in Covent Garden, 12 January 1762;

The Orators, London, Little Theatre in the Hay-Market, 28 April 1762;

The Trial of Samuel Foote, Esq. for a Libel on Peter Paragraph, London, Little Theatre in the Hay-Market, 11 May 1763;

The Mayor of Garratt, London, Little Theatre in the Hay-Market, 20 June 1763;

The Patron, London, Little Theatre in the Hay-Market, 26 June 1764;

The Commissary, London, Little Theatre in the Hay-Market, 10 June 1765;

An Occasional Prologue, London, Theatre Royal in the Hay-Market, 29 May 1767;

The Devil upon Two Sticks, London, Theatre Royal in the Hay-Market, 30 May 1768;

Dr. Last in his Chariot, by Isaac Bickerstaff, with scenes by Foote, London, Theatre Royal in the Hay-Market, 21 June 1769;

The Lame Lover, London, Theatre Royal in the Hay-Market, 22 June 1770;

The Maid of Bath, London, Theatre Royal in the Hay-Market, 26 June 1771;

The Nabob, London, Theatre Royal in the Hay-Market, 29 June 1772;

Piety in Pattens, a skit surviving from Foote's *Primitive Puppet Show*, London, Theatre Royal in the Hay-Market, 15 February 1773;

The Bankrupt, London, Theatre Royal in the Hay-Market, 21 July 1773;

The Cozeners, London, Theatre Royal in the Hay-Market, 15 July 1774;

The Capuchin, Foote's revision of his *A Trip to Calais*, for which he had been refused a license, London, Theatre Royal in the Hay-Market, 19 August 1776.

BOOKS: *The genuine Memoirs of the life of Sir John Dinely Goodere, Bart, who was murder'd by the contrivance of his own brother, on board the Ruby Man of War, in King Road near Bristol, Jan. 19, 1740* [OS]. *Together with the Life, history, tryal and last dying words of his brother Capt. Samuel Goodere, who was executed at Bristol on Wednesday the 15th day of April 1741, for the horrid Murder of the said Sir John Dinely Goodere, Bart. Dedicated to the Right Worshipful Henry Combe, Esq. Mayor of Bristol. By S. Foote, of Worcester-*

Samuel Foote, circa 1767 (portrait from the studio of Sir Joshua Reynolds; by permission of the Garrick Club)

College, Oxford, Esq; and Nephew to the late Sir John Dinely Goodere, Bart. (London: Printed & sold by T. Cooper, 1741?);

The Roman and English Comedy Consider'd and Compar'd. With remarks on The Suspicious Husband. And an examen into the Merit of the Present Comic Actors (London: Printed for T. Waller, 1747);

A Treatise on the Passions, so far as they Regard the Stage; with a critical enquiry into the Theatrical Merit of Mr. G–k, Mr. Q–n, and Mr. B–y. The first considered in the part of Lear, the two last opposed in Othello (London: Printed for C. Corbett, 1747);

Taste. A Comedy, Of Two Acts. As it is Acted at the Theatre-Royal in Drury-Lane (London: Printed for R. Francklin, 1752);

The Englishman in Paris. A Comedy in Two Acts. As it is performed at the Theatre-Royal in Covent-Garden (London: Printed for Paul Vaillant, 1753);

The Knights. A Comedy, in Two Acts. As it is Performed At the Theatre-Royal in Drury-Lane (London: Printed for P. Vaillant, 1754);

The Englishman return'd from Paris, Being the Sequel To the Englishman in Paris. A Farce in Two Acts. As it is perform'd at the Theatre-Royal in Covent-Garden (London: Printed for Paul Vaillant, 1756);

The Author; A Comedy of Two Acts. As perform'd at the Theatre Royal in Drury-Lane (London: Printed for R. Francklin & sold by P. Vaillant, 1757);

The Minor, A Comedy. Written by Mr. Foote. As it is now acting at the New Theatre in the Hay-Market. By Authority from the Lord Chamberlain (London: Printed & sold by J. Coote, G. Kearsly, T. Davies, and others, 1760);

A Letter from Mr. Foote, To The Reverend Author Of the Remarks, Critical and Christian, on The Minor (London: Printed for T. Davies, 1760);

The Orators. As it is now performing at the New Theatre in the Hay-Market (London: Printed for J.

Samuel Foote, "Orator and Mimick" (artist unknown)

Coote, G. Kearsly & T. Davies, 1762);

The Comic Theatre. Being a Free Translation of all the Best French Comedies. By Samuel Foote, Esq. and Others, 5 volumes (London: Printed by Dryden Leach for J. Coote, G. Kearsly & S. Crowder, 1762);

The Mayor of Garret. A Comedy, In Two Acts. As it is Performed at the Theatre-Royal in Drury-Lane (London: Printed for P. Vaillant, 1764);

The Lyar. A Comedy in Three Acts. As it is Performed at the Theatre in the Hay-Market (London: Printed for G. Kearsly, 1764);

The Patron. A Comedy in Three Acts. As it is Performed at the Theatre in the Hay-Market (London: Printed for G. Kearsly, 1764);

The Commissary. A Comedy in Three Acts. As it is Performed at the Theatre in the Hay-Market (London: Printed for P. Vaillant, 1765);

Wilkes: An Oratorio. As Performed at The Great Room in Bishopsgate-Street. Written by Mr. Foote. The Music by Signor Carlos Francesco Baritini, authorship uncertain (London: Sold by F. Richards & S. Woodgate, 1769);

The Lame Lover, A Comedy in Three Acts. As it is Performed at the Theatre-Royal in the Hay-Market (London: Printed for Paul Vaillant & sold by P. Elmsly and Robinson & Roberts, 1770);

Apology for the Minor. In a Letter to the Rev. Mr. Baine. To which is added, The original epilogue (Edinburgh: Printed for J. Wood, 1771);

The Maid of Bath, a Comedy in Three Acts, As it is Performed at the Theatre-Royal, in the Haymarket [unauthorized edition] (London: Printed for George Allen, 1771); authorized edition, published by George Colman the Elder (London: Printed by T. Sherlock for T. Cadell, 1778);

The Bankrupt. A Comedy, in Three Acts (London: Printed for G. Kearsly & T. Evans, 1776);

The Devil Upon Two Sticks; A Comedy, in Three Acts. As it is performed at the Theatre-Royal in the Haymarket. Written by the Late Samuel Foote, Esq. and Now Published by Mr. Colman (London: Printed by T. Sherlock for T. Cadell, 1778);

The Nabob; A Comedy, in Three Acts. As it is Performed at the Theatre-Royal in the Haymarket. Written by the Late Samuel Foote, Esq. and Now Published by Mr. Colman (London: Printed by T. Sherlock for T. Cadell, 1778);

The Cozeners; A Comedy, in Three Acts. As it is Performed at the Theatre-Royal in the Haymarket. Written by the Late Samuel Foote, Esq. and Now Published by Mr. Colman (London: Printed by T. Sherlock for T. Cadell, 1778);

A Trip to Calais; A Comedy in Three Acts. As Originally Written, and Intended for Representation, By the late Samuel Foote, Esq. To which is annexed, The Capuchin; as it is performed at the Theatre-Royal in the Haymarket. Altered from the Trip to Calais, by the late Samuel Foote, Esq. and Now Published by Mr. Colman (London: Printed by T. Sherlock for T. Cadell, 1778);

The Second Act of Diversions of the Morning–see under OTHER;

As Acted 1763, At the Hay-Market Theatre. Tragedy a-la-Mode–see under OTHER;

The Trial of Samuel Foote, Esq. for a Libel on Peter Paragraph–see under OTHER;

An Occasional Prologue, Performed at the Opening of the Theatre-Royal in the Haymarket, 1767–see under OTHER;

Samuel Foote's Primitive Puppet-Shew Featuring Piety in Pattens–see under OTHER.

Collections: *The Works of Samuel Foote, Esq.*, 2 volumes (London: G. Robinson, 1799);

The Dramatic Works of Samuel Foote, Esq., to which is prefixed a life of the author, 2 volumes (London: Printed for W. Lowndes & S. Bladon, 1809);

The Works of Samuel Foote, With Remarks on each Play and an Essay on the Life, Genius, and Writings of the Author, edited by John Bee (John Badcock), 3 volumes (London: Sherwood, Gilbert & Piper, 1830);

The Plays of Samuel Foote, 3 volumes, edited by Paula R. Backscheider and Douglas Howard (New York & London: Garland, 1983).

OTHER: *The Second Act of Diversions of the Morning, as Acted at The Theatre-Royal, Drury-Lane, 1758-9*, in *The Wandering Patentee; or, A History of The Yorkshire Theatres, from 1770 to the Present Time*, by Tate Wilkinson, 4 volumes (York: Printed for the author by Wilson, Spence & Mawman, 1795), IV: 237-250;

As Acted 1763, At the Hay-Market Theatre. Tragedy A-La-Mode, Being the Second Act of Mr. Foote's Diversions of the Morning, and Substituted in Lieu of the Former Second Act in his Farce Called Tea. Acted by Mr. Foote and Mr. Wilkinson, in Drury-Lane Theatre, 1758-9, in *The Wandering Patentee*, I: 285-299;

The Trial of Samuel Foote, Esq. for a Libel on Peter Paragraph. Performed at The Theatre-Royal in the Haymarket, 1763. Written by Mr. Foote. Printed from his own Hand-Writing, in *The Wandering Patentee*, IV: 251-260;

An Occasional Prologue, Performed at the Opening of the Theatre-Royal in the Haymarket, 1767. Written by Samuel Foote, Esq., in *The Monthly Mirror*, 17 (January 1804): 44-51;

Samuel Foote's Primitive Puppet-Shew Featuring Piety in Pattens: A Critical Edition, edited by Samuel N. Bogorad and Robert Gale Noyes, in *Theatre Survey*, 14, no. 1a (Fall 1973): 1-129.

Samuel Foote was a mimic and playwright whose caricatures of London life gained him a reputation as the English Aristophanes and the Hogarth of the stage. Sometimes writing two or three parts for himself in a single comedy, Foote regularly played the predatory wit opposite the sorts of dullards he must have despised in real life. A modern purveyor of "old comedy," he mimicked friend and foe alike, and his contemporaries seem to have longed for him to imitate them, even though they feared the result. Acting in his own plays at the theater in the Haymarket, Foote successfully competed with the Drury Lane and Covent Garden patent houses for nearly thirty years. His antics were immensely popular, and many greater literary voices testified to his brilliance. When James Boswell argued that Foote would seem merely foolish in the company of Thomas Betterton, Samuel Johnson disagreed: "Foote, Sir, quatenus Foote," he said, "has powers superior to them all." Even Edward Gibbon considered him a worthy diversion. On being urged by his sister to flee London's tedious and stultifying summer, Gibbon refused, observing that "when I am tired of the Roman Empire I can laugh away the Evening at Foote's Theatre."

Born in Truro, Cornwall, in 1721, Foote was named for his father, an apparently genial man who held several public offices, including Member of Parliament for Tiverton and mayor of Truro. Foote's mother, Eleanor, was the daughter of a baronet, Edward Goodere of Hereford. Like her son, she was short and plump, and even in her seventy-ninth year was said to possess the sharp tongue and quick wit that Foote seems to have inherited. Early biographers emphasized the eccentricity of the Goodere family, whose peculiarities ranged from the harmless to the malevolent. Indeed, Foote's first published work was a pamphlet describing the murder of one of his maternal uncles by another. At Oxford, Foote seems to have been an irrepressible prankster, and he left Worcester College in 1740 without taking a degree. He dabbled in law at the Inner Temple, but as was his habit, he never applied himself seriously so long as he had ready cash to spend on the more pleasurable pursuit of being a bon vivant.

Soon weighed down by debt, Foote took the expedient of marriage to Mary Hickes, a former neighbor from Truro, on 10 January 1741. She came to him with a dowry that he promptly squandered. Contemporary accounts suggest that he treated his wife badly, even deserting her when his financial situation became less precarious. Mary Hickes appears to have died prematurely, and though she and Foote had no children, he did have two natural sons by a mistress, both of whom were provided for in his will. On the whole, however, his reactions to women were characterized by extremes of effusiveness and debasement, a fact which later helped fuel allegations that Foote was homosexual. In any case, Foote's marriage kept him out of debt only temporarily, and he eventually resorted to acting as a means of support. His wit had made him numerous wealthy and aristocratic friends who encouraged him to turn his talents in the direction of the theater.

Foote's initial appearance on the London stage was an unlikely one. He played Othello to Charles Macklin's Iago at the Haymarket, and Macklin himself observed that "neither his figure, voice, nor manners, corresponded with the character." Critics and biographers are no doubt correct in asserting that tragedy was simply an inappropriate vehicle for Foote's gift of mimicry. It is worth remembering, however, that this *Othello* was Foote's acting debut, and as a novice he might have stumbled even in comedy. Furthermore, given the vanity of Macklin, who was Foote's tutor as well as fellow actor, it is possible that Macklin's assessment of Foote's performance was less than generous. In any case Foote did act the part several more times, including a benefit at Drury Lane.

More significant than Foote's actual performance in *Othello* was the fact that Macklin's production, like Foote's later managerial efforts, was intended to evade the Licensing Act. Advertisements maintained that tickets were available gratis and that Shakespeare's play would be performed "by a set of Gentlemen for their own Diversion." This attempt to justify unauthorized competition with the patent houses anticipated Foote's similar ruse, beginning with *The Diversions of the Morning* in 1747. Macklin's lessons in oratory and elocution may have been superfluous in light of Foote's natural gifts, but this initial experience at the Haymarket clearly prepared Foote to follow in the steps of Theophilus Cibber and William Gifford as a successful evader of the Licensing Act and a plague upon the managers of Covent Garden and Drury Lane.

Foote's career as a comic actor seems to have been launched at the Smock Alley Theatre in Dublin during the 1744-1745 season. Upon his return to Drury Lane, on 1 November 1745, he played a series of comic parts, the majority of which he must have acted during the previous season in Dublin. These included Sir Harry Wildair in George Farquhar's *The Constant Couple*, Lord Foppington in Sir John Vanbrugh's *The Relapse*, and most significant, Bayes in George Villiers, duke of Buckingham's popular burlesque, *The Rehearsal*. This last part, in which Foote continued David Garrick's tradition of improvisation and mimicry, proved an enduring vehicle for the future playwright. He appears to have delighted audiences by his mocking portrayal, or "taking off," of his contemporaries. The part was suggestive of the direction Foote's own dramatic efforts would take, and it was one to which he returned in the final years of his career, playing it to great acclaim at the Haymarket from 1772 to 1776.

In spite of his inroads at Drury Lane, Foote was not in demand as an actor during these early years, and it is doubtful that any amount of work could have financed his ostentatious life-style. Whether the mercurial Foote despaired over his lack of success is uncertain, but a letter from Garrick, dated 18 August 1746, says, perhaps in jest, that Foote "has renounced the Stage for Ever." In any case the nascent dramatist momentarily turned his attention to theatrical criticism, producing two unremarkable essays, *A Treatise on the Passions* and *The Roman and English Comedy Consider'd and Compar'd*, both published early in 1747. Although these offer nothing new in a scholarly vein, the latter is of interest to theater historians because of Foote's extended, if irrelevant, comparison of the acting styles of Garrick and Colley Cibber.

By December 1746 Foote was again acting at the Haymarket, but this time he followed Macklin's example by renting the house and organizing his own theatrical troupe. In defiance of the patent theaters, he not only performed *Othello* once more, but on 22 April 1747, offered the first entertainment of his own devising, *The Diversions of the Morning; or, A Dish of Chocolate*. In a variation on the transparent ruse of advertising a musical concert with a play included gratis, Foote proceeded to advertise his new entertainment along with a farce called *The Credulous Husband*, which consisted of scenes from Congreve's *The Old Bachelor*. On the day after his *Diversions of the Morning* opened, however, the authorities locked the theater and turned the audience away, probably at the instigation of one of the owners of Drury Lane.

Having sampled Foote's abilities as a mimic in his Drury Lane stint as Bayes in *The Rehearsal*, actors at the patent houses had reason to fear his satiric jabs. Whether they dreaded ridicule or were merely annoyed at Foote's pilfering from the standard repertoire, the actors at the patent theaters were undoubtedly behind the effort to stop Foote's Haymarket venture. Foote was equally determined to stay open, and apparently with the help of well-placed friends (who would have occasion to rescue him more than once), the fledgling playwright was allowed to continue his *Diversions of the Morning*, so long as no direct infringement on the rights of the patent theaters was observable. The compromise, as Foote's notice in *The Daily Advertiser* for 24 April made clear, was to move his *Diversions of the Morning* to midday, on pretense of his audience's drinking "a dish of chocolate" with the author. No such dish was ever served, of course, nor was the similarly fictitious "dish of tea" offered by Foote on 1 June 1747, when he once more risked treading on the wary toes of the patent houses by moving his entertainment to half-past-six in the evening.

Foote's *Cup of Tea* continued his unparalleled success in drawing audiences to the Haymarket. His own makeshift company had given thirty-five performances by 6 June 1747, and Foote took his entertainment to Drury Lane at the end of the year. The precise content of these early performances is impossible to discern, even though two versions of the second act of Foote's *Diversions* are extant. The first of these was printed by Tate Wilkinson in *The Wandering Patentee* and represents the second act as performed at Drury Lane in 1758-1759. The second version of act 2 of *Diversions*, also printed by Wilkinson, was called *Tragedy a-la-Mode; or Lindamira in Tears* and was acted at the Haymarket in 1763. Foote's medium was a fluid one and his jests highly topical, but these two printed texts give a general idea of Foote's early technique. Each is a variation on the *Rehearsal* format, and each was probably accompanied in performance by a more topical piece in which Foote satirized contemporary events and individuals.

Foote celebrated his success by disappearing from the theatrical scene, probably to spend his

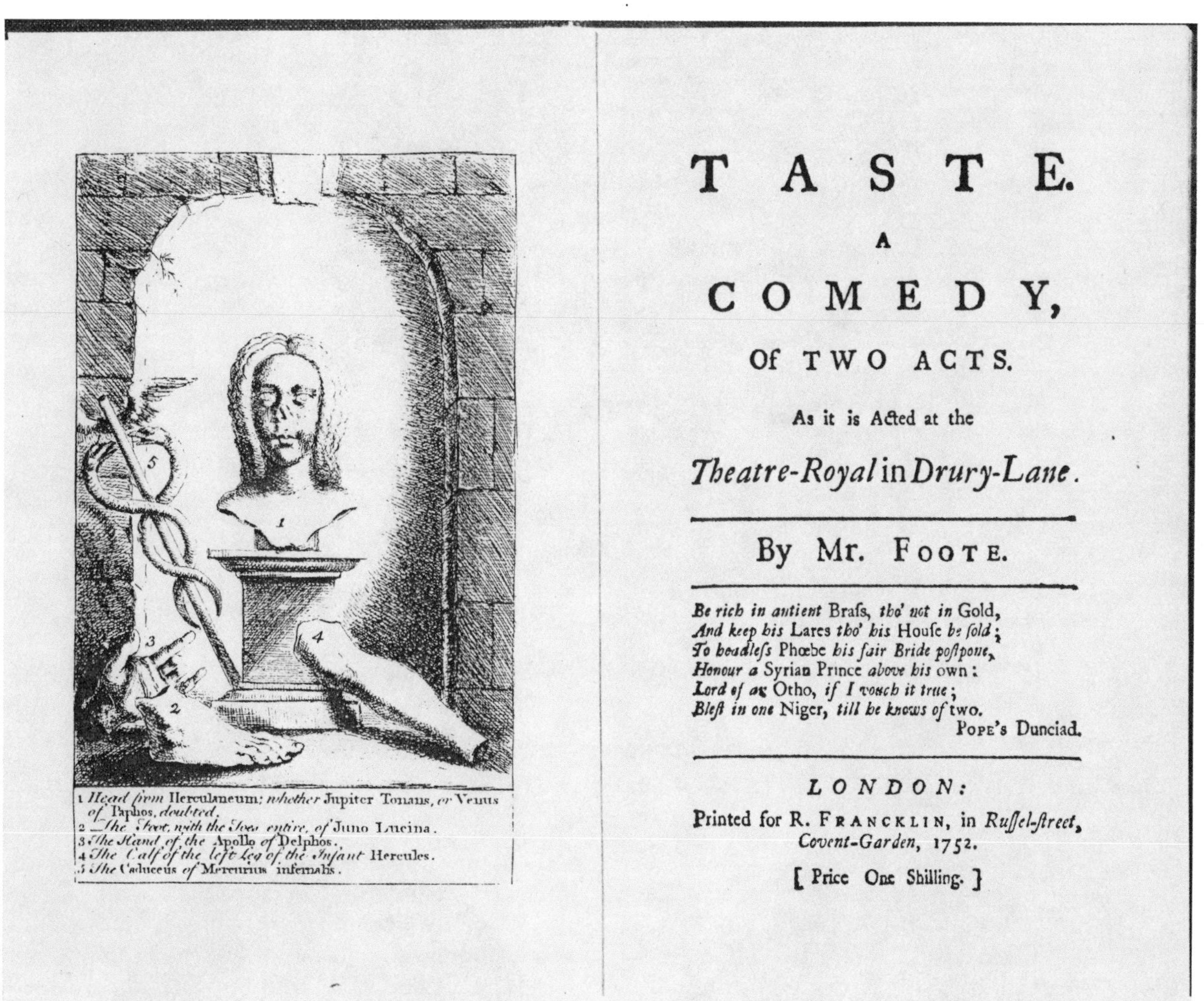

TASTE.

A

COMEDY,

Of TWO ACTS.

As it is Acted at the

Theatre-Royal in *Drury-Lane*.

By Mr. FOOTE.

Be rich in antient Brass, *tho' not in* Gold,
And keep his Lares *tho' his* House *be sold*;
To headless Phœbe *his fair Bride postpone*,
Honour a Syrian Prince *above his* own:
Lord of an Otho, *if I vouch it true*;
Blest in one Niger, *till he knows of* two.
POPE's Dunciad.

LONDON:

Printed for R. FRANCKLIN, in *Russel-street*, *Covent-Garden*, 1752.

[Price One Shilling.]

Frontispiece and title page for Foote's satire on would-be antiquarians

profits vacationing in France. He did not return until 4 November 1747, when he again performed his *Cup of Tea* at the Haymarket and then as an afterpiece at Covent Garden. Interest in his satiric jabs had begun to wane, however, and early 1748 found Foote in Dublin once more. His next appearance at the Haymarket was on 18 April 1748 with *An Auction of Pictures*, in which he offered a satiric portrait of Henry Fielding, among others. The result was a small theatrical war in which Foote and Fielding fought skirmishes in print as well as on the stage. In addition to offering a puppet show in regular competition with Foote's Haymarket fare, Fielding lambasted him in *The Jacobite's Journal*, entering the judgment that "you *Samuel Fut* be p-ssed upon, with Scorn and Contempt, as a low Buffoon; and I do, with the utmost Scorn and Contempt, p-ss upon you accordingly."

The quarrel with Fielding was followed the next year by an even more heated one with the actor Henry Woodward, which resulted in a small riot that seriously damaged the Haymarket. Foote's attention was eventually deflected by his work on *The Knights*, his first real play. Unlike his earlier mixtures of adaptation and mimicry, *The Knights* was a comic love intrigue with a country setting. It was still the occasion for satire, however, including targets so unlikely as Italian opera and the gentry of Cornwall. Foote opened *The Knights* at the Haymarket on 3 April 1749, and by 1 June it had received twenty performances.

With the end of the Haymarket season, Foote again left the stage, apparently to spend money he had recently inherited. He did not return until his production of *Taste*, which was first performed at Drury Lane on 11 January 1752. Continuing the direction toward full-blown comedy that he had begun with *The Knights*, Foote wrote *Taste* as a sat-

"Buck Metamorphos'd or Mr. Foote," Foote (at left) in a scene from The Englishman Returned from Paris *(drawn and engraved by G. Smith)*

George Anne Bellamy and Peg Woffington, the actresses whose feuding on and off the stage was the subject of Foote's lost skit The Green-Room Squabble *(portrait of Woffington: Jones Bequest, Victoria and Albert Museum)*

ire on the burgeoning antiquarian trade. The play ridicules those who unthinkingly prefer the ancient and exotic over the modern and familiar. The frontispiece to the first edition illustrates the range of "ancient" artifacts by means of which would-be connoisseurs were duped. Chief among the gullible collectors is Lady Pentweazel, whose nouveau-riche pretensions were acted to great acclaim by the comedian Jeremy Worsdale. Only the first act of *Taste* seems to have had enduring appeal, however, and later performances often substituted a burlesque ultimately deriving from Foote's successful formula in *Diversions of the Morning*.

After the production of *Taste*, Foote again took to travel and did not return to the stage until 24 March 1753, for the opening of *The Englishman in Paris* at Covent Garden. Having mocked the aesthetic pretensions of his countrymen in *Taste*, Foote turned in his new play to the doltishness they exhibited in travels abroad. Although the play remained in the Drury Lane and Covent Garden repertoires for more than two decades, its satire is weighty and didactic compared with Foote's more mature efforts. Foote himself, who followed Macklin in the role of Buck, seems to have tired of the part by the end of the next season and rarely performed it afterward. Perhaps Foote saw the inadequate characterization of his rowdy Englishman. The title role of Buck presents an oddly contradictory individual, at once generous and gullible, courageous and rash. To link these opposites required deftness and range of the sort that Farquhar and Richard Brinsley Sheridan possessed but that Foote did not. As Simon Trefman observes, "Foote was a master of the many tongues of roguery, but knew only one heavy monotone for virtue."

The 1753-1754 season found Foote back at Drury Lane acting a variety of parts, including numerous, widely acclaimed performances as Buck in *The Englishman in Paris*. By February, however, he was back at Covent Garden, where he also returned for the next season. Foote acted few parts and offered no new plays in the 1754-1755 season, and by 12 November 1754 he was out of work. Never at a loss for ingenious ways to lure the public, however, Foote rented the Haymarket in order to give mock lectures ridiculing Macklin's recently opened school of oratory. The result was just the sort of theatrical war that seems to have bolstered Foote's career whenever its demise seemed imminent. Audiences for Foote's "lectures" were large, and Macklin himself added to their success by appearing in person and being subjected to further ridicule.

During the summer of 1755, Foote encouraged Arthur Murphy in the latter's plan to write a sequel to *The Englishman in Paris*. Inspired by Murphy's idea, however, Foote secretly wrote his own sequel, *The Englishman Returned from Paris*, which opened at Covent Garden on 3 February 1756, two months before Murphy's play. Early biographers insisted that Foote plagiarized wholesale from Murphy's work, but the discovery of Murphy's *Englishman from Paris* in the Newberry Library, and its publication in 1969 by the Augustan Reprint Society, put such accusations to rest. Foote was certainly duplicitous in simultaneously encouraging and competing with Murphy, but he did not steal Murphy's material, and his own play is clearly superior. In fact, Foote's foppish Buck and wily Lucinda were more successful in this play than in the original. *The Englishman Returned* saw nineteen performances by the end of its first season, and it was acted regularly at Covent Garden until 1760.

Foote occupied himself during the summer of 1756 by dramatizing a widely publicized feud between Peg Woffington and George Anne Bellamy. The two actresses had apparently taken to heart their competing roles in Nathaniel Lee's *The Rival Queens*, and a quarrel over one of Bellamy's sumptuous Parisian gowns ended with Woffington driving her from the stage with a wooden dagger. The text of Foote's Haymarket farce on the subject does not survive, but he called it *The Green-Room Squabble or a Battle Royal between the Queen of Babylon and the Daughter of Darius*.

On 5 February 1757, Foote's new play *The Author* opened at Drury Lane and was widely praised. The plot, one Sheridan was to adapt in *School for Scandal* (1777), involves a father who is presumed dead and who disguises himself in order to spy on his son, the impoverished author of the play's title. In addition to having a thoroughly worked out comic plot, *The Author* provided an appealing vehicle for Foote's own talents as a mimic. The ostensibly secondary part of Cadwallader was a satiric portrait of the boisterous John Apreece (or ApRice), whose vanity had led him to encourage Foote to portray him on the stage. Foote drew large audiences as Cadwallader, even though some critics objected to the blatantly ad hominem attack on Apreece. Although Foote's talent for mimicry insured the success of *The Author*, the play also showed that Foote could build character and sustain plot, skills that he had begun to manifest in

Foote as Mother Cole (left) and as Shift imitating Dr. Squintum (right) in the play whose satire on evangelist George Whitefield angered his Methodist admirers

his previous play, *The Englishman Returned.*

Foote began the 1757-1758 season at Drury Lane, but the terms of his agreement with Garrick included plans for a two-month stint in Dublin with Thomas Sheridan's company. In October, therefore, Foote set sail for Dublin with the young Tate Wilkinson, whose talents as a mimic Foote promoted, only to have Wilkinson win acclaim in a devastatingly accurate imitation of Foote himself. Upon his return to London in January, Foote took up the part of Cadwallader again, but Apreece objected so vociferously that Garrick did not offer the play after the 1 February performance. Foote was thus out of work at mid season again, though he seems to have had the financial resources to survive until the beginning of the 1758-1759 season. By autumn, however, he still had no regular contract with either patent house and no new play to offer. Wilkinson, whose career was temporarily linked to Foote's, found himself in similar straits, and the two were rescued only by the unexpected departure of Woodward and several of his friends for Ireland. Woodward had quarreled with Garrick, and Foote used the breach to negotiate an agreement that stipulated employment for Wilkinson as well.

The season began well for Foote, as Garrick agreed to a revival of *Diversions of the Morning*, beginning on 17 October, with Foote as Puzzle and Wilkinson as Bounce. Foote no doubt expected to use the elastic material of *Diversions* as a vehicle for his own and Wilkinson's imitations, but other members of the Drury Lane company persuaded Garrick to insist that they be exempted from being "taken off." Foote and Wilkinson agreed to the exemption, but the audience cried out for the newcomer Wilkinson's imitations, and in order to appease the crowd, Garrick was forced to relent. Despite persistent objections from the other actors, subsequent performances of *Diversions of the Morning* that season were dominated by Wilkinson's imitations of everyone from Isaac Sparks and Spranger Barry to Foote and Garrick. All this delighted Foote, of course, because he was reaping the profits from Wilkinson's sudden success.

Wilkinson's success was a stroke of badly needed luck for Foote, since he had written nothing new since *The Author*, and since *Diversions of the Morning* was given new life only as a vehicle for Wilkinson's fresh talent. Foote's luck seemed to be running out by mid season, however, as he planned his benefit for 18 December. He intended to begin the evening by playing Shylock in *The Merchant of Venice* and to finish by reviving *The Author* with a new scene for Wilkinson. On the day of the performance, however, Apreece managed to persuade the lord chamberlain to forbid the performance of the play, and Foote had no choice but to substitute his well-worn *Diversions of the Morning*.

Penniless and without employment in London, Foote resorted to his usual emergency measure of seeking a contract elsewhere. Instead of Dublin, however, Foote this time chose the unlikely venue of Edinburgh. On 15 March 1759, he presented *The Author*, which he had been unable to stage in London; performances of *Diversions of the Morning* and *The Englishman Returned* followed, along with Foote in his usual repertoire of parts, including Bayes in *The Rehearsal*.

By the end of April, Foote was back in London, apparently having made enough money to keep himself afloat until the beginning of the 1759-1760 season. Lacking a contract with either major theater, however, Foote again left town, this time for Barry and Woodward's Crow-Street Theatre in Dublin. Foote may have acted briefly with Barry and Woodward, but by 9 November 1759 he was back at the Haymarket. Unable to draw an audience there, Foote returned to Dublin, but by this time Garrick had sent Wilkinson to Barry and Woodward's competitors at Smock Alley. Wilkinson's mimicking of Foote drew large houses, and the direct competition made an already bad season worse for Foote. His new play, the original two-act version of *The Minor*, opened at the Crow-Street Theatre on 28 January 1760, but the production was a failure, and by mid February Foote had left Ireland.

Back in London, Foote was still in serious financial trouble, though his lively conversation made him new friends, including Laurence Sterne, who was in London enjoying the success of the first two volumes of *Tristram Shandy*. Desperate for money, Foote decided to offer *The Minor* as summer fare at the Haymarket. Even Foote must have known that the prospects for success were not good. The play had already failed in Dublin, and Foote was mounting it again with a much less experienced cast. Working against the odds, however, Foote revised the play into the extant three-act version and, as if to ensure its success, chose to play the parts of Shift and Mother Cole himself. Foote's work on the Haymarket production of *The Minor* paid off handsomely, for the play opened on 28 June 1760 and was an instant success. It had a remarkable run of thirty-five performances and resulted in Garrick's engaging Foote to play *The Minor* at Drury Lane during the 1760-1761 season.

The Minor is an interesting example of Foote's gifts and limitations as a playwright. Like *The Author*, it is held together by an unremarkable plot involving a profligate though good-hearted son and his reclamation through the efforts of a disguised father. To this main plot, Foote added the two ingredients that usually accounted for his theatrical successes. First, he chose an object of satire that would create immediate controversy, in this case the well-known Methodist preacher George Whitefield. Second, he provided a vehicle for his own imitative skills, in this case the parts of Mother Cole and Shift. Though Foote does not bring Whitefield, alias Mr. Squintum, onstage, he does allow Shift to imitate him in the epilogue. Further jabs at the itinerant preacher are taken in the part of Mother Cole, whose portrait Foote drew in the likeness of a notorious London bawd, Mother Jennie Douglas. Foote's Mother Cole is an enthusiastic convert to Methodism and constant espouser of Whitefield's pieties. In addition to delighting audiences with his transvestism and mimicry, Foote fueled the controversy caused by the play in a paper war with defenders of Methodism.

The string of objections to *The Minor* no doubt increased its popularity, but the furor eventually worked against Foote. Prior to the play's Drury Lane opening in the fall of 1760, serious efforts were underway to have it suppressed. Selina Hastings, countess of Huntington, Whitefield's patroness, intervened on his behalf, first with the lord chamberlain and then with the archbishop of Canterbury. The lord chamberlain, who had already licensed the play, initially seemed unwilling to require major alterations, but the death of George II on 25 October, the day *The Minor* was to have

THE MINOR. 41

LOADER.

What, and bilk thee of thy ſhare?

Mrs. COLE.

Ah, don't mention it, Mr. Loader. No, that's all over with me. The time has been, when I could have earn'd thirty ſhillings a day by own dry drinking, and the next morning was neither ſick nor ſorry: But now, O laud, a thimbleful turns me topſy turvey.

LOADER.

Poor old girl!

Mrs. COLE.

Ay, I have done with theſe idle vanities; my thoughts are fix'd upon a better place. What, I ſuppoſe, Mr. Loader, you will be for your old friend the black-ey'd girl, from Roſemary-Lane. Ha, ha. Well, 'tis a merry little tit. A thouſand pities ſhe's ſuch a reprobate!——But ſhe'll mend; ~~her time is not come; all ſhall have their call, as Mr. Squintum ſays, ſooner or later; regeneration is not the work of a day. No, no, no.~~——Oh!

Sir GEORGE.

Not worſe, I hope.

Mrs. COLE.

Rack, rack, gnaw, gnaw, never eaſy, a bed or up, all's one. Pray, honeſt friend, have you any clary, or mint water in the houſe?

DICK.

A caſe of French drams.

G Mrs. COLE.

Page from the copy of the third edition of The Minor *submitted for licensing prior to a Drury Lane revival of the play on 22 November 1760. This copy contains corrections by David Garrick and passages marked for deletion by the Examiner of Plays (Larpent Collection, LA 177; by permission of the Henry E. Huntington Library and Art Gallery).*

[20] W: I shall curb your ~~imp~~ impertinence ~~but since~~
the Story is got abroad, I will my Dear Freind
treat you with all the particulars
S.J.: I shall hear it with pleasure ~~h~~ this is a
lucky adventure but he must not know he
is my Rival
W: Why Sir between Six and Seven my Goddess
embark'd at Somerset Stairs in one of
the Companys Barges gilt and hung with
Damask expressly for the Occasion
P: Mercy on us
W At the Cabbin Door she was accosted
by a beautiful Boy who in the Garb of a
Cupid paid her some Complements in
~~Verse~~ of my own composeing the conceits
were pretty allusions to Venus and the
Sea the Lady and the Thames, no great
matter but however well timed and what
was better well taken
S.J. Doubtless
P At what a rate he runs
W: As soon as we had gaind the Center
of the River two Boats full of Trumpets
French Horns and other Marshal Music
struck up their spritely Strains from the
Surry side, which were echoed by a
suitable number of lutes flutes & Hautboys
from the opposite shore in this state
the Oars keeping time we majestically saild
along till the Arches of the new Bridge gave
a pause and an oportunity for an Elegant

Page from act 1, in Foote's hand, of the copy of The Lyar *that was submitted to the Examiner of Plays for licensing prior to the first performance, on 12 January 1762 (Larpent Collection, LA 200; by permission of the Henry E. Huntington Library and Art Gallery)*

Robert Baddeley as Sir Jacob Jollop and Samuel Foote as Major Sturgeon in a late 1763 production of The Mayor of Garratt *(engraving by J. G. Haid, based on a painting by Johann Zoffany)*

opened at Drury Lane, gave Whitefield's supporters three weeks in which to pursue their case. As a result, the lord chamberlain was persuaded to forbid many of the play's satiric thrusts, including Shift's "taking off" of Whitefield in the epilogue. By the time the newly expurgated version of *The Minor* opened at Drury Lane on 22 November, however, Foote's play had already gone through several printed editions, all of which represent the earlier version of the play. In fact, a copy of the third edition, with corrections in Garrick's hand and with passages marked by the examiner for omission, was submitted for licensing prior to the Drury Lane opening. This corrected copy of *The Minor*, marked by Garrick and the censor, is among the Larpent manuscripts in the Huntington Library.

Following the success of *The Minor* in the regular season, Foote sought to rent the Haymarket for the summer of 1761, but found that he was too late. As an alternative, he joined Murphy in an arrangement whereby they rented Drury Lane from Garrick and promised to provide three new plays each, all of which Garrick would have the option of producing in the regular season. Murphy was quite prolific and met his end of the bargain, but Foote was unable to turn out a single play. In fact, his next work, *The Lyar*, was not ready until fall, and he arranged for Rich to produce it at Covent Garden, where it opened on 12 January 1762. This play is an exception to the usual pattern of Foote's work, since it was not particularly topical and offered him no successful vehicle as an actor. The story involves the London adventures of a mendacious hero, Young Wilding, and Foote's prologue alleges that it is based on Lope de Vega. As Mary Megie Belden has pointed out, however, the play actually derives from Corneille's *Le Menteur* (1643), to which Sir Richard Steele had also turned for his play *The Lying Lover*. Although Foote had little success in the title role at Covent Garden, the play held the stage longer than any other of his works. Among revivals of *The Lyar* was one at the Olympic Theatre in 1879 that played more than a hundred performances.

In his next play, *The Orators*, Foote returned to his usual method of creating a vehicle for mimicry and satiric comment on the issues of the day. The play is a loose amalgam of mock lecture and trial followed by a skit satirizing the Robin Hood Society, an amateur debating club. First billed as a "Course of Comic Lectures on English Oratory,"

Samuel Foote (engraving by Brookshaw, based on a 1765 portrait by Cotes)

Foote's play recalls his earlier jabs at Macklin, but this time his target was Thomas Sheridan, who had begun a series of lectures on oratory. *The Orators* opened at the Haymarket on 28 April 1762, and its success as summer fare rivaled that of *The Minor* two years earlier. The loose construction of the play allowed fairly regular variation in its content. One such variation, *The Trial of Samuel Foote, Esq. for a Libel on Peter Paragraph*, performed on 11 May 1763, was subsequently printed.

Following the poor showing of *The Lyar* during the previous season at Drury Lane, *The Orators* must have convinced Foote that his best venue, both artistically and financially, was the Haymarket. Except for a handful of performances at Drury Lane the next season, and an occasional performance in Scotland or Ireland, Foote was to remain at the Haymarket, playing exclusively in the summer months, until the end of his career in 1776.

In preparation for the 1763 season at the Haymarket, Foote managed to reingratiate himself with Wilkinson, whom he hired to play Shift in *The Minor*. Through Wilkinson he also acquired the services of Thomas Weston, who was to play the role of Jerry Sneak in Foote's new play, *The Mayor of Garratt*. The play treats an historical event, a mock election held periodically in the hamlet of Garratt in Surrey. Its satire on political corruption, military incompetence, and wedded misery produced an enduring and accessible play. There are satiric portraits of Thomas Pelham-Holles, duke of Newcastle and Thomas Sheridan, among others, but the strokes of satire are generally broader, as when Crispin Heel-Tap commands the electorate to proceed "with all the decency and confusion usual upon these occasions." Originally presented as an afterpiece to *The Minor*, Foote's *The Mayor of Garratt* opened on 20 June 1763 to great acclaim. It was acted twenty-four consecutive times, ended the season with a total of thirty-six performances, and went on to become Foote's most popular play.

Foote left for Paris after the summer season, but he was back playing *The Mayor of Garratt* at Drury Lane on 30 November 1763. These performances, ending on 9 December, marked Foote's last appearance at either of the major London theaters. Beginning with the summer season at the Haymarket in 1764, his energy was devoted to the Little Theatre there, where he had offered plays and entertainments intermittently for nearly two decades, since his first *Cup of Tea* in 1747. Foote's meticulous planning for the 1764 season included preparation of his new play, *The Patron*, a three-act comedy based on Jean-François Marmontel's story "Le Connaisseur," from his *Contes moraux* (1761), which Foote followed quite closely. *The Patron* ran for seventeen performances, an indication of moderate enthusiasm, and the season as a whole was a successful one for Foote.

By the summer season of 1765, Foote had begun to make adjustments in his company that suggest a manager tinkering with an essentially successful arrangement. He reduced the number of actors from thirty to nineteen while increasing the number of performances from forty-three to fifty-three. Foote's new offering for the season was *The Commissary*, a three-act comedy about a military supplier and would-be gentleman, Zachary Fungus. The general satiric target suggested by the title was commissaries who had amassed large fortunes during the Seven Years' War and were now returned from France to find a niche for themselves. The social pretensions of Zachary Fungus required a wife with an appropriate pedigree, and much of Foote's satire is directed at Mrs. Mechlin, the bawd and marriage broker who bilks the gullible commissary. The play was popular and saw more than one hundred performances by the end of Foote's Haymarket career in 1776.

Foote had enjoyed four lucrative summer seasons at the Haymarket, and the end of the 1765 season found him keeping company with the aristocratic friends into whose circle his theatrical success had brought him. Unfortunately, a visit to Lord and Lady Mexborough in nearby Hampshire ended in an accident that nearly cost Foote his life. On a dare, Foote attempted to ride a temperamental horse belonging to the duke of York. No skilled horseman, he was promptly thrown and suffered a compound fracture of the lower leg. Amputation above the knee was the only remedy, and though he survived the ordeal, Foote seemed to think his career was at an end.

Never one to be undone by misfortune, Foote soon recovered his good spirits as well as his health. Within a few weeks of the accident, which occurred on 3 February 1766, Foote had turned the gruesome event to his own advantage. Long desirous of a royal patent for the Haymarket theater, Foote used the incident and the duke of York's distress over his involvement in it as means to the end of securing a patent. To the duke's offers of assistance, Foote replied that a patent right to the theater in the Haymarket during his lifetime would relieve his sole remaining distress, poverty. The duke's intervention led to the bestowing of a royal patent on 5 July 1766. Much to Foote's dismay, however, the grant restricted his Haymarket performances to the summer season, from 15 May through 15 September. Since Foote had specifically complained of his inability to compete with the existing patent houses, the limitation naturally came as a bitter disappointment. Moreover, Foote could not help but suspect Garrick of double-dealing in the whole matter, publicly supporting Foote's right to a competing enterprise, but privately seeking the seasonal limitation that the lord chamberlain finally authorized.

Foote's unhappiness with the terms of the patent did not keep him from setting about to plan the next summer season at the Haymarket. Aided by a wooden leg and a gold-headed crutched cane, Foote managed to perform twenty-eight times during the summer of 1766. His roles included Mother Cole in *The Minor* and Zachary Fungus in *The Commissary*, both of which parts allowed him to mock his own infirmity. Mother Cole limps because of her "rheumatism," and Fungus subjects himself to a riding lesson in which he falls off a wooden horse. Contemporary accounts suggest that Foote's stage antics masked the pain and anger he felt at his misfortune, but his return to the Haymarket was nothing less than a triumph, both personally and professionally.

In preparation for the 1767 season under his new patent, Foote bought the theater at the Haymarket and set about refurbishing it. He also purchased an adjacent house in order to have additional costume storage, a green room, and living quarters for himself. Busying himself with these efforts, Foote wrote no new play for the season,

Foote in one of the parts he created for himself after a riding accident forced the amputation of one of his legs

though he did offer an immensely popular *Occasional Prologue* (or *Occasional Prelude*, as it is sometimes called) to celebrate the newly equipped Haymarket. The only new play was *The Tailors*, sometimes attributed to Foote in spite of his insistence that it was not his own. Even though he hired Spranger Barry and Ann Dancer to stifle competition from the Opera house, Foote's season was less than spectacular. The Haymarket saw fifty-eight performances that summer, but Foote's own contribution included only twenty-five appearances in mainpieces and fifteen in afterpieces.

Undaunted by a lackluster season, Foote made preparations for the summer of 1768 with his usual gusto. Barry and Dancer were gone, but Foote retained the superior core of comic actors he had put together the previous season. These included not only Weston but Edward Shuter, Charles Bannister, and John Palmer. Foote's new vehicle for himself was *The Devil upon Two Sticks*, a satire based on an English translation of Alain-René Lesage's *Le Diable boiteux* (1707). A parody of sentimental love plots, the play involves the efforts of Harriet, a young woman of means, to circumvent her authoritarian father and marry the man of her choice, a clerk named Invoice. In their flight from Madrid, where the play begins, the couple finds a lame devil in a bottle who agrees to transport them to England. The devil's effort to reacquaint them with their native land becomes the occasion for Foote's witty assessment of the various professions they might choose to follow. Medicine is the chief object of satire, and Foote devotes the last two acts almost entirely to a parody of the current dispute between the Licentiate and the Royal College of Physicians over voting privileges in the college. The play was an immense success and very profitable for Foote. He wrote his own infirmity into the part of the lame devil, and he addressed enough topical matters to allow improvisation in the lines he spoke. As is so often the case with Foote's work, the printed version does not reflect the immensely fluid medium in which he performed.

With the close of the 1768 Haymarket season, Foote took a respite at Bath. The waters may have been good for his health, but Foote also used the vacation to gamble away all his available cash. This might have spelled disaster had he not already contracted to play *The Devil upon Two Sticks* in Ireland. Foote repeated his London success in the title role, and with the proceeds he spent time in Paris before returning to London in February 1769. The following summer brought no new plays, but Foote had a successful season nonetheless. This was the year of Garrick's attempt at a Jubilee in honor of Shakespeare, and though Foote spent much time satirizing it as an instance of Garrick's self-promotion, he himself hired Thomas Sheridan to act in a series of Shakespeare plays at the end of the 1769 Haymarket season.

For the 1770 summer season, Foote wrote *The Lame Lover*, a satire on the legal profession. The attack on lawyers was too arcane to generate real enthusiasm, but Foote was well received in the part of Luke Limp. Widely recognized as a portrait of John Skrimshire Boothby, Luke is a social climber preoccupied with establishing aristocratic connections for himself. *The Lame Lover* was acted only fifteen times by summer's end, and Foote rarely offered it afterward.

In August 1770, Foote set about plans to lease the Edinburgh Theatre during the winter season. No major London actor had been to Scotland since Foote's own trip a decade before, but the Haymarket actors made a success of Foote's venture. "We have been kept laughing all this winter by Foote," Boswell wrote to Garrick, but though Foote had a three-year lease, he did not choose to make the difficult trip to Scotland for a second season.

Foote's new comedy for the next season at the Haymarket was *The Maid of Bath*. The play is highly topical and was eagerly awaited by the London audience. It is the story of Kitty Linnet, a beautiful young woman whose parents insist on marrying her to the aging but wealthy Solomon Flint. As usual, Foote's dramatic situations reflected contemporary events, in this instance the case of Elizabeth Linley, an actual maid of Bath whose parents attempted a forced match of their daughter with Sir Walter Long, a man old enough to be her grandfather. *The Maid of Bath*, which opened on 26 June 1771, was an immediate critical and popular success. Its favorable reception was largely attributable to the cause célèbre on which Foote drew, and not on the quality of the play itself. Untouched by the scandal it reports, modern readers find it less remarkable than did Foote's original audience.

The end of the Haymarket season was marred for Foote by the death of his most abiding friend, Sir Francis Delaval. Though not one to maintain friendships easily, Foote had been remarkably intimate with Delaval for twenty-five years. Foote provided evidence of his attachment by taking his friend's illegitimate son under his wing. Foote's generosity could hardly keep pace with the youth's extravagance, however, and Foote spent large sums of money to keep Delaval *fils* from imprisonment for debt.

For the 1772 season, Foote incurred additional expenses by further remodeling the Haymarket and hiring eleven more players than the previous year. Foote's company now numbered fifty-one, and its summer fare included fifty-six performances. Foote himself, his wooden leg having become a part of the show instead of an impediment, acted in fifty-two mainpieces and twelve afterpieces. Foote's new play, *The Nabob*, satirized unscrupulous individuals who had made large fortunes in India and then returned to England, where they sustained their wealth and position by the same corrupt means. One such nabob, Lord Robert Clive, had in fact been investigated by Parliament, and was thus a celebrated case. The plot of the play in some sense reverses the situation of *The Maid of Bath*, as young Sophy Oldham tries to save her family from debt by offering to marry their creditor, Sir Matthew Mite, a nabob just returned from India. A generous uncle finally saves the day, and the sentimental plot concludes with Sophy's marriage to her cousin.

The Nabob was a great success, but Foote was troubled by the fact that Drury Lane had extended its season well into June, thus interfering with his Haymarket offerings. Garrick's friend Torré also provided further competition for Foote with his fireworks at Mary-le-Bone Gardens. Such encroachments rekindled Foote's desire for a year-round venue, and he petitioned George III for permission to extend the Haymarket season. Such permission was not forthcoming, as Foote could hardly have expected it would be. Nonetheless, Foote competed with the winter houses by such means as were at his disposal. Since puppet shows were not forbidden under his patent, he began work on *The Handsome Housemaid; or Piety in Pattens*, the first offering of his *Primitive Puppet Show*, which opened on 15 February 1773.

Foote used the *Primitive Puppet Show* to satirize both the current state of English theater and

The Theatre Royal in the Hay-Market, circa 1768

to have another jab at the Methodists. Wooden puppets, he argued, were the only suitable vehicle for the sentimental plots and lifeless acting to which the stage had been reduced. With his emphasis on "primitive," Foote also suggested that his puppets were the means by which theater would be returned to the prestige it enjoyed in Roman times. Of course, this pseudohistorical explanation merely emphasized the fact that "primitive" was meant to satirize Methodism's insistence on a return to the simple ways of the early Church. The actual skit, *Piety in Pattens*, is a spoof of Samuel Richardson's *Pamela* (1740), and hardly primitive in any sense. In fact, Foote's audience appears to have disliked the playlet because it lacked the broad strokes of a Punch and Judy show. Opening night produced a near riot as a rowdy audience damaged the gallery, insisting that what they had seen was not worth the price of admission. Foote revised his puppet show, however, and managed to give seventeen performances before the end of the regular season on 16 April. During the summer season, *Piety in Pattens* was performed by real actors as a "Comic Interlude," but Foote did not publish it. The sketch survives in two manuscript copies, one in the Larpent Collection and the other in the Folger Shakespeare Library.

Always on the brink of financial disaster himself, Foote seems to have been keenly interested in the subject of his next play, *The Bankrupt*, which he wrote for the 1773 Haymarket season. London had recently witnessed a series of failed commercial ventures, and Foote followed with great attention the case of Alexander Fordyce, an investor whose speculations had reduced him to bankruptcy. Going so far as to attend the sale of Fordyce's belongings, Foote bought one of the man's pillows, alleging that it had a narcotic effect on him. "For if the original proprietor could sleep so soundly on it, at the time of owing so much as he did," Foote said, "it may be of singular service to me on many occasions." *The Bankrupt* was not particularly well received, but it was only one feature of Foote's generally successful season of more than fifty performances.

During November and December 1773, Foote was back in Dublin, where he acted in *The Maid of Bath* and *The Nabob*. Just after the New Year, he returned to London, but he was soon on his way to Edinburgh, where he also played for several weeks before returning to prepare his next season at the Haymarket. Retreating from the generally sentimental subjects he had parodied in recent works, Foote wrote *The Cozeners*, a satiric play that allowed him to mimic a whole range of knaves and gulls. The plot involves the exploits of Flaw, a lawyer, and Mrs. Fleece'em, a thief recently returned from exile in America. Their clients, whom they dupe with various schemes of procurement, include an Irishman, a Jew, a preacher's wife, and a country family with a doltish son. The play is full of references to contemporary scandal, and it satirizes a variety of individuals, from Lord Chesterfield to the well-known adventuress Caroline Rudd.

Now at the height of his career, Foote had obviously settled into something of a routine at the Haymarket. He was offering a new play each year, and he invariably provided a full slate of performances between 15 May and 15 September. Although he had not been successful in his effort to renegotiate the Haymarket patent so that he could compete directly with the two major houses, his original grant had marked him as the only manager to offer regular theatrical fare outside the confines of Drury Lane and Covent Garden. Furthermore, he had become a consistently successful playwright. Although always open to the charge that his characters and their predicaments were much the same from play to play, Foote had mastered the art of topical satire and witty dialogue. If his plots were thin, audiences generally ignored the fact, focusing instead on his humor and admiring his relentless assaults on the hypocritical and the inane.

In spite of his successes, Foote left for Paris at the end of the 1774 season in what appeared to be a weary state. He wrote to Garrick indicating that he would vacate the Haymarket if he could find an appropriate tenant. By the time he returned from his vacation, however, Foote seems to have been ready to reimmerse himself in work. He set about writing *A Trip to Calais*, inspired perhaps by the fact that his subject was one of the most delicious scandals to attract London's attention in years.

The first part of *A Trip to Calais* is actually about a clandestine marriage, and it is based on the elopement of R. B. Sheridan and Elizabeth Linley, the latter of whom Foote had already portrayed in *The Maid of Bath*. Their marriage had been the subject of public comment, but it never reached the scandalous proportions of Foote's second object of satire, Elizabeth Chudleigh. A maid of honor to the Princess of Wales, Elizabeth was secretly married to Augustus John Hervey. When she later became mistress to Evelyn Pierrepont, the second duke of Kingston, she conspired with him to have her marriage to Hervey invalidated so that she might marry the aging duke and thus become the duchess of Kingston. The scheme was a temporary success, and the new duchess lived securely until the duke's death in 1773. Soon after, however, a disgruntled relative of the duke sought to reopen the question of Chudleigh's marriage to Hervey as a means of challenging the duke's will, which had left nearly the entire estate to the duchess. The effort resulted in the duchess's flight to Calais where she prepared her case before being tried in England for bigamy.

The duchess was awaiting trial when she learned that Foote was planning to caricature her as Lady Kitty Crocodile in his new play. She managed to keep the play from being licensed, and a highly publicized dispute between her and Foote lasted through the summer of 1775. The duchess was finally convicted of bigamy in April 1776 and stripped of her title, but she had managed to reclaim her title as countess of Bristol and thus escaped punishment. By this time, however, Foote had made other enemies, chief among them the journalist William Jackson, who accused him publicly of being homosexual. Jackson's allegations were supported by one of Foote's former servants, John Sangster, who testified that Foote had sexually assaulted him. Foote's Haymarket audience was astonishingly loyal, and his 1776 season there was an immense success. Nonetheless, his sodomy case finally came to trial on 9 December 1776, and though he was acquitted, the ordeal took a devastating toll on Foote.

Before his trial, Foote had revised *A Trip to Calais*, substantially altering the second act and calling the work *The Capuchin*. He deleted Lady Kitty Crocodile and put Dr. Viper, a caricature of Jackson, in her place. Audiences seemed to find the play too closely connected to the ugly quarrel between the two men, however, and it received only ten performances in the 1776 season. *The Capuchin* was to be Foote's last play. At the conclusion of his grueling trial, he completed plans for selling his interest in the Haymarket to George Colman the Elder. The transaction was completed on 16 January 1777, and although Foote acted for Colman during the summer of 1777, he was stricken on three occasions with convulsive seizures. After the third bout, on 6 August, he took his doctor's advice and went to Brighthelmstone to recuperate. He returned to London in September and was advised to spend the winter in the south of France, but his journey took him only so far as Dover, where another seizure resulted in his death on 21 October 1777.

Because he created vehicles chiefly for his own mimicry and improvisation, Foote's comedies did not in most cases outlast him. A few, including *The Minor* and *The Devil upon Two Sticks*, were acted during the next decade, but nineteenth-century performances of his plays, except for *The Lyar*, were virtually nonexistent. Besides being works that demanded their author to act them, Foote's comedies were filled with references to contemporary events and people. This fact contributed to their popularity, but it also ensured that they would be forgotten. Since his works are not often read today, Foote is more readily granted a place in theatrical than in literary history. Certainly, he was second only to Garrick as an actor-playwright-entrepreneur, and he singlehandedly broke the stranglehold of the patent houses on London theater. But Foote was also a superb wit and raconteur. He was an intellectually acute if often strident individual, and his plays were admired by contemporaries whose literary judgments were virtually unquestioned in their day.

Biographies:

William Cooke, *Memoirs of Samuel Foote*, 3 volumes (London: Richard Phillips, 1805);

John Forster, "Samuel Foote," in his *Historical and Biographical Essays*, 2 volumes (London: John Murray, 1858);

Percy H. Fitzgerald, *Samuel Foote, A Biography* (London: Chatto & Windus, 1910);

Mary Megie Belden, *The Dramatic Work of Samuel Foote*, Yale Studies in English, no. 80 (New Haven: Yale University Press, 1929);

Simon Trefman, *Sam. Foote, Comedian, 1720-1777* (New York: New York University Press, 1971).

References:

Martin C. Battestin, "Fielding and 'Master Punch' in Panton Street," *Philological Quarterly*, 45 (January 1966): 191-208;

Elizabeth N. Chatten, *Samuel Foote* (Boston: Twayne, 1980);

Arthur H. Scouten, "On the Origin of Foote's Matinees," *Theatre Notebook*, 7 (1953): 28-31;

Mary Margaret Stewart, "Fielding and Foote, Once More," *Notes and Queries*, 230 (June 1985): 218-219;

Simon Trefman, "Arthur Murphy's Long Lost *Englishman from Paris:* A Manuscript Discovered," *Theatre Notebook*, 20 (Summer 1966): 137-141;

Edward H. Weatherly, "Foote's Revenge on Churchill and Lloyd," *Huntington Library Quarterly*, 9 (November 1945): 49-60;

Robert Verner Wharton, "The Divided Sensibility of Samuel Foote," *Educational Theatre Journal*, 17 (March 1965): 31-37;

W. K. Wimsatt, "Foote and a Friend of Boswell's: A Note on *The Nabob*," *Modern Language Notes*, 57 (May 1942): 325-335;

Christopher Wood, "An Eighteenth-Century Satire on the Art Market," *Connoisseur*, 163 (December 1966): 240-242.

Papers:

Fifteen of Foote's plays survive in manuscript versions that were submitted to the lord chamberlain for licensing. These are part of the Larpent Collection in the Henry E. Huntington Library. The Larpent Collection also includes a copy of the third edition of *The Minor* with changes required by the examiner incorporated in Garrick's hand. Only two Foote plays are known to exist in manuscripts other than those in the Larpent Collection, and both are in the Folger Shakespeare Library. One is a second version of the skit *Piety in Pattens*, and the other is an incomplete manuscript copy of *The Devil upon Two Sticks*. Neither is in Foote's hand. The Larpent manuscripts are also written out by amanuenses, although several have corrections and additions in Foote's hand. The only extended autograph in the Larpent Collection is the first act of *The Lyar*. Few letters by Foote survive, and these are scattered among research libraries and other archives in Britain and America. The eleven letters in the Folger Library represent the largest single holding. Although several letters have been printed or excerpted in biographies, there is no published collection.

Oliver Goldsmith

(10 November 1730?-4 April 1774)

Richard Bevis
University of British Columbia

See also the Goldsmith entry in *DLB 39: British Novelists, 1660-1800.*

PLAY PRODUCTIONS: *The Good-Natured Man*, London, Theatre Royal in Covent Garden, 29 January 1768;

She Stoops to Conquer, London, Theatre Royal, Covent Garden, 15 March 1773;

The Grumbler, London, Theatre Royal, Covent Garden, 8 May 1773.

SELECTED BOOKS: *The Memoirs of a Protestant, Condemned to the Galleys of France for His Religion*, by Jean Marteilhe, translated by Goldsmith as James Willington, 2 volumes (London: Printed for R. Griffiths & E. Dilly, 1758);

An Enquiry into the Present State of Polite Learning in Europe (London: Printed for R. & J. Dodsley, 1759);

The Bee, nos. 1-8 (London: 6 October-24 November 1759); republished as *The Bee. Being Essays on the most Interesting Subjects* (London: Printed for J. Wilkie, 1759);

The Citizen of the World; or Letters from a Chinese Philosopher, Residing in London, To His Friends in the East, 2 volumes (London: Printed for J. Newbery, 1762);

The Mystery Revealed: Containing a Series of Transactions and Authentic Testimonials Respecting the Supposed Cock-Lane Ghost (London: Printed for W. Bristow, 1762);

Plutarch's Lives, Abridged from the Original Greek, Illustrated with Notes and Reflections, 7 volumes (London: Printed for J. Newbery, 1762);

The Life of Richard Nash, of Bath, Esq. Extracted Principally from His Original Papers (London: Printed for J. Newbery & W. Frederick, 1762);

An History of England in a Series of Letters from a Nobleman to His Son, 2 volumes (London: Printed for J. Newbery, 1764);

The Traveller; or, A Prospect of Society (London: Printed for J. Newbery, 1764);

Essays. By Mr. Goldsmith (London: Printed for W. Griffin, 1765);

Edwin and Angelina: A Ballad by Mr. Goldsmith, Printed for the Amusement of the Countess of Northumberland (London: Privately printed, 1765);

The Vicar of Wakefield: A Tale, 2 volumes (London: Printed by B. Collins for F. Newbery, 1766);

A Concise History of Philosophy and Philosophers, by Jean Henri Samuel Formey, translated anonymously by Goldsmith (London: Printed for F. Newbery, 1766);

The Good Natur'd Man: A Comedy. As Performed at the Theatre-Royal in Covent Garden (London: Printed for W. Griffin, 1768);

The Roman History, From the Foundation of the City of Rome, To the Destruction of the Western Empire, 2 volumes (London: Printed for S. Baker & G. Leigh, T. Davies & L. Davis, 1769);

The Deserted Village, A Poem (London: Printed for W. Griffin, 1770);

The Life of Thomas Parnell, D. D. (London: Printed for T. Davies, 1770); also published in Thomas Parnell, *Poems on Several Occasions* (London: Printed for T. Davies, 1770);

The Life of Henry St. John, Lord Viscount Bolingbroke (London: Printed for T. Davies, 1770); also published in Henry St. John, Lord Viscount Bolingbroke, *A Dissertation upon Parties* (London: Printed for T. Davies, 1770);

The History of England, from the Earliest Times to the Death of George II, 4 volumes (London: Printed for T. Davies, Becket & De Hondt & T. Cadell, 1771);

Threnodia Augustalis: Sacred to the Memory of Her late Royal Highness, The Princess Dowager of Wales, Spoken and Sung in the Great Room at Soho-

Oliver Goldsmith, 1766 (portrait by Sir Joshua Reynolds; by permission of the National Portrait Gallery, London; Copyright Photograph, Reg. No. 828)

Square, on Thursday the 20th of February (London: Printed for W. Woodfall, 1772);

Dr. Goldsmith's Roman History, Abridged by himself for the Use of Schools (London: Printed for S. Baker & G. Leitch, T. Davies & L. Davis, 1772);

She Stoops to Conquer: or, The Mistakes of a Night. A Comedy. As it is acted at the Theatre-Royal in Covent-Garden (London: Printed for F. Newbery, 1773);

The Retaliation: A Poem (London: Printed for G. Kearsly, 1774);

The Grecian History, from the Earliest State to the Death of Alexander the Great, 2 volumes (London: Printed for J. & F. Rivington, T. Longman, G. Kearsley, W. Griffin, G. Robinson, R. Baldwin, W. Goldsmith, T. Cadell & T. Evans, 1774);

An History of the Earth, and Animated Nature, 8 volumes (London: Printed for J. Nourse, 1774);

An Abridgement of the History of England from the Invasion of Julius Caesar to the Death of George II (London: Printed for B. Law, G. Robinson, G. Kearsly, T. Davies, T. Becket, T. Cadell & T. Evans, 1774);

The Comic Romance of Monsieur Scarron, translated by Goldsmith, 2 volumes (London: Printed for W. Griffin, 1775);

The Haunch of Venison: A Poetical Epistle to Lord Clare (London: Printed for J. Ridley & G. Kearsly, 1776);

A Survey of Experimental Philosophy, Considered in Its Present State of Improvement, 2 volumes (London: Printed for T. Carnan & F. Newbery jun., 1776);

The Grumbler: a Farce, adapted by Goldsmith from Sir Charles Sedley's translation of David Augustin de Brueys's *Le Grondeur,* edited by

Alice I. Perry Wood (Cambridge, Mass.: Harvard University Press, 1931).

COLLECTIONS: *The Miscellaneous Works of Oliver Goldsmith,* edited by James Prior, 4 volumes (London: J. Murray, 1837);

Collected Works of Oliver Goldsmith, edited by Arthur Friedman, 5 volumes (Oxford: Clarendon Press, 1966).

OTHER: Richard Brookes, *A New and Accurate System of Natural History,* preface and introductions to volumes 1-4 by Goldsmith, 6 volumes (London: Printed for J. Newbery, 1763-1764);

C. Wiseman, *A Complete English Grammar on a New Plan,* preface by Goldsmith (London: Printed for W. Nicoll, 1764);

Poems for Young Ladies. In Three Parts. Devotional, Moral, and Entertaining, edited anonymously by Goldsmith (London: Printed for J. Payne, 1767);

The Beauties of English Poesy, edited by Goldsmith, 2 volumes (London: Printed for William Griffin, 1767);

Charlotte Lennox, *The Sister: A Comedy,* epilogue by Goldsmith (London: Printed for J. Dodsley & T. Davies, 1769);

Joseph Cradock, *Zobeide. A Tragedy,* prologue by Goldsmith (London: Printed for T. Cadell, 1771).

Oliver Goldsmith, a writer who (as Dr. Johnson said) left no genre untouched, and touched none that he did not adorn, gave us two of the most characteristic poems, the best-loved novel, the most delightful stage comedy, and much of the best periodical writing of his day. His friends, distracted by his clowning and ineptitude, could never quite decide which was greater: their admiration for the writer, or their bemusement at the buffoon. Joshua Reynolds found it necessary to assert that "such a genius could not be a fool." But posterity, spared the spectacle of the genial bumbler, has been less ambivalent. At eighty, Goethe said that *The Vicar of Wakefield* (1766) had formed him when he was twenty. William Butler Yeats envisioned Goldsmith "sipping at the honey-pot of his mind." For Virginia Woolf, he had "the born writer's gift of being in touch with the thing itself and not with the outer husks of words." If *The Vicar of Wakefield* is no longer on every pious bookshelf, it is still taught, along with *The Deserted Village* (1770) and some of the essays, and *She Stoops to Conquer* (1773) is often revived. Goldsmith now appears one of the most enduring, as well as the most versatile, of eighteenth-century writers, valued for his warmth of style, his balance of reason and feeling, and his ability to evoke an almost prelapsarian innocence.

He was born at Pallas, County Longford, Ireland, on 10 November, probably in 1730 (although 1728 and 1731 are also possible), the second son of Charles Goldsmith, a goodhearted but rather feckless clergyman, and Ann Jones Goldsmith. Oliver would fictionalize his father as the Reverend Primrose in *The Vicar of Wakefield* and as the Man in Black's father (in *The Citizen of the World,* 1762); he was estranged from his mother before he emigrated in 1752, and that proved to be an enduring breach and trauma. Soon after Oliver's birth, the Reverend Goldsmith took up a new living at Lissoy (the Auburn of *The Deserted Village*), where the boy spent a rural childhood that he later tended to idealize, though a case of smallpox at eight or nine left ugly pockmarks which, along with a protrusive brow, receding chin, and stocky figure, gave him a lasting conviction of his own ugliness. Between the ages of about six and fifteen Oliver attended four different schools in the vicinity. In the first the village schoolmaster Thomas Byrne, a colorful veteran, fired his imagination and gave him a lifelong love of storytelling; in the last, the Reverend Patrick Hughes of Edgeworthstown gave him friendship as well as a good grounding in the Latin classics.

As a child Oliver occasionally demonstrated a flair for wit and verse, which (along with some scholastic aptitude) convinced his mother and a benevolent uncle, the Reverend Thomas Contarine, that he should follow his brother Henry to university. At this point, however, the Goldsmith penchant for imprudence began to affect Oliver's prospects. Henry, who was to have helped the family, suddenly married and left Trinity College to become a humble teaching curate (1743); then sister Catherine eloped with one of Henry's pupils (1744). When the Reverend Goldsmith's anger cooled, he engaged himself to provide a £400 dowry, which he could not afford except by mortgaging a property to the couple, and was unable to pay off in his lifetime. Oliver's future was likewise mortgaged: when he entered Trinity College, Dublin (11 June 1745), it was not, like his father and brother before him, as a gentlemanly pensioner, but as a menial sizar waiting on the pensioners.

Trinity, with a good library and an assiduous

Statue of Goldsmith, by Foley, at the gate of Trinity College, Dublin

faculty, was superior to Oxford and Cambridge in some respects, but Goldsmith had an undistinguished and turbulent career there; his statue at the gates is an irony. His manners and appearance were described as coarse, he was adequately but not overly well prepared, and his father had placed him with a tutor, Dr. Theaker Wilder, who was so sadistic that he had no other students. Under such a professor Goldsmith's academic motivation and performance were not strong, and Dublin, then the second largest city in the British Isles, offered many distractions: the life of the streets, women, musical concerts, and–a favorite Trinity resort–the Theatre Royal in Smock Alley, which, under Thomas Sheridan's direction, presented David Garrick, Charles Macklin, George Ann Bellamy, and other London stars. Goldsmith also enjoyed playing his flute and lounging, or rioting, with his fellow students. The sizar's uniform was a constant humiliation, and his poverty worsened after his father's death (1747), despite occasional benefactions from the Reverend Contarine. Yet even when reduced to pawning books and composing topical street ballads for a few shillings (his first employment with the booksellers), he would dispense charity to some of Dublin's numerous poor. He was "publicly admonished" after participating in a fatal riot, competed for a scholarship but obtained only an "exhibition," took to gambling–splurging any winnings–and ran off toward Cork after an especially bad row with Wilder. Returned by Henry and reaccepted on probation, he failed an important examination and finished his B.A. a year late (February 1750).

If his mother expected that "Noll" would now begin to help the straitened family in their cottage at Ballymahon, she was disappointed; he showed little inclination to do anything constructive. Pressed to take holy orders (for which he felt no call), he went to the interview his uncle had arranged with the Bishop of Elphin wearing scarlet breeches–possibly an effect of color blindness–and came away empty-handed. What he really enjoyed, it appears, was holding forth at the local inn like Tony Lumpkin at the Three Pigeons. "Something must be done for Noll" became the family watchword. He tutored briefly but decamped after a row, probably over gambling, and headed for Cork with a good horse and thirty pounds, reportedly to immigrate to America. Six weeks later he returned home on a nag, penniless, with a tall story about giving all his money and his horse for his passage, then missing the boat and receiving enough charity to get home–a story he then denied but later affirmed. Again "something must be done for Noll." Uncle Thomas donated fifty pounds for study of the law in London; Oliver gambled it away in Dublin. At this point his mother understandably gave up on him, but the rest of the family took up a new collection and sent him to Edinburgh to study medicine (fall 1752). Joining the ranks of poor Irish emigrants, he never returned to Ireland.

In Goldsmith's earliest surviving letters, from Edinburgh to Ireland, we see him, like any student away from home, inventing his persona: the serious medical student, the grateful recipient of benefactions. He did enjoy the lectures of the celebrated Alexander Monro and join the Medical Society, but much of what interested him was social or preliterary. He traveled in the Highlands and was not impressed, bought finer clothes than he could afford so he could attend the balls, compared the Scots to the Irish, and accepted invitations to James, duke of Hamilton's until he realized that he had been assigned the role of court jester. To his other traits–good nature, imprudence, self-consciousness about being ugly and poor, a penchant for clowning–can now be added pride, and a sense of being an outsider.

After a year Goldsmith felt that he had drunk sufficient of Edinburgh, and early in 1754 he sailed to Leyden, Holland–narrowly missing arrest and shipwreck if his letters can be credited–ostensibly to continue his medical studies. In retrospect it looks more like a *Wanderjahr* or two inspired by Baron Ludwig Holberg's travels, or what Goldsmith later called "philosophic vagabondage," during which he gathered the materials he would use in *An Enquiry into the Present State of Polite Learning* (1759), *The Traveller* (1764), and a hundred essays. He seems to have regarded Leyden's teachers lightly: he put more energy into observing the Dutch, attending the commedia dell'arte, gambling, teaching English, borrowing money, and writing cheerful misrepresentations of his existence to his relatives. Typically, he sent some expensive tulip bulbs to his uncle on his way out of town.

Late in 1754 or early in 1755 he traveled toward Paris. We have no primary evidence (letters, journals) about Goldsmith's travels in Europe, only hearsay, recollection, and what can be deduced from *Polite Learning, The Traveller*, and George Primrose's rambles in *The Vicar of Wakefield.* He certainly traveled in great poverty, using his flute to obtain money or hospitality whenever possible. In Paris he lodged with Irish monks and became acquainted with the Théâtre Français and Comédie Italienne as well as with the Sorbonne's lecturers. Thence he proceeded via Strasbourg down the Rhine to Switzerland, enjoyed a summer tour of the Alps, and crossed into Italy, visiting the northern cities and spending some months in Padua, though there is no proof that he attended the old university there (or any other European institution). By now Goldsmith had outrun his lines of supply: Thomas Contarine had died and, despite Goldsmith's letters, no other remittances reached him. Come winter, he begged his way back across France, reached Dover in February 1756 and made his way to London, henceforth his home.

That first year Goldsmith probably tried a number of occupations: pharmacist's assistant, school usher, proofreader at Samuel Richardson's print shop (where he met Edward Young), and perhaps even physician. He began to call himself "Doctor" around this time, and may have petitioned Trinity College for his B.M., though his friend and biographer Thomas Percy found no evidence that it was ever granted. One gauge of his restlessness and frustration is that he apparently aspired to win a £300 prize by deciphering the "Written Mountains" of the Middle East, despite his complete ignorance of Oriental languages. His "break" came, well disguised, when an ailing schoolkeeper, the Reverend Milner, asked Goldsmith to assume his teaching duties at Peckham. The position itself proved at best a mixed blessing. Milner's pledge to place Goldsmith with the East India Company as a physician came to nothing, but at Milner's table Goldsmith met the publisher of John Cleland's *Fanny Hill* (1748-1749) and the *Monthly Review*, Ralph Griffiths, who (by early 1757) offered him work as a reviewer. Although the connection soon soured, it opened many doors. The years of preparation were finally over; the years of hack work were beginning.

For a hundred pounds per annum and lodging above Griffiths's shop at the Sign of the

Dunciad on Paternoster Row, Goldsmith wrote reviews for five hours a day. At once he displays a balanced judgment, a measured, cadenced style, and an intellectual self-assurance totally at odds with the impression of fecklessness he had made on everyone except, presumably, Griffiths. "He had only to take his pen," observed Virginia Woolf, "and he was revenged . . . upon the fine gentlemen who sneered at him, upon his own ugly body and stumbling tongue." In the May 1757 *Monthly Review* he pronounces John Home's tragedy *Douglas*, the Edinburgh success which had just come to town, full of "languor, affectation, and the false sublime" as well as deficient in moral fable and poetry. Edmund Burke's *Philosophical Enquiry into . . . the Sublime and the Beautiful* is judged "agreeable" rather than "instructive": it simply replaces the system it explodes with the author's own feelings. Moving comfortably among his future friend's ideas, which are summarized with some dissent, Goldsmith maintains his independence, exhibiting generosity but never subservience. He went on to give Tobias Smollett's *History of England* a mixed review (June) and Thomas Gray's *Odes* a mostly negative one (September) before rather mysteriously leaving Griffiths and the *Monthly Review* that autumn.

In 1758 Goldsmith taught again at Peckham, freely translated the *Mémoires* of the French Protestant refugee Jean Marteilhe, and extended his literary acquaintance to Smollett and the Dodsley brothers, for whom he engaged to write a survey of European literature. He still hoped to be a doctor on the Coromandel coast of India, and had paid a fee to some East India Company "Lofty," but could not afford to purchase his kit and in December failed his medical exam before the College of Surgeons. The entire exercise was academic anyway, since the French had now taken Coromandel, and in March 1759 he finally abandoned the idea.

Although it was a winter of discontent for Goldsmith, who was discovering that he could publish without achieving fame or profit and was being pursued by Griffiths for debt, 1759 was as crucial a year in his career as for England in the Seven Years' War. He began to write for Smollett's *Critical Review*, perhaps contributing the notice of Arthur Murphy's *The Orphan of China* (May), which takes a dim view of chinoiserie and of Chinese literature in general. In February he met Thomas Percy the antiquarian, his future biographer, who left a graphic account of a visit to Goldsmith's one-chair room at Green Arbor Court during which the landlady's daughter came curtseying to beg "a chamberpot full of coals." He also met Burke, almost as versatile a man as he but more brilliant, Murphy, another Irish man of letters, and John Newbery, the "philanthropic bookseller" who would be one of his most important patrons.

In April 1759 Dodsley published Goldsmith's anonymous *Enquiry into the Present State of Polite Learning in Europe*. It did not meet with much favor, being the kind of galloping compendium by one writer in one volume that would soon become obsolete, but it may shed light on his travels and states his broad critical views more clearly than any other document. Goldsmith surveys no less than ancient and modern literature and criticism, and, although the familiar theme of "modern decline" is present, an antipathy to criticism is more prominent. It was "Critics, sophists," and others who brought down "ancient polite learning," so the rise of criticism in modern France and England is ominous. An inflexible application of foreign rules threatens to stifle the natural British genius, as a doctrinaire objection to anything "low" is in effect banishing humor from the stage (here Goldsmith anticipates his problems with *The Good-Natur'd Man*, 1768). The booksellers must share the blame for wit and poetry being discouraged, a subject on which Goldsmith (who had not met Newbery when he wrote this) could speak personally. To these views, which can be paralleled in the Scriblerians and Samuel Johnson, Goldsmith adds material from his travels, especially the valuable remarks on Continental universities and on Holberg's wanderings.

The chapter "Of the Stage" is particularly interesting and had significant consequences. It portrays a theater torn between the devotees of "decoration and ornament" and the advocates of "regularity and declamation," wherein new plays "must be tried in the manager's fire, strained through a licenser," and purged by the critics. Under such conditions, it might be better if plays "were read, not acted." Since avarice rules the London theater, old plays whose dead authors do not have to be paid are preferred. (David Garrick took this as a personal attack, and Goldsmith softened the discussion in the second edition.) Few writers, he concludes, will look to the stage "for either fame or subsistence." His own experience a decade later would do little to change this verdict.

That fall Goldsmith edited a weekly, *The Bee*, in the manner of *The Spectator, The Rambler,* and *The Idler,* but it did not catch on, running only eight numbers. The contents are a potpourri of

Oliver Goldsmith (sketch by Henry Bunbury; by permission of the Trustees of the British Museum)

original observations, poetry, bits of political and natural history, and translations of contemporary European authors. "A City Night-Piece" (no. 4) is a sympathetic evocation of London's dark side–robbers, suicides, street people–that turns up again in *The Citizen of the World.* Remarkably for its period, it takes the stillness of the empty streets at 2 A.M. as foreshadowing the "desart" that London will eventually become. The pieces "On Our Theatres" in numbers 1 and 2 show that Goldsmith was observing the English stage as closely as he had the European: he protests against rolling out the "death carpet" at Drury Lane before a tragedy's final bloodbath, and against a fat heroine pretending to die of famine in *Jane Shore.* Numbers 5 and 8 also treat the theater, the latter noting opera's decline.

During much of his career Goldsmith lived the frenetic existence of a hack, with plenty of low-paying work, much of it anonymous and in periodicals. As he was not a careful manager, his own affairs were often chaotic. But for much of 1760-1761 he was a salaried employee of Newbery, and his life was relatively stable. His most important production in this period was a series of 119 "Chinese letters" in Newbery's *Public Ledger* (24 January 1760-14 August 1761), which were revised and collected as *The Citizen of the World* (1762). The central figure is a cultivated Chinese visitor to London, Lien Chi Altangi, who reports, to a correspondent in China, his serious or amusing reflections on England and his friends, especially the Man in Black and Beau Tibbs. Incoming letters provide an exotic countermelody: the romantic adventures of Lien's son Hingpo and his ladylove Zelis, who proves to be the niece of the Man in Black.

There is potential for an epistolary novel or two here, but Goldsmith worked out the plots and themes as he went along; his approach is journalistic and derivative. The basic idea had appeared in Montesquieu's *Lettres persanes* (1721), which Lord Lyttelton had imitated; in the Marquis D'Argens's *Lettres chinoises* (1755 edition), which Horace Walpole had used in *Letter of Xo-Ho* (1757); and in Giovanni Paolo Marana's *L'Espion turc à Paris* (1684); and he drew his Chinese lore from books by two French Jesuits, Le Comte and Du Halde. But for the English materials–mildly satiric observations on manners, fads (including chinoiserie), books and institutions (including the theater), the portraits of a shabby beau and a fine lady–Goldsmith depended on his own eye, and he shared his expatriate sensibility between the peripatetic Chinese and the gruff but charitable Man in Black. *The Citizen of the World* is one of the most underwritten opportunities in the history of prose fiction; yet it has its moments and its value.

The period of the "Chinese letters" gave Goldsmith the fleeting illusion of prosperity. In 1760 he moved to new lodgings in Wine Office Court off Fleet Street, joined the Robin Hood Debating Society, and met the poet Chris Smart and the dramatist Isaac Bickerstaff. His acquaintance widened in 1761 to include two of his greatest friends, Joshua Reynolds and Dr. Johnson (who had admired the Chinese letters), and probably David Garrick and William Hogarth as well. Now a part of London's artistic and literary inner circle, he serialized his "Memoirs of Voltaire" in *The Lady's Magazine*, which he was editing, and made a start on *The Vicar of Wakefield*.

Yet overall 1761 was not a productive year–the Voltaire memoir had been written in 1759–and the bills came due in 1762, a low point in some ways. Despite publication of his *Life of Richard Nash*, an interesting "low" biography, and various periodical essays, Goldsmith's affairs were again in disarray, and once more he dreamed of a new start in the East. On 28 October 1762 Dr. Johnson had to rescue him from house arrest by his landlady, who had summoned the bailiffs because the rent was in arrears. Casting about for something of value, Johnson skimmed the (perhaps unfinished) manuscript of *The Vicar of Wakefield*, carried it to Newbery, and returned with, probably, twenty pounds for a one-third share. Newbery now undertook to manage Goldsmith's chaotic life, installing him in new premises at Canonbury House, Islington, and arranging for him to draw cash advances against payments for future works. He may have completed *The Vicar of Wakefield* under this regime, but Goldsmith was mortgaging his literary prospects, and, though a staunch Tory, he would not supplement Newbery's allowance by writing for the government.

When James Boswell met Goldsmith at Christmas 1762, the latter was still only a curio, a minor constellation scarcely worth recording, and 1763 added nothing more significant than a translation of Plutarch's *Lives* to the record. It was 1764 that made Goldsmith a literary celebrity. In February he became, with Johnson, Burke, Reynolds, and others, a co-founder of The Club, which met at the Turk's Head on Mondays to dine and talk. Although his inclusion in this elite group–an outgrowth of Joshua Reynolds's literate dinner parties–testifies as much to Goldsmith's bonhomie, his "clubability," as to his literary credentials, it was an outward and visible sign that he had arrived. In June he published *An History of England in a Series of Letters from a Nobleman to His Son*, for which Newbery had already paid him in full. Goldsmith's aristocratic persona emphasizes the moral utility of studying the history that the real-life author found it expedient to compile from David Hume, Paul de Rapin de Thoyras, and other recent historians. By September, feeling able to manage without Newbery's protection, Goldsmith had moved into congenial new quarters at Garden Court in the Temple, long the resort of law students, scholars, and wits. And in December (1764) he published the poem he had begun in Europe in 1755 as *The Traveller*, the first work to carry his name.

Dr. Johnson, who had encouraged Goldsmith to publish the poem, wrote a favorable review and later said that he had contributed some of the concluding couplets. These are natural affinities: *The Traveller; or, A Prospect of Society* is the same kind of Augustan verse essay, providing "observation with extensive view," as Johnson's own *Vanity of Human Wishes* (1749) and Joseph Addison's *Letter from Italy* (1703). There is also an obvious parallel with Montesquieu's *L'Esprit des lois* (1748) in the connections made between climate and national character. But Goldsmith gives this geopolitical survey of Europe–the poetic counterpart of his *Enquiry into the Present State of Polite Learning*–a personal stamp, dedicating it to his brother Henry, and referring to his own tribulations:

> Where'er I roam, whatever realms to see,
> My heart untravell'd fondly turns to thee;
> Still to my brother turns, with ceaseless pain,
> And drags at each remove a lengthening chain.

This is not Childe Harold, not a fall upon the thorns of life; if it is a step away from the Augustan

Oliver Goldsmith (portrait by Benjamin West; Temple Scott, Oliver Goldsmith Bibliographically and Biographically Considered, *1928)*

"norm" of generalization, it is no greater a one than Pope had taken in the 1730s.

The poem made Goldsmith's reputation and dazzled The Club, and its enthusiastic reception encouraged the publication of *Essays. By Mr. Goldsmith* (1765), a collection that included the well-known "Reverie at the Boar's-Head-Tavern" and the encounter with the strolling player, both from the *British Magazine* of 1760. Yet despite his success–he moved to new rooms in the Temple that year–Goldsmith still needed more income than he could generate, still envied Johnson and Boswell their resources. He tried doctoring one last time, and visited Hugh Percy, earl of Northumberland, to be inspected for patronage, but reportedly either delivered his prepared speech to the footman by mistake or asked the earl to help his brother Henry.

The prestige accruing from *The Traveller* probably also prompted Francis Newbery (John's nephew) to risk publishing *The Vicar of Wakefield* (purchased in 1762) in March 1766. Initial reaction was as mixed as subsequent criticism; only the terms have changed. Reviewers praised its style and humor, and the pastoral idyll of the first half, while faulting the extravagance and carelessness of the latter portions of the tale. Even The Club was divided, with Burke coming down in favor, Johnson (despite his earlier support) against. But through translations it made its way into Europe, and after Goldsmith's death became almost a cult novel, evoking eulogies from Goethe, von Schlegel, Washington Irving, Dickens, Thackeray, George Eliot, and more. The paradoxes of the novel, and our century's puzzlement over it, John Bender's recent article notwithstanding, were best summed up by Henry James: only the "miracle of style" and its "exquisite" tone could have saved a work "almost infantine in its awkwardness, its funny coincidences. . . ."

The modern tendency is to stress the satiric, ironic, and/or theological aspects of the Primroses' initial happiness, farfetched disasters, and even more absurd recovery. The story can be viewed parabolically, as a version of the book of Job. At first the Reverend Primrose and his innocent family exist in a rural paradise, wrought out of nostalgia for an Irish childhood. Then come the disasters: the vicar is defrauded of his money; the eldest son must leave to seek his fortune; the family must move and retrench; one daughter is deceived by a villain; the house catches fire; the vicar is imprisoned for debt and told horrible stories of the fate of his children. Only the most diehard realist is still reading on that level when Parson Primrose delivers his prison sermon on "unequal providence," asserting that God's goodness and justice will be seen–but only in a future life. Then, his point seemingly well made, Goldsmith turns and restores the Primroses to felicity as improbably as Job's creator, largely through the agency of a benevolent squire, Sir William Thornhill (the villain's uncle), who has lived among them incognito, and who finally marries Sophia Primrose. Apparently forgotten, and certainly undercut, in this triumphant theodicy is the argument of the vicar's sermon. Was he then wrong? But the novel, like its author, has triumphed over such paradoxes.

The Vicar of Wakefield apart–and it was several years old–this was not a productive period for Goldsmith. In 1766 he anonymously translated Jean Henri Samuel Formey's *Histoire abrégée de la philosophie* and edited an anthology of *Poems for Young Ladies*; another anthology, *Beauties of English Poesy*, followed in 1767. Truth is, he had acquired a new social interest: Reynolds, now his best friend, introduced him in 1766 to the widow Mrs. Horneck and her two pretty daughters. The younger, Mary, aged fourteen, soon became, and remained, Goldsmith's favorite female. Reynolds and the Hornecks were as near as the adult Goldsmith ever came to a domestic circle; he was always ready to spend time, money, and energy diverting them, especially Mary. At about the same time he turned to the most social of the arts, beginning his first comedy, *The Good-Natured Man* (1768), soon after meeting the Hornecks. His residence at the Temple, traditionally the haunt of avid theatergoers and even of playwrights (for instance, Henry Fielding and Arthur Murphy), and his acquaintance with several professional actors, may have stimulated his interest in the stage, and the success of Garrick and George Colman the Elder's *The Clandestine Marriage* (1766) would have encouraged him about the prospects for staging new comedies.

The Club, which heard or read Goldsmith's play in manuscript, supported Goldsmith through the trials of getting it staged. Reynolds brought together Goldsmith and Garrick, who made politely encouraging noises, then temporized, then asked for revisions, suggesting William Whitehead, the poet laureate and a "house" playwright, as referee. Goldsmith instead carried it to George Colman the Elder who, pressured by Burke and Reynolds, accepted it for Covent Garden. Next came problems with the actors, especially William Powell, who warned that his character, Young Honeywood, would not "play" onstage. Either by accident or design, Goldsmith's play was delayed until 29 January 1768: six days after Garrick premiered a rival comedy, Hugh Kelly's *False Delicacy*, at Drury Lane. In this head-to-head competition *The Good-Natured Man* finished second; although its respectable run of ten performances was sufficient to give Goldsmith his three "benefit" nights, his grandiose expectations were disappointed. Public disapproval of the "bailiff scene" as "low" forced its omission in performance, and the greater success of Kelly's comedy caused a breach between the two Irish playwrights. Goldsmith printed his play with a combative preface–and the bailiff scene.

The title character, Young Honeywood, is that cliché of Georgian fiction and drama, the generous but thoughtless and imprudent young man. For example, he will indulge himself in private charities to the needy, yet leave his tradesmen's bills unpaid. He is also as falsely "delicate" as are the principal lovers in Kelly's comedy, refusing to declare his love for the heiress Miss Richland out of a sense of his own unworthiness (and doubts of her love), even courting her on behalf of the lying, namedropping influence-peddler Lofty. Secretly, though, she pays Honeywood's debts. In the subplot, Leontine tries to pass off his unauthorized fiancée, Olivia, to his parents, the Croakers, as their long-absent daughter, and for several acts is incredibly successful. The two plots converge when Honeywood, in a characteristic piece of well-meant bungling, spoils their planned elopement, causing Leontine to draw on him. Only then does Sir William Honeywood, the hero's benevolent uncle, who has returned from his travels to watch the proceedings incognito, resolve the complications. He vouches for Olivia's family, qualifying her as Leontine's wife; discredits Lofty; wags a reforming finger at Young Honeywood, and joins him with Miss Richland.

Goldsmith's diverse sources and inspirations included some of his own work. He borrowed the character of Lofty and some dialogue from a couple of French plays, quite a common practice at the time. Sir William, the kindly relative who observes anonymously, resembles Gov. Cape in Samuel Foote's *The Author* (1757). Croaker was modeled on Johnson's Suspirius in *The Rambler* (1750-1752), though he can be paralleled to characters in Ben Jonson's and Roman comedies as well. Goldsmith wrote in the preface that he was "prepossessed in favour of the poets of the last age," and certainly Miss Richland owes much to the strong women of William Shakespeare, William Congreve, and George Farquhar. Even the bailiff scene had a parallel in Richard Steele's personal life. On the other hand, Lofty resembles Goldsmith's own Beau Tibbs in *The Citizen of the World* as nearly as he does the title character of David-Augustin de Brueys's *L'Important* (1694), and Young Honeywood is a type that Goldsmith had himself developed, chiefly through the stories that Beau Tibbs and Sir William Thornhill (in *The Vicar of Wakefield*) tell of their well-intentioned but misguided and disastrous youths. For that matter, Thornhill is as good a model as Foote's Gov. Cape for the benevolent spying of Sir William Honeywood.

The exact nature of *The Good-Natured Man* has puzzled and divided critics. In his preface, Goldsmith declared his theoretical allegiance to the old comic ideals of "nature and humour," as opposed to the "genteel comedy," descended from Steele, that had been produced in the 1760s by Frances Sheridan, Elizabeth Griffith, William Whitehead, and most recently Hugh Kelly. He refers specifically to the bailiff scene, whose humor proved too broad for "the public taste, grown of late, perhaps, too delicate," but many of Croaker's and Lofty's scenes also purvey humours comedy or situation comedy. Much of the plot does consist of such comic staples as mistaken identities, deception, and cross-purposes dialogue, and some passages are downright farcical; moreover, satire on Young Honeywood's abuse of good nature is inherent in the plot, and points of manners are also satirized, as in the bailiff scene (III.i). On the other hand, some speeches, and especially the moralizing close, seem to fall into just the sentimentality that Goldsmith said he wanted to avoid, and these sections tend to leave spectators and commentators wondering whether the play achieves the author's intentions, or whether those intentions were as clear and monolithic as he professed.

The uncertainty of tone that has caused the play to be labeled both sentimental and antisentimental is one of several related weaknesses clustering around Young Honeywood. Whereas Beau Tibbs and Sir William Thornhill speak as *reformed* philanthropes recounting follies long past, Young Honeywood is there before us in the fullness of his folly, hurting himself and others with his naiveté. How are we meant to react to him? His steward assures us that "his faults are such that one loves him still the better for them" (I.i), but even if this is true it is not the traditional comic agenda of scourging vice and folly that Goldsmith said he supported, and most audiences have difficulty balancing exasperation at his foolishness with admiration for his benevolence. It looks as if Goldsmith could not finally distance a character based on some aspects of his father and himself. There are other kinds of problems too: scenes that are decidedly *un*comic, behavior even from main characters that seems downright obtuse, speeches as sententious as those in the genteel comedies, and stretches of laborious writing, notably in the exposition (act 1) and in the heavy, moralizing finale. Only in flashes do we see the playwright Goldsmith would become.

Having made four or five hundred pounds on the staging and printing of the play, Goldsmith soon moved into better rooms in Brick Court, Middle Temple, above the great legal scholar William Blackstone, whom he disturbed with noisy dinner parties. The recklessness with which Goldsmith expended his windfall on clothes, furniture, and hospitality fixed his reputation for extravagance, and guaranteed his continuance in financial straits. In part he may have been compensating for private griefs: John Newbery, his longtime publisher, friend, and imposer of discipline, had died in December, and his beloved brother Henry in May. With a new friend, the Irish barrister Edmund Bott, Goldsmith rented a cottage near Edgeware, eight miles from London, where he worked on his history of Rome and began *The Deserted Village* in the summer of 1768. Most of his time still went to hack work, though. He published *The Roman History* so admired by Dr. Johnson in 1769, and contracted with booksellers to write a natural history and a history of England. That year also brought a nominal professorship of ancient history in the new Royal Academy, of which Reynolds had been named head, and a trip to Oxford with Dr. Johnson, who received an honorary degree. There is no firmer evidence that Goldsmith was given a degree here, however, than that he received one anywhere else.

The Deserted Village, published in May 1770, lifted Goldsmith's reputation to new heights. Yet while reviewers admired the construction, movement, and language of the poem, as T. S. Eliot has done, they rejected its sociopolitical assertions. Goldsmith blames the depopulation of "sweet Auburn" on two unquestioned phenomena of his time, growing prosperity and Enclosure Acts (without proving any necessary connection between them), and his dedication to Reynolds insists that, whatever critics thought, the ills described are not imaginary. Later he told William Cooke that he had been collecting materials during excursions to the country for four or five years, and the 1762 article on "The Revolution in Low Life" shows his early concern at the eradication of villages by wealthy landlords. Here Goldsmith was ahead of his time: the next generation would vindicate his alarm.

Modern critics concentrate on the poem's personal aspects: the idealizing of scenes from his childhood around Lissoy, the subtext of coming to terms with guilt over his *own* desertion of family and village, and the difficulty of reconciling his professed love of rural innocence and hatred of luxury with his observed love of dress and masquerade in London. But these are biographers' concerns: general readers respond to the nostalgia–and anger–over something beautiful that is being destroyed. Everyone regrets the loss of some aspect of childhood, and whether or not we have a village in our individual pasts, collectively we came from them. Goldsmith taps into these archetypes, as well as intuiting the imminent demise of the whole medieval agricultural order that still persisted in the English countryside.

The popularity of the new poem and Goldsmith's central location in the Middle Temple made his social life more frenetic than ever. Besides his Club friends, there were the delightful Horneck ladies, whom he escorted on an almost farcical tour to France (July 1770), discovering ruefully that travels in Europe by himself at twenty-five and with respectable ladies at forty were two quite different undertakings. (If he had other, more rakish relations with women, as friends sometimes hinted, we have no evidence of them.) There were gentlemen of means, including Robert Nugent, lord Clare, the Irish peer for whom he wrote (in 1770 or 1771) *The Haunch of Venison* (1776), and Joseph Cradock, an amateur writer, first drawn to him, perhaps, by his reputation, but held by his humor and humanity. And there were those whom he succored, such as McVeagh McDonnell, a poor student who would recall his "flow, perhaps an overflow, of the milk of human kindness," and Paul Hiffernan, a minor writer who became a dependent. If Goldsmith could not get a pension, he could give one. Charity that he could ill afford to anyone more needy than he (including the street singer whom he left a card game to relieve because she sounded distressed) was a given of Goldsmith's nature. Yet when he learned of his mother's death in 1770, he ordered only a half-mourning suit, telling Reynolds's sister it was for "a distant relation." Even death did not reconcile them.

To the booksellers he was always, and increasingly, in arrears; the dark side of being paid in advance was that he must then write prodigiously knowing that he had already spent his fee on last month's (or last year's) indulgence. (Yet he may have refused another invitation to write on behalf of the Ministry in 1770; it could have led to a pension, but he did not believe in party writing.) So he turned out biographies of Thomas Parnell and Henry St. John, lord viscount Bolingbroke in 1770, an abridgment of his *History of England* in 1771 and another, of his *Roman History*, in 1772, without getting ahead at all. The prospects for more of the same cycle of servitude cannot have been good for his increasingly precarious health. In 1772 he began the natural history for which he had contracted with Griffin in 1769, but he was seriously ill with a bladder infection, which required surgery, even before he returned to London for the winter. Since his summer sojourns in the country were supposed to be salubrious, this was an ominous development.

Still he found time to do work of his own choosing. In the summer of 1771 he wrote *She Stoops to Conquer* (1773), appropriately "in the country": a rented room at the Selby farm near Hyde, six miles from London. Typically he had to sell the copyright to meet his debts in 1772, months before it was staged; he had accepted an advance from Newbery on a (lost) novel, perhaps a version of *The Good-Natured Man*, which the bookseller then rejected. In February 1772, a *Threnodia Augustalis*, with libretto by Goldsmith, music adapted from Henry Purcell and George Frideric Händel, was sung in honor of the late Princess Dowager of Wales. And he probably wrote "An Essay on the Theatre" for the *Westminster Magazine* (January 1773) before packing his expensive new clothes and going down to spend Christmas with the Hornecks at Barton in Suffolk.

"An Essay on the Theatre; or, A Comparison Between Laughing and Sentimental Comedy" was not the first critical polemic on the types of comedy now called "hard" and "soft," but it was the fullest general treatment that had appeared. The author–

Dear Sir

I ask you many pardons for the trouble I gave you of yesterday. Upon more mature deliberation and the advice of a sensible friend I begin to think it indelicate in me to throw upon you the odium of confirming Mr. Colman's sentence. I therefore request you will send my play by my servant back, for having been assured of having it acted at the other house, tho' I confess yours in every respect more to my wish, yet it would be folly in me to forego an advantage which lies in my power of appealing from Mr. Colman's opinion to the judgement of the town. I entreat, if not too late, you will keep this affair a secret for some time. I am Dear Sir

your very humble servant

Oliver Goldsmith.

Goldsmith's 6 February 1773 letter to David Garrick, manager of the Drury Lane theater, requesting the return of She Stoops to Conquer *so that George Colman the Elder could stage it at Covent Garden (Temple Scott,* Oliver Goldsmith Bibliographically and Biographically Considered, *1928)*

assumed to be Goldsmith, though the anonymous essay was not ascribed to him until 1798–insists that "laughing comedy," the "natural portrait of Human Folly and Frailty" sanctioned by Aristotle, Boileau, and Voltaire, is the true line (the essay draws heavily on Voltaire's *Dictionnaire philosophique*, 1764). Comedy should expose and ridicule the faults of the low and middle ranks of society: that is the view of "all the Great Masters." In the "Weeping Sentimental Comedy" (French *comédie larmoyante*) currently fashionable, however, our distresses and virtues are portrayed and our foibles flattered. If the author was Goldsmith–and the evidence is strong–he had progressed considerably since 1768 in clarifying his convictions. The polarity he now sees is not only between the low and the genteel or even the classical and the nouveau, but between the moral and the amoral, between genuine comedy and "bastard tragedy." If these views are taken seriously, of course, *The Good-Natured Man*, which centers on the calamities, virtues, and lovable faults of Young Honeywood, must be classified as a sentimental comedy.

"An Essay on the Theatre" also served as theoretical preparation for *She Stoops to Conquer*, just the kind of "laughing and even low comedy" recommended there, but Goldsmith again encountered various obstacles in getting his play produced. This time he naturally offered it first to George Colman, sometime in 1772. Colman, how-

Recitative 2
Who ~~with~~ mimic their passion, and who, grimly smiling,
Still thus address the fair with voice beguiling.
Air. Cotillon

Turn, my fairest; turn, if ever
Strephon caught thy ravish'd eye.
Pity take on your swain so clever,
Who without your aid must die.
Yes, I shall die, hu hu hu hu
Yes, I must die, ho ho ho ho.
Da Capo.

Mrs Bulkley Let all the old pay homage to your merit:
Give me the young, the gay, the men of spirit.
Ye travelled tribe, ye Maccaroni train,
Of French Friseurs, and nosegays justly vain,
Who take a trip to Paris once a year
To dress, and look like awkward French men here
Lend me your hands. O fatal news to tell
Their hands are only lent to the Heinelle

Mrs Catley Ay, take your travellers, travellers indeed!
Give me my bonny Scot, that travels from the Tweed.
Where are the Cheels? Ah Ah I well discern
The smiling looks of each bewitching Bairne
Air A bonny young lad is my Jockey

I'll sing to amuse you by night and by day,
And be unco merry when you are but gay,
When you with your bagpipes are ready to play,
My voice shall be ready to carrol away
With Sandy, and Sawney, and Jockey,
With Sawney, and Jarvie and Jockey

Page from one of Goldsmith's rejected epilogues for She Stoops to Conquer *(Parke-Bernet Galleries, Inc., sale number 665, 24-25 April 1945). When Mary Bulkley and Ann Catley both insisted on delivering the epilogue, Goldsmith attempted to compromise by writing a dialogue to be spoken by both actresses, but Catley refused.*

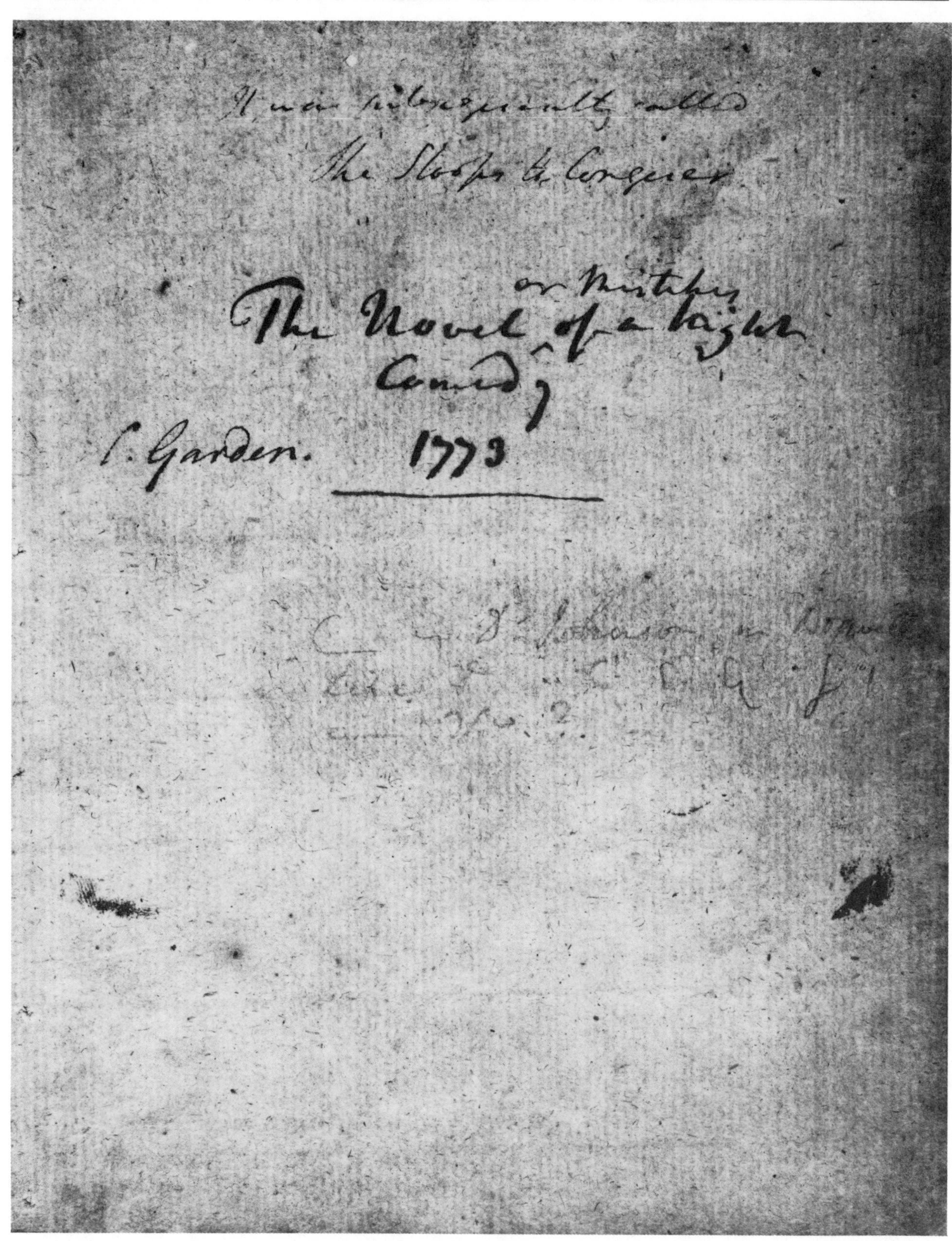
It was subsequently called
She Stoops to Conquer

The Novel or Mistakes of a Night
Comedy

C. Garden. 1773

Title and text pages from the playhouse copy of the Goldsmith comedy submitted to the Examiner of Plays for licensing prior to its first performance, on 15 March 1773 (Larpent Collection, LA 349; by permission of the Henry E. Huntington Library and Art Gallery). After considering several other titles, Goldsmith decided to call his play She Stoops to Conquer.

something. Sir, about hypocrisy— 43

Marlow: Yes. Madam. in this age of hypocrisy, there are few, who, upon strict enquiry, do not—a-a-a—

Miss H. I understand you perfectly. Sir.

Marlow: (aside) Egad. and that's more than I do myself.

Miss H. You mean that in this hypocritical age. there are few that do not condemn in public, what they practice in private.—and think they pay every debt to virtue, when they praise it.

Marlow. True. Madam, those who have most virtue in their Mouths, have least in their bosoms. But I'm sure I fatigue you, Madam.

Miss H. Not in the least. Sir, There's something so agreeable and spirited in your manner—Such life, and force—Pray Sir go on.

Marlow. Yes. Madam. I was saying—That there are some occasions—when—a total want of Courage. Madam destroys all the—and puts us—upon—a-a-a

Miss H. I agree with you entirely, a want of courage upon some occasions, assumes the appearance of ignorance, and betrays us when we most want to excell. I beg you'll proceed.

Marlow. Yes. Madam—morally speaking Madam—But I see Miss Neville expecting us in the

ever, perhaps recalling Goldsmith's 1768 remark about London's theater managers being "blockheads," temporized, as Garrick had in 1767, and in January 1773 Goldsmith was reduced to writing Colman a note begging him to touch up the play and stage it so that he could pay a large debt. By February Goldsmith was sufficiently desperate to offer the play to Garrick. At this point The Club intervened: Johnson used "a kind of force" to induce Colman to proceed with the play, however reluctantly, and Goldsmith retrieved his copy from Garrick. Rehearsals began with friends, including the Hornecks, in attendance.

But this was only the beginning. No one liked the working title, "The Mistakes of a Night," which had connotations of "Spanish intrigue" novels and might focus attention on the play's farcical aspects. Friends suggested "The Old House a New Inn" and "The Belle's Stratagem": still not quite right. Finally Goldsmith himself hit on *She Stoops to Conquer,* perhaps recollecting a line in Dryden or adapting a phrase from one of his epilogues. That was another problem: it took five tries, three by Goldsmith, to produce a satisfactory epilogue. Moreover the actors were again balky. Two experienced hands, William Smith and Henry Woodward (probably influenced by Colman's pessimism), rejected major roles, which devolved upon less established performers, while two actresses bickered over the epilogue. (Attending a performance of the Italian *fantoccini* puppets in 1772, Goldsmith had remarked wistfully how manageable they must be.) The Club's offer of membership–and perhaps the success of Samuel Foote's *The Handsome Housemaid; or, Piety in Pattens,* a satire on sentimentalism, in February–brought Garrick over, more or less. He contributed a valuable though double-edged prologue, which, while it makes fun of sentimental comedy, also jokes about Goldsmith's medical credentials: the audience is to "pronounce him *regular,* or dub him *quack.*"

Despite all of this–Goldsmith's own last-minute revisions, and an unusually late opening (the Ides of March)–the play was produced successfully. Goldsmith's friends formed a claque, but the audience was generally friendly, all the parts being well acted. Too nervous to eat dinner or attend the performance at first, Goldsmith arrived backstage in time to hear someone hiss the "horsepond scene." "What's that?" he cried. "Psha! Doctor," snapped Colman, "don't be fearful of *squibs,* when we have been sitting almost these two hours upon a barrel of gunpowder." The play's run was long enough–twelve nights that season, plus more in the summer and fall–to turn Colman's well-publicized doubts to journalistic ridicule and earn the playwright more than five hundred pounds. The published version (quite properly dedicated to Johnson) also sold well, though its reviews were less favorable than those given the performance, and Goldsmith, having sold the copyright, could not profit from the sales. He did, however, discharge some debts.

The story, for all its onstage complications, is simple enough. To the Hardcastles' country manor come two young suitors from London: Marlow has been sent to woo Kate, the only daughter of an old friend of his father; his friend Hastings is panting to court his love Miss Neville, the Hardcastles' ward. Comedy being what it is, there are many impediments. Marlow, a shy, sheltered collegian, is the "double gallant" type, impudent with lower-class females but terrified of ladies; and Mrs. Hardcastle, who holds Miss Neville's fortune in trust until her majority, intends her for her son (by her first marriage) Tony Lumpkin. "Squire" Tony, a mischievous but good-natured bumpkin, is the play's prime mover: encountering the lost Londoners first at a tavern, he directs them to the manor, but tells them it is an inn. Hastings is soon undeceived by Miss Neville, but Marlow is fooled until near the end. Kate cures his shyness by playing a barmaid, then a "poor relation," whom he courts ardently, and then revealing herself. Tony, who has his own girlfriend, helps Miss Neville and Hastings elope, but they dutifully return, ask clemency, and are given blessing and fortune. Kate and Marlow are joined by the two fathers, and Tony receives his inheritance and his freedom.

As usual, Goldsmith borrowed from or alluded to a wide spectrum of printed sources, mostly French and English drama; yet these are so smoothly integrated with his own experiences and so deeply informed by his own values that the end product seems perennially fresh, lively, and original. The basic premise of sending two London men to a country house to win brides, for example, is that of Farquhar's *The Beaux Strategem* (1707), but its working-out overthrows every expectation except that of a happy ending. Tony Lumpkin resembles both Hodge in Isaac Bickerstaff's *Love in a Village* (1762, based partly on a play by Pierre Carlet de Chamblain de Marivaux) and the ambitionless Goldsmith of 1751; significantly, Tony and his mother are one another's biggest problems. In Restoration comedies countrymen appeared as fools in London drawing rooms; here Tony, on his

Edward Shuter and Jane Green as Mr. and Mrs. Hardcastle, with John Quick as Tony Lumpkin, in act 5, scene 1, of She Stoops to Conquer *(engraving by W. Humphrey, based on a painting by T. Parkinson)*

own turf, easily hoodwinks the city dudes into mistaking an old house for an inn: a mistake Goldsmith himself once made in Ireland, probably less grossly than Marlow, but also one used in Florent Dancourt's *Maison de campagne* (1688). Tony's descriptions of the countryside, here and later, give us more of a sense of the outdoors than any English comedy since Farquhar, and reflect Goldsmith's own love of rural life and country excursions.

At the Hardcastles' house the allusions and the surprises continue. The awkward rusticity of the inmates and the ladies' interest in London would have been what audiences expected, but the obvious warmth and fondness within the family circle (including the servants) were unconventional. Kate's "pretty smooth dialogue" with Marlow (II.i) parodies the sententious conversations of young lovers in the genteel comedies, though there is probably some of Goldsmith in Marlow's agony here too, and some of Mary Horneck in Kate. Kate's scheme to win him in disguise had many precedents, including Rosalind in *As You Like It* (circa 1600) and Amanda in Colley Cibber's *Love's Last Shift* (1696), but Goldsmith's handling is unique, and quite in keeping with his age's search for a humane solution to the problem of forced or arranged marriages. Marlow does not, like Cibber's Loveless, announce his love after the revelation of the lady's identity shows him his self-interest; rather, like Aimwell in *The Beaux Stratagem*, he declares his feelings at the most inopportunistic moment. Kate's strategy solves three problems simultaneously: Marlow's schizoid treatment of females from different classes, the impersonality of the arranged marriage, and the scarcity of good suitors for a country girl like herself at a time when marriage was a woman's best option.

As Garrick warned a young actor, comedy is a serious matter: *She Stoops to Conquer* joined a debate over the nature of man that had agitated comedy for a century. Thomas Hobbes's influential *Leviathan* (1651), depicting man as a selfish, power-hungry savage requiring strict controls, provided a philosophical basis for Restoration comedy to portray an urban jungle ruled by cynical, predatory, and dangerously attractive rakes who use wit to manipulate others and achieve dominance. Marriage is a defeat; the country is exile. Beginning in the 1690s, however, John Locke and his followers argued that man has a "moral sense," that even in the "state of nature" he was innately good and happy. These notions–and the strident moral-reform movement–spawned the "soft" or "sentimental" or "reform" comedy, pioneered by Cibber, which focuses on educating and reforming an erring character. Some of the reforms were ludicrous, however, and some of the moralized comedies, es-

For the Benefit of Mr. QUICK.

At the Theatre-Royal, Covent-Garden,

This preſent SATURDAY, MAY 8, 1773,

KING LEAR.

King Lear by Mr. ROSS,

Edgar by Mr. SMITH,

Gloſter by Mr. HULL,

Baſtard by Mr. BENSLEY,

Albany by Mr. OWENSON,

Cornwall by Mr. GARDNER,

Kent by Mr. CLARKE,

Gentleman Uſher by Mr. QUICK,

Being his FIRST APPEARANCE in that Character.

Goneril by Mrs. VINCENT,

Regan by Miſs PEARCE,

Cordelia by Miſs MILLER.

End of the Play, An Interlude, written by S. FOOTE, Eſq.

Lady Pentweazle, Mr. QUICK, Carmine, Mr. DAVIS.

After the Interlude, the WHIM,

By Mr. ALDRIDGE and Signora MANESIER.

To which will be added a new Farce (never performed) called

The GRUMBLER.

The PRINCIPAL PARTS by

Mr. QUICK,

Mr. DAVIS, Mr. OWENSON,

Mr. KING, Mr. SAUNDERS,

Miſs PEARCE and Miſs HELME.

On Monday, MACBETH.

With the Occaſional PRELUDE. And the MUSICAL LADY.

For the Benefit of Miſs BARSANTI.

Playbill advertising the only performance of the afterpiece Goldsmith wrote for John Quick, whose portrayal of Tony Lumpkin in She Stoops to Conquer *had helped to insure the play's success (by permission of the Henry E. Huntington Library and Art Gallery)*

pecially after Steele's *The Conscious Lovers* (1722), stiflingly genteel.

She Stoops to Conquer tries to correct both of these stylistic extremes. The triumphs of Tony, the attractiveness of the country, the warm yet moral relationships, and the happy prospects for young love put the Restoration "comedy of manners" in its narrowly circumscribed place. At the same time the laughter, particularly the "low" humor, the freedom of manners, the earthiness of the principals, and the lively courtship of Kate and Marlow show the moralists how their point should be made. The play is a virtual School for Comedy, yet it is also entertaining and farcical.

"Farcicality" was just the accusation made by the play's detractors, such as Walpole, and admitted by some of its friends, including Johnson. Even today, when the play is criticized, the word "farce" generally turns up. Less often it is called "sentimental"; rarely, and less probably, it is called both. Others have been able to see the farcing as part of a larger design. Virginia Woolf observed that "amusement of so pure a quality will never come our way again . . . [it is] perfect of its kind." A more typical modern defense is Ricardo Quintana's argument that *She Stoops to Conquer* is a masterpiece of irony. One of its best ironies came after the fact: in 1779 it was produced for the Quakers of Philadelphia as "A Lecture on the Disadvantages of Improper Education Exemplified in the History of Tony Lumpkin."

Though by now heartily sick of theatrical politics, Goldsmith undertook to provide something for the "benefit night" of John Quick, who, as Tony Lumpkin, had helped put across his comedy. It need not be much: Goldsmith's name would ensure a good turnout, and the piece would play only once. He seized upon *Le Grondeur* by de Brueys and La Palaprat (1691), which the Théâtre Français had cut from five acts to three; Charles Sedley had translated it as *The Grumbler* (1702), and an anonymous hand had altered and further reduced it, to two acts, in 1754. Goldsmith performed additional surgery: his version, with half the original plot, has one act. The Grumbler himself is a Theophrastan type (the self-tormentor) used as a blocking character, a *senex amans*: he wants to marry his son's fiancée because he finds her irascible manner (adopted to please him and get his consent) attractive. So she reverses her strategy, sends him a rough dancing master, and gets him to resign his pretensions. His brother then moralizes against "turbulence of temper." *The Grumbler* is what Georgian critics called "mere farce": a sketchy treatment of a conventional and absurd situation.

Goldsmith's last year was by no means easy. Enraged by a newspaper attack (probably by William Kenrick) that dragged in Mary Horneck, he caned the publisher and had to settle out of court for fifty pounds, then published a letter about freedom of the press that Johnson thought "a foolish thing well done." He envied Hugh Kelly the success of his new play, and Johnson and James Beattie their pensions, while he remained poor, overworked, and unwell. Gambling and other extravagances worsened his situation, and the booksellers were growing more cautious. Foregoing the amenities of Hyde to stay in London, he slaved away at his compilations, one imagines rather hopelessly, finishing volume one of his *Grecian History* in June, and making progress on his huge *History of the Earth* and an abridgment of his English history. There were brighter moments: Thomas Percy agreed to write his biography; he met Edward Gibbon; and General Pasquale Paoli, the Corsican patriot, paid him an elegant compliment: "M. Goldsmith est comme la mer, qui jette des perles et beaucoup d'autres belles choses, sans s'en appercevoir." But his mind ran on suicide: he argued about it with Johnson, went to view the room where Thomas Chatterton had killed himself, and lingered over Socrates' death in the *Grecian History*.

With his friends he grew testy when provoked, quarreling (but making up) with Johnson, reproaching Reynolds for glorifying Beattie in a portrait; and he paused to meditate a riposte after Garrick spoke his witty but harsh epitaph:

> Here lies Nolly Goldsmith, for shortness call'd Noll,
> Who wrote like an angel, but talked like poor Poll.

The result of this accumulated irritation was an unfinished poem, written early in 1774, called *Retaliation*: verse epitaphs for several friends who frequented the St. James coffeehouse. Though the tone varies, Goldsmith pulled few punches. With Burke (who played practical jokes on him) he is sharp: Burke, who "to party gave up, what was meant for mankind." Cumberland is smoothly flattered while his sentimental comedies are critiqued: "wherefore his characters thus without fault?" (Answer: he "drew from himself.") Reynolds is treated kindly, while Garrick receives the longest and, predictably, most cutting treatment. Superbly talented,

> On the stage he was natural, simple, affecting,
> 'Twas only that when he was off he was acting,

21

they spare nothing for their Pleasures, and the ease with which most of them throw away Money, makes it suspected that it is not got with much trouble.

Enter Scamper.

Scam. Sir a Gentleman would speak with you.

Jenny. Good here comes Scamper. he'll manage you I'll warrant me. [Aside]

Sour. Who is it.

Scam. He says his name is Monsieur Ri — Ri — Stay, Sir. I'll go and ask him again..

Sour. [pulling him by the Ears] Take that Sirrah, by the way.

Scam. Ahi! ahi. . . . Exit.

Jenny. Sir you have torn off his hair, so that he must now have a wig, you have pulled his Ears off; but there are none of them to be had for money

Sour. I'll teach him — 'tis certainly Mr. Rigaut my Notary, I know who it is, let him come in: Could he find no Time but this to bring me Money? Plague take the blockhead!

Enter Dancing Master and his fidler.

Sour. This is not my man; Who are you with your Compliments

Page from the playhouse copy of The Grumbler *submitted to the Examiner of Plays for licensing prior to its only performance, on 8 May 1773 (HM 23; by permission of the Henry E. Huntington Library and Art Gallery)*

a thing of trick, finesse, and (metaphorical) rouge. (It should be noted, however, that Garrick lent Goldsmith money to spend his final New Year's holiday with the Hornecks at Barton.)

The end came with unexpected swiftness; there was no time to mellow. Goldsmith's intestinal malaise worsened, but even as he was arranging to leave London and settle permanently with the Selbys in Hyde Lane, Garrick was writing retaliatory couplets that called him an "odd fellow" and, three times, a rake, bestowed on the world "For the joy of each sex," whatever that might mean. (When their mutual friend Isaac Bickerstaff fled England on a charge of homosexuality in 1771, a scurrilous poem connected him with Garrick.) Goldsmith's remove to the country came too late: he had to return to London in March to seek treatment for cystitis, dysuria, bladder stone, and kidney infection. There he was greeted by "Humourous Anecdotes of Dr. Goldsmith" in the March *Westminster Magazine*, for which he had written the previous year; they helped confirm his reputation as an eccentric and a buffoon. Though he called in Dr. William Hawes, he insisted on overdosing himself with "James's Fever Powder," a popular remedy he had tried before, against two physicians' advice. Vomiting and diarrhea followed and persisted. A third doctor was called in, who asked him, "Is your mind at ease?" "No," replied Goldsmith, "it is not." Those were his last recorded words: he died in convulsions at 3 A.M. on 4 April 1774 in his Temple rooms.

Burke wept, Johnson grieved, and Reynolds painted no more that day, but when they discovered that Goldsmith was some two thousand pounds in debt (Johnson: "Was ever poet so trusted before?"), they abandoned plans for a grand funeral. Goldsmith was buried quietly at the Temple church on 9 April, virtually without close friends in attendance–although the coffin was opened so that Mary Horneck could have the lock of hair she requested. There were discordant notes: his old enemy William Kenrick issued some unrepentant doggerel calling Goldsmith a "blundering, artless suicide," and *The Retaliation* appeared on 19 April. Such had been Goldsmith's industry right to the last that his bibliography, like the fingernails, kept growing after death: his two-volume *Grecian History*, an abridgment of his *History of England*, and his eight-volume *History of the Earth, and Animated Nature* were all published in June and July. Johnson wrote a mutual friend that "He had raised money and squandered it, by every artifice of acquisition, and folly of expence. But let not his frailties be remembered; he was a very great man." Yet he omitted him from his *Lives of the English Poets*, and Percy's thin memoir was not published until 1801.

Goldsmith's development as a writer was certainly stunted by the years of hack work; yet he managed to grow from a competent journalist to an acknowledged artist in the major literary forms of his age. Johnson (who insisted on composing his Westminster Abbey epitaph in Latin) hailed him as a "powerful yet kindly master of the emotions," a "versatile" genius who tried, and adorned, every genre. This last tribute has stuck as a label; his opus does have a breadth and competence that a Renaissance gentleman might admire. He could tune in various modes as well: if his writing sometimes seems essentially Augustan, as in *The Traveller*, at other times he sounds pre-Romantic (*The Deserted Village*). His reputation was higher in the nineteenth century, while his histories were still used, than it is today. *The Vicar of Wakefield* has lost its position as a classic, and his fiction and poetry are valued chiefly as poignant tokens of "the world we have lost." Only *She Stoops to Conquer* seems undiminished; it synthesizes much of what the Georgian enlightenment had to say about human values, its ironies are now appreciated, and it has attracted many of the greatest actors of this century: Laurence Olivier, Helen Hayes, Peggy Ashcroft, John Mills, Tom Courtenay, and many more. Through his second comedy Oliver Goldsmith seems likely to live a good while longer.

Letters:

The Collected Letters of Oliver Goldsmith, edited by Katharine C. Balderston (Cambridge: Cambridge University Press, 1928).

Bibliographies:

Temple Scott, *Oliver Goldsmith Bibliographically and Biographically Considered* (New York: Bowling Green Press, 1928);

Samuel Woods, *Oliver Goldsmith: A Reference Guide* (Boston: G. K. Hall, 1982).

Biographies:

Thomas Percy, Memoir of Goldsmith, in volume 1 of *The Miscellaneous Works of Oliver Goldsmith, M.B.* (London: Printed for J. Johnson by H. Baldwin & sons, 1801); modern edition of Percy's memoir: *Thomas Percy's Life of Dr. Oliver Goldsmith*, edited by Richard L. Harp (Salzburg: Institut für Englische Sprache und Literatur, 1976);

James Prior, *The Life of Oliver Goldsmith, M.B.*, 2 volumes (London: Murray, 1837);

John Forster, *The Life and Times of Oliver Goldsmith*, 3rd edition (London: Bradbury & Evans, 1848);

Washington Irving, *Oliver Goldsmith. A Biography* (New York: Putnam/London: John Murray, 1849);

Henry Austin Dobson, *The Life of Oliver Goldsmith* (London: Scott, 1888);

Ralph M. Wardle, *Oliver Goldsmith* (Lawrence: University of Kansas Press, 1957);

A. Lytton Sells, *Oliver Goldsmith: His Life and Works* (London: Allen and Unwin, 1974);

A. Norman Jeffares, "Goldsmith: The Good Natured Man," *Hermathena*, no. 119 (1975): 5-19;

John Ginger, *The Notable Man: The Life and Times of Oliver Goldsmith* (London: Hamilton, 1977).

References:

William W. Appleton, "The Double Gallant in Eighteenth-Century Comedy," in *English Writers of the Eighteenth Century*, edited by John H. Middendorf (New York: Columbia University Press, 1971);

John Bender, "Prison Reform and the Sentence of Narration in *The Vicar of Wakefield*," in *The New Eighteenth Century*, edited by Felicity Nussbaum and Laura Brown (New York & London: Methuen, 1987);

Marlies K. Danziger, *Oliver Goldsmith and Richard Brinsley Sheridan* (New York: Ungar, 1978);

Oliver W. Ferguson, "Antisentimentalism in *The Good Natur'd Man*: The Limits of Parody," in *The Dress of Words: Essays on Restoration and Eighteenth Century Literature in Honor of Richmond P. Bond*, University of Kansas Publication, Library Series 42, edited by Robert B. White, Jr. (Lawrence: University of Kansas Libraries, 1978), pp. 105-116;

Ferguson, "Sir Fretful Plagiary and Goldsmith's 'An Essay on the Theatre,' " in *Quick Springs of Sense: Studies in the Eighteenth Century*, edited by Larry S. Champion (Athens: University of Georgia Press, 1974), pp. 113-120;

W. T. Gallaway, Jr., "The Sentimentalism of Goldsmith," *PMLA*, 48 (December 1933): 1167-1181;

Byron Gassman, "French Sources of Goldsmith's *The Good Natur'd Man*," *Philological Quarterly*, 39 (January 1960): 56-65;

Morris Golden, "The Family-Wanderer Theme in Goldsmith," *ELH*, 25 (September 1958): 181-193;

Golden, "Goldsmith's Reputation in His Day," *Papers on Language and Literature*, 16 (Spring 1980): 213-238;

Mary Elizabeth Green, "Oliver Goldsmith and the Wisdom of the World," *Studies in Philology*, 77 (Spring 1980): 202-212;

Bernard Harris, "Goldsmith in the Theatre," in *The Art of Oliver Goldsmith*, edited by Andrew Swarbrick (London: Vision Press, 1984);

Robert B. Heilman, "The Sentimentalism of Goldsmith's *Good Natur'd Man*," in *Studies for William A. Read: A Miscellany Presented by Some of his Friends*, edited by Nathaniel M. Caffee and Thomas A. Kirby (University: Louisiana State University Press, 1940), pp. 237-253;

Richard Helgerson, "The Two Worlds of Oliver Goldsmith," *Studies in English Literature*, 13 (Summer 1973): 516-534;

Robert H. Hopkins, *The True Genius of Oliver Goldsmith* (Baltimore: Johns Hopkins Press, 1969);

Robert D. Hume, "Goldsmith and Sheridan and the Supposed Revolution of 'Laughing' Against 'Sentimental' Comedy," in *Studies in Change and Revolution*, edited by Paul Korshin (London & Menston: Scolar Press, 1972), pp. 237-276;

A. Norman Jeffares, *A Critical Commentary on She Stoops to Conquer* (London: Macmillan, 1966);

Jeffares, *Oliver Goldsmith* (London: Longmans, 1959);

Clara M. Kirk, *Oliver Goldsmith* (New York: Twayne, 1967);

Louis Kronenberger, *The Thread of Laughter* (New York: Hill & Wang, 1952);

Sean Lucy, ed., *Goldsmith, The Gentle Master* (Cork: Cork University Press, 1984);

Munro MacLennan, *The Secret of Oliver Goldsmith* (New York: Vantage, 1975);

Ricardo Quintana, "Goldsmith's Achievement as a Dramatist," *University of Toronto Quarterly*, 34 (January 1965): 159-177;

Quintana, *Oliver Goldsmith: A Georgian Study* (New York: Macmillan, 1967);

Quintana, "Oliver Goldsmith: Ironist to the Georgians," in *Eighteenth-Century Studies in Honor of Donald F. Hyde*, edited by W. H. Bond (New York: Grolier Club, 1970), pp. 297-310;

Joshua Reynolds, *Portraits by Sir Joshua Reynolds, Character Sketches of Oliver Goldsmith, Samuel Johnson, and David Garrick, together with Other*

Manuscripts of Reynolds Discovered among the Boswell Papers and now First Published, edited by Frederick W. Hilles (New York: McGraw-Hill, 1952), pp. 44-59;

Allen Rodway, "Goldsmith and Sheridan: Satirists of Sentiment," in *Renaissance and Modern Essays Presented to Vivian de Sola Pinto*, edited by G. R. Hibbard (London: Routledge & Kegan Paul, 1966), pp. 65-72;

G. S. Rousseau, ed., *Goldsmith: The Critical Heritage* (London & Boston: Routledge & Kegan Paul, 1974);

Virginia Woolf, "Oliver Goldsmith" (1934), in her *Collected Essays*, 2 volumes (London: Hogarth Press, 1966), I: 106-114.

Papers:

The Haunch of Venison, in the New York Public Library, is one of the few literary manuscripts extant in Goldsmith's hand. The Huntington Library has playhouse copies of *She Stoops to Conquer* (with the title "The Novel or Mistakes of a Night"; Larpent Collection, LA 349) and *The Grumbler* (HM 23).

Elizabeth Griffith

(11 October 1727?-5 January 1793)

Susan Staves
Brandeis University

PLAY PRODUCTIONS: *The Platonic Wife*, London, Theatre Royal in Drury Lane, 24 January 1765;

The Double Mistake, London, Theatre Royal in Covent Garden, 9 January 1766;

The School for Rakes, London, Theatre Royal in Drury Lane, 4 February 1769;

A Wife in the Right (also known as *Patience the Best Remedy*), London, Theatre Royal, Covent Garden, 9 March 1772;

The Times, London, Theatre Royal in Drury Lane, 2 December 1779.

BOOKS: *A Series of Genuine Letters between Henry and Frances*, by Elizabeth Griffith and Richard Griffith, volumes 1 and 2 (London: Printed for W. Johnston, 1757); volumes 3 and 4 (London: Printed for W. Johnston, 1766); volumes 5 and 6 (London: Printed for W. Richardson & L. Urquhart, 1770);

The Memoirs of Ninon de L'Enclos, with Her Letters to Monsr. de St. Evremond and to the Marquis de Sevigné, by Douxménil (and probably Louis Damours), translated by Griffith, 2 volumes (London: Printed for R. & J. Dodsley, 1761);

Amana. A Dramatic Poem. By a Lady, dedication signed Eliza Griffith (London: Printed by T. Harrison for W. Johnston, 1764);

The Platonic Wife. A Comedy. As it is Performed at the Theatre-Royal in Drury-Lane. By a Lady (London: Printed for W. Johnston, J. Dodsley & T. Davies, 1765);

The Double Mistake. A Comedy. As it is Performed at the Theatre-Royal in Covent-Garden (London: Printed for J. Almon, T. Lowndes, S. Bladon, & J. Williams, 1766);

The School for Rakes: A Comedy. As it is Performed at the Theatre-Royal in Drury-Lane (London: Printed for T. Becket & P. A. De Hondt, 1769);

Two Novels. In Letters. By the Authors of Henry and Frances, by Elizabeth Griffith and Richard Griffith, 4 volumes (London: Printed for T. Becket & P. A. De Hondt, 1769)–comprises *The Delicate Distress* by Elizabeth Griffith (two volumes) and *The Gordian Knot* by Richard Griffith (two volumes);

Memoirs, Anecdotes, and Characters of the Court of Lewis XIV, by Marie-Marguerite, marquise de Caylus, translated by Griffith, 2 volumes (London: Printed for the editor & sold by J. Dodsley, J. Murray, and Richardson & Urquhart, 1770);

The Shipwreck and Adventures of Monsieur Pierre Viaud, a Native of Bordeaux, and Captain of a Ship, by Jean Gaspard Dubois-Fontanelle, translated by Griffith (London: Printed for T. Davies, 1771);

The History of Lady Barton, A Novel, in Letters, 3 volumes (London: Printed for T. Davies & T. Cadell, 1771);

A Wife in the Right: A Comedy (London: Printed for the author & sold by E. & C. Dilly, J. Robson & J. Walter, 1772);

The Fatal Effects of Inconstancy, or, Letters of the Marchioness de Syrcé, the Count de Mirbelle, and Others, by Claude Joseph Dorat, translated by Griffith, 2 volumes (London: Printed by J. Bew, 1774);

The Morality of Shakespeare's Drama Illustrated (London: Printed for T. Cadell, 1775);

The Story of Lady Juliana Harley. A Novel. In Letters, 2 volumes (London: Printed for T. Cadell, 1776);

A Letter from Monsieur Desenfans to Mrs. Montagu, by Noel Desenfans, translated by Griffith (London: Printed for T. Cadell, 1777);

The Princess of Cleves. An Historical Novel, by Marie-Madeleine, comtesse de La Fayette, perhaps translated by Griffith (London: Printed for J. Wilkie, 1777);

The Times: A Comedy. As it is now Performing at the

Elizabeth Griffith

Theatre Royal in Drury-Lane (London: Printed for Fielding & Walker, J. Dodsley, T. Becket & T. Davies, 1780);

Novellettes, Selected for the Use of Young Ladies and Gentlemen, by Griffith, Oliver Goldsmith, and Mr. McMillan (London: Printed for Fielding & Walker, 1780)–comprises one story by McMillan, two stories by Goldsmith, and thirteen stories by Griffith first published in *The Westminster Magazine, or the Pantheon of Taste* between 1773 and 1779;

Essays, Addressed to Young Married Women (London: Printed for T. Cadell & J. Robson, 1782).

OTHER: *A Collection of Novels, selected and revised by Mrs. Griffith*, 3 volumes (London: Printed for G. Kearsly, 1777);

François Marie Arouet (Voltaire), *Works, Translated from the French; with Notes, Critical and Explanatory*, translated by Griffith and others, 14 volumes, edited by W. Kenrick (London: Printed for Fielding & Walker, 1779-1781).

Like Elizabeth Inchbald, Elizabeth Griffith was a professional actress who later had success as a playwright and novelist. Her plays mix conventional comedy with sentiment, topical satire, and

to surfeit him. He has had a dozen Amours at least, within these twelve Months.

Ld.y Frank– A dozen, did you say, Lady Fanshaw?

Ld.y Fan– I did indeed; & your Ladyship may be assured I have spoken within bounds.

Clar– I dare say so too– And yet he has behaved with honour to them all.

Ld.y Frank– How you amaze me! With honour said you? I thought till now that Constancy in Love had been a Virtue.

Ld.y Fan:– I have met with some such musty Morals, among the metaphysics of old Romances, but ye. Bonton of later times, have exploded it long since I assure yr. Ladyship.

Enter Fontange

Font– I humbly beg a mille pardon of your Ladyship, & of all dé Ladyships, for me Entre here, but I have a beg of Nicodumpus this half hour, to bring a this Lettre to your Ladyship; but he pretend a he does not entendez moy, & I am forced to bring it myself; for which I beg a mille pardon again.

Ld.y Frank– Give it me, Madem.le; I shall return immediately. {Exeunt Ld.y F. & Font.

Sr. Wm. Bel– Each Word each Glance discovers some new Charm; And dead, not cold is her, she cannot warm. [Looking after her.]

Ld.y Fan– O fye, Sir William! what a mere whining Inamorato you are! Why don't you say all these fine things to her face? What signifies you sighing them out after she has got beyond Ear shot?

Sr. Wm. Bel– The delicate & high Respect I bear toward her Ladyship's unhappy Situation, must seal my Lips in everlasting Silence,— Nor shall I ever breath a Sigh or Wish that may offend her.

Ld.y Fan: & Clar– Ha, ha, ha!

Clar– And so you think she would be offended– Lord, Sr. William! tho' you are very young, you need not pretend to be quite so innocent. Offended! Ha, ha, ha!

Enter Ld.y Frankland—

I am pleas'd to hear you are so merry Ladies; prithee Communicate the Occasion, for I should be glad to try if there be Sympathy in Mirth, as well as Contagion in Sorrow. Do tell me what you laugh at?

Sr. Wm. Bel:– Lady Fanshaw & Clarinda, madam, were saying—

Page from the playhouse copy of The Platonic Wife *submitted to the Examiner of Plays for licensing prior to the first performance, on 24 January 1765 (Larpent Collection, LA 244; by permission of the Henry E. Huntington Library and Art Gallery)*

explicit didactic advice to women. Like her Georgian contemporaries, Hugh Kelly and Richard Cumberland, she wrote comedy descended from the earlier English exemplary comedy of Colley Cibber and Richard Steele but given new life by the sentimental and enlightenment commitments of the 1760s and 1770s in both England and France. Those modern historians of the drama who have mentioned her plays have generally found them undistinguished, often dramatically inept and tediously sententious; her contemporaries gave her plays more mixed reviews, sometimes complaining about poor plotting or lack of incident, but usually finding her sentiments and her morals admirable. Domestic issues, particularly the proper conduct of wives and husbands, important in many Georgian comedies, are especially so to Griffith, who endeavored, despite complaint from some of her audiences and critics, to present women characters as serious moral beings. Her mixing assertions of women's abilities with relentless respectability and an acceptance of the propriety of women's subordination to men is not likely to appeal to the casual modern reader, but nevertheless represents an important kind of eighteenth-century feminism.

Griffith first achieved public notice as an actress at the Smock Alley Theatre, Dublin, debuting in the role of Juliet in *Romeo and Juliet* on 13 October 1749. Among her other Dublin roles were Cordelia in *Lear*, Calista in Nicholas Rowe's *Fair Penitent*, Lucinda in Richard Steele's *Conscious Lovers*, and Jane Shore in Rowe's she-tragedy of that name. Although there has been some doubt about the place of Griffith's birth, she seems to have been born in Dublin on 11 October 1727 to Thomas and Jane Foxcroft Griffith. Her father (1680-1744) was an actor, as was her brother Richard. In a period when women were denied access to the formal literary education available to gentlemen, Griffith's professional familiarity with the roles she played was an important part of her literary education and preparation for her later career as a writer.

Griffith's romance with Richard Griffith (1716-1788), an educated Irish gentleman-farmer, led to the publication of what contemporaries regarded as one of her most interesting works, *A Series of Genuine Letters between Henry and Frances*, published in six volumes between 1757 and 1770. These *Letters* appear to be edited versions of actual letters Richard, as "Henry," and Elizabeth, as "Frances," wrote to each other over years of courtship, and, later, marriage. During the troubled years of their courtship, Henry is reluctant to propose marriage, pleading that neither of them has an adequate fortune, and Frances is in some danger of becoming his mistress. At one point she writes to him, "I am not so unreasonable to take it ill, that you do not offer what, I know, is not, at present, within your Power and Prudence; but, I have really great Reason to resent, that you should attempt to offer me any thing short of it." Many of the letters touch on literary and philosophical subjects of mutual interest, like the letters of Jonathan Swift and Alexander Pope or Cicero's *Offices*; Griffith clearly values the opportunity to supplement her limited education. After five years of this correspondence, alternately affectionate and embittered, the two were privately married in Dublin on 12 May 1751, with Lady Orrery as a witness. Subsequent letters deal with the marital relationship of the two and with their ideas for various literary projects. The advertised "genuineness" of the *Letters* encouraged eighteenth-century readers to believe in the possibilities of sentiment in everyday life, and provided for some women readers a useful model of the intelligent, reflective woman. The young Fanny Burney professed to like the *Genuine Letters* better than *The Vicar of Wakefield* (1766), writing in her diary, "Those Letters are doubly pleasing, charming to me, for being genuine–they have encreased my relish for *minute, heartfelt* writing, and encouraged me in my attempt to give an opinion of the books I read."

Amana, Griffith's first play, is the least typical of her dramatic works. It is the only tragedy, the only verse drama, and the only unperformed play she published. Basing her plot on an Oriental tale by John Hawkesworth, Griffith retains much of Hawkesworth's exotic Orientalism and some of his moral warning against presumptuous attempts "to direct the hand of Providence." Osmin, the sultan of Egypt, bored despite his seraglio, sends his slave Caled to find a beautiful virgin capable of rousing his soul "to a sense of pleasure." Caled seizes Amana just as she is about to marry her lover, Nouradin, a young Egyptian merchant. Despite Osmin's worst threats, Amana makes it clear that she will die rather than submit to him–and obtains poison to effect her purpose. Nouradin, to rescue Amana, disguises himself as Osmin, but by the time he can reveal himself to her, she has already drunk the poison. Griffith departs from Hawkesworth by giving Amana an English father, Abdalla, by making Amana's resistance to Osmin more active, and by developing contrasts between British liberty and Oriental despotism. The more villainous male characters offer negative

Kitty Clive, who created the roles of Lady Fanshaw in The Platonic Wife *and Mrs. Winifred in* The School for Rakes *(engraving by Charles Mosley)*

characterizations of the female sex, which the play then shows are untrue "libels" on the sex. Thus, Osmin on women:

> But what are they? The very sport of nature;
> Formed solely for our use, like the fair flower
> That blooms but to be cropt, then cast away.

That a relatively uneducated female actress should attempt her debut as a playwright with a verse tragedy shows surprisingly high literary ambition. The *Monthly Review* considered *Amana* "not .... unacceptable as a poem to those who love refined sentiments and morals." *The Critical Review*, however, did what it could to discourage Griffith from further effort in this vein, complaining that the author "seems to have a fine lady's disease, the vapours; as appears by her fancying herself a POETESS, and her performance a dramatic poem."

Perhaps discouraged by the reception of *Amana*, Griffith then turned to comedy, a genre in which she was to have more success. Her first comedy, *The Platonic Wife*, is based on one of the elegant stories of Jean-François Marmontel, "L'hereux divorce," from the popular *Contes moraux*. The female protagonist, Lady Frankland, makes such extravagant demands for romance of her husband that she forces a separation. While separated, she attempts to show that a married woman can have male friends, but the lesson of the play is that such Platonic friendship is impossible. *The Platonic Wife* yields a double moral: overtly, Lady Frankland must learn that she is not entitled to have her demands for romance within marriage met and that she requires the protection of her husband to live with happiness and reputation; covertly, however, the play suggests that as soon as a good woman relinquishes her demand for romance within marriage as an entitlement, her husband will give her romance, indeed, romantic adulation as a free gift. Among the characters added to the Marmontel story by Griffith are two sophisticated and cynical ladies who are so jealous of Lady Frankland's reputation for virtue and of her happiness with her husband that they conspire against her. Such characters are rather common in Griffith's plays; their lives add a harsher realism to plays in which the main plots can sometimes seem cloyingly sentimental. Griffith also adds a lively set of servants–English, French, Irish, and West Indian–who vividly demonstrate the social conflicts that resulted when fashionable Londoners in the age of empire filled their households with both domestic and foreign servants. Her Irish servant turns out to have more conscience than stage Irishmen usually did, while the less scrupulous French maid is used to point a patriotic moral about the folly of Britons who buy foreign products or employ foreigners "while there are persons in our own country, both in trade and service, sufficient to supply our uses." On opening night (24 January 1765), *The Platonic Wife* was greeted with applause from some but "catcalls, hisses, groans, and horselaughs" from others; certain quick alterations, including apparently the repainting of a badly done portrait of Lady Frankland crucial to the couple's reconciliation, earned the play a respectable six-day run.

It appears from the epilogue to *The Platonic Wife* that Griffith was in the audience to witness the fate of her first play. According to Benjamin Victor, when she was ready for the presentation of her next comedy, *The Double Mistake* (1766), "Her private friends advised her very prudently to conceal herself." *The Double Mistake* is Griffith's only experiment with the Spanish *capa y espada* play, being ultimately based on Calderón's *No siempre lo peor es cierto* (1652), probably through the mediation of George Digby's loose translation of Calderón, *Elvira: or the worst not always certain* (1667). Her heroine, Emily Southerne, successfully resists her father's attempt to make her marry an old man and manages to marry instead her lover, Sir Charles Somerville, although it takes all five acts before Sir Charles has a satisfactory explanation for his discovery of a strange man in Emily's bedroom. The strange man turns out to have been Harry Freeman, the younger and lazier son of a Lombard Street banker who "formerly sold rum and hops in Bishopsgate-street." Harry hopes to enrich himself by eloping with Louisa Belmont, a romantic young sister of Lord Belmont. Harry's older brother, however, is presented as the ideal type of the businessman. Lord Belmont moralizes about the pleasures of conscientiously settling one's accounts, and Lord Belmont and the Elder Freeman engage in mutual admiration, including even an invitation from the nobleman to his banker to visit him in the country as a friend. Incidental comedy is provided in the satire of a learned lady fond of Greek and Latin and of an elderly bachelor antiquarian, torn between his cravings for Roman antiquities and natural curiosities including talking parrots and black tulips. Despite Emily's invocation of "the rights of human kind" in her resistance to forced marriage, she also articulates what the play recommends as the correct attitude for women: "by nature and by providence designed, our helpless sex's strength lies in dependence; and where we are so blest to meet with generous natures, our servitude is empire. . . ."

Issues of proper conduct for women and a forced marriage also figure in Griffith's most popular play, *The School for Rakes* (1769), the only one of her plays to be anthologized in *Bell's British Theatre*. Lord Eustace, in love with Harriet Evans, has tricked her into an invalid marriage, then been commanded by his father to marry a wealthy young woman and threatened with disinheritance should he attempt to defy his father's command. Once Harriet and her father, Sir William Evans, learn, through a newspaper announcement, of Lord Eustace's impending wedding, a moral and prudential dilemma arises: even should Lord Eustace repent his treachery to Harriet, ought she to be willing to forgive him and to marry him? In the end, however, Lord Eustace's contrition and bravery effect a reconciliation. Sir William, changing his mind on the vexed question of whether rakes can make acceptable husbands, declares: "The man who sincerely repents of error, is farther removed from vice, than one who has never been guilty." *The School for Rakes* was Griffith's adaptation of Pierre-Augustin Caron de Beaumarchais's first play, *Eugénie* (1767), an adaptation done with the assistance of David Garrick. In *Eugénie* the heroine has both been tricked into a false marriage and made pregnant by a count. Griffith elected to omit the pregnancy and generally to soften the character of her rake, observing in her advertisement that she hoped "his compunction, for the crime he had committed, will render him more worthy the favour of a British audience, whose generous natures cannot brook the repre-

Thomas King, who created the role of William Woodley in The Times *(portrait by Benjamin Wilson; by permission of the Garrick Club)*

sentation of any vice, upon the stage, except in order to have it punished, and reclaimed."

Not only adaptation but also translation from the French was an important part of Griffith's literary career. The worldliness of some of the French texts she elected to translate contrasts strikingly with the sometimes repressive didacticism and domestic sentiment of her more original drama and fiction. Her *Memoirs of Ninon de L'Enclos* (1761), a libertine woman, are prefaced by a commendatory poem likening the translator to asbestos, capable of passing through dangerous fire only to gain in purity. *The Shipwreck and Adventures of Monsieur Pierre Viaud* (1771), very probably an authentic narrative of a Frenchman shipwrecked off the coast of Florida, is an exciting account of the struggle to survive under harrowing conditions. Madame La Coutre, a bourgeois matron stranded with the narrator, displays considerable practical energy, helping to kill an alligator the narrator has stunned, then making leggings from rawhide to protect their legs from the underbrush. Griffith, who probably decided to translate this adventure partly to gratify nationalistic pride and curiosity during the brief time when Florida was a British possession, must also have been intrigued by the adventures of Madame La Coutre, who shows such courage. Griffith's reading and translation of French novelists such as Marie-Madeleine, comtesse de La Fayette, and Claude Joseph Dorat helped shape her practice as a novelist. The influence of the French *drame*, the new bourgeois form, on her plays is equally evident, and not only in her adaptation of Beaumarchais. We also know from her 1767 correspondence with Garrick that she prepared a version of Denis Diderot's *Père de famille* (1758) that seems never to have been produced, although it is less clear whether her version was one of the anonymous ones published or whether she also translated Diderot's *Fils naturel* (1758).

The only one of Griffith's plays not to have

a known source, *A Wife in the Right* (1772), also had the most disastrous stage history. Lady Seaton, a wife for only a few months, has reason to believe that her husband has already been unfaithful to her and that his mistress is Miss Charlotte Melville, a friend of Lady Seaton's who has been staying with Lady Seaton but who has suddenly and mysteriously left the house. Considerably less refined comedy is provided by Governor Anderson, Lady Seaton's uncle, recently returned from India and intent on buying a seat in Parliament, in part so that his enjoyment of Indian food and loose Indian dress may be made more general through the passage of an act "that curry and pellow shall be the common food, and that there shan't be a button worn in all England." The governor is victimized by a set of contemporary low characters including Squeezem, a borough jobber who claims to have spent one thousand pounds in a single day on food and drink for voters; Bull, a stockbroker who touts inside-trader information on the value of East India stock; and Mrs. Frankley, a cynical and greedy young widow who raises money by pawning the diamonds the governor has given her and wearing paste instead. In the upper plot, Charlotte Melville is discovered to have been faithful to her lover, Colonel Ramsey, who returns hoping to marry her after two years abroad. Lord Seaton, we eventually learn, had loved Charlotte and wished to break his engagement to marry her, but she fled rather than betray either her love for Colonel Ramsey or her friendship with Lady Seaton. Among the erroneous views Lord Seaton has to recant is his early declaration that "Female friendships . . . are not among the perennials of life." For her part, Lady Seaton, despite the correctness of her conduct in not upbraiding her husband either for his apparent infidelity or for his occasional rudeness to her, has to repent that, although she loved Lord Seaton when she married him, she was aware that he did not love her. The candid disclosures of husband and wife to each other, their self-recrimination and requests for forgiveness, lead first to Lord Seaton's assuring his wife that she had his "confidence and esteem" and then, rapidly, to the awakening in him of a genuine "tenderness" toward her. *A Wife in the Right*, however, was doomed to have only one performance. The opening scheduled for 5 March 1772 had to be postponed because Edward Shutter, cast as the governor, was too drunk to appear. When, on 9 March, the play did open, Shutter offered a confession and apology to the audience, but this colloquy with the audience, according to Griffith, "threw him into such confusion, that he was not able to get the better of it, throughout the whole performance," forgetting much of his part and ad-libbing wildly. At the conclusion of the performance, when a second performance the following night was announced, shouts for and against broke out, apples and half-pence were thrown, a chandelier broken, and, finally, the comedy withdrawn. Thus deprived of the usual opportunity to publish her play during its first run, Griffith had recourse to publishing *A Wife in the Right* by subscription; subscribers included–besides Gertrude Russell, duchess of Bedford, her early patron–Edmund Burke, James Boswell, Elizabeth Montagu, and Sir Joshua Reynolds.

Griffith's comedies all suggest the later eighteenth-century imperial London of conspicuous consumption: of portraits painted by fashionable Italian or English artists, of pleasure gardens at Vauxhall and Ranelagh, of gambling at cards, and of auctions of fine china or Oriental curiosities at Mr. Longford's or Christie's. The expensiveness of this conspicuous consumption is the central subject of her final play, *The Times* (1779). Simply by indulging themselves in conventional fashionable expenses, Mr. William Woodley and Lady Mary Woodley, a sympathetic and loving young married couple, have run through his estate of four thousand pounds a year. Mr. Woodley is contrite, but so uxorious that even as his wife sends him out to buy another thousand-pounds' worth of jewels to be added to her earrings, he cannot bear to tell her that the bailiffs are virtually at the door. When Mr. Woodley finally has no alternative but to tell his wife of their approaching ruin, she astonishes him by volunteering to sign over her jointure as security for their debts and expressing her willingness to embark instantly on a simpler country life. Lady Woodley's sacrifice of her jointure, romantically rejected by her husband, is shortly made unnecessary when Sir William Woodley, a crotchety but kindly uncle who has been waiting for them to reform, undertakes to pay the debts himself. Equal sensibility and even superior morality are to be found in a subplot where Mr. Belford, a virtuous middle-aged lawyer, offered a match with the pretty and wealthy eighteen-year-old Louisa Woodley, gallantly declines to force her inclination and generously assists her in gaining her relatives' consent to her marriage with the equally virtuous, and younger, Colonel Mountfort. *The Times* is based on *Le Borru bienfaissant* by the great Italian playwright Carlo Goldoni; Goldoni moved to Paris late in his career and wrote this successful play in

French for a Paris audience of 1771.

Among Griffith's miscellaneous prose works, *The Morality of Shakespeare's Drama Illustrated* (1775) and *Essays, Addressed to Young Married Women* (1782) are worth noting. *The Morality*, praised by contemporaries, along with Charlotte Lennox's *Shakespear Illustrated* (1753-1754) and Elizabeth Montagu's *An Essay on the Writings and Genius of Shakespeare* (1769), is one of the earliest attempts at literary criticism by a woman. Shakespeare, who, like these women, had never been to a university, was an especially tempting subject, a leading candidate for the position of British Bard in a period of new national self-confidence, a great writer about whom they could dare to write. *Essays*, Griffith's last book, is a fairly conventional compendium of advice for the period, urging women to accept the responsibilities of behaving like morally serious people and emphasizing obligations to the family. The *Monthly Review* began its account by announcing, "Mrs. Griffith's reputation, as an elegant Moralist, is so perfectly established, that it wants no succor from our applause." In the *Essays* Griffith speaks in part as the successfully married woman whose marriage has been documented in *The Genuine Letters* and whose comedies have presented sympathetic married couples solving problems of contemporary marriage.

After this productive and quite celebrated literary life, Griffith, with her husband, retired from London to live in Ireland on an estate acquired by their son Richard, who had made his fortune in the East India trade. Richard, her husband and fellow author, died in 1788; Griffith followed on 5 January 1793. Her obituary in the *Gentleman's Magazine* noted her "excellence in composition, intended to reach the heart," and quoted a late poet to call her "A second Sappho, with a purer flame." With very few early advantages beyond her family's place in the minor theatrical world of Dublin, and battling the usual money and health anxieties so commonly attendant on literary lives in the eighteenth century, Griffith preserved her self-respect and made herself into a contemporary female literary celebrity. She has left us a set of works which illuminate both her own remarkable life and the struggles of more ordinary women to lead imaginatively and morally fulfilling lives in the eighteenth century.

Letters:

The Private Correspondence of David Garrick, 2 volumes, edited by James Boaden (London: Colburn & Bentley, 1831-1832).

Bibliography:

J. E. Norton, "Some Uncollected Authors XXII: Elizabeth Griffith, 1727-1793," *Book Collector*, 8 (1959): 418-424.

References:

Ellen Argyros, " 'Intruding Herself Into the Chair of Criticism': Elizabeth Griffith and *The Morality of Shakespeare's Drama Illustrated*," in *Proceedings of the Conference on Eighteenth-Century Women and the Arts*, edited by Frederick R. Keener and Susan E. Lorsch (New York: Greenwood Press, 1988), pp. 283-289;

Susan David Bernstein, "Ambivalence and Writing; Elizabeth and Richard Griffith's *A Series of Genuine Letters between Henry and Frances*," in *Proceedings of the Conference on Eighteenth-Century Women and the Arts*, pp. 269-276;

Dorothy Hughes Eshleman, *Elizabeth Griffith: A Biographical and Critical Study* (Philadelphia: University of Pennsylvania, 1949);

Marla Harris, " 'How Nicely Circumspect Must Your Conduct Be': Double Standards in Elizabeth Griffith's *History of Lady Barton*," in *Proceedings of the Conference on Eighteenth-Century Women and the Arts*, pp. 277-282;

Gordon Ruesch, "On Editing Elizabeth Griffith's *Platonic Wife*," in *Proceedings of the Conference on Eighteenth-Century Women and the Arts*, pp. 263-276.

Papers:

Most of the surviving letters of Griffith to David Garrick are at the Victoria and Albert Museum; a few Griffith letters are at Harvard. The Larpent Collection at the Huntington Library includes manuscripts for *The Platonic Wife, The Double Mistake, Patience the Best Remedy* (also known as *A Wife in the Right*), and *The Times;* Larpent manuscripts are generally written by professional copyists rather than authors, although some revisions may be authorial.

Thomas Holcroft

(10 December 1745-23 March 1809)

Sid Sondergard
St. Lawrence University

See also the Holcroft entry in *DLB 39: British Novelists, 1660-1800.*

PLAY PRODUCTIONS: *The Crisis; or, Love and Fear,* London, Theatre Royal in Drury Lane, 1 May 1778;

Duplicity, London, Theatre Royal, Covent Garden, 13 October 1781; revised as *The Mask'd Friend,* London, Theatre Royal, Covent Garden, 6 May 1796;

The Noble Peasant, London, Theatre Royal in the Hay-Market, 2 August 1784;

The Follies of a Day; or, The Marriage of Figaro, translated from Pierre-Augustin Caron de Beaumarchais's play, London, Theatre Royal, Covent Garden, 14 December 1784; reduced to three-act afterpiece, London, Theatre Royal, Drury Lane, 7 November 1789;

The Choleric Fathers, London, Theatre Royal, Covent Garden, 10 November 1785;

Seduction, London, Theatre Royal, Drury Lane, 12 March 1787;

The German Hotel, adapted from Johann Christian Brandes's *Der Gasthoff,* attributed to Holcroft, London, Theatre Royal, Covent Garden, 11 November 1790;

The School for Arrogance, London, Theatre Royal, Covent Garden, 4 February 1791;

The Road to Ruin (also known as *The City Prodigals; or, the Widow Bewitched*), London, Theatre Royal, Covent Garden, 18 February 1792;

Love's Frailties; or, Precept Against Practice, London, Theatre Royal, Covent Garden, 5 February 1794;

The Rival Queens; or, Drury-Lane and Covent-Garden, London, Theatre Royal, Covent Garden, 15 September 1794;

The Deserted Daughter (also known as *'Tis a Strange World*), London, Theatre Royal, Covent Garden, 2 May 1795;

The Man of Ten Thousand, London, Theatre Royal, Drury Lane, 23 January 1796;

The Force of Ridicule, adapted from Pierre Claude Nivelle de la Chausée's *Le Préjugé à la mode,* London, Theatre Royal, Drury Lane, 6 December 1796;

Knave or Not? (also known as *Knave or No Knave?*), London, Theatre Royal, Drury Lane, 25 January 1798;

He's Much to Blame (also known as *The Disloyal Lover*), London, Theatre Royal, Covent Garden, 13 February 1798;

The Inquisitor, London, Theatre Royal in the Hay-Market, 23 June 1798;

The Old Clothesman, London, Theatre Royal, Covent Garden, 2 April 1799;

Deaf and Dumb; or, The Orphan Protected, translated from Jean Nicolas Bouilly's *L'abbé de l'Epée,* London, Theatre Royal, Drury Lane, 24 February 1801;

The Escapes; or, the Water Carrier, London, Theatre Royal, Covent Garden, 14 October 1801;

A Tale of Mystery, adapted from Charles Guilbert de Pixerécourt's *Coelina,* London, Theatre Royal, Covent Garden, 13 November 1802;

Hear Both Sides (also known as *The Lawyer*), London, Theatre Royal, Drury Lane, 29 January 1803;

The Lady of the Rock, London, Theatre Royal, Drury Lane, 12 February 1805;

The Vindictive Man, London, Theatre Royal, Drury Lane, 20 November 1806.

BOOKS: *Elegies. I. On the Death of Samuel Foote, Esq. II. On Age. By Thomas Holcroft, of the Theatre Royal, Drury-Lane* (London: J. Bew, 1777);

A Plain and Succinct Narrative of the Late Riots and Disturbances in the Cities of London and Westminster, and Borough of Southwark . . . with an Account of the Commitment of Lord George Gordon

Thomas Holcroft (portrait by John Opie; by permission of the National Portrait Gallery, London; Copyright Photograph, Reg. No. 512)

to the Tower, and Anecdotes of His Life, as William Vincent of Gray's Inn (London: Printed for Fielding & Walker, 1780);

Alwyn; or The Gentleman Comedian, 2 volumes (London: Printed for Fielding & Walker, 1780);

Duplicity: A Comedy. As it is Performed at the Theatre-Royal, Covent Garden (London: G. Robinson, 1781);

The Trial of the Hon. George Gordon commonly called Lord George Gordon, for High-Treason, at the Bar of the Court of King's Bench, on Monday, the 5th of February, 1781.... Taken in Shorthand, as William Vincent (London: Printed for Fielding & Walker, 1781);

Human Happiness; or The Sceptic. A Poem, in Six Cantos (London: Printed for L. Davis, 1783);

The Family Picture; or, Domestic Dialogues on Amiable and Interesting Subjects: Illustrated by Histories, Allegories, Tales, Fables, Anecdotes, &c. Intended to Strengthen and Inform the Mind, 2 volumes (London: Printed for Lockyer Davis, 1783);

The Noble Peasant; A Comic Opera in Three Acts (London: G. Robinson, 1784);

Philosophic Essays on the Manners of Various Foreign Animals; with Observations on the Laws and Customs of Several Eastern Nations. Written in French by Foucher d'Obsonville, translated by Holcroft (London: Printed for J. Johnson, 1784);

The Follies of a Day; or, The Marriage of Figaro. A Comedy, as it is Now Performing at the Theatre-Royal, Covent-Garden. From the French of M. De Beaumarchais, translated by Holcroft (London: G. G. J. & J. Robinson, 1785);

Tales of the Castle: or, Stories of Instruction and Delight. Being Les veillées du château, Written in French by Madame la Comtesse de Genlis, 5 volumes, translated by Holcroft (London: Printed for G. Robinson, 1785);

The Choleric Fathers. A Comic Opera. Performed at the Theatre-Royal in Covent-Garden (London: G. G. J. & J. Robinson, 1785);

Sacred Dramas Written in French by Madame la Comtesse de Genlis, translated by Holcroft (London: G. G. J. & J. Robinson, 1786);

Caroline of Lichtfield: A Novel, Translated from the French, 2 volumes, by Isabelle, baroness de Montolieu, translated by Holcroft (London: Printed for G. G. J. & J. Robinson, 1786);

Seduction: A Comedy. As it is Performed at the The-

atre-Royal in Drury-Lane (London: Printed for G. G. J. & J. Robinson, 1787);

The Present State of the Empire of Morocco. Its Animals, Products, Climate, Soil, Cities, Ports, Provinces, Coins, Weights, and Measures. With the Language, Religion, Laws, Manners, Customs, and Character, of the Moors; the History of the Dynasties Since Edris; the Naval Force and Commerce of Morocco; and the Character, Conduct, and Views, Political and Commercial, of the Reigning Emperor. Tr. from the French of M. Chénier, 2 volumes, by Louis de Chénier, translated by Holcroft (London: G. G. J. & J. Robinson, 1788);

The Life of Baron Frederic Trenck; Containing His Adventures; His Cruel and Excessive Sufferings, During Ten Years Imprisonment, at the Fortress of Magdeburg, by Command of the Late King of Prussia; also, Anecdotes, Historical, Political, and Personal. Tr. from the German, 4 volumes, translated by Holcroft (London: G. G. J. & J. Robinson, 1788-1793);

Posthumous Works of Frederic II, King of Prussia, 13 volumes, translated by Holcroft (London: Printed for G. G. J. & J. Robinson, 1789);

Essays on Physiognomy; for the Promotion of the Knowledge and the Love of Mankind, by Johann Caspar Lavater, translated by Holcroft, 3 volumes (London: Printed for G. G. J. & J. Robinson, 1789);

The German Hotel; a Comedy. As Performed at the Theatre Royal, Covent Garden, by Johann Christian Brandes, translated by Holcroft (London: G. G. J. & J. Robinson, 1790);

The School for Arrogance: A Comedy. As it is Acted at the Theatre Royal, Covent Garden (London: G. G. J. & J. Robinson, 1791);

The Road to Ruin: A Comedy. As it is Acted at the Theatre Royal, Covent-Garden (London: Printed for J. Debrett, 1792); modern edition, edited by Ruth I. Aldrich (Lincoln: University of Nebraska Press, 1968);

Anna St. Ives; A Novel, 7 volumes (London: Printed for Shepperson & Reynolds, 1792);

The Adventures of Hugh Trevor, 6 volumes (volumes 1-3, London: Printed for Shepperson & Reynolds, 1794; volumes 4-6, London: Printed for G. G. & J. Robinson and Shepperson & Reynolds, 1797);

Love's Frailties: A Comedy in Five Acts, as Performed at the Theatre Royal, Covent-Garden (London: Printed for Shepperson & Reynolds, 1794);

The Deserted Daughter: A Comedy. As it is Acted at the Theatre Royal, Covent-Garden (London: Printed for G. G. J. & J. Robinson, 1795);

A Narrative of Facts, Relating to a Prosecution for High Treason; Including the Address to the Jury, Which the Court Refused to Hear; with Letters to the Attorney General, Lord Chief Justice Eyre, Mr. Serjeant Adair, the Honourable Thomas Erskine, and Vicary Gibbs Esq. and the Defence the Author Had Prepared, if He Had Been Brought to Trial (London: Printed for H. D. Symonds, 1795);

A Letter to the Right Honourable William Windham on the Intemperance and Dangerous Tendency of His Public Conduct (London: Printed for H. D. Symonds, 1795);

The Man of Ten Thousand: A Comedy. As it is Acted at the Theatre Royal, Drury Lane (London: Printed for G. G. & J. Robinson, 1796);

Travels through Germany, Switzerland, Italy, and Sicily. Tr. from the German of Frederic Leopold Count Stolberg, 2 volumes, translated by Holcroft (London: Printed for G. G. & J. Robinson, 1796, 1797);

Knave; or Not? A Comedy: in Five Acts. As Performed at the Theatre Royal, Drury-Lane (London: Printed for G. G. & J. Robinson, 1798);

He's Much to Blame, a Comedy: in Five Acts. As Performed at the Theatre Royal, Covent Garden (London: Printed for G. G. & J. Robinson, 1798);

The Inquisitor; a Play, in Five Acts. As Performed at the Theatre-Royal in the Hay-market (London: G. G. & J. Robinson, 1798);

Herman and Dorothea. A Poem from the German of Goethe, translated by Holcroft (London: Printed for T. N. Longman & O. Rees, 1801);

Deaf and Dumb: or, The Orphan Protected: an Historical Drama. In Five Acts. Performed by Their Majesties Servants of the Theatre Royal, in Drury-Lane, February 24th, 1801, by Jean Nicolas Bouilly, translated by Holcroft (London: Printed for J. Ridgway by J. D. Dewick, 1801);

A Tale of Mystery, a Melo-drame: as Performed at the Theatre-Royal Covent Garden (London: R. Phillips, 1802);

Hear Both Sides: a Comedy, in Five Acts. As it is Performed at the Theatre-Royal, Drury-Lane (London: R. Phillips, 1803);

Travels from Hamburg, through Westphalia, Holland, and the Netherlands, to Paris, 2 volumes (London: R. Phillips, 1804);

Memoirs of Bryan Perdue: A Novel, 3 volumes (London: Longman, Hurst, Rees & Orme, 1805);

The Lady of the Rock: a Melo-Drame, in Two Acts; as it is Performed at the Theatre Royal, Drury-Lane

[278]

SONG CXXXVIII.

Down the bourn, or thro' the mead, His golden locks
wav'd with the wind, John - ny, lilt-ing, tun'd his
reed, And ſought his An - nie fair and kind. Dear
ſhe lov'd the weel knawn ſong, While her John - ny,
blithe and bon - ny, Sung her praiſe the whole day
long. Down the bourn, or thro' the mead, His gold-

[279]

gold - en locks wav'd with the wind, John-ny, lilt - - - ing,
tun'd his reed, And ſought his An - nie fair
and kind.

Of coſtly claiths ſhe had bit few,
Of pearls or jewels nae grat ſtore;
Fair was her face, her love was true,
And Johnny wiſely wiſh'd nae more:
Love's the pearl that ſhepherds prize,
O'er the mountain,
By the fountain,
Wins the heart, and wiles the eyes.
Down the bourne, &c.

Gowd and titles give not halth,
Johnny cou'd nae theſe impairt;
Youthſoo Annie's greateſt walth
Was her faithſoo Johnny's heart:
Sweet the joys the lover's find,
Great the treaſure,
Sweet the pleaſure,
Where the heart is always kind.
Down the bourne, &c.

B b 2 SONG

"Johnny and Mary," lyrics by Holcroft with music by Shield (from The Vocal Enchantress, 1783)

(London: Longman, Hurst, Rees & Orme, 1805);

Tales in Verse; Critical, Satirical, and Humorous (London: Published for the author by H. D. Symonds, 1806);

The Vindictive Man: a Comedy, in Five Acts, as it was Performed at the Theatre Royal, Drury Lane (London: H. D. Symonds, 1806);

Memoirs of the Late Thomas Holcroft, Written by Himself and Continued to the Time of His Death [by William Hazlitt] *from His Diary, Notes and Other Papers,* 3 volumes (London: Longman, Hurst, Rees, Orme & Brown, 1816); republished as *The Life of Thomas Holcroft, Written by Himself; Continued to the Time of His Death from His Diary, Notes & Other Papers, by William Hazlitt,* edited, with introduction and notes, by Elbridge Colby (London: Constable, 1925).

Collection: *The Plays of Thomas Holcroft,* 2 volumes, edited by Joseph Rosenblum (New York: Garland, 1980)–comprises, volume 1: *Duplicity, Seduction, The Road to Ruin, Love's Frailties,* and *The Deserted Daughter;* volume 2: *The Man of Ten Thousand, The Force of Ridicule, Knave; or Not?,* and *He's Much to Blame.*

OTHER: *The Theatrical Recorder,* 2 volumes, edited by Holcroft (London: H. D. Symonds, 1805).

PERIODICAL PUBLICATIONS:

FICTION

The History of Manthorn, the Enthusiast, Town and Country Magazine, 10-11 (March 1778): 129-132; (April 1778): 171-175; (July 1778): 363-368; (September 1778): 469-471; (November 1778): 588-592; (January 1779): 13-15; (March 1779): 144-146.

NONFICTION

"The Philosopher," *Town and Country Magazine,* 9-10 (October 1777): 544-546; (December

Thomas Holcroft (engraving by Condé, from the December 1792 issue of the European Magazine*)*

1777): 636-638; (February 1778): 73-75; (March 1778): 115-118; (May 1778): 241-242; (June 1778): 283-285; (July 1778): 348-351; (September 1778): 465-467; (November 1778): 585-586; (December 1778): 619-621; (January 1779): 25-27; (February 1779): 94-96.

Perhaps the most notorious playwright of the eighteenth century's closing decade, Thomas Holcroft was a professional writer in the broadest sense: a prolific translator, journalist, novelist, and critic, whose opinions of the theater were frequently consulted by the age's literati. A synthesist in the great tradition of actors who become playwrights, Holcroft profited from his experience as a strolling player, incorporating others' plots, characters, and stylistic affectations into his own dramatic pieces (*The School for Arrogance*'s Lady Peckham and *The Deserted Daughter*'s Mrs. Sarsnet are modeled on Sheridan's Mrs. Malaprop). Observing in *The Monthly Review* that "Mere sentimental comedy is indeed a puling, rickety, unhealthy brat, and no fair offspring of the muse," and acutely feeling the aristocratic elitism of the comedy of manners, Holcroft wrote "elegant comedy" that mixes sentimentality and caricature to dramatize human error in the hope of effecting change. A domestic moralist in his fictions, Holcroft remained quiet on the subject of his private life, avoiding public comment about having been married four times (1765, circa 1772, 1778, and 1799) and widowed three, and about the suicide of his only son, William (after stealing forty pounds from his father), in 1789. Though branded a political subversive at the peak of his career, he achieved popular prominence and saw his works produced at London's Drury Lane, Covent Garden, and Haymarket playhouses.

Thomas Holcroft the Elder kept a shoemaker's shop in Orange Court, Leicester Fields, London, where his son Thomas was born 10 December 1745; though the elder Thomas tried horse trading and in 1751 dragged his family into the country to assist his efforts at peddling, he ultimately returned to his original vocation. Young Thomas was taught by his father to read at about age six and, after devouring the Bible, was thrilled to be given his first two books, one of them Richard Johnson's *The Most Famous History of the Seven Champions of Christendom* (1596-1597). He never forgot its heroic inspiration and determined to make a success of himself if given the chance. His first opportunity for social mobility came in 1757 when he was apprenticed to Mr. John Watson, groom at Captain Vernon's Newmarket stable. From the money earned by grooming and exercising horses, Holcroft paid five shillings a quarter for lessons in "the art of psalmody," and somewhat less for three months of mathematics tutoring; when he was not actively working, he was enthusiastically applying himself to his latest lessons. He returned to work as an apprentice shoemaker with his father in 1758, and while in Liverpool in 1764, he instructed children in reading at a small school. Soon forced to return to London, Holcroft's first published writing appeared in *The Whitehall Evening Post,* at the rate of five shillings per column.

After he was accepted into the employ of the abolitionist Granville Sharpe, his fortune seemed assured; but once his frequenting of a spouting club in Cripplegate was discovered, he was dismissed. On the verge of enlisting as a soldier for the East India Company, Holcroft was advised to apply to Charles Macklin, then assembling a company to play Dublin. Interviewing first with Samuel Foote, who could offer him little salary at the Haymarket since he was inexperienced, Holcroft applied to and was accepted by Macklin. The thirty shillings per week promised him was reduced steadily after he arrived in Dublin, so he returned in 1771 to England, where he joined a series of traveling companies–including those of Roger Kemble, Cockran Joseph Booth (where he met Elizabeth Inchbald), and Samuel Stanton–acting a wide variety of mostly comic roles.

Applying for work at London playhouses without success, Holcroft finally coerced Richard Sheridan's wife into reading his comic opera *The Crisis; or, Love and Fear.* For this and his basic musical talents, the new Drury Lane manager hired him in 1778 at twenty shillings a week; unfortunately, *The Crisis* was not well received and closed after one performance. Disgruntled with his meager wages, unable to convince Sheridan to mount another production of *The Crisis,* Holcroft again called upon Mrs. Sheridan to add her voice to other influential women in support of another comic opera, "The Shepherdess of the Alps" (not to be confused with Charles Dibdin's play). Holcroft had also translated the Puccini opera based on Carlo Goldoni's *La buona figliuola* as "The Maid of the Vale," but neither work received production–largely because the author's financial condition and ambition led him to demand too large a percentage of potential profits.

Holcroft began writing pieces on the theater for *The Westminster Magazine* and *The Town and Country Magazine* as well as song lyrics for a variety of periodicals. Several of the latter were set to music by William Shield, whose friendship provided Holcroft with much of his later comic operas' best music. His first novel, *Alwyn; or The Gentleman Comedian,* was published in 1780 and introduced the character Hilkirk, a thinly disguised persona for the author and his experiences as a strolling player. Thanks to a marginally regular income generated by various writing projects, Holcroft finally abandoned an acting career that had rarely risen above mediocrity.

He was encouraged in his ambition of becoming a professional writer by the relative success of his comedy *Duplicity* (1781), which opened at Covent Garden, then under the managership of Thomas Harris, to whom the play is dedicated. Capitalizing on the continuing success of Edward Moore's *The Gamester* (1753), Holcroft shapes his dramatic treatment of fashionable gaming to his moralist vision, declaring in the preface, "I would rather have the merit of driving one man from the gaming-table, than of making a whole theatre merry." Sir Harry Portland, a compulsive gentleman gambler, is apparently being swindled by Mr. Osborne, whom he befriended after rescuing him from banditti while traveling through Italy. As Sir Harry ultimately faces the shame of having gambled away his sister Melissa's dowry, Osborne admits to having cozened young Portland of his fortune, but only in order to protect him–and he returns a box containing deeds and money to Sir Harry, who is thereby cured of "the detestable vice of gambling." While such a reversal might be construed as amateurish clumsiness, it functions as one of Holcroft's most prominent stylistic patterns, allowing him extensive commentary on a given social evil before returning abruptly to an idyllic comic resolution.

Holcroft landed two jobs guaranteeing him a chance to visit Europe in 1783: as Paris correspondent for *The Morning Herald* and as an agent for printer John Rivington. When his income abroad proved irregular, he returned to England, where

Charles Mathews as Goldfinch in an early nineteenth-century production of The Road to Ruin

he had left the manuscript of his comic opera *The Noble Peasant* (1784) in the hands of George Colman the Younger, the son of Foote's successor at the Haymarket. Covent Garden's successful revival of Leonard Macnally's *Robin Hood; or, Sherwood Forest* in April 1784 helped to stimulate audience appetite for medieval fantasies and rewarded Holcroft's effort sufficiently to inspire Colman himself to write later two similar pieces, *The Battle of Hexham; or, Days of Old* (1789) and *The Mountaineers* (1793). Holcroft's Leonard, a modest but fierce warrior, defends Earl Walter and his daughter Edwitha from the forces of Anlaff the Dane and the machinations of the miles gloriosus Earl Hubbard, revealing himself finally to be heroic Leoline the Briton. While the plotting of the piece is predictable, Holcroft's skill with naturalistic dialogue also extends to his lyrics, which often seem as elegant as they are functional. The year 1784 also marked the composition of "Ellen; or, the Fatal Cave," apparently Holcroft's only tragedy; he was never able to secure its production or publication.

Moved by the Paris triumph of Pierre-Augustin Caron de Beaumarchais's *Mariage de Figaro* (1784), Holcroft again left England for France in September 1784. There, with his poet friend Nicholas de Bonneville, he attended the opera every night until he had compiled a pirated manuscript, which Harris secured upon his return; it proved an unqualified success at Covent Garden under the title of *The Follies of a Day.* As both a mainpiece and afterpiece, it earned twenty-eight performances in its first season. Holcroft acts primarily as translator here, and the opera's popularity derives from its hectic stage business and constant flow of comic intrigues, fueled by Figaro's plots to protect the virtue of his wife-to-be Susan from the powerful Count Almaviva. This success was not contagious, however, and Holcroft's next comic opera, *The Choleric Fathers,* had a disappointing run of seven performances the following year at Covent Garden. Again employing Spanish char-

If I should be brought to the bar to be acquitted without trial, I wish to state to the Jury the exact evidence that was given before the Privy Council, by the persons who were examined relative to me. Mr Sharp is the principal of them; but I believe Messrs Blake Symonds and probably Frost gave some evidence. I wish to know accurately if they did what it was, and should be obliged to you if you would apply to each of them personally lead them to the subject in the best manner you can conceive, show them the importance of exposing the iniquity of the prosecution, and after having made memorandums yourself of what they have said, if they say anything, prevail on as many of them as you can to write, separately to me, the substance of what they would have deposed had they been called upon to give evidence before a jury.

I take it for granted I need not detail the reason of all this— Mr Sharp I recollect gave me twice information of what he had said. The first time as I remember it was that, when questioned by the Privy Council concerning me on the meeting of the Committee, "I had made a speech, and talked a great deal about peace and benevolence, as I always did;" or something to this purpose: and the

Pages from a letter to William Godwin, written from Newgate in late 1794 while Holcroft was imprisoned on charges of high treason (Foster Bequest, by permission of the Victoria and Albert Museum)

second that he had informed them, "I was a natural Quaker; that is, that I had all the pacific principles of the Quakers, but none of their religion"; or to that effect. Pray extract all this as fully and as accurately as you can. Arthur Blake, I think, informed me of something very essentially to the same purpose; though I have forgotten what. Of Symmonds too either I am deceived or I have a similar recollection. I do not imagine I shall see Frost, now Tooke is gone. Blake did live in Devonshire Street; Symmonds in Crown Office Row, Inner Temple: Frost I suppose has lodgings in town. But Sharp perhaps can give you information concerning any of them. He may likewise happen to know some other witness, examined at the Privy Council, that has spoken concerning me. Be as full in your inquiries as you can. I know I need not apologize to you for wishing to communicate serious and beneficial facts to the public — The reason of my wishing them to write to me is the effect that it would have upon the Jury if given under their own hands

T Holcroft

Newgate
Nov.r 24th

acters, and featuring another Figaro-like intriguer, Holcroft's portrayal of two irascible fathers oafishly opposing the marriage of their children was not revived after the 1785-1786 season.

Harris had accepted the script of the comedy *Seduction* along with *The Choleric Fathers* in summer 1785, and Holcroft expected to see it produced in January or February 1786–when this failed to happen, he turned to Drury Lane. Produced nine times toward the end of the 1786-1787 season, *Seduction* again asserted Holcroft's didactic intentions in its preface: "If I have written a comedy which, perfectly moral in its tendency, and counteracting a fashionable vice that is in danger of becoming a vulgar one, has charms sufficient to attract spectators, I am of opinion I have done my country an essential service." As in *Duplicity,* the drama condemns Lord Morden's slavish adherence to "fashionability," which exposes his wife to the seductions of the unscrupulous Sir Frederic Fashion. Its appeal to audiences may have been restricted by the author's obsession with the "classical unities" (the action covers twelve hours; the stage is never vacant; and the setting never deviates from Lord Morden's house), a topic later discussed at great length in his "Essay on Dramatic Composition," from *The Theatrical Recorder* (1805).

Over three years elapsed before Holcroft's next production, and he returned to translation to support his family, earning twelve hundred pounds for his voluminous rendering of Frederic II's *Posthumous Works* (1789). Holcroft's disputes with critics from the *Analytical Review,* who attacked some of his translation work, may have necessitated his use of a pseudonym to shield his next two dramatic productions from automatic disapproval. Covent Garden records note that payment for *The German Hotel* was made to "Marshall, author," though the comedy is ordinarily attributed to Holcroft. Primarily an adaptation of Johann Christian Brandes's *Der Gasthoff; oder Trau, Schau, Wem!* (1776), the play's prelude ironically features an authorial persona–M'Carnock–who vents his spleen on the fickle theater audience, complaining that "The poet may rack his brains and waste his days and nights" only to unveil his work before a forum "predetermined to condemn, because to damn an author is damned high fun!"

Holcroft's admonitions to the wealthy continued in 1791 with *The School for Arrogance* (advertised its first two nights as the work of "James Marshall"), which William Hazlitt calls "the first of the author's pieces, in which there appear a marked tendency to political or philosophical speculation." The arrogance of the title is that displayed by nouveau riche Lady Peckham, who values only what is British, and by Count Connolly Villars, who has made a pretentious claim to nobility in France thanks to the secret support of his father, Mr. Dorimont. After revealing the harm bred by such prejudices, Dorimont closes the play by declaring, "Truth alone can make men wise and happy." A year later Holcroft's most popular play, *The Road to Ruin,* debuted at Covent Garden and went through eleven published editions within twelve months. While the play is concerned with reforming dissolute youth and continues its author's previous crusade to reveal the moral flaws of affluent English society, its composition recognizes popular taste. It features comedy-of-manners satire by providing the pretentious fop Goldfinch with a vocabulary of cant phrases that individuate him and make him ridiculous. The "hero," Harry Dornton, initially charges debts against his father's banking firm with utter nonchalance, but in sentimental convention, goes nearly mad with remorse when he comprehends the harm he has done his loving father's business. The reconciliations that are a regular feature of Holcroft's comedy are more gradual and occur in the last two scenes of the play. The year's triumphs were crowned by the publication and popular acknowledgment of his novel *Anna St. Ives.*

Reception of the first part of *The Adventures of Hugh Trevor* in 1794 was far less enthusiastic than Holcroft expected, and he found the six performances of *Love's Frailties; or, Precept Against Practice* in the latter half of the 1793-1794 season no less disappointing–particularly as he was forced to omit passages such as Craig Campbell's revelation, "I was bred to the most useless, and often the most worthless of all professions; that of a gentleman." The play treats Sir Gregory Oldwort's opposition to his nephew, Charles Seymour, and niece, Louisa, who fall in love with characters of inferior rank and wealth. Sir Gregory, however, in attempting to seduce Charles's Paulina, exhibits the corruption of affluence. In doing so, he denies that there is a moral hierarchy concomitant to social stratification. Unfortunately, influential London playgoers were not in the mood for a sermon on virtue as the true determinant of nobility.

Proving himself a neophyte in political as well as social theory, Holcroft had joined the Society for Constitutional Information in November 1792 in order to gain a forum for his views on the natural superiority of virtue, truth, and reason; he never advocated violent reform, but insisted repeatedly

Thomas Holcroft and William Godwin at the 1794 treason trial of John Thelwall, a fellow member of the Society for Constitutional Information (collection of Dr. Kenneth J. Garlick)

that the society's function was merely to provide *information* to further their republican designs. A warning against such potentially seditious societies had been issued 21 May 1792, and, on 7 October 1794, Holcroft was delivered into custody at Newgate to appear before the court on charges of high treason as one of the so-called Twelve Reformers, including John Horne Tooke, John Thelwall, and the supposed mastermind, shoemaker Thomas Hardy. Outraged by the nebulous nature of the charges brought against him, Holcroft demanded his day in court: the 9 October 1794 *St. James's Chronicle* reported "We do not understand he is in any imminent danger; and suppose, from his behaviour, he has the idea of obtaining the reputation of a martyr to liberty at an easy rate." After anticipating the opportunity to vindicate himself publicly for nearly two months, he was denied it when brought to face the indictment against him on 1 December. Freed, Holcroft was unable to shake the stigma of the accusations against him despite publication the following year of *A Narrative of Facts, Relating to a Prosecution for High Treason* and *A Letter to the Right Honourable William Windham,* written in response to Windham's description of him in a Parliament speech as "an acquitted felon."

Holcroft's prelude *The Rival Queens; or, Drury-Lane and Covent-Garden* played only once before his trial and was never revived. As a commentary on the dynamics of theater life in the last decade of the century, however, it is full of interesting observations: Tim Half-Price, a self-proclaimed "box lobby buck," revels in his disruption of performances, proclaiming himself "Quarrel-master General to you both"; meanwhile carpenters, servants, and stage men argue the merits of their competing houses, which hinge on their respective attitudes toward Drury Lane's glamorous decor. Holcroft ostensibly acts as spokesman for the healthy competition of the rival playhouses, but he is also protecting his own interests when Queen Covent-Garden pleads, "My Sister's powers are indisputable: I would be the first to see and own them: but while I own, shall I not emulate? She deserves your love; but may I not deserve it too! Without it, I must sink, pine and expire. Does she wish my destruction? No; she is too generous; too noble-minded!"

Lady Vib. 66
No. He is here.
Lady J.
Here! And has he not thought proper to let me know of his arrival?
Lady V.
No, no. The haughty Gentleman has only thought proper to reproach Lord Vibrate for admitting the pretensions of Sr George. He is too proud to endure a Competitor.
Lady J.
Indeed! Such pride is the very way to insure his Competitor success. Insulted my father!
Lady V.
I will leave you to judge how deeply, when I tell you that, fluctuating & undecided as Lord Vibrate is, he was so offended, that he pledged his honor in favour of Sir George.
Lady J.
Insult my father! And not deign to let me know of his arrival!
Lady V.
I hope, when Sir George comes, you will admit him

Page from the playhouse copy of He's Much to Blame *submitted to the Examiner of Plays for licensing prior to the first performance, on 13 February 1798 (Larpent Collection, LA 1195; by permission of the Henry E. Huntington Library and Art Gallery)*

Holcroft managed to remain in Harris's favor at Covent Garden, and even his notoriety did not deter audiences from viewing *The Deserted Daughter* (offered anonymously on opening night) or hinder its many revivals following the 1794-1795 season. Mordent is another corrupt man of wealth who has abandoned his daughter in order to facilitate a profitable second marriage and then has arranged for the girl to become part of Mrs. Enfield's house of prostitution; but the innocent daughter, Joanna, possesses a sixth sense that allows her to assess an individual's relative goodness or evil. She falls in love with Cheveril, the ward of Mordent, who has just reached majority and inherited a large sum: he wants to become a man of fashion, but not at the expense of other people–"If I cannot be wicked without being criminal, damme if I do not live and die an honest dull dog!" These relationships are further complicated by an unscrupulous accountant, Item, who schemes to secure the wealth of Mordent and Cheveril for himself, while his honest nephew, Clement, tries to restore the wealth embezzled by his uncle. As deliberately developed as *The Road to Ruin,* the success of this sentimental comedy preceded a period of theatrical disappointments, the nadir of Holcroft's career.

The Man of Ten Thousand is superficially *Timon of Athens* revised, with comedy exchanged for tragedy and the misanthrope replaced by a stoic. The generous Dorington is Holcroft's model of the perfectly virtuous individual: in the face of financial ruin, abandonment by false friends, and dissolution of an engagement, Dorington never varies in temper from perfect affability. Dorington's servant Herbert and friend Hairbrain offer to rescue the bankrupted gentleman when they unexpectedly come into sizable fortunes, but Dorington–in a serious plotting blunder–is rescued by fate instead. Drury Lane followed this run of only seven performances with another Holcroft comedy at the end of 1796, *The Force of Ridicule.* Its prologue openly confesses that the entire piece is taken from Pierre Claude Nivelle de la Chausée's *Le Préjugé à la mode* (1735): "Who is the Plagiarist? Why he that steals / From secret hoards; and while he robs, conceals." The story of Lord Dorville, who claims (despite his own discreet affairs) to love his wife, Constantia, and becomes violently jealous when she appears to be courted by his friend Melford, revived *Seduction*'s campaign against fashionability and was performed only once.

Holcroft seems to have suffered from public identification with his character Monrose in *Knave or Not?,* produced at the end of Drury Lane's 1797-1798 season. The play's advertisement notes the complaint that has "most generally been made against him is that he thinks men capable of gradations of virtue, which others affirm they can never attain," while accusations against him include "faction, commotion, and anarchy." Harry Monrose is a misanthrope who justifies his attitude as the best tool for avoiding poverty. He berates wealthy Sir Job Ferment and continues to rail against lords at the end of act 2, lawyers ("legal robbers") in act 3, and men of wit who treat their friends to food and drink in order to "pick their pockets at hazard and faro" at the opening of act 4. In the closing scenes, Monrose is prevented from succeeding in his self-serving scheme to improve his station by marrying the heiress Aurelia; his only punishment, however, is to witness her marriage to a worthier man. Holcroft's diary entry for 29 October 1798 reveals his anger at Drury Lane for abruptly ending *Knave or Not?*'s run–though a reasonably competent comedy of manners, its termination came as a surprise, apparently, to no one but himself.

Following this unhappy string of Drury Lane productions, Holcroft's *He's Much to Blame* played frequently during Covent Garden's 1798-1799 season. Hazlitt called it Holcroft's finest example of "what is commonly understood by *genteel comedy.*" Unlike those of its immediate predecessors, its characters have virtues to balance their vices, and Holcroft's theories of human perfectibility are demonstrated rather than simply asserted. Sir George Versatile is another man of fashion, but he is as generous to others as to himself, and he genuinely repents his abandonment of Maria Delaval when she arrives on the scene in male disguise. He relinquishes his interest in Lady Jane Vibrate to Paul Delaval, who, after following Maria, determined to revenge her wrongs in blood, reveals his own generosity by forgiving Sir George. This pleasant formula was not repeated that summer when *The Inquisitor* played the Haymarket for only three performances. Holcroft complains in his diary 17 July 1798 that "though the Inquisitor was certainly no more than a trifling effort, I still do not think it a contemptible one." Audiences disagreed, finding his synthesis of Spanish Inquisition and *Romeo and Juliet* motifs completely distasteful. When wickedly ambitious Padre Francisco attempts to dissolve the unconsummated marriage of Don Alberto and Leonora, niece of the Chief Inquisitor, in order to recommend instead his own brother, Don Fernando, the two lovers vow a suicide pact to drink poison; but at the last possible

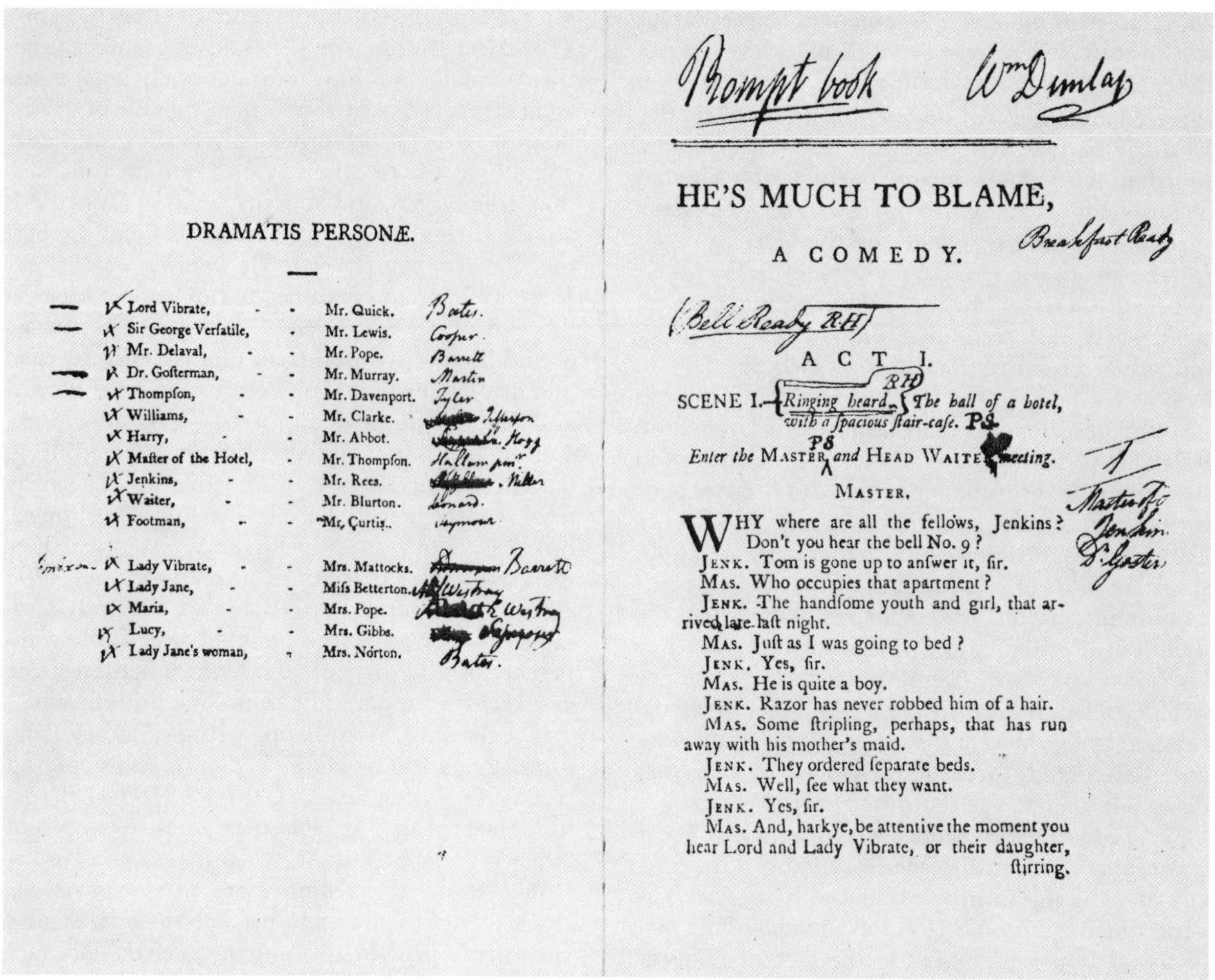

Prompt book Wm Dunlap

DRAMATIS PERSONÆ.

Lord Vibrate,	-	Mr. Quick.
Sir George Verfatile,	-	Mr. Lewis.
Mr. Delaval,	-	Mr. Pope.
Dr. Gofterman,	-	Mr. Murray.
Thompfon,	-	Mr. Davenport.
Williams,	-	Mr. Clarke.
Harry,	-	Mr. Abbot.
Mafter of the Hotel,	-	Mr. Thompfon.
Jenkins,	-	Mr. Rees.
Waiter,	-	Mr. Blurton.
Footman,	-	Mr. Curtis.
Lady Vibrate,	-	Mrs. Mattocks.
Lady Jane,	-	Mifs Betterton.
Maria,	-	Mrs. Pope.
Lucy,	-	Mrs. Gibbs.
Lady Jane's woman,	-	Mrs. Norton.

HE'S MUCH TO BLAME,

A COMEDY.

ACT I.

SCENE I.—The hall of a hotel, with a fpacious ftair-cafe.

Enter the MASTER *and* HEAD WAITER.

MASTER.

WHY where are all the fellows, Jenkins? Don't you hear the bell No. 9?

JENK. Tom is gone up to anfwer it, fir.

MAS. Who occupies that apartment?

JENK. The handfome youth and girl, that arrived late laft night.

MAS. Juft as I was going to bed?

JENK. Yes, fir.

MAS. He is quite a boy.

JENK. Razor has never robbed him of a hair.

MAS. Some ftripling, perhaps, that has run away with his mother's maid.

JENK. They ordered feparate beds.

MAS. Well, fee what they want.

JENK. Yes, fir.

MAS. And, harkye, be attentive the moment you hear Lord and Lady Vibrate, or their daughter, ftirring.

Pages from prompter William Dunlap's copy of the first edition of the play William Hazlitt called Holcroft's finest "genteel comedy" *(Elbridge Colby, ed.,* The Life of Thomas Holcroft, Written by Himself; Continued to the Time of His Death from His Diary, Notes & Other Papers, by William Hazlitt, *1925)*

second Francisco is overcome by guilt and prevents the tragedy that theatergoers might well have preferred.

The Old Clothesman, a delightful comic opera that should have been an ideal afterpiece, faced an even more disheartening reception. More than two months ahead of its opening, Holcroft reports in his diary, 26 January 1799, that Thomas Attwood, composer for the new opera, had reported "the performers gave high applause at the reading of 'the Old Clothesman.' " Its comic conflict unfolds between wealthy Mr. Morgan, sitting in his countinghouse scheming investments in lottery tickets and sugar, and Dewberry, peddler of old clothes, who insists gleefully that his son Frank, Morgan's sharpest clerk, will definitely marry the boss's daughter Clara. The fathers' fortunes are reversed, however, when Morgan's investments fail, and Dewberry reveals himself recipient of a recent windfall from having outfitted his brother for trade in the Indies. There is enough money for all, the children marry, and Dewberry is content to continue working outdoors, selling old clothes. Despite the inoffensive plot and jolly lyrics throughout, the opera played only twice and was never published.

A series of bad investments and disappointments at the playhouses provoked Holcroft to sell off his library and art collection to finance another trip abroad. He treated this turn of events as political exile, writing in public explanation, "My income has always been the produce of my labour; and that produce has been so reduced, by the animosity of party spirit, that I find myself obliged to sell my effects for the payment of my debts, that I may leave the kingdom till party spirit shall sub-

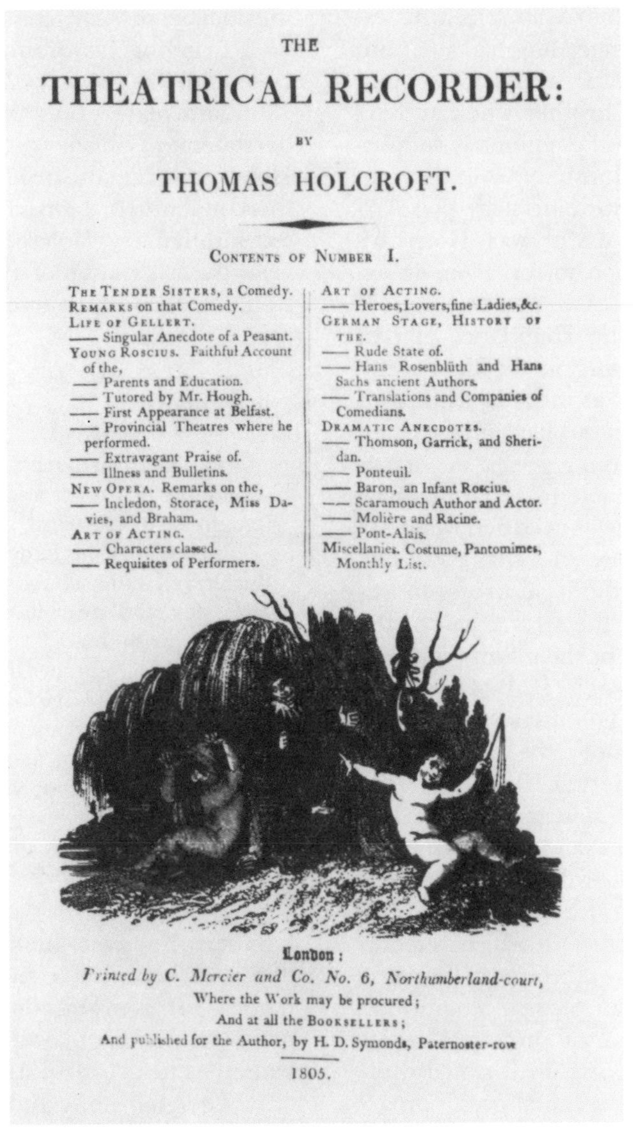

THE

THEATRICAL RECORDER:

BY

THOMAS HOLCROFT.

CONTENTS OF NUMBER I.

THE TENDER SISTERS, a Comedy.
REMARKS on that Comedy.
LIFE OF GELLERT.
—— Singular Anecdote of a Peasant.
YOUNG ROSCIUS. Faithful Account of the,
—— Parents and Education.
—— Tutored by Mr. Hough.
—— First Appearance at Belfast.
—— Provincial Theatres where he performed.
—— Extravagant Praise of.
—— Illness and Bulletins.
NEW OPERA. Remarks on the,
—— Incledon, Storace, Miss Davies, and Braham.
ART OF ACTING.
—— Characters classed.
—— Requisites of Performers.
ART OF ACTING.
—— Heroes, Lovers, fine Ladies, &c.
GERMAN STAGE, HISTORY OF THE.
—— Rude State of.
—— Hans Rosenblüth and Hans Sachs ancient Authors.
—— Translations and Companies of Comedians.
DRAMATIC ANECDOTES.
—— Thomson, Garrick, and Sheridan.
—— Ponteuil.
—— Baron, an Infant Roscius.
—— Scaramouch Author and Actor.
—— Molière and Racine.
—— Pont-Alais.
Miscellanies. Costume, Pantomimes, Monthly List.

London:
Printed by C. Mercier and Co. No. 6, Northumberland-court,
Where the Work may be procured;
And at all the BOOKSELLERS;
And published for the Author, by H. D. Symonds, Paternoster-row
1805.

Table of contents for the first number of Holcroft's compendium of theater writings

side." He sailed in May 1799 for Hamburg, where he started the journal *European Repertory,* which lasted only two issues. Holcroft moved to Paris in May 1801 (where he was popularly branded an espionage agent), and that year marked the debut of two new pieces at Drury Lane: *Deaf and Dumb; or, The Orphan Protected* and *The Escapes; or, the Water Carrier,* an unpublished musical entertainment played regularly as an afterpiece in subsequent seasons. *Deaf and Dumb,* billed "an historical drama," opened with a run of nine consecutive nights and was frequently revived thereafter because it satisfied the audiences' growing appetite for emotional entertainment. The drama details the efforts of the Abbé De l'Epée to restore the deaf-mute "Theodore," cheated of his inheritance by his uncle, Darlemont, to his legal title as Count Julio of Harancour. Julio's attempts to express his love for those around him, particularly for his long-lost brother, St. Alme, and his gratitude to De l'Epée, are copiously accompanied by tearful admiration and commentary on the youth's inherent nobility.

Holcroft continued to gratify the desires of London theatergoers following his return to England in October 1802, for Covent Garden played his *A Tale of Mystery,* the first English "melodrame," essentially a musical afterpiece with orchestral voicings to cue audience response to certain characters or situations. Like *Deaf and Dumb,* it features a mute individual, Francisco–in reality Count Bianchi–who has been the object of assassination attempts by the brother who seized his estates and has been masquerading as a Count Romaldi in order to kill him. Driven mad by guilt, Romaldi is shielded by his brother when archers come to arrest him. Short and emotionally simplistic, the piece also included dumb shows in recognition of the pantomime's continuing stage popularity. Considerably less successful was Holcroft's comedy *Hear Both Sides,* which suffers from an excess of exposition, a confusing proliferation of characters, and a maddening abundance of plot complications before revealing in the final scene that the lawyer Fairfax is not as wickedly avaricious as his fellow advocate Quillet but has, in fact, acted in the best interests of the young profligate, Harry Headlong. Having been unable to reach financial agreement with Harris at Covent Garden when negotiating terms for the play in February 1799, Holcroft's chastisement of the legal profession finally played Drury Lane in the second half of the 1802-1803 season; glancing at the infamy continuing to plague the playwright as a result of his political trial, Fairfax counsels, "To mistake is the lot of man: since then errors are not to be avoided, may they be pardoned, and forgotten."

Holcroft's final novel, *Memoirs of Bryan Perdue,* and *The Theatrical Recorder* were published in 1805. The latter is a compendium of theatrical documents including play translations (several written by his daughter, Fanny); treatises such as "The Art of Acting," "Some Account of the Rise and Progress of the German Stage"; biographies of Samuel Foote and his most successful comic actor, Thomas Weston; reports on regional theater; as well as anecdotes and general gossip on actors throughout the kingdom and Europe. Drury Lane produced his second melodrame, *The Lady of the Rock,* with music by Fanny Holcroft. The afterpiece was advertised for only eight performances that season, and the author's attempts to please failed: the play's published advertisement explains "I intended to convey a public moral, and teach parents the vice of encouraging their children to be spies, when I conceived and gave a sketch of a lovely little girl, innocently betraying her mother, for whom she had the tenderest affection: but this likewise gave a slight degree of offence, and I curtailed the part of the child: for dramatic authors must not reason, but comply with the public feeling." Ever the moralist rather than the ambassador, Holcroft remains torn between proving himself an author as gauged by theatrical success or proving himself a man of superior values who will sacrifice material success to receive the satisfaction of instructing others.

Bringing his dramatic career to an inauspicious end, *The Vindictive Man* opened 20 November 1806 and played only twice; Hazlitt in polite understatement calls it "certainly not the best of Mr. Holcroft's dramatic productions" and concedes "It was condemned at Drury-Lane." Guilty of extreme self-indulgence, Holcroft's persona Lambert reveals the frustration of a man who wanted nothing so much as to be a successful writer:

> Poor and obscure of birth, at my native village I learned to read, the seven Champions of Christendom fired my blood, I determin'd to adventures, eloped in green boyhood, and made my way to London. . . . hunger and thirst sharped the sense, taught me a little truth, and even forced me to beg . . . a course of servitude followed, and books that luckily fell into my hands inspired me with a reverence for and dear love of Virtue and Knowledge. . . . Oh how I exulted that Shakespeare, Spencer [*sic*], Milton, Dryden, Bacon, Locke, and Newton were all English men! . . . Convinced I was a man of genius, I stripped the lace from my livery, hired a garret, and commenced author. . . . Here I remained four years, scribbling and starving, abused by Review [*sic*], neglected by the public, imposed upon by the Booksellers, and dreadfully convinced of being a blockhead.

Lambert, however, finally rejects the lure of the pen and becomes a successful lawyer: "a petty fogger." It is ironically appropriate that at the play's resolution, playwright and persona cry together, "The dreadful struggle's over! hatred is extinct. Love harmony and happiness to all."

That Holcroft was well-read and intelligent is clear, reflected in a circle of friends including personages as diverse as author William Godwin and anatomist Sir Anthony Carlisle. His lifelong ambition to be esteemed an educated gentleman inspired the overcompensation for a working-class background that produced his prolific literary output. Though he influenced Godwin's *Political Justice* (1793) and assisted in securing publication of the first part of Thomas Paine's *Rights of Man* (1791), his political sense was that of a Romanticist; he believed that man's inherent goodness had simply been warped by corrupt aristocratic values. Never slow to express his opinions, the assertion of his values and personal worth as a dedicated author often led to disputes, some occurring with theatrical managers who responded by refusing or limiting the performance of certain main pieces. As a known and sporadically profitable dramatist, however, he was repeatedly welcomed back into the graces of the rival playhouses. Though his plots are rarely original, Holcroft's plays are supported by an individual wit and feature dialogue that is always competent, at times strikingly natural. And with the exception of those moments when the moralist in him demands a platform, transforming speeches into sermonettes on vice or social injustice, the plays are also vividly entertaining.

Bibliography:

Elbridge Colby, *A Bibliography of Thomas Holcroft* (New York: New York Public Library, 1922).

References:

Elbridge Colby, "Holcroft: Translator of Plays," *Philological Quarterly,* 3 (July 1924): 228-236;

Colby, "Thomas Holcroft–Man of Letters," *South Atlantic Quarterly,* 22 (January 1923): 53-70;

John Eva, "Mrs. Inchbald and Thomas Holcroft in Canterbury 1777," *Notes and Queries,* 199 (April 1954): 173-174;

Stewart S. Morgan, "The Damning of Holcroft's *Knave or Not* and O'Keefe's *She's Eloped," Huntington Library Quarterly,* 22 (November 1958): 51-62;

Janie Senechal-Teissedon, "Thomas Holcroft et le mélodrame en Angleterre," *Bulletin de la Société d'Études Anglo-Américaines des XVIIe et XVIIIe Siècles,* 10 (1980): 109-125;

Virgil R. Stallbaumer, "Holcroft: A Satirist in the Stream of Sentimentalism," *ELH,* 3 (March 1936): 31-62;

Peter Thomson, "Thomas Holcroft, George Colman the Younger and the Rivalry of the Patent Theatres," *Theatre Notebook,* 22 (Summer 1968): 162-168;

Paul M. Zall, "The Cool World of Samuel Taylor Coleridge: Thomas Holcroft, Hyperhack," *Wordsworth Circle,* 11 (Autumn 1980): 212-214.

Papers:

Manuscript transcriptions of Holcroft plays by playhouse personnel may be found in the Larpent Collection of the Huntington Library, San Marino, California (including unpublished works, with the exception of *The Crisis, Shepherdess of the Alps, Maid of the Vale,* and *The Escapes).* The Forster Bequest at the Victoria and Albert Museum includes a small holding of Holcroft letters.

Elizabeth Inchbald

(15 October 1753-1 August 1821)

Patricia Sigl

PLAY PRODUCTIONS: *A Mogul Tale,* London, Theatre Royal in the Hay-Market, 6 July 1784;

I'll Tell You What!, London, Theatre Royal in the Hay-Market, 4 August 1785;

Appearance Is Against Them, London, Theatre Royal, Covent Garden, 22 October 1785; revived as *Mistake upon Mistake, or Appearance Is against Them,* London, Theatre Royal, Covent Garden, 1 May 1804;

The Widow's Vow (also called *The Neuter*), adapted from *L'Heureuse erreur* by Joseph Patrat, London, Theatre Royal in the Hay-Market, 20 June 1786; rewritten in entirety by William Dimond and produced as a comic opera: *Brother and Sister,* with music by Henry R. Bishop and William Reeve, London, Theatre Royal, Covent Garden, 1 February 1815;

Such Things Are, London, Theatre Royal, Covent Garden, 10 February 1787;

The Midnight Hour, adapted from *Guerre ouverte, ou Ruse contre ruse* by Dumaniant (Antoine Jean Bourlin), London, Theatre Royal, Covent Garden, 22 May 1787; revised by Thomas Simpson Cooke as *The Wager, or the Midnight Hour,* a comic opera, London, Theatre Royal, Drury Lane, 23 November 1825;

All on a Summer's Day, London, Theatre Royal, Covent Garden, 15 December 1787;

Animal Magnetism, adapted from *Le Médecin malgré tout le monde* by Dumaniant, London, Theatre Royal, Covent Garden, 29 April 1788;

The Child of Nature, adapted from *Zélie, ou l'Ingénue* by Stéphanie Félicité Ducrest de Saint Aubin, comtesse de Genlis, London, Theatre Royal, Covent Garden, 28 November 1788; shortened to three acts, London, Theatre Royal, Covent Garden, 8 December 1788; compressed into two acts by Inchbald, London, Theatre Royal, Covent Garden, 23 April 1800;

The Married Man, adapted from *Le Philosophe marié,* by Destouches (Philippe Néricault), London, Theatre Royal in the Hay-Market, 15 July 1789;

The Hue and Cry, adapted from *La Nuit aux aventures* by Dumaniant, London, Theatre Royal, Drury Lane, 11 May 1791; produced by John Cartwright Cross (with the addition of songs and with some alteration of the text) as *An Escape into Prison,* a Musical Farce, London, Theatre Royal, Covent Garden, 13 November 1797;

Next Door Neighbours, adapted from *L'Indigent* by Louis Sébastien Mercier and from *Le Dissipateur* by Destouches, London, Theatre Royal in the Hay-Market, 9 July 1791;

Young Men, and Old Women (also called *Lovers No Conjurors*), altered and adapted from *Le Méchant* by Jean-Baptiste-Louis Gresset, London, Theatre Royal in the Hay-Market, 30 June 1792;

Every One Has His Fault, London, Theatre Royal, Covent Garden, 29 January 1793;

The Wedding Day, London, Theatre Royal, Drury Lane, 1 November 1794;

Wives as They Were, and Maids as They Are (also called *The Primitive Wife and Modern Maid*), London, Theatre Royal, Covent Garden, 4 March 1797;

Lovers' Vows, adapted from *Das Kind der Liebe* by August Friedrich von Kotzebue, London, Theatre Royal, Covent Garden, 11 October 1798;

The Wise Man of the East, adapted from *Das Schreibepult, oder Die Gefahren der Jugend* by Kotzebue, London, Theatre Royal, Covent Garden, 30 November 1799;

To Marry, or Not to Marry, London, Theatre Royal, Covent Garden, 16 February 1805.

BOOKS: *Appearance is Against Them. A Farce, in Two Acts, as it is Acted at the Theatre Royal, Covent Garden* (London: G. G. J. & J. Robinson, 1785);

The Widow's Vow. A Farce, in Two Acts, as it is Acted

Elizabeth Inchbald (engraving by Wooding, based on a portrait by J. Russell)

at the Theatre Royal, Hay-Market (London: Printed for G. G. J. & J. Robinson, 1786);

I'll Tell You What. A Comedy, in Five Acts, as it is Performed at the Theatre Royal, Haymarket (London: Printed for G. G. J. & J. Robinson, 1786);

The Midnight Hour. A Comedy, in Three Acts. From the French of M. Damaniant, called Guerre Ouverte; ou Ruse contre ruse. As it is now performing at the Theatre Royal, Covent Garden (London: Printed for G. G. J. & J. Robinson, 1787);

Such Things Are; A Play, in Five Acts. As Performed at the Theatre Royal, Covent Garden (London: Printed for G. G. J. & J. Robinson, 1788);

The Mogul Tale; or, The Descent of the Balloon. A Farce. As it is Acted at the Theatre-Royal, Smoke-Alley (Dublin: Printed for the Booksellers, 1788); republished in *The London Stage,* volume 4 (London: Sherwood, Jones & Co., circa 1824-1827);

The Child of Nature, A Dramatic Piece, in Four Acts. From the French of Madame the Marchioness of Sillery. Formerly Countess of Genlis. Performing at the Theatre Royal, Covent Garden (London: Printed for G. G. J. & J. Robinson, 1788);

Animal Magnetism, A Farce, in Three Acts, As Performed at the Theatre Royal, Covent-Garden (Dublin: Printed for P. Byron, 1788?); republished in *The London Stage,* volume 4 (London: Sherwood, Jones & Co., circa 1824-1827);

The Married Man. A Comedy, in Three Acts. From Le Philosophe Mariè [sic] of M. Nericault Destouches. As Performed at the Theatre Royal, Hay-Market (London: Printed for G. G. J. & J. Robinson, 1789);

A Simple Story. In Four Volumes (London: G. G. J. & J. Robinson, 1791);

Next Door Neighbours, A Comedy; In Three Acts. From the French Dramas L'Indigent *&* Le Dissipateur. *As Performed at the Theatre-Royal, Hay-Market* (London: Printed for G. G. J. & J. Robinson, 1791);

The Massacre: Taken from the French. A Tragedy of Three Acts, in Prose, altered and adapted from *Jean Hennuyer, Évêque de Lizieux; drame en trois actes,* by Louis Sébastien Mercier (London: Printed for G. G. J. & J. Robinson, 1792);

Every One Has His Fault: A Comedy, in Five Acts, as it is Performed at the Theatre Royal, Covent-Garden (London: Printed for G. G. J. & J. Robinson, 1793);

The Wedding Day, A Comedy; In Two Acts. As Performed at the Theatre Royal, Drury Lane (London: Printed for G. G. & J. Robinson, 1794);

Nature and Art, in Two Volumes (London: G.G. & J. Robinson, 1796);

Wives As They Were, And Maids as They Are. A Comedy in Five Acts: Performed at the Theatre Royal, Covent-Garden (London: Printed for G. G. & J. Robinson, 1797);

Lovers' Vows. A Play, in Five Acts, Performing at the Theatre Royal, Covent-Garden. From the German of Kotzebue (London: Printed for G. G. & J. Robinson, 1798);

The Wise Man of The East. A Play, in Five Acts, Performing at the Theatre Royal, Covent Garden. From the German of Kotzebue (London: Printed for G. G. & J. Robinson, 1799);

A Case of Conscience: A Play, in Five Acts–see under OTHER;

To Marry, or not to Marry; A Comedy, in Five Acts. As Performed at the Theatre-Royal, Covent-Garden (London, Longman, Hurst, Rees, and Orme, 1805).

Collections: *The Plays of Elizabeth Inchbald,* edited by Paula R. Backscheider, 2 volumes (New York: Garland, 1980);

Selected Comedies, edited by Roger Manvell (Lanham, Md.: University Press of America, 1987).

OTHER: *The British Theatre; Or, A Collection of Plays, which are Acted at the Theatres Royal, Drury-Lane, Covent Garden, And Haymarket . . . with Biographical and Critical Remarks, by Mrs. Inchbald,* 25 volumes (London: Longman, Hurst, Rees & Orme, 1806-1808; facsimile, Hildesheim & New York: Olms, 1970);

"Novel Writing," *Artist,* 14 (13 June 1807): 9-19;

A Collection of Farces and Other Afterpieces Which are Acted at the Theatres Royal, Drury Lane, Covent Garden, and Hay-Market . . . Selected by Mrs. Inchbald, 7 volumes (London: Longman, Hurst, Rees & Orme, 1809; facsimile, Hildesheim & New York: Olms, 1969);

"Letter on the present state of our Drama," signed "A CHRISTIAN, but no FANATICK" (not avowed but probably by Inchbald), *Artist,* new series 9 (1809-1810): 138-153;

The Modern Theatre; A Collection of Successful Modern Plays, As Acted at the Theatres Royal, London, selected by Mrs. Inchbald, 10 volumes (London: Longman, Hurst, Rees, Orme & Brown, 1811; facsimile, New York: Blom, 1968);

A Case of Conscience: A Play, in Five Acts, edited by James Boaden, in his *Memoirs of Mrs. Inchbald,* 2 volumes (London: Bentley, 1833), II: 295-352.

Elizabeth Inchbald infused a vigor into some of the stock characters and motifs of sentimental comedy that made them last until the time of T. W. Robertson in the 1860s. A dramatist with an actress's inside knowledge of the theater, she excelled at stagecraft. At the least she was an admirably skillful adapter. At her best she was able to give her characters a charm that was distinctively hers. One of her creations, Mr. Harmony the family peacemaker, became a household word. In the theater of high comic naïveté she was supreme. Writing plays was her steady and lucrative business, but the publication of two novels, at the height of her career, brought her new literary fame. It was not until 1806, when she embarked on her prefaces to the *British Theatre* series that she attempted to act as a critic.

Inchbald's familiarity with the working theater gave her a great advantage over Hannah Cowley or any genteel dramatist. Even in her mature years she could not equal the elegant dialogue or the refinement of Hannah Cowley, but she was able to move her audience to laughter and to tears in a way Cowley never managed. She had spent her life behind the scenes watching actors, studying audiences, and observing plays, old or new. She combined knowledge of stage effect with a sense of craftsmanship. From 1784 to 1805 she applied her skills to English broad farce and to French *petite comédie,* to the *drame* and to experimenting with a wide range of patterns for five-act seriocomedy.

Though not born in the playhouse, Inchbald–the daughter of John and Mary Simpson–grew up in a family of theatrical enthusiasts. Her brother George Simpson acted with the Norwich company. In their farmhouse at Stanningfield, near Bury St. Edmunds, Suffolk, plays and novels were the favorite reading. She had no formal schooling and taught herself the rudiments of grammar, history, and science, but she did have a French tutor in Edinburgh in 1776. She read the classics–in English translation. She never tried to learn German. Compared to Thomas Holcroft, her achievements were perhaps modest, but the

Mrs Inchbald.

1785 Aug: 13 — I'll tell you what! & Hunt the Slipper.

Paid		Money	Tickets	Value
330	Box - -	84 .. 10 .. 0	- - -	— — —
253	Pit - -	37 .. 19 .. 0	- - -	— — —
314	Gall. - -	31 .. 8 .. 0	—	— — —
190	Gall. - -	9 .. 10 .. 0	—	— — —
	Odd Money	- - - - -	—	— — —
		163 .. 7 .. 0	Tickets	- - - - -
	After money	1 .. 10 .. 0	Money	164 .. 17 .. 0
	£	164 .. 17 .. 0	Total	164 .. 17 .. 0
	Charges	63 .. 0 .. 0		
	Ballance £	101 .. 17 .. 0		

Treasurer's account for an author's benefit performance of the play that established Inchbald's reputation as a dramatist (Harvard Theatre Collection; by permission of Harvard College Library)

idea of earning a living as a critic or translator in Grub Street was alien to her way of life in the performing theater.

After 1772, when she married the actor Joseph Inchbald and began to tour the provincial circuits, her life centered in the playhouse. Her looks seemed to qualify her to play the tall beauties of tragedy. Country audiences applauded her Jane Shore, her Calista, her Zara, and her Lady Randolph. In comedy, she acquired a fame in parts such as Bellario and Rosalind, which showed off her excellent breeches figure. London critics thought differently when she came out at Covent Garden in October 1780. She had a speech impediment that made her stage delivery monotonous. She settled down in London to a round of second- or third-rate roles, but had hopes that the managers would accept one of the farces she had in manuscript. Her husband had died in 1779, and she needed the money. At that time she turned her writing ambitions, previously only exercised on a draft of an early novel, to the drama. Her first attempts were a group of farces, "A Peep into a Planet," "The Ancient Law," and "Polygamy," refused by the theaters, and for which no manuscript copies are known to exist. They were probably in the same broad farcical style as her surviving farces.

Broad English farce–not genteel *petite comédie*–was Inchbald's point of departure as a dramatist, judging from her earliest known work, *A Mogul Tale* (1784). She seized upon the most vigorous form in vogue in the 1780s, the theater of equivoque and double entendre that John O'Keeffe had made overwhelmingly popular in *The Son-in-Law* (1779) and in *The Agreeable Surprise* (1781). The love of fun, which was as fundamental in Inchbald's work as was her grasp of the affecting and the pathetic, is abundantly evident in *A Mogul Tale,* which remained a stock piece in the summer Haymarket repertory long after the balloon rage was over. A Wapping cobbler and his wife, Fan, take off from Hyde Park Corner in a balloon with a quack balloon doctor and land in the garden of the Great Mogul, where their outrageous assumed identities lead to a hilarious trial scene. Written probably in early 1784, at a time when affairs in India were under discussion, the farce carries a slight philanthropic message in the Mogul's clemency, but it was for its rich, whimsical humor that it became a favorite of Haymarket audiences. George Colman the Elder, the Haymarket manager, added some touches and strokes that ensured bursts of applause. Still, the framework of comic equivoque and the wealth of comic detail are wholly characteristic of Inchbald in her first phase.

Only two other examples of Inchbald's early broad farces are known to survive–*Appearance Is Against Them* and *The Widow's Vow,* brought out in the 1785 and 1786 seasons. They made the galleries laugh heartily, but critics in the pit and boxes were apt to detect indecencies and double entendres and to type Inchbald as an Aphra Behn "who fairly puts all characters to bed." The early farces are evidence of her knowledge of comic situation and her thorough experience in the acting theater. The scenes are written for her fellow actors. She knew how to play off Mary Wells's naïveté, William Parsons's mime, John Edwin's country boobies, and John Quick's irascible old men. All of her early farces sustained themselves without the support of songs, by the simple counterpointing of one actor against another.

If Inchbald knew how to make her audience laugh, she could also make them cry–or both laugh and cry. The cornerstone of her reputation as a dramatist was laid in 1785-1787 with a comedy, *I'll Tell You What!*, and *Such Things Are,* a play that pushed the boundaries of laughing and crying comedy into sharper and more powerful contrast than anyone could remember seeing before. Few critics bothered to mount a serious attack on crying comedy in the face of the complete success of these plays in the theater, and particularly since *Such Things Are* carried a tribute to the philanthropist John Howard, whose reputation in 1787 had never been higher.

I'll Tell You What! had its inspiration in the kind of sentimental comedies Colman the Elder was producing at the Haymarket about 1780. Inchbald left London in the summer of 1781 to spend the months of June to September with her mother and sister at their farm in Stanningfield, and there she wrote this first comedy. Its scenes recall now Colman's *Separate Maintenance* (1779) or *The English Merchant* (1767), or Sir Richard Steele's *The Conscious Lovers* (1721), but the combination was fresh and forceful. Colman the Elder helped materially to blend her two plots together. In performance, the pathetic tale of the destitute wife rescued, unknowingly, by her father-in-law, was the most powerful scene in the play. The actress Elizabeth Farren lent a fashion to the role. Inchbald's name was made as a dramatist who could rivet her audience's attention by a tale of pathos and, in the next scene, send them into bursts of laughter by a new comic impasse.

In 1786 and 1787 philanthropy became very

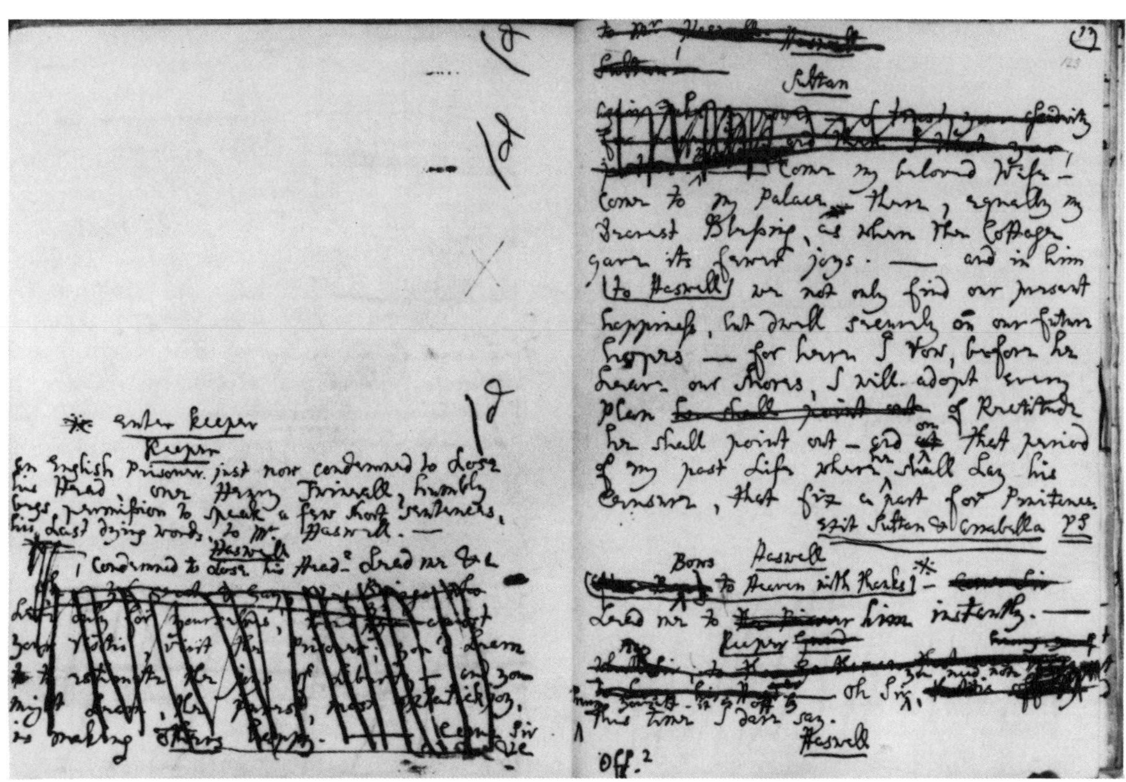
Enter Keeper

Keeper

An English Prisoner just now condemned to lose his Head, one Henry Twinall, humbly begs permission to speak a few short sentences, his last dying words, to Mr. Haswell.—

Sultan

Come my beloved Wife—Come to my Palace—there, equally my dearest Blessing, as when thy Cottage gave its sweetest joys.—and in him (to Haswell) we not only find our present happiness, but dwell securely on our future hopes—for here I vow, before he leaves our shores, I will adopt every plan of Rectitude he shall point out—and on that period of my past Life where he shall lay his Censure, that fix a part for Penitence.

Haswell

Lead me to him instantly.—

Pages from act 5, scene 3, of Inchbald's manuscript for Such Things Are *(Add. 27575, ff 122v-123r; by permission of the Trustees of the British Library)*

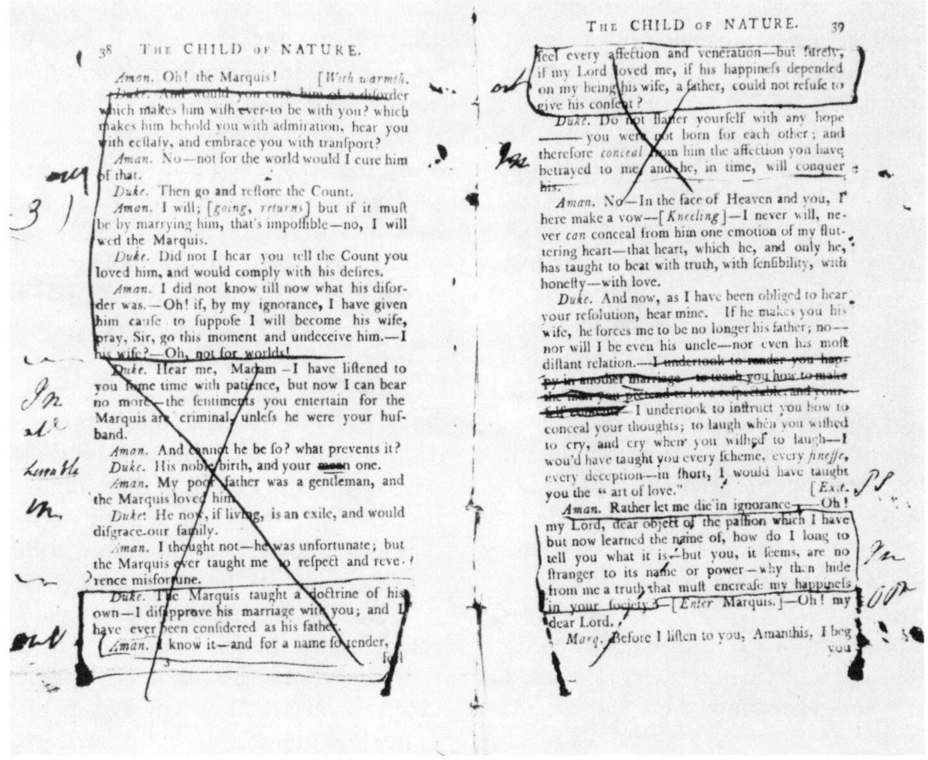
38 THE CHILD OF NATURE.

Aman. Oh! the Marquis! [*With warmth.*

Duke. And would you cure him of a diforder which makes him wish ever to be with you? which makes him behold you with admiration, hear you with ecftafy, and embrace you with tranfport?

Aman. No—not for the world would I cure him of that.

Duke. Then go and reftore the Count.

Aman. I will; [*going, returns*] but if it muft be by marrying him, that's impoffible—no, I will wed the Marquis.

Duke. Did not I hear you tell the Count you loved him, and would comply with his defires.

Aman. I did not know till now what his diforder was.—Oh! if, by my ignorance, I have given him caufe to fuppofe I will become his wife, pray, Sir, go this moment and undeceive him.—I his wife?—Oh, not for worlds!

Duke. Hear me, Madam—I have liftened to you fome time with patience, but now I can bear no more—the fentiments you entertain for the Marquis are criminal, unlefs he were your hufband.

Aman. And cannot he be fo? what prevents it?

Duke. His noble birth, and your mean one.

Aman. My poor father was a gentleman, and the Marquis loved him.

Duke. He now, if living, is an exile, and would difgrace our family.

Aman. I thought not—he was unfortunate; but the Marquis ever taught me to refpect and reverence misfortune.

Duke. The Marquis taught a doctrine of his own—I difapprove his marriage with you; and I have ever been confidered as his father.

Aman. I know it—and for a name fo tender, I feel

THE CHILD OF NATURE. 39

feel every affection and veneration—but furely, if my Lord loved me, if his happinefs depended on my being his wife, a father, could not refufe to give his confent?

Duke. Do not flatter yourfelf with any hope ——you were not born for each other; and therefore *conceal* from him the affection you have betrayed to me, and he, in time, will conquer his.

Aman. No—In the face of Heaven and you, I here make a vow—[*Kneeling*]—I never will, never *can* conceal from him one emotion of my fluttering heart—that heart, which he, and only he, has taught to beat with truth, with fenfibility, with honefty—with love.

Duke. And now, as I have been obliged to hear your refolution, hear mine. If he makes you his wife, he forces me to be no longer his father; no—nor will I be even his uncle—nor even his moft diftant relation.—I undertook to render you happy in another marriage—to teach you how to make the man you pretend to love refpectable, and yourfelf contented—I undertook to inftruct you how to conceal your thoughts; to laugh when you wifhed to cry, and cry when you wifhed to laugh—I wou'd have taught you every fcheme, every *fineffe*, every deception—in fhort, I would have taught you the "art of love." [*Exit.*

Aman. Rather let me die in ignorance—Oh! my Lord, dear object of the paffion which I have but now learned the name of, how do I long to tell you what it is—but you, it feems, are no ftranger to its name or power—why then hide from me a truth that muft encreafe my happinefs in your fociety?—[*Enter* Marquis.]—Oh! my dear Lord.

Marq. Before I liften to you, Amanthis, I beg you

Pages from the copy of The Child of Nature *used by prompter J. Patterson at the Theatre Royal, Liverpool, circa 1801-1818 (Collection of P. Sigl)*

fashionable, and praise of John Howard's work as a prison reformer was sung at public meetings. Enlightened though Inchbald's views always were, *Such Things Are,* her play about Howard, is directly prompted by the philanthropy craze at that time and not by any personal crusade for prison reforms.

Such Things Are was frankly an exploitation of the laughing and crying theater she had formulated in *I'll Tell You What!,* making the most of the full repertory of tragedy and comedy actors of the Covent Garden company, a larger winter theater. She set her scene in Sumatra in the dungeons of an Oriental tyrant. Her portrayal of the visit of John Howard to the sultan's prison was not a heavy documentary but scenes of melting pathos and one electrical moment as Howard reformed the would-be thief, Zedan. Alexander Pope, the young tragedian, gave a performance of Haswell (the John Howard of the play) that was vigorous and not sententious. Throughout, Inchbald's stage experience in eighteenth-century Oriental tragedies stood in good use to her. She alternated the prison scenes with a plot of mistaken identity that unfolded as ludicrously as Goldsmith's house mistaken for an inn. It introduced the irrepressible flatterer Twineall, played by William Lewis, probably the strongest high-comic actor at Covent Garden.

Thus she intertwined two plots in a manner that recalled the old tragicomedy of Thomas Southerne. Fanny Burney saw "great merit . . . both in the serious and the comic plots" (*Diary,* 19 February 1787). *Such Things Are* had a success that was the talk of theatrical circles for months. By the summer of 1787 every provincial company that could get a copy of the as-yet-unpublished text was performing it.

Behind Inchbald's proficiency in broad-comic equivoque or in staging a gripping recognition scene lay an awkwardness and inexperience in writing genteel comedy. The lord chamberlain's copy of *All on a Summer's Day,* which she withdrew after one performance on 15 December 1787, reveals her lack of knowledge in handling high-comic characters to suit the refinement of the times. The indiscretions of the play's witty wife, Lady Carrol, provoked the censure of the audience. The composition date of this early comedy cannot be established with any certainty. Inchbald stated only that it had been lying by her "above two years."

The Midnight Hour, from Dumaniant's *Guerre ouverte* (1786), inaugurated in 1787 a new direction in Inchbald's theater in which she trained herself in the refined motifs and characters of the French drama. At first sight, *The Midnight Hour* is just another version of the familiar old plot, usually set in Spain, of a lover's stratagems to outwit a guardian. This was used countless times, but most memorably in Isaac Bickerstaff 's *The Padlock* (1768), Richard Brinsley Sheridan's *The Duenna* (1775), and George Colman the Elder's *The Spanish Barber* (1777). What is new about *The Midnight Hour* is precisely what gave *Guerre ouverte* such popularity in Paris in 1786–the pace of the action unrolled with such rapidity and interest that it gave the audience no time to think of double entendre. It employed the full repertory of low-comic actors but drew its humor from their blundering simplicity in a tense intrigue plot of stratagems and counterstratagems. It was harmless to morals and highly entertaining–this is what kept it in the repertories season after season.

Inchbald's craftsmanship as an adapter and as a dramatist can be perceived for the first time in the skill with which she realized Dumaniant's plan. Amateurs, such as the anonymous author of *The Midnight Hour; or, War of Wits* (1787), tried to improve their translations of *Guerre ouverte* by adding witty points. Inchbald was a professional who calculated in terms of stage performance. Brilliant dialogue was not her aim. She reduced Dumaniant's text to nearly half its length and naturalized it into familiar, everyday English. She compressed monologues and broke down the stretches of one- and two-line interchanges that scintillate in French but drag in English. Her end product is a dialogue less verbally focused than the French, more interwoven with gesture, pantomime, and stage situation. Her version does not strike the reader at first glance as possessing the novelty that her rival adapters gave theirs, but the momentum it acquired in the theater is proved by its thirty-four performances in the 1787-1788 season and its permanent place in the acting lists.

The success of this new kind of intrigue comedy is proved by the fact that Inchbald carried out not one but three adaptations from Dumaniant plays and took her laughable *Animal Magnetism* (1788) from his *Le Médecin malgré tout le monde* (1786). This farce was never printed, except in pirated Irish editions, and the French source was never specified, though it was openly avowed to be taken from the French. Inchbald repeated the same technique she had used in *The Midnight Hour*–she kept up a fast intrigue pace where all depended on the timing of exits and entrances and a quick clothes change. The plot about a quack

Inchbald as the Lady Abbess in The Comedy of Errors *(engraving by E. Scriven, based on a portrait by H. Ramberg)*

doctor and lovers who pretend to be mesmerized was in Charles Dickens's words "one of the most ridiculous things ever done " (letter to Hon. Mrs. Richard Watson, 24 September 1850). He himself played the doctor at Knebworth in 1850, at Tavistock House Theatre in 1857, and elsewhere. *Animal Magnetism,* as much as *The Midnight Hour,* was established as a stock piece.

A third adaptation from Dumaniant, which Inchbald called *The Hue and Cry,* was considered by managers to be too similar to *The Pannel* (1788), John Philip Kemble's alteration of Bickerstaff 's *'Tis Well It's No Worse* (1770), and was shelved in 1789. The farce has many comic touches that are genuinely Inchbald's. With a good cast it might have succeeded, but it made no impression when it was got up for a benefit in 1791 at Drury Lane, and John Cartwright Cross's effort to stage it as a comic opera, *An Escape into Prison* (Covent Garden, 13 November 1797)–with alteration of one of Inchbald's main comic characters–fell flat.

The Child of Nature (1788) was just another French translation, but in it Inchbald stumbled on a character that became an integral part of her mature theater–the ingénue. She took the play from Madame de Genlis's *Zélie, ou l'Ingénue,* an exquisitely refined dressing up of Molière's *L'École des femmes* (1662). *Zélie,* part of Genlis's *Théâtre de so-*

ciété (1781), was probably never performed on the commercial stage. When Inchbald began cutting and altering it, she decided she liked working with the ingénue, whom she called Amanthis, and she began to improvise new dialogue for her. She found that the character could be used with touching pathetic, as well as comic, effect.

She had discovered a high-comic character perfectly keyed to her own talent for naïveté. Offstage, her friends relished and repeated her naïve strokes. There were not many roles of ingenuous women Inchbald could play on the stage–her comic delivery was slow because of her speech impediment–but in a small circle her simplicity and her stutter charmed. As Frances Ann Kemble said, "Mrs. Inchbald had a singular uprightness and unworldliness, and a childlike directness and simplicity of manner, which, combined with her personal loveliness and halting, broken utterance, gave to her conversation, which was both humorous and witty, a most peculiar and comical charm. . . ." Inchbald was a woman of the theater, trained to think always in terms of theatrical pose. She cultivated naïveté in the London drawing rooms and in her writings, where the ingénue, either in the form of a child or a young girl, is a stand-by.

The comedy she drafted from *Zélie* was originally five acts. Before the first night it was cut to four acts and in subsequent nights to three. On 23 April 1800 she reduced the text to two acts for Harriet Siddons and printed this version in her *Collection of Farces* (1809). The French ingénue was a little too refined and too sentimental for the English; yet the play remained perennially attractive, in three or two acts. The innocence and delicacy of Amanthis were what the box audience wanted. Her sensibility afforded a good recognition scene with a long-separated father. For the next generation Inchbald's play was frequently used for a theatrical début because the appealing simplicity of the heroine helped to ease the awkwardness of a first-night performance. Maria Foote played Amanthis on 26 May and 14 September 1814 for her London début.

For refinement and for comic piquancy, Inchbald's ingénues outdid anything Hannah Cowley ever attempted in that line of character. It occurred to Anne Brunton, who created the role of Amanthis, to take for her benefit Cowley's *More Ways than One* (1783; an adaptation of *L'École des femmes*) and to play Arabella (Cowley's version of Molière's Agnès). The revival had only one performance, on 19 May 1789. David Garrick's *The Country Girl* (1776) and Mrs. Dorothy Jordan were certainly more fun, but *The Child of Nature* possessed a new refinement that outdated previous adaptations of Molière, in a guardian who was tender and genteel, and an ingénue too innocent to intrigue at all.

Throughout 1788-1792, Inchbald continued to shop for her plays in the French theater and to cut them down to size for the summer Haymarket audience. She improved her reputation as a genteel and elegant dramatist by announcing that Destouches or Jean-Baptiste-Louis Gresset was her source. But their five-act verse comedies required large-scale reworking to interest an English audience. In *The Married Man* (1789) she trimmed *Le Philosophe marié* (1727), a comedy by Destouches, down to three acts of simple prose, sometimes abandoning the French and improvising her own dialogue. She tailored her adaptation to suit the action and mime of John Bannister, Junior, cast in the role of the husband ashamed to be married. Elizabeth Kemble was perfect as the tender wife. Inchbald managed to bring life to a very old and stale play without having to draw on low-comic actors. The summer audience applauded, gave her credit for neat dialogue and elegant character, but really preferred the verve and pace of *The Midnight Hour*.

Inchbald had always been a woman of liberal sympathies. She had at her disposal in the plays of Louis Sébastien Mercier material for powerful pathetic reversals and also for outright attacks on the rich and on religious intolerance. Writing in 1791, with her reputation in the theater and as a novelist just made, she does not in *Next Door Neighbours* (nor does she ever in future years) risk her good standing with audiences. She gave them a portrait of Mercier's weavers which she outlined for its pathetic effect, with no embellishment of humanitarian sentiments. She needed some lighter scenes in the drawing room and took them from Destouches's *Le Dissipateur* (1753). All in all, in this composite of two French plays, she affirms the soundness of her basic formula for comedy, such as she had laid it out as early as 1781 in *I'll Tell You What!:* scenes of comic high life interwoven with a tale of distress, and both plots presided over by one of those gruff moralists so dear to eighteenth-century audiences. In *Next Door Neighbours* he is Bluntly. Acted by John Bannister, Junior, Bluntly was the hub of the play who kept the old plots moving and who could speak a sentiment with an energy and conviction that brought a volley of applause.

Elizabeth Inchbald (engraving based on a portrait by S. Drummond)

A second debt to Mercier Inchbald did not avow, though she did own on the title page of *The Massacre* (1792) that it is "Taken from the French." Her source lay concealed under the multitude of changes she introduced. It is unidentified in all bibliographies and theses and no Inchbald editor has attempted to list it. Now it can be established that she took her play from another drama by Mercier–*Jean Hennuyer, Évêque de Lizieux* (1772). Probably translating sometime in 1791, Inchbald was certainly following the London newspaper reports of the butchering of venerable citizens by French mobs. *Jean Hennuyer* is about a family of Protestants saved from the Saint Bartholomew's Day massacre (1572). Inchbald dropped Mercier's historical framework, set her scene in the present, added new pathetic incidents, and rewrote most of the final act with a new tragedy ending. She paints the horrors of the French Revolution of 1789, and she makes a final plea for Christian charity. *The Massacre* is in no sense the work of a political reactionary. Had she wished to attack royalty, she would have chosen to adapt Marie-Joseph Chenier's *Charles IX* (1789), which was having a sensational success in Paris. Instead she chose an old *drame* of Mercier's, and she concentrated on creating effects of pathos, by drawing pathetic characters and adding pathetic coups de théâtre. But one could not be too careful in such times. In 1792, after *The Massacre* had been rejected by both George Colman the Younger and Thomas Harris–for reasons unexplained–Inchbald first printed her tragedy and then suppressed the edition. She could not run the risk of involving herself in "political disputes."

The 1792 season was Inchbald's last as a dramatist at the small summer Haymarket. *Young Men, and Old Women* was a grossly simplified two-act farcical version of the French classic, *Le Méchant* (1745), by Jean-Baptiste-Louis Gresset. A new character she added, Mrs. Ambilogy–a woman who had once been detected in a lie and who is never afterward believed–was novel but failed to amuse strongly, even as acted by Ludia Webb. The situation of the young men disguised as old women brought to mind too much the lover's contrivance in Hannah Cowley's *Who's the Dupe?* (1779). Inchbald's farce had only six performances, one of the worst records of Inchbald's whole career. Even at their best, her neat and sprightly adaptations from the French–though they upheld the Haymarket's reputation for legitimate comedy and provided her with the modest sums that managers paid for translations–could not compete with *The Battle of Hexham* (1789) or with any of the other historical melodramas George Colman the Younger had begun to bring out, and they put her work at a disadvantage beside his.

From 1789, when Inchbald retired as an actress, she was no longer tied to the routine of nightly performances, and she stayed home and finished her novel. The publication of *A Simple Story* in 1791 made her famous not only in the theater but in the world of letters and in the London drawing rooms. But there was much more money to be made by writing for the stage. It had taken her ten months of steady toil to finish her novel, she complained to William Godwin, but she "had frequently obtained more pecuniary advantage by ten days labour in the dramatic way." Between 1793 and 1805 she brought out, mainly at Covent Garden, that group of comedies that were to please audiences most and would become stock pieces in her day and in the nineteenth century.

Inchbald's later comedies appeared during the most turbulent years of the French Revolution. Had she preached a serious doctrine of brotherly love and humanitarianism, her plays might have died stillborn, as did *The Massacre*. Her comedies flourished because she found memorable comic embodiment for amiable characters. In an ambiance of harmless fun, with now and then a tear to add interest, the piquant lesson they teach is one of forgiveness, reconciliation, and resolving discords into harmony. Thus she pushed an indulgent sentimental ethic to an extreme not reached before by Colley Cibber or Hugh Kelly.

Every One Has His Fault, which came out on 29 January 1793, in the same week Louis XVI was executed, is her most finished seriocomic compound. Amid family breaches and quarrels and marriage infidelities, there moves the whimsical figure of the compulsive philanthropist Mr. Harmony, who resorts to benevolent lies in order to bring disputing parties together. Charles-Albert Demoustier produced on 29 September 1791, in Paris, *Le Conciliateur, ou l'homme aimable* (a comedy in five acts), which may well have given Inchbald the idea for a character like Harmony, but the form she gave him is wholly hers. Never before in a high-comic frame had the benevolent liar been used to such advantage. Harmony's humor is drier, less farcical, than Reynolds's caricatures. As originally created by the comedian Joseph Munden, Harmony's lines were spoken in a tone of comic satire, even on the first night, when, in the mood of political crisis, one ultraconservative paper, *The True Briton,* claimed it caught Munden trying to mouth democratic sentiments with his line "Provisions are so scarce!" Inchbald replied with a letter denying the charge; the other papers rallied to her side, and audiences applauded more loudly on the following nights. She had nothing to gain by playing with politics in the theater. Nineteenth-century critics were amused that the comedy could ever have been considered revolutionary. *Every One Has His Fault* seemed to them to be merely a satisfying combination of domestic drama and drawing-room comedy, for which Harmony served as an ingenious pivot. He was also an embodiment of an amiable ethics. With his way of glossing over people's faults, he was as representative of Inchbald's theater as anything she ever created.

The remaining mature plays illustrate Inchbald's skill in a few other types of character. She wrote a two-act sketch with the ingénue for Dorothy Jordan; *The Wedding Day* (1794) became a favorite afterpiece. Although *The Child of Nature*'s gentility had stifled some of her prudish critics, Inchbald adopted here a contrapuntal dialogue between the ingénue and her husband that was thoroughly English. It recalls the Teazles or Peggy and Moody, but has enough of Amanthis's ingenuous ignorance of love to satisfy later refinement. The farce–or rather *petite comédie*–shows Inchbald's virtuosity in the naïve question and reply, and her perfect knowledge of the high-comic actors who spoke her lines. It is a good example of the contrast between Inchbald's and Sheridan's theater. She could not approach his brilliancy of dialogue, and she did not attempt to do so. She aims only to counterpoint the ingénue with her husband–with the rake–or with the unexpectedly returned first wife–in a series of amusing short exchanges that make the most of a situation.

The engraved portrait of Inchbald that was published as the frontispiece to James Boaden's Memoirs of Mrs. Inchbald *(1833)*

With *Wives as They Were, and Maids as They Are* Inchbald submitted to the London audience her mature and most finished stage portrait of the seriocomic heroine. She proved that she could now match Hannah Cowley in elegant drawing-room comedy and even surpass her for genuine fun, but she never tried to rival the innocent vivacity so important in Cowley's women. Inchbald's heroine, Miss Dorrillon, is more culpable and more interesting. She is the Lady Townly of 1797 and a votary of dissipation. With this character's mixture of virtues and vices, Inchbald could obtain a wide range of effects. She had plotted in her novel, *A Simple Story,* a series of contests between Miss Milner and her guardian. It is Inchbald's own familiar repertory, tried and tested, that she brings back to the theater, in a ripe form. The stage motif Inchbald chooses is the old one of the father who comes back in disguise to watch over his child. But the sentimental formula was sound and always built up to a strong climax. When *Wives as They Were, and Maids as They Are* first appeared, it was called "the *feminine gender* of the Road to Ruin." The actor Joseph Munden, originally a low comedian but well established in high comedy, played the father with flourishes of pathos, an innovation he had made when he created Old Dornton in Holcroft's comedy. Miss Dorrillon was played by Maria Foote and Elizabeth Yates in the 1820s, and later by Mary Ann Stirling, Louisa Nisbett, and Amy Sedgwick. *Wives as They Were* remained a steady favorite, with a good role for a leading actress, plus several memorable eccentrics: the audacious rake, Bronzely; the martinet husband, Lord Priory, who makes his wife rise at five; and the wife who obediently does so.

On 24 March 1798, Benjamin Thompson's adaptation of August Friedrich von Kotzebue's *Menschenhass und Reue* (1789) was produced at Drury Lane as *The Stranger,* with John Philip Kemble and Sarah Siddons, and the vogue of the German drama set in. Kotzebue's plays about misanthropic husbands and abandoned mistresses were powerful novelties, but they usually lacked the

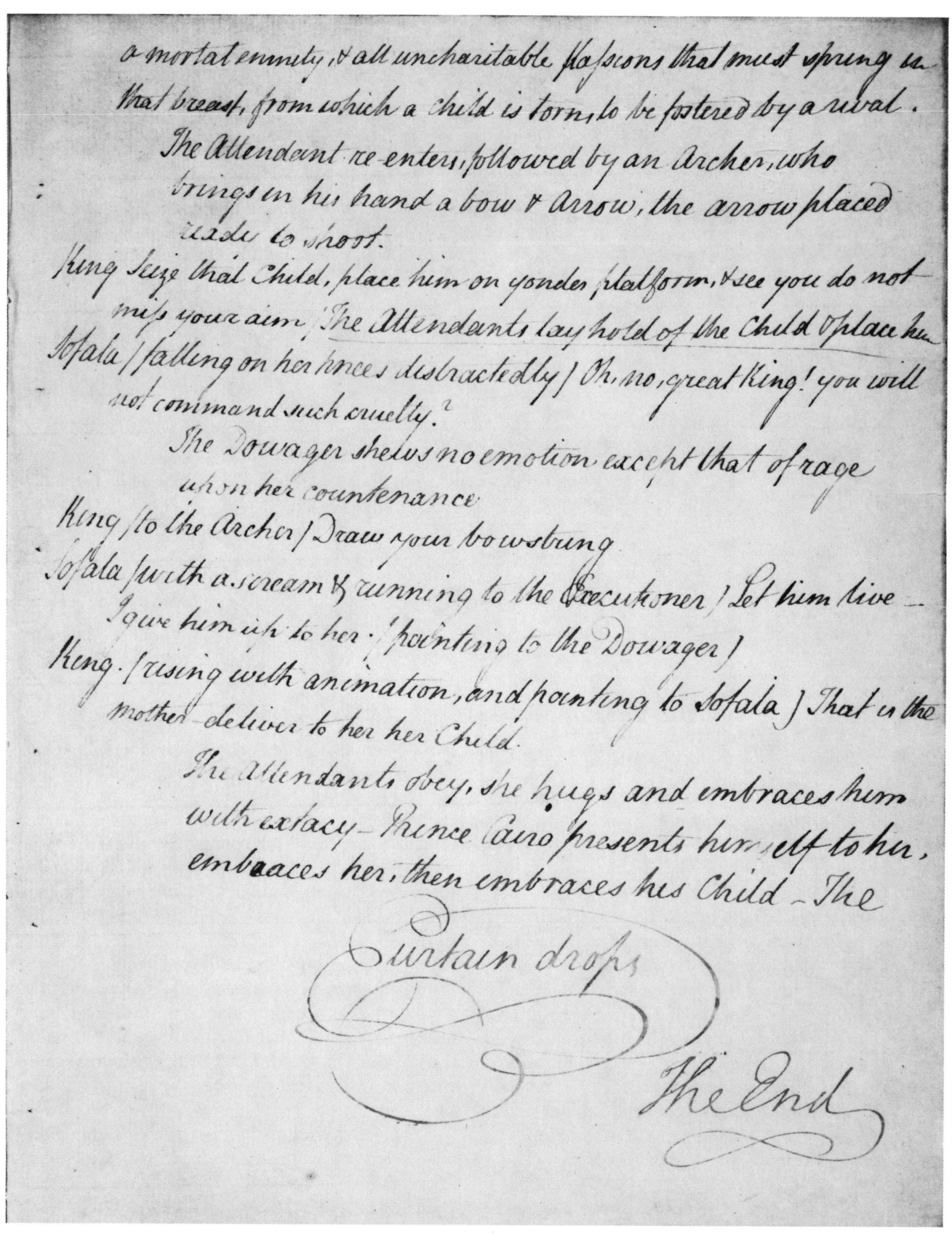

a mortal enmity, & all uncharitable passions that must spring in
that breast, from which a child is torn, to be fostered by a rival.

The Attendant re-enters, followed by an Archer, who
brings in his hand a bow & Arrow, the arrow placed
ready to shoot.

King Seize that Child, place him on yonder platform, & see you do not
miss your aim. (The Attendants lay hold of the Child & place him

Sofala (falling on her knees distractedly) Oh, no, great King! you will
not command such cruelty?

The Dowager shews no emotion except that of rage
upon her countenance

King (to the Archer) Draw your bowstring

Sofala (with a scream & running to the Executioner) Let him live —
I give him up to her — (pointing to the Dowager)

King (rising with animation, and pointing to Sofala) That is the
mother — deliver to her her Child.

The Attendants obey, she hugs and embraces him
with extacy — Prince Cairo presents himself to her,
embraces her, then embraces his Child — The

Curtain drops

The End

Page from the playhouse copy of "The Egyptian Boy" submitted to the Examiner of Plays for licensing in 1802 (Larpent Collection, LA 1348; by permission of the Henry E. Huntington Library and Art Gallery). Never produced or published, this play has been only recently attributed to Inchbald.

fuller measure of comic relief an English audience expected, and they challenged the ingenuity of the adapter. One of the greatest receipt grossers of the whole Kotzebue period, along with *Pizarro* (1799) and *The Stranger*, was Inchbald's *Lovers' Vows* (1798). It was a case of the right play at the right time for the right adapter. No one else could have made as much of the pathos or of the ingénue's naïveté. She did not write the butler's verses (she got the journalist, John Taylor, to produce some of his rimes), but she conceived correctly the support Munden would bring by speaking them. The text of this adaptation was one of her great triumphs as a craftsman. Two rival amateur translators, Anne Plumptre and Stephen Porter, could claim that their versions were more literal and more correct. They attacked her in the press, in handbills, and in the prefaces to their translations. She neither knew German nor cared about the fine points of the German text. Working from a literal translation of *Das Kind der Liebe* (1790), she had only aimed to convey the sense in a forceful, shortened, simple, natural, and unstilted English–and in this she excelled.

The Kotzebue plays are an inseparable part of Inchbald's work, though their morals were not what she would have chosen in 1798 for her own theater. She was aware, too, along with Jane Austen, of the notoriety of Kotzebue's heroines. It was a tour de force of the adapter's art to make such characters please in the theater, and to do so as adeptly as the butler does with his "Loss of innocence never sounds well except in verse." *Lovers' Vows* is a repository of the skills, both comic and serious, that played an essential part in her craft. The laying out of the pathetic scenes is a task she executes with energy and with marked success.

Of the next Kotzebue play her manager Thomas Harris sent her, perhaps in manuscript, *Das Schreibepult* (1800), Inchbald could make little. It was a heavy domestic drama about a sum of money concealed in a writing desk. She reworked the entire plot, introduced a situation similar to Stockwell and Belcour's in Richard Cumberland's *The West Indian* (1771), invented a disguise for the father as Ava Thoanoa, an Indian sage, and added a family of Quakers. *The Wise Man of the East* was a laborious and able piece of stagecraft that built up to a stirring recognition scene, but it did not thrill and delight as did *Lovers' Vows*. In a season when Kotzebue was still the rage, *The Wise Man of the East* (1799) only managed fourteen performances. One journalist, Thomas Dutton, ridiculed her alterations of Kotzebue in a satirical poem addressed to "the Theatrical Midwife of Leicester Fields."

A Case of Conscience dates from the 1801-1802 season if the casting for Drury Lane and Covent Garden, included in Inchbald's hand in her manuscript copy, is any guide. It may have been written a year or two earlier. The play seems to have been intended for Sarah Siddons and J. P. Kemble, and the misanthropic husband recalls the embittered Dorriforth in Inchbald's own novel. A distinctive feature of *A Case of Conscience* is the orthodox turn of the plot: the wife is innocent, but the machinations of a villain have made the husband believe that she is faithless and that their child is not his son. This is the new turn Jacques-Marie Boutet de Monvel gave to his dramatization of *A Simple Story*, part two, produced as *Mathilde, drame en prose et en cinq actes*, in Paris on 27 June 1799, and Inchbald may owe a small debt to him. Managers do not seem to have taken Inchbald's attempt at Gothic drama seriously; yet *A Case of Conscience* shows her readiness to take up Gothic materials and use them with flamboyant theatrical effect.

In 1802 Inchbald adapted for Thomas Harris a little three-act French melodrama, *Le Jugement de Salomon* by Louis Charles Caigniez, but before it could be performed, James Boaden produced a rival version, *The Voice of Nature*, at the Haymarket on 31 July 1802. Inchbald called her adaptation "The Egyptian Boy." Unpublished, unperformed, and permanently shelved, her play lay forgotten with the lord chamberlain's manuscripts with no note of the author. "The Egyptian Boy" is the work of a professional adapter. Had it been performed, it would have reaffirmed her skill in making the most of a tender sentimental situation. The seduced mother and the repentent lover were as good as *Lovers' Vows*, and there was a charming role for a small child.

J. P. Kemble never produced *A Case of Conscience*. Instead he brought out in 1805 at Covent Garden another Inchbald comedy, *To Marry, or Not to Marry*–her final play, and one that seemed wholly characteristic of the fun, the elegance, and the simplicity of style that had pleased in her theater. Kemble played the leading role of a bachelor reluctant to marry until a pretty girl–another of Inchbald's ingénues–takes refuge in his house from a lover, and he unexpectedly falls in love with her. The combination of bachelors and old maids eager to marry or escape from marriage gave rise to a fund of amusing scenes that still delighted audiences in the mid-nineteenth century. The melodramatic episode in a moonlit wood still had good

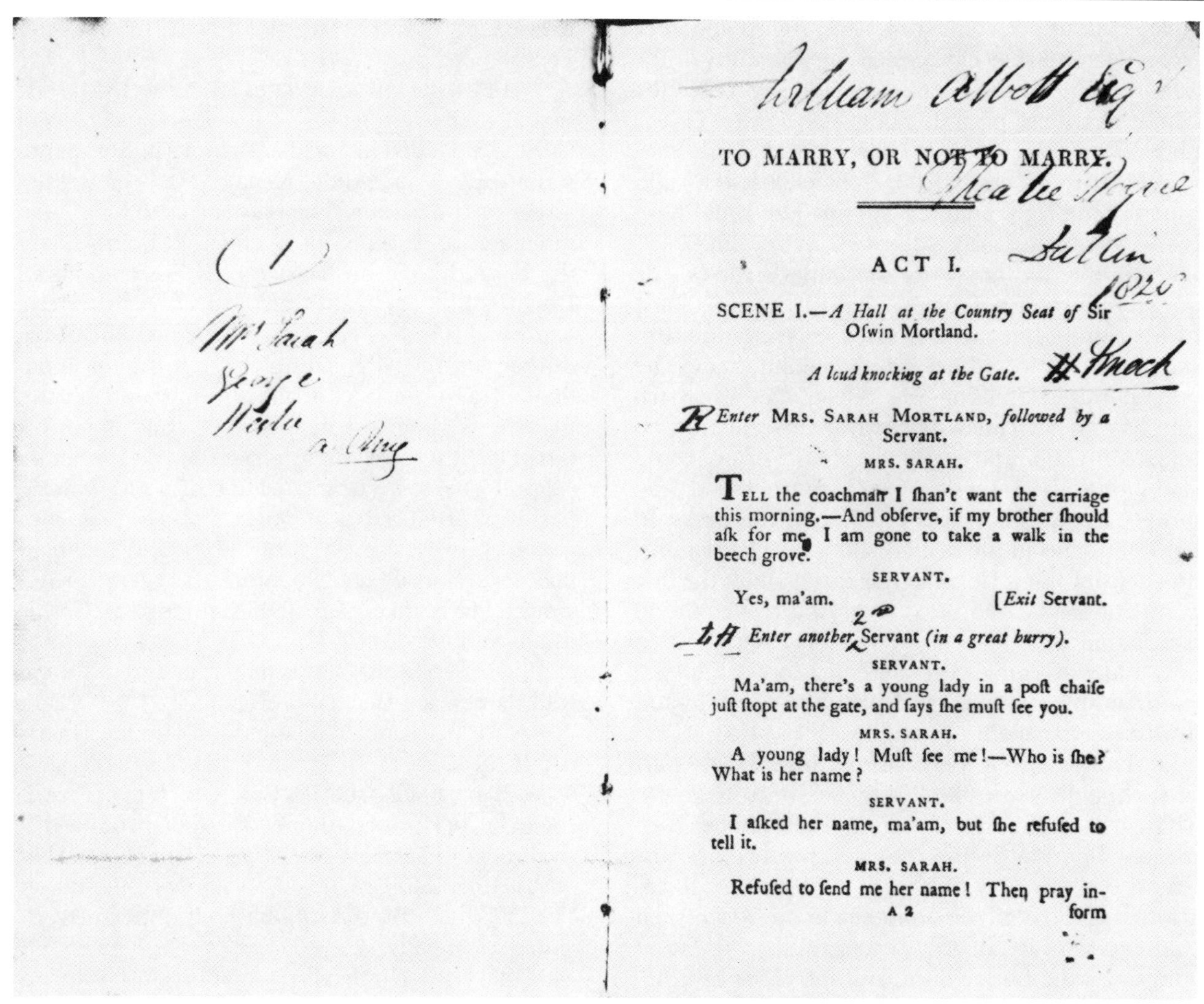

TO MARRY, OR NOT TO MARRY.

ACT I.

SCENE I.—*A Hall at the Country Seat of* Sir Oſwin Mortland.

A loud knocking at the Gate.

Enter MRS. SARAH MORTLAND, *followed by a* Servant.

MRS. SARAH.

TELL the coachman I ſhan't want the carriage this morning.—And obſerve, if my brother ſhould aſk for me, I am gone to take a walk in the beech grove.

SERVANT.

Yes, ma'am. [*Exit* Servant.

Enter another Servant *(in a great hurry).*

SERVANT.

Ma'am, there's a young lady in a poſt chaiſe juſt ſtopt at the gate, and ſays ſhe muſt ſee you.

MRS. SARAH.

A young lady! Muſt ſee me!—Who is ſhe? What is her name?

SERVANT.

I aſked her name, ma'am, but ſhe refuſed to tell it.

MRS. SARAH.

Refuſed to ſend me her name! Then pray in-

A 2 form

Pages from a stage manager's copy of To Marry or Not to Marry *prepared by actor William Abbott in 1826 while he was leasing the Theatre Royal, Dublin (collection of P. Sigl)*

effect in the 1820s but it dated more quickly than the rest of the comedy.

After a lifetime spent exclusively in the acting theater, Inchbald in 1805 was persuaded by her publishers, Longman, Hurst, Rees, and Orme, to write remarks for *The British Theatre,* a series of plays they proposed to publish. She had no experience as a critic and had never criticized for the monthly press. And of course she had no academic training. She undertook the job to compensate for the money she lost by refusing to publish her memoirs. "I own myself so ignorant of the subject I could have written on Law, Physick, or Divinity with almost as much knowledge and with less pain. . . ," she insisted, but Longman assured her that no learning was expected of a woman.

On Saturday, 15 February 1806, the first play appeared–Colman the Younger's *The Mountaineers*–at one shilling in royal 18mo with an engraving from a scene in the play, or at two shillings on superfine paper with the addition of a portrait of the author. Thereafter, the plays continued to appear weekly. The collected edition, published in 1808, comprised 125 plays in twenty-five volumes. Her observations of the playhouse made interesting reading. She knew an abundance of anecdotes about the actors. She had a shrewd knowledge of which plays were vigorous and which moribund, which scenes and which roles were best. A few male competitors cavilled at her judgments. Colman the Younger attacked her in a sarcastic letter. Inchbald made a conciliating reply. But most enthusiasts of the theater, though they might disagree with her about a scene or a character, approved her remarks–even clergymen, such as James Plumptre.

Elizabeth Inchbald, circa 1808-1814 (drawing by George Dance; by permission of the National Portrait Gallery, London)

The British Theatre was an ambitious undertaking. It included the plays of Shakespeare, which *Bell's British Theatre* had omitted, and it extended up to Thomas Morton, Holcroft, and Inchbald, the latest modern dramatists. The editors did not print prologues and epilogues. They also established a new policy of excising text not spoken in the theater instead of printing it in inverted commas. It is impossible to say if Inchbald helped to make these cuts. As far as we know for certain, she only wrote remarks.

Her comments carried a weight beyond her modest role as a playhouse observer, and they served as a standard of the acting drama for her generation. She took a fresh view of Shakespeare's plays as they were performed in the repertory and did not hesitate to criticize Samuel Johnson's remarks on such plays as *Julius Caesar, Measure for Measure*, and *The Tempest*. Thus she paved the way for later critics. One of her most important tasks was to censure. Her sense of what was immoral in early comedy was sharply in the mind of Francis Place when he wrote his unpublished history of the theater. Of a performance of *Rule a Wife and Have a Wife* on 20 October 1826, he says, "many passages were omitted and many expressions changed from those in Mrs. Inchbald's edition." Bound up in attractive volumes, Inchbald's play sets were read by the Victorians. Anthony Trollope owned *The British Theatre* and *A Collection of Farces* (1809).

One last effort by Inchbald was a "Letter on the present state of the drama" which she did not avow and signed only "A CHRISTIAN, but no FANATICK." This letter appeared in Prince Hoare's *Artist* in 1810. Inchbald attacks the superstition of some Methodists who had seen the burning of the theaters in 1808 and 1809 as a fulfillment of a divine judgment, and she defends the theater's role in furnishing amusement and instruction. Her love for the theater was as ardent as ever in 1809, though she lived increasingly in retreat. She was no Hannah More who decried the sinfulness of the stage.

Much was made by Victorian biographers of Inchbald's piety in her final years and her generosity to her family. Her executrix, Frances Phillips, who assembled her papers and listed them for the publisher Richard Bentley, has one lot labeled, "21 common Letters to prove Mrs. Inchbald's general benevolence of character." Her biographer James Boaden used the papers Frances Phillips put at his disposal.

For the theater it is enough perhaps to see Inchbald as her audience liked her, in gentle, amiable roles. She was the beautiful Mrs. Inchbald, whose lovely features and touching airs were perfect in the roles of virtuous, innocent wives. Her amiability might be as much of a fiction as Mr. Harmony and the sentimental fabric of all her comedies, but the pathos of her plays was exquisite, and her admirers paid her tribute in words like these:

> Yet I neglect not, Inchbald, worth like thine,
> Because no pathos in thy *voice* appears;
> 'Tis in thy *writings* melting beauties shine
> 'Tis *there* thy pathos each racked bosom tears.
> (*Public Advertiser*, 10 May 1786).

As late as the 1860s, her comedies continued to amuse and to touch audiences. For originality and vigor–and for number of performances–Holcroft's *The Road to Ruin* (1792) and Colman the Younger's *John Bull* (1803) surpassed anything she ever wrote. Her specialties lay elsewhere, in the school of genteel sensibility of Cibber and Kelly. Into the old genteel theater, she instilled a new element of pathos and a comic buoyancy. She created an elegant drawing-room theater, but one without brilliant wit. She does not, by her pathetic scenes and characters, provide the bridge to a new problem drama, as has sometimes been suggested. She remains keyed to eighteenth-century seriocomic patterns, which she adapted skillfully to produce more powerful effects. Contemporaries testify to the singular simplicity and force of her pathos. Her comedy was equally good, sometimes original. Her characterization of the benevolent liar Harmony was remembered for generations. In the portrayal of the high-comic ingénue and the employ of the naïve question and reply she was unequaled in her day.

Letters:

Letters, edited by James Boaden, in volume 2 of his *Memoirs of Mrs. Inchbald,* 2 volumes (London: Richard Bentley, 1833).

Bibliography:

G. Louis Joughin, "An Inchbald Bibliography," *Studies in English* (University of Texas), 14 (July 1934): 59-74.

Biographies:

James Boaden, *Memoirs of Mrs. Inchbald,* 2 volumes (London: Richard Bentley, 1833);

Roger Manvell, *Elizabeth Inchbald* (Lanham, Md.: University Press of America, 1987).

References:

E. S. de Beer, " 'Lovers' Vows': The Dangerous Insignificance of the Butler," *Notes and Queries,* 207 (November 1962): 421-422;

James Shackelford Dugan, "A Critical Study of the Plays of Elizabeth Inchbald," Ph.D. dissertation, University of Toronto, 1979;

G. Louis Joughin, "The Life and Work of Elizabeth Inchbald," Ph.D. dissertation, Harvard University, 1932;

Samuel Robinson Littlewood, *Elizabeth Inchbald and Her Circle* (London: O'Connor, 1921);

Françoise Moreux, *Elizabeth Inchbald et la comédie "sentimentale" anglaise au xviiie siècle* (Paris: Aubier-Montaigne, 1971);

Bruce Robertson Park, "Thomas Holcroft and Elizabeth Inchbald: Studies in the Eighteenth Century Drama of Ideas," Ph.D. dissertation, Columbia University, 1952;

William Reitzel, "*Mansfield Park* and *Lovers' Vows,*" *Review of English Studies,* 9 (October 1933): 451-456;

Gary James Scrimgeour, "Drama and the Theatre in the Early Nineteenth Century," Ph.D. dissertation, Princeton University, 1968;

Patricia Sigl, "The Elizabeth Inchbald Papers," *Notes and Queries,* 227 (June 1982): 220-224;

Sigl, "The Literary Achievement of Elizabeth Inchbald (1753-1821)," Ph.D. dissertation, University College of Swansea, 1981;

Sigl, "Mrs. Inchbald's 'Egyptian Boy' " *Theatre Notebook,* 43 (1989): 57-69.

Sigl, "Prince Hoare's *Artist* II and the Theatres. What Mrs. Inchbald contributed," *Theatre Notebook* (forthcoming 1990).

Research Note:

Patricia Sigl is arranging publication of a study of Mrs. Inchbald's dramatic works.

Papers:

The body of papers left by Inchbald at her death passed into the hands of her executrix, Frances Phillips, who in 1832 assembled and listed all letters, diaries, manuscripts, and accounts, as well as playbills, newspaper cuttings, and miscellanea. Her list is in the papers of the publisher Richard Bentley, British Library Add. 46611, ff. 262-263. Bentley accepted her proposal that a biography of Inchbald be written, and the Inchbald papers passed into his hands, some of them remaining there until his death in 1871. The Folger Library holds nine of her diaries (all that appear to have survived) for the years 1776, 1780, 1781, 1783, 1788, 1807, 1808, 1814, and 1820, plus one small memoranda book for 1793. Autograph manuscripts of *Animal Magnetism* and *I'll Tell You What!* are in the Harvard College Library, while that of *Such Things Are* and part of *The Wedding Day* (act 2), are in the British Library. Inchbald's correspondence with the Colmans, with the Kembles, and with Godwin, is in the Victoria and Albert Museum Library. The lord chamberlain's manuscripts of her plays, including her unpublished plays, are in the Huntington Library, San Marino, California. The York Public Library has unpublished letters from Inchbald to Tate Wilkinson. The Lord Abinger MSS. contain copies of letters from Inchbald to Godwin, 1792-1817. The Bodleian Library, Oxford, has copies of thirteen letters from Inchbald to John Taylor, 1789-1818. Letters to her York relatives are in the Leeds Archives. The Becks Collection, New York Public Library, includes prompt books.

Robert Jephson

(1736-31 May 1803)

Temple J. Maynard
Simon Fraser University

PLAY PRODUCTIONS: *Braganza*, based on René Aubert de Vertot's *The History of the Revolutions of Portugal*, London, Theatre Royal in Drury Lane, 17 February 1775;

The Law of Lombardy, based on cantos 4, 5, and 6 of Ariosto's *Orlando Furioso*, London, Theatre Royal in Drury Lane, 8 February 1779;

The Count of Narbonne, adapted from Horace Walpole's *The Castle of Otranto*, London, Theatre Royal, Covent Garden, 17 November 1781;

The Hotel; Or, The Servant With Two Masters, based on Carlo Goldoni's *Il Servitore di Due Padroni*, Dublin, Theatre Royal, Smock Alley, 8 May 1783; abridged as *Two Strings to Your Bow*, London, Theatre Royal, Covent Garden, 16 February 1791;

The Campaign; Or, Love in the East Indies, Dublin, Theatre Royal, Smock Alley, 30 January 1784; London, Theatre Royal, Covent Garden, 12 May 1785;

Julia; Or, The Italian Lover, London, Theatre Royal, Drury Lane, 14 April 1787;

Conspiracy, based on Pietro Metastasio's *La Clemenza di Tito*, London, Theatre Royal, Drury Lane, 15 November 1796.

BOOKS: *Considerations Upon the Augmentation of the Army. Address'd to the Publick* (Dublin: Printed for H. Bradley, 1768);

The Batchelor; Or, Speculations of Jeoffry Wagstaffe, Esq., by Jephson, John Courtenay, and Francis Burroughs, 2 volumes (Dublin: Printed by James Hoey, Junior, 1769);

An Epistle to Gorges Edmond Howard, Esq., with Notes Explanatory, Critical, and Historical, by George Faulkner, Esq. (Dublin: Pat Wogan, 1771);

An Epistle from G----- E----- H---rd, Esq., to Alderman George Faulkner. With Notes Explanatory, Critical, and Historical. By the Alderman and Other Learned Authors (Barataria [i.e., Dublin]: Printed by Andrew Ferrara, 1772);

The Speech Delivered by Robert Jephson, Esq., on the 11th of February, 1774, In the Debate on the Committing Heads of a Bill, for "The better Encouragement of Persons professing the Popish Religion *to become* Protestants, *and for the further Improvement of the Kingdom"* (Dublin: James Hoey, Junior, 1774);

Braganza. A Tragedy. Performed at the Theatre Royal in Drury-Lane (London: Printed for T. Evans & T. Davies, 1775);

The Law of Lombardy; A Tragedy: As it is performed at the Theatre-Royal in Drury-Lane (London: Printed for T. Evans, 1779);

The Count of Narbonne, A Tragedy. As it is acted at the Theatre Royal in Covent Garden (London: Printed for T. Cadell, 1781);

The Hotel: Or, The Servant With Two Masters (Dublin: Printed for W. Wilson, 1784); abridged as *Two Strings to your Bow, A Farce, In Two Acts, as now performed at the Theatre-Royal Covent-Garden, with Distinguished Applause* (London: Printed for C. & G. Kearsley, 1791);

Songs, Chorusses, &c., in The Campaign; Or, Love in the East-Indies. A Comic Opera (London: T. Cadell, 1785); transcript of the manuscript in *The Plays of Robert Jephson*, edited by Temple J. Maynard (New York & London: Garland, 1980);

Julia; Or, The Italian Lover. A Tragedy. As it is acted at the Theatre-Royal, in Drury-Lane (London: Charles Dilly, 1787);

The Confessions of James Baptiste Couteau, Citizen of France; Written by Himself: and Translated From the Original French, by Robert Jephson, Esq., 2 volumes (Dublin: Printed by Zachariah Jackson, 1794; London: J. Debrett, 1794);

Roman Portraits, A Poem, in Heroick Verse (London: Printed by Henry Baldwin, for G. G. & J. Robinson, 1794);

Conspiracy, A Tragedy (Dublin: Printed by Graisberry & Campbell for John Archer, 1796).

Collection: *The Plays of Robert Jephson*, edited by

Robert Jephson (frontispiece to Roman Portraits, *1794; courtesy of the Thomas Cooper Library, University of South Carolina)*

Temple J. Maynard (New York & London: Garland, 1980).

OTHER: "A Tour to Celbridge, in Ireland (Written in Imitation of the Style of Dr. Johnson)," *Scots Magazine*, 45 (October 1783): 517-520.

Robert Jephson was regarded by his contemporaries, including such knowledgeable critics as Horace Walpole and David Garrick, as one of the greatest dramatists of the last quarter of the eighteenth century. His early tragedies were especially successful: *Braganza* exploiting a political interest, and *The Count of Narbonne* achieving significant popularity as one of the first among the many dramatic adaptations in the Gothic mode. If Jephson was not the rival of Shakespeare, as Arthur Murphy, at least, was prepared to claim, still his blank verse was a very creditable eighteenth-century version of a style inspired and augmented by Shakespearean allusion. Jephson's other writings, in a satiric or humorous mood, indicate a wit and inventiveness at least as fertile as his dramatic writings make manifest.

Robert Jephson was born in Dublin in 1736. He was the younger son of the venerable John Jephson, archdeacon of Cloyne. Robert was educated first at Ryder's Grammar School; then, when he was eleven, he went to the school kept by the Reverend Roger Ford on Molesworth Street, where he met Edmond Malone, who was to become his lifelong friend. At Ford's school the boys were encouraged to participate in dramatic productions, which were sometimes supervised by the actor Charles Macklin, inculcating a lasting fascination with the stage on the part of both Jephson and Malone. In 1751 Robert entered Trinity College, Dublin, where his tutor was Mr. Radcliffe. The records of his academic career are scanty, but it appears that he was censured for negligence in attending morning lectures. He left the university without a degree two years later, in favor of a career in the army, in which he attained the rank of captain. In 1761 Jephson took part in the military

Plate from the May 1778 issue of Walker's Hibernian Magazine *(courtesy of The Newberry Library)*

expedition to Belle Isle, but when his regiment was ordered to the attack on Havana, Jephson's precarious health induced him to retire. A certificate of ill health from his friend Sir Edward Barry, Physician General to the Army, secured him a maintenance on half pay.

In 1762 Jephson removed to London, where for the next five years he associated with such literary and theatrical personalities as Thomas and Frances Sheridan, Edmund Burke, Edmond Malone, Horace Walpole, James Boswell and Samuel Johnson, Sir Joshua Reynolds, Oliver Goldsmith, Mrs. Susannah Maria Cibber, and David Garrick. Jephson's friendships with Sir William Hamilton and Edmund Burke, especially, seem to demonstrate his social aplomb. Burke had been employed by Hamilton as his literary adviser, and had been rewarded in 1763 with a pension of three hundred pounds. In 1765, as a result of a quarrel over his obligations to Hamilton, Burke sought to resign his pension, and Jephson's name was suggested as a possible recipient. Eventually the pension was reassigned to Jephson by Matthew Colthurst, Hamilton's lawyer. Despite this potentially difficult transaction Jephson contrived to stay on friendly terms with both men. Jephson's friendship with David Garrick survived another awkward financial situation. Garrick lent Jephson five hundred pounds, but without any formal security. When in 1765 Garrick requested some form of written bond, Jephson was offended and apparently refused. The subject recurs in the correspondence between them until Jephson offers to cancel his debt from the author's proceeds from the production of *Braganza* in 1775. Garrick spared no pains or expense to make that production a success, as it certainly was.

Boswell mentions Jephson in the *London Journal* as "a lively little fellow and the best mimic in the world." Jephson's skill in mimicry may have been the means of securing him his appointment at Dublin Castle. Sir James Prior records the event in his *Life of Edmond Malone* (1860):

> He had several qualifications for social enjoyment: one particularly in being an admirable mimic. . . . Well received in the upper circles of London, he found an introduction to Charles Townshend, then a member of the ministry. One of the occasions proved to be a convivial entertainment protracted till the dawn of morning. The chief provocative to this excess was an amusing display of the talents of Jephson. He exhibited with remarkable fidelity and humour representations of persons with whom the parties present were familiar–the Duke of Newcastle, Lord North, Lord Northington, Alderman Beckford, Glover (author of *Leonidas*), and others of note. So well was this done that Charles Townshend, in a fit of admiration, started from his chair, embraced him with rapture, and vowed to make him his secretary. This enthusiasm passed away with the moment; but he was not forgotten. When his brother, Lord Townshend, went to Ireland as viceroy, Jephson was put upon the list for an office in the household, and soon became Master of the Horse.

The post of master of the horse was worth five hundred pounds a year, and on the strength of this employment Jephson married Jane Barry, daughter of his friend Sir Edward Barry, in 1767. They lived first in Dublin Castle, as a part of the establishment of George Townshend, the lord lieutenant, later at a house in Black Rock. The couple had no children. Jephson supported the administration by his writing and also in his elected capacity of M.P., for Johnstown (1775-1776), for Old Leighlin (1777-1782), and for Granard (1783-1788). His gifts of mimicry and satire, apparent socially and in the House, earned him the nickname of the "Mortal Momus." Jephson contrived to retain his office of master of the horse through thirteen successive administrations until his death in 1803.

In 1768 Jephson published his *Considerations Upon the Augmentation of the Army*, in which he argues in favor of the proposal to increase the establishment by an additional 3,235 men. He maintains that the expense of "near seventy Thousand Pounds, and the annual Expence afterwards, of about thirty-five Thousand" is not too great to be borne, and that the dangers to which Ireland is exposed are extreme. He notes that the recent reverses of France in North America and her inability to contend with the British navy in the West Indies and the Leeward Islands make an invasion of unprotected Ireland seem likely:

> What Object then remains so inviting? What enterprize so practicable as a Descent upon *Ireland*? Abounding with Harbours, Bays and landing Places; unfurnished with Forts and Soldiers: Where too, the unhappy Prevalence of the Religion of our Enemies . . . renders their Loyalty suspicious. . . .

Jephson adds that numerous discontented natives could be found to serve as levies or mariners to assist an enemy, and security can be found only in an augmented military presence. Jephson's knowledge of the requirements of military maneuvers is in evidence in this rational discourse.

The Batchelor; Or, Speculations of Jeoffry Wagstaffe, Esq. (1769) consists of a series of articles in the manner of Joseph Addison's *Spectator* or Jonathan Swift's *Bickerstaff* papers. The essays originally appeared in the *Mercury*, published in Dublin by James Hoey, Jr., between 29 March 1766 and 30 January 1768. They were written by Robert Jephson, John Courtenay, Francis Burroughs, and others. The persona adapted is that of Jeoffry Wagstaffe, an elderly bachelor, cousin of Swift's Isaac Bickerstaff. Some of the papers inveigh against extravagance in dress and hairdressing, against ruinously expensive entertaining, against the French taste in fashions or cooking. The authors seek to improve the morals and manners of their Irish contemporaries, and to encourage the patronage of Irish manufactures, such as the use of Irish silks instead of those imported from France. Letters and poetry, ostensibly submitted by readers such as Miss Letitia Love-Youth, Barnaby Brittle, and Obadiah Plaincoat, contrive to satirize the themes of personal foolishness and social excess. Some numbers ironically or directly support the administrative policies of Lord Townshend, the lord lieutenant.

In 1771 Jephson published *An Epistle to Gorges Edmond Howard, Esq., with Notes Explanatory, Critical, and Historical, by George Faulkner, Esq.* In this satire Jephson imitates Faulkner's style to pillory both Howard and Faulkner. The hoax was all

		Feb^y				
108	Thurs	2	Matilda	7	Rival Candidates	2
109	Fry	3	D^o	8	Mayor of Garratt	4
	20					
110	Sat	4	Maid of the Oaks	21	Cath & Petruchio	2
111	Mond	6	Distress'd Moth^r	5	Rival Candidates	3
112	Tues	7	Matilda	9	Harl: Jacket	14
113	Wed	8	Cholerick Man	11	Rival Candidates	4
114	Thurs	9	School for Wives	3	D^o	5
115	Fry	10	Jane Shore	3	D^o	6
	21					
116	Sat	11	Rule a Wife	2	Harl: Jacket	15
117	Mond	13	Matilda	10	Rival Candidates	7
118	Tues	14	Cholerick Man	12	D^o	8
119	Wed	15	D^o Command	13	D^o	9
120	Thurs	16	Maid of Oaks	22	High Life	3
121	Fry	17	Braganza	1	Anatomist	3
	22					

This Tragedy having been read by the Authors Friends in most of the great Family's in Town & puff'd up in Such a Manner that the Expectations of the Audience were so much rais'd that it fell far Short of what they imagin'd — The four first Acts are heavy & want incident & Plott, the Writing is Clear & Nervous — the 5 Act has more incident & Plot but the Writing not so nervous. No Play had ever more Justice in the getting of it up M^r G was not Sparing of his Labour & attendance nor was any Expence deny'd for the Cloaths & Scenes both of which were Superb and it

Pages from the diary of William Hopkins, prompter at the Theatre Royal in Drury Lane, including his assessment of the first performance of Braganza *(by permission of the Folger Shakespeare Library)*

		Feb	received with very great applause			
122	Sat	18	Braganza	2	Cath & Petr	3
123	Mond	20	Do	3	Deserter	10
124	Tues	21	Do	4	Irish Widow	10
125	Wed	22	Do	5	Rival Candidates	10
126	Thurs	23	Brothers	1	Harlequins Jack	16
127	Fry	24	Braganza	6	Trip to Scotland	2
	23					
					Rival Candidates	11
128	Sat	25	Do	7		
129	Mond	27	Do	8	Do	12
130	Tues	28	Maid of the Oaks	23	Deuce is in him	3
			Lent begins			
		March				
131	Thurs	2	Braganza	9	Peep behind Curtn	1
	24					
132	Sat	4	Braganza	10	Rival Candidates	13
133	Mond	6	West Indian	2	Harl: Jacket	17

Mr Reddish being a little out of his Senses he could not play Morcar in Matilda therefore notwithstanding the Bills were up for it we were oblig'd to change it to the West Indian & about Two o'Clock we put up fresh Bills for West Indian & as Mrs. Abington was not in humour to play at so Short notice we was oblig'd to borrow Miss Barsanti to play Miss Rusport

134	Tues	7	Zara	3	Rival Candidates	14
135	Thurs	9	Braganza	11	Do	15
	25					
136	Sat	11	Do	12	Harlequins Jacket	18
137	Mond	13	Do	13	Note of hand	5

the more effective in that these men were already at variance. The epistle is in octosyllabic verse, but a major strength of the work is found in the notes, which purport to explain topical allusions throughout:

> My muse the Architect now greets,
> Whose lofty domes adorn our streets;
> Who, Vanburgh like, claims double bays,
> For piling stones, and writing plays.

These lines, which ironically compare Howard to John Vanburgh, are the occasion for extensive and witty notes on Howard's real-estate ventures, on Faulkner's building of his own house without a staircase, and on the resemblance of Vanburgh's design for Blenheim palace to the Bastille. In 1772 Jephson continued the jest with his *Epistle from G----- E----- H---rd, Esq.*, in which once again he exposed both Faulkner and Howard to the great amusement of their fellow citizens.

The Speech Delivered by Robert Jephson . . . for "The better Encouragement of Persons professing the Popish Religion *to become* Protestants . . ." was published in 1774. Here Jephson in an address to the House of Commons condemns the outmoded and inhumane penal laws against adherents of the Roman Catholic faith. He offers both moral and pragmatic reasons for a change: "In what history of any country has it been found, that persecution rooted out religious heresies, or terrified men into the pale of establishment?" The thesis is well argued, showing Jephson's humanity as well as his command of his native tongue.

Robert Jephson's play *Braganza* was first produced in London at the Theatre Royal in Drury Lane, on Friday, 17 February 1775. It is based on Abbé René Aubert de Vertot's *The History of the Revolutions of Portugal* (1711). Jephson follows his source fairly closely, except that he makes the duke, Don Juan, more heroic than history would have him. Vertot suggests that he was not ambitious but rather lethargic and hesitant. Jephson also heightens the character of "bright Louisa," the duchess of Braganza. Her courage and resolution may be in part a reflection of Lady Macbeth. Though Vertot has her persuade her reluctant husband to countenance the conspiracy, Jephson accentuates her fortitude.

As the play opens, Ribiro, one of the Portuguese nationalists, is confirming the faith of several other conspirators. It is the eve of the revolution designed to throw off Spanish domination and the cruel exactions of Velasquez, the minister of Spain, who is the virtual dictator of Portugal. Velasquez himself is plotting to consolidate his power by having the duke of Braganza assassinated. He boasts, "The precious mischief swells my exulting breast. . . ." Like other Gothic villains, he enjoys his role.

In act 2, we are offered the first verbal depiction of the duchess, one of Jephson's most appealing heroines:

> from her lucid eyes
> Stream'd the pure beams of soft benevolence,
> And glories more than mortal shone around her.
> Harmonious sounds of dulcet instruments
> Swell'd by the breath, or swept from tuneful wire,
> Floated in air–while yellow Tagus burn'd
> With prows of flaming gold; their painted flags
> In gaudy frolick fluttering to the breeze.

In this depiction Louisa seems compounded of part goddess, part Shakespeare's Cleopatra. But courage is her salient characteristic, and she labors to stiffen her husband's resolve in sentiments reminiscent of Lady Macbeth:

> I have a woman's form, a woman's fears,
> I shrink from pain and start at dissolution.
> To shun them is great Nature's prime command;
> Yet summon'd as we are, your honour pledg'd,
> Your own just rights engag'd, your country's fate,
> Let threat'ning death assume his direst form,
> Let dangers multiply, still would I on,
> Still urge, exhort, confirm thy constancy,
> And though we perish'd in the bold attempt,
> With my last breath I'd bless the glorious cause,
> And think it happiness to die so nobly.

The duchess is truly heroic, though her husband is not. The development of the action depends largely on her.

The devious and impious character of the tyrant Velasquez is clearly indicated by his plot to have Braganza assassinated by poisoning the wafer which will be administered to the duke as he takes communion. This attempt fails only because Braganza is interrupted by the alarmed confederates. It is interesting that the conspirators try to prevent Braganza from hazarding his own person in the revolt. He seems to accede, but in the event does become involved in the fray. Here Jephson departs from history. As the Spanish guards are defeated in act 5, Louisa, left alone, gives sanctuary to a fugitive who turns out to be Velasquez in disguise. He seizes Louisa and defies the returning rebels to come near him. His desperate action nearly

John Henderson as Bireno, Elizabeth Younge as Princess Sophia, and William Smith as Paladore in the first production of The Law of Lombardy

succeeds, as the duke is paralyzed by his fears when his wife is threatened. Only Louisa retains her fortitude in this situation:

> Give me a thousand deaths;
> Here let me fall a glorious sacrifice,
> Rather than buy my life by such dishonour.
> (*To the Duke*) If thy fond love accept these shameful terms,
> That moment is my last–these hands shall end me.
> (*To Velasquez*) Blood thirsty tyger, glut thy fury here.

Louisa's defiance and a fortuitous interruption by Ramirez, the monk whom Velasquez has suborned, so distract this ingenious villain that he drops his dagger! Jephson's other villains are less inept.

His contemporaries thought highly of Jephson's *Braganza*. In 1774 David Garrick wrote to George Steevens, "We have a Tragedy of great Merit, from a Mr. Jephson of Ireland; there is a wonderful flow of Poetry, & something we have not seen in our time." Horace Walpole's response to the play was even more enthusiastic: "Braganza was acted last night with prodigious success. . . . I trust if this tragedy does not inspire better writers, that it will at least preserve the town from hearing with patience the stuff we have had for these fifty years." The prompter William Hopkins's notes concerning *Braganza* relate, "No Play had ever more Justice in the getting of it up. Mr. G. was not Sparing of his Labour & Attendance nor was any Expence deny'd for the Cloaths & Scenery both of which were Superb. . . ." As Jephson had proposed repaying to Garrick his debt of £500 from the proceeds of the author's nights, the manager may have been especially interested in the fate of this tragedy. In any event *Braganza* was performed fifteen times between 17 February 1775 and 9 May 1775. It grossed £3282.3.0, and Jephson's share on the

3.

Abandon us to Grief and misery,
Yet I will wander with thee o'er the World
I will not wish my reason may forsake me,
Nor sweet oblivious dulness steal my Senses,
While thy soft age may want a Mother's Care,
a Mother's tenderness to wake and Guard thee.
Ade: And if the love of your dear Adelaide,
Her reverence, duty, endless Gratitude
For all your angel Goodness now can move you,
Oh for my sake, (lest you quite break my heart)
Wear but a little outward shew of Comfort,
awhile pretend it tho' you feel it not,
And I will bless you for deceiving me.
Count: I know 'tis weakness, folly to be mov'd thus,
And these, I hope are my last Tears for him.
Alas, I little knew, deluded Wretch!
His riotous fancy Glow'd with Isabel,
That not a thought of me possess'd his mind
But Coldness and aversion; how to shun me,
And turn me forth a friendless Wanderer.
Aust: Vain were the attempt to palliate Injuries
Too foul in their own Nature to receive
Whiteness from words, but Lady! for your peace

Page from the playhouse copy of The Count of Narbonne *submitted to the Examiner of Plays for licensing prior to the first performance, on 27 November 1781 (Larpent Collection, LA 575; by permission of the Henry E. Huntington Library and Art Gallery)*

Two depictions of Elizabeth Younge as Hortensia in The Count of Narbonne *(courtesy of The Lewis Walpole Library, Yale University)*

author's nights was £475.13.6. *Braganza* was performed another five times between 3 October 1782 and 22 May 1783. Thereafter it was revived about once each year.

The Law of Lombardy premiered in London at the Theatre Royal in Drury Lane, on Monday, 8 February 1779. The story is drawn from cantos 4, 5, and 6 of Ariosto's *Orlando Furioso;* it bears only a superficial resemblance to Shakespeare's *Much Ado About Nothing* (circa 1598), although it shares with the latter work the theme of a slandered bride. The law in question, which demands the death penalty for any woman shown to be unchaste, is identical with the "Scottish law" of Ariosto's fable:

> Our impious Scottish law, severe and dread,
> Wills, that a woman, whether low or high
> Her state, who takes a man into her bed,
> Except her husband, for the offence shall die.
> Nor is there hope of ransom for her head,
> Unless to her defence some warrior hie;
> And as her champion true, with spear and shield,
> Maintain her guiltless in the listed field.

With such a law on the books, not even virtue itself is safe.

As the play opens Bireno wishes to marry the Princess Sophia in order to recoup his fortune. He explains his situation to his mistress, Alinda, the handmaid of Sophia, "My possessions, / The means of pleasure to my thriftless youth, / Moulder in confiscation." Alinda, pregnant with Bireno's child, is naturally reluctant, but agrees to assist his suit. The princess virtuously loves Paladore, an English knight, and is loved by him. But the aged king sanctions Bireno's addresses to the princess, hoping to stabilize his realm through such a marriage. When the princess rejects Bireno's advances, he plots to convince Paladore of her unworthiness by pretending to be her accepted lover. Bireno stations Paladore below the princess's apartments, while Alinda, in the clothes of the princess, lets down some "cordage" and welcomes him to her arms. Paladore, convinced, contemplates suicide, but settles for leaving town.

At this point in act 2, Bireno's malignity predominates over his earlier plans. In order to maintain his deception, Bireno determines to accuse the princess of unchastity and occasion her death through a public invocation of the sanguinary law. It is unclear how this will help him attain the fortune he had desired, but perhaps he is caught up in his own machinations. He sends Alinda off into the forest with two of his henchmen, who are instructed to kill her and ensure her silence. Paladore, wandering through the forest, drives off her murderers and hears her dying confession that it was she whom Paladore had observed welcoming Bireno into the palace. Paladore returns to Pavia in time to appear as Sophia's champion at the trial by combat and to kill Bireno.

Jephson's reputation after the success of *Braganza* was so high that *The Law of Lombardy* was dedicated, with permission, to King George III. However, the play did not receive the critical acclaim accorded to *Braganza*, although it was performed ten times between 8 February 1779 and 21 April 1779, grossing £1543.13.0 of which Jephson received £103.17.0.

The Count of Narbonne was performed at the Theatre Royal, Covent Garden, on Saturday, 17 November 1781. The play was the first of the dramatic adaptations of Horace Walpole's *Castle of Otranto* (1764). Jephson greatly simplified the plot and changed the names of the characters for those used by Walpole in his unacted drama *The Mysterious Mother* (1768). Thus, Manfred, prince of Otranto, becomes Raymond, count of Narbonne, while Hippolita, his wife, is renamed Hortensia. The role of Isabel, beloved by the hero and the count, is so reduced that she does not appear onstage at all! Most significantly, Jephson cut out most of the supernatural omens and appearances. The giant helmet and other prodigies would have been difficult to manage onstage, but their absence drastically changes the nature of this Gothic tale. Walpole praised Jephson's accomplishment, though he regretted the necessity of such drastic alteration. Jephson was unable to leave Ireland to oversee the productions of his plays in London, but Walpole was sufficiently interested in the success of *The Count of Narbonne* that he left his retirement at Strawberry Hill in order to oversee the production. He attempted to instruct the actors, and adjust the costuming, even lending an "authentic" costume from his collection to the actor John Henderson, who was to play the priest. Walpole's involvement over the question of the statue in act 5 severely affected the friendly relations between himself and Jephson. The scene was constructed with the statue recumbent on the tomb. Jephson's lines called for it to be erect, in part so that its likeness to the hero, Theodore, should be more apparent. Walpole maintained that the statue was more correctly constructed as it was, and Jephson's angry response severely strained their friendship. The 1781 Dublin production of *The Count of Narbonne* was more auspicious, in that it gained the author a friend rather than losing him one. In 1781 Jephson met John Philip Kemble at a dinner given by Richard Daly, the manager of the Smock Alley theater. He was impressed with Kemble's classical knowledge, but the actor was still unsure of himself at this early point in his career. In *A History of the City of Dublin* (1859) John T. Gilbert records that Kemble's "negligent delivery and heaviness of deportment impeded his progress, until these defects were removed by the instruction of his friend Captain Jephson, in whose 'Count of Narbonne' his reputation was first established."

The play begins with the count lamenting the escape of Isabel from his Gothic hall. Since the recent death of his son, named Edmund in the play, the count has determined to wed Isabel himself to secure his dynasty. In order to achieve this, he must divorce his wife, Hortensia, countess of Narbonne. He is already aware of the rumors to the effect that his father had acquired his inherited lands in some underhanded fashion. The appearance of the young peasant Theodore in the castle precipitates the series of revelations that reestablishes the rightful family and occasions the death of the count's daughter, Adelaide, stabbed by Narbonne, who in his frenzy mistakes her for Isabel.

The Count of Narbonne was a success at the box office, grossing £3634.1.6 in its first season, not including the receipts for the three author's nights. It was performed twenty-one times between 17 November 1781 and 13 May 1782, and it was performed an additional five times between 3 October 1782 and 22 May 1783.

The Hotel; Or, The Servant With Two Masters was acted in Dublin only, at Smock Alley, on 8 May 1783. However, a shortened version, entitled *Two Strings to Your Bow*, had a considerable success in London in 1791. *The Hotel* is based on a play by Carlo Goldoni, *Il Servitore di Due Padroni* (*The Servant of Two Masters*), which Jephson follows quite

11

Maria— a hundred—but they were kill'd in Battle or grew inconstant, so, I lost or forgot them. they succeeded to my smiles, as fast as to each other's Commiss-ions, ~~and the list of my Gallants wou'd make~~ almost as large a Volume, ~~as the list of success-ions in the Army.~~

Song—

Yet, know that pity's tender sighs
Can this soften'd bosome swell,
For when one faithfull lover dies,
Thus I ring his knell—
Farewell —Farewell—
Ding ding dong bell—
But when another swain appears,
Doom'd to fill the vacant place,
I dry my eyes, for constant tears
Serve but to spoil the face.

Lucy —Yet there is one, Maria at this moment—

Maria— I know who you mean, Farquar—

Page of act 1, scene 1, from the playhouse copy of The Campaign *submitted to the Examiner of Plays for licensing prior to the first London performance, on 12 May 1785 (Larpent Collection, LA 703; by permission of the Henry E. Huntington Library and Art Gallery)*

closely. It also resembles a play by Thomas Vaughan, *The Hotel; Or, The Double Valet* (1776), itself derived from Goldoni's comedy. Jephson's play was, as he says, never intended for publication, but a spurious edition having been printed in Cork, he published his own edition in Dublin in 1784.

In act 1 Don Sandro, father of Ferdinand, and Don Pedro, father of Leonora, are finalizing plans for a wedding between their children. Leonora had been betrothed to Don Felix of Salamanca, but news of his death has opened the way for her marriage to Ferdinand. However, a few lines into the first scene of act 1 a servant, Lazarillo, announces the arrival of Don Felix in Granada. We soon learn that the newcomer is Donna Clara masquerading as her dead brother. She has assumed this disguise in order to follow her lover, Octavio, who had fled Salamanca after being somehow involved in the death of Don Felix. Donna Clara soon reveals her true identity to Leonora, and the understanding between them allows for some potentially amusing scenes, such as when Donna Clara outbraves Ferdinand, who wants to fight his supposed rival. There is a lot of swaggering as Donna Clara, in this amusing breeches role, defies him to his chagrin. Ferdinand blusters in dismay:

> What means that piece of steel dangling there by thy effeminate side? Is thy soft hand too weak to touch it? Death! to be rivall'd by a puppet, by a thing made of cream! Why, thou compound of fringe, lace and powder, darest thou pretend to win a Lady's affections? Answer, stripling, can'st thou fight for a Lady?

The major thrust of the play, however, is based on the complexities of the relations of the servant Lazarillo with Donna Clara (as Don Felix) and with Octavio. Lazarillo is hired by each of them, and they take nearby rooms in the same hotel. Since he cannot read, Lazarillo runs into farcical complexities in delivering mail and bank drafts to the wrong person, trying to order dinner at the same time for each of them, and mixing up the required dishes. Much of the slapstick humor involves Lazarillo's compulsive sampling of the food he has ordered for his two masters. This situational comedy is not developed as much as it might have been in order to figure as a main piece, but cut down it served very well as an afterpiece for years. *The Hotel* was never performed in its entirety in London, but in its reduced form as *Two Strings to Your Bow* it was performed eight times between 16 February 1791 and 13 June 1791.

The Campaign; Or, Love in the East Indies was first produced at the Theatre Royal, Covent Garden, on 12 May 1785, having earlier been produced in Dublin, at the Smock Alley theater, on 30 January 1784. It is a comic opera, with "A new Overture by the celebrated Haydn. The Airs by David Rizzio, [J. C.] Bach, Paisiello, Duni, Carolan, Shield and Tenducci." *The Campaign* was not published in full in Jephson's lifetime, though the *Songs, Chorusses, &c., in The Campaign* were published twice, once by Jephson in 1785, and again as *Songs and Chorusses in Love and War* in 1787 after a production by John O'Keefe. The manuscript for the entire work is in the Larpent Collection in the Huntington Library, and a transcript of this manuscript is to be found in *The Plays of Robert Jephson* (1980), edited by Temple Maynard. The attribution on the title page of the manuscript of the "poetry" to Sir Nathaniel Barry is interesting, as Jephson was an accomplished poet himself.

The Campaign opens with the "Officers and Soldiers returning with flying Banners from a Successful Action." We see General Howitzer, Captain Farquar, Lieutenant Sulphur, and Ensign Flag discussing a recent encounter. General Howitzer remarks:

> A Soldier without wounds is a kind of discredit to the profession. He's like a will without witnesses, or a uniform without trimmings. A flesh wound is nothing, a mere scratch of a Pin, a ragged remnant of a scramble. The Loss of a limb, indeed, is something, it sticks by a Man always.

Though the setting is a fortress, the main theme is love. Sulphur rebukes Farquar for paying his addresses to both Miss Seymour, the heiress, and to Maria, the commissary's daughter. Farquar justifies his conduct:

> FARQUAR: So, because I have a Town House, I must not have a Villa? Sulphur, stick to you Artillery, calculate Elevations, and devise Smoke Balls. A head full of triangles is a very improper recepticle for Ideas of Modern Gallantry.

The other romantic lead is that of Saib, an East Indian. This is a breeches role, first played in London by Mrs. Kennedy. Saib is in love with Miss Lucy Seymour. Their love is expressed most affectingly in the numerous songs.

> SAIB: If you wou'd know what pain it is to part
> Ask, ask this bleeding heart

That almost breaks, when I must leave thee.

Humor is added in the songs and dialogue of Susan, a maid, and Gregory, a new recruit.

The Campaign was performed only three times, on 12, 14, and 19 May 1785. Receipts are unknown for these performances. In its altered form as *Love and War*, produced by O'Keefe, it was more successful, and had a run of eleven productions in the 1787 season.

Julia; Or, The Italian Lover was first performed at the Theatre Royal, Drury Lane, on 14 April 1787. It is a tragedy in five acts. The story was supposedly based on an actual event that occurred in the Isle of Guernsey, but Jephson transfers the locale to Italy. The play was written for Mrs. Sarah Siddons, who had taken the lead in each of Jephson's tragedies, while the star role, that of the villain, Mentevole, was taken by Mrs. Siddons's brother, John Philip Kemble. The part was so exacting that although it showed off Kemble's dramatic powers, it took too much out of him, and he declined any further representations at the time.

In *Julia* Jephson found a theme sufficiently Gothic to display the full powers of a virtuoso artist. Mentevole, the villain, loves or desires Julia. He has murdered Claudio, who was engaged to her. As the play opens Marcellus, Claudio's twin brother, returns to Genoa, and we witness the complexities of Mentevole's devious plotting in his last desperate attempt to win Julia's hand.

Julia was performed only once in its first season, grossing £217.2.6. However, it was performed eight times in the following season between 11 December 1787 and 1 January 1888, grossing £1360.14.6. Jephson received £157.14.0 for the three author's nights benefits. Despite its moderate success at the box office, some contemporary critics considered it the best of Jephson's tragedies.

Conspiracy was produced at Drury Lane on 15 November 1796. It is a reworking of "Vitellia," a tragedy that Jephson had offered to Garrick as early as 1775. Garrick had rejected it then as unworthy of Jephson's abilities; it was not especially well received upon its production as *Conspiracy*. Jephson based this work on *La Clemenza di Tito* by Pietro Metastasio. He seems also to have been aware of an earlier translation from the same source, that is, John Cleland's *Titus Vespasian* (1760). In some passages Jephson follows his source quite closely. In others he is more original, and these are frequently the better lines. The dialogue is often lively, but the motivations of his tragic heroine, Vitellia, seem forced.

Vitellia conspires with her admirer, Sextus, to incite an uprising in Rome and to assassinate the noble emperor, Titus. Her motive is jealousy on two counts. Her father had been emperor but was deposed and condemned. Titus, although not implicated in the coup, profits by it. More significantly, Vitellia is sexually jealous; she is in love with Titus, who favors Berenice or Cornelia, rather than she. Vitellia attempts to cajole Sextus into killing the emperor when she believes that he will marry Berenice. Then, hearing that Titus has sent Berenice away, she seeks to restrain Sextus's hand. No sooner is this done, than Vitellia learns that Titus is considering taking Cornelia as his wife, so she again urges Sextus to implement his assassination. However, Cornelia is in love with Annius and begs to be excused. In the bloody aftermath of the conspiracy, first Sextus, then Annius, are condemned by Titus, and Vitellia poisons herself just before she learns that Titus had finally chosen her to be his consort.

Conspiracy was performed only twice in 1796; on 15 November it grossed £237.10.0, but on 17 November, at its second performance, it made only £158.17.0 and was discontinued. Garrick's theatrical instincts in refusing it twenty years earlier were confirmed when it finally reached the stage.

In *Roman Portraits* (1794) Jephson recounts in heroic couplets the history of Rome, and the characters of her leaders from Numa Pompilius to Augustus. He tells as well of the accomplishments of her major writers, such as Virgil, Horace, and Ovid. Throughout the poem Jephson bases his descriptions on the accounts of such Roman historians as Sallust, Tully, and Tacitus. As his preface points out, the author seeks to compare the actions and shortcomings of the Roman republic with the excesses of the French nation after the French Revolution. Jephson writes a flowing verse, inspired by the examples of John Dryden and Alexander Pope.

In *The Confessions of James Baptiste Couteau* (1794) the hero's encomiums on his own unstinting debauchery and unrestrained vice reveal the motivations of a monster. The author's ironic enthusiasm for Couteau's magnificent excesses may recall Henry Fielding's technique in his *Life of Mr. Jonathan Wild the Great*, but here such an attitude is less forced in being offered as the natural egotism of the villain himself. Couteau suggests that his *Confessions* are modeled on those of "John James Rousseau," but he denigrates the paucity of the crimes Rousseau has to relate as "wretched trifles." This work may have been written in response to *The*

Present State of the Manners, Arts, and Politics, of France and Italy; In a Series of Poetical Epistles, From Paris, Rome, and Naples, addressed to Robert Jephson (in 1792-1793) by his friend and literary associate John Courtenay. Courtenay's verse epistles likewise satirize the moral shortcomings and the criminal excesses of the leaders of the French Revolution. However, Courtenay directly criticizes such figures as Couteau in a rather halting verse, while Jephson's similar moral and political stance is couched in a carefully modulated prose, replete with a consistent ironic perspective, "in the present age the way to honours and felicity is open to all persons who have spirit, and who by the mere force of genius will venture to emancipate themselves from vulgar prejudices. . . ." In discussing his classical education, received during his sojourn in a convent, Couteau exclaims, "The Rape of the Sabine Women was to me a ravishing subject," and he further relates, "my hero was Cataline."

The travels of the hero allow for Couteau's descriptions of Dublin and London. In the latter city he indulges his libidinous propensities by his employment in Dr. Graham's Temple of Health, an "edifice erected to rationalized incontinence." Later, back in France, Couteau's amorous inclinations lead him to drug and ravish the beautiful daughter of a farmer when her virtue, or her repugnance at his ugliness, makes her repudiate his advances. Afterward Couteau notes, "she was fast verging to a state of insanity," and he is compelled to kill her, but not without regret:

> Poor Claudine! I did not wish to destroy her; I loved her, tenderly loved her, and she died an oblation, not to my inhumanity, but to a mistaken faith, and to prejudices imbibed from the nipple. Let the indignant world cry out with me, "These are the effects of superstition; *tantum religio potuit suadere malorum.*"

At least Couteau's stance is consistent! As he takes us further into the perverse psychology of his hero, Jephson is not averse to borrowing from Swift's *Modest Proposal* (1729) to display the amoral nature of this revolutionary:

> It is a vulgar error to suppose that human flesh is not palatable. I have tasted it often, and never without pleasure. Even a woman of Seventy, provided she has not been what is called an Old Maid, eats well with vinegar, mustard, and red pepper. . . . An Irish Child which has been fed on milk and potatoes . . . is a nicer dish with spinach than any houselamb. . . .

The tone of *The Confessions,* so different from Jephson's dramatic writing, links this final work to his earlier style in *The Batchelor* (1769) or *An Epistle to Gorges Edmond Howard* (1771), in both of which a delightful irony is exhibited. Nowhere else, however, is so perverse an ironic stance maintained with such obvious gusto.

In the prologue to *Braganza,* Arthur Murphy asserts on Jephson's behalf, "Vigorous he comes, and warm from Shakespeare's school. / Inspir'd by him. . . ." The theatergoing public was disposed to agree, and the playwright enjoyed a considerable success throughout most of his dramatic career. Only his last play was notably a failure; but curiously, *Conspiracy* actually reads quite well, and might play well even today before an accepting audience. His other tragedies enjoyed a well-deserved triumph on the London stage, and in Dublin all his plays were perennial favorites. Jephson's diction varied with his subject. In *The Campaign* it is colloquial and witty, in *Braganza* heroic, in *Julia* powerful, and in *Conspiracy* inflated with bombast. Significantly, Jephson's adaptation of Walpole's *Castle of Otranto* as *The Count of Narbonne* may be said to have inaugurated the popular genre of Gothic drama, and, if much of its verse seems overly solemn, that was the mode to which the dramatist felt committed. His contemporaries admired Jephson for his command of the language and his poetic skill, though they might criticize his plots. He demonstrated an assured facility in each of the genres he assayed, correctly assessing the current mode and the topical subject that would appeal.

Letters:

David Garrick, *The Private Correspondence of David Garrick with the Most Celebrated Persons of his Time* . . . , 2 volumes, edited by James Boaden, includes some of Jephson's letters to Garrick (London: Henry Colburn & Richard Bentley, 1831);

Historical Manuscripts Commission, *The Manuscripts of The Duke of Beaufort, K.G., The Earl of Donoughmore, and Others,* Twelfth Report, Appendix, part 9, includes three of Jephson's letters to John Hely Hutchinson (London: Her Majesty's Stationery Office, 1891).

Biographies:

Arnold Lätt, *Robert Jephson and His Tragedies* (Zurich: Dissert.-Druckerei Gebr. Leemann & Co., 1913);

Martin Severin Peterson, *Robert Jephson (1736-*

1803): A Study of His Life and Works, University of Nebraska Studies in Language, Literature, and Criticism, no. 11 (Lincoln: University of Nebraska, 1930);

Maurice Denham Jephson, *An Anglo-Irish Miscellany: Some Records of the Jephsons of Mallow* (Dublin: Allen Figgis, 1964).

References:

James Boaden, *Memoirs of Mrs. Siddons. Interspersed With Anecdotes of Authors and Actors*, 2 volumes (London: Henry Colburn, 1827);

Boaden, *Memoirs of the Life of John Philip Kemble, Esq., Including a History of the Stage, From the Time of Garrick to the Present Period*, 2 volumes (London: Printed for Longman, Hurst, Rees, Orme, Brown & Green, 1825);

John Courtenay, *The Present State of the Manners, Arts, and Politics, of France and Italy; In a Series of Poetical Epistles, From Paris, Rome, and Naples, In 1792 and 1793: Addressed to Robert Jephson, Esquire* (London: Printed for G. G. & J. Robinson, 1794);

Percy Fitzgerald, *The Kembles: An Account of the Kemble Family* . . . , 2 volumes (London: Tinsley Brothers, 1871);

Arnold Lätt, *Robert Jephson and His Tragedies* (Zurich: Dissert.-Druckerei Gebr. Leemann & Co., 1913);

Temple J. Maynard, Introduction and notes to *The Plays of Robert Jephson*, edited by Maynard (New York & London: Garland, 1980);

[John O'Keeffe], *Songs, Chorusses, &c. in Love and War*, a shortened version of Jephson's *Songs and Chorusses in The Campaign* . . . (London: Printed for T. Cadell, 1787);

Martin Severin Peterson, *Robert Jephson (1736-1803): A Study of his Life and Works*, University of Nebraska Studies in Language, Literature, and Criticism, number 11 (Lincoln: University of Nebraska Press, 1930).

Papers:

The manuscripts of five of Jephson's plays are in the Larpent Collection of the Huntington Library. These are: *The Law of Lombardy* (LA 466), *The Count of Narbonne* (LA 575), *The Campaign; Or, Love in the East Indies* (LA 703), *Julia; Or, The Italian Lover* (LA 768), and *The Conspiracy* (LA 1120). Collections of holograph letters are to be found in the British Library, the Bodleian Library at Oxford, the National Library of Ireland, and the Public Record Office of Northern Ireland.

Hugh Kelly

(1739-3 February 1777)

Gretchen Foster
Albion College

PLAY PRODUCTIONS: *False Delicacy: A Comedy*, London, Theatre Royal in Drury Lane, 23 January 1768;

A Word to the Wise: A Comedy, London, Theatre Royal in Drury Lane, 3 March 1770;

Clementina: A Tragedy, London, Theatre Royal, Covent Garden, 23 February 1771;

The School for Wives: A Comedy, London, Theatre Royal in Drury Lane, 11 December 1773;

The Romance of an Hour: A Comedy of Two Acts, London, Theatre Royal, Covent Garden, 2 December 1774;

The Man of Reason (published as *The Reasonable Lover*), London, Theatre Royal, Covent Garden, 9 February 1776.

SELECTED BOOKS: *L'Amour à-la-mode, or Love à-la-mode, a Farce in Three Acts*, by Louis du Tem, possibly translated by Kelly (London: Printed for William Johns, 1760);

Thespis; or, a Critical Examination into the Merits of all the Principal Performers belonging to the Drury-Lane Theatre (London: G. Kearsley, 1766; second edition, with "corrections, and additions," 1766);

Thespis: or, A Critical Examination into the Merits of all the Principal Performers belonging to Covent Garden Theatre. Book the Second (London: G. Kearsley, 1767);

The Babler. Containing a Careful Selection from Those Entertaining and Interesting Essays, Which Have Given the Public So Much Satisfaction under That Title during a Course of Four Years, in Owen's Weekly Chronicle, 2 volumes (London: Printed for J. Newbery, L. Hawes, W. Clark, R. Collins & J. Harrison, 1767);

Memoirs of a Magdalen, or the History of Louisa Mildmay, 2 volumes (London: W. Griffin, 1767);

False Delicacy: A Comedy; as It Is Performed at the Theatre-Royal in Drury-Lane, by His Majesty's Servants (London: Printed for R. Baldwin, W. Johnson & G. Kearsly, 1768);

A Word to the Wise, A Comedy, as It Was Performed at the Theatre Royal, in Drury-Lane (London: Printed for the Author & sold by Dodsley, J. & E. Dilly, G. Kearsley, and T. Cadell, 1770);

Clementina, a Tragedy, As it is Perform'd with universal Applause at the Theatre-Royal in Covent-Garden (London: Printed for Edward & Charles Dilly and T. Cadell, 1771);

The School for Wives. A Comedy. As It Is Performed at the Theatre-Royal in Drury-Lane (London: Printed for T. Becket, 1774);

The Romance of an Hour, A Comedy of Two Acts, As it is performed, with Universal Applause, at the Theatre Royal in Covent-Garden (London: Printed for G. Kearsley, 1774);

The Works of Hugh Kelly (London: Printed & sold by T. Cadell, 1778);

Plays of Hugh Kelly, edited by Larry Carver (New York & London: Garland, 1980)–includes first printing of *The Reasonable Lover* (also known as *The Man of Reason*).

Hugh Kelly, born poor and Irish, died poor and in London. But for about eight years he was famous and, by his moderate standards, rich. His circle of friends included Oliver Goldsmith, David Garrick, and Samuel Johnson. A successful journalist, novelist, and playwright, Kelly is remembered mainly for his six plays–five comedies and one tragedy. He specialized in sentimental or "weeping" comedies, as opposed to the "laughing" comedies of the Restoration wits. Sentimental comedy sets the heart over the head. According to Arthur Sherbo, in *English Sentimental Drama* (1957), these plays are artificial and improbable, appeal to the essential goodness of human nature, and greatly emphasize pathos. Kelly's plays contain all these features but, at their best moments, also have wit and verve. Kelly attempted to combine the best features of sentimental and comic drama. He de-

scribes his goals in the preface to *The School for Wives:*

> His chief study has been to steer between the extremes of sentimental gloom, and the excesses of uninteresting levity; he has some laugh, yet he hopes he has also some lesson; and, as fashionable as it has been lately for the wits, even with his friend Mr. Garrick at their head, to ridicule the Comic Muse, when a little grave, he must think that she degenerates into farce, where the grand business of instruction is neglected, and consider it as a heresy in criticism, to say that one of the most arduous tasks within the reach of literature, should, when executed, be wholly without utility.

Kelly's experiments in mingling pathos and comedy are not generally seen as successful. They lead to artificial dialogue and improbable action. Scenes that promise comedy switch course for no apparent reason and end in tear-dimmed moralizing. Because Kelly's comedies both practice and ridicule the sentimental genre, he cannot be classed as a purely sentimental dramatist. Arthur Sherbo points out in *English Sentimental Drama* such ridicule was fairly common during this period and Kelly "affords evidence of [its] fashionableness." Kelly's preface to *The School for Wives* makes this clear, at the same time that it tries to distinguish his method from the usual ridicule which "degenerates into farce." Kelly seems entirely sincere in his attempt both to please and to instruct in a new way that touches the hearts and appeals to the wit of an increasingly heterogeneous British audience, and he succeeds in doing just that.

Kelly arrived in London ill-educated and trained to use his hands rather than his wits. In a very few years, with the help of the circulating library, his own observation, and above all his keen sense of what would captivate the public, he found himself the author of a successful play that netted

Frances Abington as Thalia, the Comic Muse (portrait by Sir Joshua Reynolds, at Waddesden Manor, Aylesbury, Buckinghamshire; James A. de Rothschild bequest; by permission of the National Trust). Mrs. Abington created the roles of Betty Lambton in False Delicacy *and Miss Walsingham in* The School for Wives.

him seven hundred pounds and when published sold ten thousand copies the first year. Such an author deserves notice by anyone interested in the eighteenth century, the history of English drama, or popular taste.

Kelly was born in Dublin, Ireland, the son of a tavern keeper. He received limited schooling and while still young was apprenticed to a staymaker. In the spring of 1760 he traveled to London to seek his fortune. At first he plied his needle, not very successfully, making stays, but he soon began to pursue what had been his goal all along–writing. After a few months working as an attorney's copy clerk and contributing articles to newspapers, his free-lance writing for the *Gazeteer* brought him an increasingly good living. He was soon submitting various kinds of pieces, including editorials, to *The Court Magazine* and *The Ladies Museum*. He wrote some political pamphlets, and Lord Chesterfield praised his "Vindication of Mr. Pitt's Administration." He also began to be known as a government spokesman, a label which caused him trouble later on. About 1761 he married a seamstress, Elizabeth (surname unknown), to whom he appeared to be devoted throughout his life; he took rooms in the Middle Temple Lane and was soon earning a living solely as a writer.

Kelly's early biographer Thomas Cooke noted that Kelly relished the public notice he was beginning to receive:

> He was vain of the character of an *author by profession*, or to use his own words, "of sitting in the chair of criticism." He was likewise fond of dress, and

though his person, which was low and corpulent, did not aid this propensity, his vanity prevailed, and he was constantly distinguished in all public places by a flaming broad silver-laced waistcoat, bag-wig, sword, &c.

Kelly began to establish a reputation as a drama critic, and in 1766 he published anonymously an imitation of Charles Churchill's *Rosciad* (1761), titled *Thespis; or, a Critical Examination into the Merits of all the Principal Performers belonging to the Drury-Lane Theatre*. His satire was rough rather than subtle. He characterized one Drury Lane actress as a "moon-eyed ideot" and, as Cooke reported, caricatured Mrs. Kitty Clive's "person and temper . . . so coarsely . . . that the public were unanimous in their disapprobation." *Thespis* also contained very flattering comments about the actor-manager David Garrick, which helped Kelly get his start in the theater. A few months later he republished *Thespis* with "corrections and additions" that he hoped would atone for what he called the "ruffian cruelty" of the first version.

During the 1760s Kelly also wrote a series of essays for *Owen's Weekly Chronicle*, a selection of which he published anonymously in two handy pocket volumes titled *The Babler* (1767). Thomas Cooke, in his brief biography of Kelly published in *The European Magazine* (1793-1794), noted that although these essays lacked the profundity and deep knowledge of human character of a *Spectator* or *Rambler*, they did "discover some quickness of observation, a fertility of invention, and no inconsiderable degree of humour." Above all, they "pleased the greater part of the public" whom Cooke characterized as "*the middle-sized in understanding*." About this time Kelly also became editor of John Newbery's *Public Ledger*, the daily paper to which he had contributed so many lucrative paragraphs. Newbery was Kelly's publisher for both *The Babler* and *Memoirs of a Magdalen, or the History of Louisa Mildmay*. This sensationally titled epistolary novel came out in 1767 and was a great success, running to three editions as well as to a version in French. Its popular appeal and financial success were considerable; its quality as a novel less so. And its patently moral purpose was, in Thomas Cooke's eye at least, diluted by the details of the heroine's seduction painted "in such *glowing colours*, and with such a *minuteness of description*, as we fear might have sometimes defeated the *moral*."

In the same year Kelly began his first play, *False Delicacy: A Comedy*. David Garrick, the manager of the Drury Lane theater, had called on Kelly after the appearance of *Thespis* and suggested that he write for the stage. Kelly, by now adept at rapid production, began the play on Easter Monday 1767, planned to have it ready by September, but, according to a letter preserved in James Boaden's *The Private Correspondence of David Garrick* (1831-1832), sent an early, still untitled, version off late in June. Garrick gave it a star cast, including the comedian Tom King and Mrs. Ann Dancer (who was persuaded to forgive Kelly's rough treatment in *Thespis*), and produced it on 23 January, timing it to compete with Oliver Goldsmith's *The Good-Natured Man*, which opened six days later at Covent Garden.

False Delicacy is all about love and the hazards that "false delicacy" creates. It comes out wholeheartedly for plainspokenness and direct action in the affairs of lovers. The young widow, Lady Betty Lambton, loves Lord Winworth, but her extreme delicacy about widows' remarrying has led her to reject his suit. Discouraged, he resolves to switch his suit to Miss Marchmont, an impoverished young woman whom Lady Betty supports and loves dearly. Miss Marchmont, however, loves Mr. Sidney (Lord Winworth's impoverished young cousin). To add to the agony, Winworth in his effort to help mend his cousin's fortunes, pushes Sidney (who secretly returns Miss Marchmont's love) into a suit for the wealthy Miss Rivers, daughter of Lady Betty's brother Lord Rivers, who is the stereotype of a "heavy" father. Lord Rivers approves the match, but, alas, Miss Rivers is unaccountably swept off her feet by the impetuous but middle-aged Sir Harry Newburg, whose morals are not of the best sort. Sir Harry's cousin, Mr. Cecil (played by comedian Tom King) is also middle-aged and also loves Miss Marchmont. However, unlike the other lovers, he takes a commonsense approach to life. In this he is joined by the robustly sensible Mrs. Harley, played by the accomplished comedienne Mrs. Dancer. When it becomes clear to him that Miss Marchmont loves Sidney, Cecil and Mrs. Harley cooperate to get the right lovers together.

The comedy arises mainly from the misunderstandings originally spawned by Lady Betty's extreme delicacy, which disseminates like a virus until it infects most of the other lovers. Unfortunately the comic potential of such scenes is never fully realized because Kelly, trying to fuse tears and laughter, dilutes them with sentiment and sententiousness. Even the witty repartée between the two plainspoken characters, Mrs. Harley and Cecil, is continually interrupted by the high-minded sentiments of the others.

PROLOGUE.

WRITTEN BY MR. KELLY.

SPOKEN BY MR. KING.

WELL, here you are, and comfortably ſqueez'd ——
But do you come *quite* willing to be pleas'd?—
Say, do you wiſh for bravo — fine — encore ——
Or — hiſs — off, off, — no more — no more — no more ——
Tho' for true taſte I know the warmth you feel,
A roaſted poet is a glorious meal ——
And oft I've known a miſerable wit,
Thro' downright laughter faſtn'd on the ſpit,
Baſted, with cat-call ſauce, for very fun,
Not till quite ready —— but till quite undone ——
And yet you ſerv'd the puppy as you ought ——
How dare he think to tell you of a fault ——
What fair one here from prudence *ever* ſtrays,
What lover here *e'er* flatters or betrays?
What huſband here is *ever* found to roam,
What wife is here that does not *doat* on home?
In yon gay circle, not a blooming face
From Club's rude king cou'd point you out the face;
No ſober trader, in that crowed pit,
'Till clear, broad day will o'er his bottle ſit;
Nor while our commerce *fatally* decays,
Erect his villa, or ſet up his chaiſe ——
Nay, you above, in cake-conſuming bow'rs,
Who thro' whole Sundays munge away your hours;

d You

PROLOGUE.

You are ſo mild, ſo gentle, that ev'n here,
Your ſweet ton'd voices never wound the ear;
Ne'er make the houſe for tune or prologue ring,
Roaſt-beef — roaſt-beef — the prologue, prologue — King —
Why then, thus weigh'd in truth's ſevereſt ſcale,
Shall each pert ſcribbler impudently rail,
With dull morality diſgrace the ſtage,
And talk of vices in ſo *pure* an age;
Your wiſe forefathers, in politer days,
Had ev'n their faults commended in their plays,
To cheat a friend, or violate a wife,
Was then true humour, comedy, and life ——
But now the bard becomes your higheſt boaſt,
Whoſe ill-bred pen traduces you the moſt;
Whoſe ſaucy muſe can hardily aver
That ſtill a *lady* poſſibly can err;
That ſtill a *lord* can trick you at a bet,
And fools and madmen are exiſting yet ——
Be rous'd at laſt — nor, in an age ſo nice,
Let theſe grave dunces teize you with advice ——
What, tho' ſome taylor's oft protracted bill
May hang all trembling on the author's quill,
Regard it not, remove the growing evil —
A well dreſt poet is the very devil ——
Do taverns dun him — What, can ſcribblers treat?
Fine times, indeed, when ſcribblers think to eat ——
Do juſtice then — to-night, ten minutes here
May blaſt the bard's whole labour of a year ——
What do I ſee! — reſentment in your eyes?
'Tis true, the fellow at your mercy lies;
And of all wreaths, the Briton's nobleſt crown,
Is ne'er to ſtrike an enemy when down ——

*

Dramatis Perſonæ.

MEN.

SIR GEORGE HASTINGS,	Mr. King.
SIR JOHN DORMER,	Mr. Reddiſh.
WILLOUGHBY,	Mr. Aickin.
CAPTAIN DORMER,	Mr. Palmer.
VILLARS,	Mr. Cautherly.
FOOTMEN,	Mr. Watkins. Mr. Wrighten.

WOMEN.

MRS. WILLOUGHBY,	Mrs. Jefferys.
MISS WILLOUGHBY,	Mrs. Baddely.
MISS DORMER,	Miſs Younge.
MISS MONTAGU,	Mrs. Barry.
JENNY,	Mrs. Smith.
LUCY,	Miſs Platt.

Prologue and cast list from the first edition of A Word to the Wise

Despite these shortcomings, the play was an immediate popular success. Critics could carp that it had neither plot, humor, nor wit and was, in Samuel Johnson's words (as recorded by James Boswell), "totally void of character." The London audiences took it to their "middle-sized" minds and easily touched hearts. The critic for *The Monthly Review* found it "a very agreeable play to *see*," but noted that "the critical reader who has not been present at the representation, will be apt to wonder what its uncommon success can be owing to." The more tolerant writer for *The Critical Review* discerned "beauties in this comedy sufficient to warrant the very favourable reception it has met with" but added that the chief reason for admiration is that Kelly "has been able to work up so pleasing a drama from such slight materials." Thomas Cooke, writing after Kelly's death, agreed that it showed no original characters or "refined turn of thinking," but he recognized its merit in exhibiting "just views of human life" and showing "the business of drama with much pleasantry and effect."

Kelly had both talent and luck. He discerned the trend in taste toward sentimental comedy's more delicate effects as opposed to the rougher humor and sharper wit of the traditional laughing comedy that Goldsmith was attempting in *The Good-Natured Man*, with which Kelly's play had been timed to compete. The critics praised Goldsmith's comedy, but the British public flocked to Kelly's sentimental drama. This was a new kind of public, larger, more diverse, and far less committed to excellence than the elite and sophisticated audiences of the Restoration and early eighteenth century. It embraced not only the well-educated and sophisticated but also that much larger, heterogeneous audience made up of middle-class husbands and wives, young apprentices and shopgirls, footmen and maids. These people did not seek wit, intellect, and comedy in the great tradition of the past, but untaxing entertainment, some easy laughter mingled with the delicate sentiments and refined manners that they were themselves seeking to attain. Kelly's *False Delicacy* suited their needs; his very situation–a poor and unknown young man on the rise–mirrored many of theirs.

Thus *False Delicacy* scored a great success. During 1768 it had twenty-one performances. It played to full houses in the English provinces and abroad in Lisbon and Paris. The London performances alone netted Kelly seven hundred pounds. The first printed edition sold thirteen thousand copies the first year. The success of the play's French and Portuguese productions caused it to be translated into both those languages as well as into German and Italian. Kelly's success brought him an opening-night celebratory dinner at the Globe Tavern, a public breakfast sponsored by his publishers, and a continuing feud with Oliver Goldsmith. Goldsmith had voiced his resentment at Kelly's success, calling his play trash and its author a blockhead. Kelly, quite understandably, resented Goldsmith's comments, and, although their friendship never recovered, he is reported to have wept at Goldsmith's funeral. Kelly's genuine good nature and desire to give the heart equal standing with the head pervaded his life as it did his plays.

When Kelly's second comedy, *A Word to the Wise*, opened two years later, his theatrical undertakings became complicated by his journalistic career. Because of his writings in the *Public Ledger* and elsewhere, Kelly had come to be seen as a spokesman for the government, which was experiencing a period of weakness and extreme unpopularity. At the same time John Wilkes, a charismatic rascal, had become a popular hero by publishing an attack on George III, which could have landed him in prison. Fearing arrest, Wilkes fled to the Continent but returned to England in secret and stood for election to Parliament in Middlesex. In his "Hugh Kelly: Contributions toward a Critical Biography" (1965), Thomas O'Leary reports that this middle-class electorate of "small shopkeepers and city workers" elected him by a large majority. Thus alerted to Wilkes's return, the government attempted to arrest him, vacillated, and finally did imprison him, making him a more popular hero than ever. When Kelly reported a trial connected with Wilkes's doings, he was accused of being a venal tool in the government's conspiracy to pillory Wilkes.

Charges that Kelly was a paid government hack in the Wilkes case were at their height when *A Word to the Wise* opened at the Drury Lane on Saturday, 3 March 1770. The opposition was organized into groups of Laughers and Yawners, spaced to bracket the audience and even draw them into their well-orchestrated disturbances. Cooke noted that most of the opening-night performance "was little better 'than inexplicable dumbshow.' " The second night was no better, so the third performance was canceled, *False Delicacy* being substituted but faring no better because the rioting was against Kelly rather than the play.

Of the play itself, Cooke observed that "from what could reach our ear the first and second night of its performance, it had little or no dramatic se-

Mary Ann Yates, who created the title role in Clementina

lection or character, and so abounded with commonplace sentiment, that, in all probability, he would not have been much a gainer had it been left to its own fate." In fact, the patently unfair treatment at the theater, which Cooke noted "drew the humanity of the public to his side," probably made the printed play more successful than it deserved. From subscriptions alone, Kelly earned eight hundred pounds. Publishing the play also allowed Kelly to remind the public of how unfairly he had been treated and to practice some of the same elevated morality which his plays preached. In his preface to the play he wrote, "Popular resentment has had it's [*sic*] victim, and the sacrifice being now over, perhaps a few words may be heard in his defence." After exonerating himself at length, he forgave his opponents because "the heated hour of prejudice however, is not the hour of sober reflection; at such a season the very virtues of our hearts frequently lead us into mistakes; and we run into excesses which our cooler reason must disapprove, from an actual rectitude of intention."

Like *False Delicacy, A Word to the Wise* was intended to elicit both laughter and tears in the cause of morality. Unlike its predecessor, which had ridiculed the folly of overstrained delicacy, *A Word to the Wise* attacked the vice of libertinism. Like all of Kelly's comedies, it centers around love and marriage and begins with everything at cross purposes. Sir John Dormer intends his daughter to marry the foppish but essentially good-hearted Sir George Hastings, made appropriately lovable and ridiculous by Tom King's comic talents. Naturally Miss Dormer resists a coxcomb who "fancies every woman must at first sight fall violently in love with him." But, as she confides to her friend Miss Montagu, an even more powerful reason is her love for her father's poor but virtuous and agreeable clerk, Mr. Villars, who returns her love but has, of course, kept this a secret.

Sir John is also engineering a match for his son, Captain Dormer, a self-professed libertine. The spirited and outspoken Miss Montagu is his target, but she not only despises young Dormer, but finds herself becoming enamored of Sir George. Captain Dormer is in love with the inexperienced Miss Willoughby but, as a rake, is contemplating not marriage but seduction. Miss Willoughby, abetted by her self-centered and discontented stepmother, returns the Captain's love and agrees to elope with him. Her father is a British Candide, determined to be cheerfully optimistic whether suffering from a broken leg (it might have been both legs) or afflicted by the mysterious disappearance of his infant son (it might have been his daughter as well).

The tangled love affairs lead to some comedy but much more sermonizing. When Sir John challenges Sir George to a duel because of the broken engagement to Miss Dormer, the very nonpugilistic Sir George extracts some comedy from the situation through speeches like "though there may be a great deal of bravery in venturing one's life, I can't say that there is a great deal of satisfaction." But when the duel is dramatically aborted by Miss Dormer's arrival and confession, the scene concludes with moralizing all around. Similarly, the potentially very funny scene in which Miss Montagu and Miss Willoughby set up the now repentant rake, Captain Dormer, to renew his addresses to Miss Montagu while Miss Willoughby waits in ambush and then confronts him ends with some pretty stiff moralizing by the captain on his own sins.

Kelly's theme causes him difficulty. Ridiculing the foible of extreme delicacy lends itself to

CLEMENTINA,

A

TRAGEDY,

As it is Perform'd with univerſal Applauſe at the

Theatre-Royal in COVENT-GARDEN.

A NEW EDITION.

LONDON:
Printed for EDWARD and CHARLES DILLY, in the Poultry,
And T. CADELL, in the Strand.
MDCCLXXI.

TO

GEORGE COLMAN, Eſq;

DEAR SIR,

WHEN I inſcribe this Tragedy to you, I mean to pay myſelf a very high compliment; the utmoſt I could poſſibly ſay of you, would by no means extend your Reputation; but it will do me much honour to declare, that ſo celebrated a writer has diſtinguiſhed CLEMENTINA with the moſt eſſential attention; and that ſo valuable a man has given me leave to ſign myſelf, what I truly am,

DEAR SIR,
His moſt faithful
and moſt obliged
humble ſervant,

The AUTHOR.

A

ADVERTISEMENT.

THE Author of this Tragedy has printed ſeveral lines for the Cloſet, which, in the Repreſentation, were omitted for the ſake of brevity. —The chief buſineſs of this advertiſement, however, is to acknowledge his obligations to the inimitable performance of Mrs. YATES, and to thank Mr. BENSLEY, Mr. SAVIGNY, and Mr. WROUGHTON, for their great good-nature, in undertaking their reſpective characters at the ſhort notice of a week, when Mr. ROSS unexpectedly returned the part of *Anſelmo**, which had been in his poſſeſſion above a fortnight, and left it no more than barely poſſible for the utmoſt diligence of theſe Gentlemen, to exhibit a piece, which the public have ſince been kindly pleaſed to honour with the moſt generous approbation.

* This circumſtance obliged Mr. BENSLEY, who was caſt for *Palermo*, to undertake Mr. SAVIGNY's part, which was originally *Granville*—Mr. SAVIGNY taking *Anſelmo*, and Mr. WROUGHTON, *Palermo*.

A 2

Dramatis Perſonæ.

ANSELMO - - - Mr. SAVIGNY.
GRANVILLE - - Mr. BENSLEY.
PALERMO - - - Mr. WROUGHTON.
ADORNO - - - - Mr. GARDNER.

CLEMENTINA - - Mrs. YATES.
ELIZARA - - - - Miſs PEARCE.

CITIZENS, GUARDS, &c.

SCENE, VENICE.

TIME—The Time of Repreſentation.

Title page, dedication, advertisement, and cast list from the second "NEW EDITION" of Kelly's third play

lightness and softness, but using laughter to confront the real vice of the libertine demands a far more deftly wielded lash than Kelly could handle. The play's title reveals its deficiency. A word, or in this instance far too many words, to the wise leads to sermons not comedy.

After the fiasco with *A Word to the Wise*, Kelly switched from comedy to tragedy and from Drury Lane to Covent Garden. As an even surer safeguard, he concealed his authorship, advertising *Clementina* as the work of an unnamed American cleric not yet arrived in England. Covent Garden's manager, George Colman the Elder, was Kelly's friend as well as sponsor and provided both a prologue and epilogue for the tragedy. Gratefully, Kelly dedicated it to Colman. The play opened on 23 February 1771, and, in Cooke's words, "lingered out its nine nights, and then was heard no more."

Clementina mingles heroic love and political idealism. Anselmo is leading the Venetian state in its attempt to throw off Spanish rule. Unknown to him, his daughter, Clementina, has married Rinaldo, with whose father Anselmo has a long-standing feud. When the play opens, Rinaldo is believed to have been killed fighting for Venice in a battle with Spain, but the audience soon learns he is alive. Unaware of this, Anselmo betroths Clementina to the Venetian patriot Palermo. She tries to refuse but finally agrees to accept Palermo. An ambassador from France, calling himself Granville but actually Rinaldo in disguise, arrives to convey to Anselmo "Royal Lewis's" offer to help Venice throw off Spanish oppression. Anselmo sees through the French king's attempt to bribe him and in a patriotic fury declares he will never "sell the brightest birthright of a people, / To gain a robber's portion of the plunder!" Such sentiments stirred the independent and freedom-loving British audience and appealed to their easily roused anti-French feelings. They applauded Kelly's sentiments and overlooked his bombastic language and improbable plot.

The tragedy ends with the deaths of both hero and heroine. Granville / Rinaldo is imprisoned by Anselmo and fatally wounded in a duel with Palermo. Clementina finally confesses her marriage, but it is too late. Granville dies in her arms, and she stabs herself. Anselmo's final speech deflates whatever pathos has been evoked through these events by pointing to the moral: "The dire effects of filial disobedience."

The plot depends on improbable actions carried out by characters whose motives stem mainly from Kelly's need to provide dramatic action dressed out with high-sounding speeches. The bombastic and limping verse coupled with relentless moralizing dissipates most of the tragic effect. Any lingering pathos vanishes with the epilogue, which pays lighthearted tribute to the beauties of Venice and then chauvinistically proclaims liberal Britain's superiority to authoritarian Venice.

Clementina brought Kelly financial, if not critical, reward. The nine-night run brought him the proceeds from three author's benefit performances, as well as two hundred pounds from publishers Charles and Edward Dilly for the publication rights. The critics were not so generous. In his *Complete History of the Stage* (1797-1800), Charles Dibdin reported:

> It set the audience asleep and therefore they had not spirit enough to damn it. . . . A gentleman was asked, after one of the representations of this play, why he did not hiss it? "How the devil could I," said he, "It was impossible! A man cannot hiss and yawn at the same time."

The anonymous writer for *The Critical Review* declared that among recent plays that had survived more than a night or two this was "by far the meanest, whether we consider its fable, characters or language." Despite excellent performances by the Covent Garden cast, especially by the talented Mrs. Mary Ann Yates as the heroine, the reviewer wrote that the play's author showed "neither genius nor learning to boast of." He should consider himself lucky for the "uncommon charity of the English audiences" which kept his drama alive through nine performances.

After a two-year respite, during which Kelly carried on his journalistic career, possibly receiving some sort of pension from the government that he apparently continued to support in his editorials, he brought out *The School for Wives*. In it he returned both to comedy and Drury Lane but again chose to hide his authorship, perhaps because he was still supporting Frederick, lord North's unpopular government in his newspaper articles and editorials. His friend William Addington, a London magistrate who was later knighted, agreed to be named as the author, a precaution that was abandoned when full houses guaranteed a successful run. The play opened on 11 December 1773 and rivaled the popularity of *False Delicacy*. From the end of 1773 through 1774 it was performed twenty-nine times, and it continued to be produced during the next two years. After Kelly's death it

on the Men. I have found them always more afraid of
ridicule from each other, than of censure from themselves
however if you dare run the risque, we'll try the sincerity
of Mr. Beville's Reformation

Mrs Belville

If I dare run the Risque— I'd stake my soul upon his honour

Lady Ra

Then your poor soul wou'd be in a very terrible situation—

Mrs Belville

By what test can we prove his sincerity

Lady R

By a very simple one You know I write so much like Miss Wal=
=singham that our hands are scarcely known a Sunder

Mrs Belville

Well—

Lady R.

Why then let me write to him as from her?

Mrs Belville

For what purpose

Lady Ra

For a purpose that can by no means injure Miss Walsingham
& yet will abundantly satisfy your curiosity— 'Tis a pretty
dramatic conceit— I have it here in my head, but you must keep
every thing a most inviolable secret—

Mrs Belville

O do you suppose that I wou'dn't be as silent as death upon every
thing that was injurous to my husbands Reputation?— I have

Page from the playhouse copy of The School for Wives *submitted to the Examiner of Plays for licensing prior to the first performance, on 11 December 1773 (Larpent Collection, LA 362; by permission of the Henry E. Huntington Library and Art Gallery)*

remained in the repertory, appearing every two years or so through 1800.

The play contains Kelly's favorite sentimental, romantic, and comic elements–the libertine who reforms, the spirited young woman who captures all hearts, the blustering father who must yield to his child's wishes, and no end of mixups and mistakes. Kelly also mixes in those rareties of the English stage, a pacific Irishman and an honest attorney, two characters which reflect Kelly himself–his Irish background and his aspiration to become a lawyer. The play dramatizes not only what wives are supposed to learn but also what sentimental drama is supposed to teach. Kelly introduces a sentimental dramatist, Lady Rachel Mildew, who helps underscore his belief in the value of sentimental comedy and is also a focus of some mild comedy herself as her name indicates. He also has some linguistic fun with the military jargon of General Savage.

The action centers around the high-spirited but impoverished Miss Walsingham and her many suitors and the libertine Mr. Belville and his many affairs. The patient endurance of his wife and his reformation are object lessons in the school for wives. Miss Walsingham and Captain Savage are secretly engaged. The captain's father, General Savage, keeps a mistress, Mrs. Tempest, who has him completely subdued though constantly hoping for liberation. General Savage is engineering a match for his son, the captain, with Mr. Belville's wealthy sister at whose house Miss Walsingham is staying. His matchmaking efforts, together with Miss Walsingham's attempt to ingratiate herself with what she hopes is her future father-in-law, cause the general to fall in love with Miss Walsingham and to fancy she returns the compliment. Mr. Belville is pursuing an affair with his mistress's niece, Miss Leeson, a stagestruck young lady who thinks Mr. Belville is interested in her acting ability. Simultaneously, he finds himself smitten with the universally captivating Miss Walsingham. To complete the circle of romantic entanglement, Miss Leeson's brother, an impoverished but virtuous young attorney, loves and is loved by Mr. Belville's wealthy sister. The lively action occasioned by these interlocking relations carries through to a happy ending for all. Belville reforms, the young people pair up, and money showers down on the virtuous but needy ones. The general does not escape Mrs. Tempest, who forces him to give Miss Walsingham's hand to his son.

Opportunities for pure comedy abound, and in this play Kelly allows them more scope than he had in the earlier comedies. As affairs are drawing to a climax, Mr. Belville, with lingering rakishness, plans to meet Miss Walsingham at a masquerade, but his fledgling conscience persuades him to go no further with his plans for seduction. The woman he meets, disguised by a blue domino, is not Miss Walsingham, but his own wife. Captain Savage, the general, and the honest attorney Torrington have also followed the woman they believe to be Miss Walsingham. With drawn sword, the captain forces an unmasking, which leads to chagrin all around, except on the part of Mrs. Belville, who has proved her husband's fidelity under extreme circumstances and who says demurely, "Is conjugal fidelity so very terrible a thing now-a-days that a man is to suffer death for being found in company with his own wife?"

Kelly's lesson for wives is more complex than the patient-Griselda character of Mrs. Belville (the only actual wife in the drama) would imply. Even she displays newfound spunk at the play's close, when, taking her final cue from the triumphant Mrs. Tempest, she conjectures, "If the women of virtue were to pluck up a little spirit, they might be soon as well treated as kept mistresses." The play also depicts a school for husbands. When Miss Walsingham hesitates to accept Captain Savage after his display of irrational jealousy, he begins with the standard lecture: "In the happiest unions, my dearest creature, there must be always something to overlook on both sides." Then, faced with Miss Walsingham's less than enthusiastic "Very civil, truly," he hastens to add "that if the lover has thro's misconception been unhappily guilty, he brings a husband altogether reform'd to your hands."

In the closing dialogue, Kelly states his version of the commonplace that literature's goal is delightful instruction, which reflects the eighteenth century's obsession with the Horatian ideal for poetry of "utile dulci." Using his surrogate, Lady Rachel, to begin an attack on "modern critics" who insist "the only business of comedy is to make people laugh," Kelly gives the final word to the bewitching Miss Walsingham: "Unless we learn something while we chuckle, the carpenter who nails a pantomine together, will be entitled to more applause than the best comic poet in the kingdom."

Audiences loved Kelly's latest blend of laughter and sentiment, and even some critics looked favorably on it. The critic for *The Westminster Magazine* enthusiastically endorsed it. Cooke found it "a comedy of some merit, both in morals and character." Although not very deep, it did exhibit "com-

Frontispiece to the 1775 edition of The School for Wives

mon foibles in a pleasing, dramatic manner." The "British Theater" column in *The London Magazine* was less complimentary, finding the play a pastiche of stage effects and sentimentalism which pandered to the public taste. Partly echoing Samuel Johnson's charges against *False Delicacy*, the reviewer concluded the play was "devoid of original characters, natural situations and comic humor."

The School for Wives was published in 1774 and ran to four editions in London and one in Ireland. The publisher brought out a new edition in 1775. Subsequently, it was included in such collections as *Bell's British Theatre* (1797), Elizabeth Inchbald's *Modern Theatre* (1811), *The London Stage* (1824-1827), and *The British Drama, a Collection*, edited by Richard Cumberland (1817).

The year after *The School for Wives* opened, Kelly produced the two-act afterpiece, *The Romance of an Hour*. Originally he conceived it as a vehicle for the Drury Lane actress Mrs. Frances Abington, who had expressed her "wish to perform a character of *perfect simplicity*," similar to the heroine in a short story by French writer Jean François Marmontel, "The Test of Friendship" (1765). The resulting play was not produced at Drury Lane, however. Kelly gave a diplomatically obscure explanation in the advertisement to the published text:

> The difficulty however of producing a new piece accurately, which is solely designed for the emolument even of the first performers, occuring to us both, Mrs. Abington generously refused to hazard any little reputation which I might possess, upon her account; and I took my trifle the more readily back, from a reflection that she could only have what she always has on her night, an overflowing theatre.

Apparently Kelly and Mrs. Abington both feared that the "trifle" would not fill the house long enough to enhance her reputation or his profits. Instead, the play was produced at Covent Garden on 2 December 1774, with Mrs. Mary Bulkley playing the innocent foreigner Zelida. In the advertisement, Kelly acknowledged his debt to Marmontel for this character but insisted that the situation itself was a stock one and that the remainder of the characters were his own creation.

The plot of the play pits the innocent but wise foreigner (an orphaned East Indian maiden, Zelida, with her faithful servant Bussora) against the corruptions of British society. Zelida is supposed to be engaged to Colonel Ormsby, who had saved her father's life numerous times in the Indian wars. But she and Ormsby's best friend, Brownlow, have fallen in love. Zelida is staying at the house of Brownlow's sister, Lady Di Strangeways, and her husband, Sir Hector. They are the stock comic mismatched pair. Sir Hector is a salty sea dog in tastes and language and is raising their bear-cub son, Ourson, to be just like him. Some rather crude comedy arises from Lady Di's unsuccessful efforts to refine her husband and son.

Ormsby's imminent return to England brings affairs to a head. Zelida flees the Strangewayses' house and takes refuge in a questionable rooming house, where Sir Hector, always on the lookout for fresh romantic conquests, accidentally happens upon her. He quickly changes his plan of seduction into a plea for Zelida to return to his house, at which Ormsby has now arrived. After an aborted duel, Zelida and Brownlow are united through the efforts of Bussora, whose wildly ungrammatical but unfailingly wise comments are supposed to evoke the usual Kelly mélange of smiles and warm feelings. Zelida and Bussora give us the simple-but-wise foreigner's critique of British society. Commenting on Lady Di's portrait, Bussora sounds like an East Indian version of Jonathan Swift:

> Yes, lady; me wonder how painter can make like of the lady's in England–um have so many complexion.–in morning um is yellow–in noon um is red–in evening um is red and white–and when em go to bed, um faces have fifty colours, just so as back of alligator upon Ganges.

The play was moderately successful. Critical response ranged from the *Critical Review*'s praise of its plot and main characters to *The London Packet*'s damnation of its stale rehashing of old themes and characters. In his memoir of Kelly, Cooke found it "a very flimsy performance," but noted that it "worked its way tolerably well, as by tacking it to good first-pieces, and opportune nights, it brought some money both to the Author and the Theatre."

During the year following this slight piece, Kelly worked on the full-length comedy which was to be his last, *The Man of Reason* (or *The Reasonable Lover* as it was alternatively titled). It opened and closed at the Covent Garden theater on 9 February 1776. Kelly had asked Garrick to read the play and had made some of the changes Garrick suggested, but had not improved it sufficiently to eliminate Garrick's original reservations about it. Covent Garden manager Thomas Harris accepted it for production, but did not provide the kind of polish that Garrick might have given had he been its producer. Thomas O'Leary ascribes the play's failure to the absence of "Little Davy," remarking that had Garrick "fidgeted over this as he had over *The School for Wives, The Man of Reason* might have been another hit and Kelly might have continued in the theater."

The play is both a sentimental comedy of mismatched lovers and a satire in the tradition of the comedy of humours. The reasonable lover, Sir James Clifford, prides himself on his rationality, which he carries to its ridiculous extreme. The overly complicated plot revolves around misunderstood motives, hidden identities, and romantic entanglements in the households of Mr. and Mrs. Freemore and of Mrs. Winterly. The Freemore ménage is composed of Mr. Freemore, a scholarly man who is nobly disinterested about money but also heavily in debt; his greedy and shrewish wife; and their very eligible daughter, Flavella, who is as good as she is beautiful. Flavella obeys her domineering mother in order to make life easier for her beloved father, who long ago elected to be henpecked rather than live in constant warfare. Miss Freemore loves Captain Cleveland, who has just arrived in London, but her mother wants her to marry the wealthy Sir James. Captain Cleveland is actually the son of the Freemore family's close friend, Dr. Wilmington, who does not recognize him because he has not seen him since he was a boy. Dr. Wilmington, who has his own reasons for disliking Miss Freemore's engagement to Sir James, is conspiring with Captain Cleveland to win Miss Freemore.

The second plot features Dr. Wilmington's daughter, who is staying with her aunt Mrs. Winterly. She has been engaged to Wyndham, a nephew of Sir James, but because of a recent fight over a woman's honor he had to flee England. He has returned in disguise and is a footman in Mrs. Winterly's house. Sir James's other nephew, Lestock, is now courting Miss Wilmington, encouraged by her father, who has been assured by Lestock that Wyndham is dead. Lestock will inherit Sir James's fortune, provided no children intervene in the meantime. Thus he and Dr. Wilmington have a sincere interest in preventing Sir James's marriage to Miss Freemore. They have circulated rumors about her attachment to Cleveland and take every opportunity to encourage their marriage. In his role as Mrs. Winterly's footman, the personable Wyndham is besieged by advances from both Mrs. Winterly and her maid Gloworm, and he is hard pressed to keep his "due distance" from both. His attempts to escape their advances while retaining his job produce some comic scenes reminiscent of Henry Fielding's *Joseph Andrews* (1742).

The seemingly unending complications are finally resolved and the young lovers united. Sir James's attempts to be rational have not only been consistently frustrated but have landed him briefly in a madhouse. As his rascally nephew Lestock, who engineers his uncle's removal to the madhouse, observes, "From the first moment my Uncle commenc'd a man of Reason, and profess'd an open Defiance to the authority of custom it struck me that some opportunity might occur to take out a commission of lunacy against him." He achieves his goal when Sir James, in preparing for his wedding with Miss Freemore, rationally prefers Turkish dress over English because "a fine Muslin [*sic*] Turban is much cleaner than a greasy Wig" and "a loose flowing Robe is much more convenient than one of those ridiculous Coats." Lestock summons a group of doctors to pronounce him crazy. Kelly takes this opportunity to satirize the medical profession as well. The doctors, whose names (Crisis, Ravage, System, and Hemlock) amply describe them, examine Sir James and pronounce him insane because, among other aberrations, he sleeps when he is tired, gets up when he is awake, and eats when he is hungry. As the madhouse keepers carry him off, Sir James brings down the act 4 curtain crying: "This is a General Conspiracy against me–but it is what a Man of Superior Wisdom deserves for living in a Country of fools." He also has the last word, finally accepting the world as it is: "From this day I bid adieu to Singularity; and shall allow myself really a lunatic, if I ever again make love to a young woman or attempt to give Society Customs, instead of receiving Customs from Society."

Sir James's acquiescence to society's customs may reflect Kelly's own recognition of the need to base his plays on what his audience wanted. In this instance, however, he failed to read the public's taste correctly. His attempt to soften the comedy of humours with sentiment was a disaster. The failure of *The Man of Reason* was so decisive that it was not published until 1980, when Larry Carver included a typed transcription of the Larpent manuscript copy of the play in his edition of Kelly's plays. The textual editor notes that the Larpent manuscript "was copied by three scribes," who "differ in handwriting, in the treatment of accidentals, and in accuracy." Thus, as printed, the text is highly inconsistent and difficult to read, which perhaps adds to the confusion of Kelly's already complicated plot.

Abandoning the theater, Kelly sought a living as a lawyer, or as Cooke put it, "to exchange light congenial reading for the severer studies of the law" and in the process giving up "what was little short of a certainty for all the precariousness of a new profession." Politics had proved too great a struggle for him, and despite his stipend and his past success in the theater, he had not really been able to penetrate the heart of London society. Law was the route by which Kelly sought to achieve this. As early as 1767, he had entered himself as a student in the Middle Temple, and, as the author of "The Life of Mr. Hugh Kelly" (*Works*, 1778) noted, "was called to the Bar so early as the year 1774." But his health was poor, and middle age was approaching. Success did not come quickly in this sterner profession, and, his income reduced, Kelly began drinking more and more to escape the dismal reality around him.

In January of 1777, he developed an abscess in his side which stemmed from tuberculosis of the bone. Eighteenth-century medical science was insufficiently advanced to cure such a disease in a man who was overweight and had neglected his health for some years. Kelly died at thirty-eight, leaving a wife and, as Cooke reported, "a family of five or six children" in straitened circumstances. Friends rallied around and raised what Cooke called "a comfortable annuity" for his widow. Samuel Johnson, Kelly's neighbor in Gough Square, whose charity was not hindered by his previous estimation of Kelly's talents, wrote a prologue for a revival of *A Word to the Wise*. This, together with publication of Kelly's works by subscription, raised additional money to support his family.

Twentieth-century critics vary in their assessment of Kelly's place in English drama. The more conservative school, which began during the 1920s and 1930s, includes G. H. Nettleton, Ernest Bernbaum, Ashley Thorndike, and Mark Schorer. These authors view Kelly as predominantly sentimental, with a mingling of the comic that often causes problems in tone and dramatic structure. A more recent view, begun by C. J. Rawson and continued by Joseph Donohue and Larry Carver, sees Kelly as at least partly, or even mainly, comic and satiric. Schorer sums up the earlier stance. In an article in *Philological Quarterly* (1933), he discusses Kelly's first three comedies, *False Delicacy*, *A Word to the Wise*, and *The School for Wives*, and concludes:

> The three comedies of Hugh Kelly are essentially alike. All find their basis in a shallow optimism that assumes goodness in all men and in the Providence that rules men. This optimism is accompanied by and closely related to a moral purpose that expresses itself in platitudinous dialogue of an extremely genteel variety and in an artificially didactic conduct of plot that gives rise to improbability in action just as the optimism gives rise to improbability in character. Finally, the real interest of the plays is not in a picture of human absurdities but in a picture of human distresses from which springs a ridiculous display of sensibilities that bear no relation to valid emotion, and which expect the audience to sympathize with and weep for that virtue and honesty made distraught by too much genteel woe.

Despite these clearly sentimental features, Schorer does find that Kelly "differed from the typical sentimentalist not only in his comic method, which attempted to mingle pathos and mirth rather than to alternate them, but, more important, in his own awareness of the fallacies in the very tradition he employed." In another age with a different kind of audience, Kelly might, "with these critical perceptions, have written good comedies."

Kelly's mingling of comedy and pathos in the same scene is the basis of Bernbaum's criticism in *The Drama of Sensibility* (1925). According to him, particularly in *False Delicacy* and *A Word to the Wise*, Kelly makes the mistake of abandoning "the usual method of lending the principal passages a consistently sentimental tone and striking the comic note only in subordinate ones." Bernbaum admits Kelly's popularity but notes that from a critical standpoint it is hard to account for his mingling of comedy and sentimentalism in the same scene "except on the ground that the playwright strove at any cost to achieve the unexpected."

As recently as the 1960s, Allardyce Nicoll in *British Drama in the Eighteenth Century* reaches a similar conclusion that Kelly's sentimental dramas, although attempting to be "realistic," "imposed upon the stage a kind of dialogue insipid and ridiculously artificial." He believes that this "strange dichotomy" of the natural and artificial parallels the awkward mingling of comedy and sentiment. The natural desire to laugh unrestrainedly at foibles is perverted by Kelly's infusion of heavy-handed and artificial sentiments into the very scenes that have the most comic promise.

C. J. Rawson, in his 1962 essay "Some Remarks on Eighteenth-Century 'Delicacy' (1768)," suggests a different approach to interpreting Kelly's method in *False Delicacy*. First, he identifies Kelly's use of delicacy as "almost the equivalent of 'sensibility.' " This is the kind of sensibility that, in its extreme form, Jane Austen satirizes in *Sense and Sensibility* (1811). Just as Austen's Marianne carries sensibility to ridiculous and dangerous extremes, most of the characters in *False Delicacy* are both ludicrous and potentially destructive in the extent to which they insist on maintaining their delicate sentiments. Undisturbed by what Schorer sees as a fatal dichotomy, Rawson welcomes the satire that underlies the sentiment in *False Delicacy*, noting that "the title alone should set us on our guard." The comparison with Austen "helps us see that sustained mockery of sensibility may coexist with strong sympathy for it" and that we should view *False Delicacy* in this line rather than as traditional sentimental comedy with bits of satire awkwardly thrown in. He cites Arthur Sherbo's *English Sentimental Drama* as support for his position. Despite Sherbo's warning against "finding deliberate ridicule where excessive sentimentalism merely 'stirs *our* sense of the ridiculous,' " Rawson feels Sherbo agrees with him that *False Delicacy* is less sentimental and more intentionally satirical than is usually believed.

Whether or not Sherbo agrees with Rawson, he disagrees strongly with Larry Carver's interpretation of Kelly's satiric intent. In his review of Carver's edition of *The Plays of Hugh Kelly* for *The Eighteenth Century: A Current Bibliography* (1980), Sherbo finds Carver's "attempt to explain much in Kelly's plays as satire, irony, parody, and pseudoparody wholly unconvincing." In his introduction to Kelly's plays Carver takes off from Rawson and gains impetus from Joseph Donohue's contention, in *Dramatic Character in the English Romantic Age* (1970), that *False Delicacy* is "a competent and entertaining comedy of manners that sets out to cast ridicule on false delicacy" but swerves from its original purpose in the fifth act, which "does not fulfill the promise of the first four." Carver admits that Kelly was a moralist who appealed to the "feeling and informed heart" but insists that he most often does so not through pathos but "through a deft use of parody and satire." This extreme reading of Kelly's purpose allows Carver to use the most sentimental scenes as evidence of satire, interpreting them as "parody and sometimes 'pseudoparody to disarm criticism.' " Carver sees this double parodic stance as "the dominant trope in Kelly's life and work." Particularly in characters that reflect himself (such as the Irishman Connolly and the sentimental dramatist Rachel Mildew in *The School for Wives*), Kelly both parodies the type of the comic Irishman and tear-drenched dramatist and asserts their value in what Carver calls "pseudo-parody." Thus Kelly has his cake and eats it too; he scores comic points and yet reminds his audience of the goodness of the Irish and the moral value of sentimental comedy. As Carver puts it: "He asserts his own values and aesthetic and corrects what he sees as the misconception of them by others, and he does so through self-effacement and self-parody." Carver admits the danger of "making Kelly say what we want him to say by claiming that he is being ironic" but still holds to his point.

Kelly has always been seen as an anomaly, most recently by Arthur Sherbo on whom Carver draws to support his contention that Kelly is more comic than sentimental. Despite the ingenuity of his arguments, Carver is not finally convincing. His best evidence comes from the play that critics agree is Kelly's best, the one in which he most successfully alternates comedy and sentimentalism. But reading through all of Kelly's plays refutes Carver's thesis. They are not witty. We may echo the critic for *The Monthly Review* who found *False Delicacy* "a very agreeable play to *see*" but acknowledged that anyone who had only read the play's text "will be apt to wonder what its uncommon success can be owing to." If the satire depends more on staging and less on dialogue, then Carver's use of the plays' texts to prove his point defeats itself. And, as Sherbo notes in *English Sentimental Drama*, "just because this excess [of sentimentality] stirs *our* sense of the ridiculous . . . it is highly questionable that it appeared ridiculous to audiences of the latter half of the eighteenth century."

Kelly's place in English drama is not of the first or even of the second rank. His plays seem to have been popular for many of the reasons that Hollywood movies are. They moved audiences to easy tears and uncritical laughter, creating an illusion that something worthwhile was being experienced. Today we flock to such unstressful movies and let television's situation comedies wash over us with their beguiling yet refreshing nonsense. Such amusements, on which large numbers of people spend their time and money, are always worth knowing about. Kelly wrote at a time when popular art appealing to large, diverse audiences was just coming into existence. As Russell Nye writes in *The Unembarrassed Muse* (1970), "Satisfying a large audience involves no less skill than pleasing a smaller or more sophisticated one; popular artists can and do develop tremendous expertise and real talent." Kelly's *False Delicacy* showed such talent in embryo, and *The School for Wives* developed it further. Had he continued to write plays, he might well have reached even higher. Thomas Cooke, perhaps overly optimistically, yet not without reason, concluded his biographical essay with this estimate:

> In short, Kelly had talents enough to keep his literary fame alive whilst he himself lived, and had his education been better, and fortune easier, so as to have enabled him to select and polish his works, his genius was such as probably might have given his name a niche amongst the first dramatic poets of this country.

Biographies:

Edward Thompson(?), "The Life of Mr. Hugh Kelly," prefixed to *The Works of Hugh Kelly* (London: T. Cadell, 1778);

Thomas Cooke, "Hugh Kelly," *The European Magazine*, 24 (November 1793): 337-340; (December 1793): 419-421; 25 (January 1794): 42-48;

"Life of Kelly," prefixed to *Memoirs of a Magdalen,*

or the History of Louisa Mildmay, 2 volumes in 1 (London: Printed by J. Wright for C. Cooke, 1795);

David Erskine Baker, Isaac Reed, and Stephen Jones, *Biographia Dramatica; or, A Companion to the Playhouse*, second revision, 3 volumes (London: Longman, Hurst, Rees, Orme & Brown, 1812), I: 419-421;

Thomas K. O'Leary, "Hugh Kelly: Contributions toward a Critical Biography," Ph.D. dissertation, Fordham University, 1965.

References:

Ernest Bernbaum, "Kelly, Goldsmith, Mrs. Griffith, and Cumberland: 1768-1772," in his *The Drama of Sensibility* (Cambridge: Harvard University Press, 1925), pp. 224-246;

Larry Carver, Introduction to *The Plays of Hugh Kelly* (New York & London: Garland, 1980);

Fances Diane Corvasce, "Hugh Kelly: a Critical Edition of *False Delicacy*," Ph.D. dissertation, New York University, 1976;

Joseph W. Donohue, *Dramatic Character in the English Romantic Age* (Princeton, N.J.: Princeton University Press, 1970), pp. 114-118;

Jean-Michel LaCroix, "Une Lecture Antisentimentale du Théâtre du Hugh Kelly," *Bulletin de la Société d'Etudes Anglo-Américaines des XVIIe et XVIIIe Siècles*, 8 (1979): 87-112;

LaCroix, *L'Oeuvre de Hugh Kelly (1739-1777)* (Lille & Talence, France: Universities of Lille & Bordeaux, 1984);

Allardyce Nicoll, *British Drama*, fifth edition, revised (New York: Barnes & Noble, 1963), pp. 186-188;

Nicoll, *A History of English Drama 1660-1900*, volume 3, fourth edition, revised (Cambridge: Cambridge University Press, 1955), pp. 129-132;

C. J. Rawson, "Some Remarks on Eighteenth-Century 'Delicacy' (1768)," *Journal of English and Germanic Philology*, 61 (1962): 6-13;

Mark Schorer, "Hugh Kelly: His Place in the Sentimental School," *Philological Quarterly*, 12 (October 1933): 389-401;

Arthur Sherbo, *English Sentimental Drama* (East Lansing: Michigan State University Press, 1957);

Ashley Thorndike, *English Comedy* (New York: Macmillan, 1929), pp. 446-450.

Papers:

There appears to be no substantial repository for Hugh Kelly's letters, notebooks, or manuscripts. Ten letters are held in the Forster Collection of the Victoria and Albert Museum, London, England. The playhouse manuscript for *The Man of Reason* exists under the title *The Reasonable Lover*. It is Larpent MS 401, held in the Huntington Library, San Marino, California. Also in the Larpent Collection at the Huntington Library fair fair-copy manuscripts for *False Delicacy*, *A Word to the Wise*, *Clementina*, *The School for Wives*, and *The Romance of an Hour*.

Charles Macklin

(May 1699-11 July 1797)

Richard B. Schwartz
Georgetown University

PLAY PRODUCTIONS: *King Henry VII. Or the Popish Impostor*, based on John Ford's *Perkin Warbeck*, London, Theatre Royal in Drury Lane, 18 January 1746;

A Will and No Will: Or a Bone for the Lawyers, London, Theatre Royal in Drury Lane, 23 April 1746;

The New Play Critiz'd: or the Plague of Envy, London, Theatre Royal in Drury Lane, 24 March 1747;

The Lover's Melancholy, adapted from John Ford's *Lover's Melancholy*, London, Theatre Royal in Drury Lane, 28 April 1748;

The Fortune Hunters, London, Theatre Royal in Drury Lane, 28 April 1748;

Covent Garden Theatre; or Pasquin Turn'd Drawcansir, Censor of Great Britain, London, Theatre Royal in Covent Garden, 8 April 1752;

Love à la Mode, London, Theatre Royal in Drury Lane, 12 December 1759;

The Married Libertine (originally titled *The School For Husbands*), London, Theatre Royal in Covent Garden, 28 January 1761;

The True-Born Irishman: or the Irish Fine Lady, Dublin, Crow Street Theatre, 14 May 1762; performed as *The Irish Fine Lady*, London, Theatre Royal in Covent Garden, 28 November 1767;

The True-Born Scotsman, Dublin, Crow Street Theatre, 10 July 1764; expanded as *The Man of the World*, London, Theatre Royal in Covent Garden, 10 May 1781;

The Whim, Dublin, Smock Alley Theatre, 26 December 1764.

BOOKS: *The Case of Charles Macklin, Comedian* [single sheet] (London, 1743);

Mr. Macklin's reply to Mr. Garrick's answer. To which are prefix'd, all the Papers, which have publickly appeared, in regard to this important dispute (London: Printed for J. Roberts & A. Dodd, 1743)–includes both The Case of Macklin, and *Mr. Garrick's answer*;

King Henry the VII. Or the Popish Imposter. A Tragedy. As it is Acted by His Majesty's servants, at the Theatre Royal, in Drury-Lane (London: Printed for R. Francklin, R. Dodsley & J. Brotherton, 1746);

The Fortune-Hunters. A Farce. To Which is Annexed, a Humourous New Ballad, called The Female Combatants; Or, Love in a Jail, As it Was Acted at Mac L-n's Amphitheatre with Great Applause (London: Printed by A. M'Culloh for L. Donnelly, 1750);

Epistle from Tully in the shades to Orator M---n in Covent Garden (London: Printed & sold by M. Cooper, 1755);

A Scotsman's Remarks on the farce of Love a la Mode, Scene by Scene. As it is acted at the Theatre Royal in Drury Lane (London: Printed for J. Burd, 1760);

An Apology for the conduct of Mr. Charles Macklin, comedian; which, it is hoped, will have some effect in favour of an aged player, by whom the public at large have for many years been uncommonly gratified (London: Sold by T. Axtell, J. Swan, 1773);

A New Comedy. Love a-al-a-Mode [sic] *in Two Acts* [pirated edition] (London, 1779); republished as *Love a la Mode. A Farce. By Mr. Charles Macklin. As performed at the Theatres-Royal, Drury-Lane and Covent-Garden* [authorized edition] (London: Printed by John Bell, 1793);

The Man of the World. A Comedy in five acts. As performed at the Theatres-Royal, Drury Lane and Covent-Garden. Regulated from the prompt-book, by permission of the Managers (Edinburgh: Oliver & Boyd, 1781?); republished as *The Man of the world. A comedy, in five acts. As performed at the Theatre-Royal Smoke-Alley. Written by Charles Macklin, Esq.* (London?: The Booksellers, 1786?);

The True-Born Irishman; Or, Irish Fine Lady. A Comedy of Two Acts (Dublin: Sold by the booksellers, 1783);

Charles Macklin, circa 1792 (portrait by John Opie; by permission of the Garrick Club)

The Covent Garden Theatre; or Pasquin turn'd Drawcasir, introduction by Jean B. Kern (Los Angeles: William Andrews Clark Memorial Library, University of California, 1965);

A Will and No Will; or, A Bone for the Lawyers and The New Play Critiz'd; or, The plague of envy, introduction by Kern (Los Angeles: William Andrews Clark Memorial Library, University of California, 1967).

During a life that spanned almost the entire eighteenth century, Charles Macklin distinguished himself as a playwright, an actor / manager, and a champion of artists' rights. Apart from his life in the theater, Macklin enjoyed a brief period as a tavern keeper, which was a short-lived mid-career venture. His plays exhibit a passionate desire to reveal society's irrationality through the use of madcap humor; his theatric style, it is said, initiated a revolution in acting technique. Besides his work as an actor and a playwright Macklin was well known for his excellent method of teaching acting, his emphasis always falling on the improvement of elocution.

He was the first actor of his generation to make a clean break from the old declamatory style, in which the words being uttered did not necessarily carry any emotional content pertinent to the psychological reality of the character the actor was portraying. Macklin attempted to wrest the process of acting from the jaws of monotony and boredom, and he started a movement for which he still receives far too little credit. His reforms in performance as well as theater etiquette, especially stage management, accelerated a trend toward professionalism in the theater world. If actors had usually been treated as second-class citizens it was often because they themselves had acted irresponsibly. Macklin valued his profession and worked diligently throughout his career to raise its stature; in the process he became known for his difficult temperament and his standards of perfection. However, his demanding efforts were not in vain. He became famous for his revolutionary interpretation of Shylock in Shakespeare's *The Merchant of*

Venice, and in his later years he increased his fame by playing two parts that he had created, that of Sir Archy Macsarcasm in *Love à la Mode* and Sir Pertinax Macsycophant in *The Man of the World*. In fact, Macklin made the better part of his fortune by using aspects of his own personality in the creation and depiction of a cast of unforgettable characters.

No stranger to controversy, Macklin's fierce independence led to a ceaseless determination to secure artistic control over creative works as personal property, a stance which would embroil him in numerous legal battles. More than once he filed suit to maintain control of the fruits of his creative labor. Macklin lived an active and provocative existence throughout his turbulent career. His life and works serve as the linkage between two eras in the history of the theater.

The background of Macklin's life is shrouded in self-created mystery. However, the most likely date of his birth is 1699 (though Macklin would not or could not acknowledge the precise date). In 1699, a son was born to Alice O'Flanagan (or Agnes Flanagan) and William McLoughlin (or Terence Melaghlin), either of which last name their son Cathal (Charles) anglicized to Macklin. It is generally believed that he was born and lived through his early teens in Culdaff, County Donegal, in northwestern Ireland. He grew up speaking Irish, and he was instructed by a stern Scots schoolmaster in his early years, a fact which may account for his unsympathetic depiction of the people of that country, notably as Macsarcasm and as Macsycophant. Through participation in a school play in which he took the role of Monimia in Thomas Otway's *The Orphan*, Macklin was introduced to the world of theater. Leaving home at an early age (probably at fourteen), he worked as a scout (also known as a badgeman or "page") at Trinity College before embarking for London. Macklin would not return to his native country until he was an established writer and actor.

The events and experiences of a number of Macklin's early years are lost to us, and one can only surmise what a young man of his age and ambitions might have done to keep body and soul together. Success did not come easy to Macklin in either his literary or his theatrical career. Some accounts report that he was in England as early as 1717, working as an actor in touring companies outside of London in such places as Bristol and Bath. As an apprentice for a number of years in the provinces, Macklin would have had a chance not only to perfect his technique but, more important, to cultivate an acceptable English accent, a requisite if he had any serious intentions about a career on the London stage. Macklin secured a position at Lincoln's Inn Fields in approximately 1730, where he most likely worked as a waiter at the coffeehouse and served as a jack-of-all-trades in the theater. Three years later, in 1733, Macklin's theatrical career began in earnest. Because of a walkout by a number of actors (among them Theophilus Cibber) Macklin was hired for an engagement at Drury Lane.

A second important event of 1733 was the birth of Macklin's first child, a daughter, Maria, born to Macklin and his common-law wife, Ann Grace Purvor. The couple finally married in late November or early December 1739. Mrs. Macklin was an actress of considerable comic talents and was a loyal companion to Charles throughout her life, both on and off the stage. They often performed together in such roles as those of Mr. and Mrs. Peachum in Gay's *The Beggar's Opera*. The daughter, Maria, became a formidable actress in her own right and performed many times with her father both in parts that he had created, as well as in common repertory roles. She died at the height of her career because of a tumor allegedly sustained by wearing a garter that was buckled too tightly. After an unsuccessful operation she died at the age of forty-eight.

In the years immediately following the fortuitous 1733 engagement, Macklin established himself as a leading actor at Drury Lane. Like many of his fellow actors, he lived in close proximity to Covent Garden, where he stayed throughout his career in order, he said, "to save coach hire."

A significant event of Macklin's life occurred in this early part of his career when he was arrested for involuntary manslaughter. Backstage at Drury Lane on 10 May 1735, Macklin got into an argument with another actor, Thomas Hallam, who had taken his wig before a performance. Angered because Hallam continued to bicker with him even after handing over the wig, Macklin swung around to point accusedly with a cane. By accident he jabbed Hallam's eye, causing an injury which resulted in death within a day. It is a testament to Macklin's popularity that, although he was found guilty, he served no time in prison. Fellow actors rallied to testify on his behalf, including his rival James Quin, and although Macklin was ordered to be branded, the brand was given as a formality with a cold iron.

Macklin continued to work at Drury Lane under the manager John Highmore and, after

Four of the many portraits of Macklin as Shylock: this page (top), by Johann Zoffany (by permission of the National Theatre), and (bottom), also by Zoffany, circa 1767-1768, Macklin at left center with Maria Macklin (on his left) as Portia (by permission of the Tate Gallery, London); next page (top), engraving by C. Grignion, based on a drawing by Thomas Parkinson and published as a plate to Bell's Shakespeare *in 1775, and (bottom) Macklin at left center with Elizabeth Pope (on his left) as Portia, engraving by William Nutter, based on a painting by John Boyne and published by W. Yolland in 1790.*

Act 4 MERCHANT of VENICE. Scene 1
M.r MACKLIN in the Character of SHYLOCK.
most learned Judge! a Sentence; come, prepare

him, Charles Fleetwood. Having garnered much favor with Fleetwood, Macklin was promoted to deputy manager. Macklin's first initiative in this position proved to be both highly successful and historically significant. It was in his capacity as deputy manager that he, in 1741, revived the original version of Shakespeare's *The Merchant of Venice*. For many years a bastardized version of the play, George Granville's *The Jew of Venice* (1701), had been performed. As deputy manager, Macklin was given the responsibility of casting the play. With less talent at his disposal than he might have wished, he continued to press for high production standards, requiring the actors to appear promptly for rehearsals and to memorize lines faithfully and scrupulously. In addition, Macklin worked assiduously on the directorial concept of the production. He also developed a striking interpretation of Shylock, which he tempered while still in rehearsal lest the manager and the other actors revolt against his conception. When the opening night arrived, he released himself from his self-imposed constraints and offered an unprecedented interpretation of Shylock, showing the character in all of his humanity, both good and bad, both comic and tragic. For this work he is hailed as one of the greatest Shylocks in the history of the theater. His calculated performance rocked Drury Lane and prompted vast critical acclaim, the most famous of which is attributed to Alexander Pope: "This is the Jew / That Shakespeare drew." Apart from the realistic emotional portrayal Macklin offered, the role was also played in authentic dress, Macklin's costume thus making sense of the lines in the play referring to Shylock's "Jewish gabardine." He also wore a red hat which, in researching the part, he found to be a characteristic element of the dress of Jewish men in the time the play was set. Hereafter and, until he acted in the great parts he wrote, he was known to his colleagues and the public as Shylock. Scholars and theater professionals alike are indebted to him for reviving the original version of Shakespeare's *Merchant of Venice*. The strength of the image created by his performance in this role is the depiction of Macklin immortalized in Maria Edgeworth's nineteenth-century novel *Harrington* (1817), in which the young protagonist is taken by his friend to see "the most celebrated Jew in all England, in all Christendom, in all the world . . . ," who is, of course, Macklin's Shylock.

The actors' strike of 1743 prompted the great split between Macklin and David Garrick, a rift that would last through most of their careers. Both had vowed to maintain solidarity with the strikers until their demands were met by the management at Drury Lane. Garrick, however, broke the strike and went back to work, thus initiating the feud between the two men. Whereas Garrick went to work at Drury Lane, Macklin, never one to compromise his integrity nor to miss a fresh chance, took advantage of another opportunity. He joined Henry Fielding's company at the Haymarket with the young Samuel Foote as his assistant. This engagement kept him employed until later in the year when Garrick went to tour in Ireland, and Macklin left the Haymarket for a suitable arrangement at Drury Lane, once again securing a job because of the untimely departure of another actor. During this period he wrote many songs for plays, prologues and epilogues, and he was involved in nearly every aspect of each production, but he himself was yet to write an entire play.

Finally, the first of Macklin's plays, *King Henry VII. Or the Popish Impostor*, debuted at Drury Lane on 18 January 1746. Based on John Ford's *Perkin Warbeck* (1634), the play was written as a patriotic piece in response to the threat of a Jacobite invasion. Little is known about this work except for the fact that it was an utter failure. As a first effort it offers hints of Macklin's gift for satire, but its principal result was to make Macklin the object of ridicule. However, though the play was defeated, the author was not. Indeed Macklin satirized himself with references to the failure of that play in the prologue to his next–*A Will and No Will: Or a Bone for the Lawyers* (one of the characters referring to his previous work as a "merry tragedy").

Macklin's second play was not a great success, but it received more critical acclaim than his first. *A Will and No Will: Or a Bone for the Lawyers* opened at Drury Lane on 23 April 1746. Based on Jean-François Regnard's *Le Legitaire universel* (1708) and Ben Jonson's *Volpone* (1606), the plot of this two-act farce is told in the prologue (spoken by actors pretending they are members of the pit). The play concerns the efforts of a nephew, Bellair, who, with the help of a few servants, sets out to secure an inheritance from his decrepit uncle, Sir Isaac Skinflint, a grotesque part played by Macklin himself. The desired ends are achieved through the use of a series of absurd disguises and manipulative conversations designed to prey upon certain peoples' basic avarice and insecurity. Lawyers are tricked into making a false will with the servant dressed as Skinflint (who has supposedly died, a fact of which the lawyers are unaware). However,

in his extravagant Manner, returns Jupiter thanks for his having liv'd in a time when such a Comedy was written.

Cank: Blockheads! Fools! Idiots! what signifies Taste or Learning, if such Wretches are Suffer'd to have Sway in the Common Wealth of Letters.

Enter Plagiary

Plag: A blundering Blockhead! he pretend to give his Judgment upon Writing!

Cank: What's the Matter Plagiary?

Plag: Why there's that Stirring Irish Barronet blundering out such fulsome Praise upon the New Play, as is enough to make a Sensible Man Sick—I did but offer an Objection or two and my Lady Critick and the whole Knot open'd upon me Like a Pack of Hounds—I was forc'd to quit the Room.

Cank: I am Amaz'd at my Lady Criticks liking it but I will soon convince her of her Error. but dear Plagiary was there no Opportunity, nor no Attempt to hinder its Success.

Plag: Not after it begun, before indeed, there was as promissing a Spirit in the Pit as ever made an Authors Heart Ake they Whistled hollow'd and Catcall'd and interrupted the Prologue for above ten Minutes.

Cank: Ay! that look'd Charming.

Plag: O Delightfull!—I wou'd not have given Sixpence to have Secur'd its Destruction,—every Body round me concluded it a gone Play.

Grub: And so they did about me I Assure you.

Plag: If they had been possess'd with the Spirit of Eolus they cou'd not have behav'd better before the Prologue was Spoke; but the Instant the Curtain was drawn up their Clamour chang'd to a fix'd Attention, and their Prejudice to burst of Applause, which made the Ring.

Cank: What no hissing at all?

Plag:

Page from the playhouse copy of The New Play Criticiz'd *submitted to the Examiner of Plays for licensing prior to the first performance, on 24 March 1747 (Larpent Collection, LA 64; by permission of the Henry E. Huntington Library and Art Gallery)*

Old Skinflint comes back to life and tries to put a wrench in their plans. Thanks to the unbending stubbornness of the lawyers, the first will cannot be dissolved. The aged man is left in confusion and vows to prove that he was insane when the will was drawn.

This play expresses some of Macklin's dark attitudes toward human nature, attitudes which are further explored in his later plays. Some of the subjects the play treats are greed and parsimony, marriages of convenience, and the hideous injustice of the legal profession, all of which are cast in bold relief by the antics of Macklin's shrewd characters. However, the servant Shark's final words present Macklin's personal judgment: "For should our Will in Westminster be tried / The Right, I fear, would fall on t'other side. / Here you are absolute; confirm my Cause. / If you approve–a Figg for Courts and Laws!" Macklin characteristically underlines his plays' themes, leaving no doubt concerning the lesson one should glean from what has been offered in apparent jest.

The critical reception and popular response to Benjamin Hoadly's *The Suspicious Husband* helped inspire Macklin to write his third play, *The New Play Critiz'd: or the Plague of Envy*, which opened at Drury Lane on 24 March 1747. The play offers much insight into whether public opinion or critical exactitude should define the success or failure of a new play. It also demonstrates, in miniature, the integral part that the theater played in eighteenth-century London society. The play calls into question the true source of a play's success: whether it be a "good play" because it entertains people or whether it must be capable of simultaneously exemplifying a certain number of Aristotelian principles or some other abstract gauge of "correct" art. The main character of the piece is a critic called "Canker." Played as an afterpiece at Covent Garden while Hoadly's *The Suspicious Husband* (featuring Garrick) played at Covent Garden, it is an interesting look at what Macklin himself may have felt as a writer in competition with other writers. The critic Canker says of envy, "All Mankind had some, but Authors most; and we can better brook a rival in our Love than in our Fame." The personal feelings of a man in competition with the likes of Quin and Garrick are not far from the surface.

The Fortune Hunters, Macklin's fourth play, made its first appearance at Drury Lane on 28 April 1748. In this play some young Irishmen go in search of wives (that is, their fortunes) in London. William W. Appleton notes in his biography of Macklin that "the farce merits its total neglect." There has been speculation concerning whether the play is actually Macklin's, since he was in Dublin for the years 1747-1749, but Macklin traveled with great frequency, and it is likely that in between engagements in Dublin he sought to further his London interests. Macklin had gone to Dublin to work with Thomas Sheridan at the Smock Alley Theatre, where he formally agreed to take the great comic roles while Sheridan would play the tragic ones. Always one to follow opportunity, Macklin would spend the better part of the next four decades shuttling between jobs in England and Ireland.

Macklin was back in London and at the height of his career in 1750, when his son, John, was born. Unlike his sister, he did not pursue a life in the theater, choosing instead a vagabond's existence. Macklin attempted to give him a proper education, and at one time John attempted to carve out a living in the military in India, but he never found a suitable profession. His life was one of excess, and it ended early.

The fifth of Macklin's dramatic endeavors is *Covent Garden Theatre; or Pasquin Turn'd Drawcansir*, which played on 8 April 1752. Macklin wrote this play in response to criticism of Fielding's role as a magistrate involved in issues of social reform. An afterpiece, it was performed at Covent Garden. The title comes from two names associated with Fielding: Pasquin was a character he had played in his own play of the same name, and Sir Alexander Drawcansir (from Buckingham's *Rehearsal*) was the assumed name he used in the *Covent Garden Journal*, the serial in which he often explored his experiences as a magistrate. The play has little plot. In two acts the follies and vices of society are paraded by a character who represents Fielding. This mini-pageant highlights once again the hypocrisy of Macklin's society. Though notable for its political passion, like his first play, it was not a theatrical success. The extent to which the play is designed to mock or defend Fielding is not entirely clear. Some have even argued that Fielding might have had a hand in the writing of the play, and, in fact, he advertised it in the *Covent Garden Journal*. Because of Macklin's penchant for reform in all aspects of the theater and the incisiveness of his wit regarding his society, it seems likely that he supported Fielding's views. Moreover, the two men had been colleagues at the Haymarket theater and they had parted on the

Caricature of Macklin

most amicable of terms.

In 1753, at a benefit for his daughter, Maria, Macklin surprised his public by announcing that he would resign from his acting career. Leaving Drury Lane and Covent Garden, he intended to commence a business venture as a tavern keeper. If Macklin, as is believed, worked as a waiter at Lincoln's Inn Fields, he had some experience upon which to build. However, it was not any ordinary tavern that Macklin intended to operate, for in it Macklin began his brief tenure as an orator. Perhaps piqued by his exposure to the intellectual life while a page at Trinity College in his youth, Macklin initiated "The British Inquisition" at his tavern on 21 November 1753. A contemporary advertisement of the event announces "The British Inquisition" as follows:

> This Institution is upon the plan of the ancient Greek, Roman, and Modern French and Italian Societies of liberal investigation. Such subjects in Arts, Sciences, Literature, Criticism, Philosophy, History, Politics, and Morality, as shall be found useful and entertaining to society, will there be lectured upon and freely debated; particularly Mr. Macklin intends to lecture upon the comedy of the Ancients, the use of their masks and flutes, their mimes and pantomimes, and uses and abuses of the Stage.

Although a master of subtlety in acting, Macklin apparently did not master that trait in real life. This series of tavern talks is now famous as the first known public lecture series on Shakespeare. The lectures were part of an evening at his tavern, and

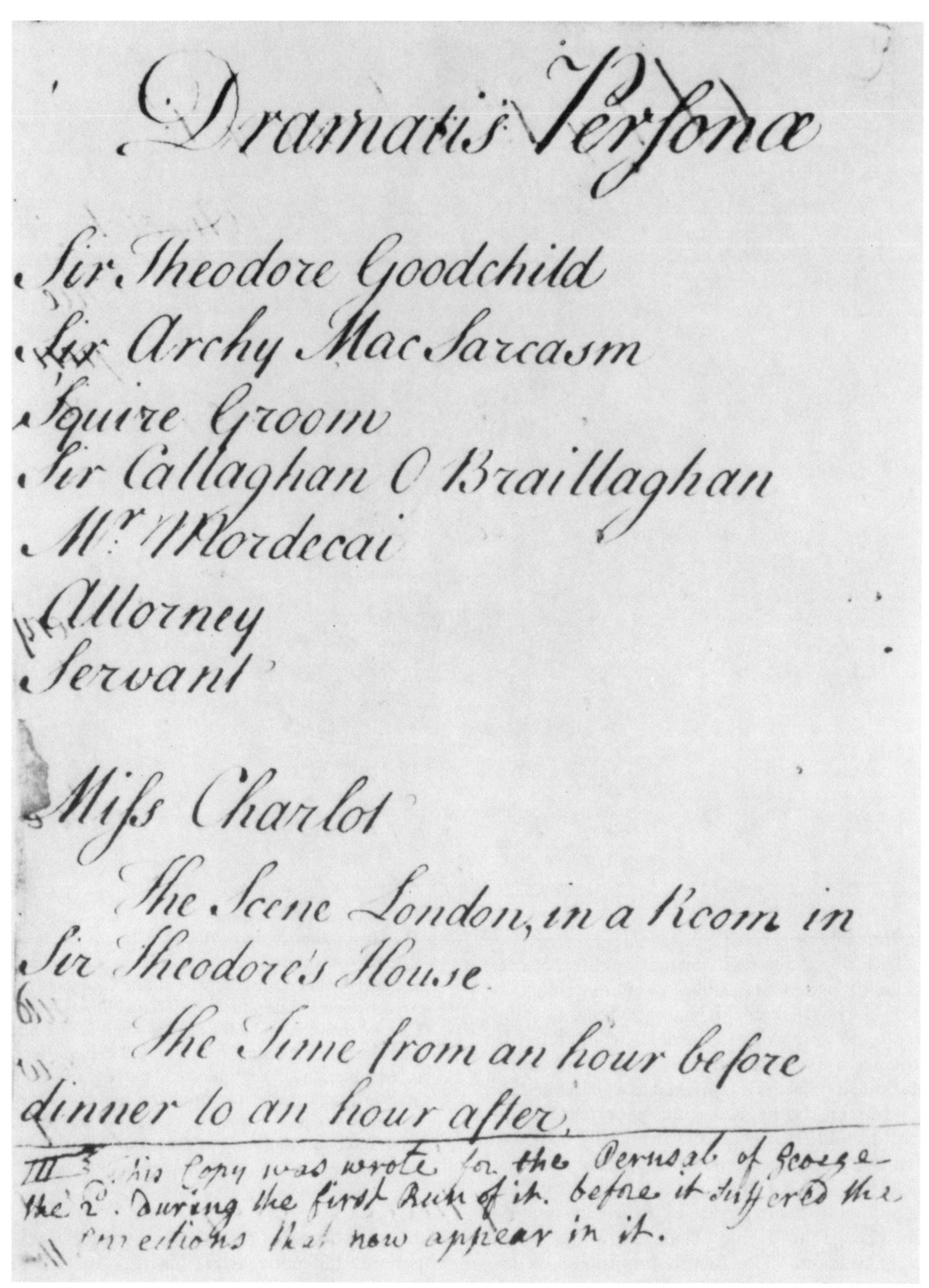

Dramatis Personæ

Sir Theodore Goodchild
Sir Archy Mac Sarcasm
Squire Groom
Sir Callaghan O Braillaghan
Mr Mordecai
Attorney
Servant

Miss Charlot

The Scene London, in a Room in Sir Theodore's House.

The Time from an hour before dinner to an hour after.

[illegible] This Copy was wrote for the Perusal of George the 2d. during the first Run of it. before it suffered the corrections that now appear in it.

Page from the manuscript for Love à la Mode, *approved by Macklin (by permission of the Garrick Club)*

Macklin had meticulously groomed his waiters and instructed them in the levels of service that he expected. After the meal, the lectures would begin, and Macklin, a man of little formal education, would hold his audience captive while he philosophized on a number of topics about which he had little authority but a great many opinions. His bombastic approach doomed the venture to failure before it ever really began.

It cannot have been easy for Macklin to survive on the wages he earned as an actor, but his business foray proved even less profitable and a critical failure as well. Once again, Macklin became the object of ridicule. This brief interlude in his theatrical career also marked the breaking point between his early halting attempts at writing and his later, highly successful full-length plays.

Returning to his theatrical career in full force in 1757, Macklin joined Spranger Barry in Dublin in a joint venture at the Crow Street Theatre. There, Macklin was able to do two things that he loved: nurture careers (Barry's as well as his own) and continue to write plays. Macklin intended to be a partner with Barry at the theater, but he had to change his plans because of the grave illness of his wife. However, he had always made a supplemental income from the teaching of acting, and he began to do so once again. Macklin was a perfectionist with regard to elocution, a field which he successfully attempted to reform. His meticulous approach to the teaching of acting was legend; James Boswell, for example, twice refers to the fact that Macklin served as an elocution teacher to Alexander Wedderbourne. It was suggested that Wedderbourne curb his Scottish accent, and Macklin was the obvious choice of instructor. He pursued his activities as an elocution and acting coach in Dublin, as well as in London. Students flocked to him because of his popularity, and he trained a great number of aspiring actors. In addition to his teaching he was fortunate enough to be able to work for Barry and the partner he had secured to take Macklin's place. In fact, the Crow Street Theatre was so successful that Sheridan was forced to close Smock Alley. Macklin's tenure in Dublin came to an end, however, with the death of his wife on 28 December 1758. Shortly after her death, Macklin moved in with Elizabeth Jones, a woman thought to have been his housekeeper. She would be his companion to the end of his days, though they did not marry until 13 February 1778.

In the time that Macklin spent commuting between the two countries he had access to two cultures and, therefore, two points of view on the societies of both England and Ireland. He sought reform not only in theater practice but also in the societies to which he and his colleagues played. He satirized English, Scottish, and Irish cultures mercilessly, and he was able to capitalize on his multiple perspectives when he wrote his first full-length play, *Love à la Mode*.

Macklin's first truly memorable play was his sixth one: *Love à la Mode* opened at Drury Lane on 12 December 1759 and marked a turning point in his literary career. This two-act play follows the efforts of a young woman and her guardian to dupe her four suitors in order to determine which one of them is truly worthy of her affections. The four suitors, a Jew, an English country squire, a Scotsman (Sir Archy Macsarcasm, a part for which Macklin was famous), and an Irishman fighting for the Prussian army, give Macklin a broad base from which to explore the narrow attitudes of his society. Each gentleman is mercilessly ridiculed by his rivals because of stereotypes associated with his nationality, and Macklin also returns to one of his favorite themes–the question of love versus money. In *The Merchant of Venice*, of course, the suitors who come to win Portia's favor are impressed by her wealth and have an overblown sense of their own importance. Ultimately, Bassanio wins her because he picks the casket of "base lead," willing to "give and hazard all he hath." In *Love à la Mode* the Irishman is the hero and, as such, is the first sympathetic Irish character that Macklin draws. While the comments of the other men lead the audience to believe that Calligan O'Bralligan will be yet another Irish stage buffoon, Macklin plays against their expectations and exhibits a (rare) personal fondness for his own people. Though the other three men forsake the woman when they learn that she has lost her wealth, O'Bralligan loves her more for her misfortune. The allure of money and power in conflict with personal integrity is an issue that Macklin addresses throughout his work. A huge popular success in London as well as in Dublin, *Love à la Mode* was also one of the chief causes prompting Macklin to struggle for control over his texts. Many theater managers were attempting to exploit the play's success and pirate copies so that they might perform the play at their own theaters. However, Macklin sued and insisted on his rights.

On the heels of the success of *Love à la Mode*, Macklin wrote *The School for Husbands, or the Married Libertine*, which first appeared at Covent Garden on 28 January 1761. The action of this farce focuses on a husband, Lord Belville (played by

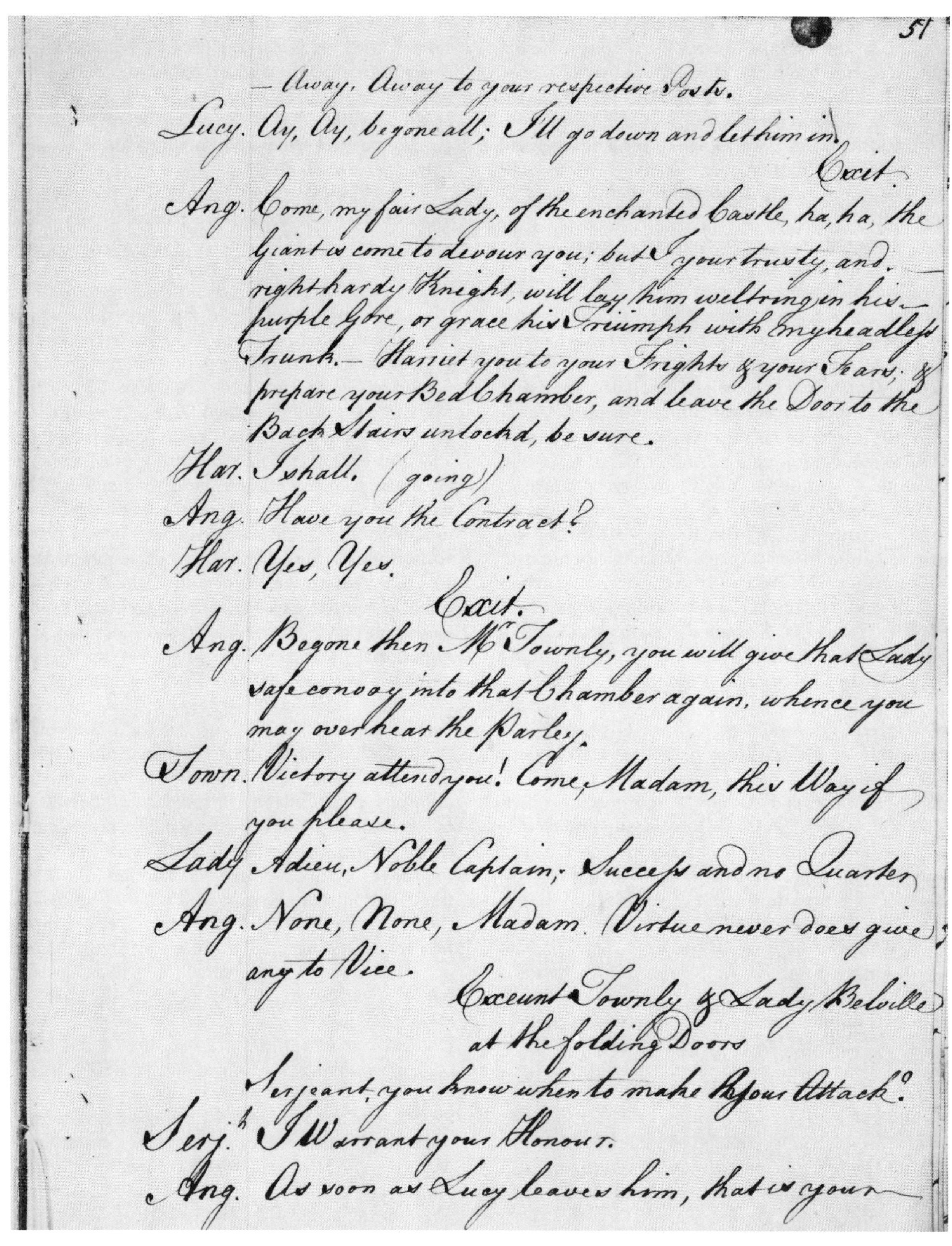
51

—Away, Away to your respective Posts.

Lucy. Ay, Ay, begone all; I'll go down and let him in.

Exit.

Ang. Come, my fair Lady, of the enchanted Castle, ha, ha, the Giant is come to devour you; but I your trusty, and right hardy Knight, will lay him weltring in his purple Gore, or grace his Triumph with my headless Trunk.— Harriet you to your Frights & your Fears; & prepare your Bed Chamber, and leave the Door to the Back Stairs unlock'd, be sure.

Har. I shall. (going)

Ang. Have you the Contract?

Har. Yes, Yes.

Exit.

Ang. Begone then Mr Townly, you will give that Lady safe convoy into that Chamber again, whence you may over hear the Parley.

Town. Victory attend you! Come, Madam, this Way if you please.

Lady Adieu, Noble Captain; Success and no Quarter

Ang. None, None, Madam. Virtue never does give any to Vice.

Exeunt Townly & Lady Belville at the folding Doors

Serjeant, you know when to make your Attack?

Serj. I Warrant your Honour.

Ang. As soon as Lucy leaves him, that is your

Page from the playhouse copy of "The School for Husbands" submitted to the Examiner of Plays for licensing prior to its first performance, as The Married Libertine, *on 28 January 1761 (Larpent Collection, LA 184; by permission of the Henry E. Huntington Library and Art Gallery)*

Charles Macklin as Sir Pertinax Macsycophant in The Man of the World *(portrait by De Wilde; by permission of the Garrick Club)*

Macklin), who is a known philanderer. Since "no ties bind him" and "no obligations, however sacred, restrain him," his wife decides to teach him a lesson, giving him a taste of his own medicine. She is aided by other family members and her servants in achieving her husband's public humiliation. In a series of hilarious plot contrivances involving absurd disguises and assumed identities, the husband is brought to his knees to beg forgiveness for his infidelities. The play exposes the double sexual standard of the time, and the husband learns the great value of a loving and forgiving wife. The action of the farce is clever and brisk, and it shows the further development of Macklin's ability to extract humor from painfully detailed depictions of human nature.

Anglophilia was rampant in eighteenth-century Dublin society, and it provoked Macklin to write *The True-Born Irishman*, which opened at the Crow Street Theatre in Dublin on 14 May 1762. In this play a wife, Mrs. O'Dougherty, is taught a lesson by her husband. The wife has fallen prey to the craze for things English to the point of having changed the family name to Diggerty. She travels to London for the coronation of George III, and she consorts with the members of Dublin society who have, through political favors, sold their dignity for a title. In addition, she has fallen under the spell of one Count Mushroom, a "coxcomb" stirring up trouble in numerous marriages in Dublin. With a little help from a family member and a consenting servant, Mr. O'Dougherty makes his wife see the error of her ways. She in turn helps her husband to humiliate Count Mushroom in front of all the people whom he has so viciously slandered. The humor comes from situations and character and also from the inappropriate use of what Mrs. Diggerty considers to be sophisticated language. This play pointedly underlines the implicit prevalence of Irish self-hatred that was perpetuated for years in the person of the stage Irishman, a phenomenon in which Macklin was personally involved, and yet able to utilize for the purpose of entertainment as well as social commentary. Macklin's play was a smashing success in Dublin because of its timeliness and topicality. However, attempts to revive the success in London a few seasons later under the title of *The Irish Fine Lady* were disastrous. Macklin's associates had warned him that the success of the play was based on a confluence of geographic and topical opportunities. In England there was no similar cultural stress in need of relief. Macklin concluded, "There's a geography in the humour as well as in the morals, which I had not previously considered."

The last play Macklin was to write began under the title *The True-Born Scotsman*, a three-act piece which first appeared at the Crow Street Theatre on 10 July 1764. The revised five-act version became the most successful of Macklin's works. *The Man of the World* was first performed in 1781 (the year of his daughter's death). In this play Macklin immortalized himself by portraying the morally repugnant incarnation of greed, Sir Pertinax Macsycophant, a character he played well into his eighties. Like Sir Archy Macsarcasm in *Love à la Mode*, Macsycophant was another nonsympathetic Scotsman. The play deals with the philosophical differences regarding love, marriage, and politics between a young man, Charles Egerton, and his father, Macsycophant. Unwilling to settle for an arranged marriage that will secure political territories (votes) for his father, the son challenges the father's wishes and desires to marry for love. As his name implies, Macsycophant is prepared to do anything to ingratiate himself and curry favor, political or otherwise. He is repulsed by the thought of moral rectitude and, for this, is estranged from his children, who symbolize the promise of a new philosophy of work, love, and marriage. Again, the play's success relies not only on well-contrived plot twists, but also on painstaking details of characterization. Regarding political parties, Macklin wrote,

> There is no reasoning with party or faction, for the first thing they attempt is to make a slave of reason;–very implicitly do whatever party or faction demands;–tyranny, disorder, injustice, violence, and habituated villainy, are the political elements of all party and factions, which, like the enraged elements of nature, never leave off quarrelling till an ancient national officer–old General Ruin–sends them all to the devil.

On the question of virtues he said, "We are prouder of our follies and our vices that are applauded by the ignorant million than of our virtues that are praised only by the thinking few." And of truth: "The world is tired of truth; it is so plain, so obvious, so simple, and so old; it gives no pleasure." The play was initially confiscated by the lord chamberlain for being slanderously offensive, but Macklin fought with persistence to have his only copy handed back over to him. In his arguments, he wrote that the "business of the stage was to correct vice and laugh at folly" and that the play was "in support of virtue, morality, decency, and the laws of the land."

The Man of the World synthesizes all of Macklin's finest traits as a mature writer. He is at his most lyrical in the voices of the young, and at his most incriminating in his depiction of the vices of the play's elder statesmen. There are the formulaic devices expected–the maid jealously conniving against another woman, a number of men in love with the same woman, the problem of mistaken identity, and, as in many of Macklin's works, a set of morally repugnant characters offering preposterous points of view with no clue that others might find fault with them. The conclusion of *The Man of the World* leaves the family unhappy and unreconciled, but the young lovers do have a vision for the future. The play has the ingratiating wisdom of an aged poet.

In 1773, after the first version of *The Man of the World* and before its authorized publication, Macklin made his famous appearance in Shakespeare's *Macbeth* at Covent Garden. This production is legendary because of the riots that it incited. *Macbeth* had already been done in tartan dress so that was not controversial. However, Macklin's age strained all credibility. Critics of his performance urged that "In act the second, scene the first, Shakespeare has made Macbeth murder Duncan; now Mr. Macklin, being determined to copy from no man, reversed this incident and in the very first act, scene the second, murdered Macbeth." He was heckled as an "old toothless dotard, with the voice of a tired boatswain." Impertinent and irreverent remarks filled the theater during his performance. Macklin publicly accused two men of hissing his performance, and he was determined to fight the issue to the end. Macklin was convinced that the hissers had been planted by Garrick, who was presumably angered by the fact that Macklin was play-

Macklin was so well known for his portrayal of Shylock that his decision in 1773 to play Macbeth inspired this caricature by an unknown engraver ("Old Envy"), based on a portrait by an unknown artist ("Young Vanity")

Another engraving of Macklin as Macbeth (artist unknown)

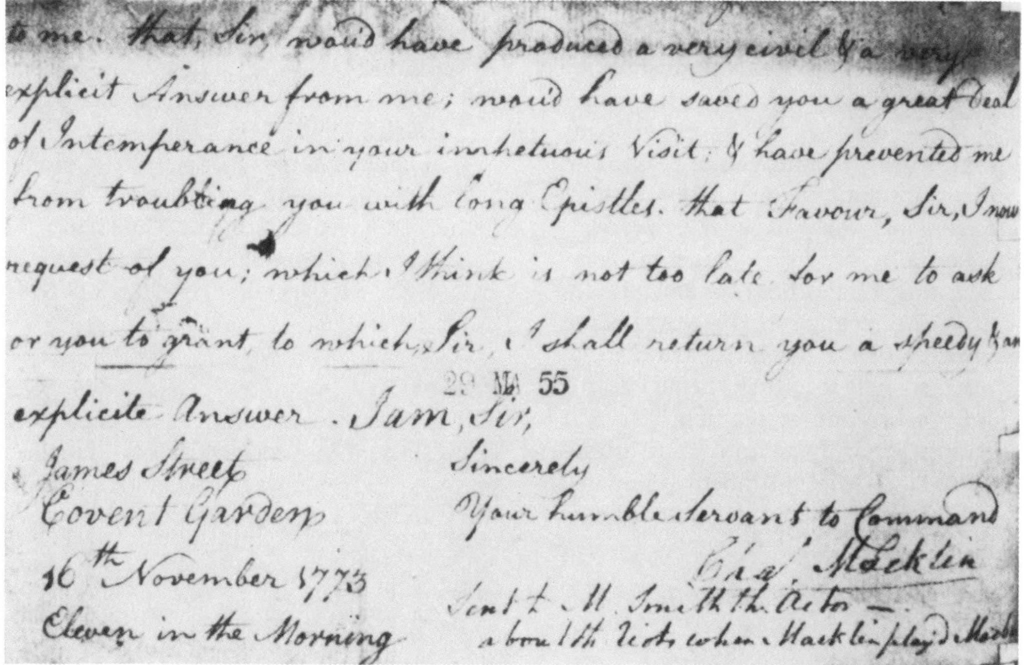

to me. that, Sir, wou'd have produced a very civil & a very explicit Answer from me; wou'd have saved you a great deal of Intemperance in your impetuous Visit; & have prevented me from troubling you with long Epistles. that Favour, Sir, I now request of you; which I think is not too late for me to ask or you to grant, to which, Sir, I shall return you a speedy & an explicite Answer. I am, Sir,

James Street
Covent Garden
16th November 1773
Eleven in the Morning

Sincerely
Your humble Servant to Command
Chas. Macklin

Sent to M. Smith the Actor — about the Riots when Macklin play'd Macb

Portion of a letter from Macklin to actor William Smith, whom Macklin had replaced as Macbeth (by permission of the Trustees of the British Library). After Macklin publicly accused him of organizing a claque to hiss Macklin's performances, Smith proposed a duel, but when Macklin accepted the challenge Smith backed down. Earlier in this letter Macklin declared, if Smith "had asked a civil or reasonable account of the matter, I should have given it him with pleasure, for that I was really a great coward and hated fighting. . . ."

ing parts in which Garrick had achieved his fame. With great difficulty Macklin got through four performances of *Macbeth*. He then returned to performing *The Merchant of Venice*. However, his enemies were not yet satisfied. They came to see Shylock, and when he entered the stage they called out for his removal. Objects were hurled, and Macklin was forced to leave. A riot ensued during which a number of spectators were injured and major structural damage was done to the Covent Garden theater. Macklin finally filed suit against six men who were accused of "riotous conspiracy to deprive Mr. Macklin of his livelihood." The case went on for two years, and Macklin ultimately triumphed. He wanted these men to be prosecuted to serve as examples to the public. The conspirators' hopes that Macklin's career would be ruined were all for naught; within a week he was back at work at Covent Garden, playing Garrick's most famous role, Shakespeare's Richard III. Macklin was nothing if not tenacious.

As far as is known, *The Man of the World* was the last of Macklin's plays. A majority of his papers were lost at sea during one of his crossings from England to Ireland. There are accounts that his notes included plans for a play which treats the theme of madness in a family, as well as a comedy set in hell. These plays were either lost at sea or never completed. He performed in a number of relief benefits for himself, but he was eventually forced to retire from the stage because of senility. It has been suggested that his funds had been seriously reduced because of excessive loans given to his vagrant son. Whatever the reason, he was able to bring in some income from authorized publications of his works in his later years.

Macklin was a reformer in stage management, in questions of intellectual property, in elocution, and in acting technique. His works serve as living indictments of the hypocrisies and social problems of the society in which he lived. Although he managed to outlive his first wife and both of his children, from 1777 until his death he lived with his second wife, Elizabeth Jones, in Tavistock Row, Convent Garden. His last appearance on the stage was as Shylock on 7 May 1789, and for the remaining eight years of his life he was a lively spirit in the theater communities of both London and Dublin, strolling through his old haunts and telling tales of the century he had witnessed. Charles Macklin died in his sleep in London on 11 July 1797.

It is ironic that a man who was such a luminary in his day could slip into such obscurity now. His work has a liveliness and a passion that rivals that of many of his contemporaries. He is now chiefly remembered for his work as an actor, and it has been said that it was Macklin who "made a science of acting." One cannot help but think of his own words in *A Will and No Will:* "Lord, how many great men have been lost for want of being thrown in a proper light?"

Biographies:

William Cooke, *Memoirs of Charles Macklin* (London: Printed for James Asperne, 1804; facsimile, New York: Benjamin Blom, 1972);

Edward Abbott Parry, *Charles Macklin* (London: Kegan Paul, Trench, Trubner & Co., 1891);

William W. Appleton, *Charles Macklin: An Actor's Life* (Cambridge, Mass.: Harvard University Press, 1960).

References:

Robert R. Findlay, "The Comic Plays of Macklin: Dark Satire at Mid Eighteenth Century," *Educational Theatre Journal*, 20 (October 1968): 398-407;

Esther M. Rauschenbush, "Macklin's Lost Play About Henry Fielding," *Modern Language Notes*, 51 (December 1936): 505-514.

Papers:

The Larpent Collection of the Huntington Library houses the manuscripts of all Macklin's extant plays except for *Love à la Mode*, which is owned by the Garrick Club.

Arthur Murphy

(27 December 1727-18 June 1805)

Robert F. Bode
Tennessee Technological University

PLAY PRODUCTIONS: *The Apprentice,* London, Theatre Royal in Drury Lane, 2 January 1756;

The Englishman from Paris, London, Theatre Royal in Drury Lane, 3 April 1756;

The Upholsterer: or What News, London, Theatre Royal in Drury Lane, 30 March 1758;

The Orphan of China, London, Theatre Royal in Drury Lane, 21 April 1759;

The Desert Island: a Dramatic Poem in Three Acts, London, Theatre Royal in Drury Lane, 24 January 1760;

The Way to Keep Him (three-act version), London, Theatre Royal in Drury Lane, 24 January 1760; (five-act version), London, Theatre Royal in Drury Lane, 10 January 1761;

All in the Wrong, London, Theatre Royal in Drury Lane, 15 June 1761;

The Old Maid, London, Theatre Royal in Drury Lane, 2 July 1761;

The Citizen (three-act version), London, Theatre Royal in Drury Lane, 2 July 1761; (two-act version), London, Theatre Royal in Covent Garden, 15 November 1762;

No One's Enemy But His Own (three-act version), London, Theatre Royal in Covent Garden, 9 January 1764; (two-act version), London, Theatre Royal in Covent Garden, 26 October 1774;

What We Must All Come To, London, Theatre Royal in Covent Garden, 9 January 1764; produced, with additional music, as *Marriage à-la-Mode, or, Conjugal Douceurs,* London, Theatre Royal in Drury Lane, 22 April 1767; slightly altered as *Three Weeks after Marriage,* London, Theatre Royal, Covent Garden, 30 March 1776;

The Choice, London, Theatre Royal in Drury Lane, 23 March 1765;

The School for Guardians, London, Theatre Royal in Covent Garden, 10 January 1767; abridged by Thomas Hull as the comic opera *Love Finds the Way,* London, Theatre Royal, Covent Garden, 18 November 1777;

Zenobia, London, Theatre Royal in Drury Lane, 27 February 1768;

The Grecian Daughter, London, Theatre Royal in Drury Lane, 26 February 1772;

Alzuma, London, Theatre Royal, Covent Garden, 23 February 1773;

News From Parnassus: a Prelude, London, Theatre Royal, Covent Garden, 23 September 1776;

Know Your Own Mind, London, Theatre Royal, Covent Garden, 22 February 1777;

The Rival Sisters, London, Drury Lane at the King's Theatre in the Haymarket, 18 March 1793.

BOOKS: *The Gray's Inn Journal. By Charles Ranger, Esq.,* 52 nos. (London: Printed for W. Faden & J. Bouquet, 29 September 1753-21 September 1754); revised and republished in 2 volumes, with nos. 1-49 from *The Craftsman* (21 October 1752-22 September 1753) and three new numbers (London: Printed by W. Faden for P. Vaillant, 1756);

The Apprentice, a Farce in Two Acts. As it is Performed at the Theatre-Royal in Drury-Lane (London: Printed for P. Vaillant, 1756);

The Spouter: or, the Triple Revenge. A Comic Farce in Two Acts. As it was Intended to be Perform'd. With the Original Prologue. Written by the author; and intended to be spoken by Mr. Garrick, dress'd in black, attributed to Murphy (London: Printed & sold by W. Reeve, 1756);

The Test, nos. 1-35 (London: S. Hooper, 6 November 1756-9 July 1757);

The Upholsterer, or What News? A Farce, in Two Acts. As it is Performed at the Theatre-Royal, in Drury-Lane. By the Author of the Apprentice (London: Printed for P. Vaillant, 1758);

The Orphan of China, a Tragedy, as it is Perform'd at the Theatre-Royal, in Drury-Lane (London:

Arthur Murphy

Printed for P. Vaillant, 1759);

The Desert Island, a Dramatic Poem, in Three Acts. As it is Acted at the Theatre-Royal in Drury-Lane (London: Printed for Paul Vaillant, 1760);

A Poetical Epistle to Mr. Samuel Johnson, A.M. By Arthur Murphy (London: Printed for Paul Vaillant, 1760);

The Way to Keep Him, a Comedy in Three Acts: as it is Perform'd at the Theatre-Royal in Drury-Lane (London: Printed for P. Vaillant, 1760); expanded as *The Way to Keep Him, a Comedy in Five Acts, As it is performed at the Theatre-Royal in Drury-Lane. By Mr. Murphy. The Fourth Edition* (London: Printed for P. Vaillant, 1761);

All in the Wrong. A comedy. As it is Acted at the Theatre-Royal in Drury-Lane. By Mr. Murphy (London: Printed for P. Vaillant, 1761);

The Examiner. A Satire. By Arthur Murphy, Esq. (London: Printed for J. Coote, 1761);

An Ode to the Naiads of Fleet-Ditch: By Arthur Murphy, Esq. (London: Printed for M. Cooper, 1761);

The Old Maid. A Comedy in Two Acts, as it is Performed at the Theatre-Royal in Drury-Lane. By Mr. Murphy (London: Printed for P. Vaillant, 1761);

The Auditor (London, 1762-1763 [lost]); also published in *The Political Controversy: or, Weekly Magazine of Ministerial and Anti-Ministerial Essays, Consisting of the Monitor, Briton, North Briton, Auditor, and Patriot, Entire; (with Select Pieces from the News-Papers) . . . By the Editor, John Caesar Wilkes, Esq.* [pseud.] (London: Printed for S. Williams, 1762-1763);

The Citizen. A farce. As it is Performed at the Theatre-Royal in Covent-Garden. By Arthur Murphy, Esq. (London: Printed for G. Kearsley, 1763);

No One's Enemy but His Own. A Comedy in Three Acts, as it is Performed at the Theatre-Royal in Covent-Garden (London: Printed for P. Vaillant, 1764);

What We Must All Come To. A Comedy in two Acts, as it Was Intended to be Acted at the Theatre-Royal in Covent-Garden (London: Printed for P. Vaillant, 1764); republished as *Three Weeks after Marriage; A Comedy, In Two Acts: as performed at the Theatre-Royal in Covent Garden* (London: Printed for G. Kearsley, 1776);

The School for Guardians. A Comedy. As it is Performing at the Theatre-Royal in Covent-Garden (London: Printed for P. Vaillant, 1767);

Belisarius. By M. Marmontel. A New Edition, by Jean-François Marmontel, translated by Murphy (London: Printed for P. Vaillant, 1768);

Zenobia: a Tragedy. As it is Performed at the Theatre-Royal in Drury-Lane. By the Author of The Orphan of China (London: Printed for W. Griffin, 1768);

The Grecian Daughter; a Tragedy: as it is Acted at the Theatre-Royal in Drury-Lane (London: Printed for W. Griffin, 1772);

Alzuma, a Tragedy. As Performed at the Theatre-Royal in Covent-Garden (London: Printed for T. Lowndes, 1773);

Know Your Own Mind: a Comedy, Performed at the Theatre-Royal, in Covent-Garden (London: Printed for T. Becket, 1778);

Seventeen Hundred and Ninety-One; a Poem, in Imitation of the Thirteenth Satire of Juvenal. By Arthur Murphy Esq. (London: Printed for G. G. J. & J. Robinson, 1791);

An Essay on the Life and Genius of Samuel Johnson, LL.D. By Arthur Murphy, . . . (London: Printed for T. Longman, B. White & Son, B. Law, J. Dodsley, H. Baldwin [and 32 others], 1792);

The Rival Sisters. A tragedy. Adapted for Theatrical Representation, as Performed at the Theatre-Royal, Drury-Lane. Regulated from the Prompt-Book, . . . (London: Printed by John Bell, 1793);

The Works of Cornelius Tacitus; with an Essay on His Life and Genius, 4 volumes, translated, with an essay, by Murphy (London: For the author, 1793);

The History of Cataline's Conspiracy, with the four Orations of Cicero; to which are added notes and illustrations, translated by Murphy as G[eorge] F[rederic] Sydney (London: Printed for T. N. Longman and Hookham & Carpenter, 1795); republished as *The Works of Sallust. Translated into English By The Late Arthur Murphy, Esq.* (London: Printed for James Carpenter and J. Cuthell and P. Martin, 1807);

Arminius; a Tragedy. By Arthur Murphy, Esq. (London: Printed for J. Wright, 1798);

The Bees. A Poem. From the Fourteenth Book of Vanière's Praedium Rusticum. By Arthur Murphy, by Jacques Vanière, translated by Murphy (London: Printed for F. & C. Rivington, 1799);

The Life of David Garrick, Esq. By Arthur Murphy, Esq., 2 volumes (London: Printed for J. Wright, 1801);

New Essays / By Arthur Murphy, edited by Arthur Sherbo (East Lansing: Michigan State University Press, 1963);

The Englishman from Paris (Los Angeles: William Andrews Clark Memorial Library, University of California, 1969).

Collections: *The Works of Arthur Murphy, Esq. In Seven Volumes* (London: Printed for T. Cadell, 1786);

The Way to Keep Him, and Five Other Plays, edited by John Pike Emery (New York: New York University Press, 1956);

The Plays of Arthur Murphy, edited by Richard B. Schwartz (New York: Garland, 1979).

OTHER: *An Essay on the Life and Genius of Henry Fielding,* in *The Works of Henry Fielding,* 4 volumes, edited by Murphy (London: A. Millar, 1762).

Arthur Murphy was one of the most popular comic dramatists of the second half of the eighteenth century. He clearly belongs in the group that today is ranked next best after Richard Sheridan and Oliver Goldsmith. From early in his career he rebelled against the contemporary fad of sentimental comedy, writing instead laughing comedies reminiscent of the comedies of the Restoration; these plays continued to be performed well into the nineteenth century, and their ability to draw large audiences is attested to by the frequency with which they were chosen by actors and actresses for their benefit-night plays. In addition he wrote tragedies that were popular onstage in their own time but seldom performed afterward; these plays reflect contemporary concepts of tragedy which have not retained critical acceptance and, from all accounts, relied heavily on the skills of particular players for their effectiveness in the original performances. His critical reputation has suffered from a mistaken classification of his comedies as "sentimental" in the nineteenth century and from the charge that he was merely a translator of contemporary French plays rather than a playwright himself. The elements of his comedies that have caused them to be misclassified are those reliant upon the fundamental goodness of mankind and the final reformation of characters who do wrong; however, Howard H. Dunbar in his *Dramatic Career of Arthur Murphy* (1956) has shown that Murphy's use of ridicule to reform the characters places his comedies in a context with Restoration comedies and makes them antithetical to methods of sentimental comedy. The charge of plagiarism through translation originated in his practice of frankly acknowledging his borrowing from French sources coupled with Charles Churchill's condemning him for that practice in *The Rosciad* (1761); it persisted well into the twentieth century. However, modern scholarship has rejected the charges of plagiarism by revealing the high percentage of original material in his plays and the degree to which borrowed material has been modified.

The son of Richard and Jan French Murphy, Arthur Murphy was born in Ireland on 27 December 1727. Before he was two years old his father died, and his mother became dependent on her brother, who moved the family to London in 1735. Arthur was sent to France to stay with his maternal aunt a year later, and when her health failed in 1738, he remained in France and was sent by his mother to the Jesuit College for English Catholics at St. Omer, where he remained for six years. He was registered under the name of Arthur French since English law forbade the education of English children at foreign Catholic schools. While there he studied humanities, especially the Greek and Latin classics, the latter of which he put to particular use in his plays and in his translations of Tacitus and Sallust, among others. When he returned to London, his uncle Jeffrey French intended to employ him in trade, but upon discovering that he knew no arithmetic in spite of his education he sent him to Webster's Academy to learn mathematics, accounting, and bookkeeping. In 1747 Murphy was sent to Cork, Ireland, to serve as an apprentice to the merchant Edmund Harrold. At first he was unhappy with both the people and the country, but he was introduced into society and eventually became reconciled to both. In spite of his having received the majority of his formal education in France, it was during his time in Cork that he developed a mastery of the French language. In 1749 he returned to London, having refused to sail to Jamaica on his uncle Jeffrey French's orders, and, as a result, was disowned by his uncle. From then until the end of 1751 he worked as a bookkeeper in a London banking house, hoping to reconcile his uncle to him through his diligence, but the hoped-for reconciliation did not come, and he left the bank, apparently intending to make his living as a writer. By 1752 Murphy was writing a regular essay for *The Craftsman* called "The Gray's Inn Journal," which after nearly a year he brought out for a second year as a separate publication. About this time he also seems to have become engaged to marry a lady whose name remains undiscovered; this lady died early in 1754, and although his name was later linked on long-term bases with several prominent actresses, Murphy never married. At the completion of *The Gray's Inn Journal* Murphy began his formal connection with the stage, being engaged to act at Covent Garden for the 1754-1755 season. His first role was Othello on 18 October, apparently successful, and he performed eight other roles there during that season.

Early in 1754 he submitted his first dramatic work, a two-act farce entitled *The Young Apprentice,* to David Garrick for production at Drury Lane. This play initiated the first of many disagreements between Murphy and Garrick concerning both the content and the scheduling for performance of Murphy's plays, Murphy usually wanting a performance date earlier than suited Garrick and Garrick procrastinating on the date by requesting changes in the text of the play. As a result Murphy withdrew his play from Garrick's consideration, an action he would take several times during his career as a playwright, and the play was not performed until it appeared as the afterpiece on 2 January 1756 under the title *The Apprentice.*

The subject of this farce is the desire of a young man named Dick to abandon his apprenticeship with the apothecary Gargle to take up a life upon the stage. The plot is further complicated by Dick's falling in love with his master's daughter, Charlotte, with whom he plans to elope so that they can both follow a thespian calling. Their plans are spoiled when they are caught by a bailiff, and Dick must promise to abandon acting in exchange for his father's going bail for himself and his would-be wife. The play is true laughing comedy satirizing the vehemence of Dick's temporary passion for acting, and the scenes and characters are drawn almost exclusively from life. There were many "spouting clubs" in London at the time of the play's performance where amateur actors, often apprentices from other occupations, could read parts of plays or sometimes even give full performances; *The Apprentice* was credited by many through the remainder of the century with making these clubs appear ridiculous and thereby keeping down their numbers. The pattern of Dick's speech is the first indication of Murphy's feeling for the effect of a play onstage, for Dick was played in the original production by Harry Woodward, a well-known impersonator, and subsequently by other actors known for their ability to mimic, and Dick's speech consists of a tissue of accurate quotations from other playwrights; thus the actors playing Dick apparently elicited laughter by delivering the quoted lines in the manner of other well-known contemporary actors.

Shortly after the performance of *The Apprentice,* another farce, *The Spouter; or, The Triple Revenge,* was published anonymously; although Murphy never listed it among his works, it seems to have been fairly well known by contemporaries that he was the author. This play has no plot and is virtually without visual action. Instead it consists of a series of vignettes each ridiculing a particular real and recognizable person and does not appear to have been intended for performance. Like a few of Murphy's other, usually nondramatic, works, it was occasioned as part of a pamphlet war, in this case to defend Garrick against a series of attacks by Theophilus Cibber.

On 3 April 1756 Garrick produced Murphy's third play, a farce called *The Englishman from Paris.* This play was intended to be a sequel to an afterpiece by Samuel Foote entitled *The Englishman in Paris* that had been extremely popular three years before. However, Murphy, as he was to do again later in his career, divulged his plan for the play to a rival playwright, and Foote wrote his own sequel called *The Englishman Returned from Paris,* which he produced at Covent Garden some two months before Murphy's play was ready for performance. Murphy's play moves rapidly and simply: Jack Broughton, the title character, having been completely made over into a French mold during his stay in Paris, comes home to find himself betrothed to Harriet, daughter of a country gentleman. Her father, Quicksett, however, dislikes things French and will not approve the marriage; Jack's father, also distressed by the folly of Jack's French behavior, threatens to disinherit him. Having had his French clothing impounded by the customs officers, Jack dresses in his old English garb; with the change of clothing comes a change of heart, so he sloughs off his acquired French behavior and gains Quicksett's approval for his marriage to Harriet.

Of Murphy's acknowledged works, *The Englishman from Paris* was the only one not published in his lifetime. In fact the play was considered lost until a copy was discovered in the Newberry Library in Chicago in 1964; that copy is the one Garrick had submitted to the lord chamberlain for approval to act, a copy that had inexplicably disappeared from the lord chamberlain's files. In his article on its discovery, Simon Trefman has traced the manuscript's curious history and come to the conclusion that Murphy may have deliberately suppressed the play, which is "not one of his better efforts." Until the discovery of the manuscript made other interpretations possible, modern critics, working from statements ultimately attributable to Murphy himself, concluded that Murphy's play and Foote's sequel were very much alike, Foote having stolen Murphy's plan, and, since Foote's play was performed first, Murphy's play was performed only the one time because the ground had already been covered. However, since the plays are not in fact very similar, it seems more likely that Murphy's play was simply not popular.

During the 1755-1756 season Murphy acted with the company at Drury Lane, his second and final year upon the stage; throughout his life he appears to have regretted having ever been an actor. By the fall of 1756 he had completed a tragedy called *The Orphan of China;* again he argued about production with Garrick, who rejected the play. He ventured into political journalism for the first time when he began producing a paper called *The Test* (6 November 1756-9 July 1757), which had the purpose of supporting the interests of Henry Fox against the government of William Pitt. Fox seems to have criticized each issue prior to publication, and when he received his sought-after office of Paymaster of the Forces, publication of the paper was suspended without its ever having become widely known that Murphy was its author. During the period of its publication *The Test* and its opposing paper *The Con-Test* were the center of much political discussion. Murphy's service for Henry Fox rewarded him with acceptance into Lincoln's Inn in 1757 through Fox's influence, after he had been refused entrance by both the Middle Temple and Gray's Inn presumably on the grounds that he was an actor. From this time on his legal and dramatic careers competed for his time. During this period Murphy also began a series of articles for *The Chronicle* called "The Theatre," in which he offered criticism of the contemporary theater and acting; these essays continued intermittently for a period of two years, and many modern critics agree with John P. Emery's estimation in his *Arthur Murphy: An Eminent English Dramatist of the Eighteenth Century* (1946) that these essays "constitute the best journalistic dramatic criticism of the eighteenth century."

His next play to be produced was another two-act farce in the manner of *The Apprentice* entitled *The Upholsterer.* The exceptionally fine cast that

Garrick chose for the first performance at Drury Lane on 30 March 1758 is an indication that the often stormy relationship between himself and Murphy was in a period of calm. The play satirizes, primarily in Quidnunc the upholsterer and to a lesser extent in the barber Razor, newsmongers whose excessive interest in ill-founded political rumors and other similarly unreliable sources of information leads them to neglect their own true interests. The satire is set against the background of a love affair between Bellmour and Quidnunc's daughter Harriet and Quidnunc's discovery of his long-lost and now independent wealthy son Rovewell; the play concludes with the promise of the lovers' marriage and the rescue of Quidnunc from bankruptcy by his son. In addition to drawing much of the play from life, Murphy is indebted to many literary sources. The main idea for the satire on newsmongers, as Murphy acknowledges in his prologue, came from Joseph Addison and Richard Steele's *Tatler;* numerous other sources can be identified as well. However, his use of those sources here is characteristic of the pattern he followed in the majority of his subsequent plays: while individual elements can be traced to definite sources, Murphy has so metamorphosed them as he combined them into his own play that they might more legitimately be described as new with him. The character Termagant, Harriet's maid, is an example of the pattern: Murphy borrowed Termagant's misuse and mispronunciation of words from Slipslop's practice in Henry Fielding's *Joseph Andrews,* although the two characters are not greatly similar in other ways, and Sheridan seems to have subsequently borrowed Termagant's speech pattern for his Mrs. Malaprop, who is also otherwise somewhat different from Murphy's character.

During 1758 Murphy planned or wrote five plays which were never acted or published. Two of these five, "The Comical Fellow" and "The Discreet Man," have disappeared entirely. The other three, "The Tender Wife," "The Graces," and "The Rout," existed in manuscript in Murphy's library when it was sold after his death but have since disappeared as well. The last of these, however, was the cause of another serious argument between Murphy and Garrick, for Murphy, having discussed *The Rout* with Garrick, accused him of giving the plot of the play to John Hill, who subsequently wrote a play with the same title that Garrick produced at Drury Lane. The disagreement was further complicated by Murphy's continuing effort to bring pressure to bear on Garrick to have him produce the once-rejected *The Orphan of China.* After accepting and then refusing the play again, Garrick finally produced it on 21 April 1759 with elaborate scenery; he played the leading role himself.

In *The Orphan of China* Zaphimri, the orphan of the title, the only surviving child of the previous emperor, has been hidden by the mandarin Zamti for the twenty years since Timurkan, a Tartar, conquered China and killed the remainder of Zaphimri's family. Zamti, having sent his real son, Etan, away, has raised the orphan in Etan's place. Etan, however, leads a rebellion, is captured, and, as a result of revelations by Zamti's wife, Mandane, is suspected of being the missing orphan. Timurkan tortures Zamti to get the truth, and Zaphimri and Etan each claim to be the true prince in order to save the other's life. Zaphimri then kills Timurkan, but Zamti dies as a result of the torture, and Mandane kills herself in grief. All of the violent action occurs offstage. The play was a success in its first performance, appealing as it did to the contemporary interest in the Orient and providing good opportunities in performance for the actors. Murphy's sources for the story are an English translation of a Chinese work and a French play by Voltaire based on the same Chinese source, both adapted rather than translated into Murphy's play; his indebtedness to, as well as his differences from, Voltaire are to some degree detailed in the letter to Voltaire that Murphy added at the end of the printed text of the play. Modern critics agree with Allardyce Nicoll's classification of the play in his *A History of Late Eighteenth Century Drama 1750-1800* (1927) as "a tragedy of mingled classic and romantic tendencies." The acceptance of the tragedy by both the critics and the theatergoing public brought Murphy to be recognized as one of the leading dramatists of the day.

In the summer of 1759 Murphy offered the three-act version of *The Way to Keep Him,* which he had written the previous year, and a new play in blank verse, *The Desert Island,* to Garrick. As usual, the two disagreed and their friendly relations ended for a time, but Garrick finally agreed to produce and act in both plays. They were performed together at Drury Lane on 24 January 1760. As with *The Orphan of China,* modern critics find a blend of the classical with the romantic in *The Desert Island.* The play deals with the reuniting of Ferdinand with his wife, Constantia, and their daughter, Sylvia. The three had been shipwrecked on a desert island sixteen years before the beginning of the play, and, unknown to Constantia, Fer-

10

Uneasy — Nor shall I ever be so again —

Bell — I wish You would keep that resolution — where do you dine?

Bever — Will you dine With me?

Bell. — I can't, It's Club day.

Bever — faith so it is — I'll attend you —

Bell — That's right; let us turn towards the Mall — & saunter there till Dinner —

Bever — No — I cant go that way yet — I must Enquire how Belinda does — And What her Father said to her — for I have not seen her since we parted in the Morning —

Bell — And now According to Custom — You will make her An Apology for leaving her when there was an absolute Necessity for it — and fall to an explanation of Circumstances that require no explanation at all, & refine upon things, and —

Bever — Nay if you begin with Your Raillery, I am off — Your servant. a l'homme —

{ Exit.

Bell — Poor Beverley! Tho a handsome fellow & of agreeable Talents — he has such a strange diffidence in himself, and such a solicitude to please, that he is allmost every Moment of his Life most heartily uneasie —

{ Enter Sr John. }

Sr John — Not yet, not yet! — Nobody like it as yet — Ha! who is that hovering About my house? If that should be he now — I'll examine him nearer — Pray Sir — What the Devil shall I say! (aside.)

Bell — Sir —

Sr John — I beg pardon for troubling you Sir — but pray what a Clock is it by your Watch?

Bell. By my Watch — Sir, I'll tell you in a moment —

Sr John Let me examine him now! — { looks at him & the Picture by turns. }

Bell — Egad, I'm afraid my Watch is not right — it must be later —

Sr John It is not like him —

Bell — It does not go — I'm afraid —

Sr John — The Eye — no! —

Bell — Yes it Goes — But sure it must be wrong — Why Sir by my Watch it wants a Quarter of three —

Sr John Sir I thank you — but pray Sir — pray Sir — { Comparing him with the Picture. } — the Nose — no, it is not he —

Bell — this seems to be an odd fellow — What is he fumbling about?

Sr John I beg Your Pardon Sir, for this trouble — Within a Quarter of three did you say, Sir?

Bell — Yes Sir, but it must be more by the day —

Sr John — Sir, I am oblig'd to you — it is not he — And yet if it should be he! — No, no, I am still to seek —

{ Enter Beverley. }

Page from the playhouse copy of All in the Wrong *submitted to the Examiner of Plays prior to the first production, on 15 June 1761 (Larpent Collection, LA 198; by permission of the Henry E. Huntington Library and Art Gallery)*

Henry Woodward as George Philpot, Michael Dyer as Young Wilding, and Edward Shuter as Old Philpot in the two-act version of The Citizen

dinand was immediately taken captive by pirates. Constantia decides he has abandoned them and as a result warns her daughter against all men. Ferdinand then returns with his friend Henrico and, after some complications, is reunited with his wife, to whom he explains his absence. In one of these complications Henrico meets and falls in love with Sylvia, who chooses to trust him in spite of her mother's warning, and the two plan to marry with her parents' blessing upon their return to England. Murphy used a contemporary Italian play as the source, greatly expanding upon and adapting the original. From the beginning critics have remarked on the virtually complete lack of action in the play, although there is ample opportunity for the conveying of emotions. The play was performed and first published with the description "a Dramatic Poem"; however, critics from its first performance to the present disagree on the genre to which it belongs, calling it a tragedy, a tragicomedy, a romance, and even a closet drama.

The Way to Keep Him, a comedy, retained its popularity a great deal longer than the play with which it was originally performed. During the year following its first performance as an afterpiece, Murphy expanded the play into a five-act version which, after some disagreements between Murphy and Garrick, was first performed at Drury Lane on 10 January 1761. The three-act version of the play has as its main source a contemporary French play, which Murphy acknowledges in the advertisement to the printed version, and in fact it owes a great deal to that source. However, the five-act version is virtually a reworking of the original idea, with the addition of several characters. The five-act version involves the movement toward happiness in their married state of two couples, the Lovemores and Sir Bashful and Lady Constant. Mrs. Lovemore has allowed herself to become dull, so her husband pursues other women. Sir Bashful loves his wife but thinks it unfashionable to reveal it, so he treats her badly and quarrels with her continually. The plot develops around Lovemore's and his friend Sir Brilliant Fashion's pursuit of the widow Bellmour, Sir Brilliant's pursuit of Mrs. Lovemore, and Lovemore's pursuit of Lady Constant, the latter complicated by her husband's reliance on Lovemore for advice about how to treat his wife. All of this is further complicated by the use of disguise and the misdirection of letters and gifts. The men of the play rely heavily on trickery and deceit to accomplish their ends, whereas the women by being straightforward and honest remain one step ahead of them. The play concludes with Mrs. Lovemore's having enlivened her behavior to the point that she now interests her husband and with Sir Bashful's confession of his true affection for his wife. The philandering of Lovemore and various other elements of the plot are reminiscent of Restoration comedy. However, there are some sentimental elements as well, for the wives here truly love their husbands, and, as Lovemore himself points out in admitting his wrongdoing, his wife's behavior after their marriage is at least a partial cause of his pursuit of other women. The five-act version was an immediate success and was performed regularly over the next thirty years, continually attracting the best actors and actresses of the time. Contemporary critics had special praise for the characterization, and modern critics consider the play to be one of Murphy's two best comedies and the equal of Sheridan's *The Rivals* (1775).

In 1761 Murphy agreed with his friend Samuel Foote to rent Drury Lane for the summer and to write three new plays each for the season. Foote did not deliver on his promise of new plays, but Murphy did, beginning with the full-length comedy *All in the Wrong,* which was performed on 15 June 1761. The play turns upon various complications resulting, at least in part, from the mutual jealousy of Sir John and Lady Restless. Their jealousy spreads among the remaining characters like a fall in a set of dominoes, affecting the relationships of two pairs of youthful lovers, Beverley and Belinda and Bellmont and Clarissa, until virtually everyone is suspicious and consequently jealous of everyone else. However, all misunderstandings, many of which result from a very effective use of dramatic irony, are cleared up at the conclusion of the play, and the young lovers are again betrothed to their desired mates. The play's source is Molière's *Sganerelle, ou le Cocu imaginaire* (1660), but Murphy adapts and develops material from the French original. Audiences clearly enjoyed the play, which continued to be performed into the nineteenth century, but contemporary critical reception of the play was mixed, partly because Murphy was involved in another pamphlet war at the time of its performance. John P. Emery finds the play to have a "Restoration atmosphere," being less sentimental and presenting its moral less emphatically than *The Way to Keep Him.* He and other modern critics praise the play for its maintenance of lively action and its development of character.

The Old Maid, the second of Murphy's promised three plays, was produced at Drury Lane on 2 July 1761. The play is a two-act comedy adapted and developed from a contemporary French play. In the play Clerimont meets a Miss and a Mrs. Harlow; he is attracted to the younger of the two and assumes that she is the unmarried lady when in fact it is the forty-three-year-old who is the spinster. He requests Miss Harlow's hand from her rather surprised brother, who gives it, and the old maid promptly breaks off her longstanding match with her fiancé, Captain Cape. The confusion is maintained by keeping the characters apart until the conclusion of the play, when all are brought together to arrange for the marriage. The old maid, having lost both her new and her old lovers, is then ridiculed for her vanity. Initially, the play was not well received by critics, in part at least because Murphy was still involved in a pamphlet war, but the audience at its first performance laughed heartily at its generous use of dramatic irony. Critical estimates of the play improved with time, and it remained a popular afterpiece into the nineteenth century.

The third new play supplied by Murphy, the three-act version of *The Citizen,* was performed on the same bill with *The Old Maid.* Murphy revised the play into a two-act version the following year by removing several scenes; this version was then printed. The source for this play is again a contemporary French play, but Murphy has so recast what he borrowed that it would be more accurate to describe *The Citizen* as original. In the two-act version Old Philpot, a businessman of the City and a miser, and Sir Jasper Wilding, a country squire, each having a son and a daughter, have arranged for the marriage of their children to each other. However, Sir Jasper's daughter Maria, who is in love with another man, Beaufort, first convinces young George Philpot that she is simpleminded and then later in the play so dazzles him with a display of her wit that she effectively discourages him from agreeing to marry her. Meanwhile, Beaufort tricks her father into giving consent for his marriage to Maria. In the course of the play George is exposed for living a double life as both a citizen and a man-about-town, and his father is exposed for his lust as well as his miserliness. Howard H. Dunbar describes the two-act version as "unquestionably one of the most successful plays of the last half of the century," often chosen by actors and actresses for their benefit nights. The contemporary critical reception, as with Murphy's other two new plays presented during this summer, was somewhat mixed.

The pamphlet war that was responsible for the mixed critical receptions of Murphy's plays during this summer season also initiated the charge from which Murphy's reputation as a playwright has suffered on into the twentieth century: that he is little more than a translator of French plays. Charles Churchill leveled this charge in *The Rosciad,* one of the more memorable sallies in this war, and although Murphy responded with *An Ode to the Naiads of Fleet-Ditch* (1761), a poem much criticized for its lack of finesse, Churchill's attack was so successful that Murphy thereafter defended himself in print against it several times.

Murphy and Foote had rented Drury Lane for the summer through an agreement with Garrick and his partner Henry Lacy that provided for a set payment to Murphy for presentations during the regular winter season of any new plays which he produced during the summer. In spite of this agreement Garrick had tried to discourage Murphy from producing any new plays during that summer, suggesting that he hold them for the winter season instead. When Murphy subsequently submitted the three new plays to Garrick, he accepted *All in the Wrong* and *The Old Maid* but rejected *The Citizen,* which he had previously accepted and then returned to Murphy at his request early in 1761 during his bereavement over the death of his mother. Additionally Garrick and Murphy quarreled over the payment Murphy was to receive for the other two plays. The result was that Murphy, who had apparently had some type of long-term understanding with Garrick that made him effectively the "house playwright" for Drury Lane, severed his connections with that theater. Therefore, when he revised *The Citizen* into the two-act version, it was presented at Covent Garden, on 15 November 1762.

Early in 1762 he completed an edition of the works of Henry Fielding for which he wrote an essay on the life of the author; the edition was almost universally praised by contemporaries and was reprinted for nearly a century. On 21 June 1762 he was admitted to the bar, although he did not practice law for another two years. In addition, he took an action that was to have a substantial, negative effect on both the public and the critical reception of his subsequent plays: he began to write a political paper called *The Auditor,* which supported the unpopular administration of John Stuart, third earl of Bute.

Murphy's next plays, *No One's Enemy But His Own* and *What We Must All Come To,* were performed at Covent Garden on 9 January 1764. Careless, a wealthy and handsome young man, is the character referred to in the title *No One's Enemy But His Own.* The plot turns on the consequences of his chief faults of fickleness and loquaciousness. In the course of the play he abandons Lucinda, pursues Hortensia, and then finally pursues Lucinda again for marriage, and he courts the young wife of his sixty-year-old friend Sir Philip Figurein for less honorable purposes. Because he freely confides his conduct of these activities to his supposed friend Wisely, he is outmaneuvered in his pursuit of all three ladies and exposed for his faithlessness to friends and mistresses alike. The source of the play is a contemporary French play by Voltaire; however, Murphy here as before so alters the original that it is more than an adaptation. The character of Sir Philip Figurein, a gentleman with a passion for dancing, has no counterpart in Voltaire's play; in fact, John P. Emery says he "seems to be unique in drama." Sir Philip is said to be drawn from life, having in fact an identifiable original, the case with many characters in Murphy's other comedies and farces as well. Modern critics find problems with the plotting of the play, particularly with several scenes that do nothing to develop the story, apparently having been intended to dazzle by means of witty language but not being sufficiently lively and polished to do so. Ten years later Murphy reduced the play from three to two acts; nevertheless it was rarely performed. The contemporary reception of the play was not positive, but for reasons which had little to do with the play itself, for the audience on the opening night was filled with enemies Murphy had made by writing *The Auditor.* However, this audience saved the real force of its disapprobation for the companion piece.

What We Must All Come To espouses marriage for the sake of happiness rather than social position. Nancy Drugget, daughter of a social-climbing mother and a gardening-enthusiast father of the merchant class, wants to marry Woodley; her mother wants her to make a socially more advantageous match by marrying Lovelace. Her parents agree and disagree alternately in the course of the play over which suitor to favor. However, their older daughter, Lady Rackett, and her husband, Sir Charles, who have come to visit, quarrel almost continuously even though they have been married a scant three weeks, so Nancy's parents choose happiness over social position for Nancy and agree to let her marry Woodley. Drugget's taste for gardening styles of the previous century provides the opportunity for a good deal of laughter as well as occasionally having some effect on the plot. Modern critics see the play as an almost wholly original

Sarah Siddons as Euphrasia in The Grecian Daughter, *a role she played in London for the first time in 1782*

work, one of Murphy's best farces, lively and with considerable wit even though it is thinly plotted. The opening-night audience, however, interrupted the performance several times, and the play was largely condemned in reviews by contemporary critics. Murphy said publicly that the play was disliked for various faults mentioned by the reviewers; however, it seems more likely that the play suffered because of Murphy's political activities rather than its own faults, for, virtually unaltered, it was subsequently and regularly produced for the rest of the century under two other titles, *Marriage à-la-Mode, or, Conjugal Douceurs* and *Three Weeks after Marriage*.

In the year following the presentation of these two plays Murphy applied himself to the practice of the law, pleading his first case in Trinity Term. He also wrote a two-act comedy entitled *The Choice,* which was acted without the author being identified at Drury Lane on 23 March 1765 while Garrick was out of the country. The play seems to have no clearly identifiable source as many of the characters and situations are stock. The plot involves the disinheriting of Young Loveworth by his father as a result of his marriage to Clarissa, who is without a fortune, and their subsequent reconciliation, which is brought about by a trick based on mistaken identity and is aided by Woodvil, a friend to both father and son. Modern critics have offered various explanations for the anonymous presentation of the play, the chief of which is the severely negative reaction to his last plays, and for the fact that Murphy gave the play outright to the actress Mary Ann Yates; however, contemporary reception of the play, both in performance and by critics, was unenthusiastic but not negative; the play was rarely performed.

Murphy's next play, a five-act comedy entitled *The School for Guardians,* which he wrote in 1763, was also acted without its author being identified when it was first presented at Covent Garden on 10 January 1767, and like his previous play, it was given outright to an actress, although this time the recipient was Murphy's mistress Ann Elliot. The play, begun as a modernization of William Wycherley's *The Country Wife* (1675), is, as Murphy acknowledged, a combination of elements from three plays by Molière. Two sisters have been educated by different guardians with differing methods, Mary Ann Richley by Oldcastle in country simplicity and Harriet by Lovibond in the ways of the world. Each guardian intends to marry his ward, but each girl is in love with a young man, Mary Ann with Young Brumpton and Harriet with Bellford. In the end each guardian is tricked into giving his consent for the marriage of his ward to the man of her choice. The play uses some disguise and coincidence and a good deal of trickery to bring about the proper matching of the girls and the thwarting of their guardians. The play was neither a critical nor a theatrical success. Many contemporary critics saw the cause in part to be Garrick's recent presentation of an adaptation of *The Country Wife* at Drury Lane, but modern critics find the play inferior to Murphy's other five-act comedies and suggest that both this and the previous play, written with the apparent intention of giving them to actresses, did not have the playwright's full attention. When Murphy published the play in his *Works* in 1786, he reduced it to three acts.

In March of 1767 Murphy published, anonymously, a translation of Jean-François Marmontel's *Belisarius* (1766), which received uniform critical approval. He also began his translation of Tacitus, which was not published until 1793, and in the fall he was brought to a reconciliation with David Garrick. As a result of this last, Murphy submitted two plays to Garrick, the tragedies *Alzuma* and *Zenobia,* both of which were accepted. Although there was some disagreement between Murphy and the management of Drury Lane over the form of payment for the two plays, Murphy and Garrick stayed on good terms, and *Zenobia* was performed on 27 February 1768.

Zenobia, a play about love set against a background of war, is complicated by having much of the causative action precede the beginning of the play and by having two characters, including Zenobia herself, appear in disguise. Zenobia, married to Rhadamistus, has been separated from her husband during the invasion of Armenia by Rhadamistus's father, Pharasmenes, whom he has never seen. Each supposes that the other is dead. Zenobia, disguised under the name Ariana, is captured by Pharasmenes, who falls in love with her. Teribazus, Pharasmenes' other son and Rhadamistus's younger brother, also falls in love with her. Rhadamistus, true heir to the kingdom of Armenia, which his father has usurped, having appealed for help to Rome, arrives as the Roman ambassador with the name Flamminius. After much jealousy and some revelations of true identities, Zenobia agrees to marry Pharasmenes as the only way to save Rhadamistus, who has been condemned to death. She poisons the wine used in the wedding ceremony, thereby killing Pharasmenes, and dies herself, leaving Rhadamistus to inherit the kingdom of Armenia. The story of Zenobia is from Tacitus's *Annales,* with a few elements added from other sources, but the development is largely Murphy's. *Zenobia* was not performed frequently after its initial run, and audience reception of the play seems to have been negatively affected by the actress playing the part of Zenobia. Contemporary critics praised the play moderately; modern critics find it superior to *The Orphan of China,* though overall not particularly good.

Alzuma was not performed at this time; the play passed between Garrick and Murphy several times over the next two years, even after Garrick had paid Murphy for it, until it was finally returned to Murphy without explanation in 1770. After the presentation of *Zenobia,* Murphy applied himself to establishing his law career and, as a result, made a comfortable income from it.

Garrick accepted Murphy's next play, a tragedy called *The Grecian Daughter,* before it was completed and performed it at Drury Lane on 26 February 1772. He seems to have had an immediate sense of the play's ability to succeed, for he expended an unusual amount of money on the scenery for it. The subject of the play is filial piety, and the source of the story is a familiar narrative found in the works of Valerius Maximus. Dionysius, having unjustly deposed Evander, king of Syracuse, has imprisoned him and is starving him to death. Euphrasia, the "Grecian daughter," has remained behind when her husband, Phocion, took their child to the safety of the approaching Greek army. When she visits her imprisoned father, she suckles him from her own breast to prevent his starvation. This act so impresses the guards that they assist in Evander's escape and avoidance of recapture by Dionysius. At the conclusion of the play the tyrant Dionysius finds Euphrasia and Evander hiding in the temple from which he plans to fight off the advancing Greek

55.

La: Bell... Verses, Aunt?

La: Jane... Verses, to you?

Mrs. Br.... Verses to me. Only hear Sir John - (reads.)

"I look'd and sigh'd, and wish'd I could speak

'And fain would have paid adoration

La: Bell... Stay, stay, stay, mine begins the same way (takes out a Paper.)

La: Jane.... The very words of mine - (takes out a Paper.)

Mrs. Br.... Will those Girls have done? - (reads.)

"But when I endeavour'd the matter to break

La: Bell - (reads.) "Still then I said least of my Passion

Mrs. Br... Will you be quiet? (reads.)

"Still then I said least of my Passion.

"I swore to myself -

La: Bell - reads fast.) - - - - - - - - "And resolv'd I would try

Mrs. Br..
La: Bell.. } (Reading together.) "Some way my poor heart to recover"

La: Jane
La: Bell } Reading eagerly together.)
Mrs. Br.

"But that was all vain, for I sooner could die

"Than live, with forbearing to love her"

La: Bell... Oh! ho, ho! Mr. Dashwould, what a piece of work has he made?

Dash.... And the Verses copied from Congreve!

La: Bell... Copied from Congreve! - (laughs heartily)

Mrs. Br.... There, Sir John, there is your Son's behaviour!

Dash.... There, Mr. Bygrove, there is the Widow's behaviour!

Byg.... And now, Mr. Dashwould, now for your wit.

Mrs. Br... (To Sir John.) I am not disappointed in the least, Sir.

Sir Jn°... I never was so covered with confusion!

La: Bell... I never was so diverted in all my days.

Page from the playhouse copy of Know Your Own Mind *submitted to the Examiner of Plays for licensing prior to the first performance, on 22 February 1777 (Larpent Collection, LA 425; by permission of the Henry E. Huntington Library and Art Gallery)*

Frontispiece to volume one of The Works of Arthur Murphy, Esq. *(1786)*

army, determines to kill them, but Euphrasia kills him instead with her dagger. The play was an instant critical and theatrical success, and its popularity survived until the end of the century. Much of the contemporary criticism of the play also emphasizes the degree to which it is dependent upon the skills of the actors and actresses for its theatrical effect. Modern critics, however, while seeing the play as one of the best eighteenth-century tragedies, qualify their praise by finding in those plays very little of any lasting literary value.

Later in the year Murphy began to negotiate with Garrick for the production of his comedy *Know Your Own Mind* while at the same time negotiating with Thomas Harris and George Colman the Elder at Covent Garden for the production of the tragedy *Alzuma.* At first it seemed that the tragedy would have to be postponed at the one theater since the comedy was to be acted at the other, but Murphy argued with Garrick for the final time and withdrew the comedy from his consideration. As a result, *Alzuma* was performed at Covent Garden on 23 February 1773. The play is set in Cuzco, Peru, shortly after Pizarro's conquest of the Incas. Pizarro has married Orazia, wife of the previous ruler whom he has killed. She has become a Christian, but her daughter Orellana, loved by Pizarro's son Don Carlos, will not. Orellana's brother, Alzuma, from whom she has been separated for ten years, is captured, and his mother, Orazia, eventually recognizes him. Don Carlos, also not knowing Alzuma's true identity, is at first jealous of Orellana's relationship with him but later learns his true identity as well. Orazia pleads with Pizarro for Alzuma's life, but since she does not reveal his identity to Pizarro, he will not rescind his condemnation unless Alzuma becomes a Christian. At first he refuses, but then afterward he agrees, using the opportunity to kill Pizarro. Orazia is accidentally killed by Alzuma as well, and at Orazia's dying request, Alzuma and Orellana become Christians. Contemporary critical opinion differs on the play; it is clear, however, that the theatrical aspects of the performance were deficient. In addition, the play was written in 1762 and contains a number of topical references to events of that time; eleven years later these references were stale. Modern critics have tended to favor the play among Murphy's tragedies, noting, however, that he was a better writer of comedy than of tragedy.

After the production of *Alzuma* Murphy announced his intentions of giving all of his time to the legal profession. He did not, however, entirely sever his relations with the theater. He was involved in a continuing dispute over the legal nature of literary copyright; he favored a limited term rather than a perpetual copyright, and his view prevailed before the House of Lords in 1774. He modified *No One's Enemy But His Own* to the two-act version which was produced at Covent Garden on 26 October 1774, and he made slight alterations to *What We Must All Come To,* which was produced as *Three Weeks after Marriage* at Covent Garden on 30 March 1776. In the same year he wrote *News From Parnassus,* a one-act farce, which was produced at the opening of the modified Covent Garden on 23 September 1776. The play relies for its effect primarily on a number of satiric pieces. The plot involves the arrival in London of Boccalini, a noted satirist, who has brought the news from Parnassus which at first he refuses to divulge. In spite of the protective efforts of his servant La Fleur, several people of different literary professions gain access to the satirist, who then proceeds to dispense his news, thereby satirizing various literary and literary-related professions. Because of the purpose of the play's production, it had a limited run, although contemporary and modern critics agree in praising it.

Murphy's *Know Your Own Mind,* which he had completed by 1760, was performed at Covent Garden on 22 February 1777. Again Murphy began with a contemporary French play for his source, but he so altered the elements that he borrowed that *Know Your Own Mind* is clearly his own creation. The play has an extremely involved plot consisting of no less than three overlapping love triangles. This structure is further complicated by conflicting parental orders to marry, an irresolute suitor (Millamour), a tyrannical, conniving widow (Mrs. Bromley), and a fortune-hunting machiavel (Malvil). By the conclusion all of the lovers are matched up with the suitors of their choice, Millamour has settled on which lady he will really marry (Lady Bell), Mrs. Bromley has admitted her wrongdoing toward her dependent Miss Neville and accepted her suitor Bygrove, and Malvil is thoroughly exposed for his hypocrisy. The play was successful in its first run, although by all accounts some members of the cast were not quite up to the demands of the roles, which were written for specific actors and actresses fifteen years earlier. After a brief period in which it was not acted, it was performed yearly well into the nineteenth century. Contemporary critics praised the play, and modern critics are almost uniform in their agreement of its value. Howard Dunbar calls it "the best comedy of manners since Congreve," and others rank it higher in many ways than Sheridan's *The School for Scandal* (1777).

In the 1780s Murphy gave most of his time to his legal work and his translations; he did, however, continue to write plays for his own entertainment. One of these, his last new play to be produced in his lifetime, was his tragedy *The Rival Sisters,* written in 1783 and printed in his *Works* of 1786, but not performed until 18 March 1793 by the Drury Lane company at the King's Theatre in the Haymarket. The source of the play is a French tragedy by Corneille, and although Murphy's play is an adaptation rather than a translation of the source, it is the closest to the original of all of Murphy's plays. The play is set in antiquity on Naxos, and the sisters of the title are Phaedra and Ariadne, daughters of King Minos of Crete, whom they have betrayed for love of Theseus. Theseus, however, loves only Phaedra. Periander, King of Naxos, loves Ariadne. In the attempt to acquire Ariadne's love, Periander attempts to separate Theseus from Phaedra and then finally imprisons him. Ariadne has him released, but Theseus betrays her, leaving her behind as he departs with Phaedra. In grief, Ariadne stabs herself. The play had a short run and did not become a stock piece. It was largely ignored by contemporary critics, probably because it had been printed long before it was performed, and modern critics disagree on its value.

In 1798 Murphy published a tragedy entitled *Arminius,* which seems to have been intended as a closet drama from the beginning. The source of the story is an account of the title character in Tacitus, which Murphy altered somewhat to make his point against civil war. The other plays written toward the end of his life were never performed or published: "The Duke of Florence," a tragedy; "The Heroic Sisters," a tragedy; "The Gardener of Sidon," a musical drama; and "The Oxfordshire Wife," a comedy which he never completed. The manuscript of "The Duke of Florence," which was sold at Murphy's death, was last sold in 1939; the remainder have disappeared.

When Murphy died on 18 June 1805, he was one of the foremost dramatists of his day and many of his plays had become stock pieces in the theaters. Modern critics have noted that his best work was in comedy and farce; his chief skill was his ability to write natural dialogue and by that means to create highly individualized characters, a skill which improved regularly during his career. These plays are often very reminiscent of Restoration comedy, both in content and method, and they avoid most of the characteristics of sentimental drama. His tragedies have not fared as well in critical estimation; modern critics find them merely adequate, at least partly because the eighteenth-century taste in tragedy has not survived, and at least partly because Murphy did not produce blank verse equivalent in quality to his prose. Several modern critics remark that Murphy should be read more than he is, but they admit as well that the very qualities that made his plays good theater make them unpopular closet drama: they contain many contemporary references that are unfamiliar to modern readers, and they were written to achieve theatrical effect by capitalizing on the skills of particular actors and actresses. However, modern critics generally agree that in *Know Your Own Mind* he wrote a play that suffers from neither of these handicaps, a play which in fact is so good that it equals or betters any other written by his contemporaries.

Biography:

Jesse Foot, *The Life of Arthur Murphy, esq.* (London: J. Faulder, 1811)–includes correspondence.

References:

Roy E. Aycock, "Shakespearian Criticism in the *Gray's-Inn Journal* and the *Craftsman:* some Publication Mysteries," *PBSA,* 67 (1973): 68-72;

Joseph M. Beatty, Jr., "The Battle of the Players and Poets, 1761-1766," *Modern Language Notes,* 34 (December 1919): 449-462;

Tuvia Bloch, "The Antecedents of Sheridan's Faulkland," *Philological Quarterly,* 49 (April 1970): 266-268;

Harold L. Bruce, "Voltaire on the English Stage," *University of California Publications in Modern Philology,* 8 (June 1918);

J. Homer Caskey, "Arthur Murphy and the War on Sentimental Comedy," *Journal of English and Germanic Philology,* 30 (October 1931): 563-577;

Caskey, "Arthur Murphy's Commonplace-Book," *Studies in Philology,* 37 (October 1940): 598-609;

Caskey, "The First Edition of Arthur Murphy's *Sallust,*" *Philological Quarterly,* 13 (October 1934): 404-408;

H. MacL. Currie, "Arthur Murphy, Actor and Author," *New Rambler,* 14 (1973): 9-13;

Howard Hunter Dunbar, *The Dramatic Career of Arthur Murphy* (New York: Modern Language Association, 1956);

John P. Emery, *Arthur Murphy: An Eminent English Dramatist of the Eighteenth Century* (Philadelphia: University of Pennsylvania Press, 1946);

Emery, "Murphy's Criticisms in the *London Chronicle,*" *PMLA,* 54 (December 1939): 1099-1104;

Martin Lehnert, "Arthur Murphy's *Hamlet*-Parodie (1772) aut David Garrick," *Shakespeare-Jahrbuch,* (1966): 97-167;

Henry Knight Miller, "Internal Evidence: Professor Sherbo and the Case of Arthur Murphy," *Bulletin of the New York Public Library,* 69 (1965): 459-470;

Susan M. Passler, "Coleridge, Fielding and Arthur Murphy," *The Wordsworth Circle,* 5 (Winter 1974): 55-58;

Robert Donald Spector, *Arthur Murphy* (Boston: Twayne, 1979);

Spector, "Arthur Murphy: Embattled Dramatist," *Notes and Queries,* 26 (February 1979): 40-41;

Simon Trefman, "Arthur Murphy's Long Lost *Englishman from Paris:* A Manuscript Discovered," *Theatre Notebook,* 20 (Summer 1966): 137-141.

Papers:

Manuscripts of many of Murphy's plays are housed in the Larpent Collection of Huntington Library. Manuscript letters are housed in the John Rylands Library, Manchester (*Eng. Mss.* 548, 891) and the Rush Rhees Library, University of Rochester.

John O'Keeffe

(24 June 1747-4 February 1833)

Frederick M. Link
University of Nebraska–Lincoln

PLAY PRODUCTIONS: *The She Gallant; or, Square Toes Outwitted,* Dublin, Smock Alley Theatre, 14 January 1767; London, Theatre Royal in the Hay-Market, 13 October 1779; revised as *The Positive Man,* London, Theatre Royal, Covent Garden, 16 March 1782;

Harlequin in Waterford; or, The Dutchman Outwitted, Waterford, 28 October 1767; produced again as *Harlequin in Derry; or, The Dutchman Outwitted,* Belfast, 9 May 1770;

The Giant's Causeway; or, A Trip to the Dargle, Belfast, 25 May 1770 (probably revised as *Harlequin Teague,* 1782);

Colin's Welcome, Belfast, 26 July 1770;

The India Ship, Cork, circa 1770;

Tony Lumpkin's Ramble thro' Cork, Cork, 17 September 1773; produced again as *Tony Lumpkin's Frolics thro' Cork,* Cork, 4 October 1780 (possibly adapted for production in Portsmouth, England, 1778);

Tony Lumpkin in Town; or, The Dilettanti, Dublin, Smock Alley Theatre, 13 April 1774; adapted version, London, Theatre Royal in the Hay-Market, 2 July 1778;

The Comical Duel; or, The Good Boy, Cork, 29 September 1775;

The Shamrock; or, St. Patrick's Day, Dublin, Crow Street Theatre, 15 April 1777; altered as *The Shamrock; or, The Anniversary of St. Patrick,* London, Theatre Royal, Covent Garden, 7 April 1783; revised, with music by William Shield, as *The Poor Soldier,* London, Theatre Royal, Covent Garden, 4 November 1783;

The Son-in-Law, with music by Samuel Arnold, London, Theatre Royal in the Hay-Market, 14 August 1779;

The Dead Alive, with music by Arnold, London, Theatre Royal in the Hay-Market, 16 June 1781;

The Agreeable Surprise, with music by Arnold, London, Theatre Royal in the Hay-Market, 4 September 1781;

The Banditti; or, Love's Labyrinth, with music by Arnold, London, Theatre Royal, Covent Garden, 28 November 1781; revised as *The Castle of Andalusia,* London, Theatre Royal, Covent Garden, 2 November 1782;

Harlequin Teague; or, The Giant's Causeway (possibly a revision of *The Giant's Causeway,* 1770), by O'Keeffe and George Colman the Elder, with music by Arnold, London, Theatre Royal in the Hay-Market, 17 August 1782;

Lord Mayor's Day; or, A Flight from Lapland, with music by Shield, London, Theatre Royal, Covent Garden, 25 November 1782;

The Maid's the Mistress, adapted from G. A. Federico's libretto for *La serva padrona,* with music by Giovanni Battista Pergolesi and Arnold, London, Theatre Royal, Covent Garden, 14 February 1783;

The Young Quaker, London, Theatre Royal in the Hay-Market, 26 July 1783;

The Birth-Day; or, The Prince of Aragon, with music by Arnold, based on Germain de Saint-Foix's *Le rival supposé,* London, Theatre Royal in the Hay-Market, 12 August 1783;

Gretna Green, by Charles Stuart, with alterations by O'Keeffe and music by Arnold, London, Theatre Royal in the Hay-Market, 28 August 1783;

Friar Bacon; or, Harlequin's Adventures in Lilliput, Brobdignag, etc., with music by Shield, London, Theatre Royal, Covent Garden, 23 December 1783; revised as *Harlequin Rambler; or, The Convent in an Uproar,* London, Theatre Royal, Covent Garden, 29 January 1784;

Peeping Tom of Coventry, with music by Arnold, London, Theatre Royal in the Hay-Market, 6 September 1784;

Fontainbleau; or, Our Way in France, with music by Shield, London, Theatre Royal, Covent Garden, 16 November 1784;

The Blacksmith of Antwerp, London, Theatre Royal, Covent Garden, 7 February 1785;

John O'Keeffe (engraving by Bragg; based on a 1786 portrait by Laurenson)

A Beggar on Horseback (sometimes *The Beggar on Horseback*), with music by Arnold, London, Theatre Royal in the Hay-Market, 16 June 1785;

Omai; or, A Trip round the World, with music by Shield, London, Theatre Royal, Covent Garden, 20 December 1785;

Love in a Camp; or, Patrick in Prussia (sequel to *The Poor Soldier*, 1783, sometimes known by subtitle), with music by Shield, London, Theatre Royal, Covent Garden, 17 February 1786;

The Siege of Curzola, with music by Arnold, London, Theatre Royal in the Hay-Market, 12 August 1786; produced again as an afterpiece, London, Theatre Royal in the Hay-Market, 2 July 1787;

The Man Milliner, London, Theatre Royal, Covent Garden, 27 January 1787;

Love and War, adapted, with music by various hands, from Robert Jephson's *The Campaign* (1785), London, Theatre Royal, Covent Garden, 12 March 1787;

The Generous Tar, Waterford, 17 October 1787;

The Farmer, with music by Shield, London, Theatre Royal, Covent Garden, 31 October 1787;

Tantara-Rara, Rogues All!, adapted from A. J. Bourlin's *Les intrigants; ou, assaut de fouberies* (1787), London, Theatre Royal, Covent Garden, 1 March 1788;

The Prisoner at Large, London, Theatre Royal in the Hay-Market, 2 July 1788;

The Highland Reel, with music by Shield, London, Theatre Royal, Covent Garden, 6 November 1788; produced again as an afterpiece, London, Theatre Royal, Covent Garden, 8 December 1788;

Aladin; or, The Wonderful Lamp, with music by Shield, London, Theatre Royal, Covent Garden, 26 December 1788;

The Toy; or, Hampton Court Frolics, London, Theatre Royal, Covent Garden, 3 February 1789; revised as *The Lie of the Day; or, A Party at Hampton Court*, London, Theatre Royal, Covent Garden, 19 March 1796;

The Pharo Table, adapted from Susanna Centlivre's *The Gamester* (1705), London, Theatre Royal, Covent Garden, 4 April 1789;

The Little Hunchback, London, Theatre Royal, Covent Garden, 14 April 1789;

St. George's Day; or, Britons Rejoice (probably the same piece as *The Loyal Bandeau*), London,

Composer Samuel Arnold, who wrote the music for many of O'Keeffe's plays (engraving based on a portrait by J. Russell)

Theatre Royal, Covent Garden, 30 April 1789;

The Czar (sometimes *The Czar Peter*), with music by Shield, London, Theatre Royal, Covent Garden, 8 March 1790; revised as *The Fugitive*, London, Theatre Royal, Covent Garden, 4 November 1790;

The Basket Maker, with music by Arnold, London, Theatre Royal in the Hay-Market, 4 September 1790;

Modern Antiques; or, The Merry Mourners, London, Theatre Royal, Covent Garden, 14 March 1791;

Wild Oats; or, The Strolling Gentlemen (sometimes *Gentleman*), London, Theatre Royal, Covent Garden, 16 April 1791;

Sprigs of Laurel, with music by Shield, London, Theatre Royal, Covent Garden, 11 May 1793; revised as *The Rival Soldiers*, London, Theatre Royal, Covent Garden, 17 May 1797;

The London Hermit; or, Rambles in Dorsetshire, London, Theatre Royal in the Hay-Market, 29 June 1793;

The World in a Village, London, Theatre Royal, Covent Garden, 23 November 1793;

Life's Vagaries; or, The Neglected Son, London, Theatre Royal, Covent Garden, 19 March 1795;

The Irish Mimic; or, Blunders at Brighton, with music by Shield, London, Theatre Royal, Covent Garden, 23 April 1795;

Merry Sherwood; or, Harlequin Forester, with music by William Reeve, London, Theatre Royal, Covent Garden, 21 December 1795;

The Lad of the Hills; or, The Wicklow Gold Mine, with music by Shield, London, Theatre Royal, Covent Garden, 9 April 1796; revised as *The Wicklow Mountains*, London, Theatre Royal, Covent Garden, 7 October 1796;

The Doldrum; or, 1803, London, Theatre Royal, Covent Garden, 23 April 1796;

The Magic Banner; or, Two Wives in a House, London, Theatre Royal in the Hay-Market, 22 June 1796;

Olympus in an Uproar; or, The Descent of the Deities, with music by Reeve, adapted from Kane O'Hara's *The Golden Pippin* (1773), London, Theatre Royal, Covent Garden, 5 November 1796;

Britain's Brave Tars; or, All to St. Paul's (referred to by O'Keeffe as *Our Wooden Walls; or, All to St. Paul's*), with music by Thomas Attwood, London, Theatre Royal, Covent Garden, 19 December 1797;

She's Eloped!, London, Theatre Royal, Drury Lane, 19 May 1798;

The Eleventh of June; or, The Daggerwoods at Dunstable, London, Theatre Royal, Drury Lane, 5 June 1798;

A Nosegay of Weeds; or, Old Servants in New Places (scenes from earlier plays by O'Keeffe), London, Theatre Royal, Drury Lane, 6 June 1798.

BOOKS: *The She Gallant: or, Square-Toes Outwitted. A new comedy of two acts. As now performing, with great applause, at the theatre in Smock-Alley, Dublin* (London: Printed for T. Lowndes & J. Williams, 1767);

Airs, duetts, trios, &c. in the musical farce of the Son-in-Law. Performed at the Theatre-Royal in the Hay-Market (London: Printed for T. Cadell, 1779);

Tony Lumpkin in Town: a farce. As performed at the Theatre-Royal in the Hay-Market (London: Printed for T. Cadell, 1780);

Songs, chorusses, &c. in the new musical farce called the Agreeable Surprise, as it is performed at the The-

atre Royal in the Hay-Market (London: Printed for T. Cadell, 1781);

Songs, duetts, trios, chorusses, &c. &c. in the comic opera of the Banditti; or, Love's Labyrinth. As it is performed at the Theatre-Royal in Covent-Garden. The music by Dr. Arnold (London: Printed for T. Cadell, 1781);

Songs, duets, trios, &c. &c. in the new musical farce of the Dead Alive. As performed at the Theatre-Royal in the Hay-Market (London: Printed for T. Cadell, 1781);

Songs, airs, &c. in The entertainment of Harlequin Teague; or, The Giant's Causeway. As it is now performing at the Theatre-Royal, Hay-Market (London: Printed for T. Cadell, 1782);

Songs, duets, &c. in the new pantomime called Lord Mayor's Day; or, a Flight from Lapland. As performed at the Theatre-Royal, in Covent-Garden (London: Printed for T. Cadell, 1782);

Songs, duets, trios, &c. in the comic opera of The Castle of Andalusia. As performed at the Theatre-Royal, in Covent-Garden (London: Printed for T. Cadell, 1782);

Gretna Green, a comic opera, in two acts. As performed at the Theatre Royal, Smoke-Alley, by Charles Stuart, with alterations by O'Keeffe (Dublin: Printed for the booksellers, circa 1783);

The Agreeable Surprise. A comic opera. In two acts. . . . The music composed by Dr. Arnold (Dublin: Sold by the booksellers, 1783); republished in volume 31, no. 4, of Cumberland's British Theatre (London: John Cumberland, circa 1833);

Airs, duets, glees, &c. in the pantomime entertainment of Friar Bacon; or, Harlequin's Adventures: as performed at the Theatre-Royal, in Covent Garden (London: Printed for T. Cadell, 1783);

The Birth-day; or, The Prince of Arragon. A dramatick piece, with songs. In two acts. As performed at the Theatre-Royal, Hay-Market (London: Printed for T. Cadell, 1783);

The Castle of Andalusia, a comic opera. In three acts. As it is performed at the theatres in London and Dublin (Dublin: Sold by the booksellers, 1783); republished as *The Castle of Andalusia. A Comic Opera. In three Acts. As performed at the Theatre-Royal, Covent-Garden* (London: Printed by H. Baldwin for T. N. Longman, 1794);

The Dead Alive: a comic opera. In two acts. As it is performed at the theatres in London and Dublin (Dublin: Sold by the booksellers, 1783);

Songs, airs, &c. in the musical farce called Gretna Green. As it is performed at the Theatre-Royal, in the Hay-Market (London: Printed for T. Cadell, 1783);

Songs, duetts, and chorusses, in the Birth Day; or the Prince of Arrogan. A new dramatic piece, now performing at the Theatre-Royal, in the Hay-Market (London: Printed for T. Cadell, 1783);

Songs, duets, trios, &c. in the Poor Soldier, a comic opera: as performed at the Theatre-Royal, in Covent-Garden (London: Printed for T. Cadell, 1783);

Songs, duetts, trios, &c. in the new musical entertainment called the Shamrock; or, St. Patrick's Day. As performed at the Theatre-Royal, Covent-Garden (London: Printed for T. Cadell, 1783);

The Son-in-Law, a comic opera; in two acts (Dublin: Sold by the booksellers, 1783; "The second edition, corrected," London: Printed for B. Bladon & H. Lownds, 1792);

Airs, duets, trios, &c. in Peeping Tom of Coventry. A musical piece of two acts. Performed at the Theatre-Royal in the Hay-Market (London: Printed for T. Cadell, 1784);

The Poor Soldier, a comic opera. In two acts. With the original songs (Dublin: Printed & sold by the booksellers, 1784; Dublin: Printed by M. Doyle, 1784; republished, London: Printed by A. Strahan for T. N. Longman & O. Rees, 1800);

Songs, duets, trios, &c. in Fontainbleau; or, Our Way in France. A comic opera. As performed at the Theatre-Royal in Covent-Garden (London: Printed for T. Cadell, 1784);

The Young Quaker; a comedy. As it is performed at the Theatre-Royal in Smock-Alley (Dublin: Printed by Pat. Wogan, 1784; Dublin: Printed by Mathew Doyle, 1784); republished in volume 37, no. 6, of Cumberland's British Theatre (London: John Cumberland, circa 1836);

Fontainbleau; or, Our Way in France. A comic opera, in three acts. As performed at the Theatres-Royal in Covent-Garden. And Smock-Alley (Dublin: Sold by the booksellers, 1785; London: "printed under the authority of the managers from the prompt book" for Longman, Hurst, Rees & Orme, 1808);

Peeping Tom, of Coventry. A comic opera. As it is performed at the Theatre-Royal, Smock-Alley (Dublin: Printed by John Smith, 1785); republished in volume 31, no. 9, of Cumberland's British Theatre (London: John Cumberland, 1830s);

A short account of the new pantomime called Omai, or, A Trip round the World; performed at the Theatre-

Maria Gibbs as Cowslip in The Agreeable Surprise *(engraving by W. Ridley, based on a portrait by Clarke)*

Royal in Covent-Garden. With the recitatives, airs, duetts, trios, and chorusses; and a description of the procession (London: Printed for T. Cadell, 1785);

The airs, duets, trios, chorusses, &c. in the new musical farce of Love in a Camp; or, Patrick in Prussia; performed at the Theatre-Royal in Covent-Garden (London: Printed for T. Cadell, 1786);

Patrick in Prussia; or, Love in a Camp: a comic opera, in two acts . . . ; as performed at the Theatres Royal Covent-Garden, and Smock-Alley (Dublin: Printed for the booksellers, 1786); republished as *Love in a Camp; or, Patrick in Prussia, in Two Acts. Performed at the Theatre-Royal, Covent-Garden in 1785* (London: Printed by A. Strahan for T. N. Longman & O. Rees, 1800);

Songs, duets, trios, &c. in the Siege of Curzola, a comic opera, performed at the Theatre-Royal in the Hay-Market (London: Printed for T. Cadell, 1786);

Songs, chorusses, &c. in Love and War (London: Printed for T. Cadell, 1787)–includes one song by O'Keeffe;

The songs, duetts, chorusses, &c. in the musical entertainment of The Farmer. As performed at the Theatre Royal, Covent Garden (London: Printed for T. Cadell, 1787);

The Farmer: a comic opera, in two acts, as it is performed at the Theatres Royal in London and Dublin (Dublin: Printed by T. M'Donnel, 1788); republished as *The Farmer. In Two Acts. Performed at the Theatre-Royal, Covent-Garden, in 1787* (London: Printed by A. Strahan for T. N. Longman & O. Rees, 1800);

The Prisoner at Large: a comedy. In two acts. As performed at the Theatre Royal in the Hay-Market (London: Printed for G. G. J. & J. Robinson, 1788);

The recitatives, airs, chorusses, &c. in Aladin; or, The

Wonderful Lamp. A pantomime entertainment. Performed at the Theatre-Royal, Covent-Garden. The music composed by Mr. Shield (London: Printed for T. Cadell, 1788);

Songs, airs, duetts, and chorusses, &c. in the Highland-Reel; a comic romance. In three acts. As performed at the Theatre-Royal, Covent-Garden (London: Printed for T. Cadell, 1788);

The Highland Reel: a comic opera. In three acts. As it is performed at the Theatres-Royal in London and Dublin (Dublin: Printed by T. M'Donnel, 1789); republished as *The Highland Reel. In three acts. As performed at the Theatre-Royal, Covent-Garden* (London: For T. N. Longman & O. Rees, 1800);

The Little Hunch-back; or, a Frolic in Bagdad. A farce. In two acts. As it is performed at the Theatre Royal, Covent-Garden (London: Printed for J. Debrett, 1789);

Airs, duets, trios, chorusses, &c. in the Czar: a comic opera, in three acts. Performed at the Theatre-Royal, Covent-Garden (London: Printed for T. Cadell, 1790);

Songs, &c. in The Basket-Maker: a musical piece, in two acts (London: Printed for T. Cadell, 1790);

Wild Oats: or, The Strolling Gentlemen. A comedy, in five acts, as performed at the Theatre Royal, Covent-Garden (Dublin: Printed for the booksellers, 1791; republished, London: Printed by G. Woodfall for T. N. Longman, 1794); modern edition, "The text as prepared and directed by Clifford Williams for the Royal Shakespeare Company" (London: Heinemann Educational Books, 1977);

Modern Antiques, or The Merry Mourners, a farce, in two acts. . . . As performed at the Theatre-Royal, Covent-Garden (Dublin: Printed for P. Byrne, 1792; republished, London: Printed by A. Strahan for T. N. Longman & O. Rees, 1800);

The London Hermit, or Rambles in Dorsetshire, a comedy, in three acts, as performed with universal applause at the Theatre Royal, Haymarket (London: Printed for J. Debrett, 1793);

Sprigs of Laurel: a comic opera. In two acts. As performed, with universal applause, at the Theatre-Royal, Covent-Garden (London: Printed by H. S. Woodfall for T. N. Longman, 1793); adapted by T. Williams, with only four O'Keeffe songs remaining, as *Who'll Serve the Queen, or Military and Naval Ardour* (London, 1838);

The World in a Village; a comedy, in five acts, as performed with universal applause at the Theatre Royal, Covent-Garden (London: Printed for J. Debrett, 1793);

Airs, duetts, and chorusses, in the operatical pantomime of Merry Sherwood, or Harlequin Forrester (London: Printed for T. N. Longman, 1795);

The Irish Mimic; or Blunders at Brighton: a musical entertainment in two acts. As performed at the Theatre-Royal, Covent-Garden (London: Printed for T. N. Longman, 1795);

Life's Vagaries, a comedy, in five acts. As performed at the Theatre-Royal, Covent-Garden (London: Printed by G. Woodfall for T. N. Longman, 1795);

Oatlands; or, The Transfer of the Laurel: A Poem (London: Debrett, 1795);

Airs, duets, glees, chorusses, &c. in the opera of the Lad of the Hills; or Wicklow Gold Mine. Now performing at the Theatre-Royal, Covent-Garden (London: Printed for T. N. Longman, 1796);

Airs, duets, trios, chorusses, &c. in Olympus in an Uproar or The Descent of the Deities. A burletta in two acts. Partly taken from the Golden-Pippin. Now performing at the Theatre-Royal, Covent-Garden (London: Printed for T. N. Longman, 1796);

The Wicklow Mountains; or, the Lad of the Hills, a comic opera, in two acts (Dublin: Printed by John Whitworth, 1797); "original complete edition," *The Wicklow Mountains; or, Gold in Ireland. A Comic Drama, in two acts. By John O'Keeffe. First produced at Covent Garden Theatre, April 11th, 1795*, Dicks' Standard Plays, no. 560 (London: John Dicks, 188-);

Lie of a Day: a comedy, in three acts. As performed at the Theatre-Royal, Covent-Garden (London: Printed by A. Strahan for T. N. Longman & O. Rees, 1800);

The Positive Man. In two acts. Performed at the Theatre-Royal, Covent-Garden, in 1784 (London: Printed by A. Strahan for T. N. Longman & O. Rees, 1800);

Recollections of the Life of John O'Keeffe, written by himself, 2 volumes (London: Henry Colburn, 1826; reprinted, 2 volumes in 1, New York: Benjamin Blom, 1969); excerpted in *The New Monthly Magazine*, 16 (1826): 345-360, and 17 (1826): 17-30; with additional anecdotes in 38 (1833): 35-45; also excerpted in *Personal Reminiscences, by O'Keeffe, Kelly, and Taylor*, edited by Richard H. Stoddard (New York: Scribner, Armstrong, 1875);

O'Keeffe's Legacy to His Daughter, being the poetical works of the late John O'Keeffe, Esq., the dramatic author (London: For the editor [Adelaide O'Keeffe], 1834).

Collections: *The dramatic works of John O'Keeffe, Esq. Published under the gracious patronage of His Royal Highness the Prince of Wales. Prepared for the press by the author,* 4 volumes (London: Printed by T. Woodfall [by subscription], 1798)–includes the only printed texts of *Alfred (The Magic Banner), The Basket-Maker, Beggar on Horseback, The Blacksmith of Antwerp, The Czar Peter, The Doldrum, Le Grenadier, The Man Milliner, Tantara-Rara, Rogues All,* and *The Toy*;

The Plays of John O'Keeffe, 4 volumes, edited, with an introduction, by Frederick M. Link (New York & London: Garland, 1981)–includes an edited typescript of the British Library manuscript of *She's Eloped,* reprints of all previously published O'Keeffe plays, and reprints of the piano-vocal scores for *The Son-in-Law, The Agreeable Surprise, The Poor Soldier,* and *The Farmer.*

OTHER: Six new songs, set by Michael Arne, for an alteration of Isaac Bickerstaff 's *The Maid of the Mill* (performed at Covent Garden on 25 September 1782), *London Chronicle,* 26 September 1782; and *Town and Country Magazine* (September 1782).

LOST PLAYS: *The Generous Lovers,* five-act comedy written circa 1763, not produced or published, presumed lost;

The Siege of Troy, two-act drama written 1788, not produced or published, presumed lost;

Valentine and Orson, two-act drama written 1788, not produced or published, presumed lost;

A Pageant; or, The Rise and Progress of the English Stage, two acts, written circa 1792 but not produced or published, sold to Thomas Harris, Theatre Royal, Covent Garden, 7 November 1803, presumed lost;

Alban and Aphanasia, five acts, written circa 1794 but not produced or published, sold to Harris, Theatre Royal, Covent Garden, 7 November 1803, presumed lost;

William Tell, "an Entertainment of show and action," probably circa 1798, not produced or published, presumed lost;

Reputation, five-act comedy, sold to Harris, Theatre Royal, Covent Garden, 7 November 1803, not produced or published, presumed lost;

Emanuel; or, The Fellow Travellers, five acts, sold to Harris, Theatre Royal, Covent Garden, 7 November 1803, not produced or published, presumed lost;

The Annuity, three-act comedy, sold to Harris, Theatre Royal, Covent Garden, 7 November 1803, not produced or published, presumed lost;

Jack and His Master, two-act afterpiece, sold to Harris, Theatre Royal, Covent Garden, 7 November 1803, not produced or published, presumed lost;

Stray Sheep, two-act afterpiece, sold to Harris, Theatre Royal, Covent Garden, 7 November 1803, not produced or published, presumed lost;

Olympia; or, Both Sides Temple Bar, five-act comedy, written 1807, submitted to Theatre Royal, Covent Garden, 1819, but rejected 1821, not published, presumed lost;

An Afterpiece. Two-acts, written 1808, not produced or published, presumed lost;

A Comedy. Five Acts, written 1809, not produced or published, presumed lost;

Another Comedy. Five acts, written 1809, not produced or published, presumed lost.

John O'Keeffe began his career as a singer and actor in Ireland, appearing both in Dublin and in the provincial theaters. He soon began writing songs, comic sketches, and pantomimes; by the time he moved permanently to London in 1781 he was a thorough professional with more than a dozen years of theatrical experience. Between his first London opening in 1778 and his last in 1798, he had more than fifty pieces, counting revisions and adaptations, produced on the London stage. His most successful works were two- and three-act comic operas: *The Son-in-Law, The Agreeable Surprise, The Poor Soldier,* and *Peeping Tom of Coventry* were enormously popular afterpieces, both in London and out of it, for two generations. They propped many a lugubrious tragedy and many a sentimental "drama" both in O'Keeffe's day and after it, and made him Isaac Bickerstaff 's successor as perhaps the most widely performed dramatist of his generation. He is known today, ironically, only because *Wild Oats,* one of his five-act comedies, was revived in 1977 by the Royal Shakespeare Company. His most typical works, however, remain relatively unknown because they are essentially theatrical rather than literary. As such, they belong to a tradition difficult to recover but fascinating to anyone interested in the history of theater.

Most of our information about O'Keeffe's life comes from his own *Recollections* (1826) and from the "Memoir" which his daughter prefixed to her edition of his poems, *O'Keeffe's Legacy to His Daughter* (1834). O'Keeffe was born in Abbey Street, Dublin, 24 June 1747; he tells us that his father, also named John, "was a native of the King's County, and my mother of the County of Wexford," and that he had an older brother, Daniel, a painter of miniatures who died in London in 1787 at the age of forty-seven. His daughter tells us that her paternal grandmother's surname was O'Connor and that both her father's parents were devoted to the royalist cause. She goes on to say that O'Keeffe was "at one time intended for foreign military service, in furtherance of which he studied fortification and drawing. . . ." O'Keeffe himself says only that he "was designed by my parents and my own inclination for a painter, and not above six years of age when I was placed at Mr. West's, The Royal Academy, . . . Dublin." He also studied "Greek, Latin, and French . . . under Father Austin," who kept a school in Cook Street.

How long his formal schooling lasted is uncertain. His father died in 1758, when he was only eleven, and the boy was sent to London in August of 1762, consigned "to an aunt." He probably continued to study art, and may have been sent to London for that purpose; he frequently mentions artistic matters and continued to draw long after returning to Ireland. Nevertheless, his attraction to the theater was strong. He saw Peg Woffington in *Jane Shore* as early as 1755 and mentions attending David Garrick performances often while in London: "the delight his acting gave me was one of the silken cords that drew me towards a theatre." He returned to Dublin in 1764 and "shortly after, at the age of eighteen, began, with best foot foremost," his dramatic career.

William Clark, who refers frequently to O'Keeffe in *The Irish Stage in the County Towns, 1720-1800* (1965), calls him "one of the century's outstanding itinerant comedians," an "expert in farce," and a "colourful singing comedian" whose songs "were regularly billed as *entr'acte* attractions." O'Keeffe refers throughout the *Recollections* to his experiences in Cork, Limerick, and the other towns various theatrical troupes visited either for an annual "season" or on specific occasions such as county fairs or race meets. Although in these references he almost never identifies himself as an actor, he played many different roles, including several in Shakespeare. Early on he also began to write for the stage. His first efforts tended to be short pieces, two-act operas like *The She Gallant* (1767), afterpieces like *The India Ship* (circa 1770), pantomimes like *Harlequin in Waterford* (1767). Some opened on tour, others at the Crow Street or Smock Alley theaters in Dublin. Nearly all were topical: Tony Lumpkin might ramble "thro' Cork" when the troupe played there or "in Town" when at the capital.

In most respects, O'Keeffe had an ideal apprenticeship. As a touring actor he had to confront every sort of stage and audience, every level of acting and preparation, a variety of managers and stage personnel, and a repertory ranging from Shakespeare to the most spectacular and ephemeral pantomime contrivances. He was able to develop his talents as an actor and singer, even as an artist, and at the same time indulge his growing interest in dramatic composition. He seems to have approximated the rollicking Irishman of countless stories, been something of a dandy in dress, and been extraordinarily fond of company. His memories of this period remained remarkably detailed and vivid after half a century.

On 1 October 1774, in Limerick, O'Keeffe married Mary Heaphy, elder daughter of Tottenham Heaphy, the theatrical manager. Mary Heaphy was seventeen, O'Keeffe ten years older. For some seven years the couple seems to have lived happily enough. They had three children in quick succession: John Tottenham (1775-1804), Adelaide (1776-1855), and Gerald, who was born circa 1777 and died in infancy. Although O'Keeffe never mentions the fact, his wife was also an actress, and the O'Keeffes frequently acted together in Dublin and in the provincial towns. In December of 1777 they went to London, where O'Keeffe got George Colman the Elder to accept a refurbished *Tony Lumpkin in Town* for production at the Little Theatre in the Haymarket. The piece opened on 2 July 1778, while O'Keeffe was acting under Mattocks at Portsmouth. The couple returned to Dublin in March 1779.

Around the time of his marriage, O'Keeffe caught a cold after he fell off "the south wall of the Liffey, Dublin, in a dark December" and "thus drenched, . . . sat up with my party for some hours in my wet clothes. " The cold led, he says, to a "violent inflammation" of his eyelids and eventually to near blindness. By 1781 he required an amanuensis; although, as his daughter notes, he "could walk miles alone, distinguish light from darkness" and sometimes "the features of a human face, . . . he could not see to read or write, or know colours, or calculate distances, depths, or heights. . . ." This handicap eventually put an end to O'Keeffe's acting career, although he continued on stage until

Fellow is in Sound Health and not above 24
Chi. All from your Good Nature, Mrs Cheshire.
Mrs Che. Oh, if my Dear Husband was alive—But he's better where he is.

Air 1st. Mrs Cheshire.

Tune the Fat Friar.

In Choice of a Husband us Widows are nice
I'd not have a Man wou'd grow Old in a Trice
Not a Bear or a Monkey a Clown or a Fop
But one that cou'd Bustle and Stir in my Shop.

2d.

A Log I'le avoid when I'm chusing my Lad
And a Stork that might Gobble up all that I had
Such Suitors I've had Sir, but off they might hop
I wan't one that can bustle and Stir in my Shop.

3d.

The Lad in my Eye, is the Man to my Mind
So handsome so Young, so polite and so kind
With such a good Soul to the Altar I'd pop
He's the Man that can Bustle and Stir in my Shop.

Exeunt

Scene Sir Felix's House
Enter Compton and Sir Felix

Sr Fel. Ha, ha, ha—She's come, Mrs Cheshires come, and brought an Attorney upon him: how he'le be surpriz'd! a Letter

Page from the playhouse copy of The Agreeable Surprise *submitted to the Examiner of Plays for licensing prior to the first performance, on 4 September 1781 (Larpent Collection, LA 568; by permission of the Henry E. Huntington Library and Art Gallery)*

about 1781, when another event proved equally decisive for his future. In June of that year, convinced that his wife had begun an affair with an actor named George Graham, he left her and moved permanently to England, soon sending for his children. He never saw either wife or native land again.

His daughter reports that no legal separation ever took place, although the couple had been married by both clergyman and priest: "Mary O'Keeffe followed her husband, to seek forgiveness for her only faults, hastiness of temper, impatience of controul, preference of society blameless in itself but disapproved of by him, and perhaps some instances of youthful extravagance beyond their means." For three years, Adelaide O'Keeffe says, the Heaphys tried to soften her father's "bitter anger," but to no avail. Although the daughter makes understandable efforts to protect her mother's reputation, stating that Mary O'Keeffe's innocence was proved by "the oath of a deathbed confession, the priest being authorized to reveal it," Mrs. O'Keeffe followed Graham to an acting career in Scotland and the north, and, being a Protestant, eventually married him. She died in Dalkeith on 1 January 1813. Contemporary gossip suggests that O'Keeffe, suspecting the infidelity or finding out about it, beat his wife in a fit of jealous rage. His daughter confirms jealousy as "the master-passion of his mind" and records that, hearing that their mother had once secretly visited her children in London, he immediately packed them off to school in France–to Adelaide's "supreme horror and surprise."

The failure of his sight and his marriage profoundly altered O'Keeffe's character. He gradually withdrew from society and became something of a recluse even before his retirement from the stage. His daughter refers to his "invincible reserve" and occasional "sternness" of character, noting that after his brother, Daniel, died in 1787, "the reserve of his character became confirmed and habitual. . . ." His son's early death in 1804 made him ever more dependent on his daughter, who was his amanuensis for the last decade of his career and who took care of him from about 1819 until he died.

No one looking at O'Keeffe's career in the 1780s, however, would have thought him either effectively blind or "a wreck of domestic happiness." He had sent George Colman the Elder *The Son-in-Law* from Dublin for production at the Haymarket in August 1779. He finished the piece "in three weeks" and read of his triumph "at the Inn at Clonmel." By the time his next piece, *The Dead Alive,* appeared in June of 1781, O'Keeffe was settled in London and hard at work on new fare. *The Dead Alive* was only moderately successful, but *The Agreeable Surprise,* which followed in September, was another hit.

All three plays are two-act musical farces with music by Samuel Arnold. Arnold provided the overture and some original music for a few of the songs. The remaining lyrics were set to popular tunes or airs from contemporary Italian opera, arranged for the voices available in the company. Arnold received a flat fee for his services and could publish his music; O'Keeffe sold the copyrights to *The Son-in-Law* and *The Agreeable Surprise* to George Colman for fifty pounds each, a superb investment for the manager but a questionable decision by the author.

The Agreeable Surprise is typical not only of these pieces but of O'Keeffe's later operatic afterpieces, and so can serve to illustrate his work in the genre. After the overture, a pastorale in 6/8 time followed by a minuet, the chorus celebrates the harvest at the country estate of Sir Felix Friendly, who is entertaining his old friend Compton, a poor but patriotic sailor. At Sir Felix's request, Compton has brought up Felix's son, Eugene, as his own, and Sir Felix has brought up Compton's daughter, Laura, as an orphan he has adopted; he intends the two to marry, thinking his scheme has kept Eugene from an heir's dissipation and given Laura the sense "to distinguish merit, though linked to poverty, and generosity to reward it with her heart." Since neither son nor daughter is aware of what Sir Felix has done, his announcement that he wishes to marry Laura to his son causes consternation; Laura loves Eugene but thinks him Compton's child.

Act 2 introduces Mrs. Cheshire and her lawyer, Chicane. The former, a rich cheese-monger's widow, plans to claim Eugene for herself or sue him for the money she has forced upon him; Sir Felix has encouraged her visit for the fun of it. Eugene starts a rumor that she is a Russian princess, and the story is comically amplified by everyone who hears it. Not without a struggle, Eugene resigns Laura to his supposed rival while the awed servants wait upon "Princess Rustifusti" until Sir Felix reveals her true identity. He then reveals this deception to the lovers, remarking simply, "I love to surprise people." He suggests that Chicane marry Mrs. Cheshire, and his "agreeable surprise" ends in a sextet finale.

The Cheshire/Rustifusti equivoque provides

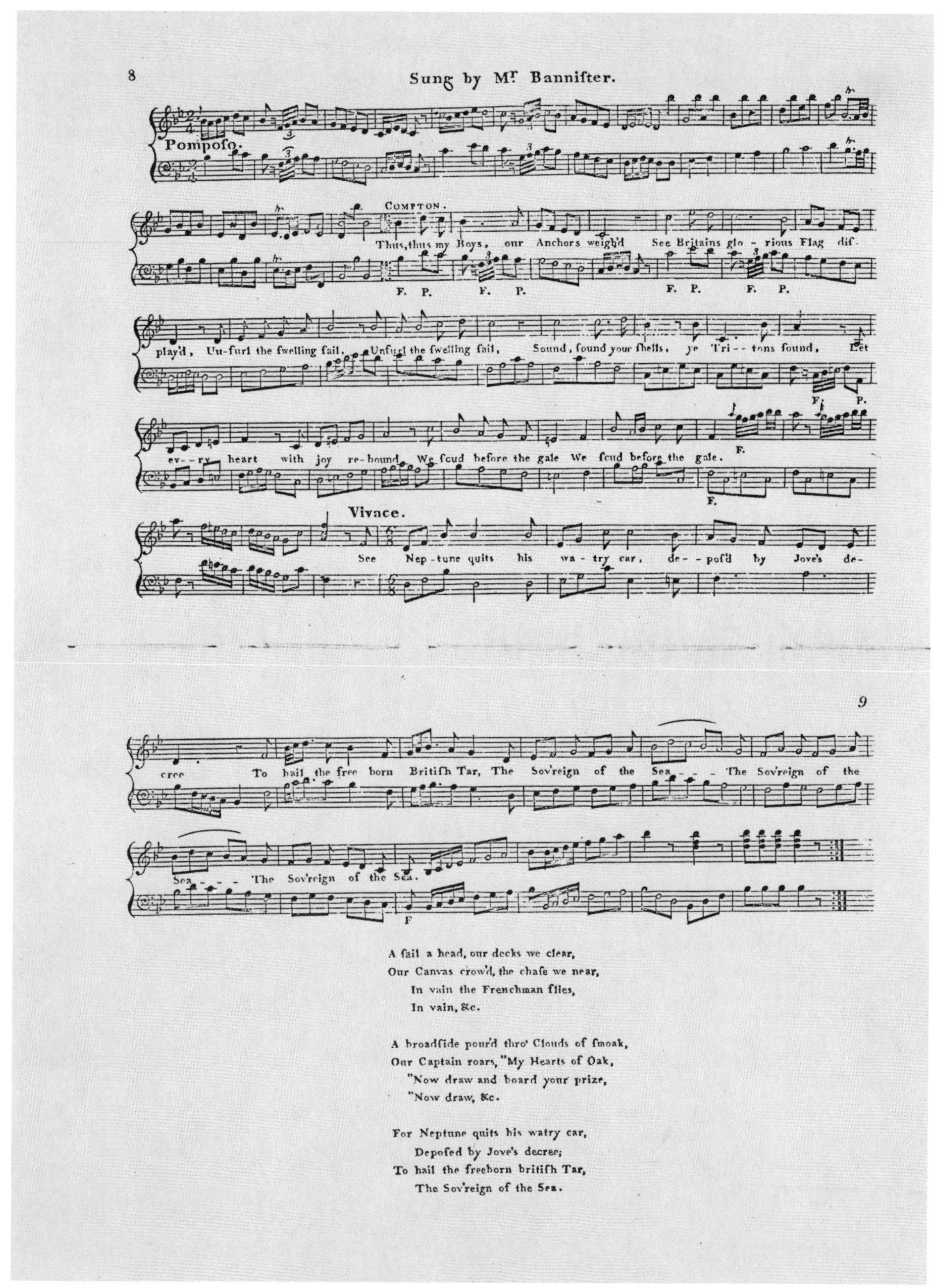

Song sung in act 1, scene 1, of The Agreeable Surprise *by Compton, a role played by Charles Bannister in the first production (from* The Agreeable Surprise, a Comic Opera in Two Acts *[score only, 1781])*

Record each tender vow;
As Night gives place to chearful day
Let hopes of future bliss allay,
The pangs we suffer now.

Ext.

Scene 4th. A Chamber.

Enter Marchioness & Francisco.

March: Now, Francisco, you understand me?

Fran: Why should I tell a lye? I do understand your Ladyship, — I am to take Inesilla to the Monesterio de las Repentidas.

March: No — to the Convent of St. Barbara.

Fran: The Convent of St. Barbara! oh, very well —

March: To morrow morning —

Fran: Ay, — a few Hours turn all our Tomorrows into Yesterdays. —

March: You take her to your own House to Night —

Fran: And in the Morning I leave her at the Monesterio de las Repentidas.

March: No — the Convent of St. Barbara.

Fran: The Convent of St. Barbara — Very well.

Page from the playhouse copy of The Banditti *submitted to the Examiner of Plays for licensing prior to the first performance, on 28 November 1781 (Larpent Collection, LA 577; by permission of the Henry E. Huntington Library and Art Gallery). In 1782 O'Keeffe revised this play as* The Castle of Andalusia.

some of the comedy, but Sir Felix's butler, Lingo, steals the show. A spouter of "balderdash Latin," Lingo practices on Cowslip the dairymaid, who rarely understands him:

> LINGO. Oh, my sweetest of Cowslips! dulces puella! by my dexter and sinister manus, your antic Caleb sings Io Poeans to see you!
> COWSLIP. What do you say–you're in pain to see me, Mr. Lingo?
> LINGO. Gerunds, declensions, verbs, and adverbs!
> COWSLIP. I should not ha' thought of your herbs.
> LINGO. Aid me, amor, the eight parts of speech–singular, plural, nouns, and pronouns!
> COWSLIP. Mr. Lingo, I doesn't love cursing and swearing!
> LINGO. Nominativo hanc, hunc, et hoc.
> COWSLIP. Hock again! You're drunk with hock, for my part, I believe. . . .

The part of Lingo, and similar parts in most of O'Keeffe's afterpieces, was written for the comedian John Edwin. His macaronic song "Amo, Amas, I Love a Lass" (II.i) is still heard occasionally, although no one remembers O'Keeffe as its author:

Oh! how bella
My puella!
I'll kiss secula, seculorum;
If I've luck, sir,
She's my uxor,
O dies benedictorum!

The songs are sprinkled throughout and were often moved, omitted, or augmented depending on the available cast and the cuts made for a particular performance. In act 1 Compton has a patriotic naval song and a typical lyric effusion; Sir Felix's "Jacky Bull" pokes fun at French fashions. Laura has her lyric, Lingo has O'Keeffe's version of a patter song, and Eugene and Laura a sentimental duet on rural love; the act ends in a quintet. Act 2 provides, besides Lingo's macaronic and the concluding sextet, a comic love song for Mrs. Cheshire, a rollicking air for Sir Felix, comic songs for Cowslip and Lingo, and "serious airs" for Laura and Eugene. The most popular songs were widely sung all over England and Ireland from piano-vocal scores.

As this synopsis suggests, the basic situation is improbable, humor is lugged in by the ears at times, and the play is farcical and sentimental by turns. O'Keeffe often returns to topical hits at the macaroni and castrati, often celebrates British naval power, usually satirizes hypocrisy and affectation without bitterness, and always rewards true love. Middle-class values are celebrated genially and usually sentimentally. Romantic comedy abounds, and happiness is often associated with a bucolic pastoralism. Audiences loved the mix, just as later audiences loved the Savoyard operas or later but still related pieces such as *Oklahoma!* and *South Pacific*.

These three afterpieces were followed by *The Poor Soldier* (1783), *Peeping Tom* (1784), *Love in a Camp* (1786), *The Farmer* (1787), *The Basket Maker* (1790), *Sprigs of Laurel* (1793), and *The Irish Mimic* (1795). O'Keeffe's first and greatest success in the operatic mainpiece category was *The Castle of Andalusia* (1782), which fed the popular taste for romantic banditti and castles in the moonlight. It was followed by *Fontainbleau* (1784), *The Siege of Curzola* (1786), *The Highland Reel* (1788), *The Czar* (1790), and *The Lad of the Hills* (1796); some of these were later reduced to afterpieces. Although the earlier of these pieces were successful, only *The Castle of Andalusia* ever approached the popularity of *The Poor Soldier* or *The Son-in-Law*.

In these years O'Keeffe also contributed to the routine work of a "house author." For example, he did lyrics for a number of the winter pantomimes produced annually at Covent Garden. These pieces depended primarily on spectacular scenic effects: *Lord Mayor's Day* (1782), for example, included an elaborate procession to Westminster and a display of the aurora borealis in Lapland. He also contributed to *Friar Bacon* (1783), *Omai* (1785), *Aladin* (1788), and *Merry Sherwood* (1795). Other routine work included alterations and adaptations of the plays of others: *The Maid's the Mistress* (1783; from G. A. Federico's libretto for *La serva padrona*, 1733), *Tantara-Rara, Rogues All!* (1788; from A. J. Bourlin's *Les intrigants*, 1787), *The Pharo Table* (1789; from Susanna Centlivre's *The Gamester*, 1705), and *Olympus in an Uproar* (1796; from Kane O'Hara's *The Golden Pippin*, 1773). Occasional pieces, usually in two acts, include *The Birth-Day* (1783), produced at the Haymarket in honor of the coming of age of the Prince of Wales, and *St. George's Day* (1789), produced in celebration of British naval victories.

Not all of O'Keeffe's plays, however, were musical. *The Young Quaker* (1783) was a successful venture into five-act comedy; Reuben Sadboy, its protagonist, is an interesting and original creation. *The Toy* (1789) was neither as successful nor as good as *The Young Quaker*, but *Wild Oats* (1791) was by John Genest's time considered "perhaps the

39

Rover. Eh! zounds my Manager

Gam: I hope her Ladyship hasn't found out that twas I had Banks arrest — would your Ladyship give leave for this here honest Man, and his Comrade to act a few plays in the Town cause I've letn my Barn, twill be some little help to me, my Lady

Rover: My Lady I understand these affairs, leave me to settle them.

Lady A: True, these are delusions, as a woman I understand not; but by my Cousins advice I will abide — ask his permission

Gam. So I must pay my respects to the young Squire — an't please your honor, if a poor man like me durst offer my humble duty

Rover. Canst thou bow to a Vagrant — ha! little hospitality

Gammon sneaks off

Lamp: Please your honor If I may presume to hope youll be graciously pleased to take our little Squad under your honors protection

Rover: Ha!

Lady A: What sayst thou Henry?

Rover. : Ay, where's Henry? — Gadso true that's me — Strange I should already forget my name, and not half an hour ago since I was Christend — Hearky, do you play yourself — Eh! Ha! Hem! fellow?

Lamp: Yes Sir — and Sir, I have just now Engaged a new Actor a Mister Rover Such an Actor!

Rover. If such is your best Actor you shan't have my Permission — my dear Madam the damndest fellow in the World — get a long out of Town, or damme I'll have all of you, man, woman, child, stick rag, and fiddle stick clapt into the whirligig

Lady A: Goodman abide not here

Rover: Eh! what you Scoundrel? how ~~you Scoundrel~~ if this new Actor you brag of that crack of your company was any thing like a Gentleman

Lamp: It isn't?

Page from the playhouse copy of Wild Oats *submitted to the Examiner of Plays for licensing prior to the first performance, on 16 April 1791 (Larpent Collection, LA 898; by permission of the Henry E. Huntington Library and Art Gallery)*

best of all O'Keeffe's pieces. Its recent revival in England and America shows that some O'Keeffe works can succeed on the modern stage but also illustrates the attendant difficulties.

The complex plot of *Wild Oats* turns on the effects of several sets of concealed or mistaken identities–on the same sort of equivoque O'Keeffe uses in many of his musical farces. This play, however, gives considerably more thematic weight to these plot devices. It opposes the hypocrisy of Ephraim Smooth to Lady Amaranth's genuine admiration and practice of Quaker principles, and the rapacity of Farmer Gammon to the generosity of Rover, Harry Thunder, Lady Amaranth, Mr. Banks, and Gammon's own children, Sim and Jane. It contrasts law with justice, the pretended with the genuine, doctrine with example, impulsive mistakes with calculated evil, the mechanical operation of institutions with the liberality of individuals.

Above all, it is a play about the theater. Harry has left school to have a fling at acting. Rover is a strolling actor, Lamp a manager who recruits him for a local performance in a barn. Despite her principles, Lady Amaranth invites the troupe to perform *As You Like It* in her home, and herself accepts the role of Rosalind. At one level, all this is one of several of O'Keeffe's attempts to present strollers in the best possible light: such actors are good people, and their playing entertains rather than corrupts. At another level, theater is metaphor. Rover is a fine actor, but he dissembles harmlessly; Ephraim Smooth is also a fine actor, but he acts for selfish purposes. The play within the play mirrors the romantic entanglements of those who are to play it and simultaneously adumbrates the happy conclusion of those entanglements. Characters are judged by their attitudes toward theater. The assumption of roles is played off against role-playing offstage, and disguises and mistaken identities have both theatrical and real-life significance.

O'Keeffe, in this as in most of his works, offers a mélange of farce, comedy, and sentiment. *Wild Oats* is based on the improbabilities, coincidences, and deliberate exaggerations of character and situation common in farce. It makes typical appeals to the interests of the contemporary audience: John Dory and his master celebrate the British navy; Lady Amaranth, Zechariah, and Smooth exploit the interest in the dialect and manners of Quakers. Sim and Jane reflect the popularity of rustics and provincial dialect. The Banks-Amelia-Sir George plot illustrates the sentimental benevolence of the day, just as Rover and Sir George exemplify current versions of the prodigal and rake-reformed motifs.

A modern director must decide how best to reconcile the farce with the sentiment, a problem contemporary audiences clearly did not feel. Today it is best to stage these works as comic romances, just as it is best to play nineteenth-century melodrama seriously. It will not do to undercut or play for laughs characters like Banks or Lady Amaranth, or to ignore O'Keeffe's insistent thesis that rank and wealth do not make the lady or gentleman. Harry says about Rover that "in this forlorn stroller I have discovered qualities that honor human nature, and accomplishments that might grace a Prince," and those qualities are exemplified when at the end of the play Rover and Lady Amaranth agree to give his newly revealed inheritance to Harry because her own fortune is enough for them.

Except for *The Young Quaker*, all of O'Keeffe's five-act comedies belong to the last years of his career. *The World in a Village* (1793) and *Life's Vagaries* (1795) were successful, although less so than *Wild Oats*. *She's Eloped!* (1798) was a complete failure. Successful, nonoperatic afterpieces included *The Blacksmith of Antwerp* and *A Beggar on Horseback* (both 1785), *The Prisoner at Large* (1788), *The Little Hunchback* (1789), and *Modern Antiques* (1791); O'Keeffe's only failures in this shorter form were *The Man Milliner* (1787) and *The Doldrum* (1796).

The onset of the French Revolution brought Adelaide O'Keeffe home in 1788 and Tottenham O'Keeffe–much Frenchified–home late in 1789. Although O'Keeffe seems never to have saved much of the money he received at the height of his career, he was proud of having paid the "two hundred pounds a-year" for his son's education "every half-year . . . beforehand"; Adelaide's convent education would have cost somewhat less, of course. It is difficult to calculate O'Keeffe's earnings over any substantial period; he sold the copyrights of five of his most successful pieces to Colman for relatively small sums, but he received some six hundred guineas for *The Castle of Andalusia* and fairly substantial sums for his best later pieces. He was able to take his family on a long vacation in Dorset in the summer of 1791 and was at Brighton and Tunbridge Wells with his daughter in 1794.

A number of factors led to O'Keeffe's retirement from the stage in 1798. George Colman the Younger took effective control of the Haymarket in 1788-1789 and seems to have had less interest in O'Keeffe than his father had had. John Edwin died in October of 1790, depriving the dramatist of his inspiration for many of his most popular comic creations. As a contemporary poem, "The Children of Apollo," said,

> For him O'Keeffe then wrote, he was his chief,
> And Edwin, all confess, play'd for O'Keeffe.

It is likely also that O'Keeffe, whose handicap increasingly kept him from theatrical as well as most other social intercourse, had written himself out and could not adapt his work to the larger theaters and changing taste of the 1790s. His last pieces are inferior to his earlier work; one has only to compare *The Young Quaker* with *She's Eloped!* to see the decline in quality.

On 6 June 1798 he saw produced a group of scenes from his most memorable plays, titled *A Nosegay of Weeds*. Thereafter, he says, "my racer, that had so often started for and won the plate, . . . quitted the course to turn into the green paddock, there to walk at his leisure and lie down at his ease." He tried to raise money to ensure his children's future by publishing his collected plays in 1798, but the venture barely paid expenses. The younger Colman refused him permission to print the five popular pieces to which he held copyright; Thomas Harris was kinder, giving O'Keeffe a benefit at Covent Garden in 1800 that produced a small annuity, and purchasing his remaining copyrights and manuscripts in 1803 for a second annuity. O'Keeffe was too proud to accept charity without making some return and, therefore, sent Harris the manuscripts of ten of his pieces, only two of which (*She's Eloped!* and *The Loyal Bandeau*) had been produced. Tottenham O'Keeffe's death in 1804, the result of "a wild scheme of obtaining a lucrative living in Jamaica, and exchanging it for one of inferior value in England," left O'Keeffe sole responsibility for his daughter. He was granted a small treasury pension of £100 per year in 1808 and an additional amount in 1826, but the Covent Garden annuity was not paid after 1825, and the government pensions stopped with his death. A subscription undertaken in 1826 produced only £188, most of which went to pay debts left behind by his son, and Adelaide O'Keeffe spent what income there was without abridging her father's comfort for her future welfare.

After retirement, O'Keeffe lived for several years in Twickenham, writing plays, occasional poems, and newspaper pieces. Five of the dramatic pieces sent to Colman in 1803 were apparently written after 1798, and he wrote four more pieces during the 1807-1809 period. None of these was ever produced or published. He moved to Chichester, Sussex, before 1819 and remained there until about 1828. His daughter joined him permanently, probably after intermittent work as a governess, about 1819. The two moved westward in 1828; O'Keeffe's declining health forced them to stop at Southampton, where he died peacefully on 4 February 1833. Adelaide O'Keeffe lived until 1855; she produced a number of novels and poems herself.

O'Keeffe's total output comes to more than sixty pieces of one kind or another in addition to a dozen or more works never produced. More than thirty are original and substantial creations; more than twenty were successful, six or eight of them spectacularly so, and only six were failures. His ten most popular pieces received nearly twelve hundred performances before 1800 in London alone and were played and published in England, Scotland, Ireland, and America well past the middle of the nineteenth century.

Nevertheless, O'Keeffe remains relatively unknown and is barely mentioned in most studies or histories of English drama. The reasons are not hard to find. History has generally taken the view expressed in "The Children of Apollo":

> Cou'd *quality* from *quantity* we reap,
> We might approve of his prodigious heap–
> If writing a great deal were writing *well*,
> O'KEEFFE would ev'ry author then excell.

Although the anonymous author excepts *Wild Oats* and a few other pieces from this condemnation, he does so because he sees in them some literary merit, and most of O'Keeffe's most successful work is essentially theatrical, not literary. Although the music for the comic operas is often charming, neither Samuel Arnold nor William Shield was more than a competent composer; one has only to remember how Mozart's music transforms the topical and pantomimic elements of Schikaneder's libretto for *The Magic Flute* (1791) to understand this limitation. Finally, most of O'Keeffe's work is heavily topical, depending for effect not only on the styles of particular actors and actresses but also on frequent allusions to contemporary people, events, and attitudes. His work belongs essentially to popular culture and to forms of that culture which no longer exist or have been greatly altered. R. B. Peake, writing of O'Keeffe in his *Memoirs of the Colman Family* (1841), puts the point well: "But alas! for the fate of a comic author, what do the public care for a man who has sent tens of thousands home to their beds laughing, year after year . . . ; his contemporaries, the nightly admirers of his effusions, have followed the creator of mirth and whim to his last home, and a succeeding generation of playgoers barely know his name!"

Yet O'Keeffe is worth study. His work represents every form of comic drama and entertainment popular in the last quarter of the eighteenth century and reflects the astonishing variety of popular taste more accurately than the work of writers now much better known. His career exemplifies the change from poetic and verbal comedy to theatrical spectacle and farce that parallels the change from the more intimate theater of the late seventeenth century to the larger halls and audiences of the 1790s. It also exemplifies the literary relationships between England and Ireland in the period and the complex interactions among writers, plays, audiences, theatrical companies, and contemporary events that make the history and sociology of theater so fascinating.

Bibliography:

Frederick M. Link, *John O'Keeffe: A Bibliography*, University of Nebraska Studies, new series 65 (Lincoln: University of Nebraska, 1983).

Biographies:

"Biographical Sketch of John O'Keeffe, Esq.," *Monthly Mirror* (London), December 1797, pp. 323-328; January 1798, pp. 13-16; February 1798, pp. 70-72;

Adelaide O'Keeffe, "Memoir," in *O'Keeffe's Legacy to His Daughter* (London: For the editor [Adelaide O'Keeffe], 1834), pp. xi-xxxviii.

Papers:

A manuscript copy of *She's Eloped!*, not in the hand of O'Keeffe or his daughter, exists in the British Library (Add. MS 25, 928). The Larpent Collection at the Henry E. Huntington Library includes the manuscript fair copies of most of O'Keeffe's dramatic pieces submitted to John Larpent, Examiner of Plays, for license. The following pieces are known to survive only in this form: *The Banditti* (original version of *The Castle of Andalusia*, 1781, LA 577), *The Maid's the Mistress* (1783, LA 616, titled "The Servant Mistress"), *The Shamrock* (1783, LA 620), *The Siege of Curzola* (1786, LA 743), *The Pharo Table* (1789, LA 860), *St. George's Day* (1789, LA 830), *The Fugitive* (1790, LA 860), *Jenny's Whim* (1794, LA 1037), *The Lad of the Hills* (1796, LA 1117), *Olympus in an Uproar* (1796, LA 1141), *Our Wooden Walls; or, All to St. Paul's* (produced 1797 as *Britain's Brave Tars; or, All to St. Paul's*, LA 1188), *The Eleventh of June* (1798, LA 1218), and *A Nosegay of Weeds* (1798, LA 1219).

Richard Brinsley Sheridan

(1751-7 July 1816)

Mark S. Auburn
Indiana University-Purdue University at Fort Wayne

SELECTED PLAY PRODUCTIONS: *The Rivals,* London, Theatre Royal, Covent Garden, 17 January 1775; revised version, London, Theatre Royal, Covent Garden, 28 January 1775;

St. Patrick's Day, London, Theatre Royal, Covent Garden, 2 May 1775;

Prelude on Opening Covent Garden next Season, London, Theatre Royal, Covent Garden, 20 September 1775;

The Duenna, London, Theatre Royal, Covent Garden, 21 November 1775;

A Trip to Scarborough, London, Theatre Royal in Drury Lane, 24 February 1777;

The School for Scandal, London, Theatre Royal in Drury Lane, 8 May 1777;

The Camp, London, Theatre Royal in Drury Lane, 15 October 1778;

Verses to the Memory of Garrick, London, Theatre Royal in Drury Lane, 11 March 1779;

The Critic, London, Theatre Royal in Drury Lane, 30 October 1779;

Pizarro, London, Theatre Royal, Drury Lane, 24 May 1799.

SELECTED BOOKS: *The Rivals, A Comedy. As it is Acted at the Theatre-Royal in Covent-Garden* (London: Printed for John Wilkie, 1775); revised as *The Rivals, A Comedy. As it is Acted at the Theatre-Royal in Covent Garden. Written by Richard Brinsley Sheridan, Esq. The Third Edition Corrected.* (London: Printed for John Wilkie, 1776);

Songs Duets, Trios, &c. in The Duenna; or, The Double Elopement. As Performed at the Theatre-Royal in Covent-Garden (London: Printed for J. Wilkie, 1775);

Verses To the Memory of Garrick. Spoken as A Monody, at the Theatre Royal in Drury-Lane (London: Published by T. Evans, J. Wilkie, E. & C. Dilly, A. Portal, and J. Almon, 1779);

The School for Scandal. A Comedy [pirated edition] (Dublin, 1780);

The Critic or A Tragedy Rehearsed. A Dramatic Piece in three Acts as it is performed at the Theatre Royal in Drury Lane. By Richard Brinsley Sheridan Esqr. (London: Printed for T. Becket, 1781);

A Trip to Scarborough. A Comedy. As Performed at the Theatre Royal in Drury Lane. Altered from Vanbrugh's Relapse; or, Virtue in Danger. By Richard Brinsley Sheridan Esq. (London: Printed for G. Wilkie, 1781);

St. Patrick's Day; or, the Scheming Lieutenant. A Comic Opera: As It is Acted at the Theatre-Royal, Smoke-Alley [pirated edition] (Dublin: Printed for the booksellers, 1788);

The Duenna: A Comic Opera. In Three Acts. As Performed at the Theatre Royal, Covent Garden: With Universal Applause. By R. B. Sheridan, Esq (London: Printed for T. N. Longman, 1794);

The Camp, A Musical Entertainment, As Performed at the Theatre Royal, Drury Lane. By R. B. Sheridan, Esq. [pirated edition] (London, 1795);

Pizarro; A Tragedy, In Five Acts; As Performed at the Theatre Royal in Drury-Lane: Taken from the German Drama of Kotzebue; and Adapted to the English Stage by Richard Brinsley Sheridan (London: Printed for James Ridgway, 1799).

Collections: *Sheridan's Plays Now Printed as He Wrote Them and His Mother's Unpublished Comedy 'A Journey to Bath,'* edited by W. Fraser Rae (London: David Nutt, 1902);

The Plays and Poems of Richard Brinsley Sheridan, 3 volumes, edited by R. Crompton Rhodes (Oxford: Blackwell, 1928);

The Dramatic Works of Richard Brinsley Sheridan, 2 volumes, edited by Cecil Price (Oxford: Clarendon Press, 1973).

Richard Brinsley Sheridan (portrait by Thomas Gainsborough)

Richard Brinsley Sheridan wrote and produced three plays that have been performed more frequently than the works of any other playwright between Shakespeare and Shaw. *The Rivals, The School for Scandal,* and *The Critic* entered the performing repertoire immediately upon their first appearance in the 1770s, and one or more of them is still performed every year. They are both timely and timeless pieces of art: timely because they reflect not only the concerns and mores but also the literary and theatrical style of late eighteenth-century England; timeless because they speak to the human condition and to the nature of artistic creation in the theater. As the basis for a major artistic reputation, three plays seem thin, particularly in comparison to the creations of Dr. Samuel Johnson, Oliver Goldsmith, Laurence Sterne, and even Tobias Smollett. Yet, because Sheridan exploited a late neoclassical style, tempered exuberant spirits with knowledge of the exigencies of theatrical production, and infused comic attack with the charitable spirit of good nature, his plays are still produced around the world.

Sheridan's pedigree forecast literary and theatrical achievement. His mother, Frances Chamberlaine Sheridan, who died while he was an adolescent student at Harrow, wrote one fairly successful play and one respected novel. His father, Thomas, was a playwright, actor, theater manager, orator, and also a scholar of English elocution who published a dictionary. His paternal grandfather Thomas Sheridan spent many intimate years with Jonathan Swift. Sheridan met and exceeded the gifts of this heritage and the expectations loaded upon his shoulders as the

Elizabeth Linley Sheridan, circa 1785-1786 (portrait by Thomas Gainsborough; Andrew W. Mellon Collection, by permission of the National Gallery of Art, Washington, D.C.)

second son, the one sent to the famous boarding school Harrow in 1762 while his favored elder brother and his two younger sisters remained with the family, the one who was to learn to shift for himself. He rose from genteel Irish poverty to become holder of the royal patent for Drury Lane theater, a Member of Parliament, a minister of government (on three occasions), and finally a landowner. His time as an active playwright covered about five years; his career as a politician spanned three decades. During all of his mature life, even the last few years, he knew material success that far exceeded anything his parents had ever experienced; he enjoyed the respect and affection of the greatest people of his day; and he served his country on a broader stage than Smock Alley (the Dublin theater his father managed) or Drury Lane (the London theater he owned). At the same time, as witnessed by his election to Johnson's Literary Club in March 1777, he became a man of letters who conversed as an equal with the principal male artists of his own generation and of the next–George Gordon, lord Byron, William Wordsworth, Samuel Taylor Coleridge, Robert Southey, Thomas Moore.

Sheridan's brief burst of literary and theatrical activity from 1775 to 1779 still commands attention and respect, while three decades of public service garner rich footnotes in histories of the stuttering growth of the British Empire. His literary and theatrical activity occurred in a context that has bequeathed to us only one other immortal play, Oliver Goldsmith's *She Stoops to Conquer* (1773); his political contributions issued forth during a tumultuous period of European history when wars and revolutions, caused by new ideas about the citizen's relationship with the social fabric and fueled by technological advances in manufacture and transportation, signaled the growth of empire. If he was only a supporting actor in the world of power, he was the star comic playwright of the Age of Garrick.

Theater in Sheridan's time appealed to the upper and middle and even lower classes, though fewer of the last could afford so little as one shilling for the upper gallery than could gentry and aristocrats the two, three, and five shillings for the first gallery, pit, and boxes. Nevertheless, the appeal encompassed all classes, and the repertoire reflected all tastes. Plays appeared in London during the winter season (September through May) mostly upon the stages of the two royal patent houses, Covent Garden and Drury Lane. Their two splendid auditoriums welcomed thousands of visitors nightly to a world more brightly lit (both by candles and by oil-fed stage devices) than anyone could see in almost any other enclosed public structure. On the stage during about 180 nights a season audiences watched versions of William Shakespeare and Ben Jonson and John Fletcher, plays by George Farquhar, Richard Steele, Colley Cibber, and Susanna Centlivre, and recent comedies by Isaac Bickerstaff, George Colman the Elder, Richard Cumberland, David Garrick, and Hugh Kelly. They did not often see plays by George Etherege, William Wycherley, Thomas Shadwell, John Dryden, or William Congreve: these century-old writers of the Restoration failed to hold a place in the British repertoire much beyond the second decade of the eighteenth century. Auditors seemed to want not only comedies, melodramas, and tragedies to their own tastes but also such entr'acte entertainments as rope dancing (tightrope walking), harlequinades, singing, monologues, and other variety pieces. And the theatrical evening had to conclude with a farce or comic operetta of an hour or so, stretching the theatrical experience into five hours or longer, from prologue, mainpiece, epilogue, entr'actes, through afterpiece.

Within its repertoire, high Georgian theater included the most stageworthy of its forebears from the early seventeenth century, the better productions of its early eighteenth-century fellow-technicians, and the recent plays of its contemporaries. High Georgian theater, especially under David Garrick's management, ignored most of the comedies and tragedies of the Caroline period (1670-1710), the plays of Farquhar and Centlivre excepted. It offered a lot of Shakespeare, though usually Shakespeare revised. A small portion of what it presented, and almost nothing of what it originated, has earned a place in literary history.

As artisans for the Georgian stage, in their published plays both Frances Sheridan and Thomas Sheridan reflect a comedic bias toward their more remote past and toward their present, just like this repertoire. Their second son, "Dick," as they called him, worked within this tradition. And when he sought subjects for his first fully developed stage works, he turned to his own experience.

While living with his father, brother, and sisters in Bath in the early 1770s, Sheridan met Elizabeth Ann Linley, the most admired singer of the period, called a "lark," a "saint," the "siren of Bath." Sheridan's father, Thomas, had made the acquaintance of the Linley family (famous musicians all) in order to expand his "Attic Entertainment," an evening of theatrical oratory and declamation which required music for balance. This presentation was Thomas Sheridan's principal means of support at Bath, and money was always tight for his growing family; Dick complained of being mocked as the "poor player's son" at Harrow. The Linleys were far more comfortable than the Sheridans; but Thomas Sheridan privately denigrated Elizabeth's father, Thomas Linley, as a mere musician, and even later he would denigrate Dick's alliance with a musician's daughter–his son was the son of a scholar, not the son of a player; his son should not marry the daughter of a "music maker."

At the start of their acquaintance, Dick seemed to have had no such pretensions. Eliza, after all, was engaged to Sir Walter Long, an older baronet of substantial revenue. Even when this alliance was broken, with much public notice, including a farce by Samuel Foote, Sheridan's part could only be advisory, particularly since Dick's older brother, Charles, was a rival for Elizabeth's affections. History has not made clear how Dick became the favored suitor, but it has left us titillating romantic hints in the form of indisputable events: a Captain Mathews addressed Eliza; the younger "Mr. S------n" assisted Miss Linley in an elopement to France; there were paragraphs in the Bath newspapers, two duels between Mathews and Sheridan (during the second of which Dick suffered severe wounds), a six-month exile for Dick at Waltham Abbey, where he was supposed to prepare himself for the bar, and at last on 13 April 1773 a clandestine wedding of the eldest Linley and the second Sheridan son. Thomas Sheridan refused to countenance the marriage for many months: he told Charles in a burst of self-indulgent affection, "I consider myself now as having no son but you," and he

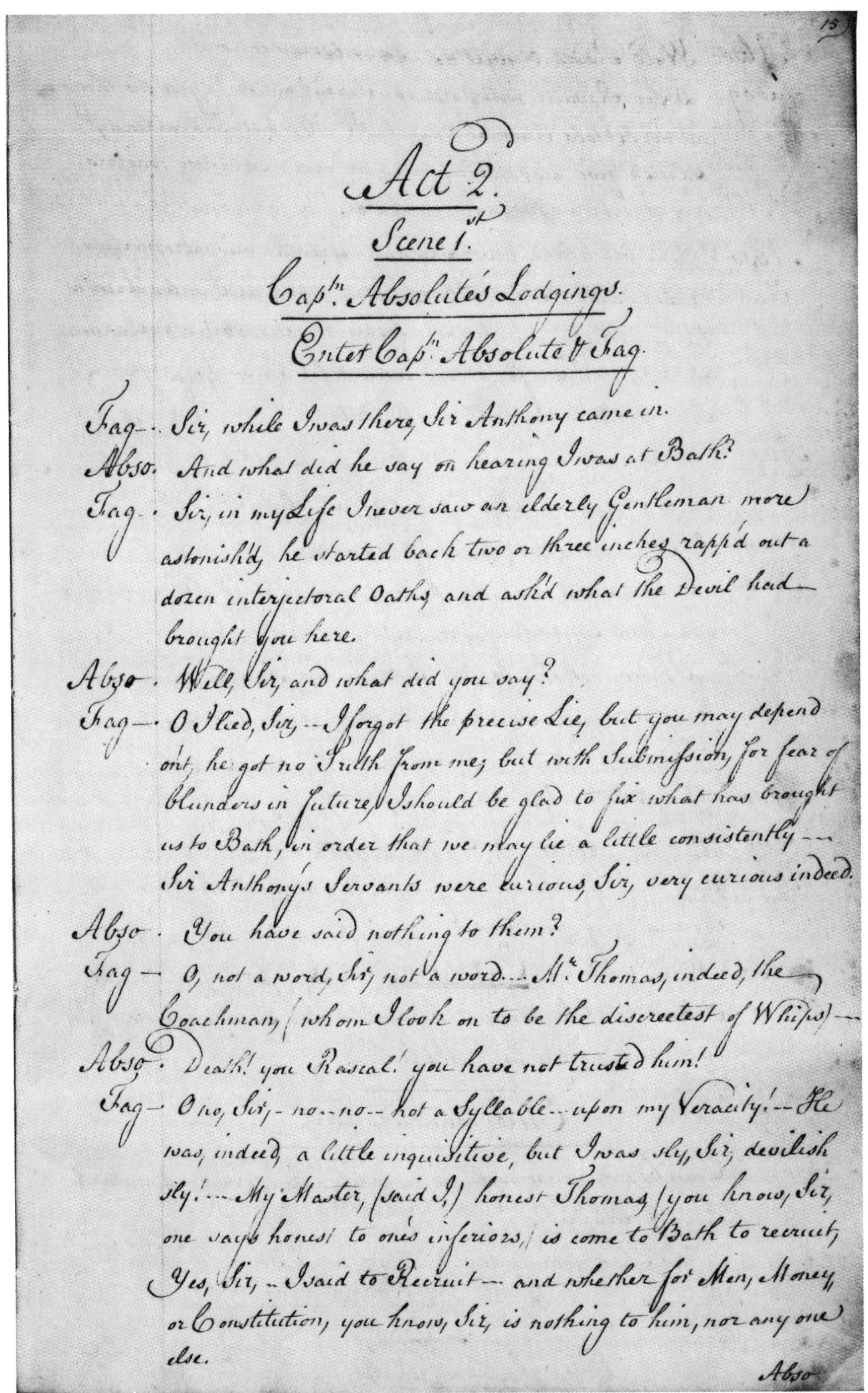

15

Act 2.

Scene 1st

Captn. Absolute's Lodgings.

Enter Captn. Absolute & Fag.

Fag — Sir, while I was there, Sir Anthony came in.

Abso. And what did he say on hearing I was at Bath?

Fag. Sir, in my Life I never saw an elderly Gentleman more astonish'd, he started back two or three inches, rapp'd out a dozen interjectoral Oaths and ask'd what the Devil had brought you here.

Abso. Well, Sir, and what did you say?

Fag — O I lied, Sir, — I forgot the precise Lie, but you may depend on't, he got no Truth from me; but with Submission, for fear of blunders in future, I should be glad to fix what has brought us to Bath, in order that we may lie a little consistently — Sir Anthony's Servants were curious, Sir, very curious indeed.

Abso. You have said nothing to them?

Fag — O, not a word, Sir, not a word — Mr. Thomas, indeed, the Coachman, (whom I look on to be the discreetest of Whips) —

Abso. Death! you Rascal! you have not trusted him!

Fag — O no, Sir, — no — no — not a Syllable — upon my Veracity! — He was, indeed, a little inquisitive, but I was sly, Sir, devilish sly! — My Master, (said I,) honest Thomas (you know, Sir, one says honest to one's inferiors,) is come to Bath to recruit, Yes, Sir, — I said to Recruit — and whether for Men, Money, or Constitution, you know, Sir, is nothing to him, nor any one else.

Abso

Page from the playhouse copy of the original version of The Rivals, *submitted to the Examiner of Plays for licensing prior to its performance on 17 January 1775 (Larpent Collection, LA 383; by permission of the Henry E. Huntington Library and Art Gallery). The play was revised extensively before it was staged again, on 28 January 1775.*

prevented his daughters, Lissy and Betsy, from seeing Dick and Eliza for three years. But Thomas Linley recognized the alliance immediately and even provided his daughter a small dowry.

And so it was that Richard Brinsley Sheridan found himself married and living in London during the 1773-1774 season without an income and soon with a growing family, for on 17 November 1775, the couple's son, Thomas, was born. Richard Sheridan would not permit Eliza to sing for money, even though she could command as much as fifteen hundred pounds for a series of concerts. James Boswell tells of Dr. Johnson's applauding the decision:

> We talked of a young gentleman's marriage with an eminent singer, and his determination that she should no longer sing in publick.... It was questioned whether the young gentleman, who had not a shilling in the world, but was blest with very uncommon talents, was not foolishly delicate, or foolishly proud.... Johnson, with all the high spirit of a Roman senator, exclaimed, "He resolved wisely and nobly to be sure. He is a brave man. Would not a gentleman be disgraced by having his wife singing publickly for hire? No, Sir, there can be no doubt here. I know not if I should not *prepare* myself for a publick singer, as readily as let my wife be one."

And so Dick turned to his "very uncommon talents," and to his mother's unpublished work, to produce his first play.

The Rivals appeared on 17 January 1775. It represents a lively if confusing imbroglio of young love triumphing over parental disapproval in the way of Roman New Comedy, with this important difference: the old parents in fact desire the marriage of the young people, and the young people create their own difficulties. Romantic Lydia Languish wants to elope rather than marry anyone with her "friends' consent." To humor her, Captain Jack Absolute has disguised himself as penniless Ensign Beverley. Lydia's aunt, Mrs. Malaprop, is negotiating with Sir Anthony Absolute about an alliance of Lydia with his son Jack Absolute. Complicating the picture are two other rivals for Lydia's affections: the foppish country booby Bob Acres and the pugnacious fortune-hunting Sir Lucius O'Trigger. Neither of these rivals ever crosses Lydia's mind, and Sir Lucius's pretensions are particularly absurd since Mrs. Malaprop herself is attracted to him. Both Mrs. Malaprop and Sir Lucius are betrayed by the scheming maidservant Lucy in the correspondence which the aunt thinks she is carrying on with Sir Lucius and which Sir Lucius thinks he is carrying on with Lydia. In a subplot which Sheridan meant to be comic but which rarely plays as such, overly delicate and emotionally insecure Faulkland tests the affections of his orphaned fiancée, Julia Melville (Sir Anthony's niece and Lydia's best friend). The difficulties are good-naturedly resolved at the scene of a six-way duel: Acres to fight "Beverley," Jack to fight Sir Lucius (either for Jack to defend his pretensions to Sir Lucius's Lydia or for Sir Lucius to avenge a slight upon Ireland which he alleges Jack made–the text gives both reasons and thereby indicates the subservience of plot to characterization), and Faulkland to fight anyone who is willing. Sir Anthony and Mrs. Malaprop arrive in time to prevent the rivals from dueling and to sort out the marriages. The key to the amiable tone of the play is Acres's resignation of any interest, Sir Lucius's offer to hold a party for everyone assembled even though he has been disappointed of a fortune and a bride, and Sir Anthony's sage advice to bring the correct couples together.

In its first performance, *The Rivals* was too long by an hour, too indelicate by a half-dozen oaths and several bawdy references, and too ill acted, especially by favorite Ned Shuter, to win the audience's approbation. Covent Garden manager Thomas Harris immediately withdrew it, and Sheridan's theatrical career might have ended then (as Eliza thought it had) except for Harris's prudent assessment of Sheridan's powers of revision. Eleven nights later, on 28 January 1775, a new version appeared, earned applause, and played steadily in the repertoire for the rest of the season and into every season thereafter. In its original performances, the play featured the best Covent Garden comedians, five of whom had created roles in Goldsmith's *She Stoops to Conquer* (1773): Jane Green was Mrs. Malaprop as well as Mrs. Hardcastle; Mary Bulkley portrayed Julia Melville as well as Kate Hardcastle; Ned Shuter, now "perfect" in his lines (that is, he knew them this time), took Sir Anthony Absolute after having created Mr. Hardcastle; perhaps John Quick as Acres incorporated features of his portrayal of Tony Lumpkin; and Lee Lewes as Jack's pompous servant, Fag, found a small but worthy successor to his formal young Marlowe. Joined by veterans like Henry Woodward (at sixty-five still acceptable in young romantic roles like Jack Absolute) and newcomers like Jane Barsanti as Lydia and Lawrence Clinch as Sir Lucius O'Trigger (in the second opening, taking the part in which John Lee had

Richard Brinsley Sheridan, 1788 (portrait by John Russell; by permission of the National Portrait Gallery, London; Copyright Photograph, Reg. No. 651)

failed on 17 January), the cast represented Covent Garden's strongest comic ensemble.

Tom Moore, Sheridan's biographer and first systematic critic, wrote that "The characters of *The Rivals* . . . are *not* such as occur very commonly in the world; and, instead of producing striking effects with natural and obvious materials, which is the great art and difficulty of a painter of human life, [Sheridan] has here overcharged most of his persons with whims and absurdities, for which the circumstances they are engaged in afford but a very disproportionate vent." Moore correctly assesses the artificial nature of these characters' idiosyncrasies, and by focusing on the characters he points as well to the essence of the play: it is a comedy of character, not a comedy of plot, and our satisfaction derives more from the exposures of foibles and absurdities for their own sakes than from a probable and necessary resolution of the difficulties in which the characters are involved or from the capacity of the artistic fabric to weave colorfully and consistently strands of truth about human existence. Subsequent critics have attributed the comedy's greatness to its exuberant play with language and with language's power to obfuscate reality, but this language emanates from, as well as serves to form, distinctly drawn, wonderfully absurd characters, stage types as ancient as

Menander's (the old father, the miles gloriosus, the amorous dowager) and as fresh as George Colman the Elder's Polly Honeycombe (1760). Sheridan's instinctive artistry took the types and complicated them–not just a country booby but also a fop, not just a romantic ingenue but a girl whose fantasies are formed by novels, not just an amorous dowager but an abuser of words so strongly portrayed that her name gave our language a new word, *malapropism*. Yet every character proves an amiable humorist, good-natured at base, a perfect stage representative of the fundamentally warm and sentimental Georgian theater.

One of Sheridan's recent critics argues persuasively that the twenty-three-year-old playwright, who denied plagiarism in the preface to the first edition of *The Rivals*, depended heavily upon Shakespeare, whether consciously or unconsciously. And both Sheridan's contemporaries and his latter-day admirers have found convincing correspondences linking his works with William Congreve's as well as with the comedies of the Garrick era. That Mrs. Malaprop's origin is Mrs. Tryfort, a character in Frances Sheridan's unpublished "A Journey to Bath," seems indisputable. But if "faded ideas float in the fancy like half-forgotten dreams," as Sheridan argued in that preface, their recombination created a stage-worthy fantasy never long off the boards. Throughout the nineteenth century and into the twentieth, in Britain and America, *The Rivals* played steadily and became by turns a starring vehicle for Mrs. Malaprop, Sir Anthony, and even Bob Acres, depending upon the acting company's resources.

Though Sheridan the fledgling playwright proved brilliant in drawing quickly and surely a range of stage characters from many walks of life and showed that he could combine them in bouncing scenes comic for their wit, their characterization, and their manifest absurdity, it is the Sheridan of comically ironic situation who proves himself more than a brilliant apprentice in *The Rivals*. His technique of empowering the audience as spectators more knowledgeable than any one of the characters permits full appreciation of every imposture and self-deception. In the third scene of the third act, for instance, Jack appears in his real character to Mrs. Malaprop but as "Beverley" to Lydia, permits thereby each woman to appear absurdly overmatched with him but foolishly pleased in her deception of the other, yet augurs his own downfall as overreaching knave. Thus, the audience anticipates the reversal that very nearly does not occur: in the second scene of the fourth act, Sir Anthony drags Jack back to Mrs. Malaprop's for the confrontation during which both niece and aunt discover the impostures played upon them, and even Sir Anthony learns how he too has been duped. Rather than surprise the audience with the probable but unexpected, Sheridan makes us coconspirators who know what must happen, who relish our more complete understanding, and who look forward to the characters' learning the truth. The only surprise arises from the artist's gratifying verbal brilliancies and unusual arrangement of familiar materials–the pleasure of the classical sonata form rather than of the tone poem.

The success of *The Rivals* led immediately to other opportunities for Sheridan. At Covent Garden on 2 May 1775 his two-act farce, *St. Patrick's Day; or, The Scheming Lieutenant*, appeared and earned for itself a minor place in the afterpiece repertoire. Written for Lawrence Clinch's benefit performance in gratitude for his having taken over Sir Lucius O'Trigger, the farce contains many of the elements of *The Rivals:* idiosyncratic but essentially good-natured characters, scenes of disguise and of revelation, amiable humorists of broad, quick, verbal strokes, and a farcical starring role rich in numerous assumed disguises for the principal male actor. Sheridan is said to have written it in forty-eight hours, but a contemporary testified that Sheridan had made a thorough review of the farcical afterpiece literature before embarking on the project, and certainly the many similarities to a variety of comedies and farces popular in the Georgian repertoire suggest ideas hardly faded in the fancy. Similarly, *Prelude on Opening Covent Garden next Season* (Covent Garden, 20 September 1775), surviving only through newspaper accounts, demonstrates the same competence as comic dramatist writing for the occasion.

In *The Duenna* (Covent Garden, 21 November 1775), however, Sheridan once more rose beyond competence to brilliance. Like *The Rivals* and *St. Patrick's Day*, the book of this comic opera reflects Sheridan's youthful experience and the typical situations of Roman New Comedy. Donna Louisa wishes to marry Antonio, but her crusty old father, Don Jerome, plans to marry her to the rich (converted) Jew Isaac Mendoza. Louisa's jealous brother, Ferdinand, wants to marry Louisa's best friend, the somewhat grave Donna Clara. Margaret, Donna Louisa's old, ugly, and clever duenna, plays upon Don Jerome's credulity and Isaac's cupidity to pass herself off as Donna Louisa, marry

Isaac secretly, and permit both young couples to wed. The characters possess the same idiosyncratic artificiality as those of Sheridan's two earlier comedies, and they appear even more artificial because the setting this time is Seville, the conventional never-never land of a number of older comedies (by Fletcher and Centlivre) and newer comic operas (by Isaac Bickerstaff) in the Georgian repertoire. But more important, the music lends a sweet poignancy to the action, cutting down thereby the manifest absurdity of character and situation.

The Duenna played an unprecedented seventy-five nights that first season and was praised by audience and critics alike. A little more than a year later, in March 1777, Johnson proposed Sheridan for membership in The Literary Club, calling him the author of "the two best comedies of his age," and Johnson meant *The Rivals* and *The Duenna*. Forty years later even William Hazlitt praised it effusively:

> The "Duenna" is a perfect work of art. It has the utmost sweetness and point. The plot, the characters, the dialogue, are all complete in themselves, and they are all [Sheridan's] own; and the songs are the best that ever were written, except those in the "Beggar's Opera." They have a joyous spirit of intoxication in them, and a strain of the most melting tenderness.

For the music, Sheridan was indebted to his father-in-law and brother-in-law, the elder and younger Thomas Linleys, though to the latter more than the former. By using in the decorative part of Don Carlos the tenor Meyer Leon, he helped guarantee a splendid musical presentation while foregoing the profits of a score of Friday performances when Leon (a Jew in real life but not in the comic opera) insisted upon retiring to his synagogue.

The Duenna was the greatest hit of many seasons, outplaying for many years even John Gay's perennially popular *Beggar's Opera* (1728), but it did not survive much beyond the early nineteenth century. Later critics have found it too slight, even putting aside the frivolity of the genre. In our century, perhaps the ridicule of Isaac because he was born a Jew offends modern sensibilities, though today we can still be amused by Louisa's comparisons of Isaac's incomplete conversion–he "stands like a dead wall between church and synagogue, or like the blank leaves between the Old and New Testament." And if Margaret's dependent position and deformed visage strike us as no subjects for comedy, her wit and cleverness earn her right to the title. Moreover, in the last decade revivals have begun to occur.

Sheridan, the "poor player's son," earned a small fortune in this first year and a half of dramatic penmanship and directing, though how much he actually earned we cannot be sure. Probably dismayed to see the money-making talents of his daughter unemployed and anxious for Eliza and Dick to find financial security, Thomas Linley had for some time urged his son-in-law to form an alliance with David Garrick, actor-manager-patentee of Drury Lane, the more profitable of the two winter Theatres Royal. But Sheridan had seen his chance after *The Rivals* to capitalize upon his growing familiarity with the talents of the Covent Garden company and gave *The Duenna* to Thomas Harris, though he also took care to cultivate Garrick's friendship. (Indeed, at that March 1777 election meeting of The Literary Club, Garrick was present along with Johnson, Edmund Burke, Adam Smith, Joshua Reynolds, and Sheridan's future political ally Charles James Fox, who was in the chair.) As the 1775-1776 season wore on, Garrick complained that "the Devil of a Duenna has laid hold upon the Town," and he even tried a revival of Frances Sheridan's *The Discovery* (1763), with himself as Sir Anthony Branville, to bring audiences home to Drury Lane. One wag remarked that "the old woman would be the death of the old man." Ill from a variety of then-incurable ailments, most particularly renal-urinary tract malfunctions, Garrick determined to make the 1775-1776 season his last as an actor and to sell his half share of the Drury Lane patent, which he valued at thirty-five thousand pounds. Sheridan, in concert with Thomas Linley, Sr., and the wealthy, fashionable physician James Ford, purchased it. In 1778 Sheridan sold his one-seventh interest to Linley and Ford and purchased the other half-interest held by Willoughby Lacy, thus becoming half owner of the patent, with Linley and Ford controlling the other half. But in order to accomplish these financial transactions, Sheridan had to borrow heavily (probably twenty-five thousand pounds) and stand surety to a thousand-pound lifetime annuity to Lacy. Thus began a pattern of leveraged finance (Sheridan put down only thirteen hundred pounds for all these transactions) that left Sheridan socially comfortable but chronically in debt. His son Tom once said that his father had changed the family name to "O'Sheridan": after all, he *owed* most of the world. Once in Tom's company Sheridan bragged to a friend that he had permitted Tom a generous allowance at college; "yes," said Tom, "you *allowed* it, but you never paid it." On another occasion, when Sheridan threatened to cut Tom off with a shilling, Tom replied, "Then, Sir, you must borrow it."

Garrick and all of London's theatergoers expected much of the twenty-four-year-old playwright when by June 1776 his accession of the Drury Lane patent was assured. Linley would be in charge of the music; Thomas Sheridan (after three years reconciled temporarily with his son and daughter-in-law) would manage the actors; Dick would keep the books and–everyone expected–write plays for his new company. Until late in the winter, however, the public must have thought that having Sheridan was small compensation for the loss of Garrick, its favorite actor. First, there was an actors' strike in which a dominant pro-Sheridan faction chaffed against Willoughby Lacy's attempts to interfere with Sheridan's management. (Thomas Sheridan had refused his son's terms and fled to Ireland; he would return as acting manager in 1778-1779 and 1779-1780, but during his fretful management profits dropped four thousand pounds from 1777-1778 and another three thousand the second year.) Next, there was no new play from Sheridan. Only one new tragedy and seven new short pieces by other hands appeared.

But Sheridan was busy, and indeed all the principal changes to the Drury Lane repertoire sprang from his creative activity. He directed Congreve's *Old Batchelor* (1693) and *Love for Love* (1695), advertising them "with alterations," even if the scripts were only purged of bawdry and suggestion. He took Garrick's popular *A Christmas Tale* and cut it for afterpiece format, garnering thirty-two performances. He refurbished the popular pantomime *Harlequin's Invasion* and earned twenty-seven presentations. He redirected *The Rivals* with a Drury Lane cast. By the time the 187 nights of the 1776-1777 season expired, 84 had featured something directly or indirectly from Sheridan's pen; and since as the principal acting manager (or artistic director) he helped to shape every new prelude, mainpiece, afterpiece, and every redirected or refurbished piece, fully 179 of the 187 nights featured some product of his creative talents.

In offering two Congreve revivals, Sheridan attempted what he would laugh at in *The Critic* as a "bungling reformation." Congreve was a greatly respected if no longer produced literary playwright, and Drury Lane was the home of "high comedy." Audiences perceived Covent Garden as the home of "low comedy." The distinctions were nice even in 1775, but (generally) low comedy portrayed old-fashioned "humours" characters and encompassed more farcical and possibly more sexually suggestive situations, whereas high comedy signified the witty, elegant, satiric, and even genteel. Sheridan of Covent Garden correctly gauged the company's talents with *The Rivals* and *The Duenna;* Sheridan of Drury Lane sputtered in his attempts to exploit his actors' best skills with revisions of literary giants like Congreve and Vanbrugh.

The first major step after Congreve was an adaptation of Sir John Vanbrugh's *The Relapse* (1696). Appearing on 24 February 1777, *A Trip to Scarborough,* Sheridan's version, shows both how greatly theatrical tastes had changed in the eighty years since Vanbrugh's comedy had appeared and how skillful Sheridan could be as a crafter of plots. Tom Moore thought Vanbrugh's original to be "luminous" only from "putrescence": to remove the "immoral" "taint" of *The Relapse* is "to extinguish" its "light." Portrayals of heterosexual libertinism and homosexual lust would offend Georgian audiences. But if Sheridan excised these, he also recrafted the plot to stand alone, divorced from its reliance upon the comedy to which Vanbrugh pretended his play to be a sequel, Colley Cibber's *Love's Last Shift* (1696); and he gave to the story an internal coherence lacking in the original. In Sheridan's version there are both probable and necessary connections among the characters of Vanbrugh's two plots, even if those connections are somewhat thin. Still, the new unified setting in a fashionable watering place remains unexploited, and the opportunity to flesh out the milieu, so brilliantly handled with servants in the Bath of *The Rivals,* passes without notice. Moore doubted that Vanbrugh's subject, even in Sheridan's hands, could "bear a second crop of wit"; and Sheridan did not sow the field he had weeded. Indeed, he did not even cast the adaptation well, for as the mildly saucy Berinthia he put forward Mrs. Mary Ann Yates, a tragic actress who was hissed off the stage at one point, prompting a noble friend from the boxes and Sheridan himself from the wings to implore her to retake the scene.

If Sheridan "spoiled" Vanbrugh's comedy (as one contemporary reported him to confess), the reason for paying less than full attention to the project became public ten weeks later, on 8 May 1777, when appeared *The School for Scandal,* the best-playing comedy of manners in the English language.

Three strands of action intertwine to make

Lady Sneerwell & Spatter

Lady Sne.— The Paragraphs you say were all inserted—

Spat. They were ma'am—

Mrs S. Did you circulate the Report — of Lady Brittle's Intrigue — with Captn Boastall—

Spat.— Madam by this Lady Brittle is the talk of half the Town — & in a week — will be toasted as a demirep—

Mrs Sneerwell. What have you done as to the innuendo — of Miss Nicely's Fondness for her own Footman—

Spatter. 'Tis in a fine train ma'am — I told it to my hair-Dresser — he courts a milliner's [illegible] in Pall-mall whose mistress has a first Cousin — who was in waiting — to Lady Clackit — I think in about fourteen hours — it must reach Lady Clackit — & then you know the Business is done—

Mrs S.— But is that sufficient do you think?

Spatter O Lud Ma'am — I'll undertake to ruin the Character of the primmest Prude in London with half as much — Ha! ha! did you never hear how poor — Miss — Wortley — lost her Lover & her character — last summer at Scarborough — this was the whole — of it — one Evening at Lady Ponyang's the conversation happen'd to turn on — the Difficulty — of breeding Nova Scotia Sheep in England — I have known instances [illegible] — says Miss Lowder —

First page of "The Slanderers" (above), one of Sheridan's early drafts for part of The School for Scandal, *and the corresponding page in the Frampton Court manuscript (right), the earliest surviving complete draft (by permission of the Princeton University Library)*

13 1.

Act 1st – Scene 1st –

– Lady – Sneerwells House –

— Lady – Sneerwell at her dressing Table with Lappet – ~~Miss~~ Verjuice drinking Chocolate –

Lady Sneerwell. The Paragraphs you say were all inserted?

Verj. – – – They were Madam – and as I copied them myself in a feign'd Hand there can be no suspicion whence they came. –

Lady Sneer. Did you circulate the Report of Lady Brittle's Intrigue with Captain Boastall?

Verj. Madam by this Time Lady Brittle is the Talk of half the Town – and I doubt not but in a Week the Men will toast her as a Demirep.

Lady Sn. What have you done as to the insinuation of a certain Baronet's Lady & a certain Cook.

Verj. – ~~That~~ is in as fine a Train as your Ladyship could wish. – I told the story yesterday to my own maid with directions to communicate it im=mediately to my Hair-dresser He I am informed has a Brother who courts a Milliner's Prentice in Pallmall whose mistress has a first cousin whose sister is Feme de Chambre to ~~Lady~~ Mrs Clackit – so that in the common course of Things it must reach ~~Lady~~ Mrs Clackit's Ears within four & twenty Hours & then you know the Business is as good as done

Robert Baddeley as Moses in the first production of The School for Scandal *(portrait by Johann Zoffany; Lady Lever Collection)*

Act 4, scene 3, of The School for Scandal: *Thomas King as Sir Peter Teazle, Frances Abington as Lady Teazle, William Smith as Charles Surface, and John Palmer as Joseph Surface in the original production (painting by James Roberts; by permission of the Garrick Club)*

the plot of *The School for Scandal.* One might be called punitive comedy of exposure, the process by which the villainous Lady Sneerwell and her scandalmongering friends and the hypocritical Joseph Surface are revealed to testy old Sir Peter Teazle, honest Sir Oliver Surface, bluff steward-manager Rowley, and lively, naive, fashion-seeking Lady Teazle as the malicious manipulators that they have been. The strand most problematic is a comedy of self-adjustment, in which the old bachelor Sir Peter and the country-bred Lady Teazle learn how to respect one another; many critics believe that their rapprochement is only a product of self-interest, but evidence in the text and what we know about the original performances suggest mutual affection to be the means of resolution. The third strand, a comedy of merit rewarded, shows how mildly libertine Charles Surface reveals himself as valuing openness, honesty, and family affection above his spendthrift habits, thereby meriting the continued support of his returning "nabob" uncle Sir Oliver and the hand of the sober, virtuous Maria, Sir Peter's orphaned ward.

If the broad, rollicking humor and sweet, touching music of *The Duenna* eighteen months before had brought all London's attention to the home of "low comedy," the witty repartee of fashionable society, the Cain-and-Abel motif, and the delightful recitation of the May-and-December theme in *The School for Scandal* now brought the town's acclamation to the house of high comedy. Sheridan had been more than customarily tardy in completing the comedy, and long-held tradition reports that the play was actually in rehearsal days before a complete final draft was in the hands of William Hopkins, prompter at Drury Lane and hence responsible for copying out parts for the actors. Sheridan scrawled out at the end of the manuscript:

> —finis—
> Thank God!
> R B S—

Then he added, again in his own hand,

> Amen!
> W. Hopkins

But even so late in the season (indeed, the actors' benefits had concluded), the play engendered wildly enthusiastic support. Passing by the outer walls of Drury Lane just as the famous screen fell and the audience exploded in laughter and applause, a journalist of the day claimed to have run for his life in fear that the building was collapsing. Twenty performances came before Drury Lane closed for the year, and in the next season forty-five were offered for a total of sixty-five in its first full year–short of *The Duenna*'s seventy-five in its first season, but grossing thirty percent more in 1777-1778 than the average evening of Sheridan's first season as manager. Intellectual observers began calling Sheridan "the modern Congreve," a sobriquet which stuck with some and which led several generations of critics beginning a century later to assess the achievement of the play not in the context of Sheridan's time but in the context of the Restoration–rather like looking exclusively at Purcell to understand Mozart, or Lely to understand Reynolds, or *Gorbuduc, Richard III.*

We have the evidence of Sheridan's "bungling reformation" of Congreve and Vanbrugh to guide our search for literary forbears, but we find in his works few if any verbal correspondences or convincing structural similarities to Restoration comedy. Further, Sheridan never wrote (or was quoted) about his literary debts. Yet, he was a conscious artist who, despite his oft-repeated claim that he never sat through the whole performance of any play, his own included, left us evidence especially in the cases of *The Critic* and *The School for Scandal* that he worked and reworked his own materials. These early materials themselves reflect literary and theatrical debts of a general nature and demonstrate not anxiety of influence but pride of craftsmanship. In the plays, as in the early jottings which were incorporated, reside situations and conventions of comedy from all times.

Schoolboy notebooks containing sketches of scenes which were shaped into the final version of *The School for Scandal* survive to this day. (Tom Moore printed generous portions in 1825, Cecil Price these and others in 1973.) In "The Slanderers" and "The Teazles" (as the two most developed portions have been called) Sheridan outlined characters and exchanges of a score or more lines which, reworked, became Joseph and Charles and Lady Sneerwell and the meetings of the Scandalous College and Sir Peter and Lady Teazle's "daily jangles." Probably composed in Sheridan's Bath years (before August 1772), the sketches are as unlike the final as "the block to the statue, or the grub to the butterfly," to quote Moore about one characterization. But in these sketches is the cynicism of the Restoration and the convolution of Jonson and Fletcher as well as a generous imagination and a faltering but occasionally firm comic touch. When

John Philip Kemble as Rolla in the first production of Pizarro

he came to amalgamate the sketches into *The School for Scandal,* Sheridan sacrificed coarseness, uncertainty, melodrama, cynicism, and diffuseness to satiric focus, wit, and sure-handed portrayal of good nature.

For the first time in his play writing career, Sheridan focused his satire on palpable social institutions as well as general human frailties. Witty abuse of those present or absent has characterized comedy of all eras and reached brilliance in the Restoration, but the Georgian period joined the love of gossip and ridicule to print publication. Journalism, whose birth many place in 1702 with the commencement of the first daily newspaper in England, was now in its adolescence and like a mischievous teenager had discovered the public's voracious appetite for scandalmongering. "The Paragraphs you say, Mr. Snake, were all inserted?" asks Lady Sneerwell in the first line of the play. In the 1760s and 1770s, unsubstantiated rumors and malicious surmise occupied the columns of British journals in the form of brief paragraphs, the names of the individuals masquerading with first and last initials interspersed by asterisks or dashes; the younger "Mr. S******n," "Miss L****y," and "Captain M*****s" had thus appeared in Bath newspapers during the eventful courtship. One monthly featured a particularly vicious column in which facing silhouette portraits of a man and a woman preceded a description of their presumed relationship identified by pseudonyms or initials. Mrs. Clackit, says Snake, has caused more than one "Tête-àTête in the Town and Country Magazine–when the Parties perhaps have never seen each other's Faces before in the course of their Lives." Sheridan's was not the first satiric attack on these practices; references to "paragraphs" form large and small parts of a half dozen Georgian comedies before *The School for Scandal,* and scurrilous journalists like Snake appear in several, most particularly Colman's Spatter in *The English Merchant* (1767), who bears the same name as Sheridan's early version of Snake in "The Slanderers."

Sheridan's originality was to dramatize the agents of scandal and slander more vividly than any purely decorative comic wits or would-be wits had been represented since the time of Congreve. Sir Benjamin Backbite, "the prince of pink heels" in his first portrayal, Mr. Crabtree, and Mrs. Candour appear only together and only in three scenes; but these appearances provide the badinage upon which much of Sheridan's play writing reputation for wit is based. What is curious about their roles as the principal agents of the comedy's satire is the process through which the audience is put by them. Lady Teazle's head (if not her heart) is turned by her misunderstanding of the social fashion of London. Like her, the audience is attracted to the quick-paced malice of the Scandal School on its first appearance, to the inventiveness of sneer, the imputation of weakness, and the innuendo of sexual frailty. When the Scandalous College meets a second time and Lady Teazle participates so gaily and maliciously, the audience may not note how her wit exceeds theirs or how Sir Peter's sly ripostes provide increasing distance and hence some objectivity. But by their third and last appearance–at Sir Peter's house following the fall of the screen–they have become more the objects than the agents of satire. Possessed of misinformation and inclined (like Fag in *The Rivals*) to fabricating elaborately circumstantial accounts rather than presenting simple forged bills, the Scandalous College now appears ridiculous in itself and a principal cause of the misunderstandings among people for whom we have come to care. The audience undergoes the same process of learning by which Lady Teazle is changed: attraction to fashionable vice, doubt, and finally enlightened, experiential rejection. Maria's wish to be granted a "double Portion of Dullness" rather than participate in slander, and Sir Peter's sarcastic cautions about Lady Teazle's "charming set of acquaintance" cannot effect the profound change in attitude toward gossip and malice that the slanderers themselves bring about.

This delicate dramatic problem challenged the young playwright even more than the eternal May-and-December story of Sir Peter and Lady Teazle. In the early version he toyed with a harsh cuckolding story like Chaucer's "Miller's Tale" and Wycherley's *Country Wife* (1675), but in the final version he sought and achieved the amiable tone of Georgian comedy. Lady Teazle learns to trust her heart, not the fashion, and Sir Peter learns to be less the father and more the husband of his young bride. To effect their mutual adjustments they must suffer considerable embarrassment, it is true, but they are no Pinchwife and Margery. As late as 1804, when he read the role of Sir Peter to an actor taking over from Thomas King, Sheridan still rejected a picture of Sir Peter as an "old fretful dotard" to be harshly chastened.

The greatest dramatic challenge, however, lay in handling the Cain-and-Abel story. Here there were three problems: how to make Joseph Surface evil but still entertaining; how to make Charles Surface culpable yet charming, essentially virtuous but not dull; and how to maximize satisfaction in the long-expected and desired reversal of fortune. Two of these problems Henry Fielding faced and overcame in *Tom Jones* (1749), the eighteenth century's greatest story of sibling rivalry. But Fielding did not face in his novel the dramatist's difficulty of portraying evil palpably before an audience without slipping into melodrama. (It is useful to know that Fielding's unperformed stage comedy on a similar theme, *The Fathers*, may have been in Sheridan's hands before the appearance of *The School for Scandal.* Sheridan would produce the play at Drury Lane on 30 November 1778, and his autograph corrections may be found in the manuscript sent to the lord chamberlain for licensing before its performance.)

Sheridan solved the first problem with the same techniques he had used in *The Rivals* and *St. Patrick's Day:* he chose a verbal characterizing device, in this case the "sentiment," not only to make Joseph entertaining but to expose him simultaneously. When Joseph utters such epigrams as "to smile at the jest which plants a Thorn in another's Breast is to become a principal in the Mischief," he expresses what he never practices and calls into doubt the motives of others who speak such "scraps of morality" and pretend to such elevation of thought and feeling. Thus, he too becomes object as well as agent of attack. And his "sentiments" join with false logic, and the dramatic soliloquy (allowed to no other character in the comedy but Sir Peter) amplifies the falseness of sentiment to maximize the contrast between Joseph's surface appearance and his real motives. Joseph becomes a comic Iago; and, like the other comic villains Mosca, Volpone, and Tartuffe, because he is complex and intelligent he is curiously attractive, even though his eventual downfall brings long-awaited pleasure.

The second problem–making Charles attractive yet mildly culpable–Sheridan solved in two ways: by keeping Charles off the stage for the first half of the representation and by characterizing him quickly and deftly, if flatly, by means of the

"Pizarro Contemplating over the Product of His New Peruvian Mine," caricature of Sheridan by James Gilray, 4 June 1799. By drawing an analogy between the playwright and the title character in his new, highly successful play, Gilray was not only commenting on Sheridan's reaction to the proceeds from it but also suggesting that his political attitudes were more like Pizarro's than those of the play's patriotic Peruvian general, Rolla.

very virtues constantly opposed to the vices of the schemers and of the Scandal School. For two-and-a-half acts we see Joseph, the calumniator, and Sir Peter, Joseph's dupe, brand Charles as spendthrift and prodigal, and though we mistrust Joseph's reports and discount Sir Peter's blind acceptance, we cannot make the final judgment ourselves. In this choice to keep Charles offstage lay peril lest he seem helpless or deserving of blame when he finally did appear. (Contrast Goldsmith's portrayal of Honeywood in *The Good-Natured Man* [1768] to see mismanagement of a somewhat similar dramatic problem.) When Charles does take the stage, in the eighth and ninth scenes of this fourteen-scene comedy, he immediately establishes himself as a hearty, vital, honest, plain-dealing young fellow, one who likes his wine but does not get drunk or abusive, one who gambles with money (offstage) but not with others' reputations, one who would sell the family silver and portraits but not the image of his benefactor. If sentimentality is a failure of feeling, then the lines in which Charles bluffly refuses to sell "that ill looking little fellow over the settee" because "hang it, I'll not part with poor Noll–The Old Fellow has been very good to me, and Egad I'll keep his Picture, while I've a Room to put it in" show that feeling supersedes rationality. Yet, they provide one means of maximizing the contrasts of dissimulation, prudential hypocrisy, avarice, and casuistry with plain dealing, honesty, familial affection, generous benevolence, and gratitude. Joseph is one pole, Lady Teazle through her affectation of fashion an intermediate latitude, and Charles is the other and true pole, the lodestar. Like Tom Jones he has faults; but unlike Tom's his are not sexual. Like Tom and Blifil, Charles and Joseph work two sides of a sentimental street.

And through this contrast, Sheridan solved his third dramatic problem: how to maximize pleasure in the inevitable comic reversal of fortune. By keeping the terms of his equation focused solely upon truth in conduct and generosity of spirit he kept from view the unknowns of self-deceit and sexual promiscuity. By bringing together both recognition and reversal at one place, the screen scene, four-fifths of the way through his play, he found a comic solution discovered as elegantly only by Molière in *Tartuffe* (1664) and Oscar Wilde in *The Importance of Being Earnest* (1895).

Dramatically, the two most important things about the long third scene of the fourth act of *The School for Scandal* are its placement within the three strands of plot and its joining of the reversal of fortunes with the revelation of essential character. In the plot, this "screen scene" comes early, though it clearly anticipates the working out of the comedy of self-adjustment (most of which occurs offstage) and the comedy of merit rewarded (much of which involves only five or six lines of affirmation) while foreshadowing the final scenes of the punitive comedy of exposure in the twelfth and fourteenth segments. As drama, the screen scene reflects three separate movements: Joseph's casuistry and Lady Teazle's temptation; Sir Peter's further duping by Joseph; and Charles's insistence upon open and honest disclosure of the truth, even to the "little milliner" supposedly behind the screen. When Charles's desire for openness and plain dealing leads to the exposure of Lady Teazle and hence of Joseph, all dramatic questions have been answered. The audience knows that Sir Oliver will be confirmed in his assessment of both nephews; that Charles will probably be rewarded with Maria; that Sir Peter will become comfortable with his decision to permit his young wife a separate maintenance (that is, an allowance, not a divorce); and that Joseph's scandalmongering friends will lose their capacity to do damage to the relationships of the Teazle and Surface families. Sheridan keeps the story going with three or four minireversals; but all significant terms of the equation have been identified, and the rest is mere ciphering.

Few disputed the artistry of *The School for Scandal* in its time. It has been presented on stage to paying audiences every year since its premiere. Henry James and George Bernard Shaw, a century after its first appearance, found fault with its sentimentality. Henry Fielding's is the greater and more serious exploration of one aspect of the comedy's subject, and one cannot dispute the essentially uncomplicated view of human nature and human relationships presented by *The School for Scandal.* But a century after James and Shaw, critics have rediscovered Sheridan's greatest play and found it worthy of serious attention.

With *The School for Scandal* Sheridan answered the expectations many had for his management of Drury Lane after Garrick. There were detractors, including his irascible and intemperate father, Thomas Sheridan, who remarked: "Talk about the merit of Dick's comedy, there's nothing to it. He had but to dip in his own heart and find there the characters both of Joseph and Charles." But most welcomed Sheridan's greatest comedy and hoped for more. In the 1777-1778 season there was nothing except Thomas Sheridan's inept direction. In the 1778-1779 season came two minor pieces: an entertainment called *The Camp* (15 October 1778) and the dramatic *Verses to the Memory of Garrick* (11 March 1779). *The Camp* exploited fears of a French invasion consequent upon that nation's recognizing the American rebels as the legitimate government of England's North American colonies. Home guards had mobilized, fashionable ladies joined them in their safe camps, and stories could be told. David Garrick had discovered one Philip De Loutherbourg, a scene painter and stage designer of great talent, and Sheridan used that talent to popular effect, particularly in this pastiche on military mobilization. Four months later Sheridan rose to the unhappy occasion offered by David Garrick's death at sixty-one to produce at Drury Lane *Verses to the Memory of Garrick,* an elegy performed by the tragic actress, Mrs. Yates. Sheridan himself headed Garrick's bier as the chief mourner.

A pastiche and a monody might carry one season during which Sheridan wrestled to gain full control of Drury Lane. But something more substantial must answer the expectations of the London audiences. Hence, *The Critic* (30 October 1779), a long afterpiece first performed following a representation of *Hamlet* and destined to replace *The Rehearsal* in the repertoire.

The Critic has no plot. Instead, it blends a variety of briefly drawn situations to burlesque the theater, theatrical literature, and the audience itself. In the first act, theatrical hangers-on Mr. and Mrs. Dangle discuss news of the Theatres Royal, receive critic Sneer, thin-skinned author Sir Fretful Plagiary (played as a caricature of Georgian dramatist Richard Cumberland in the original performances), a troupe of Italian singers for audition, and Mr. Puff, author of "The Spanish Armada," a tragedy then supposed to be in rehearsal. This first act, set in the Dangles' lodgings, recalls the opening scenes of *The School for Scandal* and *Love for Love* as a mannered presentation of interesting characters who, in Sheridan's and Congreve's comedies, would become involved in increasingly complicated situations to be unraveled only by a startling and satisfactory denouement. But the flavor of this appetizer bears little relationship to the main course of the farce, acts two and three, in which Mr. Dangle and Mr. Sneer observe a rehearsal of Puff's play, comment upon it sardonically, and serve only to direct the audience's attention to the most egregious of its absurdities. (Why Puff is the author of "The Spanish Armada" rather than Sir Fretful Plagiary, presented so brilliantly in the first act and then excused, cannot be satisfactorily explained. But Puff's original portrayer, Thomas King, had in real life presented a grand entertainment on the same topic during the preceding summer of 1779 at Sadler's Wells, where he was the manager-impresario.)

Theatrical self-reflection–drama which calls attention to itself as drama–intrigued Sheridan. Five years or so before *The Rivals* he and school friend Nathaniel Brassey Halhed had projected a farce on the Amphitryon myth using a rehearsal format, and among Sheridan's papers Moore found and reprinted numerous scenes and sketches about the theater and theatrical craftsmanship. Georgian audiences, too, evidently relished this inversion of dramatic convention, given the record of plays about the theater in the repertoire. Four entertainments and burlesques from the 1770s probably influenced Sheridan's final design, most particularly Garrick's *A Peep behind the Curtain* (1767). But his design surpassed all other examples in the repertoire, including Buckingham's perennially popular (and constantly updated) *The Rehearsal* (1671), and two centuries passed before *The Critic* itself would be replaced as the quintessential play about the theater by the comedies of Tom Stoppard.

That *The Critic* endured so long surprises in light of its topicality, for it is every bit as timely as *The Camp*. On 18 June 1779 Spain declared war with England; by 16 August 1779 reports circulated that French and Spanish fleets had slipped by a British squadron into the Channel. Newspapers reprinted Queen Elizabeth's 1588 speech to the army at Tilbury Fort as fears of a new Spanish armada mounted. If invasion anxiety lessened as autumn approached, the memory was still fresh in late October.

Moreover, Sheridan tied *The Critic* to numerous other local phenomena. The manager who "writes himself" is Sheridan, of course, and Mrs. Dangle resembles Eliza Sheridan, who was probably aiding her husband in the management of the King's Opera house, which Dick and Covent Garden manager Thomas Harris had recently acquired. The actors took occasion to mimic their peers: Dangle was recognized as Thomas Vaughan, author of a Sheridan-directed farce, theatrical amateur, and "dangler" about the green room; Miss Pope's rendition of Tilburina took off Mrs. Ann Crawford's tragic acting; and young Bannister as Don Ferolo Whiskerandos mimicked William Smith in the role of Richard III. Sheridan had gained a reputation for writing "puffs" for Drury Lane, and Puff's "puff direct" may be a "puff preliminary" for Elizabeth Griffith's *The Times*, a comedy then in rehearsal. And everyone recognized in William Parsons's portrayal of Sir Fretful Plagiary a caricature of the sentimental dramatist, Richard Cumberland, whose tragedy *The Battle of Hastings* Sheridan had produced 24 January 1778.

A favorite but probably apocryphal story places Cumberland with his children at a performance of *The Critic*. As the audience laughs at Sir Fretful, so do the younger Cumberlands. "Keep still, you little dunces, there is nothing to laugh at!" says the father, pinching them soundly. Hearing a report of Cumberland's response, Sheridan remarked that he could not understand why Cumberland would not laugh at his comedy: after all, said Sheridan, I laughed a great deal at his tragedy.

But if *The Critic* is time bound because of its local and domestic references, its art arises from its timelessness. Unlike its predecessors, *The Critic* burlesques not specific examples of theatrical literature but serious drama in general. Few if any lines in "The Spanish Armada" echo stage tragedies of the Georgian period. Instead, Sheridan focuses on ineptitude in dramatic craftsmanship divorced from any time or place. And not content merely to attack poor plotting, characterization, and dialogue, Sheridan includes inception, production, and reception as well as theatrical literature. This comprehensiveness is why the first act, so different in tone and focus, is an integral part of the farce. It is why Dangle is the amateur of dubious influence, unsure tastes, and uncertain loyalties; why Sneer is the cynical, self-interested critic; why Sir Fretful every thin-skinned playwright and Puff every spectacle monger.

One key to the informing principle of *The Critic*, to burlesque the theater in all aspects, is to be found in its grand finale, full of "magnificence!

Hester Ogle Sheridan with her son, Charles Brinsley Sheridan (engraving based on a painting by John Hoppner)

battle! noise! and procession!" The presentation of the defeat of the Spanish Armada by the English fleet, chorused by the patriotic song "Britons Strike Home" and the procession of *"all the English rivers and their tributaries,"* evoked surprised delight. And early critics lavishly praised De Loutherbourg's scenes and effects for their realism, not their mockery of theatrical effect. Thus the audience, with its appetite for spectacle, becomes the unspoken object of satire, satisfied with noise, battle, and claptrap. What better conclusion to five years of building a theatrical career dependent upon the fickle tastes of theatergoers?

When *The Critic* appeared on 30 October 1779 Sheridan was just twenty-eight years old. It would be his last comedy and his last important dramatic work. On 12 September 1780 he was elected Member of Parliament for Stafford. Horace Walpole remarked in October 1781 that "Sheridan has the opera and all the nation to regulate, and some plays to write." He would be a legislator for thirty-two years, representing Stafford and other constituencies, until in 1812 when Stafford at last turned him out of Parliament. Sheridan, M.P., was the Sheridan of his own devising, his own ambition. He returned once to dramatic literature with an adaptation of the translation of a translation–August von Kotzebue's *Die Spanier in Peru* (1796), based on Jean-François Marmontel's *Les Incas* (1777)–for *Pizarro, a Tragedy* (1799). The major interest of *Pizarro* is not literary but theatrical and political–and it was a crowd-pleasing, money-generating success. John Loftis (1977) has written convincingly about the oratorical extravaganza.

Throughout his busy career as politician and his distracted management of Drury Lane, Sheridan was constantly projecting a new play, particu-

A contemporary engraving of the fire that destroyed Sheridan's Drury Lane theater

Samuel Whitbread, who rebuilt the Drury Lane theater and bought out the Sheridan family's interest, set out to convince potential investors not to associate his enterprise with the Sheridans'. Charles Williams's 1811 caricature shows Sheridan in a wheelbarrow of rubbish pushed by Whitbread, whose assistant follows with the playwright's son Thomas.

larly when money was tight. Fragments and titles survive–"Affectation," "The Statesman." There is a grand entertainment or two like *The Camp,* one from 1794, two years after the death of Elizabeth on 28 June 1792 and shortly before his marriage to Hester Jane Ogle on 27 April 1795. Michael Kelly, a talented musician in Sheridan's employ at Drury Lane, who for thirty-five years maintained his friendship, tells of the king and queen chatting with Sheridan after a performance of *The School for Scandal,* probably sometime in the late 1780s or early 1790s. King George praised the comedy but professed greater affection for *The Rivals.* The queen asked when they could expect another comic work from Sheridan's pen, to which he replied that he "expected very shortly to finish" one. Kelly took occasion later to rehearse the conversation; you will not write another comedy because you are afraid. Afraid of whom? asked Sheridan. "You are afraid of the author of the 'School for Scandal,' " said the musician.

During the last four decades of his life, Sheridan was no further from the theater than his literary friends were from their publishers and his aristocratic friends were from their landed estates. Drury Lane was, after all, *his* estate. It provided him with income and with capital upon which to borrow. It was a great investment of which nearly every financier wanted a piece, until Sheridan's inability to manage it made clear how very overextended was the investment. Still, Drury Lane permitted Sheridan to buy several expensive elections, according to the practices of his day, and it provided him the capital (twelve thousand pounds) to purchase Polesden Lacey, a 341-acre estate with a seventeenth-century mansion, after his marriage to Hester in 1795, thus bringing into his life the "dirty acres" his chronically poor parents had never enjoyed. Polesden was settled upon his and "Hecca's" child, Charles Brinsley, born 14 January 1796, and although Sheridan died a man beset by bailiffs, he always had the small profits of Polesden to supplement his other schemes.

Many stories are told about the later years–his sexual adventures, his excessive drinking, his financial profligacy. Each tendency was clear even in his younger days. Eliza complained to her closest confidants of Dick's philandering and probably took the only revenge in her power by having an affair with Lord Edward Fitzgerald a year or two before her death. Sheridan's complicated financial transactions rode an erratic course from the heights of extravagance to the valleys of penury. And though stories of Sheridan's drunkenness multiplied as he aged, his behavior was not uncharacteristic of his age. But, always, even in his later years, we hear of a Sheridan who was charming and witty, who at forty-three with a red nose and ravaged countenance could still win the hand of the young daughter of the Dean of Winchester, become in their mutual baby talk her "poor Dan," and enjoy a second twenty-year marriage. It is a Sheridan who brushes off his creditors with humor. Hazlitt reports on one contrivance: a dun brings him a bill, often presented before, and complains of its soiled and tattered condition. "I tell you what I'd advise you to do, my friend," said Sheridan. "Take it home and write it on parchment." In another story an agent demands interest for a long overdue bill. Sheridan responds, "My dear sir, you know it is not my *interest* to pay the *principal;* nor is it my *principle* to pay the *interest.*"

It is Sheridan the Member of Parliament about whom most stories are told. The famous "Begum Speech," his exhaustive and exhausting attack upon Warren Hastings, administrator of the British East India Company (1787), excited his contemporaries. In that two-day speech, Sheridan, M.P., praised historian Edward Gibbon, then recanted later–"Did I say 'luminous'? I meant 'voluminous.' " On another occasion Sheridan, M.P., said on the floor about a fellow that "the gentleman owes his facts to his imagination and his jests to his commonplace book." Sheridan, M.P., told Charles James Fox that while it was good to take the bull of opportunity by the horns, "you need not have drove him into the room" first. Sheridan, M.P., extemporaneously put Lord Belgrave to rights on an exact quotation of Demosthenes, but there is reason to think that he imitated the sounds of Greek without the substance, thereby silencing every member who could not understand the language–that is, the whole house. Sheridan, M.P., it was who on the night of 24 February 1809 sat in the Piazza Coffee House watching the Drury Lane theater burn to the ground and remarked to a meddling interlocutor, "A man may surely take a glass of wine by his own fireside."

And while Sheridan, M.P., Under-Secretary of State (1782), Secretary of the Treasury (1783), Navy Treasurer (1806) in the "Ministry of All Talents," lover of Lady Duncannon and others of the most beautiful women of his day, and doting father to his elder son, Tom, and his young son, Charles, may seem a queer candidate for elevation to the peerage of great writers, his production as a young man of the theater beggars comparison with any of his contemporaries and with most of his successors. Byron put it well:

> Whatever Sheridan has done or chosen to do has been, *par excellence,* always the *best* of its kind. He has written the *best* comedy *(School for Scandal)*[,] the *best* drama [*The Duenna*] (in my mind, far before that St. Giles's lampoon, the Beggar's Opera), the best farce (the *Critic*–it is only too good for a farce), and the best Address (Monologue on Garrick), and, to crown it all, delivered the very best Oration (the famous Begum Speech) ever conceived or heard in this country.

Byron wrote these words in his journal only three years before Sheridan died in London on 7 July 1816 in the sixty-fifth year of his life. Sheridan expired in poverty, according to many accounts with bailiffs around him to protect their clients' interests should some money or goods be sent to succor the fading playwright-politician. Six days after his death his remains were interred at Westminster Abbey, in the Poets' Corner, the bier followed by numerous noble acquaintances and friends including two princes of the blood royal. Byron's appreciation of Sheridan's contribution to English cultural history was shared by most of their contemporaries.

But Byron could not have our perspective, which rates Sheridan as the finest British playwright between Shakespeare and Shaw. Sheridan eschewed the didactic, the melodramatic, the coldly cynical, and the violently satiric, choosing instead the middle, good-natured course of his time. He strove for original characterization, tight construction, and brilliant dialogue. He never achieved the poetic unity or intellectual penetration of Congreve, but he never sought them. He boosted the fresh boisterousness of Farquhar and avoided the cold cynicism of Vanbrugh, the tears of Steele in his decline, and the coincidences of Goldsmith.

Always Sheridan's subject matter reflected his own experience: young love, the battle of youth with age, the natural conflicts of the sexes, and (after he became a member of it) high society. In the five brief years of his active involvement as playwright he seems to have mellowed a bit as he moved from low comedy to high. But he always found self-deception to be central to the human condition.

Sheridan's plots are often so complex that readers find them hard to follow, but they work wonderfully in the theater. In that five-year burst of comic creativity Sheridan eschewed the bifurcated plot forms of his contemporaries, avoided simple coincidence, put aside duels and elopements as resolution devices, and chose instead (in *The School for Scandal*) the full unification of plot lines that point toward a single comic catastrophe in which recognition and reversal are one. Character for its own sake–as in *The Rivals* and *The Duenna*–yields to character for the drama's sake in *The School for Scandal.*

Yet Sheridan was a sentimentalist. Beneath all his comic excoriations of folly there flows a tolerance of a human nature which he believes, finally, will support social good rather than individual self-interest. Well-intentioned folks, aided by a benevolent providence, will expel the vicious from society.

Sheridan's characters are complicated psychologically only in *The School for Scandal.* Before that play, and sometimes in that play, he created stage types whose characteristics we can all recognize as part of the theatrical context rather than as natural human beings. And his dialogue for these characters represents his greatest achievement. On the one hand it marked each person as unique: it was "characteristic," to cite his contemporaries' praise. On the other it was complex and original–not just epigrammatic like Congreve but brilliantly different–witness Malaprop, Acres, Joseph Surface. We remember these characters more than the comedies in which they appear.

Sheridan's comic theatrical achievement everywhere relies upon the technique of drawing the audience in as a part of the unfolding presentation. As auditors we do not sit upon the sidelines; instead we are privileged to know much more than the players and the cheerleaders. We understand the "comedy of situation" of which we have been partners. We revel in the "how" of reaching agreement more than the "what" of the action. We pride ourselves upon the knowledge that resolution will occur because of what we know.

William Hazlitt understood Sheridan's achievement well: "Whatever he touched he adorned with all the ease, grace, and brilliancy of his style. . . . He was assuredly a man of first-rate talents."

Letters:

The Letters of Richard Brinsley Sheridan, 3 volumes, edited by C. J. L. Price (Oxford: Clarendon Press, 1966).

Bibliography:

Jack D. Durant, *Richard Brinsley Sheridan: A Reference Guide* (Boston: G. K. Hall, 1981).

Biographies:

Thomas Moore, *Memoirs of the Life of the Right Honourable Richard Brinsley Sheridan* (London: Longman, Hurst, Rees, Orme, Brown & Green, 1825);

W. Fraser Rae, *Sheridan, A Biography* (London: Richard Bentley, 1896);

Walter Sichel, *Sheridan* (London: Constable, 1909);

R. Crompton Rhodes, *Harlequin Sheridan* (Oxford: Blackwell, 1933);

Stanley Ayling, *A Portrait of Sheridan* (London: Constable, 1985);

James Morwood, *The Life and Works of Richard Brinsley Sheridan* (Edinburgh: Scottish Academic Press, 1985).

References:

Mark S. Auburn, "The Pleasures of Sheridan's *The Rivals*: A Critical Study in the Light of Stage History," *Modern Philology,* 72 (February 1975): 256-271;

Auburn, *Sheridan's Comedies: Their Contexts and Achievements* (Lincoln: University of Nebraska Press, 1977);

F. W. Bateson, "The Application of Thought to an Eighteenth-Century Text: *The School for Scandal,*" in *Evidence in Literary Scholarship. Essays in Memory of James Marshall Osborn,* edited by René Wellek and Alvaro Ribeiro (Oxford: Clarendon Press, 1979), pp. 321-335;

Peter Davidson, ed., *Sheridan: Comedies* (London: Macmillan, 1986);

Christian Deelman, "The Original Cast of *The School for Scandal,*" *Review of English Studies,* new series 13 (1962): 257-266;

Joseph W. Donohue, Jr., "Sheridan's *Pizarro:* Natural Religion and the Artificial Hero," in his *Dramatic Character in the English Romantic Age* (Princeton: Princeton University Press, 1970), pp. 125-156;

Jean Dulck, *Les Comédies de R. B. Sheridan: Étude Littéraire* (Paris: Didier, 1962);

Jack D. Durant, "The Moral Focus of *The School for Scandal,*" *South Atlantic Bulletin,* 31 (November 1972): 44-53;

Durant, "Prudence, Providence, and the Direct Road of Wrong: *The School for Scandal* and Sheridan's Westminster Hall Speech," *Studies in Burke and His Time,* 15 (Spring 1974): 241-251;

Durant, *Richard Brinsley Sheridan* (Boston: G. K. Hall, 1975);

Durant, "Sheridan's 'Royal Sanctuary': A Key to *The Rivals,*" *Ball State University Forum,* 14 (Winter 1973): 23-30;

Durant, "Truth for Sheridan: The Biographical Dilemma," in *A Fair Day in the Affections: Literary Essays in Honor of Robert B. White,* edited by Durant and Thomas Hester (Raleigh, N.C.: Winston, 1980), pp. 119-130;

Roger Fiske, "The Linleys 1775-1780," in his *English Theatre Music in the Eighteenth Century* (Oxford: Oxford University Press, 1973), pp. 413-421;

Fiske, "A Score for *The Duenna,*" *Music and Letters,* 42 (April 1961): 132-141;

Arthur Friedman, "Aspects of Sentimentalism in Eighteenth-Century Literature," in *The Augustan Milieu: Essays Presented to Louis A. Landa,* edited by Henry Knight Miller, Eric Rothstein, and G. S. Rousseau (Oxford: Clarendon Press, 1970), pp. 247-261;

Robert D. Hume, "Goldsmith and Sheridan and the Supposed Revolution of 'Laughing' Against 'Sentimental' Comedy," in *Studies in Change and Revolution,* edited by Paul J. Korshin (Menston, U.K.: Scolar Press, 1972), pp. 237-276;

J. R. De J. Jackson, "The Importance of Witty Dialogue in *The School for Scandal,*" *Modern Language Notes,* 76 (November 1961): 601-607;

Henry James, "*The School for Scandal* at the Boston Museum," *Atlantic Monthly,* 34 (December 1874): 754-757;

Philip K. Jason, "A Twentieth-Century Response to *The Critic,*" *Theatre Survey,* 15 (May 1974): 51-58;

A. N. Kaul, "A Note on Sheridan," in his *The Action of English Comedy: Studies in the Encounter of Abstraction and Experience from Shakespeare to Shaw* (New Haven: Yale University Press, 1970), pp. 131-149;

Louis Kronenberger, "Sheridan," in his *The Thread of Laughter: Chapters on English Stage Comedy from Jonson to Maugham* (New York: Knopf, 1952), pp. 191-202;

Leonard J. Leff, "The Disguise Motif in Sheridan's *The School for Scandal,*" *Educational Theatre Journal,* 22 (December 1970): 350-360;

Leff, "Sheridan and Sentimentalism," *Restoration and 18th Century Theatre Research,* 12 (May 1973): 36-48;

John Loftis, *Sheridan and the Drama of Georgian En-*

gland (Cambridge: Harvard University Press, 1977);

Oliver Lutaud, "Des acharniens d'Aristophane au critique de Sheridan," *Les Langues Modernes,* 60 (1966): 433-438;

Samuel L. Macey, "Sheridan: The Last of the Great Theatrical Satirists," *Restoration and 18th Century Theatre Research,* 9 (November 1970): 35-45;

R. D. Nussbaum, "Poetry and Music in *The Duenna,*" *Westerly* (June 1963): 58-63;

Cecil Price, "Pursuing Sheridan," in *Evidence in Literary Scholarship. Essays in Memory of James Marshall Osborn,* edited by René Wellek and Alvaro Ribeiro (Oxford: Clarendon Press, 1979), pp. 309-320;

Richard Little Purdy, Introduction to *The Rivals, A Comedy. As it was first Acted at the Theatre-Royal in Covent-Garden. Written by Richard Brinsley Sheridan, Esq. Edited from the Larpent MS.* (Oxford: Clarendon Press, 1935), pp. xi-lii;

Allan Rodway, "Goldsmith and Sheridan: Satirists of Sentiment," *Renaissance and Modern Essays Presented to Vivian de Sola Pinto,* edited by G. R. Hibbard (New York: Barnes & Noble, 1966), pp. 65-72;

Andrew Schiller, "*The School for Scandal*: The Restoration Unrestored," *PMLA,* 71 (September 1956): 694-704;

George Bernard Shaw, "The Second Dating of Sheridan," *Saturday Review,* 81 (1896): 648-650;

Dane Farnsworth Smith, "*The Critic,* Its Sources, and Its Satire," in *The Critics in the Audience of the London Theatres from Buckingham to Sheridan: A Study of Neoclassicism in the Playhouse, 1671-1779* (Albuquerque: University of New Mexico Press, 1953), pp. 115-143;

Arthur C. Sprague, "In Defence of a Masterpiece: *The School for Scandal* Reexamined," *English Studies Today,* 3rd Series, edited by G. E. Duthie (Edinburgh, 1964), pp. 125-135;

Garland F. Taylor, "Richard Brinsley Sheridan's *The Duenna,*" Ph.D. dissertation, Yale University, 1940;

Linda V. Troost, "The Characterizing Power of Song in Sheridan's *The Duenna,*" *Eighteenth-Century Studies,* 20 (Winter 1986-1987): 153-172.

Papers:

Sheridan materials are scattered throughout England and the United States, both at research libraries and in private hands. Yale, Georgetown, Harvard, and Princeton University libraries house particularly rich collections. Cecil Price in *Letters* and in *Dramatic Works* details holdings known to him through 1973.

Checklist of Further Readings

Bateson, Frederick. *English Comic Drama (1700-1750).* Oxford: Clarendon Press, 1929.

Bevis, Richard W. *The Laughing Tradition: Stage Comedy in Garrick's Day.* Athens: University of Georgia Press, 1980.

Braunmiller, A. R. and J. C. Bulman, eds. *Comedy from Shakespeare to Sheridan: Change and Continuity in the English and European Dramatic Tradition.* Newark: University of Delaware Press, 1986.

Brown, Laura. *English Dramatic Form, 1660-1760.* New Haven: Yale University Press, 1981.

Donaldson, Ian. *The World Upside-Down: Comedy from Jonson to Fielding.* Oxford: Clarendon Press, 1970.

Donohue, Joseph. *Dramatic Character in the English Romantic Age.* Princeton: Princeton University Press, 1970.

Donohue. *Theatre in the Age of Kean.* Oxford: Blackwell, 1975.

Fiske, Roger. *English Theatre Music in the Eighteenth Century.* London, New York & Toronto: Oxford University Press, 1973.

Gagey, Edmond McAdoo. *Ballad Opera.* New York: Columbia University Press, 1937.

Genest, John. *Some Account of the English Stage from the Restoration in 1660 to 1830,* 10 volumes. Bath: H. E. Carrington, 1832.

Griswold, Wendy. *Renaissance Revivals: City Comedy and Revenge Tragedy.* Chicago: University of Chicago Press, 1986.

Hogan, Charles B. *Shakespeare in the Theatre 1701-1800.* Oxford: Clarendon Press, 1957.

Holland, Peter. *The Ornament of Action: Text and Performance in Restoration Comedy.* Cambridge: Cambridge University Press, 1979.

Hotson, Leslie. *The Commonwealth and Restoration Stage.* Cambridge, Mass.: Harvard University Press, 1928.

Hughes, Leo. *The Drama's Patrons: A Study of the Eighteenth-Century London Audience.* Austin: University of Texas Press, 1971.

Hume, Robert D. *The Development of English Drama in the Late Seventeenth Century.* Oxford: Clarendon Press, 1976.

Hume. *Henry Fielding and the London Theatre, 1728-1737.* Oxford: Oxford University Press, 1988.

Hume. *The Rakish Stage: Studies in English Drama, 1660-1800.* Carbondale: Southern Illinois University Press, 1983.

Hume, ed. *The London Theatre World, 1660-1800.* Carbondale: Southern Illinois University Press, 1980.

Kenny, Shirley S., ed. *British Theatre and the Other Arts.* Washington, D.C.: Folger Books, 1984.

Kern, Jean B. *Dramatic Satire in the Age of Walpole 1720-1750.* Ames: Iowa State University Press, 1976.

Leach, Robert. *The Punch and Judy Show: History, Tradition and Meaning.* Athens: University of Georgia Press, 1985.

Leacroft, Richard. *The Development of the English Playhouse.* Ithaca: Cornell University Press, 1973.

Lewis, Peter. *Fielding's Burlesque Drama: Its Place in the Tradition.* Edinburgh: Edinburgh University Press for the University of Durham, 1987.

Liesenfeld, Vincent J. *The Licensing Act of 1737.* Madison: University of Wisconsin Press, 1984.

Lindley, David, ed. *The Court Masque.* Manchester & Dover, N.H.: Manchester University Press, 1984.

Loftis, John. *Comedy and Society from Congreve to Fielding.* Stanford: Stanford University Press, 1959.

Loftis. *Politics of Drama in Augustan England.* Oxford: Clarendon Press, 1963.

Loftis. *Sheridan and the Drama of Georgian England.* Cambridge, Mass.: Harvard University Press, 1977.

Loftis, ed. *Restoration Drama: Modern Essays in Criticism.* New York: Oxford University Press, 1966.

Lynch, James J. *Box, Pit, and Gallery.* Berkeley: University of California Press, 1953.

Mander, Raymond, and Joe Mitchenson. *The Theatres of London,* revised and enlarged edition. London: New English Library, 1975.

Manifold, John S. *The Music in English Drama from Shakespeare to Purcell.* London: Rockcliff, 1956.

Milhous, Judith, and Robert D. Hume. *Producible Interpretation: Eight English Plays 1675-1707.* Carbondale & Edwardsville: Southern Illinois University Press, 1985.

Mills, John A. *Hamlet on Stage: The Great Tradition.* Westport, Conn.: Greenwood Press, 1985.

Nicoll, Allardyce. *A History of English Drama, 1660-1900,* 6 volumes, fourth edition revised. Cambridge: Cambridge University Press, 1952-1959.

Odell, George C. *Shakespeare from Betterton to Irving,* 2 volumes. New York: Scribners, 1920.

Pedicord, Harry William. *The Theatrical Public in the Time of Garrick.* New York: King's Crown Press, 1954.

Price, Curtis A. *Henry Purcell and the London Stage.* London, New York & Cambridge: Cambridge University Press, 1984.

Price. *Music in the Restoration Theatre.* Ann Arbor, Mich.: UMI Research Press, 1979.

Prior, Moody. *The Language of Tragedy.* New York: Columbia University Press, 1947.

Rosenfeld, Sybil M. *A Short History of Scene Design in Great Britain.* Oxford: Blackwell, 1973.

Sherbo, Arthur. *English Sentimental Drama.* East Lansing: Michigan State University Press, 1957.

Smith, Dane Farnsworth. *The Critics in the Audience of the London Theatres from Buckingham to Sheridan: A Study of Neoclassicism in the Playhouse, 1671-1779.* Albuquerque: University of New Mexico Press, 1953.

Southern, Richard. *Changeable Scenery: Its Origin and Development in the British Theatre.* London: Faber & Faber, 1952.

Stone, George Winchester, ed. *The Stage and the Page: London's "Whole Show" in the Eighteenth-Century Theatre.* Berkeley: University of California Press, 1981.

Stratman, Carl J., and others, eds. *Restoration and Eighteenth Century Theatre Research: A Bibliographical Guide, 1900-1968.* Carbondale: Southern Illinois University Press, 1971.

Styan, J. L. *Restoration Comedy in Performance.* New York: Cambridge University Press, 1986.

Taney, Retta. *Restoration Revivals on the British Stage, 1944-1979.* Lanham, Md.: University Press of America, 1985.

Van Lennep, William, and others. *The London Stage 1660-1800: A Calendar of Plays, Entertainments, and Afterpieces,* 5 parts. Carbondale: Southern Illinois University Press, 1960-1970.

Winton, Calhoun. "The Tragic Muse in Enlightened England," in *Greene Centennial Studies,* edited by Paul J. Korshin and Robert R. Allen. Charlottesville: University Press of Virginia, 1984.

Worthen, William B. *The Idea of the Actor: Drama and the Ethics of Performance.* Princeton: Princeton University Press, 1984.

Contributors

Mark S. Auburn .... *Indiana University–Purdue University at Fort Wayne*
Richard Bevis .... *University of British Columbia*
Robert F. Bode .... *Tennessee Technological University*
Gretchen Foster .... *Albion College*
Jean Gagen .... *University of Kansas*
Douglas Howard .... *St. John Fisher College*
Joseph J. Keenan, Jr. .... *Duquesne University*
Frederick M. Link .... *University of Nebraska–Lincoln*
Temple J. Maynard .... *Simon Fraser University*
Laura Morrow .... *Louisiana State University in Shreveport*
Valerie C. Rudolph .... *Purdue University*
Richard B. Schwartz .... *Georgetown University*
Patricia Sigl .... *London, England*
Sid Sondergard .... *St. Lawrence University*
Susan Staves .... *Brandeis University*
Martin J. Wood .... *University of Wisconsin–Eau Claire*

Cumulative Index

Dictionary of Literary Biography, Volumes 1-89
Dictionary of Literary Biography Yearbook, 1980-1988
Dictionary of Literary Biography Documentary Series, Volumes 1-6

Cumulative Index

DLB before number: *Dictionary of Literary Biography,* Volumes 1-89
Y before number: *Dictionary of Literary Biography Yearbook,* 1980-1988
DS before number: *Dictionary of Literary Biography Documentary Series,* Volumes 1-6

A

B

C

D

E

F

G

H

I

J

K

L

M

N

O

P

Q

R

S

T

U

V

W

Y

Z

(Continued from front endsheets)

71: *American Literary Critics and Scholars, 1880-1900,* edited by John W. Rathbun and Monica M. Grecu (1988)

72: *French Novelists, 1930-1960,* edited by Catharine Savage Brosman (1988)

73: *American Magazine Journalists, 1741-1850,* edited by Sam G. Riley (1988)

74: *American Short-Story Writers Before 1880,* edited by Bobby Ellen Kimbel, with the assistance of William E. Grant (1988)

75: *Contemporary German Fiction Writers,* Second Series, edited by Wolfgang D. Elfe and James Hardin (1988)

76: *Afro-American Writers, 1940-1955,* edited by Trudier Harris (1988)

77: *British Mystery Writers, 1920-1939,* edited by Bernard Benstock and Thomas F. Staley (1988)

78: *American Short-Story Writers, 1880-1910,* edited by Bobby Ellen Kimbel, with the assistance of William E. Grant (1988)

79: *American Magazine Journalists, 1850-1900,* edited by Sam G. Riley (1988)

80: *Restoration and Eighteenth-Century Dramatists,* First Series, edited by Paula R. Backscheider (1989)

81: *Austrian Fiction Writers, 1875-1913,* edited by James Hardin and Donald G. Daviau (1989)

82: *Chicano Writers,* First Series, edited by Francisco A. Lomelí and Carl R. Shirley (1989)

83: *French Novelists Since 1960,* edited by Catharine Savage Brosman (1989)

84: *Restoration and Eighteenth-Century Dramatists,* Second Series, edited by Paula R. Backscheider (1989)

85: *Austrian Fiction Writers After 1914,* edited by James Hardin and Donald G. Daviau (1989)

86: *American Short-Story Writers, 1910-1945,* First Series, edited by Bobby Ellen Kimbel (1989)

87: *British Mystery and Thriller Writers Since 1940,* First Series, edited by Bernard Benstock and Thomas F. Staley (1989)

88: *Canadian Writers, 1920-1959,* Second Series, edited by W. H. New (1989)

89: *Restoration and Eighteenth-Century Dramatists,* Third Series, edited by Paula R. Backscheider (1989)

Documentary Series

1: *Sherwood Anderson, Willa Cather, John Dos Passos, Theodore Dreiser, F. Scott Fitzgerald, Ernest Hemingway, Sinclair Lewis,* edited by Margaret A. Van Antwerp (1982)

2: *James Gould Cozzens, James T. Farrell, William Faulkner, John O'Hara, John Steinbeck, Thomas Wolfe, Richard Wright,* edited by Margaret A. Van Antwerp (1982)

3: *Saul Bellow, Jack Kerouac, Norman Mailer, Vladimir Nabokov, John Updike, Kurt Vonnegut,* edited by Mary Bruccoli (1983)

4: *Tennessee Williams,* edited by Margaret A. Van Antwerp and Sally Johns (1984)

5: *American Transcendentalists,* edited by Joel Myerson (1988)

6: *Hardboiled Mystery Writers,* edited by Matthew J. Bruccoli and Richard Layman (1989)

Yearbooks

1980, edited by Karen L. Rood, Jean W. Ross, and Richard Ziegfeld (1981)

1981, edited by Karen L. Rood, Jean W. Ross, and Richard Ziegfeld (1982)

1982, edited by Richard Ziegfeld; associate editors: Jean W. Ross and Lynne C. Zeigler (1983)